Triumph

SPITFIRE IV

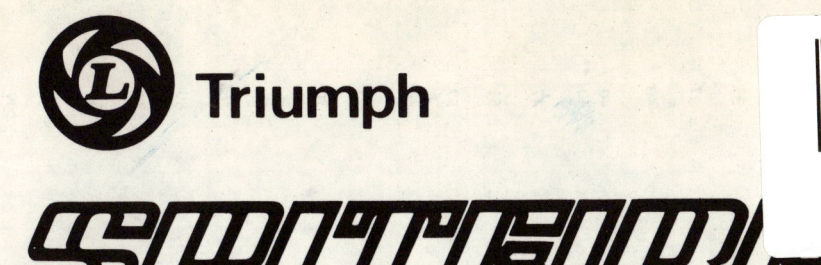

ISBN 1 869826 752

Publication Part No. 545254
Third Edition

Repair Operation Manual

Published by
Leyland Cars Ltd.

CONTENTS

General Specification Data	04
Engine Tuning Data	05
Torque Wrench Settings	06
Recommended Lubricants, Fuel and Fluids – Capacities	09
Maintenance	10
Engine	12
Anti-Pollution System	17
Fuel System	19
Cooling System	26
Manifold and Exhaust System	30
Clutch	33
Gearbox	37
Overdrive	40
Overdrive **'D' Type	40
'J' Type	40J**
Propeller and Drive Shafts	47
Rear Axle and Final Drive	51
Steering	57
Front Suspension	60
Rear Suspension	64
Brakes	70
Wheels and Tyres	74
Body	76
Heating and Ventilation	80
Windscreen Wipers and Washers	84
Electrical	86
Instruments	88
Service Tools	99

Purchasers are advised that the specification details set out in this Manual apply to a range of vehicles and not to any one: For the specification of a particular vehicle, purchasers should consult their Distributor or Dealer.

The Manufacturers reserve the right to vary their specifications with or without notice, and at such times and in such manner as they think fit. Major as well as minor changes may be involved in accordance with the Manufacturer's policy of constant product improvement.

Whilst every effort is made to ensure the accuracy of the particulars contained in this Manual, neither the Manufacturer nor the Distributor or Dealer, by whom this Manual is supplied, shall in any circumstances be held liable for any inaccuracy or the consequences thereof.

© TRIUMPH MOTORS BRITISH LEYLAND UK LIMITED

All rights reserved. No part of this publication may be reproduced, stored in a retrieval system or transmitted, in any form, electronic, mechanical, photocopying, recording or other means without prior written permission of Triumph Service Division.

INTRODUCTION

The purpose of this manual is to assist skilled mechanics in the efficient repair and maintenance of British Leyland vehicles. Using the appropriate service tools and carrying out the procedures as detailed will enable the operations to be completed in the time stated in the 'Repair Operation Times'.

Indexing

For convenience, the manual is divided into a number of divisions. Page 01-3 list the titles and reference number of the various divisions.

A list of the operations within each division appears in alphabetical order on the page preceding each division.

Operation Numbering

A master index of numbered operations has been compiled for universal application to all vehicles manufactured by the British Leyland Motor Corporation and, therefore, because of the different specifications of various models, continuity of the numbering sequence cannot be maintained throughout this manual.

Each operation described in the manual is allocated a number from the master index and cross-refers with an identical number in the 'Repair Operation Times'. The number consists of six digits arranged in three pairs.

Each instruction within an operation has a sequence number and, to complete the operation in the minimum time, it is essential that the instructions are performed in numerical sequence commencing at 1 unless otherwise stated. Where applicable, the sequence numbers identify the relevant components in the appropriate illustration.

Emission Control

With the exception of Section 17, all remaining sections of this manual relate to basic vehicles not fitted with *anti-pollution* equipment. Where an operation is affected by the presence of this equipment, refer also to Anti-pollution (Section 17) as appropriate.

Service Tools

Where performance of an operation requires the use of a service tool, the tool number is quoted under the operation heading and is repeated in, or following, the instruction involving its use. An illustrated list of all necessary tools is included in section 99.

References

References to the left- or right-hand side in the manual are made when viewing from the rear. With the engine and gearbox assembly removed, the 'timing cover' end of the engine is referred to as the front. A key to abbreviations and symbols is given on page 01-5.

Amendments

Revised and additional procedures resulting from changes in the vehicle specifications will be issued as revised or additional pages.

The circulation of amendments will be confined to Distributors and Dealers of British Leyland Motor Corporation Limited.

REPAIRS AND REPLACEMENTS

When service parts are required it is essential that only genuine British Leyland Stanpart or Unipart replacements are used.

Attention is particularly drawn to the following points concerning repairs and the fitting of replacement parts and accessories.

Safety features embodied in the car may be impaired if other than genuine parts are fitted. In certain territories legislation prohibits the fitting of parts not to the vehicle manufacturer's specification. Torque wrench setting figures given in the Repair Operation Manual must be strictly adhered to. Locking devices, where specified, must be fitted. If the efficiency of a locking device is impaired during removal it must be renewed. Owners purchasing accessories while travelling abroad should ensure that the accessory and its fitted location on the car conform to mandatory requirements in their country of origin.

The car warranty may be invalidated by the fitting of other than genuine British Leyland parts. All British Leyland Stanpart or Unipart replacements have the full backing of the factory warranty.

British Leyland Distributors and Dealers are obliged to supply only genuine service parts.

Triumph Spitfire Mk IV Manual. Part No. 545254

01.4

ABBREVIATIONS AND SYMBOLS

Across flats (bolt size)	A.F.
After bottom dead centre	A.B.D.C.
After top dead centre	A.T.D.C.
Alternating current	a.c.
Amperes	amp
Ampere-hour	Ah
**Atmospheres	Atm**
Before bottom dead centre	B.B.D.C.
Before top dead centre	B.T.D.C.
Bottom dead centre	B.D.C.
Brake horse-power	b.h.p.
Brake mean effective pressure	b.m.e.p.
British Standards	B.S.
Carbon monoxide	CO
Centigrade (Celsius)	C
Centimetres	cm
Cubic centimetres	cm³
Cubic inches	in³
Cycles per minute	c/min
Degree (angle)	deg. or °
Degree (temperature)	deg. or °
Diameter	dia.
Direct current	d.c.
Fahrenheit	F
Feet	ft
Feet per minute	ft/min
Fifth	5th
Figure (illustration)	Fig.
First	1st
Fourth	4th
Gallons (Imperial)	gal
Gallons (U.S.)	U.S. gal
**Grammes (force)	gf
**Grammes (mass)	g**
High compression	h.c.
High tension (electrical)	h.t.
Horse-power	hp
Hundredweight	cwt
Inches	in
Inches of mercury	inHg
Independent front suspension	i.f.s.
Internal diameter	i.dia.
Kilogrammes (force)	kgf
Kilogrammes (mass)	kg
Kilogramme centimetre	kgf cm
Kilogramme metres	kgf m
Kilogrammes per square centimetre	kgf/cm²
Kilometres	km
Kilometres per hour	km/h
Kilovolts	kV
King pin inclination	k.p.i.
Left-hand	L.H.
Left-hand steering	L.H.Stg.
Left-hand thread	L.H.Thd.
Low compression	l.c.
Low tension	l.t.
Maximum	max.
Metres	m
Microfarad	mfd
Midget Edison Screw	MES
Miles per gallon	m.p.g.
Miles per hour	m.p.h.
Millimetres	mm
Millimetres of mercury	mmHg
Minimum	min.
Minus (of tolerance)	−
Minute (of angle)	′
Negative (electrical)	−
**Newton metres	Nm**
Number	No.
Ohms	ohm
Ounces (force)	ozf
Ounces (mass)	oz
Ounce inch (torque)	ozf in
Outside diameter	o.dia.
Overdrive	O/D
Paragraphs	para.
Part Number	Part No.
Percentage	%
Pints (Imperial)	pt
Pints (U.S.)	U.S. pt
Plus (tolerance)	+
Plus or minus	±
Positive (electrical)	+
Pounds (force)	lbf
Pounds (mass)	lb
Pounds feet (torque)	lbf ft
Pounds inches (torque)	lbf in
Pounds per square inch	lb/in²
Radius	r
Ratio	:
Reference	ref.
Revolutions per minute	rev/min
Right-hand	R.H.
Right-hand steering	R.H.Stg.
Second (angle)	″
Second (numerical order)	2nd
Single carburetter	SC
Society of Automobile Engineers	S.A.E.
Specific gravity	sp. gr.
Square centimetres	cm²
Square inches	in²
Standard	std
Standard wire gauge	s.w.g.
Synchronizer/synchromesh	synchro.
Third	3rd
Top dead centre	T.D.C.
Twin carburetters	TC
United Kingdom	UK
Volts	V
Watts	W

Screw threads

American Standard Taper Pipe	N.P.T.F.
British Association	B.A.
British Standard Fine	B.S.F.
British Standard Pipe	B.S.P.
British Standard Whitworth	B.S.W.
Unified Coarse	U.N.C.
Unified Fine	U.N.F.

Triumph Spitfire Mk IV Manual. Part No. 545254

01.5

LOCATION OF COMMISSION AND UNIT NUMBERS

THE COMMISSION NUMBER
is the identification number which is required for registration and other purposes. It is stamped on a plate attached to the left hand bulkhead panel (not U.S.A.), and is visible when the bonnet is raised. On vehicles for the U.S.A. type markets this plate is attached to the body adjacent to the left hand door striker plate and the Commission Number is also stamped on a small plate visible through the left hand side of the windscreen.

The significance of the Commission Numbers and suffix is as follows:

- **FH** — this prefix denotes 'Spitfire Mk IV' model range.
- **FK** — is an alternative prefix for U.S.A. market only. **
- **FM** }
- **FL** — is an alternative prefix for Swedish market (pre 1972 condition only).
- **1234** — is the accumulated total build of this model.
- **L** — denotes left hand steering.
  (No letter is given to right hand steering models).
- **U** — denotes U.S.A. type markets 1972 condition onwards.

THE ENGINE NUMBER
is stamped on a machined flange on the left hand side of the cylinder block. The significance of the Engine Numbers and suffix is as follows:

- **FH** — this prefix denotes model range.
- **FK** } an alternative prefix for U.S.A. market only.
- **FM** } **
- **FL** — an alternative prefix for Swedish market (pre 1972 condition only).
- **1234** — is the accumulated total build of this type.
- **H** — denotes High Compression. Alternatively.
- **L** — denotes Low Compression. Alternatively.
- **U** — denotes U.S.A. type markets 1972 condition onwards.
- **E** — denotes engine unit.

The Commission Number plate also bears code symbols for identification of the vehicle's exterior colour, trim material and trim colour. Refer to page 04-6.

THE GEARBOX NUMBER
is stamped on the right hand side of the gearbox casing. The significance of the Gearbox Numbers is as follows:

- **FH** — this prefix denotes model range.
- **FK** — an alternative prefix for U.S.A. market only 1972 condition.
- **1234** — is the accumulated build of this type. There are no suffix letters.

THE REAR AXLE NUMBER
is stamped on the bottom flange of the axle housing. The significance of the Axle Numbers is as follows:

- **FH** — this prefix denotes model range.
- **FK** — an alternative prefix for U.S.A. market only 1972 condition.
- **1234** — is the accumulated total build of this type. There are no suffix numbers.

IMPORTANT: In all communications relating to Service and Spares it is essential to quote Commission Number, paint and trim codes and unit numbers (if applicable).

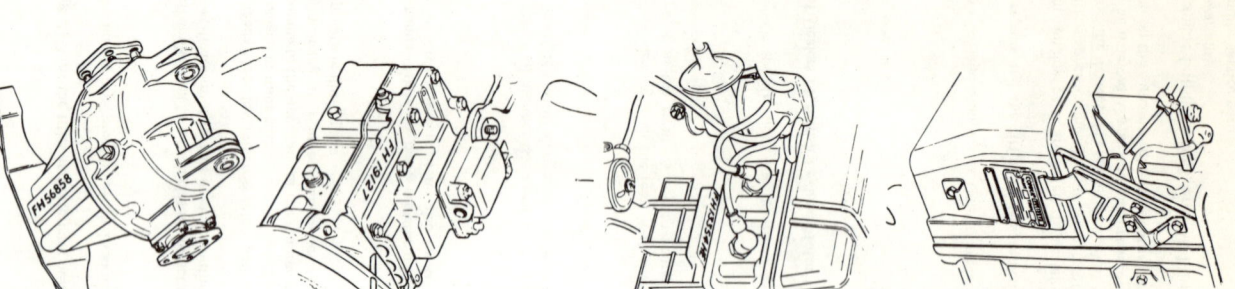

GENERAL SPECIFICATION DATA

ENGINE
		U.S.A. Market differences
Number of cylinders	4 in line	
Bore of cylinders	2·9 in (73·7 mm)	3·44 in (87·5 mm)
Stroke of crankshaft	2·992 in (76 mm)	
Capacity	79·2 in³ (1296 cc)	91 in³ (1493 cc) } (1973 models only)
Compression ratio	9·0 : 1	7·5 : 1 (1973 models only)
		8·0 : 1 (1972 model only)
Maximum Power		
1974 model }	61 bhp nett at 5500 rev/min	57 bhp SAE nett at 5000 rev/min
1973 model }		48 bhp SAE nett at 5500 rev/min
1972 model	63 bhp nett at 6000 rev/min	58 bhp nett at 5200 rev/min
Maximum Torque		
Pre 1972 model	818 lbf/in² at 2900 rev/min equivalent to 130 lb/in² bmep	885 lbf/in² SAE nett at 3000 rev/min equivalent to 122 lb/in² bmep
1974 model }		730 lbf/in² SAE nett at 2900 rev/min equivalent to 116 lb/in² bmep
1973 model }		860 lbf/in² at 3000 rev/min equivalent to 137 lb/in² bmep (1973 model only)
1972 model	837 lbf/in² at 3500 rev/min equivalent to 133 lb/in² bmep	

LUBRICATION
Type	High capacity, eccentric lobe type
Oil pump	
Oil filter	Full flow type, replaceable element
Oil warning light	Extinguishes at 3 to 5 lb/in² (0·21 to 0·35 kg/cm²) oil pressure

COOLING SYSTEM
Type	Water, "No Loss" system
Circulation	By impeller type pump, Vee belt drive
Pressure	13 lb/in² (0·91 kg/cm²)
Thermostat	Opens at 82°C (180°F) normal 88°C (190°F) cold climate
Fan	7 blades 11½in. diameter (292mm) ** 7 blades 12½in. diameter (304mm) from engine number FM10,001 UE ** and U.S.A. market only from engine number FK 33745UE

FUEL SYSTEM
Tank	Tank at rear
Pump	Mechanically operated, diaphragm type. Tank at rear with separate overflow tank
Carburetter	
1974 model }	Single, Stromberg 1·50 C.D.S.E.V. Exhaust emission controlled
and 1973 model }	Two, SU HS2E side draught exhaust emissions controlled
1972 model	Two, SU HS2E side draught Single, Stromberg 1·50 C.D.S.E. Exhaust emission controlled
Pre 1972 model	Two, SU HS2E side draught
Air cleaner	Combined air cleaner and silencer with replaceable paper elements
Crankcase ventilation	Closed circuit breathing from rocker cover to constant depression side of carburetters
Evaporative emission control	** Sealed tank filler cap. Vapour emissions from the tank are vented via a separator tank (or canister — 1974 model) to a charcoal canister located in the engine compartment. Canister purged by carburetter depression. An exhaust gas recirculating valve is located in the inlet manifold — 1974 model.

CLUTCH
Make/type	Borg and Beck single dry plate, diaphragm spring type
Release mechanism	Hydraulically operated
Plate diameter	6½ in (165 mm) ***7¼ in (184 mm) } (1973/74 model only) **
Facing material	Mintex M19 H-K Porter 11046 }

GEARBOX

Manual

Synchromesh: On forward gears

		O/D Top 'D'	Top 'J'	Top	O/D 3rd 'D'	3rd 'J'	3rd	2nd	1st	Rev.
** Gear Ratios		–		1·00	–		1·39	2·16	3·50	3·99
Overall ratios	U.S.A. 1972 only	3·29		4·11	4·58		5·71	8·87	14·40	16·39
	other U.S.A. and other markets	3·12	3·10	3·89	4·34	4·31	5·42	8·40	13·62	15·51 **

Overdrive (optional)

Make/type	Laycock, Type D	Laycock, Type J
Operative on	Top & 3rd. gears	Top & 3rd gears
Overall ratios	0·802 : 1	0·797:1

FINAL DRIVE

Type: Hypoid bevel gears in rear axle

Ratio: 3·89 : 1   4·11 : 1 (U.S.A. 1972 condition only)

** EFFECTIVE GEARING (Approximate values depending on type and condition of tyre fitted)

Engine speeds (rev/min) at road speeds of:		O/D Top 'D'	Top 'J'	Top	O/D 3rd 'D'	3rd 'J'	3rd	2nd	1st	Rev.
10 m.p.h.	U.S.A. 1972 only	503		628	701		872	1356	2202	2511
	Other U.S.A. and other markets	482	471	599	669	.656	834	1295	2100	2395
10 km/h	U.S.A. 1972 only	313		390	436		542	842	1360	1555
	Other U.S.A. and other markets	301	295	372	417	410	518	803	1304	1488 **

ROAD SPEED DATA (Approximate values depending on type and condition of tyre fitted)

** Road speed at 1,000 rev/min engine speed:

O/D Top . . . 'D' { U.S.A. 1972 only 19·9 m.p.h. (32·0 km/h)
Other U.S.A. and other markets 20·8 m.p.h. (33·5 km/h)

. . . 'J' 21·2 m.p.h. (34 km/h)

Top Gear: U.S.A. 1972 only 15·9 m.p.h. (26·0 km/h)
Other U.S.A. and other markets 16·7 m.p.h. (27·0 km/h) **

STEERING

Make/type: Alford and Alder, Rack and pinion

Turning Circle: 24 feet (7·3 metres)

Steering wheel diameter ** 1974 and 1973 model **: 14·5 in (368 mm) } – turns, lock to lock 3¾

Pre 1973 model: 15 in (381 mm)

BRAKE SYSTEM

Operation:

Foot pedal: Hydraulic on all four wheels.
U.S.A. market only: Tandem master cylinder operating front and rear brakes indépendantly

Handbrake: Mechanical on rear wheels only

Front

Type: Caliper disc

Dimensions: Disc diameter 9 in (229 mm)

Lining area: 14·8 in² (95 cm²)

Swept area: 150·0 in² (967 cm²)

Rear

Type: Drum with leading and trailing shoes

Dimensions: 7 in dia. x 1¼ in. wide (178 mm x 32 mm)

Lining area: 34·0 in² (220 cm²)

Swept area: 55·0 in² (355 cm²)

WHEELS AND TYRES

Wheels: ** Steel disc type, 4½J rims. Wire wheels optional for earlier cars. **

Tyres: ** 5.20S – 13 cross ply tubeless (with narrow white side band) or 155SR – 13 radial ply tyres for U.S.A. Market **
145SR – 13 radial ply tyres optional (except Home Market after Commission Number FH38271)
155SR – 13 radial ply tyres standard fitment to all Home Market cars after Commission Number FH38271

Tyre pressures: front: 21 lb/in² (1·476 kg/cm²) } Cross ply and
rear: 26 lb/in² (1·828 kg/cm²) } radial ply tyres

CHASSIS DATA

Wheelbase	6 ft 11 in (2110 mm)
Track: (2 up condition) front	4 ft 1 in (1244 mm) – Disc wheels
1973 model	4 ft 1¼ in (1251 mm) } – Wire wheels
Pre 1973 model	4 ft 1½ in (1257 mm) } – Wire wheels
rear ** 1974 and 1973 model **	4 ft 2 in (1270 mm) } – Disc wheels
Pre 1973 model	4 ft 0 in (1220 mm) } – Disc wheels
1973 model	4 ft 2¼ in (1276 mm) } – Wire wheels
Pre 1973 model	4 ft 0½ in (1232 mm) } – Wire wheels
Wheel alignment: (2 up condition) front	0 to 1/16 in toe in (0 to 1·5875 mm)
rear	0 to 1/16 in toe in (0 to 1·5875 mm)
Ground clearance: (2 up condition)	5 in (127mm)
Camber: (2 up condition) front	2° positive ± ½°
rear	3¾° negative ± 1°
Caster: (2 up condition)	4½° ± ½°
King pin inclination (2 up condition)	6¾° ± ¾°

ELECTRICAL EQUIPMENT

Electrical system	12 volt negative earth
Battery capacity	40 amp hour at 20 hour rate
Alternator: type ** 1973 model	Lucas 16 ACR output 34 amps
Pre 1973 model	Lucas 15 ACR output 28 amps **
Starter motor	M 35 J inertia type

OVERALL DIMENSIONS

Length	12 ft 5 in (3785 mm) 12 ft 11¼ in (3943 mm) U.S.A. – 1974 model
Width	4 ft 10½ in (1488 mm)
Height (unladen) to top of windscreen	3 ft 8¼ in (1125 mm)
Soft top, hood erect	3 ft 11½ in (1205 mm)

WEIGHTS (approx)

Dry (excluding extra equipment)	14½ cwt **(743 kg)
Basic kerb (including water, oil, fuel & tools)	15¼ cwt (778 kg)
Kerb (including optional extras, water, oil etc)	16¼ cwt (825 kg)
Maximum gross vehicle weight	20 cwt (1017 kg) **

TOWING INFORMATION

Maximum recommended trailer weight: 12 cwt (610 kg) when the trailer being towed is equipped with brakes.
3·94 cwt (200 kg) when the trailer being towed is not equipped with brakes – providing that the total car and trailer laden weights do not exceed 20·89 cwt (1112 kg)

Maximum starting gradient (fully laden car and trailer): 5·5 } with car engine in peak condition

Maximum climable gradient (fully laden car and trailer): 4·3 } with car engine in peak condition

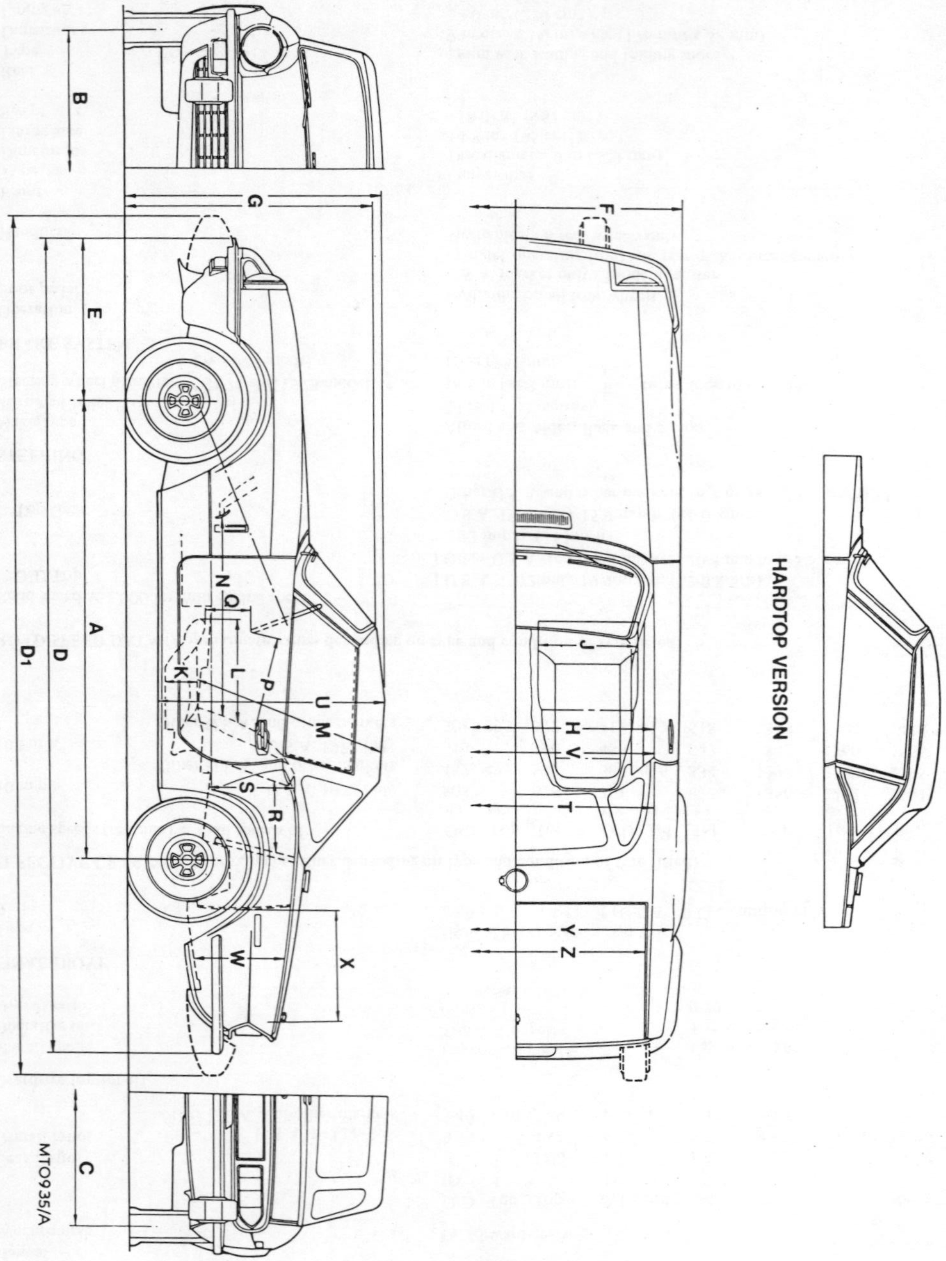

GENERAL SPECIFICATION DATA

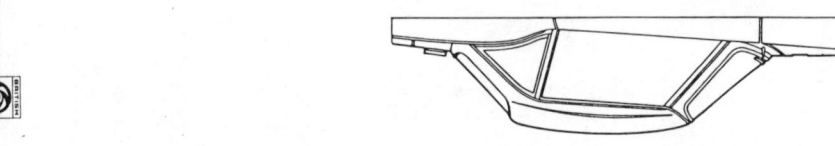

HARDTOP VERSION

VEHICLE DIMENSIONS (Approximate)

Dim.	Description	inches	mm
A	Wheelbase	83.00	2108
B	Front track:		
	Disc wheels	49.00	1244
	Wire wheels	49.50	1257
C	Rear track:		
	Disc wheels	48.00	1220
	Wire wheels	48.50	1232
D	Overall length	149.00	3785
D1	Overall length—U.S.A. market—1974 condition	155.25	3943 **
E	Front overhang	31.06	788
F	Overall width	58.50	1488
G	Height:		
	Soft top hood erect	47.50	1205
	to top of windscreen	44.25	1125
H	Width — door to door (shoulder height)	45.50	1156
J	Seat width	18.00	457
K	Seat height — floor to cushion	7.50	191
L	Seat depth	20.00	508
M	Headroom from seat cushion	35.00	889
N	Seat squab to clutch pedal:		
	Max.	41.50	1055
	Min	35.50	902
P	Seat squab to steering wheel:		
	Max.	18.00	457
	Min.	12.00	305
Q	Seat cushion to steering wheel	7.00	178
R	Length of luggage space behind seats		
	Max.	18.00	457
	Min.	12.00	305
S	Height-floor to top of seat squab	16.00	406
T	Width between wheel arches	35.50	902
U	Maximum interior height	40.00	1016
V	Maximum interior width at hip point	47.50	1208
W	Luggage compartment height:		
	Max.	17.00	432
	Min.	7.00	178
X	Luggage compartment depth:		
	Max.	22.00	560
	Min.	17.00	432
Y	Luggage compartment width:		
	(between wheel arches) Max.	48.00	1220
	Min.	35.50	902
Z	Luggage compartment effective opening width	42.00	1068

GENERAL SPECIFICATION DATA

PAINT AND TRIM CODING SYSTEM

The commission number plate bears code symbols for identification of the vehicle's exterior colour, trim material and trim colour.

Colour Code

Nine basic colours are allocated a number as shown in the table. Shades of these colours are classified as 1st shade, 2nd shade, 3rd shade, etc. The number of each shade change prefixes the basic colour to indicate the shade colour. Dual colours are identified by two code numbers separated by a stroke, e.g. 19/26 denotes 'White' and 'Wedgwood', the predominant colour being white, this symbol being quoted first.

The main trim material is identified by prefixing the colour code number with a letter, e.g.:

Leathercloth — No prefix letter
Leather — Prefix letter H
Cloth — Prefix letter C

Basic colour	Basic colour number	1st shade	2nd shade	3rd shade	4th shade	5th shade	6th shade	7th shade	8th shade	9th shade	10th shade	11th shade	12th shade
Black	01	11											
Red	02	12 Matador	22 Cherry	32 Signal	42 Burgundy	52 Scarlet	62 Inca Red	72 Pimiento	82 Carmine	92 Magenta			
Brown	03	13 Light Tan	23 Sienna	33 New Tan	43 Saddle Tan	53 Dark Brown	63 Chestnut	73 Maple **					
Yellow	04	14 Jonquil	24 Wimpey	34 Jasmine	44 Beige	54 Saffron	64 Mimosa						
Green	05	15 Cactus	25 Conifer	35 Olive	45 Lichfield	55 Laurel	65 Emerald						
Blue	06	16 Midnight Blue	26 Wedgwood	36 Dark Blue	46 Renoir	56 Royal	66 Valencia	76 Print Blue	86 Navy	96 Sapphire	106 Mallard	116 Ice	126 French
Purple	07	17 Damson	27 Shadow Blue										
Grey	08	18 Gunmetal	28 Dark Grey	38 Phantom	48 Dolphin	58 Shadow Blue	68 Slate	78 Grey					
White	09	19 White	29 Sebring White	39 Honeysuckle									

Thus: Paint 19/26 Trim 16 denote that the vehicle is painted 'White' and 'Wedgwood', and trimmed in leathercloth coloured Midnight Blue.

NOTE: Acrylic paints bear the suffix 'A'.

04.6 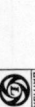 Triumph Spitfire Mk IV Manual Part No. 545254

ENGINE TUNING DATA

ENGINE
Firing order . . . . 1—3—4—2
No. 1 cylinder . . . . at front
Idle speed . . . . 800 to 850 rev/min U.S.A. market only, 750 to 800 rev/min other markets
Fast idle speed . . . . 1100 to 1300 rev/min all markets
Valve clearance (cold) . . . . . . 0·010 in (0·25 mm) inlet and exhaust
Valve clearance adjustment . . . . screw and locking nut on rocker
Location of timing marks . . . . . scale on front engine cover, mark on crankshaft pulley.
Valve timing . . . . Engine No. Eng. No. F.M.I. Engine No. 25001 and upwards
  Inlet opens . . . . U.S.A. market 18° B.T.D.C. other markets 10° B.T.D.C. U.S.A. markets 18° B.T.D.C. other markets 25° B.T.D.C.
  closes . . . . 58° A.B.D.C. 58° A.B.D.C. 50° A.B.D.C. 25° A.B.D.C.
  Exhaust opens . . . . 58° B.B.D.C. 58° B.B.D.C. 50° B.B.D.C. 65° B.B.D.C.
  closes . . . . 18° A.T.D.C. 18° A.T.D.C. 10° A.T.D.C. 25° A.T.D.C.
Ignition timing:
  static . . . . Up to Eng. No. F.M.1 8° B.T.D.C. Eng. No. F.M. 1 onwards 10° B.T.D.C. Below Engine No. 25001 8° B.T.D.C. 6° B.T.D.C.
  dynamic . . . . See No. 86.35.00

CARBURETTER
Make/type . . . . Twin S.U. HS2E Single Stromberg 150 C.D.S.E. Single Stromberg 150 C.D.S.E. Twin S.U. HS2 Single Stromberg 150 C.D.S.E.
  Up to 1973 condition
  Single Stromberg 150 C.D.S.E. (V)
  1973 condition 150 C.D.S.E.V.X.
  1974 condition
Main jet . . . . 0·090 in 0·090 in
Needle . . . . B 5 CH B 5 AV
  AAN AAN
Float height . . . . 16 to 17 mm 16 to 17 mm

IGNITION COIL
Make/type . . . . Lucas 16C6 Lucas 15C6
Primary winding resistance . . . . 1·43 to 1·58 ohms 1·30 to 1·45 ohms

BALLAST RESISTOR (Fitted up to 1973 condition only. 1973 models onwards have a resistance wire built into the harness as an alternative to the ballast resistor) **
Make/type . . . . Lucas 3BR
Resistance . . . . 1·3 to 1·4 ohms

IGNITION DISTRIBUTOR
Make/type . . . . A.C. Delco, D 204 (different to each model)
Rotation viewed on rotor . . . . . anti-clockwise
Dwell angle . . . . 38° to 40°
Capacitor capacitance . . . . . . 0·18 to 0·23 mfd
Contact breaker gap . . . . 0·014 in to 0·016 in (0·35 to 0·40 mm)
Centrifugal advance . . . . See 86.35.00
Vacuum advance . . . . See 86.35.00

SPARKING PLUGS
Make/type . . . . Champion N12Y U.S.A. market only Eng. No. FM1349 onwards
  Champion UN12Y U.S.A. market only Up to Eng. No. FM1349
  Champion N9Y other markets
Gap . . . . 0·025 in (0·64 mm)

Triumph Spitfire Mk IV Manual Part No. 545254

05.1

TORQUE WRENCH SETTINGS

SPITFIRE MkIV TIGHTENING TORQUES

Operation	Description	Specified Torque (lbf. ft.)	(kgf. m.)
ENGINE			
Air cleaner to backplate	1/4" UNF × 1/2" setscrew	8	1·1
Air cleaner to carburettor	5/16" UNF × 2 1/8" bolt	8	1·1
Alternator to mounting bracket & front engine plate	5/16" UNF × 4 7/8" bolt	22	3·0
Alternator to adjusting link	5/16" UNC × 1" setscrew	20	2·8
Clutch attachment to flywheel	5/16" UNF × 5/8" setscrew	22	3·0
Connecting rod bolt {Colour Dyed / Phosphated}	3/8" UNF × 1·65" bolt	50	6·9
	3/8" UNF × 1·65" bolt	46	6·4
Chainwheel to camshaft	5/16" UNF × 1" bolt	24	3·3
Crankshaft pulley nut	1" × 16 T.P.I.	150	20·7
Cylinder block drain plug	1/2" × 20 NPT	35	4·8
Cylinder head to block	3/8" UNF stud	46	6·4
Distributor to pedestal	1/4" UNF × 2" bolt	20	2·8
Fan attachment	5/16" UNF × 3/4" setscrew	20	2·8
Flywheel to crankshaft	3/8" UNF × 1·03" bolt	9	1·2
Fuel pump to cylinder block	5/16" UNF × 1·16" bolt	40	5·5
Gearbox & rear engine plate to block	5/16" UNF × 1·56" stud**	45	6·2
Manifold inlet to exhaust	5/16" UNF stud	14	1·9
Manifold to head	3/8" UNF stud	25	3·5
Main bearing cap bolts	3/8" UNF × 3" stud	65	9·0
Oil sump drain plug	3/8" Dryseal taper plug	25	3·5
Oil sump to block	5/16" UNF × 5/8" setscrew	20	2·8
Oil pressure switch plug to cylinder head	3/8" × 18 NP Tapered plug	14	1·9
Oil seal block attachment	5/16" UNF × 0·94" screw	14	1·9
Rocker cover to head	5/16" UNF × 4·13" stud	2	0·3
Rocker pedestal to cylinder head	3/8" UNF × 3·09" stud	34	4·7
Rear crankshaft seal	5/16" UNF × 1 1/8" setscrew	20	2·8
Rear engine mounting platform on frame	5/16" UNF × 5/8" setscrew	20	2·8
Sealing block to engine plate	5/16" UNF × 5/8" setscrew	20	2·8
Spark plug to head	14mm × 3/4" long thread	34	4·7
Starter motor attachment	3/8" UNF × 2 1/8" bolt	20	2·8
Timing cover to front engine plate	5/16" UNF × 3/8" setscrew	10	1·4

* Cad. Plated   ** Parkanised

Operation	Description	Specified Torque (lbf. ft.)	(kgf. m.)
Selector fork attachment	5/16" UNF setscrew	10	1·4
Top cover to gearbox	1/4" UNF × 7/8" setscrew	10	1·4
	1/4" UNF × 1 3/8" bolt	10	1·4
OVERDRIVE – 'D' TYPE **			
Top cover attachment	1/4" UNF × 7/8" bolt	9	1·2
Support bracket attachment	1/4" UNF × 5/8" setscrew	20	2·8
Overdrive to rear engine mounting	5/16" UNF × 7/8" setscrew	20	2·8
Support bracket to overdrive	5/16" UNF × 7/8" setscrew	20	2·8
** OVERDRIVE – 'J' TYPE			
Adaptor to gearbox	1/4" UNF setscrew	9	1·2
Overdrive to adaptor	1/4" stud	7	1·0
Overdrive to rear engine mounting	3/8" UNF/UNC stud	25	3·5
Rear engine mounting attachment	7/16" UNF bolt	38	5·2
Steady strap to overdrive unit	5/16" UNF × 7/8" setscrew	20	2·8 **

PROPELLOR SHAFT AND REAR AXLE

Operation	Description	Specified Torque (lbf. ft.)	(kgf. m.)
Axle mounting plate to hypoid housing	3/8" UNF	38	5·2
Back plate attachment (axle shaft & hub)	5/16" UNF	20	2·8
Bearing cap to housing	3/8" UNF × 1·84" bolt	38	5·2
Crown wheel to differential unit	3/8" UNF × 0·72" bolt	46	6·4
Front and rear attachment of prop. shaft	3/8" UNF × 1" bolt	34	4·7
Hub to axle shaft	5/8" UNF	120	16·6
Hypoid housing to rear axle housing	5/16" UNF × 1" setscrew	20	2·8
Hypoid flange to pinion	5/8" UNF	120	16·6
Plugs, drain and filler	3/8" × 18 dryseal	25	3·5
Rear axle to frame	7/16" UNF × 7·4" bolt	45	6·2
Rear axle nose mounting to frame	3/8" UNF Special stud	34	4·7
Road spring attachment	3/8" UNF stud	34	4·7
Shaft joint to inner axle shaft	3/8" UNF bolt	46	6·4

FRONT SUSPENSION

Operation	Description	Specified Torque (lbf. ft.)	(kgf. m.)
Anti-roll bar attachment to chassis	5/16" UNF 'U' bolt	4	0·6
Anti-roll bar link assembly	7/16" UNF	45	6·2
Anti-roll bar stud	3/8" UNF stud	32	4·4
Ball assembly to upper wishbone	5/16" UNF × 2 1/4" bolt	20	2·8
Ball pin to vertical link	7/16" UNF ball pin	14	1·9
Brake caliper to mounting plate	7/16" UNF × 1·31" bolts	38	5·2
Brake disc	3/8" UNF × 1" bolt	65	9·0
Damper attachment	7/16" UNF	34	4·7
Front suspension and engine mounting bracket to frame	3/8" UNF × 1" bolt	46	6·4
Fulcrum bracket to lower wishbone	3/8" UNF × 1 1/2" setscrew	32	4·4
Fulcrum bracket to upper wishbone	3/8" UNF × 2 5/8" bolt	32	4·4
Stub axle to vertical link	3/8" UNF × 2 1/2" bolt}	32	4·4
	1/2" UNF on stub shaft	65	9·0
Tie rod end ball joint assembly	3/8" UNF	32	4·4
Tie rod lever & dust cover to vertical link	7/16" UNF × 1·88" bolt	65	9·0
Trunion to wishbone	7/16" UNF × 2 1/2" bolt	45	6·2
Wishbone assembly to frame	3/8" UNF stud	25	3·5

GEARBOX

Operation	Description	Specified Torque (lbf. ft.)	(kgf. m.)
Drain plug	3/8" NP Taper	25	3·5
Extension to gearbox	5/16" UNF × 7/8" setscrew	20	2·8
Filler Plug	3/8" NP Taper	25	3·5
Flange to mainshaft	5/8" UNF	120	16·6 **
Gearbox case to clutch housing	1/4" UNF × 1" bolt	32	4·4
Hand lever to operating shaft	1/4" UNF × 1" bolt	9	1·2
Slave cylinder to boss	5/16" UNF × 2 1/4" bolt	** 9	1·2 **

Operation	Description	Specific Torque (lbf. ft.)	(kgf. m.)
REAR SUSPENSION			
Damper fulcrum pin	½" UNF fulcrum pin	48	6·6
Damper lower attachment	7/16" UNF	38	5·2
Pivot bracket to body floor	3/8" UNF X 1 7/8" setscrew	32	4·4
Radius arm attachment to pivot brackets and links	3/8" UNF X 2¼" bolt	32	4·4
Spring to pivot bracket	5/16" UNF X 2 5/8" bolt	20	2·8
Spring ends to vertical links	7/16" UNF bolt	48	6·6
Vertical link plates to rear hub inner	7/16" UNF X 3 3/8" bolt	48	6·6
STEERING			
Ball joint to tie rod lock nut	½" UNF on tie rod	38	5·2
Column Lower assembly to bracket	¼" UNF X ½" setscrew	9	1·2
Coupling Lower to upper clamp	¼" UNF bolt	9	1·2
Coupling pinch bolt	5/16" UNF X 1¼" bolt	14	2·0
Rack mounting to frame	5/16" UNF 'U' bolt	16	2·2
Road wheel to hub	3/8" UNF stud	48	6·6
Safety clamp socket setscrew	7/16" UNF setscrew	20	2·8
Steering column lock attachment	5/16" UNF torque head screw	Tighten to shear	
Steering column safety clamp	¼" UNF bolt	9	1·2
Steering wheel to column	9/16" UNF on column	34	4·7
BODY			
Accelerator mounting bracket	5/16" UNF X 1½" bolt	20	2·8
Accelerator mounting bracket to dash	¼" UNF X ½" setscrew	9	1·2
Bonnet hinge pivot to support bracket	3/8" UNF X 1 7/8" setscrew	32	4·4
Bumper to rear body wing sides	5/16" UNF X ¾" setscrew	14	1·9
Bumper assembly to rear support and support attachment	3/8" UNF setscrew	32	4·4
Clutch and brake pedal mounting bracket	¼" UNF X 5/8" setscrew	9	1·2
Clutch and brake master cylinder attachment	5/16" UNF X 7/8" setscrew	20	2·8
Door hinge to body	5/16" UNF X 7/8" setscrew	20	2·8
Door hinge to door	5/16" UNF X ¾" setscrew	14	1·9
Seat slide attachment	¼" UNF X 7/8" setscrew	9	1·2
Seat slide to floor	¼" UNF X ¾" setscrew	9	1·2
Seat belt attachment to tunnel & sill	7/16" UNF special bolt	32	4·4
Seat belt attachment to rear wheel arch	7/16" UNF special bolt	32	4·4
** **U.S.A. Markets – 1974 condition**			
Front bumper to impact shock absorber	¼" UNF x 7/8" setscrew	9	1·2
Front impact shock absorber to pivot support bracket	¼" UNF x 5/8" setscrew	9	1·2
Rear bumper impact shock absorber attachment	¼" UNF x 7/8" / ¼" UNF x 1" } setscrew	9	1·2
Rear bumper to support brackets	5/16" UNF x 5/8" setscrew	20	2·8
Rear impact reinforcements to trunk floor	3/8" UNF x 7/8" setscrew / 3/8" UNF x 1½" bolt }	32	4·4
Rear impact shock absorber side wall stiffening	¼" UNF x ¾" setscrew	9	1·2 **

RECOMMENDED LUBRICANTS – BRITISH ISLES

(The products recommended are not listed in order of preference)

COMPONENT	BP	CASTROL	DUCKHAMS	ESSO	MOBIL	PETROFINA	REGENT	SHELL
††ENGINE CARB. DASHPOTS AND OIL CAN	Super Visco-static 20-50	Castrol GTX	Duckhams Q20-50	Esso Uniflo	Mobiloil Super 10W/50 or Mobiloil Special 20W/50	Fina Super Grade Motor Oil SAE 20W/50	Havoline Motor Oil 20W-50	Shell Super Multigrade
GEARBOX OVERDRIVE REAR AXLE LOWER STEERING SWIVELS	BP Gear Oil SAE 90 EP	Castrol Hypoy	Duckhams Hypoid 90	Esso Gear Oil GX 90/140	Mobilube HD 90	Fina Pontonic XP 90-140	Multigear Lubricant EP 90	Shell Spirax 90 EP
FRONT & REAR HUBS BRAKE CABLES GREASE GUN	BP Energrease L2	Castrol LM Grease	Duckhams LB 10	Esso Multi-purpose Grease H	Mobilgrease MP	Fina Marson HTL 2	Marfak All purpose	Shell Retinax A

RECOMMENDED LUBRICANTS – OVERSEAS

(The products recommended are not listed in order of preference)

COMPONENT	Air temp. °C	Air temp. °F	API Designation	BP	CASTROL	DUCKHAMS	ESSO	MOBIL	PETROFINA	SHELL	TEXACO
†† ENGINE	over 30	over 80	SD or SE	† BP Super Visco-Static	Castrol GTX Castrol Super 20W/50	Q20/50; Q10-50	Esso Extra Motor Oil 20W/50; Uniflo	Mobiloil Super 10W/50 Mobiloil Special 20W/50	Fina Supergrade Motor Oil 20W/50	†	Havoline 20W/50
CARB. DASHPOTS	30 to 0	80 to 30	SD or SE								
AND OIL CAN	0 to −20	30 to −4	SD or SE		Castrolite or Castrol GTZ	Q 10-40	Esso Extra Motor Oil 10W/30	Mobiloil Super 10W/50	Fina Supergrade Motor Oil 10W/40	Shell Super Motor Oil	Havoline 10W/30
	below −20	below −4	SD or SE		Castrol 5W/20	Q5-30	Esso Extra Motor Oil 5W/20	Mobiloil 5W/20	Fina Supergrade 5W/30		Havoline 5W/20
GEARBOX OVERDRIVE AND REAR AXLE	over 0	over 30	GL4	BP Gear Oil SAE 90 EP	Castrol Hypoy	Duckhams Hypoid 90	Esso Gear Oil GX 90	Mobilube HD 90	Fina PONTONIC MP SAE 90	Shell Spriax 90 EP	Multigear Lubricant EP 90
LOWER STEERING SWIVELS	below 0	below 30	GL4	BP Gear Oil SAE 80 EP	Castrol Hypoy 80	Duckhams Hypoid 80	Esso Gear Oil GX 80	Mobilube HD 80	Fina PONTONIC MP SAE 80	Shell Spirax 80 EP	Multigear Lubricant EP 80
FRONT AND REAR HUBS BRAKE CABLES SUSPENSION BALL JOINTS (SWEDISH MARKET ONLY) GREASE GUN				BP Energrease L2	Castrol LM Grease	Duckhams LB 10	Esso Multi-purpose Grease H	Mobilgrease MP	Fina Marson HTL 2	Shell Retinax A	Marfax All-purpose

† OILS MARKED THUS ARE AVAILABLE IN MULTIGRADE FORMS WITH VISCOSITY CHARACTERISTICS APPROPRIATE TO THE AMBIENT TEMPERATURE RANGE IN INDIVIDUAL MARKETS.

†† WHERE CIRCUIT RACING OR OTHER SEVERE COMPETITIVE EVENTS ARE CONTEMPLATED IT IS ADVISABLE, IN VIEW OF THE INCREASED OIL TEMPERATURE ENCOUNTERED, TO USE OILS OF HIGH VISCOSITY.

RECOMMENDED LUBRICANTS AND ANTIFREEZE SOLUTIONS – U.S.A. MARKET

COMPONENT	SERVICE CLASSIFICATION	AMBIENT TEMPERATURE RANGE	SAE VISCOSITY CLASSIFICATION
ENGINE	API – SE	Above 14° (−10°C)	10W/50 20W/50 10W/40 20W/40
		−5°F to 50°F (−20°C to +10°C)	10W/50 10W/40 10W/30
		Below 14°F (−10°C)	5W/30 5W/20
GEARBOX, OVERDRIVE AND FINAL DRIVE	API – GL4	Above 32°F (0°C)	Hypoid 90
		Below 32°F (0°C)	Hypoid 80
STEERING RACK, HUBS & CHASSIS GREASE POINTS	NLGI 2 multipurpose grease		
BRAKE & CLUTCH FLUID	DOT 3 Type brake fluid (FMVSS No. 116) also meeting SAE J 1703		
ANTIFREEZE	Permanent type ethylene glycol base with suitable inhibitor for mixed metal systems		
WINDSHIELD WASHER	Windshield Washer Antifreeze Fluid (Proprietary Brands)		

RECOMMENDED LUBRICANTS, FUELS AND FLUID-CAPACITIES

RECOMMENDED HYDRAULIC FLUIDS

Clutch and Brake Reservoirs: Castrol Girling Brake and Clutch Fluid – Crimson or Unipart 550 Brake Fluid. Where these proprietary brands are not available, other fluids which meet the S.A.E. J.1703 specification may be used.

RECOMMENDED FUEL

The Triumph Spitfire engine is designed to operate on fuel having a minimum octane rating of 97 (High compression engines) OR 91 (Lower compression engines): this is equivalent to the British 4 star and 2 star ratings respectively. Where such fuels are not available and it is necessary to use fuels of lower or unknown rating, the ignition timing must be retarded from the specified setting, just sufficiently to prevent audible detonation (pinking) under all operating conditions, otherwise damage to the engine may occur.

IMPORTANT: When cars for the U.S.A. market enter the "United States" the ignition timing must be set to suit the use of the recommended grade of fuel AND TO COMPLY WITH REGULATIONS ON EMISSIONS FROM THE CRANKCASE AND EXHAUST.

ANTI-FREEZE SOLUTIONS

Only solutions which meet B.S.I. 3151 or 3152 specifications may be used.

		25%	30%	35%	50%
SPECIFIC GRAVITY OF COOLANT AT 15·5°C (60°F)		1·039	1·048	1·054	1·076
ANTI-FREEZE QUANTITY (Cooling system with heater)	PINTS IMP.	2·0	2·4	2·8	4·0
	PINTS U.S.A.	2·4	2·9	3·4	4·8
	LITRES	1·1	1·4	1·6	2·3
DEGREE OF PROTECTION					
Complete Car may be driven away immediately from cold		−12°C 10°F	−16°C 3°F	−20°C −4°F	−36°C −33°F
Safe Limit Coolant in mushy state. Engine may be started and driver away after short warm-up period		−18°C 0°F	−22°C −8°F	−28°C −18°F	−41°C −42°F
Lower Protection Prevents frost damage to cylinder head, block and radiator. Thaw out before starting engine.		−26°C −15°F	−32°C −26°F	−37°C −35°F	−47°C −53°F

CAPACITIES

Fuel tank . . . . pre 1972 condition   8¼ gal. (9·9 U.S. gal.) (37·6 litres)
. . . . ** 1974/1973/1972 condition **   7¼ gal. (8·7 U.S. gal.) (33·0 litres)
Engine sump and oil filter . . . .   8 pints (9·6 U.S. pints) (4·5 litres)
Engine sump (drain and refill) . . . . . .   7 pints (8·4 U.S. pints) (4·0 litres)
Gearbox (from dry) . . . .   1½ pints (1·8 U.S. pints) (0·85 litres)
Gearbox and overdrive (from dry) . . . . **'D' Type   2½ pints (2·8 U.S. pints) (2·4 litres)
. . . . 'J' Type   2·7 pints (3·25 U.S. pints) (1·5 litres)**
Rear axle (from dry) . . . .   1 pint (1·2 U.S. pints) (0·57 litres)
Cooling system (including heater) . . . . .   8 pints (9·6 U.S. pints) (4·5 litres)
Heater . . . .   1 pint (1·2 U.S. pints) (0·57 litres)

Triumph Spitfire Mk IV Manual. Part No. 545234

09.2

MAINTENANCE

MAINTENANCE OPERATIONS

Lubrication Chart	10.00.01
Pre-Delivery Inspection	10.10.01
Routine Maintenance Operation	
1,000 miles (1600 km) Free Service	10.10.03
3,000 miles (5000 km) Service	10.10.06
6,000 miles (10000 km) Service	10.10.12
12,000 miles (20000 km) Service	10.10.24
Summary Chart	10.00.02

10.1

MAINTENANCE

LUBRICATION CHART

Every 3,000 miles (5,000 km)
1. Check/top up cooling system level.
2. Check/top up engine oil level.
6. Check/top up brake and clutch fluid reservoirs.

Every 6,000 miles (10,000 km)
1. Check/top up cooling system level.
2. Change engine oil.
3. Lubricate steering rack and pinion.
4. Using OIL lubricate lower steering swivels. Swedish market only: Grease suspension/steering balls joints.
5. Check/top up carburetter piston damper(s) and lubricate throttle linkage.
6. Check/top up brake and clutch fluid reservoirs.
7. Lubricate accelerator, brake and clutch pedal pivots.
8. Check/top up gearbox oil level.
9. Check/top up rear axle oil level.
11. Lubricate handbrake linkage and cable.
12. Lubricate all door, bonnet and boot locks and hinges.
13. Lubricate battery terminals (petroleum jelly).
14. Lubricate distributor.

Every 12,000 miles (20,000 km)
1. Check/top up cooling system level.
2. Change engine oil.
3. Lubricate steering rack and pinion.
4. Using OIL lubricate lower steering swivels. Swedish market only: Grease suspension/steering ball joints.
5. Check/top up carburetter piston damper(s) and lubricate throttle linkage.
6. Check/top up brake and clutch fluid reservoirs.
7. Lubricate accelerator, brake and clutch pedal pivots.
8. Check/top up gearbox oil level.
9. Check/top up rear axle oil level.
10. Lubricate rear hubs.
11. Lubricate handbrake linkage and cable.
12. Lubricate all door, bonnet and boot locks and hinges.
13. Lubricate battery terminals (petroleum jelly).
14. Lubricate distributor.
15. Renew oil filter element.

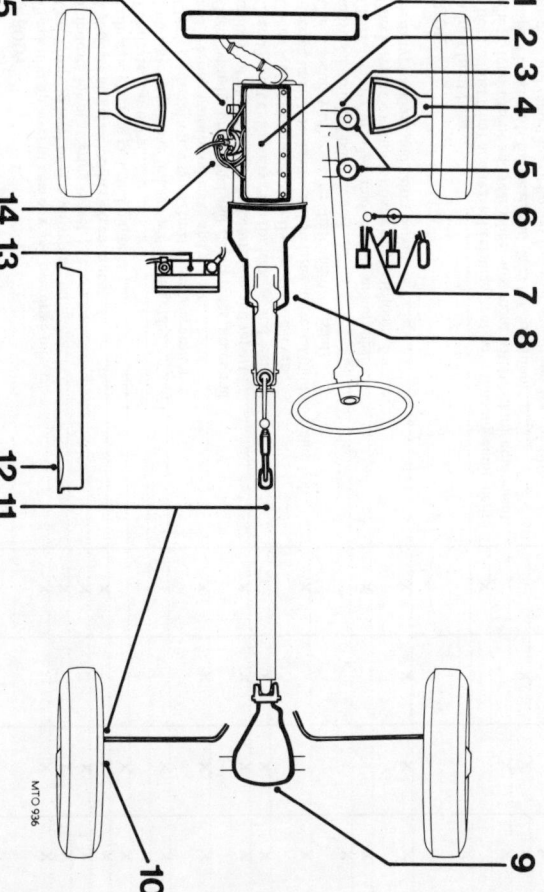

10.00.01

MAINTENANCE

SUMMARY CHART

The Summary Chart below lists general recommendations for Service Operations and Intervals. Overseas Service Engineers are advised to consult the "Passport to Service" booklet supplied with the car for amendments to these recommendations that may be specially applicable to their local operating conditions OR that may be obligatory to meet Regulations for a specific Country.

Operation Description	10.10.03 1 1.6	10.10.06 3 5	10.10.12 6 10	10.10.24 12 20
Operation Number **Interval in miles × 1,000** **Interval in Kilometres × 1,000**				
ENGINE COMPARTMENT				
1. Check/top up engine oil level (E)	X	X	X	X
2. Check/top up cooling system (E)	X	X	X	X
3. Check/top up brake fluid reservoir	X	X	X	X
4. Check/top up clutch fluid reservoir	X	X	X	X
5. Check/top up windscreen washer fluid reservoir	X	X	X	X
6. Check/top up battery	X	X	X	X
7. Check/top up carburetter piston(s) damper(s) (E)	X	X	X	X
8. Drain engine oil and refill (E)		X	X	X
9. Renew oil filter element (E)		X	X	X
10. Clean fuel pump sediment bowl		X	X	X
11. Lubricate distributor and check automatic advance (E)		X	X	X
12. Check/adjust/report condition of distributor points (E)		X	X	X
13. Distributor points — renew (E)			X	X
14. Check/adjust ignition timing using electronic equipment (E)		X	X	X
15. Check/report ignition wiring for fraying, chafing and deterioration (E)		X	X	X
16. Condenser and coil check for breakdown on oscilascope tune (E)		X	X	X
17. Clean/adjust sparking plugs (E)		X	X	X
18. Renew sparking plugs (E)			X	X
19. Check/adjust torque of cylinder head nuts/bolts (E)		X	X	X
20. Check/report cylinder compression (E)			X	X
21. Check/adjust valve rocker clearances (E)		X	X	X
22. Clean engine oil filler cap (E)		X	X	X
23. Clean carburetter air cleaner elements (E)		X	X	X
24. Renew carburetter air cleaner elements (E)			X	X
25. Check/adjust/report condition of all driving belts (E)		X	X	X
26. Check security of starter motor and alternator retaining bolts			X	X
27. Check security of engine mountings			X	X
28. Check/adjust carburetter settings (E)		X	X	X
29. Carburetter — overhaul — at 24,000 miles (E)				X
30. Fuel filter — change (E)			X	X
31. Fuel system — check for leaks (E)		X	X	X
32. Lubricate accelerator linkage/pedal fulcrum and check operation		X	X	X
33. Check battery condition: clean and grease connections		X	X	X
34. Check/report for oil/fuel/fluid leaks (general) (E)		X	X	X
35. Check/report leaks from cooling and heater systems (E)		X	X	X
36. Evapourative and crankcase ventilations systems — check hoses and restrictors for blockage, security and deterioration (E)			X	X
37. Carbon cannister — renew filter (E)				X
38. Carbon cannister — renew 48,000 miles (E)				X

Operation Description	10.10.03 1 1.6	10.10.06 3 5	10.10.12 6 10	10.10.24 12 20
Operation Number **Interval in miles × 1,000** **Interval in kilometers × 1,000**				
UNDERBODY				
39. Check/top up level of gearbox and overdrive oil		X	X	X
40. Check/top up level of final drive unit oil		X	X	X
41. Lubricate lower steering swivel		X	X	X
42. Lubricate all grease points except hubs		X	X	X
43. Lubricate steering rack and pinion		X	X	X
44. Lubricate rear hubs			X	X
45. Lubricate handbrake linkage and cable guides		X	X	X
46. Check transmission, engine, final drive, suspension and steering unit for oil leaks and report		X	X	X
47. Check visually brake, fuel and clutch pipes, hoses and unions for chafing, leaks and corrosion and report		X	X	X
48. Check/report exhaust system for leakage and security (E)		X	X	X
49. Check security of suspension fixings, tie-rod levers, steering unit attachments and steering universal joint coupling bolts			X	X
50. Check security of propeller shaft and drive shaft universal coupling bolts			X	X
51. Check security of sub-frame or body mountings			X	X
52. Check/report condition of steering unit/joints for security, backlash and gaiter condition			X	X
EXTERIOR				
53. Adjust front hubs		X	X	X
54. Check/adjust front and rear wheel alignment with tracking equipment	X			
55. Check/report front and rear wheel alignment with tracking equipment			X	X
56. Inspect brake pads for wear, and discs for condition		X	X	X
57. Inspect and report brake linings for wear and drums for condition			X	X
58. Check security of road wheel fastenings		X	X	X
59. *Check that tyres are in accordance with manufacturers specification		X	X	X
60. *Check visually and report depth of tread, cuts in tyre fabric, exposure of ply or cord structure, lumps or bulges		X	X	X
61. Check/adjust tyre pressures (including spare wheel)		X	X	X
62. Check/adjust/report headlamp alignment		X	X	X
63. Check, if necessary replace windscreen wiper blades		X	X	X
64. Fuel tank filler cap — check seal for security (E)		X	X	X
INTERIOR				
65. Check brake pedal travel and hand brake operation adjust if necessary		X	X	X
66. Check/report brake pedal travel and handbrake operation		X	X	X
67. Check operation of window controls, locks and bonnet release		X	X	X
68. Check function of all electrical systems and windscreen washer		X	X	X
69. Lubricate clutch and brake pedal pivots		X	X	X
70. Lubricate all locks, door hinges, strikers and bonnet release		X	X	X
71. Check/report condition and security of seats and seat belts		X	X	X
72. Check/report rear view mirrors for looseness, cracks and crazing		X	X	X
ROAD TEST				
73. Road/roller test and report additional work required		X	X	X
74. Ensure cleanliness of controls, door handles, steering wheels etc		X	X	X

*Important — If the tyres do not conform with legal requirements report to the owner.

Items marked (E) are particularly relevant to the emmission and evaporative control systems and must receive attention at the recommended intervals to keep these systems in good order.

MAINTENANCE

The maintenance summary list on pages 10.00.02 and 10.00.03 gives details of mile and kilometer intervals for the following operations. The figure in parenthesis to the left of each heading refers to the item number on the summary list.

(1) Check/top up engine oil level

NOTE: Allow time for oil to drain back into sump after running engine. Stand vehicle on level ground.

1. Withdraw dipstick, wipe it clean and replace in position.
2. Withdraw dipstick again and note oil level.
3. Wipe dipstick clean and replace in position. If topping up is necessary:—
4. Remove oil filler cap.
5. Add recommended grade of oil, via filler cap, to bring level just below high mark on dipstick. **DO NOT OVERFILL.**
6. Replace filler cap.
7. Allow time for added oil to drain into sump, then check final oil level using the procedure in 1 to 3 above.

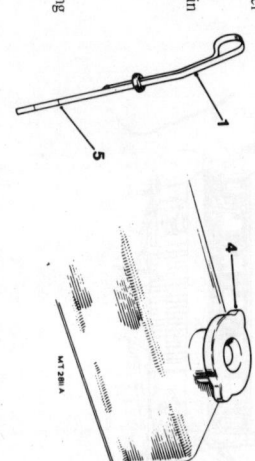

(3) Check/top up brake fluid reservoir

1. Wipe clean the reservoir cap and surrounding area.
2. Remove the reservoir cap.
3. Check fluid level against mark on side of reservoir.
4. If necessary, add fluid to bring level up to mark on side of reservoir.

WARNING: Use only new fluid of the correct specification. Do NOT use fluid of unknown origin, or fluid that has been exposed to the atmosphere, or fluid that has been discharged during bleeding operations.

5. Replace reservoir cap.
6. Remove any spilled fluid with a clean cloth.

CAUTION: Paintwork can be damaged by direct contact with brake fluid.

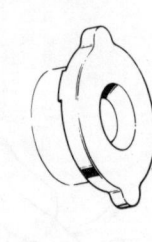

(2) Check/top up cooling system

WARNING: Do NOT remove cooling system filler caps or plugs when engine is hot.

1. Remove radiator expansion tank cap.
2. If necessary, top up expansion tank with soft water to maintain level at approximately half full.
3. Replace cap.

If the expansion tank is empty:—
4. Remove the cooling system filler cap.
5. Add soft water, via filler cap, until the system is full.
6. Replace filler cap.
7. Half fill expansion tank with soft water using the procedure in 1 to 3 above.
8. Run the engine until normal operating temperature is reached, allow engine to cool and re-check cooling system level.

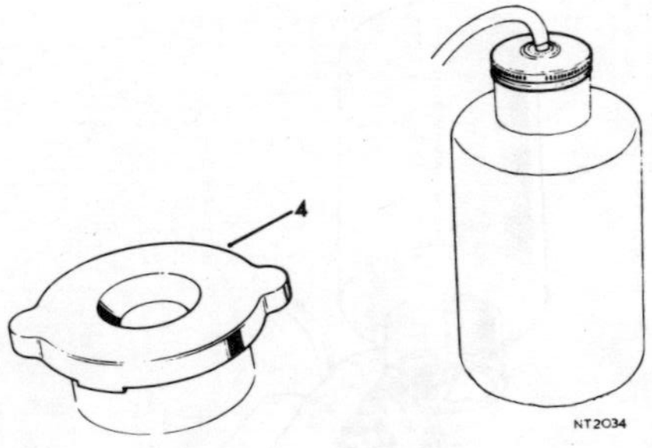

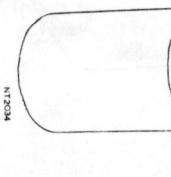

(4) Check/top up clutch fluid reservoir

1. Wipe clean the reservoir cap and surrounding area.
2. Remove the reservoir cap.
3. Check fluid level against mark on side of reservoir.
4. If necessary, add fluid to bring level up to mark on side of reservoir.

WARNING: Use only new fluid of the correct specification. Do NOT use fluid of unknown origin, or fluid that has been exposed to the atmosphere, or fluid that has been discharged during bleeding operations.

5. Replace reservoir cap.
6. Remove any spilled fluid with a clean cloth.

CAUTION: Paintwork can be damaged by direct contact with clutch fluid.

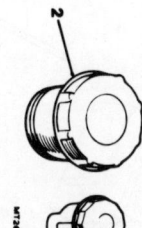

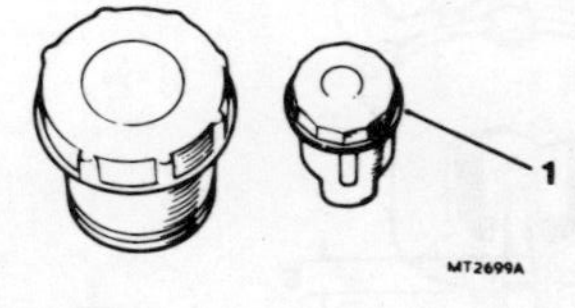

MAINTENANCE

(5) Check/top up windscreen washer fluid level

1. Check fluid level in translucent reservoir.

   If topping up is necessary:-
2. Wipe clean the reservoir cap and surrounding area.
3. Remove the reservoir cap.
4. Add soft water to bring level up to approximately 1 in (25·4 mm) from top of reservoir.
5. Replace reservoir cap.

CAUTION: As a precaution against freezing conditions, fill the reservoir with a mixture of one part methylated spirits and two parts water.
Do NOT use glycol anti-freeze solutions in the washer reservoir, as these may discolour paintwork and damage wiper blades and sealing rubbers.

(6) Check/top up battery

NOTE: Alternative procedures are given for each of the two battery types that may be fitted.

1. Lift and tilt battery cover.
2. Check electrolyte level, which if correct should just cover the seperators.

   If topping up is necessary:-
3. Add DISTILLED WATER until the filler tubes are full and the trough is just covered.
4. Replace battery cover.

Alternatively:

1. Remove battery filler plugs.
2. Check electrolyte level, which if correct should just cover the seperators.

   If topping us is necessary:-
3. Add DISTILLED WATER until the seperators are just covered. DO NOT OVERFILL.
4. Replace filler plugs.

CAUTION: Paintwork can be damaged by direct contact with the base of filler plugs.

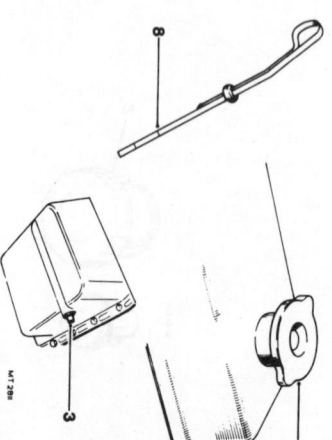

MAINTENANCE

(7) Check/top up carburetter piston dampers

Procedure for S.U. Carburetters

1. Unscrew hexagon plug from top of carburetter.
2. Withdraw plug and damper assembly from carburetter.
3. Check dashpot oil level, which if correct will be ½ in (13 mm) above the top of the hollow piston rod.
4. If necessary, add a recommended engine oil, using an oil can, until the level is correct.
5. Replace plug and damper assembly.
6. Screw hexagon plug firmly in position.

Procedure for Stromberg Carburetters

1. Unscrew hexagon plug from top of carburetter.
2. Withdraw plug and damper assembly from carburetter.
3. Replace plug and damper assembly to check oil level, which if correct will offer resistance to the assembly when the bottom of the plug threads are ¼ in (6 mm) above the rim of the dashpot.
4. If necessary, again withdraw plug and damper assembly and add a recommended engine oil, using an oil can, until the oil level is correct.
5. Replace plug and damper assembly.
6. Screw hexagon plug firmly in position.

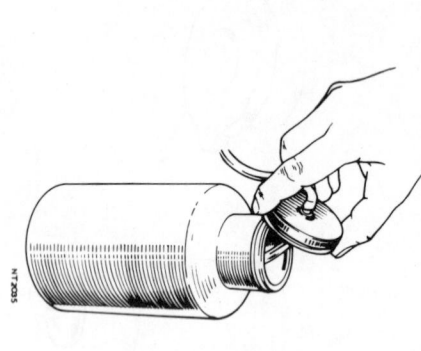

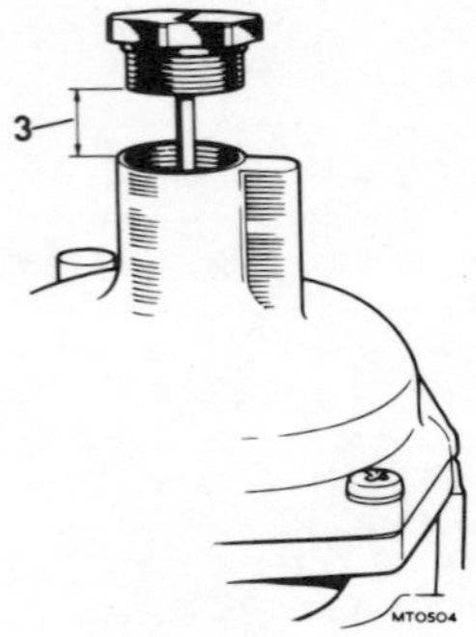

(8) Drain engine oil and refill

NOTE: This operation is best carried out when the engine is warm and with the vehicle standing level on a ramp or over a pit.

1. Wipe clean the engine drain plug and surrounding area.
2. Place a suitable receptical under the drain plug.
3. Unscrew the drain plug slowly until oil begins to escape.
4. When the rate of oil flow lessens, remove drain plug from sump and allow oil to drain completely.
5. Wipe clean the drain plug and replace it in sump.
6. Tighten drain plug to 20 to 25 lbf ft. (2·8 to 3·5 kgf m).
7. Remove oil filler cap.
8. Add a recommended engine oil, via filler cap, to bring level just below high mark on dipstick. **DO NOT OVERFILL.**
9. Replace oil filler cap.
10. Allow time for added oil to drain into sump, then check final oil level on dipstick.

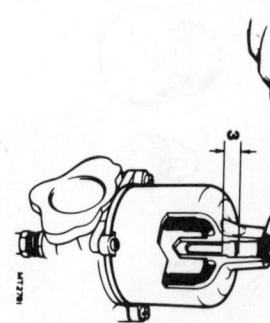

MAINTENANCE

(9) Renew oil filter element
See 12.60.01 and 12.60.08.

(10) Clean fuel pump sediment bowl
See 19.45.05

(11) Lubricate distributor and check automatic advance
Lubricate distributor — See 86.35.18

Check automatic advance
1. Fit a strobe Timing Light in accordance with the Timing Light manufacturers instructions.
2. Disconnect vacuum pipe between distributor and induction side of engine.
3. Start engine.

Check centrifugal advance
4. Using a second operator to vary engine speed, check apparent movement of timing marks under strobe light.
5. Reconnect vacuum pipe.

Check vacuum advance
6. Repeat the procedure in 4 above, comparing engine timing with and without vacuum pipe connected.
7. Stop engine.

NOTE: If more accurate results are required electronic tuning equipment may be used in conjuction with the data on page 86.35.00. This is extra to normal service requirements.

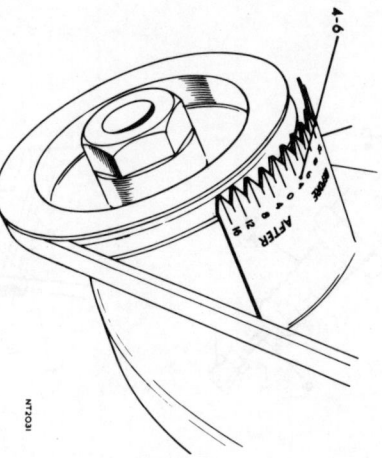

(12) Check/adjust/report condition of distributor points
See 86.35.14.

(13) Renew distributor points
See 86.35.13

(14) Check/adjust ignition timing
See 86.35.16

(15) Check/report ignition wiring for fraying, chaffing and deterioation

Low tension circuit.
1. Check exposed wiring between coil and ignition switch.
2. Check ignition coil connections.
3. Check wiring between coil and distributor.
4. Check distributor external connections.
5. Remove distributor cap and check internal wiring.
6. Check internal distributor connections.
7. Replace distributor cap.

High tension circuit.
8. Check lead between coil and distributor.
9. For each sparking plug in turn:—
   Check lead between plug and distributor.
10. Check high tension lead connections.
11. Report wiring condition.

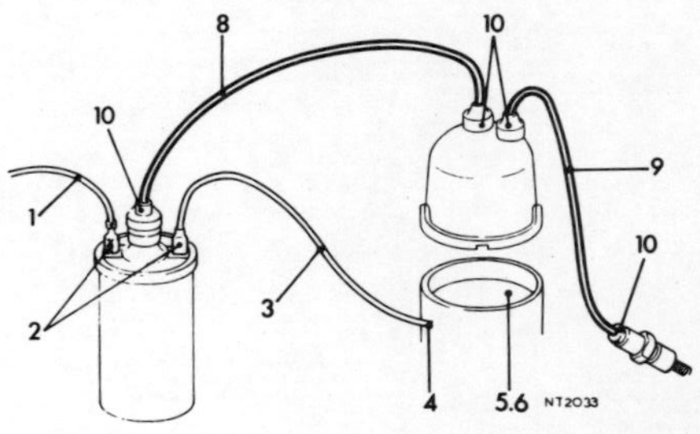

(16) Check condensor and coil for breakdown on oscilascope

Using proprietory electronic testing equipment
1. Check distributor condensor performance.
2. Check ignition coil performance.

MAINTENANCE

(17) Clean/adjust sparking plugs

For each sparking plug in turn

1. Remove ignition high tension lead from plug.
2. Unscrew plug from engine using a special plug spanner or a box type spanner.
3. Wipe clean ceramic body of plug.
4. Visually check plug body for cracks, and renew plug if cracks are present.
5. Unscrew end terminal cap from plug.
6. Clean plug terminal threads with a wire brush.
7. Clean cap threads using a low pressure air line.
8. Screw end terminal cap firmly into position on plug.
9. Clean electrode area and plug threads with a wire brush or sand blasting machine.
10. Visually check electrode surfaces for damage, and renew plug if damage is present.
11. Check electrode gap, which if correct will just allow a 0·025 in (0·64 mm) feeler gauge to slide slowly between the electrodes under light pressure.

If adjustment is necessary.

12. (a) Using a suitable tool, carefully move the side electrode.
    (b) Recheck the gap and repeat this procedure until the gap is correct.
13. Check sealing washer for cracks and distortion, and renew washer if necessary.
14. Refit sparking plug to engine.
15. Tighten plug to 14 to 20 lbf ft (1·9 to 2·8 kgf m).
16. Refit high tension lead to plug.

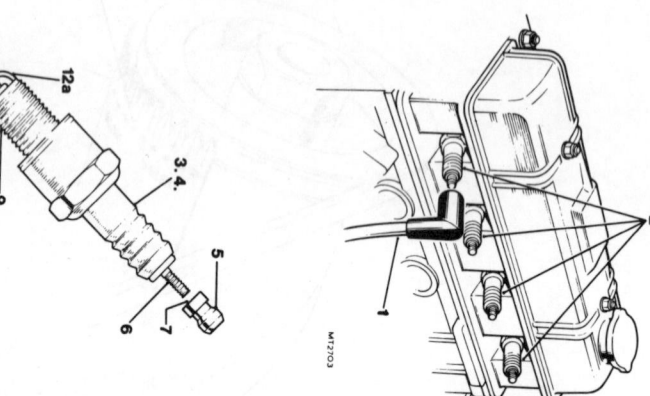

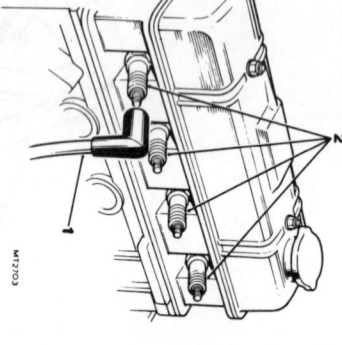

10.00.10

Triumph Spitfire Mk IV Manual. Part No. 545254.

MAINTENANCE

(18) Renew sparking plugs

For each sparking plug in turn

1. Remove ignition high tension lead from plug.
2. Unscrew plug from engine using a special plug spanner or a box type spanner.
3. Discard plug.
4. Visually check new plug for damage to body and electrodes, discard plug if damage is present.
5. Check electrode gap on new plug, which if correct will just allow a 0·025 in (0·64 mm) feeler gauge to slide slowly between the electrodes under light pressure.

If adjustment is necessary.

6. (a) Using a suitable tool, carefully move the side electrode.
   (b) Recheck the gap and repeat this procedure until the gap is correct.
7. Check sealing washer for cracks and distortion, and renew washer if necessary.
8. Fit new sparking plug to engine.
9. Tighten plug to 14 to 20 lbf ft (1·9 to 2·8 kgf m).
10. Refit high tension lead to plug.

(19) Check/adjust torque of cylinder head nuts/bolts

1. Remove rocker cover — See 12.29.42.
2. Using the sequence shown, tighten cylinder head nuts to 38 to 46 lbf ft (5·2 to 6·4 kgf m).
3. Check/adjust valve rocker clearances — See 12.29.48
4. Check rocker cover gasket for damage, and renew if necessary.
5. Refit rocker cover — See 12.29.42.
6. With gears in neutral, handbrake on, start engine and check for leaks from rocker cover gasket.

(20) Check/report cylinder compression

See 12.25.01

(21) Check/adjust valve rocker clearances

See 12.29.48

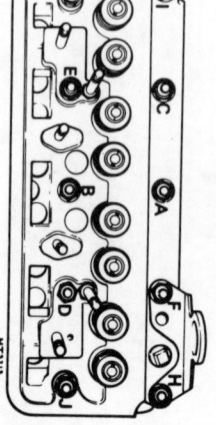

10.00.11

Triumph Spitfire Mk IV Manual. Part No. 545254.

MAINTENANCE

(22) Clean engine oil filler cap

1. Remove filler cap.
2. Clean cap with clean petrol.
3. Allow to dry.
4. Refit filler cap.

(23) Clean carburettor air cleaner elements

See 19.10.08

(24) Renew carburettor air cleaner elements

See 19.10.08

(25) Check/adjust/report condition of driving belts

1. Check and adjust – See 26.20.01.
2. Report condition where belt is visably
   (a) worn or
   (b) damaged

(26) Check security of starter motor and alternator retaining bolts

1. Check security of starter motor retaining bolts, which if correct should be tightened to 26 to 34 lbf ft (3·6 to 4·7 kgf m).
2. Check security of alternator to adjusting link bolt, which if correct should be tightened to 15 to 20 lbf ft (2·1 to 2·8 kgf m).
3. Check security of alternator mounting bracket bolt, which if correct should be tightened to 16 to 22 lbf ft (2·2 to 3·0 kgf m).

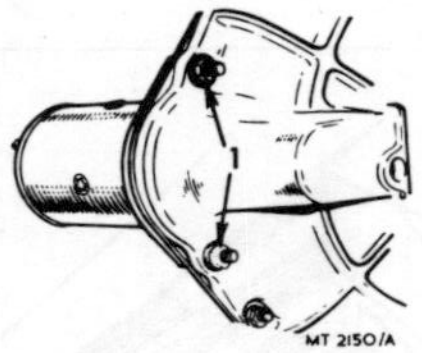

(27) Check security of engine mountings

1. Check security of front engine mountings, which if correct should be tightened to 24 to 32 lbf ft (3·3 to 4·4 kgf m).
2. Check security of rear engine mountings, which if correct should be tightened to 15 to 20 lbf ft (2·1 to 2·8 kgf m).

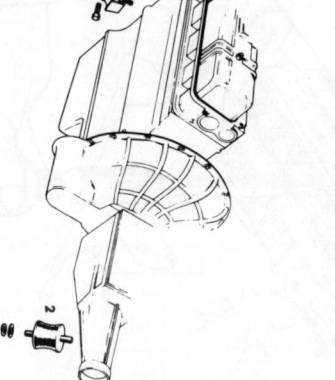

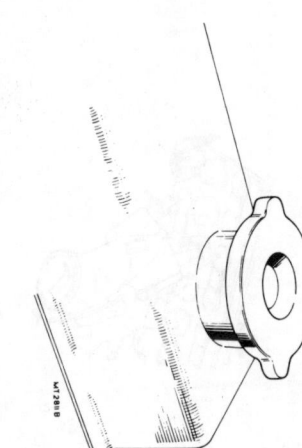

(28) Check/adjust carburettor settings

See 19.15.02

(29) Overhaul carburetter

See 19.15.18

(30) Change fuel filter

See 19.25.01

(31) Check fuel system for leaks

1. Check for leaks from fuel system connections.
2. Check fuel pipes for fractures and damage.
3. Check for leaks from fuel tank(s), pump and carburetter(s).
   On vehicles fitted with an evaporative control system, additional checks are given under 17.15.01.

(32) Lubricate accelerator linkage/pedal fulcrum and check operation

1. Lubricate accelerator linkage on carburetter(s), using an oil can.
2. Wipe away surplus oil from linkage.
3. Check for roughness in linkage operation.
4. Lubricate accelerator pedal fulcrum, using an oil can.
5. Wipe away surplus oil from pedal fulcrum.

CAUTION: Surplus oil on the pedal fulcrum can cause staining of the carpet.

6. Check carburetter throttle response to initial movement of the accelerator pedal.

   If adjustment is necessary – see 19.20.05

7. Check carburetter throttle position with accelerator pedal fully depressed.

   If adjustment is necessary – See 19.20.05.

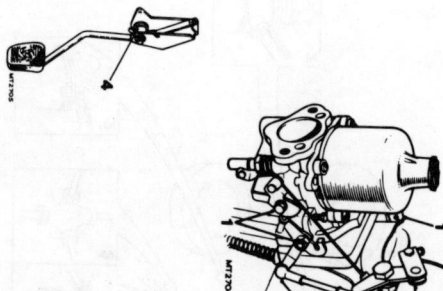
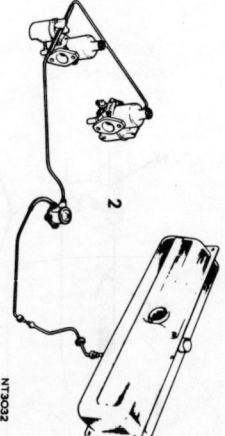

MAINTENANCE

(33) Check battery condition: clean and grease connections

With battery in location

1. Check battery and surrounding area for corrosion from battery chemicals.
2. Clean off any corrosion found.
3. Check visually for cracks in battery case.
4. Report any case cracks found.
5. Check security of terminal connections.
6. Coat terminals with petroleum jelly.

For each cell in turn:—

7. Check electrolyte specific gravity, using an hydrometer, which if correct will approximate to the tabled readings below.

NOTE *(a)* Do NOT check S.G. immediately after adding distilled water as a false reading may be obtained. *(b)* S.G. readings approximately equal for each cell indicate a battery in good condition. Conversely, if one or more cells show a reading lower than the others the battery is approaching the end of its usefull life.

Charge condition of cell — temperate climate			
Ambient Temperature °C	Specific Gravity of Electrolyte		
	Charged	Half-Charged	Discharged
5	1·287	1·207	1·117
15	1·280	1·200	1·110
25	1·273	1·193	1·103
35	1·266	1·186	1·096

Charge condition of cell — tropical climate			
15	1·250	1·180	1·100
25	1·243	1·173	1·093
35	1·236	1·166	1·086
52	1·224	1·154	1·074

8. Check voltage, using a heavy discharge tester, which if correct will give approximately equal readings for each cell.

CAUTION: This check should NOT be made on a battery in a low state of charge as shown by procedure 7 as damage to the battery can result.

NOTE *(a)* Before making this check on a battery that has just completed an operational journey, the headlamps should be switched on for 2 or 3 minutes to remove any surface charge. *(b)* Voltage readings approximately equal for each cell indicate a battery in good condition. Conversely, if one or more cells show a reading lower than the others, or a reading that falls during the test, the battery is approaching the end of its usefull life.

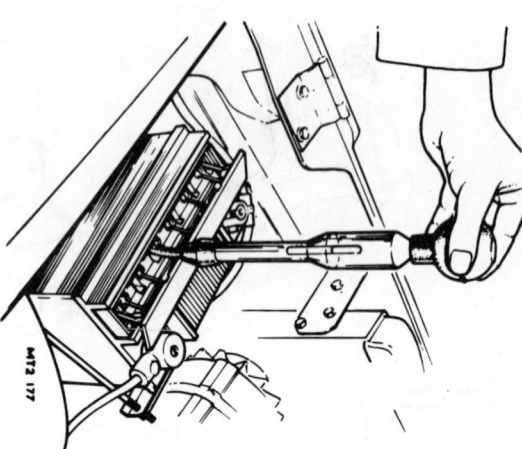
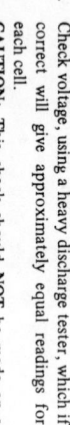

(34) Check/report oil/fuel/fluid leaks

1. Check for oil leaks from engine and transmission.
2. Check for fuel leaks from pump, carburetter, pipes, joints and unions.
3. Check for fluid leaks from brake master cylinder, pipes, joints and unions.
4. Check for fluid leaks from clutch master cylinder, pipes, joints and unions.
5. Report any leaks found.

(35) Check/report leaks from cooling and heater systems.

1. Check for leaks from engine and radiator drain taps/plugs (where fitted).
2. Check for leaks from water hose joints.
3. Check for leaks from water hoses through damage or porosity.
4. Check for leaks from water pump, thermostat housing, radiator and heater unit.
5. Report any leaks found.

(36) Evaporative and crankcase ventilation systems-check hoses and restrictors for blockage, security and deterioration.

See 17.15.01 and 17.15.36

(37) Carbon cannister — renew filter

See 17.15.07

(38) Carbon cannister — renew at 48,000 miles

See 17.15.13

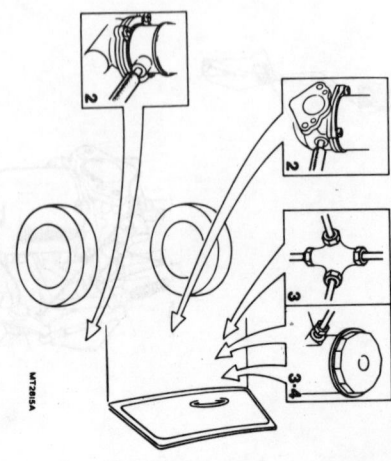
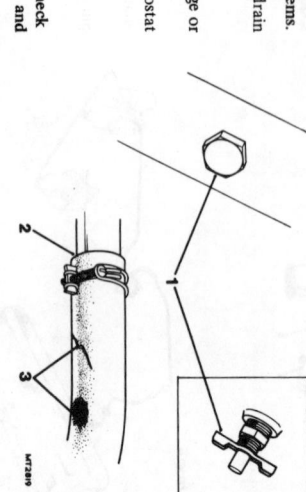

MAINTENANCE

NOTE: OPERATIONS 39 to 52 ARE BEST CARRIED OUT WITH THE CAR ON A RAMP OR OVER A PIT.

(39) Check/top up level of gearbox and overdrive oil

With vehicle standing level

1. Wipe clean gearbox filler plug and surrounding area.
2. Remove filler plug.
3. Add new oil of the recommended grade, via the filler plug hole, until the oil level reaches the bottom of the hole.
4. Allow surplus oil to drain.
5. Replace filler plug.
6. Tighten plug to 20 to 25 lbf ft (2·8 to 3·5 kgf m).
7. Wipe away surplus oil.

(40) Check/top up level of final drive unit oil

With vehicle standing level

1. Wipe clean final drive unit filler plug and surrounding area.
2. Remove filler plug.
3. Add new oil of the recommended grade, via the filler plug hole, until the oil level reaches the bottom of the hole.
4. Allow surplus oil to drain.
5. Replace filler plug.
6. Tighten plug to 20 to 25 lbf ft (2·8 to 3·5 kgf m).
7. Wipe away surplus oil.

(41) Lubricate lower steering swivel

WARNING: OIL must be used for the operation. Do NOT use grease.

1. Wipe clean the plug and surrounding area.
2. Remove the plug.
3. Fit a suitable grease nipple to the plug hole.
4. Using a grease gun, CHARGED WITH A RECOMMENDED OIL, lubricate the lower steering swivel, via the grease nipple, until oil exudes from the bearing.
5. Remove grease nipple.
6. Refit plug.
7. Wipe away surplus oil.

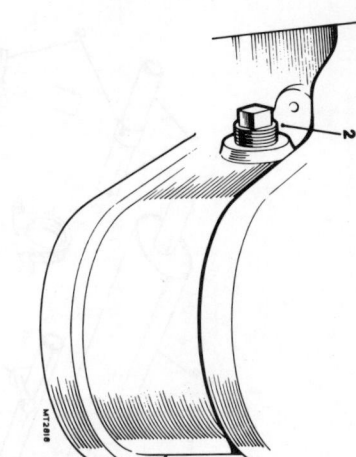

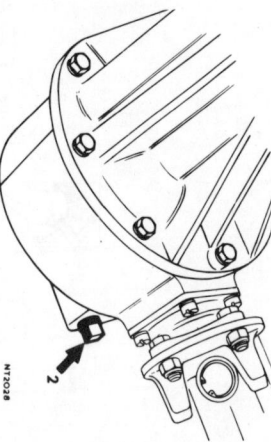

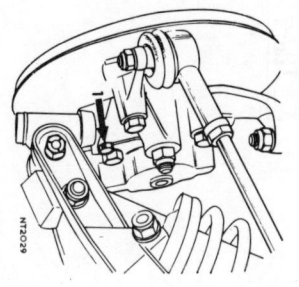

10.00.16 Triumph Spitfire Mk IV Manual. Part No. 545254.

MAINTENANCE

(42) Lubricate all grease points except hubs

Suspension/steering ball joints — Swedish Market Only.

1. Wipe clean the grease nipples and surrounding areas.
2. Apply a grease gun to nipples and grease exudes from joint.
3. Wipe away surplus grease.

(43) Lubricate steering rack and pinion

1. Wipe clean the plug and surrounding area.
2. Remove the plug.
3. Fit a suitable grease nipple to the plug hole.
4. Apply a grease gun to nipple and stroke for 5 times only.

CAUTION: Over greasing can cause damage to the rubber bellows.

5. Remove grease nipple.
6. Refit plug.
7. Wipe away surplus grease.

(44) Lubricate rear hubs

1. Wipe clean the plug and surrounding area.
2. Remove the plug.
3. Fit a suitable grease nipple to the plug hole.
4. Apply a grease gun to nipple and stroke until grease exudes from the bearing.
5. Remove grease nipple.
6. Refit plug.
7. Wipe away surplus grease.

(45) Lubricate handbrake linkage and cables

1. Lubricate handbrake pivot.
2. Smear grease around handbrake lever cable connections, working it well into the clevis.
3. Smear grease around brake drum cable connections, working it well into the clevis pin.
4. Grease exposed sections of inner cable to resist corrosion.

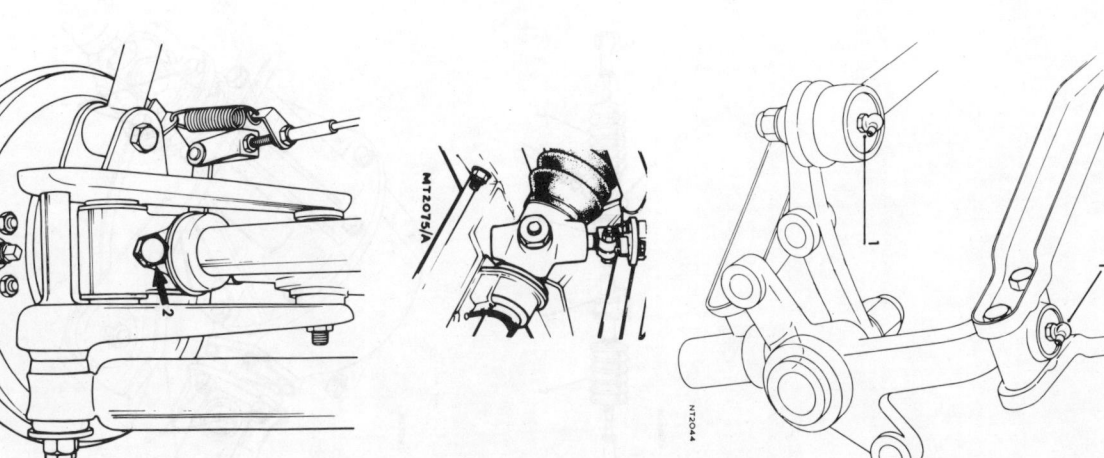

10.00.17 Triumph Spitfire Mk IV Manual. Part No. 545254.

MAINTENANCE

(46) Check engine, transmission, final drive, suspension and steering unit for oil leaks and report.

(47) Check visually brake, fuel and clutch pipes, hoses and unions for chaffing leaks and corrosion and report.

Check visually

1. Brake and clutch pipes,
2. Brake and clutch hoses,
3. Brake and clutch pipe and hose unions,
4. Fuel pipes,
5. Fuel pipe unions,

for chaffing leaks and corrosion.

6. Report any defects found.

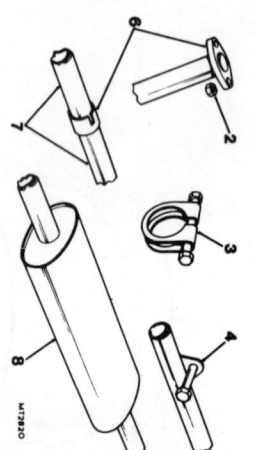

(48) Check/report exhaust system for leakage and security

1. Place car on ramp or over a pit.
2. Check security of exhaust pipe to manifold nuts, which if correct should be tightened to 12 to 14 lbf ft (1·7 to 1·9 kgf m).
3. Check security of exhaust pipe joint clips.
4. Check security of exhaust system mounting bolts.
5. Using a second operator, run engine at fast idle speed.
6. Check exhaust system joints for leaks.
7. Check exhaust pipes for leaks arising from damage or deterioration.
8. Check exhaust silencers for leaks arising from damage or deterioration.
9. Stop engine.
10. Report any defects found.

(49) Check security of suspension fixings, tie-rod levers, steering unit attachment and steering universal joint coupling bolts.

Check security of

1. Suspension fixings,
2. Tie-rod levers,
3. Steering unit attachment,
4. Steering universal joint coupling bolts.

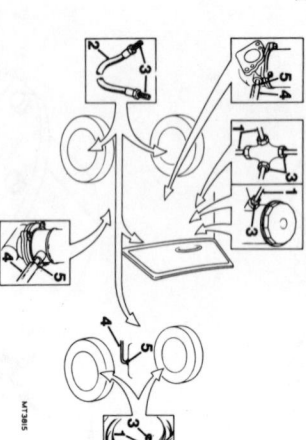

(50) Check security of propeller shaft and drive shaft universal coupling bolts

1. Check security of propeller shaft coupling bolts, which if correct should be tightened to 26 to 34 lbf ft (3·6 to 4·7 kgf m).
2. Check security of half shaft to final drive unit coupling bolts, which if correct should be tightened to 38 to 46 lbf ft (5·2 to 6·4 kgf m).

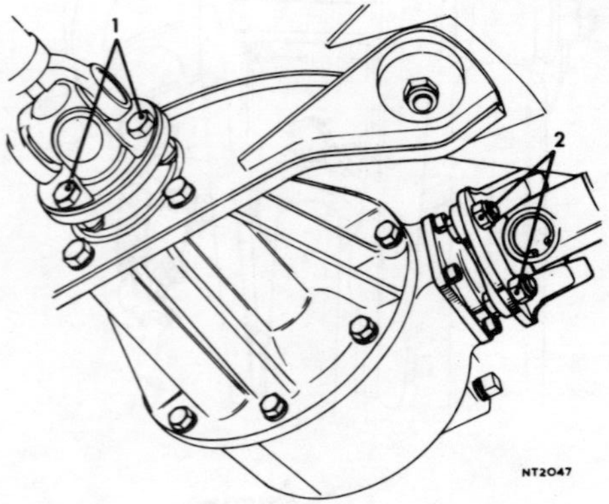

(51) Check security of sub-frame to body mountings

Using page 06 as a guide

1. Check security of sub-frame mounting bolts/nuts.

(52) Check/report condition of steering unit/joints for security, backlash and gaiter condition

1. Check security of steering unit mounting and steering joints, using page 06 as a guide.
2. Check steering for backlash.
3. Check condition of steering gaiters.
4. Report any defects found.

(53) Adjust front hubs

See 60.25.13

(54)(55) Check/adjust/report front and rear wheel alignment with tracking equipment.

Front wheel alignment — See 57.65.01
Rear wheel alignment — See 64.25.17

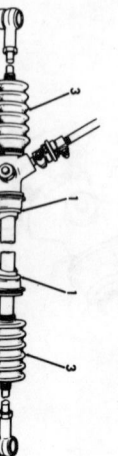

MAINTENANCE

(56) Inspect brake pads for wear and discs for condition

Front brakes

1. Jack up front of car and place safely on stands.
2. Remove front brake pads – See 70.40.02.

   CAUTION: Do NOT depress the brake pedal while pads are removed.

3. Report pad condition if the friction lining has been reduced to 0·125 inch (3 mm) or if there is not sufficient material to provide a thickness of 0·125 in (3 mm) at the completion of a further 3,000 miles (5,000 km) motoring.
4. Check brake discs for excessive scoring and report this if present.
5. Check brake discs for run out and report this if it exceeds 0·007 in (0·178 mm).
6. Refit front brake pads – See 70.40.02
7. Lower car off stands.

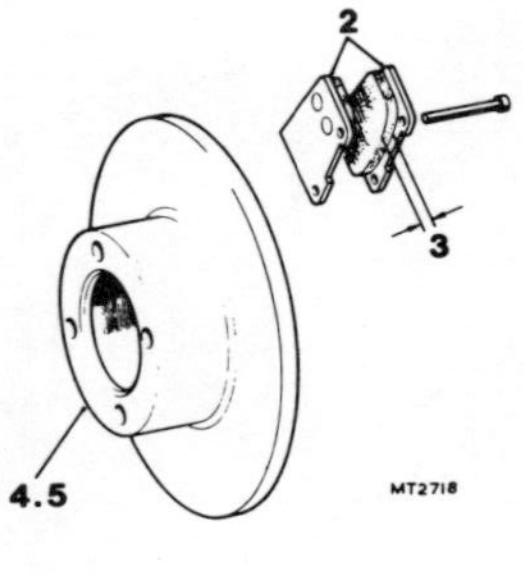

(57) Inspect and report brake linings for wear and drums for condition

1. Jack up car and place safely on stands.
2. Remove road wheel – See 74.20.01.
3. Remove brake drum – See 70.10.02 (front) or 70.10.03 (rear).
4. Check brake linings for wear and report if linings are excessively worn.
5. Check brake linings for damage and contamination by oil or grease and report if linings are damaged or contaminated.
6. Check brake drums for wear, scoring or other damage and report if drums are excessively worn, scored or damaged.
7. Remove dust, oil and grease from brake drum and backplate.
8. Refit brake drum – See 70.10.02 (front) or 70.10.03 (rear).
9. Refit road wheel – See 74.20.01.
10. Lower car off stands.

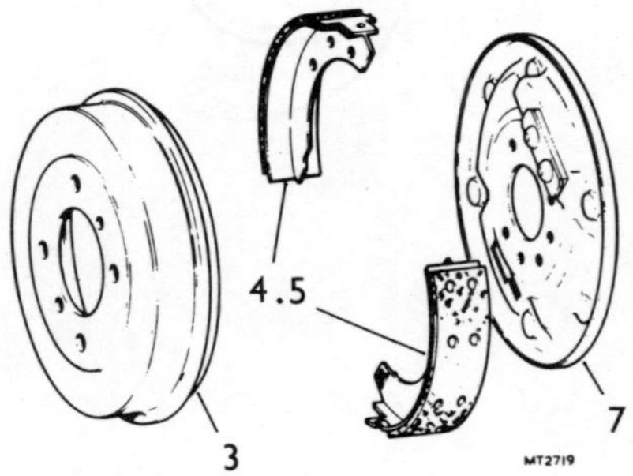

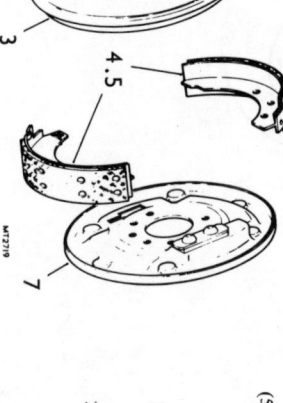

(58) Check security of road wheel fastenings.

Disc Wheels

For each wheel in turn:-

1. Check tightness of road wheel securing nuts, which if correct should be tightened to 38 to 48 lbf ft (5·2 to 6·6 kgf m).

Wire Wheels

For each wheel in turn

1. Visually check that adaptor is fitted on the correct side.
2. Remove road wheel – See 74.20.01
3. Check tightness of the adaptor securing nuts, which if correct should be tightened to 38 to 45 lbf ft (5·2 to 6·2 kgf m).
4. Replace road wheel – See 74.20.01 ensuring that the centre nut is correctly secured.

(59) Check that tyres are in accordance with manufacturers specification

For each road wheel and spare wheel:–

1. Check that tyres are in accordance with vehicle manufacturers recommendations for type and size and report any deviation.
2. Check for mixing of cross ply and radial ply tyres and report if both types are present on the vehicle (including spare wheel).

WARNING: It is illegal in the U.K. and highly dangerous to mix cross ply and radial ply tyres on the same axle or to fit radial ply tyres to the front wheels only.

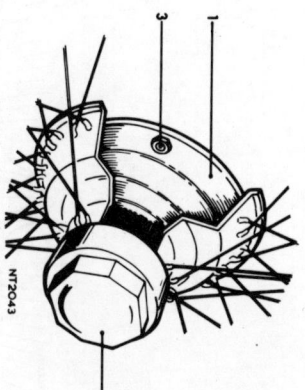

MAINTENANCE

(60) Check visually and report depth of tread, cuts in tyre fabric, exposure of ply or cord structure, lumps or bulges

For each road wheel and spare wheel:—

1. Check tread depth, which if correct should show 1mm (0·039 in) of tread (excluding wear bars) over three quarters of the bredth for the entire circumference of the tyre.

WARNING: It is illegal in the U.K. to use a car of this type fitted with tyres that have a tread depth below this minimum or tyres on which the tread is worn level with the wear indicator bars.

Check for

2. Cuts in the tyre fabric,
3. Exposure of ply or cord structure,
4. Lumps or bulges on tyre circumference,
5. Lumps, bulges or other damage on tyre walls.

WARNING: It is illegal in the U.K. to use a car fitted with tyres in a damaged condition.

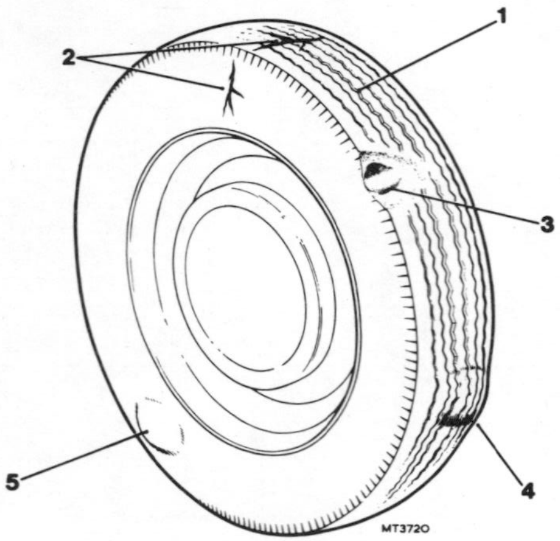

(61) Check/adjust tyre pressures (including spare wheel)

With all tyres at ambient temperature:-

1. Remove protective dust cap.
2. Using a tyre pressure gauge, tested for accuracy, check tyre rpessure.

Recommended tyre pressures: 21 lb/in² Front
26 lb/in² Rear

3. Adjust tyre pressure as necessary.
4. Replace dust cap or renew if missing.

WARNING: It is illegal in the U.K. to use a car with the tyres inflated to a pressure that is not suitable for the use to which the vehicle is put.

10.00.22

Triumph Spitfire Mk IV Manual. Part No. 545254.

MAINTENANCE

(62) Check/adjust/report headlamp alignment

See 86.40.18

(63) Check, if necessary replace windscreen wiper blades

1. Examine each wiper blade in turn for damage.
2. With wiper blades in position and windscreen wet, operate wiper motor.
3. Check wiper blade operation for smearing and adequate removal of dirt.
4. Stop wiper motor.
5. If the checks in procedures 1 and 3 are not satisfactory, replace one or both wiper blades as necessary — See 84.15.05.

(64) Fuel tank filler cap — check seal for security

See 17.15.01

(65) Check brake pedal travel and handbrake operation, adjust if necessary.

1. With handbrake in 'off' position, check brake pedal for spongyness and excessive travel.
2. If brake pedal has spongy operation, bleed and adjust brakes - See 70.25.01.
3. If brake pedal travel is excessive, adjust brakes — See 70.25.03.
4. With foot clear of brake pedal, check handbrake for excessive travel.
5. If handbrake travel is excessive, adjust handbrake — See 70.35.10.

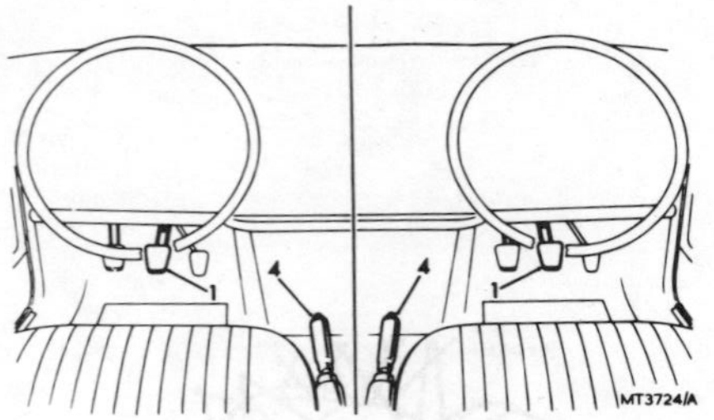

(66) Check/report brake pedal travel and handbrake operation.

1. With handbrake in 'off' position, check brake pedal for spongy operation and excessive travel.
2. Report brake pedal condition.
3. With foot clear of brake pedal, check handbrake for excessive travel.
4. Report handbrake operation.

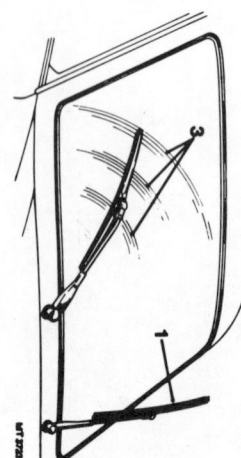

Triumph Spitfire Mk IV Manual. Part No. 545254.

10.00.23

MAINTENANCE

(67) Check operation of window controls, locks and bonnet release.

Check operation of:-

1. Window raising and lowering controls,
2. Internal door locks,
3. External door locks,
4. Luggage compartment lock,
5. Bonnet release controls,
6. Report any defects found.

(68) Check function of all electrical systems and windscreen washer.

In sequence, check operation of:-

1. Side, tail and headlamps (including headlamp dip/main beam and 'flash' controls),
2. Instrument panel illumination,
3. Interior light,
4. Horn(s),
5. Auxiliary lights,

With ignition circuits energised, check operation of:

6. All warning lights (including 'hazard' warning lights if fitted),
7. Fuel level indicator,
8. Heater blower motor,
9. Windscreen washers,
10. Windscreen wipers,
11. Direction indicators,
12. Brake lights,
13. Reversing lights.
14. Start engine and note that oil pressure warning light has extinguished.

Check operation of:-

15. Charging system warning light in relation to engine speed,
16. Temperature indicator,
17. Radio (if fitted)
18. Switch off engine and return ignition switch to the auxiliary position, then recheck the function of any fitted accessories e.g. a radio, that are supplied with power from this switch position.
19. Report any defects found.

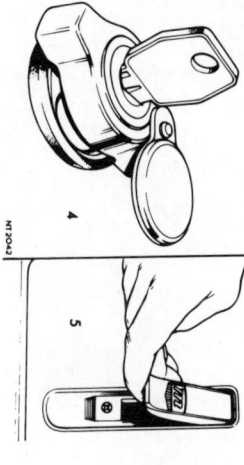

MAINTENANCE

(69) Lubricate clutch and brake pedal pivots.

Using an oil can, lubricate

1. Clutch pedal pivot.
2. Brake pedal pivot.
3. Wipe away surplus oil to prevent staining the carpet.

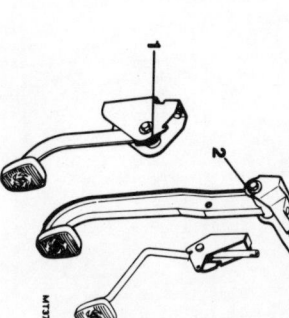

(70) Lubricate all locks, door hinges, strikers and bonnet release.

Using an oil can, lubricate

1. Door locks.
2. Door hinges.
3. Door strikers.
4. Luggage compartment lock.
5. Bonnet release mechanism.
6. Wipe away surplus oil.

(71) Check/report condition and security of seats and seat belts.

1. Move driver's seat back to its fullest extent.
2. Check security of front bolts holding seat runner to floor.
3. Move driver's seat forward to its fullest extent.
4. Check security of rear bolts holding seat runner to floor.
5. With seat in middle position, check security of seat in runner.
6. Repeat the procedure in 1 to 5 for passenger seat.
7. Check seat tipping and lock mechanisms.
8. Check seat belts for wear and damage.
9. Check seat belt connections for wear and damage.
10. Check security of seat belt anchorage bolts, which if correct should be tightened to 24 to 32 lbf ft (3·3 to 4·4 kgf m).
11. Report any defects found.

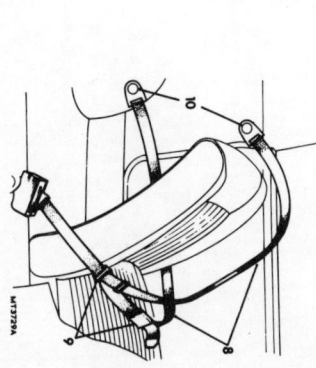 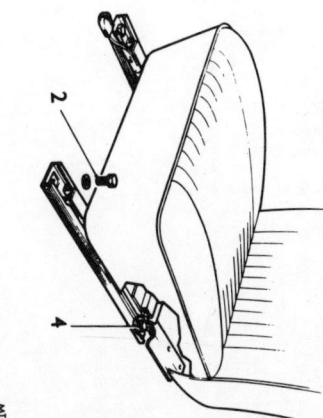

MAINTENANCE

(72) Check/report rear view mirrors for looseness, cracks and crazing.

1. Check interior mirror for looseness, cracks and crazing.
2. Check external mirrors (when fitted) for looseness, cracks and crazing.
3. Report on condition of mirrors.

(73) Road/Roller test and report additional work required

In addition to the general road test, pay particular attention to:—

1. The efficiency and function of the footbrake and handbrake.
2. The function of the steering mechanism.
3. The function of the speedometer.

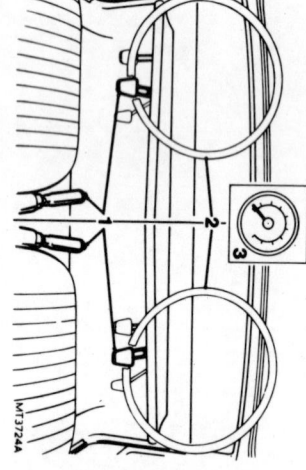

(74) Ensure cleanliness of controls, door handles, steering wheel etc.

1. Check steering wheel, gear lever, bonnet release control and fascia controls etc. for dirt and damage attributable to the service just completed.
2. Check door trims, locks and window controls for dirt and damage attributable to the service just completed.
3. Check seats, carpets and pedal rubbers for dirt and damage attributable to the service just completed.

ENGINE

ENGINE OPERATIONS

Cam followers – set – remove and refit	12.29.57
Camshaft – remove and refit	12.13.01
Centre and rear main bearings – remove and refit	12.21.42
Connecting rod bearing	
– set – remove and refit	12.17.16
– one – remove and refit	12.17.17
– extra each – remove and refit	12.17.18
Connecting rods and pistons	
– remove and refit	12.17.01
– overhaul	12.17.10
Crankshaft – remove and refit	12.21.33
Crankshaft end-float – check and adjust	12.21.26
Crankshaft pulley – remove and refit	12.21.01
Crankshaft rear oil seal – remove and refit	12.21.20
Crankshaft spigot bush – remove and refit	12.21.45
Cylinder block drain tap – remove and refit	12.25.07
Cylinder block front mounting plate gasket – remove and refit	12.25.10
Cylinder block – rebore	12.25.23
Cylinder head	
– overhaul	12.29.18
– remove and refit	12.29.10
– renew casting	12.29.22
Cylinder head gasket – remove and refit	12.29.01
Cylinder head nuts – tighten	12.29.27
Cylinder pressures – check	12.25.01
Decarbonize, reface all valves and seats, grind-in valves, tune engine	12.10.22
Distributor drive shaft – remove and refit	12.29.21

continued

ENGINE

Engine assembly – strip and rebuild	12.41.05
Engine and gearbox assembly	
– remove, change ancillary equipment and refit	12.37.03
– remove and refit	12.37.01
Engine mounting	
– front L.H. – remove and refit	12.45.01
– front R.H. – remove and refit	12.45.03
– front set – remove and refit	12.45.04
– rear L.H. – remove and refit	12.45.07
– rear R.H. – remove and refit	12.45.09
– rear set – remove and refit	12.45.10
Engine tune – check and adjust – valve clearance, distributor points, ignition timing, tune carburetters, clean fuel pump filter, road test	12.49.02
Exhaust valve seats – remove and refit	12.29.77
Engine rear gearbox adaptor plate	12.53.03
Flywheel – remove and refit	12.53.07
Gudgeon pin bush – each – remove and refit	12.17.13
Inlet valve seat – remove and refit	**12.29.76**
Main bearing	
– set – remove and refit	12.21.39
– each – remove and refit	12.21.40
– front – remove and refit	12.21.41
Oil filter assembly – remove and refit	12.60.01
Oil pick-up strainer – remove and refit	12.60.20
Oil pressure relief valve – remove and refit	12.60.56
Oil pump	
– overhaul	12.60.32
– remove and refit	12.60.26
Oil sump – remove and refit	12.60.44
Piston and/or rings	
– engine set – remove and refit	12.17.03
– extra each – remove and refit	12.17.06

continued

ENGINE

Push rods – set – remove and refit	12.29.59
Rocker adjusting screws – set – remove and refit	12.29.56
Rocker cover – remove and refit	12.29.42
Rocker shaft assembly – overhaul	12.29.55
Rocker shaft – remove and refit	12.29.54
Starter ring gear – remove and refit	12.53.19
Timing chain – remove and refit	12.65.14
Timing chain and gears – remove and refit	12.65.12
Timing chain tensioner – remove and refit	12.65.28
Timing cover oil seal – remove and refit	12.65.05
Timing gear cover – remove and refit	12.65.01
Valve clearance – check and adjust	12.29.48
Valve guides	
– exhaust – remove and refit	**12.29.71
– inlet – remove and refit	**12.29.70**
Valve timing – check	12.65.08
Valves	
– exhaust – remove and refit	**12.29.60
– inlet and exhaust – remove and refit	12.29.62
– inlet – remove and refit	12.29.63**

DISTRIBUTOR DRIVE SHAFT AND GEAR

— Remove and refit   12.10.22

Removing

1. Remove the distributor 86.35.20.
2. Remove the two nuts and washers securing the pedestal to the cylinder block studs.
3. Remove the pedestal and gasket.
4. Lift out the drive shaft and gear.

Refitting

NOTE: An end-float of 0·005 in ±0·002 in (0·13 mm ±0·05 mm) must exist between the end of the distributor pedestal and the drive gear. The end-float is controlled by the selective use of gaskets on the pedestal/cylinder block interface. To measure the end-float adopt the following procedure.

5. Measure, note the thickness of, and fit a plain washer 0·5 in (12·7 mm) i.dia over the drive shaft below the gear.
6. Insert the shaft assembly and washer into position in the bush, ensuring that the oil pump drive is mated with the shaft.

NOTE: Use a screwdriver to turn the oil pump drive: try the drive gear in a different position in order to be sure that it is down correctly.

7. Fit the distributor pedestal into position without gasket.

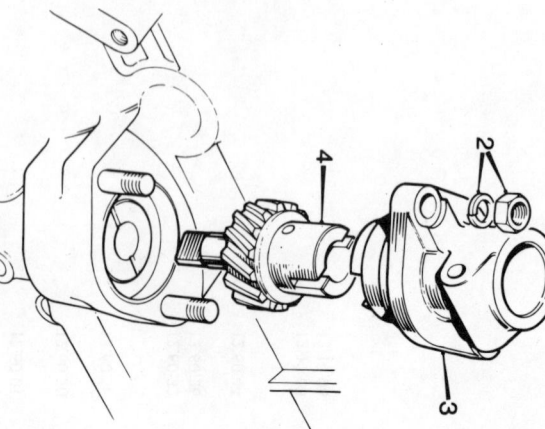

ENGINE

8. Measure the gap between the pedestal and cylinder block (a) and subtract from (b) the thickness of the washer. The result is gear end-float (or load) which must be adjusted, by gaskets, to give a mean end-float of 0·005 in (0·13 mm).

EXAMPLE 1

	in	mm
Thickness of washer (b)	0·100	2.54
Pedestal/cylinder block gap (a)	1·098	2·49
= gear end-float	+0·002	+0·05
add gasket of	0·003	0·08
for correct end-float of	0·005	0·13

continued

EXAMPLE 2

	in	mm
Thickness of washer (b)	0·100	2·45
Pedestal/cylinder block gap (a)	0·110	2·79
= Gear load of	−0·010	−0·25
add gasket of	0·015	0·38
for correct end-float of	0·005	0·13

9. Remove the pedestal, shaft assembly and washer.
10. Turn the crankshaft to bring No. 1 piston to T.D.C. on compression stroke.
11. Lower the drive gear into the bush, allowing it to turn as it meshes with the camshaft gear and ensuring that it engages with the oil pump drive dog.
12. The gear is correctly positioned when the offset slot is as shown in illustration.
13. Fit the pedestal and selected gasket.
14. Fit and tighten the nuts and washers.
15. Fit the distributor 86.35.20.

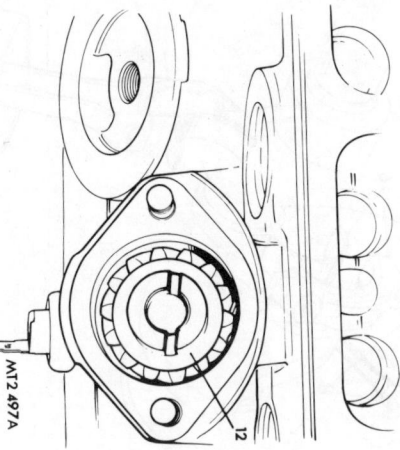

DATA

Drive gear end-float	0·003 to 0·007 in (0·08 to 0·18 mm)
Spindle diameter	0·4980 to 0·4985 in (12·65 to 12·67 mm)
Bush bore	0·5005 to 0·5010 in (12·71 to 12·73 mm)

12.10.22 Sheet 2

Triumph Spitfire Mk IV Manual. Part No. 545254.

ENGINE

CAMSHAFT

— Remove and refit **12.13.01**

Removing

1. Isolate the battery.
2. Remove the radiator 26.40.01.
3. Remove the cylinder head 12.29.10.
4. Withdraw the cam followers, identifying for re-assembly.
5. Remove the distributor drive shaft and gear. 12.10.22.
6. Remove the fuel pump. 19.45.08.
7. Remove the timing chain and sprockets 12.65.12.
8. Remove the two bolts and withdraw the camshaft location plate.
9. Withdraw the camshaft.

Refitting

10. Reverse instructions 1 to 9, and in addition:
    a. Check the camshaft end float and reduce if necessary by fitting a new camshaft plate. See instruction 55, 12.41.05.
    b. Time the valves. 12.65.08.

NOTE: Engines prior to No. 25000 used camshaft bearings.

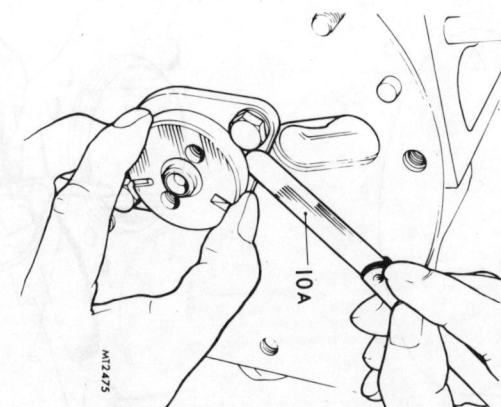

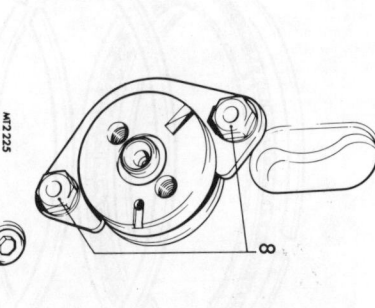

DATA

Journal diameter (Up to Engine No. 25000)	1·9649 to 1·9654 in (49·91 to 49·92 mm)
Journal diameter (from Engine No. 25001)	1·8402 to 1·8407 in (46·74 to 46·75 mm)
End-Float	0·0042 to 0·0085 in (0·110 to 0·216 mm)
Bore in block	1·9680 to 1·9695 in (49·980 to 50·025 mm)

Triumph Spitfire Mk IV Manual. Part No. 545254.

12.13.01

ENGINE

CONNECTING RODS AND PISTONS

— Remove and refit   12.17.01

Removing

1. Isolate the battery.
2. Place the car on a ramp or over a pit.
3. Remove the cylinder head. 12.29.10
4. Remove the oil sump. 12.60.44.
5. Remove the oil pick-up strainer. 12.60.20. 2 to 4.
6. Turn the crankshaft to bring Nos. 1 and 4 connecting rod bolts to an accessible position.
7. Check the identifying marks on the connecting rods and bearing caps. Mark if necessary.
8. Remove the connecting rod bolts.
9. Withdraw the bearing caps and lower half bearing shells complete with the bolt bushes.
10. Push the connecting rods and pistons upwards and carefully withdraw, identifying for reassembly.
11. Mate up the top and bottom bearing shells and caps with their respective connecting rods and piston assemblies.
12. Repeat instructions 6 to 11 on Nos. 2 and 3 bearings.

Refitting

13. Position Nos. 1 and 4 crankpins at B.D.C. and lubricate them with clean engine oil.
14. Smear the pistons and cylinder bores with clean engine oil.
15. Carefully insert the connecting rods and pistons into the bores, ensuring that the arrow (thus ▲) is pointing to the front of the engine.
16. Ensure that the open face of the big-end bearing is towards the non thrust side of the cylinder bore.
17. Stagger the piston ring gaps, avoiding a gap on the thrust side of the piston.
18. Using a piston ring compressor, gently push the pistons into the bore.
19. Fit the upper bearing shells to the connecting rod big-ends and pull the connecting rods onto the crankpins.
20. Check that the connecting rod bolt bushes are correctly positioned.
21. Fit the bearing shells to the bearing caps and fit to the connecting rods, securing with new bolts and tighten evenly** (see 06-1 for correct torque). **
22. Repeat instructions 13 to 21 on Nos. 2 and 3 cylinders.
23. Reverse instructions 1 to 5.
24. Replenish the sump with correct grade of engine oil.

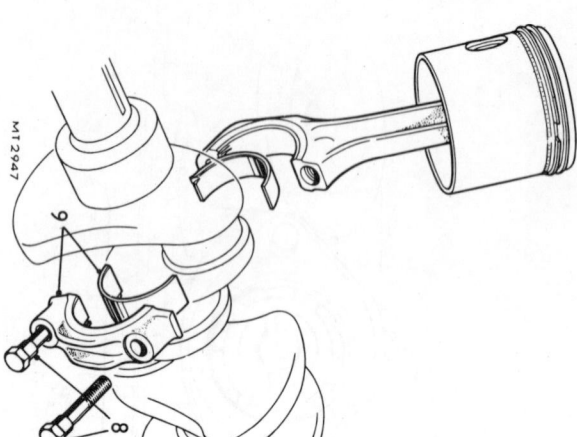

ENGINE

PISTONS AND/OR RINGS — ENGINE SET

— Remove and refit   12.17.03

Pistons and/or rings — extra each   12.17.06

See 12.17.10.

CONNECTING RODS AND PISTONS

— Overhaul   12.17.10

Gudgeon pin bush — each — remove and refit   12.17.13

NOTE: Do not mix components during this operation

Service tools: 335, S336-4

1. Remove the connecting rods and pistons 12.17.01.
2. Remove the circlips from the pistons.
3. Remove the gudgeon pin.
4. Remove the piston from the connecting rod.
5. Remove the piston rings with the expander tool and clean.
6. Clean the pistons, removing all carbon deposits, particularly from the piston ring grooves.
7. Remove the big-end bearing shells.
8. Examine the gudgeon pin and check for wear — see Data.
9. Check the piston dimensions to grade and bore — see Data.
10. Check the dimensions of piston ring grooves — see Data.
11. Check the piston ring gaps in the bores — see Data.

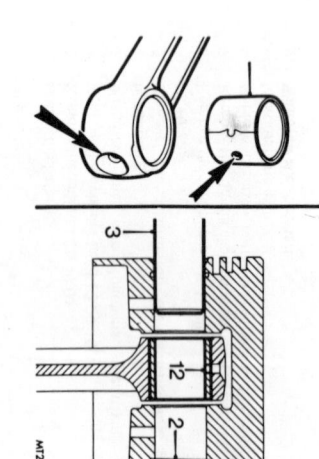

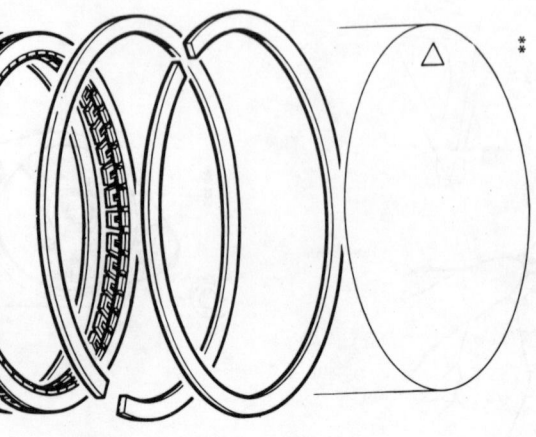

ENGINE

12. Check the small end bushes for wear, and if necessary renew using a suitable hand press to remove the old bush and fit new. Ensure that the oil hole in the bush corresponds with the connecting rod. Ream the new bush to size – see Data. When assembled dry, the gudgeon pin is a thumb push fit at 68°F room temperature. If the pin passes through the bore under its own weight, it is too slack.
13. Check the connecting rods for bend and twist. Use tools 335, and arbor adaptor S336-4 – see Data. Rods that exceed the tolerances in both conditions should be renewed or re-aligned.

Refitting

14. Reverse instructions 2 to 5:
    a. Fitting oversize pistons as necessary.
    b. Fitting the piston rings with care and in the following order: (A) expander ring into bottom groove, ensure that ends are butting but not overlapping, (B) bottom rail of expander from bottom of piston, (C) top rail from top of piston, (D) scraper ring – step uppermost to second groove, (E) compression ring to top groove.
    c. Separating the ring gaps equally on the non-thrust side of piston.
15. Refit the connecting rods and pistons 12.17.01.

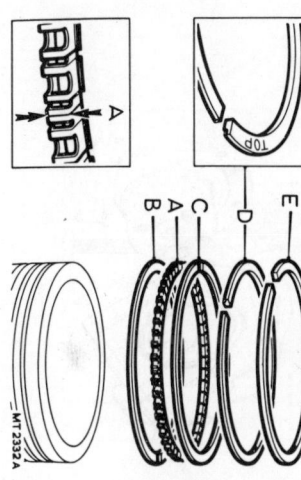

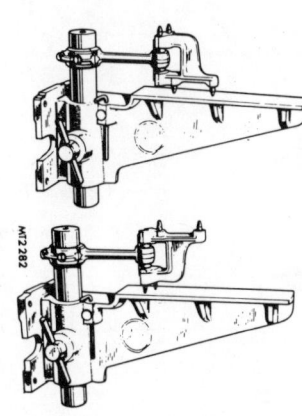

DATA
**Unless otherwise stated data is applicable to all engines.

Pistons
Bore size: Grade F .. .. 2·899 to 2·900 in (73·64 to 73·66 mm)
Grade G .. .. 2·9010 to 2·9005 in (73·86 to 73·67 mm)
Piston top diameter: Grades F and G up to Eng. No. FH/FK25001 2·875 to 2·880 in (73·03 to 73·15 mm)
From Eng. No. FH/FK25001 2·871 to 2·874 in (72·93 to 73·01 mm)
Piston Bottom diameter: Grade F Eng. Nos. Prefix FH/FK 2·870 to 2·873 in (72·90 to 72·98 mm)
From Eng. No FM 1 2·8976 to 2·8981 in (73·59 to 73·61 mm)
Grade G Eng. Nos. Prefix FH/FK 2·8984 to 2·8989 in (73·62 to 73·63 mm)
Eng. Nos. Prefix FM 2·8982 to 2·8987 in (73·617 to 73·620 mm)
Eng. Nos. Prefix FM. 2·8990 to 2·8995 in (73635 to 73·647 mm).. **
Groove width: bottom 0·020 in (0·52 mm) oversize
centre and top 0·1578 to 0·1588 in (3·99 to 4·01 mm)
Ring width: bottom (oil control) 3-part 0·064 to 0·065 in (1·625 to 1·650 mm)
centre and top (compression) 0·1540 to 0·1560 in (3·90 to 3·96 mm)
Rings available .. .. 0·0620 to 0·0625 in (1·575 to 1·587 mm)
0·010, 0·020, 0·030 in (0·25, 0·52, 0·76 mm) oversize

Connecting rods
Small end bush (fitted) i.dia .. .. 0·8126 to 0·8129 in (20·64 to 20·65 mm)
Gudgeon pin diameter .. .. 0·8123 to 0·8125 in (20·63 to 20·64 mm)
Connecting rod bend not to exceed .. .. 0·0015 in (0·04 mm)
Connecting rod twist not to exceed .. .. 0·0045 in (0·114 mm)

Connecting rod and piston assemblies
Weight variation between heaviest and lightest assembly Max. 4 drams. **

12.17.13 Sheet 2  Triumph Spitfire Mk IV Manual, Part No. 545254

ENGINE

CONNECTING ROD BEARINGS – SET
– Remove and refit 12.17.16
Connecting rod bearing – one 12.17.17
Connecting rod bearing – extra each 12.17.18

Removing
1. Remove the oil sump 12.60.44.
2. Remove the oil pick-up strainer. 12.60.20. 2 to 4.
3. Turn the crankshaft to bring the connecting rod bearing to be removed to an accessible position.
4. Remove the connecting rod bolts.
5. Remove the bearing cap complete with the shell bearing and connecting bolt bushes.
6. Push the connecting rod and piston upwards sufficiently to clear the crankpin to enable the upper shell bearing to be removed.

NOTE: Do not push the piston higher than T.D.C. or the top piston ring may be released necessitating removal of the cylinder head.

7. Remove the upper shell bearing.

Refitting
8. Insert the shell bearing in the connection rod big-end.
9. Lubricate the crankpin with clean engine oil.
10. Fit the connecting rod onto the crankpin.
11. Fit the shell bearing to the bearing cap and fit to the connecting rod.

NOTE: When fitting the bearing shells, ensure that the lug on the bearing locates correctly in the recess in the connecting rod big-end and cap.

12.** Fit and tighten the bolts (see 06-1 for correct torque)**.
13. Repeat the instructions on the remaining assemblies if necessary.
14. Reverse instructions 1 to 2.
15. Replenish the sump with the correct grade of engine oil.

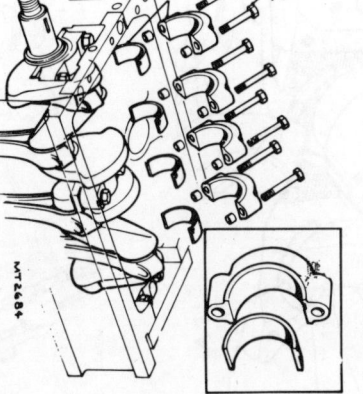

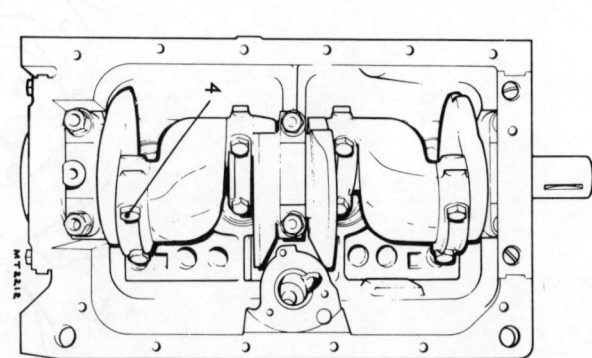

12.17.16
12.17.18 Triumph Spitfire Mk IV Manual, Part No. 545254.

ENGINE

CRANKSHAFT PULLEY
— Remove and refit
12.21.01

Removing
1. Slacken the alternator mountings.
2. Remove the fan belt.
3. Working from below vehicle, remove pulley retaining nut.
4. Withdraw pulley, if necessary use extractor, bearing on the centre nut, loosely replaced.

Refitting
5. Reverse 1 to 4, ensuring:
   a. Drive key is square in the crankshaft keyway an' is not burred.
   b. Drive belt is correctly tensioned 86.10.05.
   c. Pulley retaining nut is tightened to 90 to 110 lbf. ft (124 to 15·2 kgf. m).

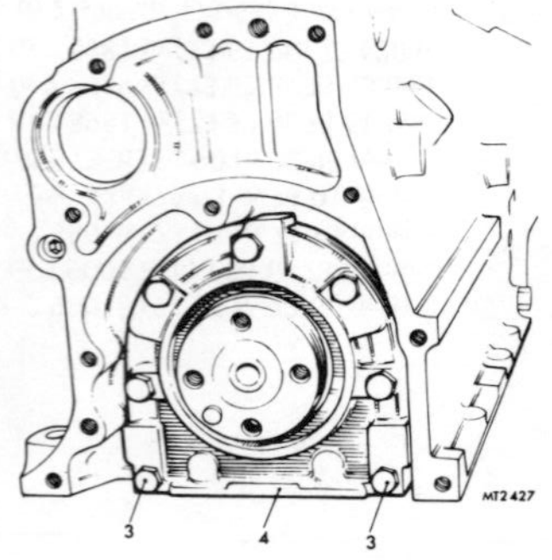

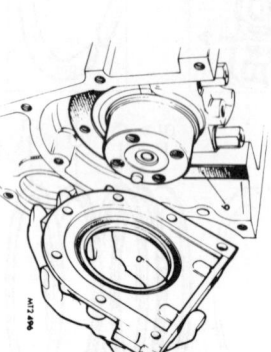

CRANKSHAFT REAR OIL SEAL
— Remove and refit
12.21.20

Removing
1. Remove the engine rear gearbox adaptor plate. 12.53.03.
2. Remove the two bolts securing the sump to the rear oil seal housing.
3. Remove the seven bolts holding the oil seal housing to the crankcase.
4. Withdraw the oil seal and housing complete, taking care not to tear the sump gasket.
5. Press out the oil seal from the housing.

Refitting
6. Smear the outside diameter of the replacement oil seal with grease and press into housing, lip face to crankshaft.
7. Clean the crankcase joint face, removing all traces of old gasket and jointing compound.
8. Coat the crankcase face with sealing compound and smear the crankshaft with oil.
9. Place a new gasket in position on the crankcase joint face.
10. Carefully slide the oil seal housing over the crankshaft. Slide the oil seal housing into contact with the crankcase joint face.
11. Fit and tighten evenly the crankcase securing bolts to 16 to 20 lbf. ft (2·2 to 2·8 kgf. m) and ensure top bolt has a plain copper washer under it.

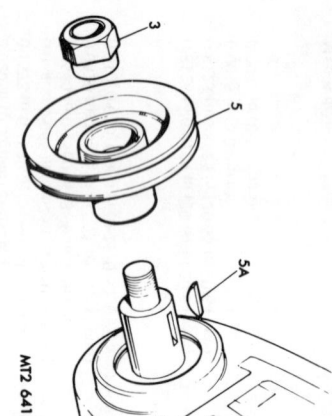

CRANKSHAFT END-FLOAT
— Check and adjust
12.21.26

Operation performed during Engine — strip and rebuild 12.41.05, Crankshaft — remove and refit 12.21.33, Front main bearing — remove and refit 12.21.41, and Centre and rear main bearing — remove and refit 12.21.42.

1. Secure a dial gauge to the crankcase so that the indicator rod rests in a loaded condition on a machined surface of a crankshaft throw.
2. Using a screwdriver between the centre main bearing cap and an adjacent crankshaft throw, force the crankshaft against the dial indicator rod.
3. Zero the dial indicator.
4. Force the crankshaft in the opposite direction and note the gauge reading, which should indicate an end-float of 0·006 to 0·014 in (0·1524 to 0·3556 mm).
5. If necessary, adjust the end-float by removing the rear main bearing cap and existing thrust washers and renewing with different washers of suitable thickness, ensuring:
   a. Thrust washers are fitted so that the thrust faces — identified by oil grooves — bear against the crankshaft faces.
   b. Locate in the register on both sides of the crankshaft bearing bore half.
6. Refit the main bearing cap complete with shell bearing and tighten the nuts to 50 to 65 lbf. ft (7 to 9 kgf. m).
7. Re-check the end-float.

NOTE: The end-float may be checked with a feeler gauge inserted between the thrust washer and crankshaft.

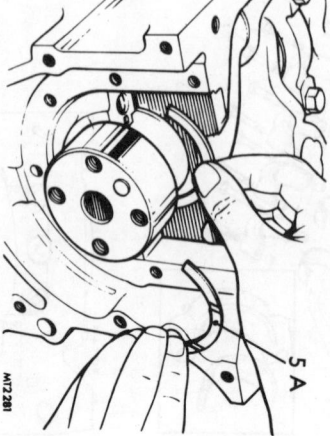

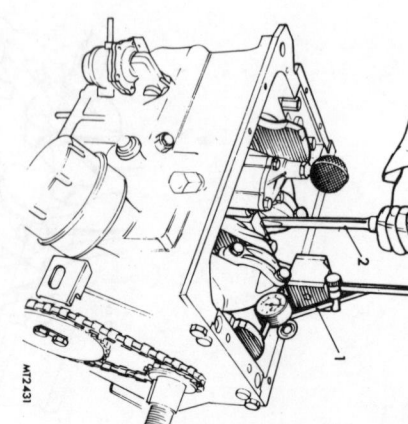

ENGINE

CRANKSHAFT

— Remove and refit   12.21.33

Removing

1. Remove the engine and gearbox assembly 12.37.01.
2. Remove the starter motor.
3. Remove the nuts and bolts securing the bell housing to the engine and lift off the gearbox assembly.
4. Remove the clutch assembly 33.10.01.
5. Remove the four bolts securing the flywheel to the crankshaft and lift off the flywheel 12.53.07.
6. Remove the seven bolts securing the engine rear adaptor to the cylinder block and remove the engine rear plate. 12.53.03.
7. Remove the alternator 86.10.02.
8. Remove the water pump housing complete with water pump, thermostat housing and fan. 26.50.03 instructions 8 to 10.
9. Remove the crankshaft pulley.
10. Remove the timing chain cover 12.65.01. instructions 5 and 6.
11. Remove the oil thrower.
12. Remove the timing chain sprocket, remove key, and then remove the shims.
13. Remove the two bolts securing the camshaft location plate and remove the plate.
14. Remove the front mounting plate. 12.25.10. instructions 9 to 12.
15. Remove the dipstick.
16. Remove the sump.
17. Remove the oil strainer 12.60.20.
18. Remove the front sealing block.
19. Remove the crankshaft rear oil seal 12.21.20. instructions 3 and 4.
20. Disconnect the connecting rods from the crankshaft, 12.17.16 instructions 4 to 7. Check the identification marks for reassembly. DO NOT MIX.
21. Remove the front centre and rear main bearing caps and shell 12.21.39. instructions 6 to 8.
22. Remove the thrust washers from the rear main bearing.
23. Lift out the crankshaft.

continued

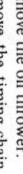

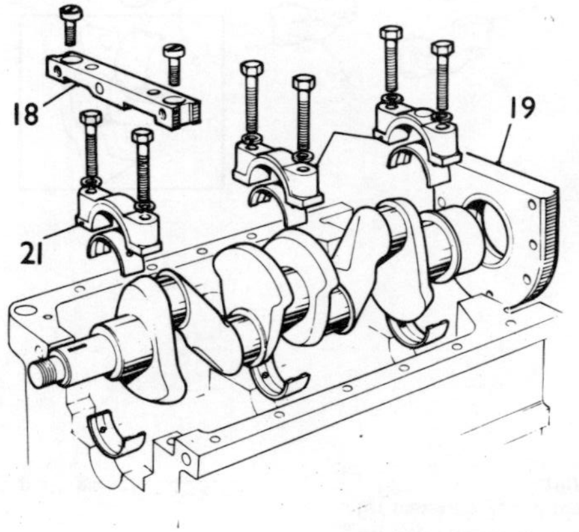

MT2 642

Triumph Spitfire Mk IV Manual. Part No. 545254.
Triumph Dolomite Manual. Part No. 545209.

12.21.33 Sheet 1

ENGINE

Refitting

24. Lubricate all parts before assembly.
25. Fit the uppper bearing shells to the crankcase and the thrust washers to the rear main bearing.
26. Fit the lower shells to the bearing caps.
27. Lower the crankshaft into the crankcase.
28. Fit the bearing caps and tighten the front and centre main bearing bolts and rear main nuts to 50 to 65 lbf. ft (7 to 9 kgf. m).
29.** Check, and adjust if necessary, the crankshaft end-float 12.21.26.
30. Reconnect the connecting rods to the crankshaft, 12.17.16 instructions 8 to 12 and fit the front sealing block, 12.21.39 instructions 14 to 17.**
31. Fit the rear main oil seal. 12.21.20. instructions 6 to 11.
32. Fit the oil pump strainer 12.60.20.
33. Fit the sump, renewing the gasket. Tighten the retaining bolts evenly to 16 to 20 lbf. ft (2·2 to 2·8 kgf. m).
34. Fit the clutch assembly 33.10.01.
35. Fit the front mounting plate and gasket, ensuring that:
    a. All traces of old gasket and jointing compound are removed from the cylinder block joint face.
    b. The cylinder block face of the new gasket is smeared with jointing compound.
    c. The mounting plate is located correctly over the dowels.
    d. The retaining bolts and screws are tightened evenly.
36. Fit the timing chain and sprockets 12.65.12. instructions 6 to 15.
37. Check the valve timing 12.65.08.
38. Fit the oil thrower, ensuring that the dished periphery faces the timing cover.
39. Fit the timing cover 12.65.01.
40.** Fit the crankshaft pulley, tightening the retaining nut to 150 lbf. ft (207 kgf. m).**
41. Fit the water pump housing complete with water pump, fan and thermostat housing. Ensure that the new gasket is fitted with jointing compound.
42. Fit the alternator and drive belt 86.10.02.
43. Fit the gearbox.
44. Fit the starter motor.
45. Fit the engine and gearbox assembly to the car. 12.37.01.
46. Fit the dipstick and check the oil sump level.

DATA

Crankshaft end-float tolerance	0·004 to 0·008 in (0·10 to 0·20 mm)
Thrust washer oversizes	0·005 in (0·13 mm)
Main bearing journals diameter (3)	2·3115 to 2·3120 in (58·713 to 58·725 mm)
Crankpins diameter (4)	1·8750 to 1·8755 in (47·625 to 47·638 mm)
Maximum run-out of centre journal (with front and rear supported)	0·003 in (0·076 mm)
Maximum out-of-balance of shaft (with key and dowel fitted)	0·3 oz. in (3·36 g. cm)
Crankshaft end-float tolerance	0·004 to 0·008 in (0·10 to 0·20 mm)
Main bearings and big-end bearings are available in the following undesizes	0·010, 0·020, 0·030 in (0·25, 0·51, 0·76 mm)

12.21.33 Sheet 2

ENGINE

MAIN BEARING – SET

– Remove and refit

Front main bearing 1 to 6, and 9 to 18	12.21.39
Centre and rear main bearing 1, 2, 7, 8, 9 to 13 and 18	12.21.41
	12.21.42

Removing

1. Remove the sump 12.60.44.
2. Remove the oil pump strainer.
3. Remove the front mounting plate gasket. 12.25.10.

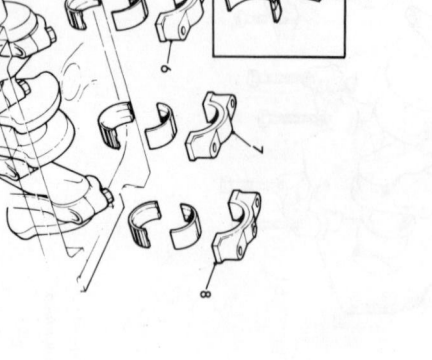

4. Remove the two screws securing the front sealing block to the crankcase.
5. Withdraw the sealing block.
6. Remove the front main bearing cap bolts and withdraw the cap complete with lower shell. Remove the upper shell and check that the cap is marked for reassembly.
7. Remove the centre main bearing bolts and withdraw the cap and lower shell. Check identification marks for reassembly and withdraw the upper shell.
8. Remove the rear main bearing cap bolts and withdraw the cap and lower shell. Check that the cap is marked for reassembly, and remove the upper shell.

continued

Refitting

9. Fit the shell bearings to the front, centre and rear main bearing caps, ensuring that the tags locate in the recesses.
10. Lubricate and feed the upper shells – tag end last – between the crankshaft journals and bearing bores, ensuring that the tags locate in the recesses.
11. Lubricate the lower shells and refit the caps, tightening the front, centre and rear main bearing cap bolts to 50 to 65 lbf. ft (7 to 9 kgf. m).
    Ensure that the identification marks coincide.
12. Check and adjust if necessary, the crankshaft end float 12.21.26.
13. Smear the front sealing block gaskets with jointing compound and fit to the crankcase, loosely tightening the screws.
14. Drive wedges into the slots.
15. Align the face of the sealing block with the crankcase and tighten the retaining screws.
16. Trim the protruding ends of the wedges flush with the crankcase – do not under-cut.
17. Reverse instructions 1 to 3, ensuring that:
    a. All gaskets are renewed.
    b. The sump is replenished with the correct grade of oil to the top mark on the dipstick.

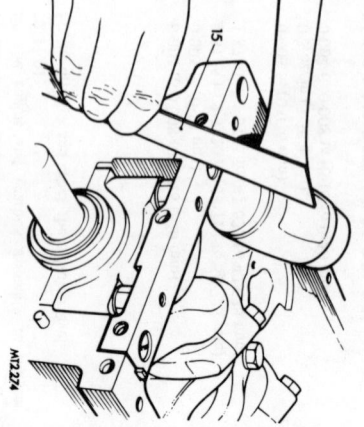

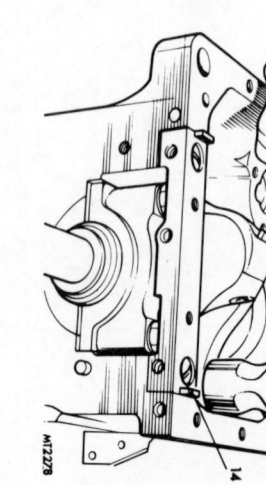

ENGINE

CRANKSHAFT SPIGOT BUSH 12.21.45

— Remove and refit

Removing
1. Isolate the battery.
2. Remove the flywheel 12.53.07.
3. Remove the spigot bush which is a sliding fit in the crankshaft flange.

Refitting
4. Smear the spigot bush with zinc oxide grease and refit.
5. Reverse instructions 1 and 2.

CYLINDER PRESSURES 12.25.01

— Check

1. Run the engine until normal temperature is attained as indicated by the temperature gauge.
2. Remove the spark plugs.
3. Fit a compression gauge to No. 1 cylinder.
4. Turn the engine over with the starter motor with the throttle wide open.
5. Note and record the gauge reading.
6. Repeat on the remaining cylinders.

NOTE: All cylinders should have pressures within 10 lb/in² (0·70 kg/cm²) Differential.

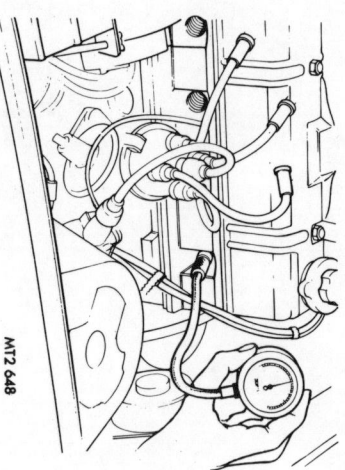

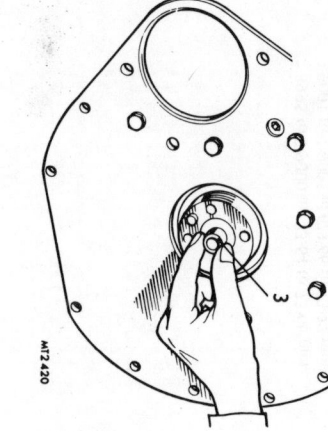

CYLINDER BLOCK DRAIN TAP 12.25.07

— Remove and refit

Removing
1. Drain the cooling system 26.10.01.
2. Remove the drain tap and adaptor assembly.

Refitting
3. Reverse instructions 1 to 2 and check for leaks.

CYLINDER BLOCK FRONT MOUNTING PLATE GASKET 12.25.10

— Remove and refit

Removing
1. Isolate the battery.
2. Remove the alternator 86.10.02.
3. Remove the water pump housing 26.50.02, 1 to 9.
4. Remove the timing chain cover 12.65.01, 3 to 6.
5. Remove the timing chain and sprockets. 12.65.12, 2 to 5.
6. Remove the two bolts securing the camshaft locating plate and remove the plate.
7. Support the engine under the sump.
8. Remove the two nuts and bolts (two each side), securing the L.H. and R.H. engine mounting bolts to the front suspension turrets.
9. Remove the four bolts securing the mounting plate to the cylinder block.
10. Remove the two screws securing the mounting plate to the sealing block.
11. Remove the front mounting plate complete with mounting rubbers.
12. Remove the front mounting plate gasket.

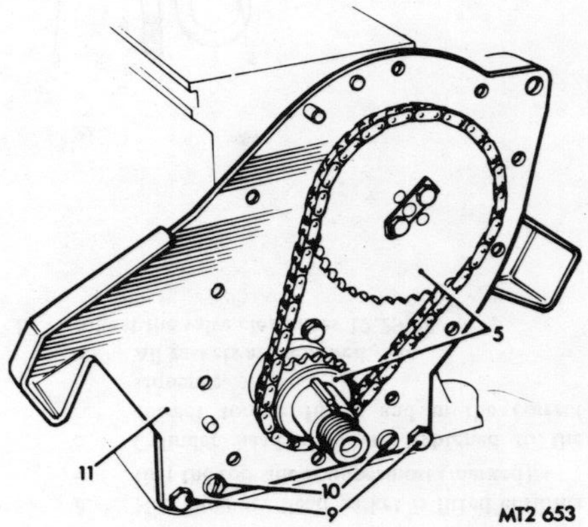

Refitting
13. Remove all traces of old jointing compound from the cylinder block face.
14. Coat the cylinder block face of the new gasket with Wellseal jointing compound.
15. Fit the new gasket.
16. Reverse instructions 1 to 11, ensuring:
    a. The camshaft sprocket is refitted in its original position and that the timing marks line up.
    b. A new water-pump housing gasket is fitted, using sealing compound.
    c. The mounting plate locates correctly over the dowels.

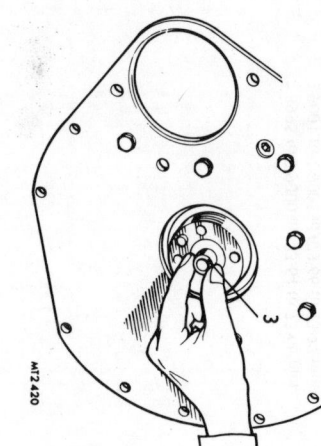

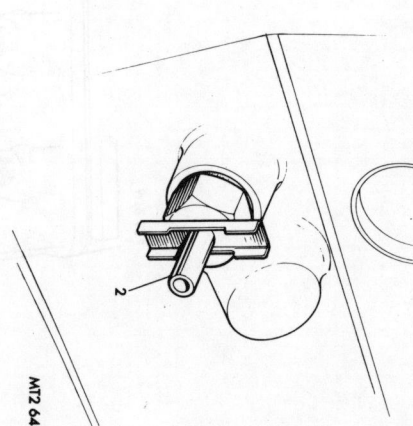

ENGINE

CYLINDER BLOCK

— Rebore   12.25.23

1. Strip engine. 12.41.05.
2. Measure bores for taper, ovality and maximum wear.
3. Rebore to dimensions in Data.

NOTE: Maximum rebore size is +0·020 in. Cylinders that cannot be rebored within this limit may be sleeved to restore them to the original size as follows:

a. 1300 engine bore out cylinders to 3·0302 to 3·0272 in. dia.

4. Rebuild engine 12.41.05.
   a. Fit new pistons to rebored dimensions, or
   b. Fit standard graded pistons to relined bores.
   c. Check alignment of connecting rods. 12.17.10. instruction 13.

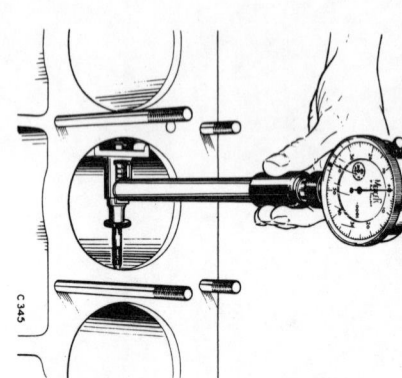

C 345

DATA

Original size bore: Grade F . . . . . 2·8995 to 2·9000 in (73·64 to 73·66 mm).
Grade G . . . . . 2·9001 to 2·9005 in (73·66 to 73·77 mm).
Maximum rebore size . . . . . +·020 in (+0·51 mm).

ENGINE

CYLINDER HEAD

— Remove and refit   12.29.10

Which includes:
Cylinder head gasket   12.29.01

Removing

1. Isolate the battery.
2. Drain the cooling system 26.10.01.
3. Remove the inlet and exhaust manifold assembly. 30.15.01.
4. Disconnect the plug leads and remove the distributor cap.
5. Remove the rocker shaft. 12.29.54.
6. Remove the push rods, suitably identifying them for reassembly in the corresponding cam followers.
7. Remove the water pump housing. 26.50.03. 1 to 7.
8. Remove the alternator. 86.10.07.
9. Slacken and remove the 10 nuts securing the cylinder head to the block reversing the tightening sequence. 12.29.27.
10. Lift off the cylinder head.
11. Remove the cylinder head gasket and discard.

Refitting

12. Reverse instructions 1 to 11, ensuring:
    a. Cylinder head and cylinder block faces are clean.
    b. New cylinder head gasket is fitted ensuring that the top side is uppermost (marked).
    c. Cylinder head nuts are tightened to the correct torque figure and in the correct sequence.
    d. All gaskets are renewed.
13. Adjust the valve clearances 12.29.48.

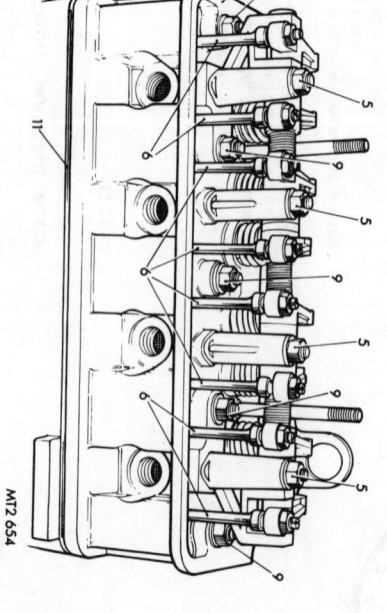

MT2 654

ENGINE

CYLINDER HEAD
— Overhaul

Which includes:

Valves — inlet and exhaust — remove and refit	12.29.18
Valves — inlet — remove and refit	12.29.62
Valves — exhaust — remove and refit	12.29.63
Valve guide — inlet — remove and refit	**12.29.64**
Valve guide — exhaust — remove and refit	12.29.71
Inlet valve seat — remove and refit	12.29.76
Exhaust valve seat — remove and refit	12.29.77

Service tools: 18G, 106, 6118B, 60A, S60A-2A or S60A-2, S60A-6.

1. Remove the cylinder head, 12.29.18.
2. Remove the spark plugs.
3. Using the valve spring compressor 18G 106 or 6118B, remove the inlet exhaust valve spring collars or split cotters.
4. Remove the inlet and exhaust valves, springs and identify for reassembly.
5. Check the inlet and exhaust valve guides for wear, and renew if necessary. Using Service tool S60A-6, assemble the replacement valve guide in the tool, with the chamfered end uppermost (leading). Position the tool on the combustion chamber face and pull the replacement guide in and the old one out. Ensure that the guide protrusion above the cylinder head top face is correct — see Data.
6. Examine the valve seats for pitting and wear. Reface where necessary, removing the minimum of material.
7. Fit valve seat inserts where the seats cannot be restored by refacing. Machine the cylinder head to the dimensions given (see Data).

NOTE: When fitting a pair of valve inserts, it will be necessary to bore the head and fit the first before boring the head and fitted inserts for the second.

8. Press in the valve insert and peen over the cylinder head casting material insert to secure.
9. Cut seats in the inserts to the dimensions given below.
10. Examine the valves and renew any with bent or worn stems (see Data) and heads where the thickness is reduced to 0·0312 in (0·8 mm). Reface where necessary.
11. Test the valve springs for fatigue to the dimensions in Data. Renew as necessary.

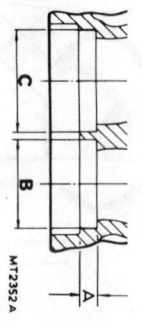

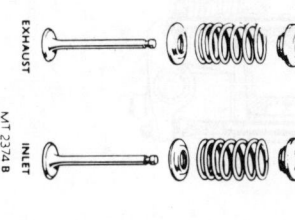

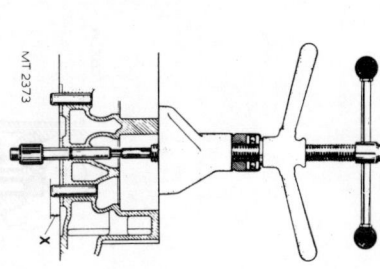

12. **Reassembling**
    Lap-in all valves, using coarse followed by fine carborundum paste, until a gas-tight seal is obtained. Remove all traces of paste and maintain identification of each valve.
13. Lubricate the valve stems with clean engine oil and assemble to the cylinder head. Ensure that the valve spring retaining collars or split collars are correctly positioned.
14. Refit the cylinder head, fitting a new cylinder head gasket.

** DATA

Unless otherwise stated data is applicable to all engines

Valves

	Inlet	Exhaust
Head diameter	Up to Eng. No. FH/FK 25001 1·304 to 1·308 in (33·12 to 33·22 mm)	From Eng. No. FH/FK 25001 and FM1 1·437 to 1·443 in (36·50 to 36·65 mm)	1·168 to 1·172 in (29·66 to 29·76 mm)
Stem diameter	0·3107 to 0·3112 in (7·87 to 7·90 mm)	0·3107 to 0·3112 in (7·87 to 7·90 mm)	0·3100 to 0·3105 in (7·874 to 7·887 mm)
Valve stem to guide clearance	0·0008 to 0·0023 in (0·02 to 0·06 mm)	0·0008 to 0·0023 in (0·02 to 0·06 mm)	0·0015 to 0·0030 in (0·03 to 0·07 mm)

Seat face angle 90° plus 30′ minus 0′

Valve guides

Length	2·0625 in (52·387 mm)
Bore	0·312 to 0·313 in (7·92 to 7·95 mm)
Outside diameter	0·501 to 0·502 in (12·72 to 12·75 mm)
Valve guide height above cylinder head	0·749 to 0·751 in (19·025 to 19·075 mm)

Valve springs — inlet and exhaust valves

	Inner	Outer
	Up to Eng. No. FH/FK 25001	From Eng. No. FK 25001	From Eng. No. FK 25001 and Eng. No. FM 1
Internal diameter	0·795 in (20·19 mm)	0·578 in (14·68 mm)	0·795 in (20·19 mm)
Working coils	3½	4	3¾
Load at length	1·074 in=105 to 115 lbf (27·28 mm=47·6 to 52·1 kgf)	0·657 in=40 to 43 lbf (16·68 mm=18·1 to 19·5 kgf)	0·989 in=123 to 133 lbf (25·1 mm=55·8 to 60·03 kgf)
Free length (approx.)	1·59 in (40·38 mm)	1·14 in (28·95 mm)	1·52 in (38·6 mm)
Solid length (max.)	0·96 in (24·38 mm)	0·552 in (14·48 mm)	0·875 in (22·2 mm)
Rate	235 lbf/in (4196 kgf/m)	85·6 lbf/in (1526 kgf/m)	240 lbf/in (4286 kgf/m)

Valve seat inserts

	Inlet		Exhaust	
	Up to	From	Up to	From
	Eng. No. FH/FK 25001	Eng. No. FH/FK 25001 and FM1	Eng. No. FH/FK 25001	Eng. No. FH/FK 25001 and FM 1
Bore into cylinder head dimension 'A'	0·216 to 0·219 in (5·48 to 5·56 mm)	0·250 to 0·255 in (6·35 to 6·48 mm)	0·248 to 0·250 in (6·30 to 6·35 mm)	0·250 to 0·255 in (6·35 to 6·48 mm)
Bore into cylinder head dimension 'B' (Exhaust)			1·5625 to 1·5635 in (39·68 to 39·71 mm)	1·249 to 1·250 in (31·72 to 31·75 mm)
Bore into cylinder head dimension 'C' (Inlet)	1·375 to 1·376 in (34·92 to 34·95 mm)			

Machined fitted inserts to 89° inclusive angle. Valve seats are to be concentric with guide bore to within 0·002 in (0·0508 mm) total indicator reading.

NOTE: When fitting valve inserts to units up to Engine No. FH 25001, FK 25001 and FM 1 it will be found that a maximum interference of 0·013 in (0·33 mm) can exist between the inlet valve and the exhaust valve insert positions. It will therefore be necessary to fit one insert first then bore into it when fitting the second insert. **

ENGINE

DECARBONIZE, REFACE ALL VALVES AND SEATS, GRIND-IN VALVES, TUNE ENGINE 12.29.21

Dismantling

1. Remove the cylinder head 12.29.10.
2. Remove the inlet and exhaust valves 12.29.62.
3. Remove the carbon deposits from combustion chambers and ports.
4. Clean the face of the cylinder head, removing all traces of carbon and high spots.
5. Clean out the water-ways.
6. Reface all seats, removing the minum of material.
7. Clean carbon from all valves and re-face.
8. Lap-in the valves, using coarse followed by fine grinding paste until a gas-tight joint is obtained. Do not mix the valves.
9. Turn the crankshaft until Nos. 1 and 4 pistons are at T.D.C.
10. Fill Nos. 2 and 3 cylinders with clean non-fluffy rag to prevent carbon falling into the bores, and cover the cam follower apertures.
11. Carefully, without scoring the piston crown, remove carbon deposits leaving a band of carbon round the periphery of the piston crown. Avoid carbon particles falling into the cylinder block water-ways.
12. Repeat instructions 9 to 11 on Nos. 2 and 3 cylinders.
13. Clean the cylinder block face, removing all traces of carbon and high spots.

Reassembling

14. Reverse instructions 1 and 2.
15. Tune the engine 12.49.02.

CYLINDER HEAD – RENEW CASTING

– Dismantle and reassemble 12.29.22

Dismantling

1. Remove the cylinder head 12.29.10.
2. Remove the inlet and exhaust valves 12.29.62.
3. Remove the spark plugs.

Reassembling to new casting

4. Fit the rocker shaft pedestal studs.
5. Fit the rocker cover studs.
6. Fit the inlet and exhaust manifold studs.
7. Lap-in all valves, removing all traces of compound.
8. Reverse instructions 1 and 2.
9. Tune the engine 12.49.02.

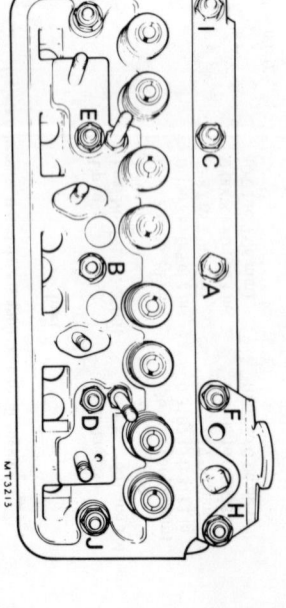

CYLINDER HEAD NUTS

– Tighten 12.29.27

1. Remove the rocker cover 12.29.42.
2. Remove the rocker shaft 12.29.54.
3. To avoid distortion, tighten the cylinder head nuts to 38 to 45 lbf. ft (5·2 to 6·2 kgf. m) in the following sequence A, B, C, D, E, F, G, H, I, J.
4. Refit the rocker shaft 12.29.54.
5. Refit the rocker cover, 12.29.42.

ROCKER COVER

– Remove and refit 12.29.42

Removing

1. Disconnect the engine breather hose from the carburetter.
2. Remove the two nuts complete with plain and fibre washers securing the rocker cover to the cylinder head.
3. Lift off the rocker cover complete with gasket.

Refitting

4. Reverse instructions 1 to 3 ensuring that the rocker cover retaining nuts are tightened evenly and not beyond 1 to 2 lbf. ft (0·14 to 0·3 kgf. m) to avoid distortion of cover. Renew the gasket.

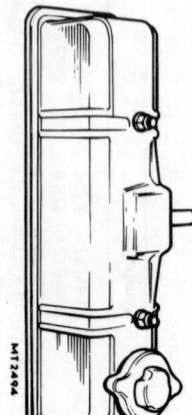

ENGINE

VALVE CLEARANCE

— Check and adjust 12.29.48

1. Isolate the battery.
2. Remove the rocker cover. 12.29.42.
3. Remove the spark plugs.
4. Counting from the front of the engin, turn the crankshaft until Nos. 8 and 6 valves are open, i.e. the valve springs fully compressed.
5. Using a 0·010 in (0.25 mm) feeler gauge, check the gap between the rocker pad and valve tip of Nos. 1 and 3 valves.
6. If adjustment is required, insert a screwdriver blade in the slot in the adjustment pin and slacken the locknut. Turn the adjustment pin clockwise to decrease and anti-clockwise to increase the gap.
7. Check and adjust the remaining valve clearances in the following sequence:
   Adjust Nos. 5 and 2 valves with Nos. 4 and 7 valves open.
   Adjust Nos. 8 and 6 valves with Nos. 1 and 3 valves open.
   Adjust Nos. 4 and 7 valves with Nos. 5 and 2 valves open.

Refitting
8. Reverse instructins 1 to 3.

ROCKER SHAFT 12.29.54

— Remove and refit

Removing
1. Remove the rocker cover 12.29.42.
2. Remove the four nuts complete with washers securing the rocker shaft pedestals to the cylinder head.
3. Lift off the rocker shaft.

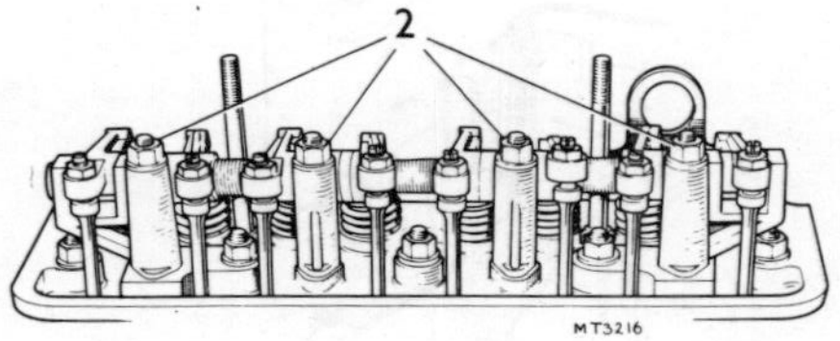

Refitting
4. Reverse instructions 1 to 3, ensuring that:
   a. The rocker adjustment screws are located correctly in the push-rod cups.
   b. The pedestal nuts are tightened evenly to 26 to 32 lbf. ft (3.6 to 4.4 kgf. m)
5. Adjust the valve clearances 12.29.48.

12.29.48
12.29.54

Triumph Spitfire Mk IV Manual. Part No. 545254.

ENGINE

ROCKER SHAFT ASSEMBLY 12.29.55

— Overhaul

1. Remove the rocker shaft 12.29.42.
2. Withdraw the cotter pin from the front end of the rocker shaft.
3. Slide off the rockers, pedestals, springs and spacers from the front end of the shaft, noting the order for reassembly.
4. Remove the screw locating the rear pedestal to the shaft.
5. Withdraw the rear pedestal and rocker.

Reassembling
6. Reverse instructions 1 to 5, observing:
   a. Renew all worn components. The grinding of worn rocker pads is not recommended.
   b. Ensure that oil-ways in rockers and shafts are clear.
   c. Ensure that the rear pedestal locating screw engages properly in the rocker shaft.
7. Adjust the valve clearances, 12.29.48.

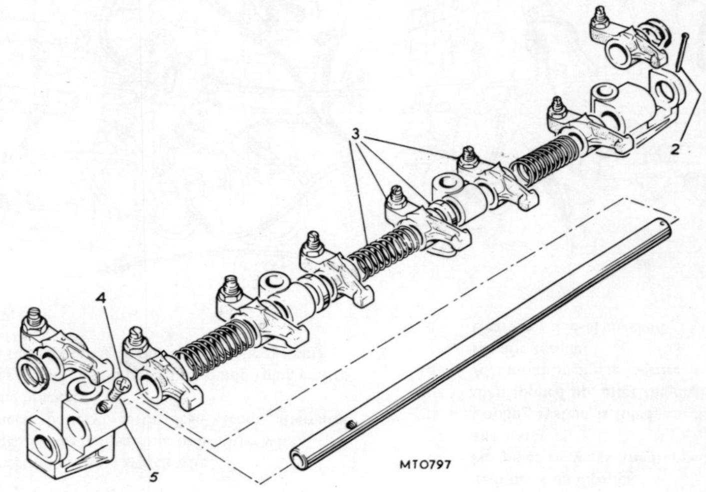

ROCKER ADJUSTING SCREWS – SET 12.29.56

— Remove and refit

Removing
1. Remove the rocker shaft assembly 12.29.54.
2. Remove the rocker adjusting screw locknuts.
3. Remove the rocker adjusting screws.

Refitting
4. Reverse instructions 1 to 3.
5. Adjust the valve clearances 12.29.48.

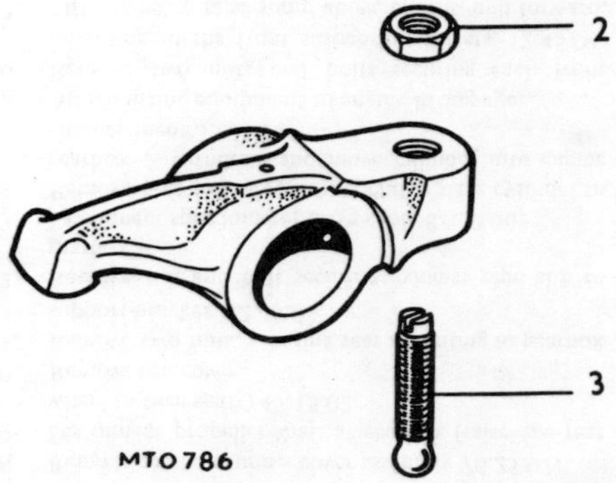

12.29.55
12.29.56

Triumph Spitfire Mk IV Manual. Part No. 545254.

ENGINE

CAM FOLLOWERS – SET
– Remove and refit   12.29.57

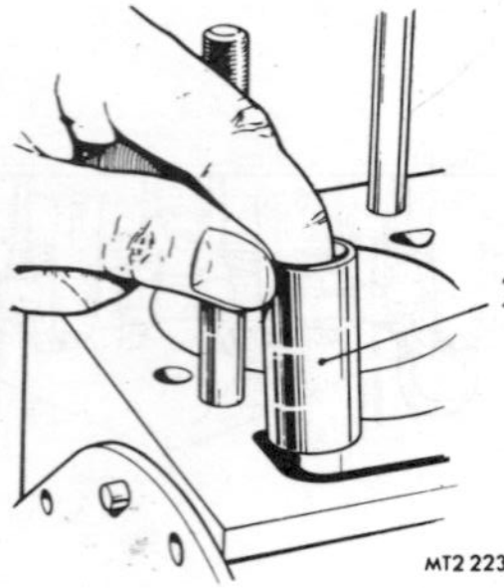

Removing
1. Remove the cylinder head 12.29.10.
2. Lift out the eight cam followers and identify for reassembly.

Refitting
3. Reverse instructions 1 and 2, ensuring:
   a. Worn or pitted cam followers are renewed.
   b. Lubricated with clean engine oil before resetting.
   c. Each follower is free to rotate and slide in its locating bore.

PUSH RODS – SET
– Remove and refit   12.29.59

Removing
1. Remove the rocker cover 12.29.42.
2. Remove the rocker shaft assembly 12.29.54.
3. Lift out the push-rods, identifying them for reassembly.

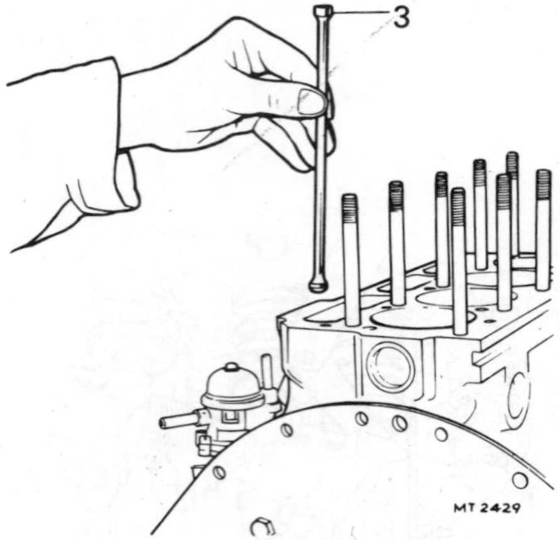

Refitting
4. Reverse instructions 1 to 3, ensuring:
   a. Push rods with worn or pitted cup and ball ends and bent shafts are renewed.
   b. Ball and cup ends are lubricated.
   c. Cup ends are located correctly in the rocker adjusting screw ball and ball ends are seated properly in the cam followers.
5. Adjust the valve clearances 12.29.48.

Valves – inlet and exhaust – remove and refit	12.29.62
Valves – inlet – remove and refit	12.29.63
Valves – exhaust – remove and refit	**12.29.64**
Valve guide – inlet – remove and refit	12.29.70
Valve guide – exhaust – remove and refit	12.29.71
Inlet valve seat – remove and refit	12.29.76
Exhaust valve seat – remove and refit	12.29.77

The above operations are included in 12.29.18.

12.29.57
12.29.77

Triumph Spitfire Mk IV Manual, Part No. 545254.

ENGINE

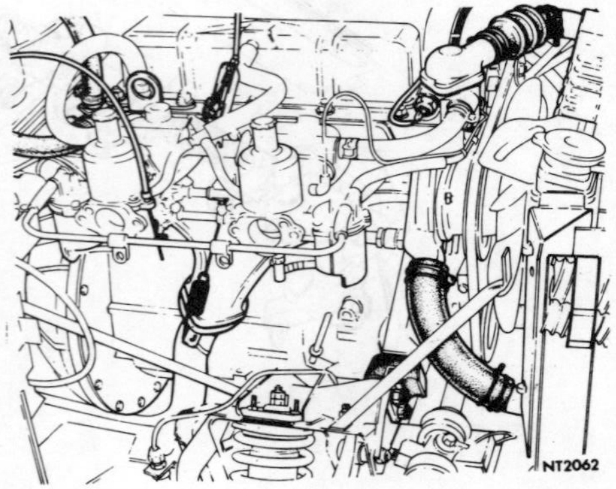

ENGINE AND GEARBOX ASSEMBLY
– Remove and refit   12.37.01

Removing
1. Remove bonnet. 76.16.01.
2. Disconnect and remove battery. 86.15.01.
3. Drain coolant. 26.10.01.
4. Drain sump oil. See 'Maintenance'.
5. Disconnect top and bottom hoses at engine, plus hose at expansion bottle. 26.30.01, 26.30.07.
6. Remove radiator – four bolts each side. 26.40.01.
7. Disconnect two heater hoses at engine.
8. Disconnect throttle cable at linkage 19.20.06.
9. Disconnect choke cable from rocker cover and carburetter.
10. Remove three nuts and washers securing exhaust front pipe to manifold. 30.10.09.
11. Disconnect at the distributor, the high and low tension leads.
12. Disconnect starter cable.
13. Disconnect multi-socket connector from the alternator.
14. Disconnect oil pressure switch wire.
15. Disconnect water temperature transmitter wire.
16. Disconnect battery earth lead from alternator mounting bracket.
17. Disconnect fuel feed pipe at fuel pump (plug end to prevent fuel siphoning or dirt entering the system).
18. Remove gearbox tunnel cover assembly 76.25.07.
19. Disconnect propeller shaft at gearbox (raise one rear wheel to turn shaft) 47.15.02.
20. Remove top cover.
21. Remove nut and bolt securing exhaust pipe clip to gearbox.
22. Remove two nuts, securing rear mounting to gearbox support bracket. 12.45.08.
23. Disconnect speedometer drive cable 88.30.06.
24. Remove bolt and nut securing clutch slave cylinder to gearbox – withdraw and move cylinder into engine compartment 33.35.01.
25. Attach lifting equipment to engine lifting eyes.
26. Remove two nuts and bolts securing each front mounting to the front suspension turrets. 12.45.04.
27. Lift engine to raise sump above chassis, pull forward, then raise and manoeuvre engine and gearbox clear of vehicle.

Refitting
28. Reverse instructions 1 to 27, ensuring:
   a. Sump filled with correct grade of engine oil to high mark on dipstick.
   b. No pipes or wires are trapped between engine and frame.
   c. Cooling system is filled, checked for leaks and then topped up, after the engine has been run.
   d. All mountings are secure and tightened to specific torque.
   e. Gearbox oil level checked.

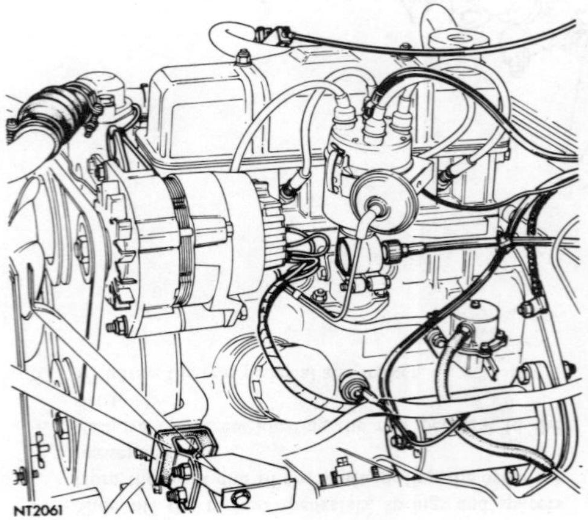

12.37.01
12.37.01

Triumph Spitfire Mk IV Manual, Part No. 545254.

ENGINE

ENGINE AND GEARBOX ASSEMBLY

— Remove, change ancillary equipment and refit 12.37.03.

Removing

1. Remove the engine and gearbox assembly 12.37.01.
2. Remove the water pump housing complete with thermostat housing, water pump, fan, pulley and belt. 26.50.03.
3. Remove the alternator and brackets.
4. Remove the air cleaner.
5. Remove the carburetters and breather pipes.
6. Remove the inlet and exhaust manifolds.
7. Remove the dipstick.
8. Remove the distributor. 86.35.20.
9. Remove the spark plugs.
10. Remove the oil filter, 12.60.01.
11. Remove the starter motor.
12. Remove the fuel pump.
13. Remove the clutch housing complete with gearbox.
14. Remove the clutch unit.
15. Remove the engine mounting rubbers.
16. Remove the oil filler cap.

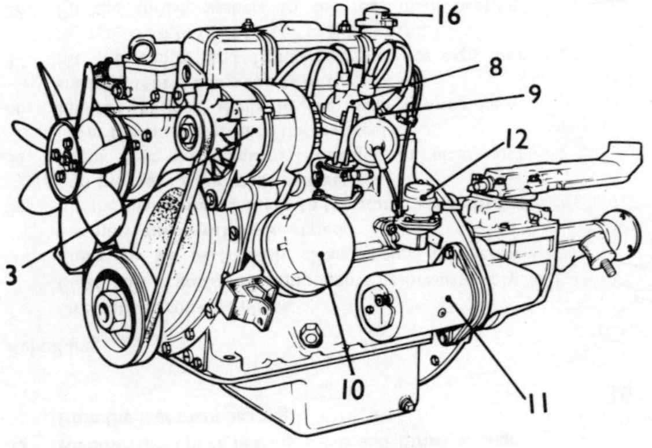

Refitting

17. Reverse instructions 1 to 16, ensuring:
    a. New gaskets and seals are fitted where applicable.
    b. Drive belt tension is adjusted 86.10.05.
    c. Distributor contact gap is adjusted 86.35.14.
    d. Check oil sump level, refill or top-up with recommended grade to high mark on dipstick.
    e. Refit the cooling system. 26.10.01.

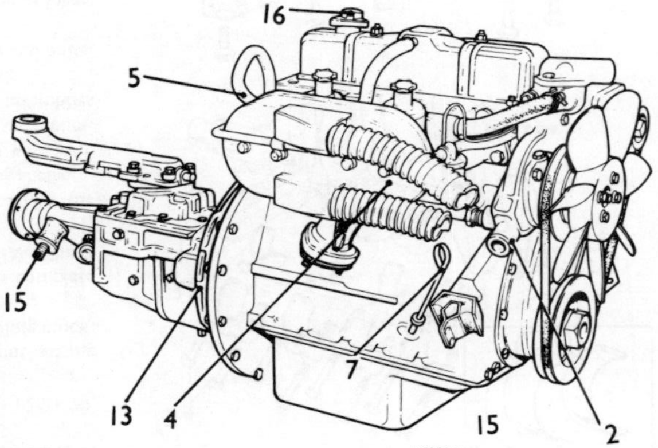

ENGINE ASSEMBLY 12.41.05

— Strip and rebuild

Stripping

1. Remove the engine and gearbox assembly and remove ancillary equipment 12.37.03.
2. Remove the rocker cover.
3. Remove the rocker shaft. 12.29.54. instructions 2 and 3.
4. Remove the cylinder head. 12.29.10 instructions 9 to 11, ensuring that the nuts are released in correct sequence 12.29.27.
5. Remove the valves and springs. 12.29.62. instructions 3 and 4, and identify for reassembly.
6. Remove the push rods and identify for reassembly.
7. Withdraw the cam followers and identify for reassembly. 12.29.57.
8. Remove the crankshaft pulley.
9. Remove the timing chain cover. 12.65.01 instructions 5 and 6.
10. Remove the timing chain and sprockets 12.65.12 instructions 2 and 5, ignoring reference to moving the crankshaft and camshaft.
11. Remove the distributor pedestal and drive gear. 12.10.22, instructions 2 to 4.
12. Remove the two bolts securing the camshaft locating plate to the cylinder block. Remove the plate and withdraw the camshaft.
13. Remove the cylinder block front mounting plate 12.25.10, instructions 9 to 12.
14. Remove the flywheel 12.53.07, instructions 3 and 4.
15. Remove the spigot bush from the crankshaft.
16. Remove the engine rear adaptor plate 12.53.03, instructions 2 and 3.
17. Turn the cylinder block over so that the sump is uppermost.
18. Remove the bolts securing the sump to the crankcase and lift off the sump complete with gasket.

ENGINE

19. Remove the oil pump strainer.
20. Remove the oil pump 12.60.26, instructions 2 and 3.
21. Remove the oil pressure relief valve 12.60.56.
22. Remove the crankshaft rear oil seal 12.21.20, instructions 3 to 5.
23. Remove the two screws securing the front sealing block to the crankcase and lift out the sealing block.
24. Remove the eight big-end bolts.
25. Withdraw the connecting rod bearing caps complete with lower bearing shells. Check identification marks for reassembly.
26. Push the connecting rods and pistons down the cylinder bores and remove the upper bearing shells.
27. Turn the cylinder block on its side and with care withdraw the pistons and connecting rod assemblies.
28. Marry-up the connecting rods and piston assemblies with their respective bearing caps and shells.
29. Remove the front and centre main bearing caps and shells.
30. Remove the rear main bearing cap bolts.
31. Withdraw the main bearing caps, complete with lower shells. Check identification marks for reassembly. DO NOT MIX.
32. Lift out the crankshaft.
33. Remove the upper bearing shells and thrust washers from the rear main bearing.

Rebuilding

34. Overhaul all sub-assemblies.
35. Clean and degrease all components before assembly. Lubricate all parts with clean engine oil before assembly, unless otherwise stated.
36. Fit the main bearing shells to the crankcase, ensuring that the tags locate in the recesses.
37. Check that the crankshaft oilways are clear, and lower the crankshaft into the crankcase.
38. Fit the bearing shells to the main bearing caps, ensuring that the tags locate in the recesses.
37. Fit the centre and front main bearing caps and tighten to 50 to 65 lbf. ft (7 to 9 kgf. m).
38. Fit the thrust washers to the rear main bearing, ensuring that the thrust faces, identified by oil grooves, bear against the crankshaft faces and locate in the registers on both sides of the crankcase bearing bore half.

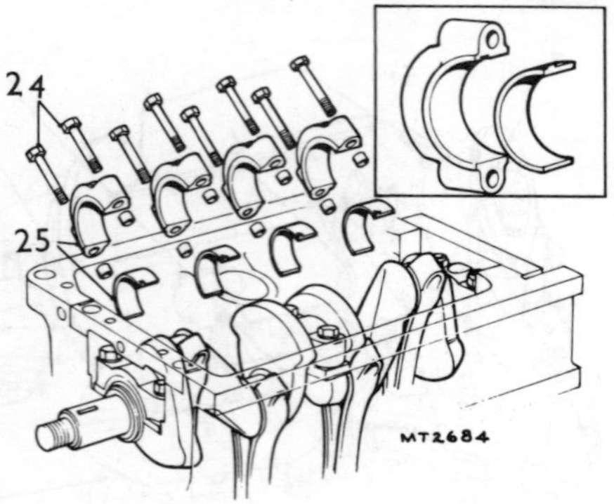

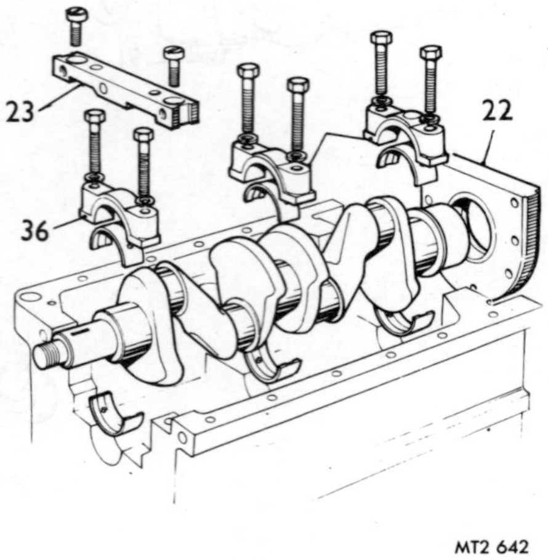

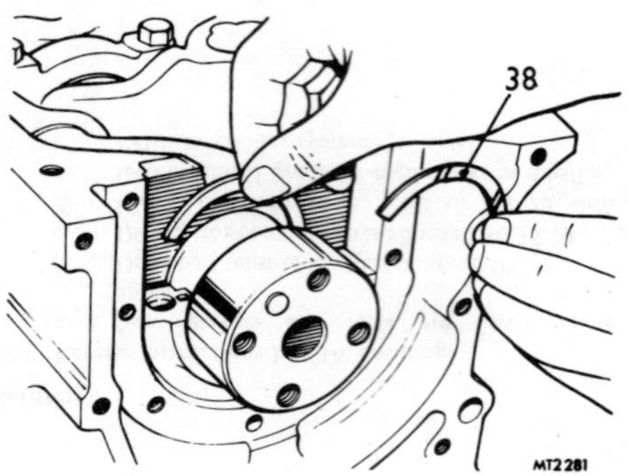

39. Check the crankshaft end-float.
40. Fit the rear main bearing cap and tighten the bolts to 50 to 65 lbf. ft (7 to 9 kgf. m).
41. Fit the piston and connecting rod assemblies to the cylinder block bores. 12.17.01, instructions 14 to 21.
42. Fit the crankshaft rear oil seal. 12.21.20, instructions 6 to 11.
43. Fit the front sealing block 12.21.39, instructions 14 to 17.
44. Fit the oil pump, ensuring that the spring washers are located under the bolt heads, tighten the bolts evenly.
45. Fit the oil strainer to the pump inlet.
46. Fit the sump with a new gasket and evenly tighten the retaining bolts.
47. Fit the oil pressure relief valve 12.60.56.
48. Turn the cylinder block over, and secure in an up-right position.
49. Fit the engine adaptor plate, ensuring correct location over the studs and dowels and that the arrow is at the top. Evenly tighten the retaining bolts.
50. Fit the crankshaft spigot bush, which should be a loose fit in the crankshaft.
51. Fit the flywheel. 12.53.07, instructions 5 to 8.
52. Coat the cylinder block face of a new front mounting plate gasket with jointing compound and place it in position on the joint face.
53. Fit the mounting plate in position over the dowels. Secure it in position with three bolts into the cylinder block and three screws into the front sealing block.
54. Assemble the camshaft into the camshaft location plate, secure it in position with the camshaft location plate, and tighten the retaining bolts.
55. Check the camshaft end-float, which should be within 0·004 to 0·008 in (0·10 to 0·20 mm). Pull the camshaft out against the location plate and insert a feeler gauge between the groove and location plate. Reduce end-float by fitting a new location plate.

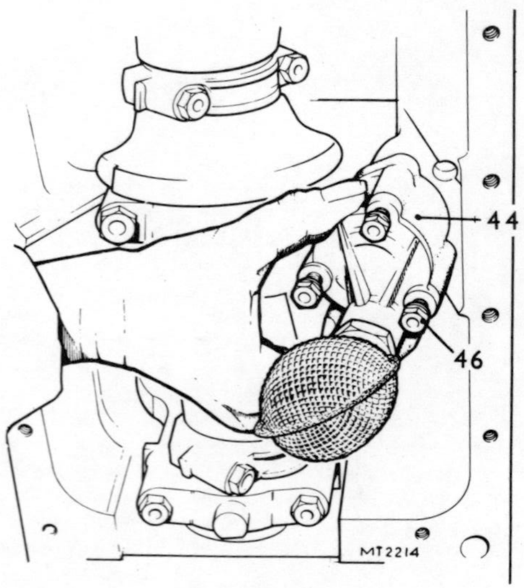

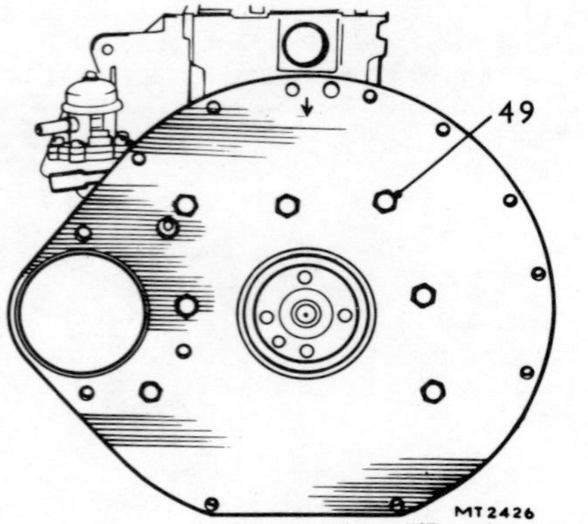

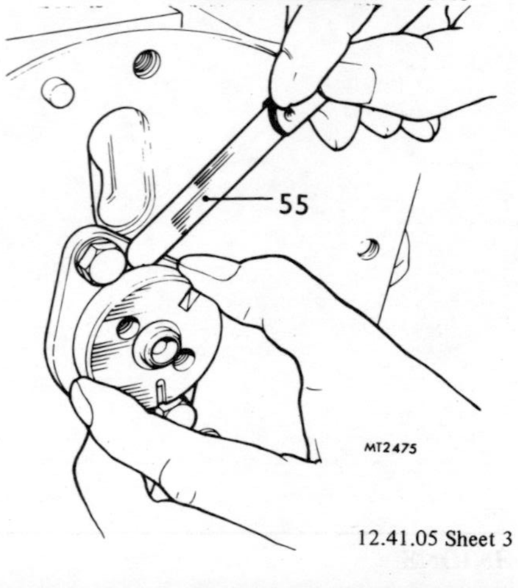

ENGINE

57. Reassemble the valves and springs to the cylinder head. 12.29.18, instructions 5 to 13.
58. Fit the cam followers to the cylinder block. 12.29.57, instruction 3.
59. Rotate the crankshaft until No. 1 piston is at T.D.C. by using a dial gauge on the piston crown. **DO NOT MOVE THE CRANKSHAFT AGAIN UNTIL THE VALVES HAVE BEEN TIMED.**
60. Fit the cylinder head assembly with a new gasket. Tighten the retaining nuts in correct sequence and torque loading. 12.29.27.
61. Fit the push-rods, ensuring that the ball ends locate in the cam followers.
62. Fit the rocker shaft assembly, ensuring that the rocker adjusting screw balls locate in the push-rods cups.
63. Tighten the rocker shaft pedestal nuts evenly to 26 to 32 lbf. ft (3·6 to 4·4 kgf. m).
64. Adjust the valve clearances of Nos. 7 and 8 valves only to 0·050 in (0·397 m) to give a working clearance. 12.29.48, instructions 6 and 7. 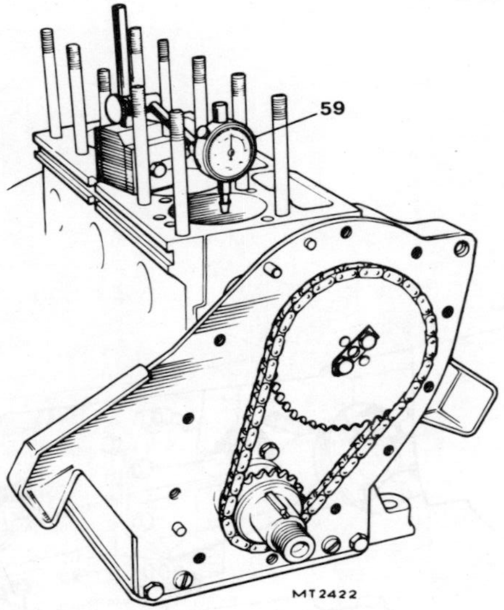
65. Turn the camshaft until Nos. 7 and 8 valves are on the 'rock', i.e. inlet valve about to open and exhaust valve about to close. This may be determined by oscillating the camshaft while measuring the rocker clearances of these two valves with feeler gauges. When the two clearances are the same, the valves and camshaft are in their correct relationship with the crankshaft.

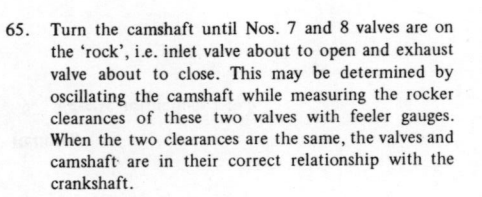

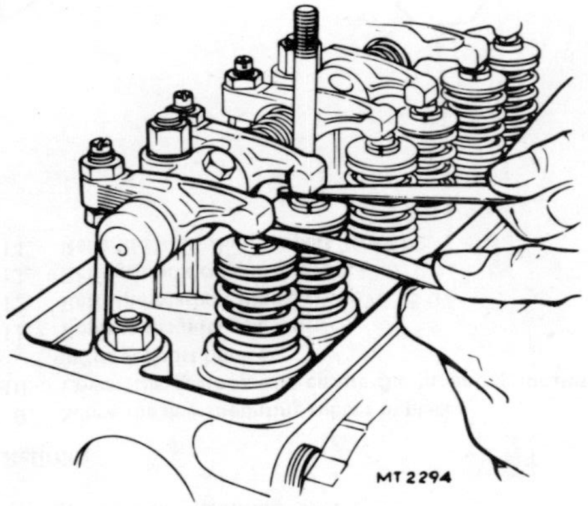

66. Encircle both sprockets with the timing chain and fit to crankshaft and camshaft respectively, keeping the chain taut on the drive side.

NOTE: The camshaft timing sprocket is provided with four holes which are equally spaced but offset from a tooth centre. Half-tooth adjustment is obtained by rotating the sprocket 90 degrees from its original position. A quarter tooth adjustment is possible by turning the sprocket 'back to front'. By rotating the sprocket 90 degrees in this position three-quarters of a tooth variation is available.

67. If new sprockets have been fitted, make a punch mark (A) on the crankshaft and camshaft sprockets on a line (C) scribed through the diameters of the two sprockets. Make also a punch mark (B) on the end of the camshaft through one of the sprocket holes and a corresponding punch mark on he sprocket. 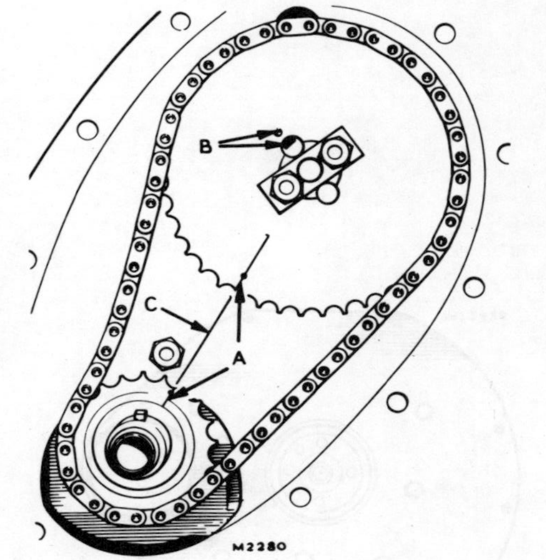
68. Check the sprockets for alignment 12.65.12.
69. Fit a new camshaft sprocket lock plate and tighten the bolts and bend over the tabs.
70. Fit the oil thrower to the crankshaft, ensuring that the dished periphery faces the timing cover.
71. Fit the timing chain cover complete with a new gasket. 12.65.01.
72. Fit the crankshaft pulley and tighten the retaining nut to 90 to 110 lbf. ft (12·4 to 15·2 kgf. m).
73. Adjust all valve clearances. 12.29.48, instructions 4 to 7.
74. Fit the distributor drive shaft and gear. 12.10.22.
75. Fit the rocker cover.
76. Fit the ancillary equipment. 12.37.03.
77. Fit the clutch assembly.
78. Fit the gearbox assembly.
79. Fit the engine and gearbox assembly to the car. 12.37.01.
80. Fill the oil sump with engine oil of the correct grade to the top mark on the dipstick, and replace the dipstick.
81. Fill the cooling system 26.10.01, instructions 5 to 10.
82. Time the ignition 86.35.16.
83. Tune and adjust the carburetters. 19.15.02.

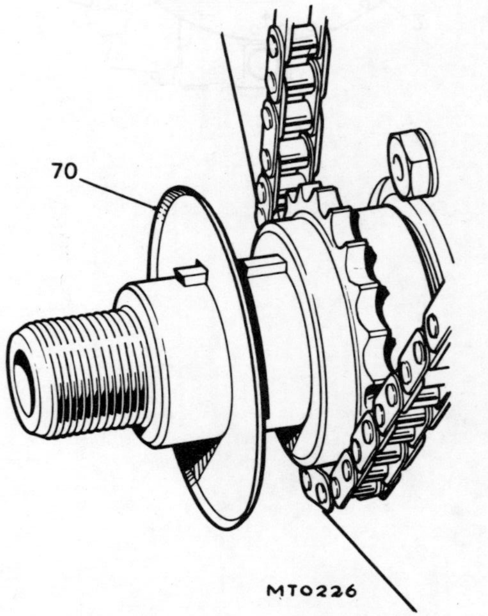

ENGINE

ENGINE MOUNTINGS – FRONT

- L.H. – remove and refit 12.45.01
- R.H. – remove and refit 12.45.03
- Set – remove and refit 12.45.04

Removing

1. Employ a jack or hoist to take the weight of the engine.
2. Remove the nuts and bolts securing the mounting to frame (two each side).
3. Remove the nut securing the mounting to the engine mounting plate.
4. Raise the engine slightly.
5. Remove the mounting(s).

Refitting

6. Reverse instructions 1 to 5.

ENGINE MOUNTINGS REAR L.H.

- LH – Remove and refit 12.45.07
- RH – Remove and refit 12.45.09
- Set – Remove and refit 12.45.10

Removing

1. Remove the front floor carpets 76.49.02.
2. Remove the gearbox cover carpet 76.49.01.
3. Remove the gearbox tunnel cover 76.25.07.
4. Place jack under gearbox.
5. Remove nuts.
6. Remove washers.
7. Jack up gearbox until the mounting rubbers are clear of the support bracket.
8. Unscrew the mounting rubber.

Refitting

9. Screw the new mounting rubber in place.
10. Lower the gearbox and ensure the mounting locates in the support bracket.
11. Replace the nuts and washers.
12. Refit the gearbox tunnel cover 76.25.07.
13. Refit gearbox cover carpet 76.49.01.
14. Refit the front floor carpets 76.49.02.

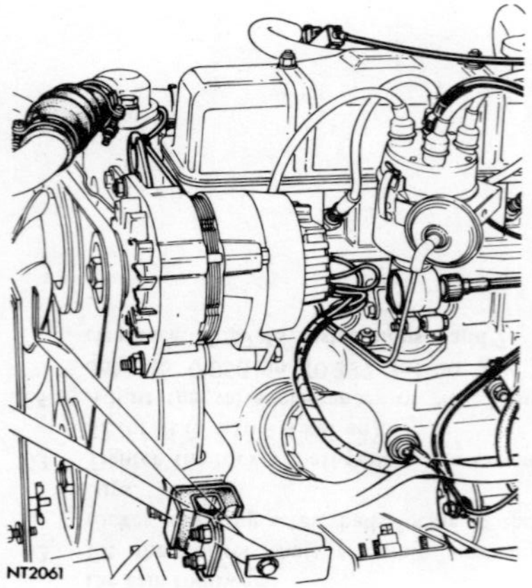

ENGINE

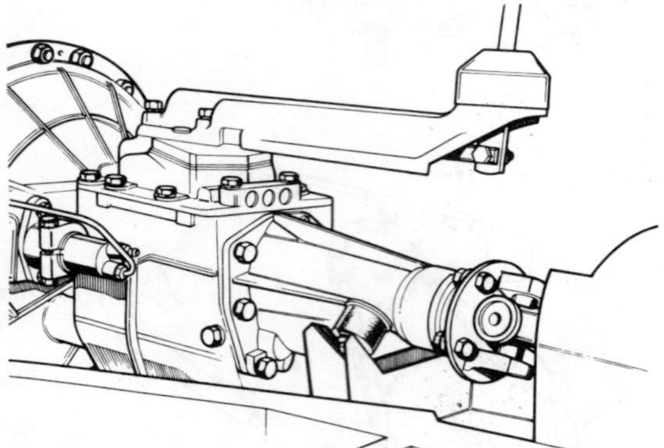

ENGINE TUNE

- Check and adjust distributor points, spark plugs, ignition timing, tune carburetters, clean fuel pump filter and road test. 12.49.02

1. Check the condition and gap of distributor points, renew or adjust as required. 86.35.13.
2. Remove the spark plugs and check their condition, renew if necessary. Clean and adjust the gaps. 86.35.01.
3. Check the ignition timing, and adjust if necessary. 86.35.16.
4. Tune the carburetters 19.15.02.
5. Clean the fuel pump filter. 19.45.02.

ENGINE REAR GEARBOX ADAPTOR PLATE

- Remove and refit 12.53.03

Removing

1. Remove the flywheel 12.53.07.
2. Remove the seven bolts securing the adaptor plate to the cylinder block.
3. Remove the adaptor plate.

Refitting

4. Reverse instructions 1 to 3, ensuring:
   a. The adaptor plate is located correctly over the dowel at the top of the cylinder block.
   b. The adaptor plate retaining bolts are tightened evenly to 16 to 20 lbf. ft (2·2 to 2·8 kgf. m).

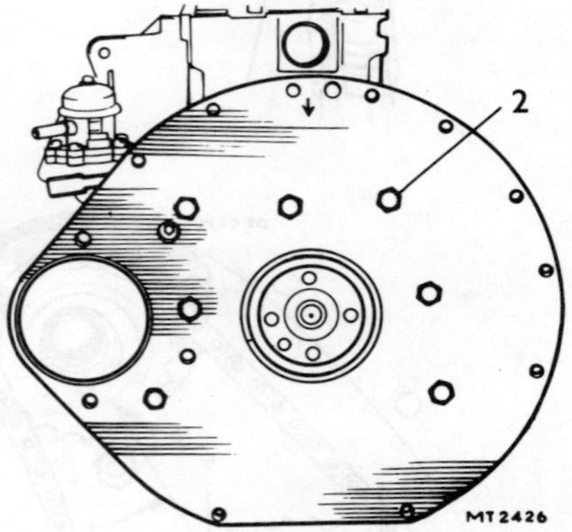

ENGINE

FLYWHEEL

— Remove and refit   12.53.07

Removing

1. Remove the gearbox 37.20.01.
2. Remove the clutch assembly 33.10.01.
3. Remove the four bolts securing the flywheel to the crankshaft.
4. Lift off the flywheel.

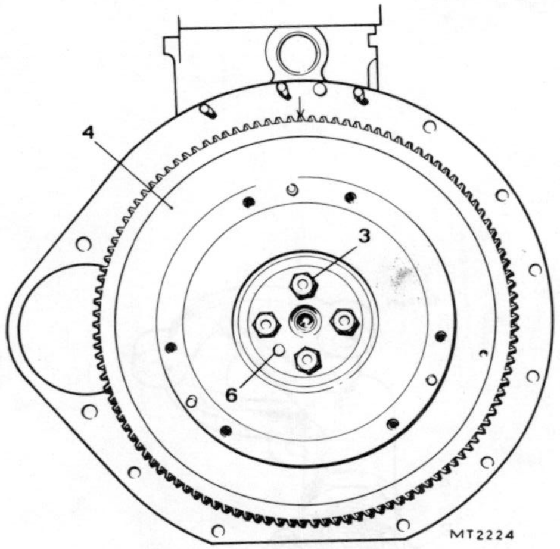

Refitting

5. Clean the flywheel mating face with the crankshaft and crankshaft flange. Check the dowel for damage, and that the crankshaft spigot bush is in position.
6. Fit the flywheel to the crankshaft, locating over the dowel in the crankshaft.
7. Tighten the flywheel retaining bolts evenly to 38 to 45 lbf.ft. (5·2 to 6·2 kgf.m).
8. Using a dial indicator gauge, check the flywheel for run-out, not to exceed 0·002 in (0·051 mm) at 3·0 in (76·2 mm) radius from spigot centre. Check concentricity, not to exceed 0·004 in (0·100 mm).
9. Refit the clutch assembly 33.10.01.
10. Refit the gearbox 37.20.01.

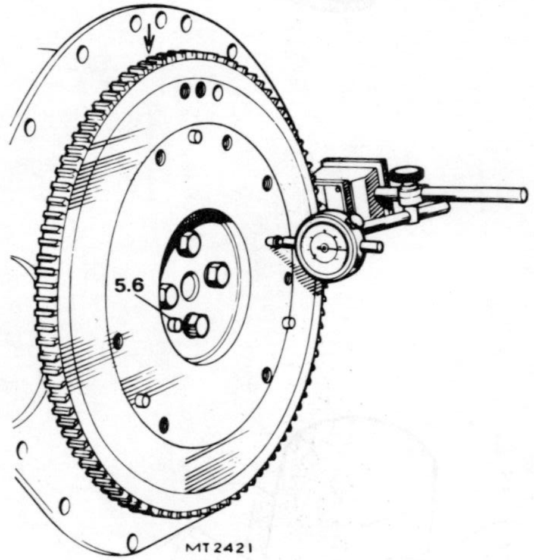

ENGINE

STARTER RING GEAR

— Remove and refit   12.53.19

Removing

1. Isolate the battery.
2. Remove the flywheel. 12.53.07.
3. Drill a hole ¼ in (6·35 mm) diameter at the point of intersection of a scribe line between any two teeth and a scribe line midway between the root diameter and inside diameter of the ring gear.
4. Hold the flywheel assembly in a soft jaw vice.
5. Place a cloth of heavy material over the ring gear for protection against flying fragments.

WARNING: Ensure adequate protection, particularly for the eyes, to prevent injury from flying fragments when the ring gear is split.

6. Place a cold chisel immediately above the centre line of the drilled hole and strike sharply to split the ring gear.

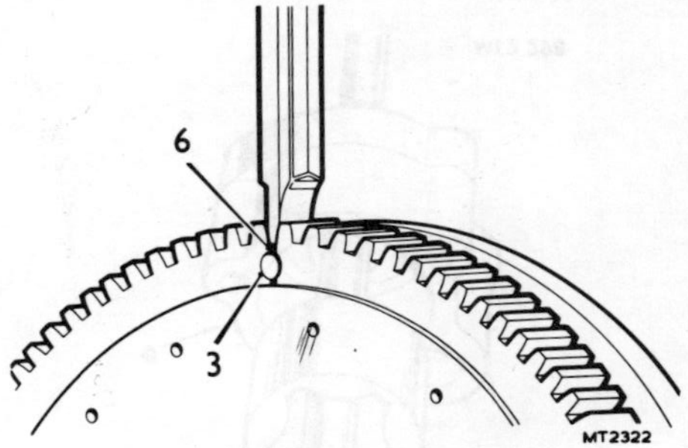

Refitting

7. Heat the replacement starter ring gear uniformly to a maximum of 200°C.
8. Place the flywheel on a flat surface, clutch face side uppermost, and clean the ring gear locating register.
9. Locate the ring gear and hold in position until it contracts sufficiently to grip the flywheel.
10. Allow the ring gear to cool gradually to avoid distortion. A maximum gap of 0·025 in (0·635 mm) is tolerable between the ring gear and the flywheel face in any one area of 6 in (15 cm) around the circumference.
11. Refit the flywheel, 12.53.07, and check that ring gear eccentricity does not exceed 0·010 in (0·254 mm).

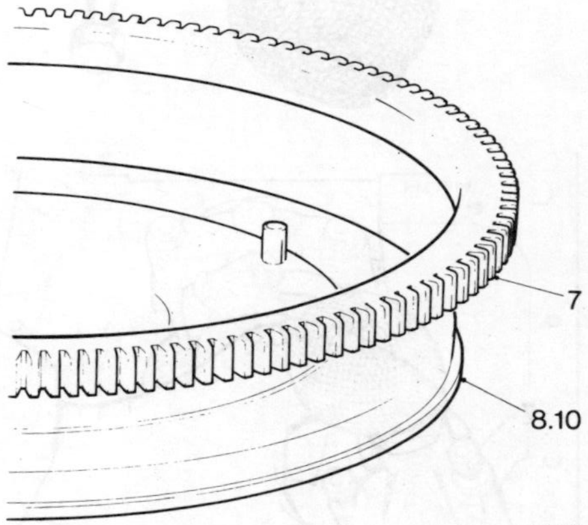

ENGINE

OIL FILTER
— Remove and refit   12.60.01

Removing
1. Isolate the battery.
2. Grasp the oil filter with both hands and turn anti-clockwise.
3. Remove the filter.

Refitting
4. Clean the cylinder block face.
5. Smear the 'O' ring with grease to prevent 'picking up'.
6. Fit the filter, turning clockwise, and tighten.
7. Start the engine and check for oil leaks between the cylinder block and filter.

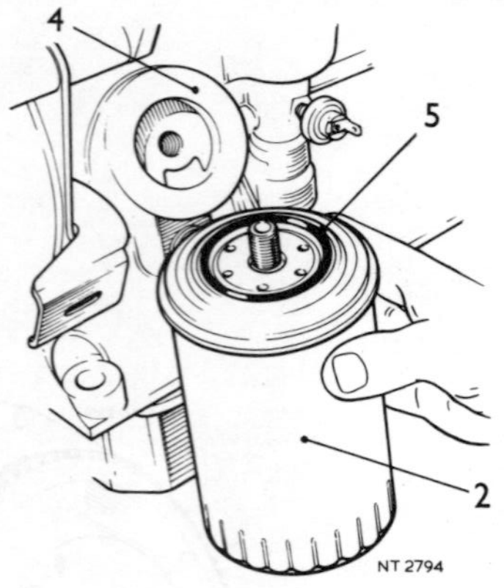

OIL PICK-UP STRAINER
— Remove, clean and refit   12.60.20

Removing
1. Remove the sump 12.60.44.
2. Release the oil strainer locknut.
3. Unscrew the oil strainer and remove it.
4. Wash the oil strainer in petrol and dry it before refitting.

Refitting
5. Reverse instructions 1 to 3.

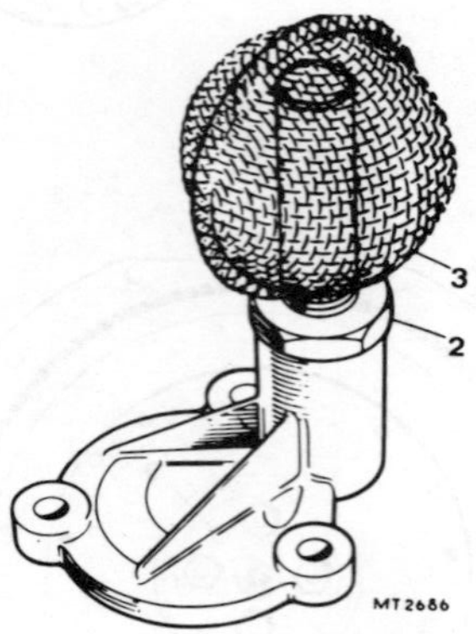

OIL PUMP
— Remove and refit   12.60.26

Removing
1. Remove the oil sump 12.60.44.
2. Slacken and remove the three bolts complete with washers securing the oil pump to the crankcase.
3. Remove the oil pump complete with cover-plate.

Refitting
4. Reverse instructions 1 to 3, ensuring:
   a. The oil pump drive shaft engages correctly into the drive gear shaft.
   b. The securing bolts are evenly tightened.
   c. Absolute cleanliness is observed.

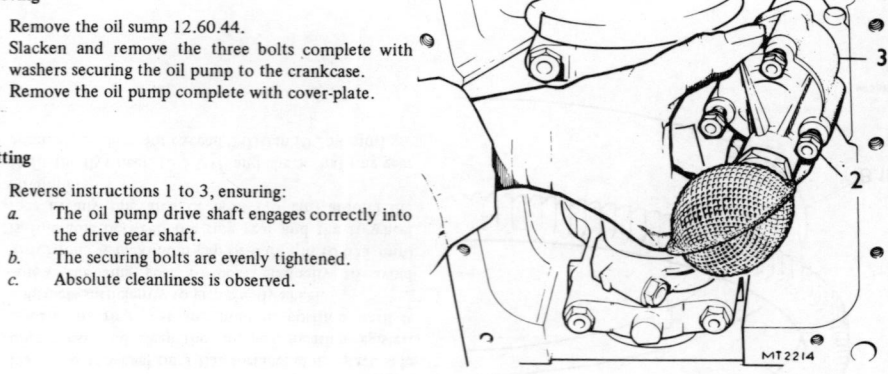

OIL PUMP
— Overhaul   12.60.32

1. Isolate the battery.
2. Remove the oil pump from the crankcase. 12.60.26.
3. Remove the cover-plate complete with strainer.
4. Remove the inner rotor and shaft assembly.
5. Remove the outer rotor.
6. Clean oil from the body and rotors, and reassemble.

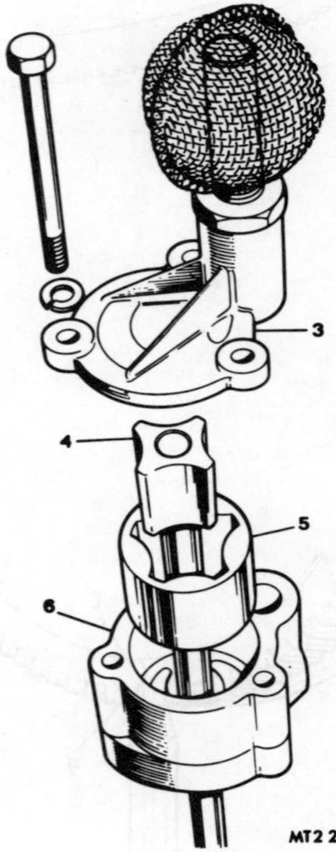

12.60.01
12.60.20

12.60.26
12.60.32 Sheet 1

ENGINE

7. Place the oil pump in a vice and using a feeler gauge:
   a. With a straight-edge across the pump body face, check the clearance between the rotors and straight-edge. This clearance must not exceed 0·004 in (0·1 mm).
   b. Check the clearance between the inner and outer rotors. This must not exceed 0·010 in (0·25 mm).
   c. Check the clearance between the outer rotor and body. This must not exceed 0·008 in (0·2 mm).
8. Check the cover-plate for scoring, and test on a surface plate for distortion. Renew if necessary.
9. Check the pump spindle bearing surface in the pump body for excessive wear.
10. Reassemble the pump, fitting any new parts necessary to satisfy the above quoted tolerances. Renew the complete pump if a satisfactory condition cannot be achieved.

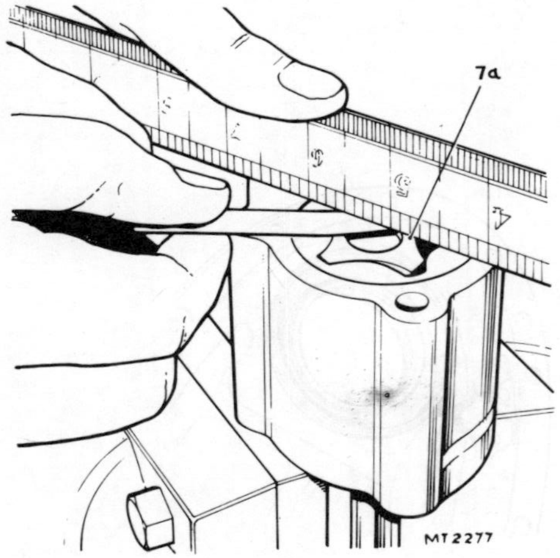

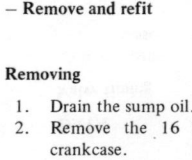

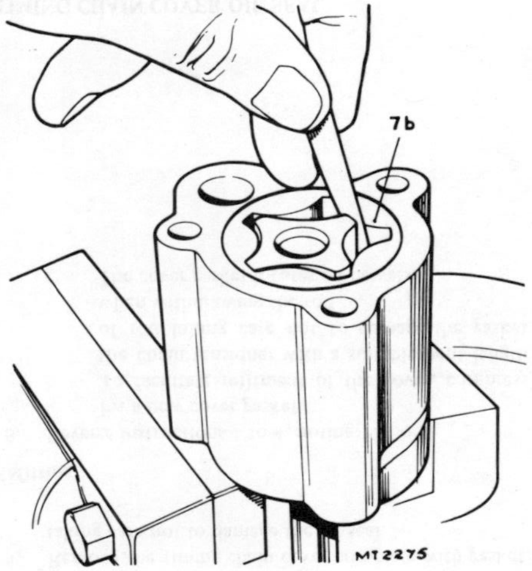

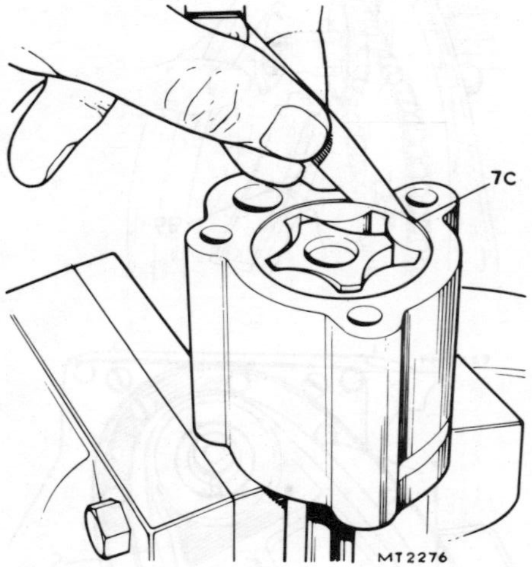

OIL SUMP
— Remove and refit   12.60.44

Removing
1. Drain the sump oil.
2. Remove the 16 bolts securing the sump to the crankcase.
3. Raise the engine sufficiently to lower the sump, turn it and withdraw.

Refitting
4. Reverse instructions 1 to 3 noting:
   a. Clean the crankcase and sump faces.
   b. Fit a new gasket
   c. The longer bolts are fitted at the rear of the sump.
   d. Tighten the retaining bolts to 16 to 20 lbf. ft (2·2 to 2·8 kgf. m).

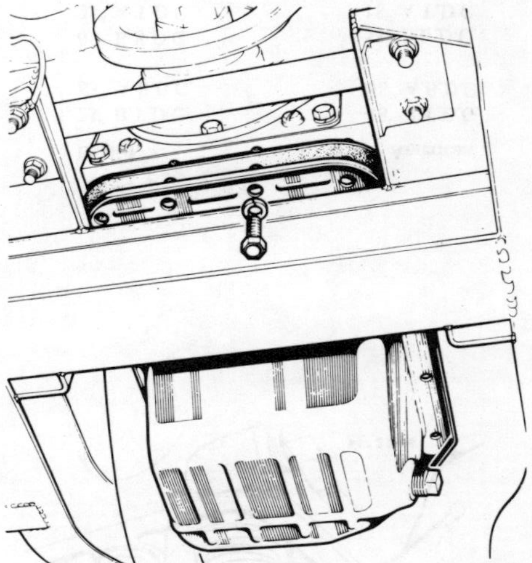

OIL PRESSURE RELIEF VALVE
— Remove and refit   12.60.56

Removing
1. Unscrew the relief valve body from the cylinder block.
2. Remove the washer.
3. Take out the plunger.
4. Remove the spring.

Refitting
5. Reverse instructions 1 to 4 ensuring:
   a. Cleanliness.
   b. A new spring is fitted if free length is not in accordance with Data.

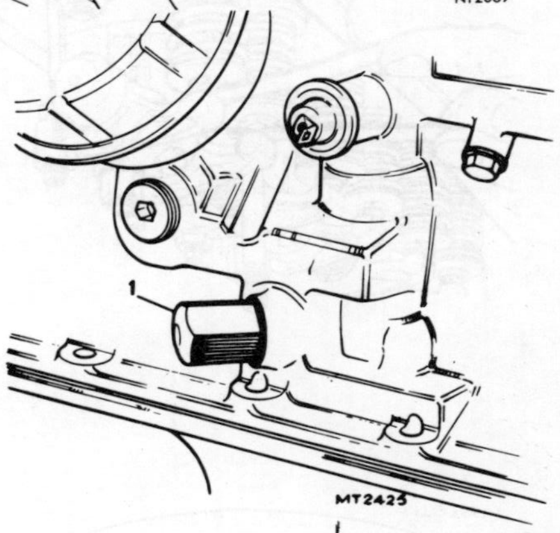

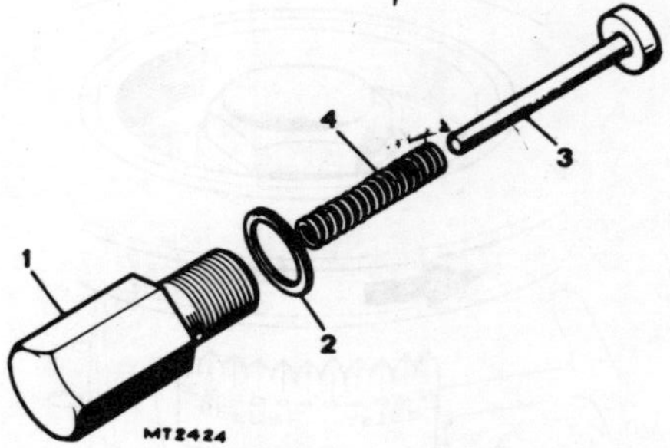

DATA
Oil pressure relief valve spring free length . . . 1·53 in (38·8 mm).

12.60.32 Sheet 2

12.60.44
12.60.56

ENGINE

TIMING CHAIN COVER
12.65.01

– Remove and refit

Removing

1. Remove the fan belt.
2. Remove the fan blades 26.25.06.
3. Remove the crankshaft pulley, 12.21.01.
4. Remove the five screws, six bolts and one nut securing the timing chain cover to the cylinder block.
5. Remove the timing chain cover complete with gasket, taking care not to damage the oil seal.

Refitting

6. Reverse instructions 1 to 4, noting:
   a. Fit a new cover gasket.
   b. To facilitate refitment of the cover, compress the chain tensioner with a suitable bent length of rod taking care not to damage the gasket when withdrawing the rod.
   c. The cover gasket locates on dowels.

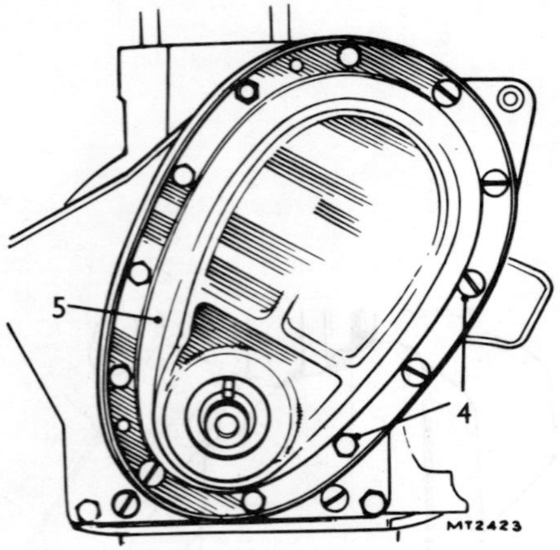

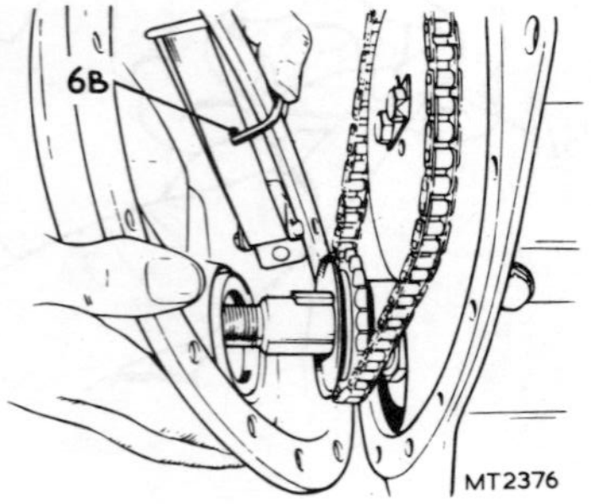

TIMING CHAIN COVER OIL SEAL
12.65.05

– Remove and refit

Removing

1. Remove the timing chain cover 12.65.01.
2. Carefully remove the oil seal, avoiding damage to the timing cover.

Refitting

3. Reverse instructions 1 and 2, ensuring that the new oil seal is:
   a. Smeared with oil before fitting.
   b. Fitted correctly, i.e. cavity face towards the engine.
   c. Pressed home squarely.

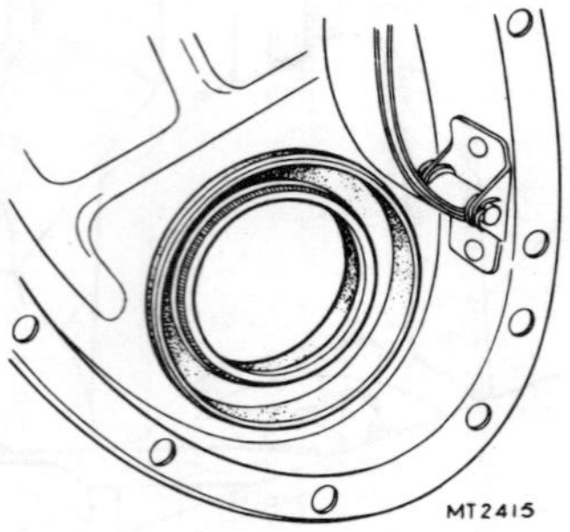

VALVE TIMING
12.65.08

– Check

1. Remove the rocker cover 12.29.42.
2. Adjust the rocker clearances of Nos. 7 and 8 valves to 0·050 in (1·27 mm) 12.29.48, instructions 6 and 7, to give a working clearance.
3. Turn the crankshaft until No. 1 piston is at T.D.C. on compression stroke, indicated by the mark on the crankshaft pulley coinciding with the pointer on the timing cover.
4. Check that Nos. 1 and 2 valves are fully closed by inserting a feeler gauge between the valve tip and rocker pad to ascertain clearance.
5. Using two feeler gauges of the same thickness, check that the rocker clearances on Nos. 7 and 8 valves are the same. Oscillate the crankshaft to achieve this condition, but ensure that when the rocker clearances are the same the conditions in instructions 3 and 4 are maintained within a few degrees.

NOTE: The actual valve clearance does not matter providing the clearances are the same.

6. Should the valve timing prove to be incorrect, retiming will be necessary, 12.41.05, instructions 59 to 67.
7. Re-adjust Nos. 7 and 8 valves to 0·010 in (0·25 mm) 12.29.48, instructions 6 and 7.
8. Refit the rocker cover 12.29.42.

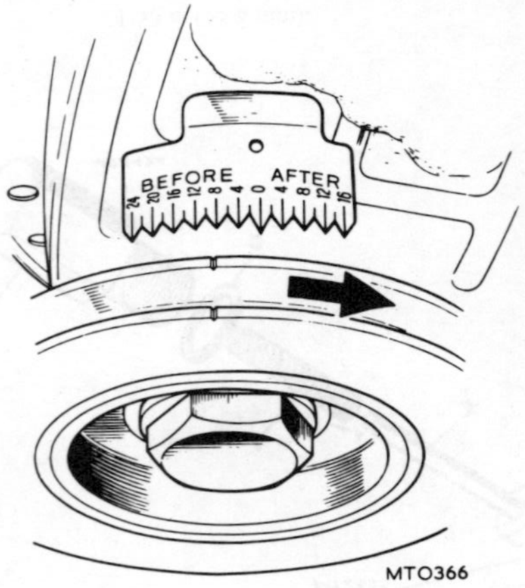

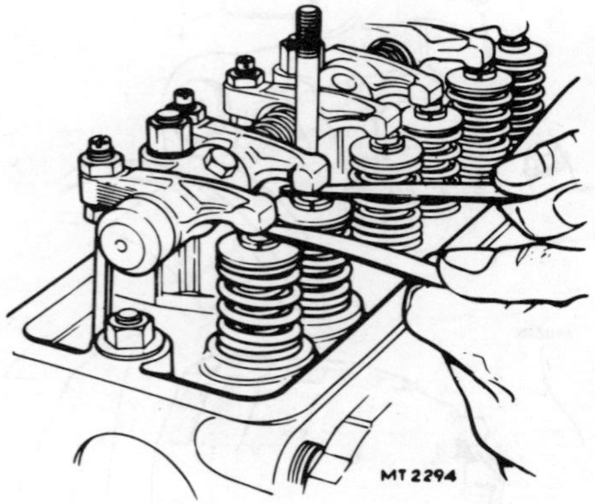

DATA

Valve timing

	English	American
inlet opens	25° B.T.D.C.	18° B.T.D.C.
closes	65° A.B.D.C.	58° A.B.D.C.
Exhaust opens	65° B.B.D.C.	58° B.B.D.C.
closes	25° A.T.D.C.	18° A.T.D.C.

ENGINE

TIMING CHAIN AND SPROCKETS

— Remove and refit

Timing chain 1 to 5, 12, and 15 to 17 12.65.12
                                        12.65.14

Removing

1. Remove the timing chain cover 12.65.01.
2. Remove the oil thrower.
3. Turn the crankshaft until the mark 'A' is in line with scribe mark 'C' and marks 'B' correspond. The crankshaft keyway should be at 12 o'clock.
4. Bend back the lock plate tabs and remove the two bolts securing the sprocket to the camshaft.
5. Taking care not to turn the crankshaft or camshaft, remove both sprockets together with the timing chain.

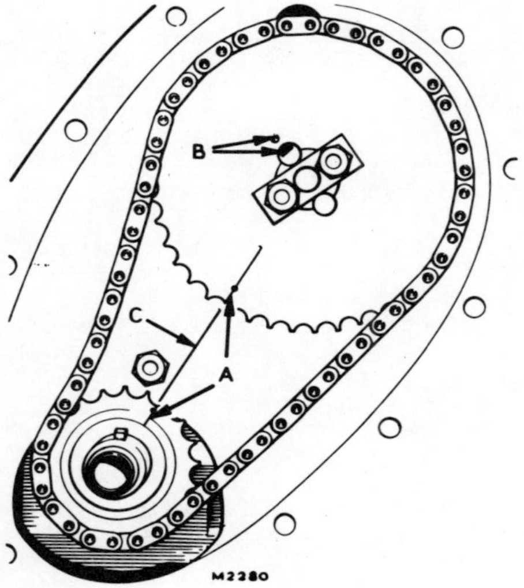

Refitting

6. Remove the crankshaft drive key.
7. Temporarily refit both sprockets.
8. Check the alignment of the sprockets by placing a straight edge across the teeth of both sprockets.

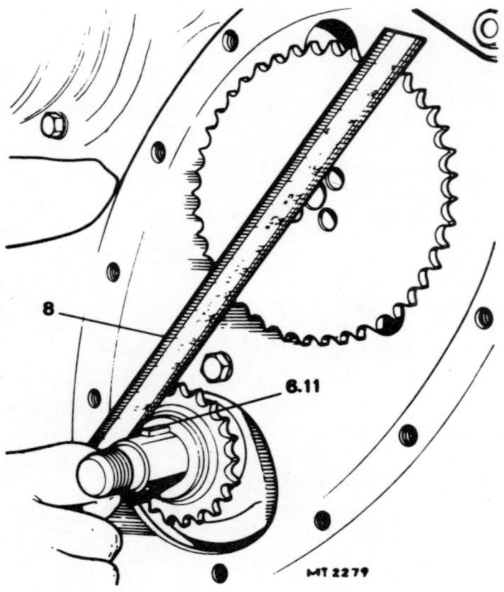

9. Correct any misalignment by fitting selective shims behind the crankshaft sprocket.
10. Remove the sprockets.
11. Refit the drive key.
12. Encircle the sprockets with the timing chain and refit ensuring that the marks on the sprockets and engine plate line up.
13. Refit the camshaft sprockets securing bolts (temporarily). 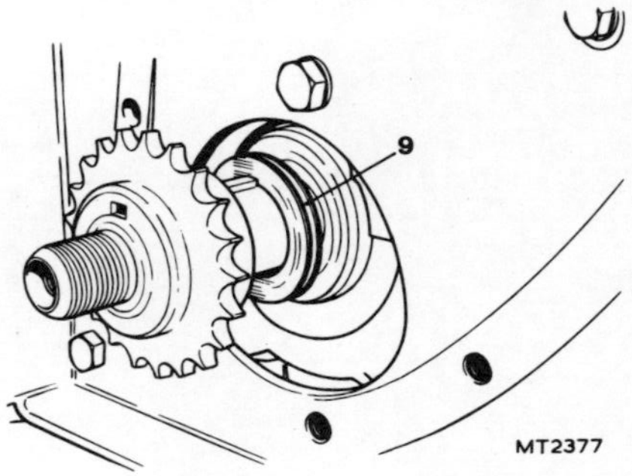
14. Check timing chain wear by placing a straight edge along the slack run of chain. If movement at the mid-point 'A' exceeds 0·4 in (10mm), renew the chain.
15. Fit a new camshaft sprocket lock plate, refit the bolts and bend the tabs.
16. Refit the oil thrower with the dished periphery towards the timing chain cover. 12.41.05
17. Refit the timing chain cover 12.65.01.

NOTE: If new sprockets are fitted see instructions 67 and 68, 12.41.05.

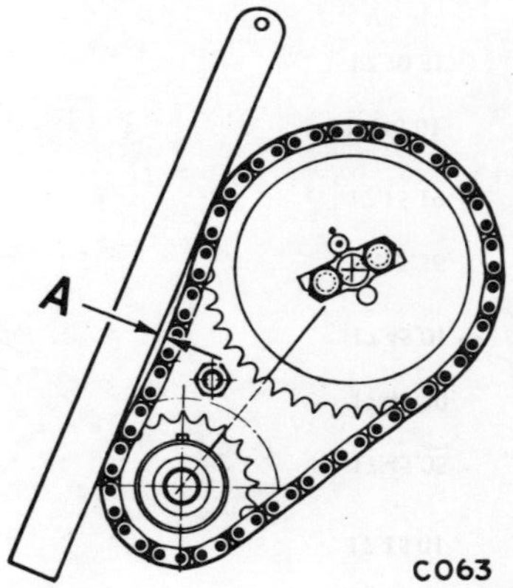

TIMING CHAIN TENSIONER

— Remove and refit 12.65.28

Removing

1. Remove the timing chain cover. 12.65.01
2. Prise open the tensioner blades.
3. Slide the tensioner off the anchor pin.

Refitting

4. Reverse instructions 1 to 3, ensuring that the tensioner is fitted correctly i.e. convex surface towards the timing chain.

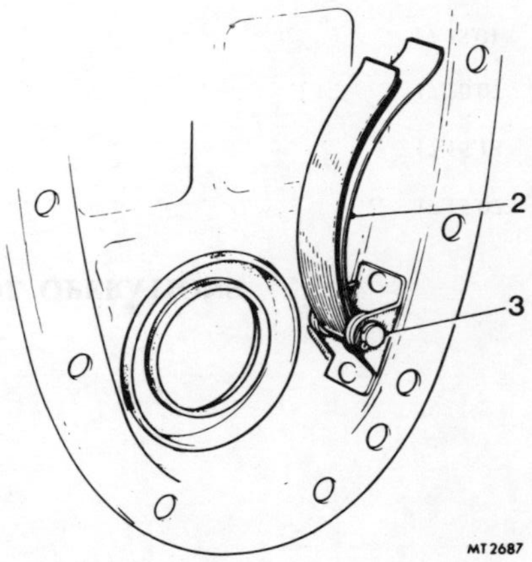

EMISSION CONTROL

EMISSION CONTROL OPERATIONS

Adsorption canister air filter — remove and refit	17.15.07
Adsorption canister — remove and refit	17.15.13
Carburetter emission pack — Red — remove and refit	17.20.07
C.O. level at idle — check	17.35.01
Control pipe, canister to fuel tank — remove and refit	17.15.24
Evaporative loss control system — leak testing	17.15.01
** Exhaust gas recirculation control valve — remove and refit	17.45.05
Exhaust gas recirculation system — check	17.45.20
Exhaust gas recirculation valve — remove and refit	17.45.01 **
Purge pipe — canister to crankcase breather — remove and refit	17.15.36
Separator tank — remove and refit	17.15.19
Running on control valve — remove and refit	17.40.01
Thermostatic switch — remove and refit	17.20.31

17.1

EMISSION CONTROL

Fault Finding Chart

CAUSE	POOR/ROUGH IDLE	LOSS OF POWER/POOR DRIVE AWAY	MISFIRING (under load conditions)	HIGH FUEL CONSUMPTION	HIGH IDLING SPEED	OVERHEATING (at idle speed)	LEAN RUNNING	ARCING AT PLUGS	SMELL OF FUEL	RICH MIXTURE	STALLING	ENGINE RUN ON	ACTION
DISTRIBUTOR C. B. POINTS	x	x	x										CHECK DWELL ANGLE/CHECK GAP & RESET/RENEW POINTS
SPARKING PLUGS	x	x	x										CHECK GAP AND RESET/RENEW DEFECTIVE PLUG
IGNITION WIRING	x	x		x									INSPECT FOR FRAYING, CHAFFING & DETERIORATION/RENEW
CHOKE MECHANISM					x								CHECK FAST IDLE ADJUSTMENT/CAM AND CABLE/ADJUST
CHOKE MECHANISM	x	x	x										REMOVE STARTER BOX AND CLEAN INTERFACE
VACUUM FITTINGS, HOSES AND CONNECTIONS		x		x									CHECK PIPING CONDITION AND SECURITY/RENEW AS NECESSARY
OIL FILLER CAP	x	x		x									CHECK FOR SECURITY/TIGHTEN CAP
VENTILATION HOSES	x	x		x	x								CHECK HOSES FOR SECURITY, BLOCKAGE & DETERIORATION
CARBURETTER	x			x									SEE CARBURETTER FAULT FINDING CHART
DISTRIBUTOR	x												LUBRICATE/CHECK OPERATION BY REMOVING PIPE & NOTING R.P.M.
CARBURETTER AIR CLEANER	x			x									CLEAN OR RENEW ELEMENT
IGNITION TIMING AND ADVANCE SYSTEMS	x		x	x									CHECK AND RESET DYNAMIC TIMING
CONDENSOR AND COIL			(x)										CHECK FOR BREAKDOWN ON OSCILLASCOPE TUNE
HOSE CONNECTIONS		x		x									CHECK FOR HOSE DAMAGE AND DETERIORATION
CARBON STORAGE CANISTER		x											RENEW CANISTER
THERMOSTATIC SWITCH			(x)										CHECK SWITCH OPERATION AND RENEW IF NECESSARY
RUNNING ON CONTROL VALVE	x												CHECK VALVE OPERATION AND RENEW IF NECESSARY
E.C.R. VALVE												x	CHECK VALVE OPERATION AND RENEW IF NECESSARY

17.00.01

EVAPORATIVE LOSS CONTROL SYSTEM

17.15.01

—Leak testing

Test apparatus: Water manometer, pressure regulating valve, pressure sealing valve and pressurized air supply. An alternative to the manometer is an accurate pressure gauge reading 0 to 30 in of water with which a pressure relief valve or weak rubber connection will be necessary to protect against over-pressurizing the system.

WARNING: During the test, pressure will be applied to the fuel tank breather system. The pressure, albeit very low, may displace pipe connections or cause an emission of fuel vapour. It is, therefore, very dangerous to allow smoking or naked lights in the test area, or exceed the pressure quoted.

Test procedure

1. At the carbon canister, detach the tube from the separator tank and insert the pressurizing tube of the test apparatus.
2. Apply 20 in of water pressure to the system and close the sealing valve. DO NOT EXCEED 25 INCHES OF WATER PRESSURE.
3. After two minutes, check the pressure in the system. If this has fallen more than 2 in of water, investigation and rectification is necessary.

17.15.01

EMISSION CONTROL

ADSORPTION CANISTER AIR FILTER
– Pre 1973 Cars only
– Remove and refit   17.15.07

Removing
1. Remove the nut and screw on the canister securing strap.
2. Lift the canister clear of the bracket.
3. Unscrew the base of the canister and lift out the filter.
4. Clean any carbon particles from the base of the canister.

Refitting
5. Fit the new filter into body of canister.
6. Reverse 1 to 3 ensuring that the canister pipes are still in position and that they present leak free joints.

WARNING: Because of the possible presence of fuel fumes, avoid naked lights or actions likely to cause sparks.

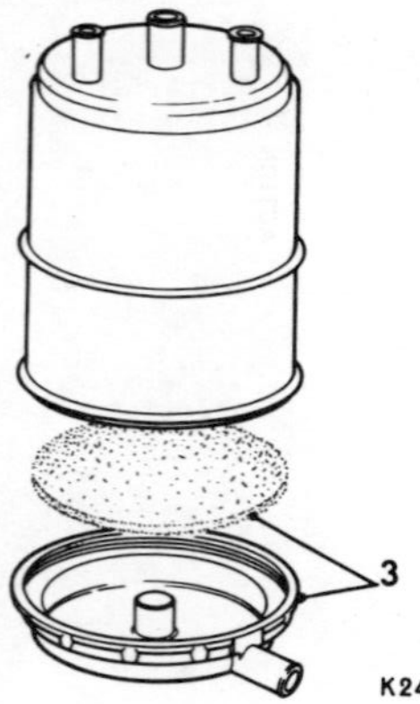

ADSORPTION CANISTER
– Remove and refit   17.15.13

Removing
1. Disconnect the two pipes into the top of the canister.
1a. 1973 vehicles – disconnect the three pipes into the top and one pipe from the bottom.
2. Remove the nut and screw on the canister securing strap.
3. Remove the canister.

Refitting
4. Reverse instructions 1 to 3 ensuring that all connections are leak free.

WARNING: Because of the possible presence of fuel fumes, avoid naked lights or actions likely to cause sparks.

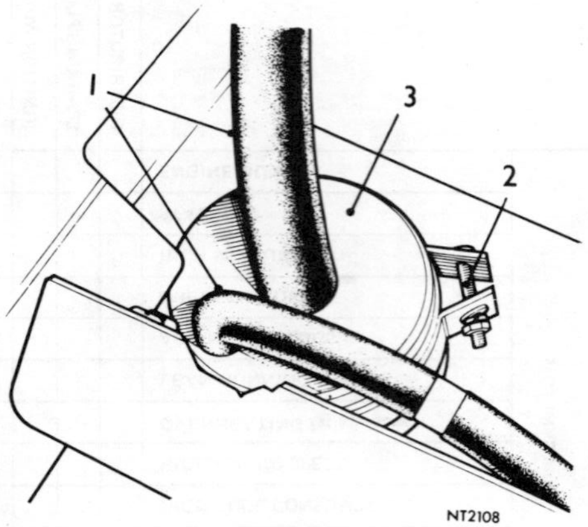

SEPARATOR TANK
– Remove and refit   17.15.19

Removing
1. From inside the driving compartment remove the six screws securing the rear squab trim pad.
2. Slacken the clamp bracket screw.
3. Disconnect and remove the separator tank.

Refitting
4. Reverse instructions 1 to 3.

NOTE: Pre 1972 models have a larger separator tank situated at the rear of the right hand trim panel in the luggage compartment. The separator tank is connected by separate pipes to each top corner of the main fuel tank.

CONTROL PIPE – CANISTER TO TANK
– Remove and refit   17.15.24

Purge pipe – Canister to crankcase breather   17.15.36

1. All piping in the evaporative control system is push fitted, access to the tank end of the control pipe is via the luggage compartment trim pad. When refitting pipes ensure that any restictor is replaced into line.

CARBURETTER EMISSION PACK – RED
– Remove and refit   17.20.07

1. Fit the gaskets and sealing washers of this pack in accordance with the overhaul procedure detailed in 19.15.17.

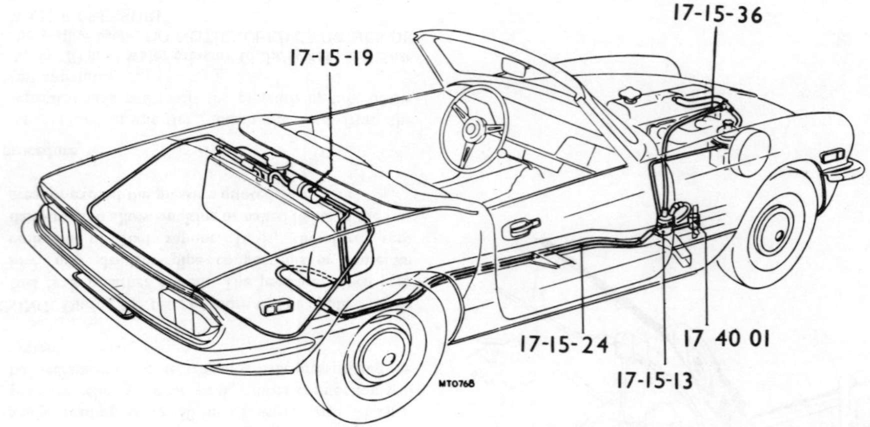

EMISSION CONTROL

THERMOSTATIC SWITCH (FITTED TO LATER CARS ONLY) 17.20.31

– Remove and refit

Removing
1. Drain the coolant.
2. Disconnect the vacuum pipes at the switch.
3. Slacken the two hose clips.
4. Remove the switch complete with mounting tube.
5. Secure the tube in a vice and unscrew the switch.

Refitting
6. Reverse instructions 1 to 5, apply sealing compound to the thread of the switch.

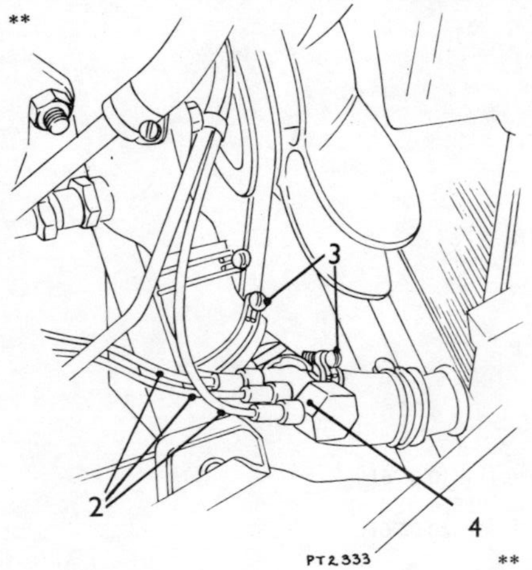

C O LEVEL AT IDLE 17.35.01

– Check

Special tools: Approved infra-red gas analyser.

1. Attain normal engine running temperature.
2. Set the idle speed to 800-850 rev/min 19.15.01 s.c.
3. Check ignition timing — reset if necessary 86.35.16.
4. Re-check idle speed — adjust if necessary.
5. Insert the exhaust gas analyser probe as far as possible into the exhaust pipe.
6. Check the CO reading. (Compare with emission control table).
7. *a)* Adjust mixture if necessary 19.15.01 s.c.
   b) Check idle speed — adjust if necessary.
8. Withdraw the analyser probe.
9. Switch off the ignition.

NOTE: Do not allow the engine to idle for longer than 3 minutes without a 'clear out' burst of 1 minute at 2,000 rev/min.

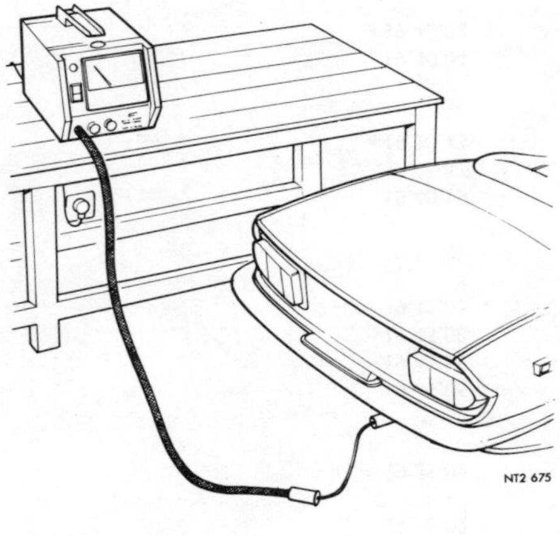

RUNNING ON CONTROL VALVE
(Not fitted to pre 1973 cars)

– Remove and refit 17.40.01

Removing
1. Remove the carbon canister 17.15.07.
2. Disconnect the two electrical leads to the solenoid at the top of the valve.
3. Disconnect the vacuum signal pipe.
4. Remove the securing bolts and lift off the valve complete with mounting bracket.

Refitting
5. Reverse instructions 1 to 4.

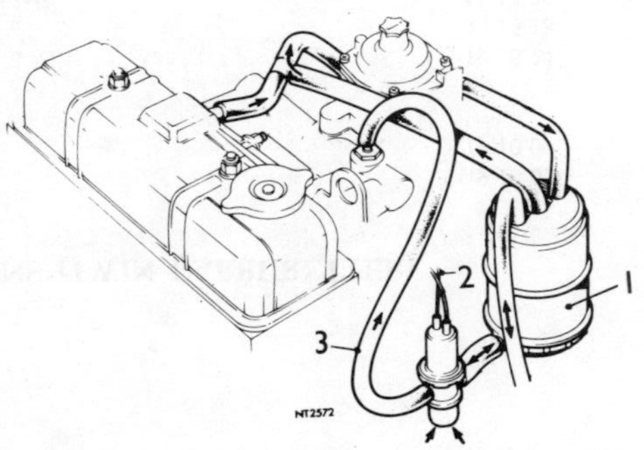

17.20.31
17.40.01

EXHAUST GAS RECIRCULATION (E.G.R.) VALVE 17.45.01

– Remove and refit

Removing
1. Disconnect the vacuum pipe at the E.G.R. valve.
2. Remove the banjo bolt securing the metal pipe to the inlet manifold.
3. Unscrew the union nut securing the metal pipe to the E.G.R. valve.
4. Slacken the locknut and unscrew the E.G.R. valve from the exhaust manifold.

Refitting
5. Reverse instructions 1 to 4.

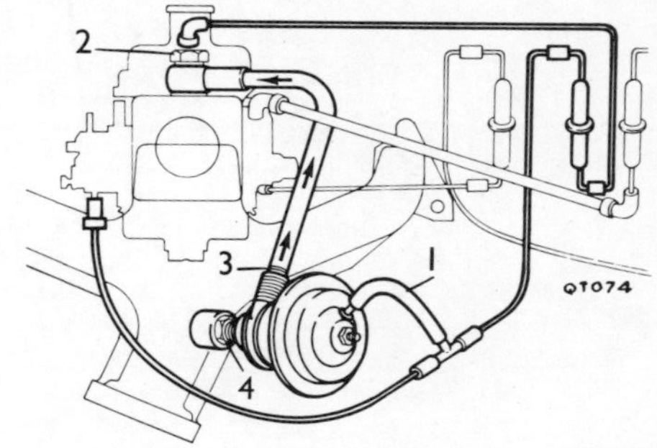

EXHAUST GAS RECIRCULATION CONTROL VALVE 17.45.05

– Remove and refit

Removing
1. Disconnect the vacuum pipe.
2. Remove the screw securing valve and bracket to carburetter.

Refitting
3. Reverse instructions 1 and 2.

EXHAUST GAS RECIRCULATION SYSTEM 17.45.20

– Check

1. Check E.G.R. valve operating line for security of push fit connections at E.G.R. valve, cut off valve, fuel trap carburetter and tee piece.
2. Renew any pipes that show signs of deterioration.
3. Check function of E.G.R. valve as follows: Warm the engine to normal running temperature and ensure that the choke control is fully home ('OFF'). Open and close the throttle several times and observe or feel the E.G.R. valve, which should open and close with the changes in engine speed. The valve should close instantly when the throttle is closed.
4. If the operation of the valve does not appear completely satisfactory, make a complete check on the operation of the valve by connecting the vacuum pipe of a distributor vacuum test unit to the valve. Ensure that the valve is actuated, held, and that there is no leak of vacuum.

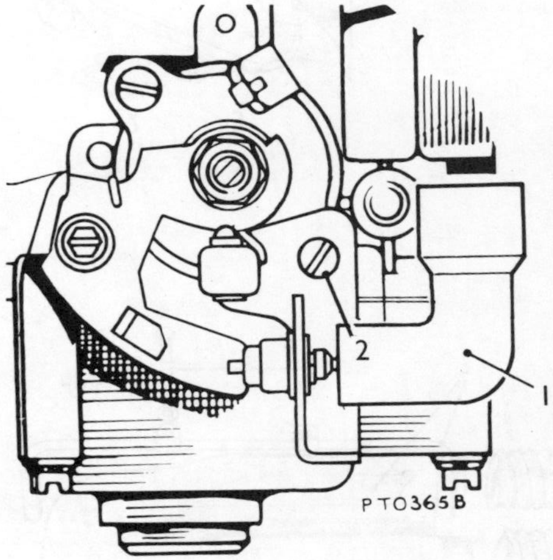

17.45.01
17.45.20

FUEL SYSTEM OPERATIONS (TWIN CARBURETTER)

Air cleaners	
— remove and refit	19.10.02
— renew elements	19.10.09
Carburetters	
— float-chamber needle and seat — remove and refit	19.15.24
— overhaul	19.15.18
— piston and suction chamber — remove and refit	19.15.30
— remove and refit	19.15.11
— tune and adjust	19.15.02
Fuel main filter — remove and refit	19.25.02
Fuel pump	
— clean filter	19.45.05
— overhaul	19.45.15
— remove and refit	19.45.08
— test on vehicle	19.45.01
Fuel tank — remove and refit	19.55.01
Hose — filler to tank — remove and refit	19.40.19
Mixture control cable — remove and refit	19.20.13
Petrol pipe	
— engine end — remove and refit	19.40.04
— tank end — remove and refit	19.40.02
Throttle cable — remove and refit	19.20.06
Throttle linkage — remove and refit	19.20.07
Throttle pedal — remove and refit	19.20.01

AIR CLEANER

— Remove and refit   19.10.02

Removing
1. Disconnect the two intake hoses.
2. Remove the four bolts and washers.
3. Remove the fuel pipe and withdraw the air cleaner complete with two gaskets.

Refitting
4. Reverse instructions 1 to 3, ensuring that new gaskets are fitted.

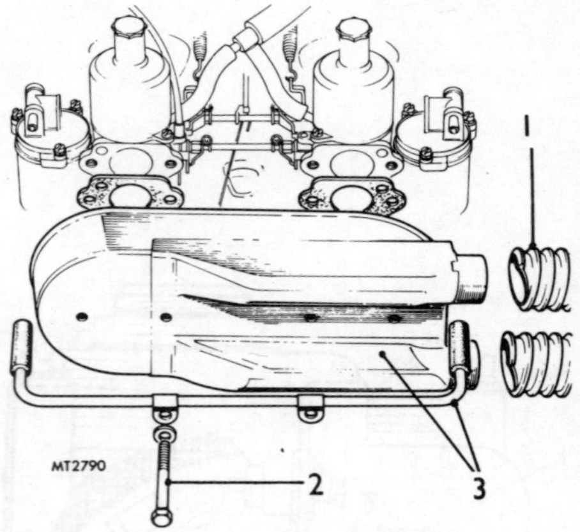

AIR CLEANER — RENEW ELEMENTS

— Remove and refit   19.10.09

Removing
1. Remove the air cleaner assembly 19.10.02
2. Remove the bolt securing the cover-plate to the container.
3. Separate the cover-plate from the container.
4. Remove and discard the paper elements.

Refitting
5. Reverse instructions 1 to 4, ensuring:
   a. New elements are fitted.
   b. Gaskets and cover-plate seal are renewed if originals are unsatisfactory.

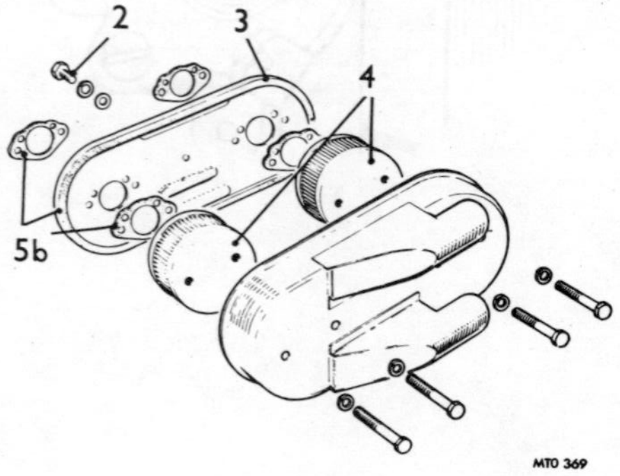

FUEL SYSTEM — TC

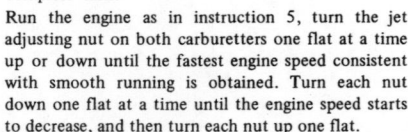

CARBURETTERS

— Tune and adjust 19.15.02

Idling — check and adjust 1 to 11 and 16
Mixture — check and adjust 1 to 20

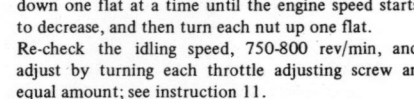

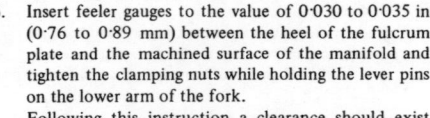

1. Check each piston damper, and top-up if necessary with a recommended engine oil until the level is ½ in (13 mm) above the top of the hollow piston rod.
2. Check the throttle action for signs of sticking, and ensure that the mixture control cable has 1/16 in (1·6 mm) free movement.
3. Remove the air cleaner. 19.10.02.
4. Connect up a suitable tachometer.
5. Start and run the engine until it reaches normal running temperature, as indicated by the temperature gauge. Continue running the engine at 2,500 rev/min for approximately one minute before commencing tuning. Repeat this operation as often as necessary.
6. Stop the engine and raise each carburetter piston with the respective lifting pins. Release the pin and check that each piston falls freely on to the carburetter bridge with a soft metallic click. Should either piston fail to fall freely, refer to 19.15.18.
7. Start the engine and check the idling speed with the tachometer, which should be 750-800 rev/min.
   a. If the reading is not correct, continue with instructions 8 to 11 and 15 and 16.
   b. If the idle speed is correct but is not consistent with smooth running, continue with instructions 8 to 21.
8. Slacken both throttle interconnection clamp nuts.
9. Slacken both jet control interconnection clamp nuts.
10. Slacken the trunnion bolts securing the mixture control inner cable.
11. With the engine running, check the carburetter balance with a meter or by comparing the intake hiss in each carburetter by holding one end of a length of small bore rubber tubing to each carburetter intake in turn and the other end to the ear. Turn the throttle adjusting screw on each carburetter until the intensity of the hiss is equal in both intakes with the correct idling speed of 750-800 rev/min as indicated by the tachometer.
    a. If with the carburetters correctly balanced the idling is still erratic, continue with instructions 12 to 20.
    b. If the idle speed is correct and consistent with smooth running, follow instructions 15 to 20.

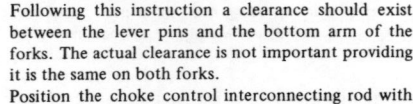

continued

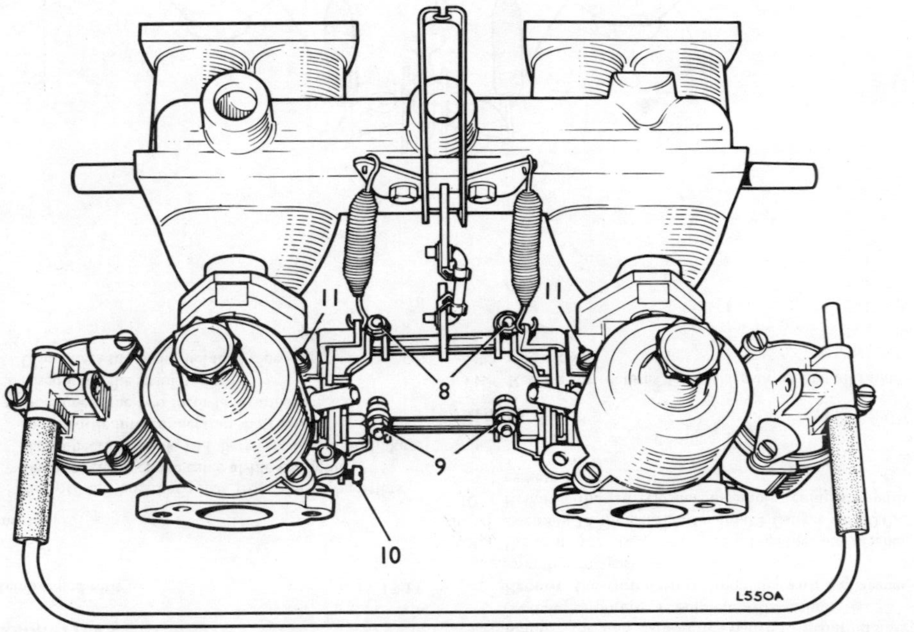

12. Tighten the jet adjusting nuts until the jet is just level with the bridge and then turn each one down two complete turns.
13. Run the engine as in instruction 5, turn the jet adjusting nut on both carburetters one flat at a time up or down until the fastest engine speed consistent with smooth running is obtained. Turn each nut down one flat at a time until the engine speed starts to decrease, and then turn each nut up one flat.
14. Re-check the idling speed, 750-800 rev/min, and adjust by turning each throttle adjusting screw an equal amount; see instruction 11.
15. Set the throttle interconnection clamping levers until the lever pins rest on the lower arm of the forks.
16. Insert feeler gauges to the value of 0·030 to 0·035 in (0·76 to 0·89 mm) between the heel of the fulcrum plate and the machined surface of the manifold and tighten the clamping nuts while holding the lever pins on the lower arm of the fork. Following this instruction a clearance should exist between the lever pins and the bottom arm of the forks. The actual clearance is not important providing it is the same on both forks.
17. Position the choke control interconnecting rod with approximately 1/32 in (0·8 mm) end clearance, and tighten the clamp nuts.
18. Pull out the mixture control approximately ½ in (13 mm) until the linkage is just about to move the jet. Start the engine and adjust the fast idle screws to give an engine speed of 1,100 to 1,200 rev/min.
19. Refit the air cleaner. 19.10.02.
20. Disconnect the tachometer.

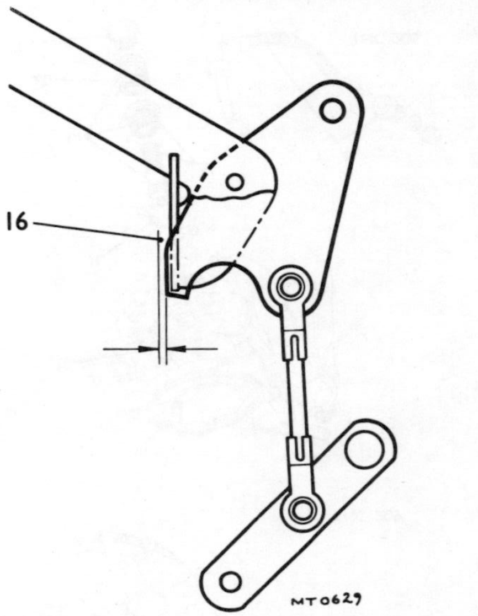

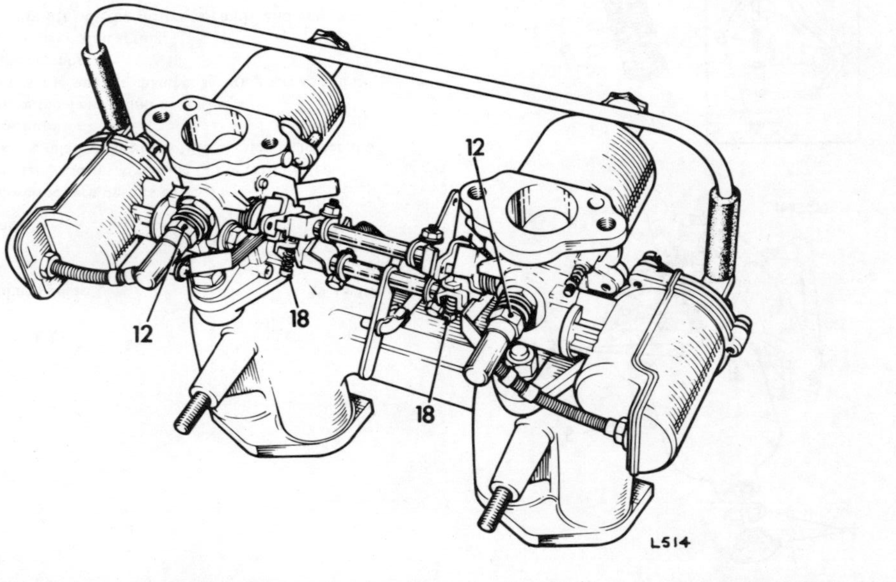

FUEL SYSTEM — TC

CARBURETTERS

— Remove and refit   19.15.11

Removing

1. Pull off the breather pipes from the carburetters.
2. Disconnect the choke cable at the trunnion.
3. Disconnect the link rod between the cable linkage and throttle interconnection shaft lever.
4. Disconnect the two throttle return springs.
5. Disconnect the vacuum pipe.
6. Disconnect the main fuel feed pipe.
7. Remove the four carburetter flange to manifold nuts (two per carburetter) complete with washers.
8. Remove the carburetters complete with air cleaner assembly and gaskets.
9. Remove the four bolts securing the air cleaner assembly to the carburetter intake flanges. 19.10.02.
10. Remove the air cleaner assembly complete with gaskets.

Refitting

11. Reverse instructions 1 to 10, ensuring that all gaskets are renewed.

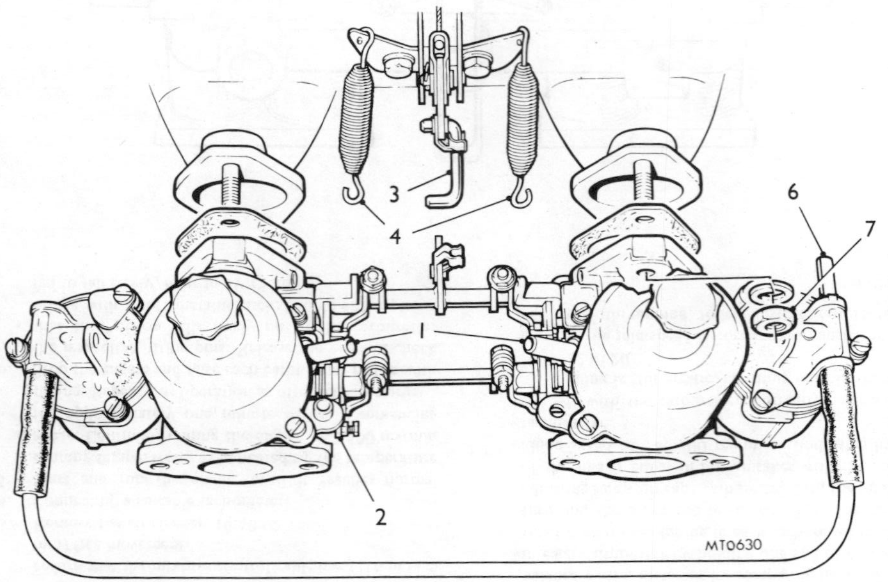

CARBURETTERS

— Overhaul and adjust   19.15.18

Dismantling

1. Remove the carburetters 19.15.11.
2. Thoroughly clean the outside of the carburetters.
3. Mark the relative position of the suction chamber and the carburetter body.
4. Remove the damper and its washer.
5. Unscrew the suction chamber securing screws and lift off the chamber.
6. Remove the piston spring.
7. Carefully lift out the piston assembly and empty the oil from the piston rod.
8. Remove the guide locking screw and withdraw the needle assembly, taking care not to bend the needle. Withdraw the needle from the guide and remove the spring from the needle.
9. Push the piston lifting pin upwards, detach its securing circlip and withdraw the pin and spring downwards.
10. Release the pick-up lever return spring from its retaining lug.
11. Support the plastic moulded base of the jet and remove the screw retaining the jet pick-up link and link bracket (when fitted).
12. Unscrew the flexible jet tube sleeve nut from the float-chamber and withdraw the jet assembly. Note the gland, washer and ferrule at the end of the jet tube.
13. Remove the jet adjusting nut and spring.
14. Unscrew the jet locking nut and detach the nut and jet bearings; withdraw the bearing from the nut.

continued

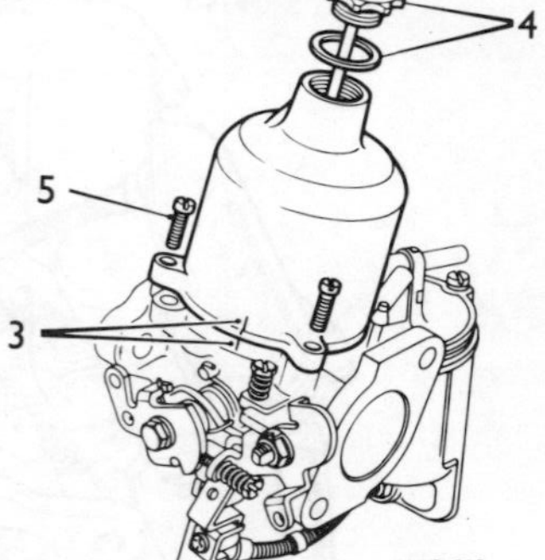

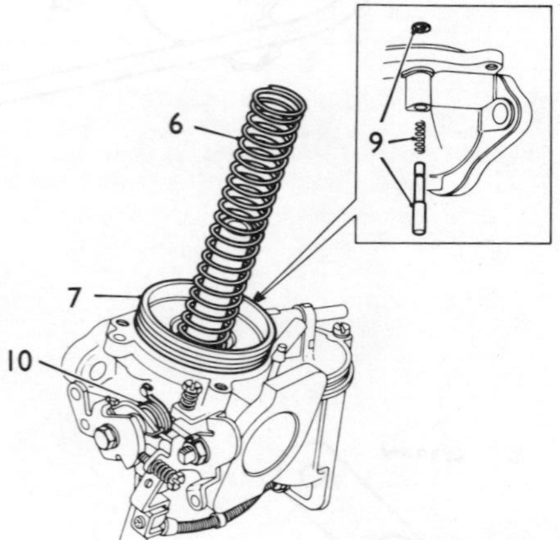

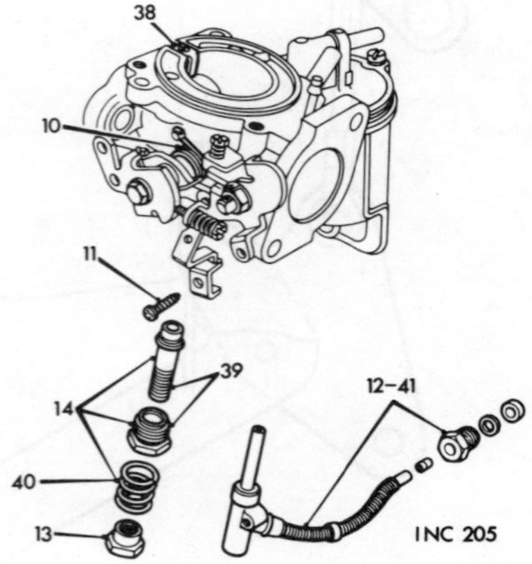

FUEL SYSTEM — TC

15. Unscrew and remove the pivot bolt and spacer.
16. Detach the lever assembly and return springs noting the pivot bolt tubes, skid washer and the location of the cam and pick-up lever springs.
17. Remove the float-chamber securing bolt and the chamber.
18. Mark the float-chamber lid location.
19. Remove the lid securing screws and detach the lid with its joint washer and float.
20. Hold the float hinge pin at its serrated end and withdraw the pin and float.
21. Extract the float needle from its seating and unscrew the seating from the lid.
22. Close the throttle and mark the relative position of the throttle disc and the carburetter flange.

CAUTION: Do not mark the throttle disc in the vicinity of the limit valve.

23. Unscrew the disc retaining screws, open the throttle and ease the disc from its slot in the throttle spindle. Store the disc in a safe place until required for assembly.
24. Tap back the tabs of the lock washer securing the spindle nut: remove the nut and detach the lever arm, washer and throttle spindle; note the location of the lever arm in relation to the spindle and carburetter body.

Inspecting

25. Examine the components as follows:
    a. Check the throttle spindle in the body for excessive play, and renew if necessary.
    b. Examine the float needle for wear, i.e. small ridges or grooves in the seat of the needle, and ensure that the spring-loaded plunger on the opposite end operates freely. Replace the needle and seating if necessary.
    c. Inspect all other components for wear and seating if necessary.
    d. Inspect all other components for wear and damage; renew unserviceable components.

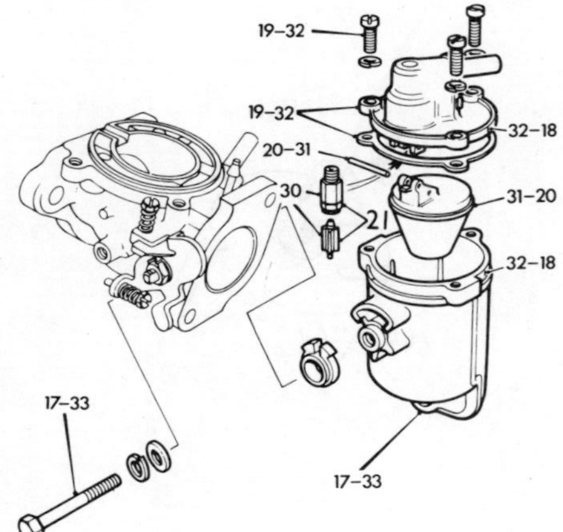

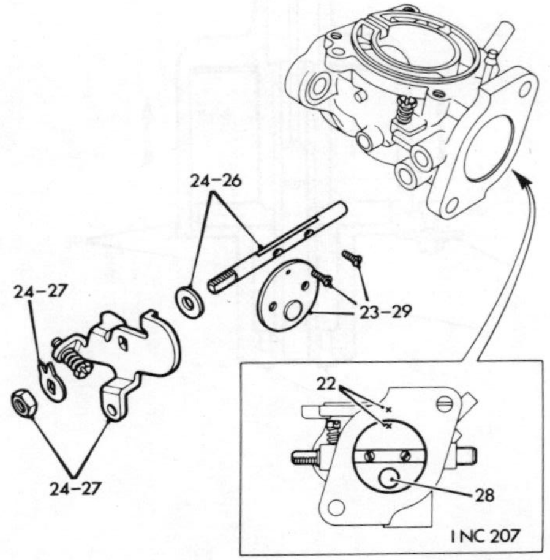

continued

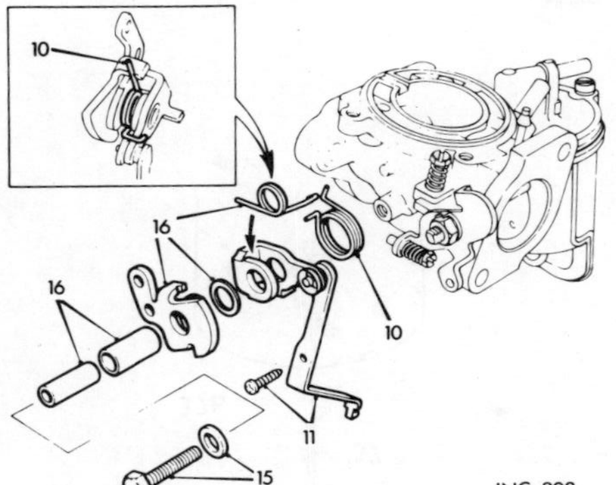

Reassembling

26. Refit the spindle to the body, with the countersunk holes in the spindle facing outwards.
27. Assemble the spacing washer, lever, lock washer and securing nut, ensure that the idling screw abutment on the lever is against the closed throttle position. Tighten the spindle nut and lock with the tab washer.
28. Insert the throttle disc into the spindle slot note the markings for reassembling, i.e. the limit valve positioned at the bottom of the spindle with the head of the valve towards the engine. Manoeuvre the disc in the spindle open and closed to centralize it in the bore of the carburetter.
29. Fit new disc retaining screws but do not fully tighten; check that the disc closes fully and adjust its position as necessary. Tighten the screws fully and spread their split ends just enough to prevent them turning.
30. Screw the seating into the float-chamber lid; do not overtighten. Insert the needle coned-end first into the seating.
31. Refit the float to the chamber lid and insert the hinge pin.
32. Refit the float-chamber lid with a new joint washer, noting the assembly markings, tighten the securing screws evenly.
33. Refit the float-chamber to the body and tighten the retaining bolt.
34. Refit the piston lifting pin, spring and circlip.
35. Clean fuel deposits off the suction chamber and piston with fuel or methylated spirit and wipe dry.

CAUTION: Do not use abrasives.

continued

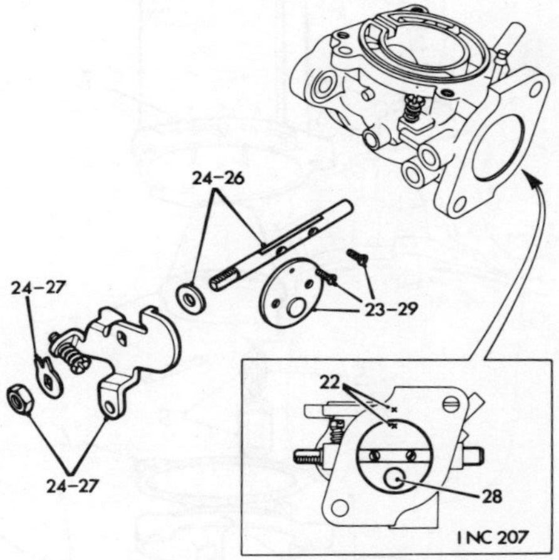

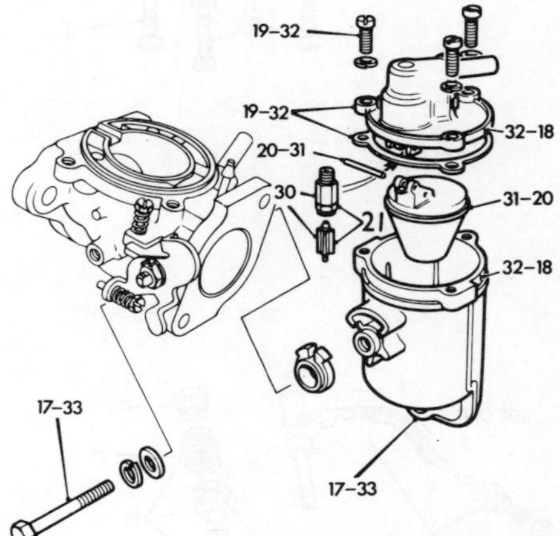

FUEL SYSTEM — TC

36. Check the operation of the suction chamber and piston (without the spring fitted) as follows:
    a. Refit the damper and washer to the suction chamber, temporarily plug the piston transfer holes with rubber plugs or Plasticine and insert the piston fully into the suction chamber.
    b. Secure a large flat washer to one of the fixing holes with a screw and nut so that it overlaps the bore.
    c. With the assembly upside-down, hold the piston and check the time taken for the suction chamber to fall the full extent of its travel. The time taken should be five to seven seconds, if this time is exceeded, check the piston and chamber for cleanliness and mechanical damage. Renew the assembly if the time taken is still not within these limits.

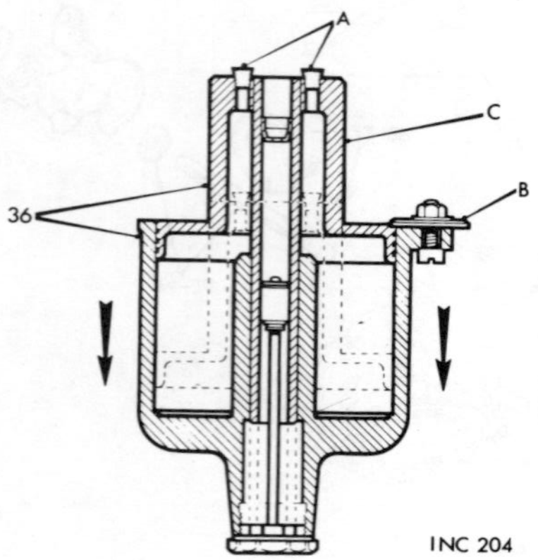

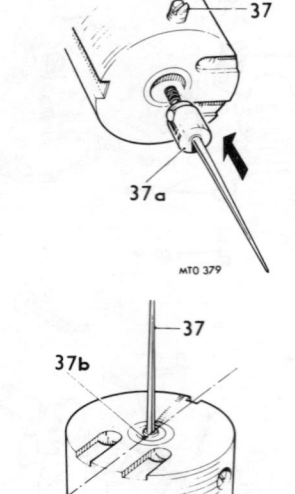

37. Fit the spring and guide to the needle and insert the assembly into the piston, ensuring:
    a. The lower edge of the guide is flush with the face of the piston.
    b. The guide is positioned so that the etched locating mark on its lower face is adjacent to, and in line with, the centre line between the two piston transfer holes.
    c. A new guide locking screw is fitted.

    NOTE: Alternative needle guides may be fitted which have a flat machined on the guide and must be positioned so that the guide locking screw tightens down on to the flat. If the guide is incorrectly positioned, the locking screw will not tighten down on the flat and will remain proud of the guide resulting in damage to the piston bore.

    continued

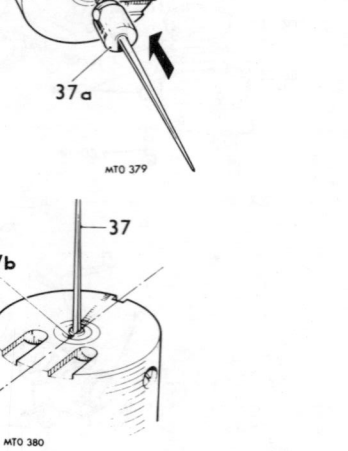

38. Check the piston key in the body for security.
39. Refit the jet bearing, fit and tighten the jet locking nut.
40. Refit the spring and jet adjustment nut, screw the nut up as far as possible.
41. Insert the jet into the bearing, fit the brass sleeve nut, washer and gland to the end of the flexible tube (if removed). The tube must project a minimum of 3/16 in (4·8 mm) beyond the gland. Tighten the brass sleeve nut until the gland is compressed; overtightening can cause leakage.
42. Refit the piston, spring and suction chamber to the body (noting the assembly marks) and tighten the securing screws evenly.
43. Reverse the instructions 15 to 14.
44. Hold up the choke lever to relieve pressure on the jet pick-up link, refit the link bracket (when fitted). Support the end of the moulded jet and tighten the securing screw.
45. Screw the jet adjusting nut down two complete turns (12 flats) to provide the initial setting.
46. Refit the carburetters 19.15.11.
47. Tune the carburetters 19.15.02.

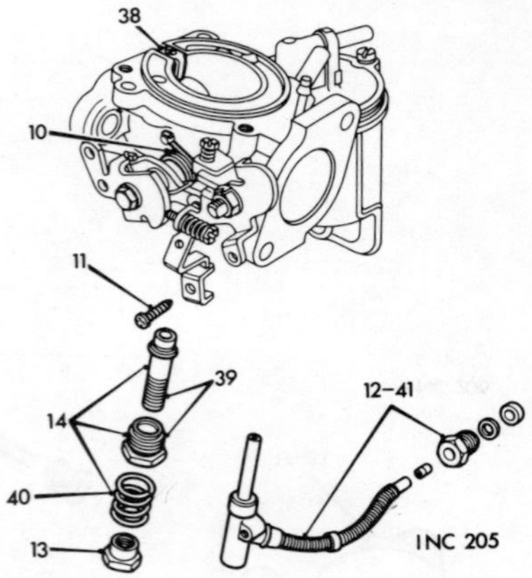

FLOAT-CHAMBER NEEDLE AND SEAT

19.15.24

— Remove and refit

Removing

1. Disconnect the fuel hose from the float-chamber.
2. Mark the lid and float-chamber for assembly.
3. Remove the lid securing screws and detach the lid.
4. Hold the float hinge pin at its serrated end and withdraw the pin and float.
5. Extract the float needle from its seating.

Inspecting

6. Examine the float needle for wear, i.e. small ridges or grooves in the seat of the needle, also check that the spring-loaded plunger on the opposite end operates freely. Renew the needle and seating if the needle is worn.

Refitting

7. Clean any sediment from the float-chamber, and fit a new joint washer, if required.
8. Reverse instructions 1 to 5.

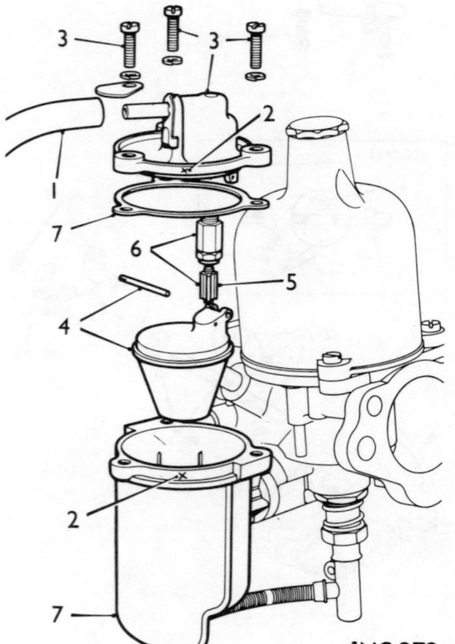

FUEL SYSTEM — TC

PISTON AND SUCTION CHAMBER   19.15.30

— Remove, clean and refit

Removing

1. Mark the relative position of the suction chamber and the carburetter body.
2. Remove the damper and its washer.
3. Unscrew the suction chamber securing screws and lift off the chamber.
4. Remove the piston spring.
5. Carefully lift out the piston assembly and empty the oil from the piston rod.
6. Clean fuel deposits off the suction chamber and piston with fuel or methylated spirit and wipe dry.

CAUTION: Do not use abrasives.

7. Check the operation of the suction chamber and piston (without the spring fitted) as follows:
   a. Refit the damper and washer to the suction chamber, temporarily plug the piston transfer holes with rubber plugs or Plasticine and insert the piston fully into the suction chamber.
   b. Secure a large flat washer to one of the fixing holes with a screw and nut so that it overlaps the bore.
   c. With the assembly upside-down, hold the piston and check the time taken for the suction chamber to fall the full extent of its travel. The time taken should be five to seven seconds, if this time is exceeded, check the piston and chamber for cleanliness and mechanical damage. Renew the assembly if the time taken is still not within these limits.

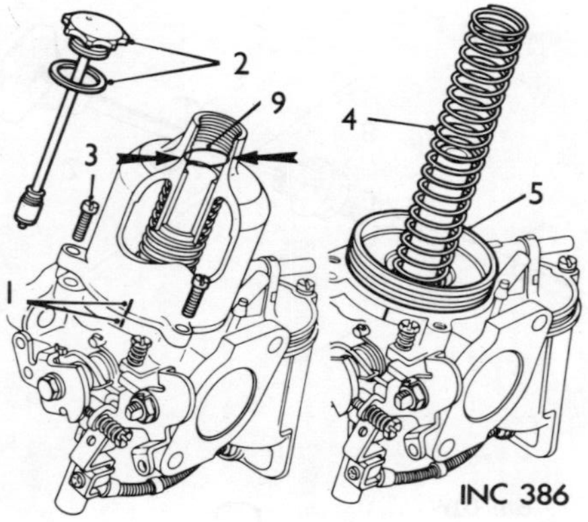

Refitting

8. Refit the piston, spring and suction chamber to the carburetter (noting the assembly marks) and tighten the screws evenly.
9. Top up each piston damper with a recommended engine oil until the level is ½ in (13 mm) above the top of the hollow piston rod.
10. Refit each piston damper with its washer.

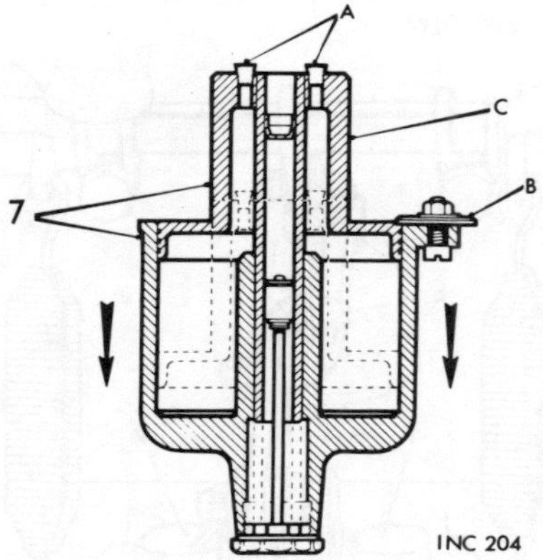

THROTTLE PEDAL   19.20.01

— Remove and refit

Removing

1. Remove the cable retaining clip.
2. Lift out the exposed inner throttle cable from the fork end of the pedal.
3. Remove the two bolts complete with plain and spring washers securing the pedal bracket to the bulkhead.
4. Remove the bracket.
5. Remove the nut, bolt and plain washer securing the pedal to the bracket.
6. Remove the pedal and return spring.

Refitting

7. Reverse instructions 1 to 6, ensuring:
   a. The return spring is positioned so that the pedal returns positively.
   b. The cable clip is correctly positioned so that the inner cable is gripped and cannot slip out.

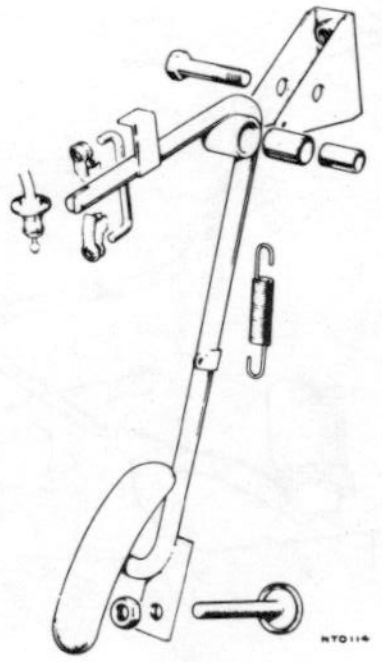

THROTTLE CABLE   19.20.06

— Remove and refit

Removing

1. Remove the cable retaining clip from the throttle pedal.
2. Withdraw the exposed end of the inner cable from the fork end of the throttle pedal.
3. Pull the outer cable complete with inner cable from the bulkhead.
4. Remove the cotter pin from the linkage clevis pin.
5. Withdraw the clevis pin complete with washer.
6. Slacken the cable adjuster locknut.
7. Screw the lower adjuster nut off the end of the cable.
8. Remove the inner and outer cable complete through the slot in the adjuster bracket.

Refitting

9. Reverse instructions 1 to 8, ensuring:
   a. The cable clip on the pedal is correctly fitted so that the cable will not slip out of the fork.
   b. The cable is not kinked or subjected to sharp bends.
   c. Cable tension is adjusted so that the heel of the fulcrum plate is just touching the machined face of the manifold.

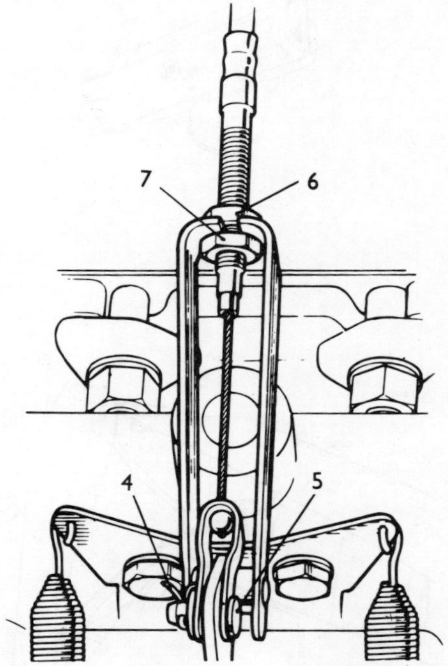

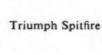

FUEL SYSTEM — TC

THROTTLE LINKAGE 19.20.07

— Remove and refit

Removing

1. Disconnect the throttle cable from the linkage. 19.20.06, instructions 4 to 8.
2. Disconnect the two return springs from the bracket attached to the manifold.
3. Release the clips securing the link rod between the throttle interconnection lever and fulcrum plate and remove the rod.
4. Remove the two bolts securing the linkage bracket to the manifold and remove the bracket complete.

Refitting

5. Reverse instructions 1 to 4.

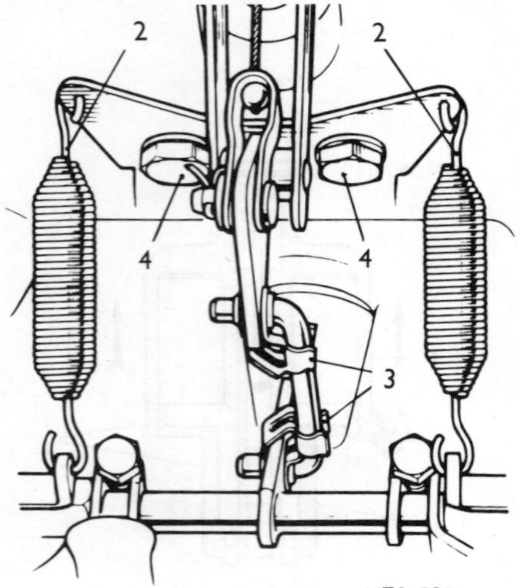

MIXTURE CONTROL CABLE 19.20.13

— Remove and refit

Removing

1. Disconnect the inner cable from the carburetter.
2. Separate the inner cable from the outer by pulling the control knob on the control panel.
3. Carefully unscrew and remove the ferrule securing the outer cable to the control panel.
4. Remove the outer cable from the control panel.
5. Drop the outer cable below the control panel and pull the cable through the bulkhead grommets into the interior of the car, and remove.

Refitting

6. Feed the control panel end of the outer cable below the panel and through the bulkhead grommets.
7. Secure the outer cable to the control panel and with the ferrule and locknut.
8. Feed the inner cable into the outer cable from the interior of the car.
9. Connect the inner cable to the carburetter.
10. Allow 1/16 in (1.6 mm) free movement of cable before the linkage is about to move the cam.

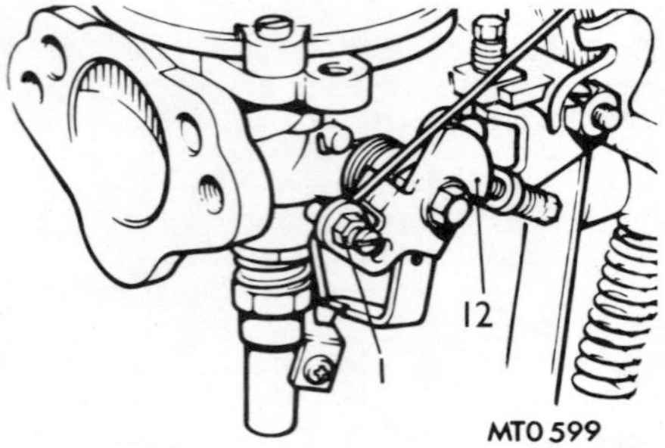

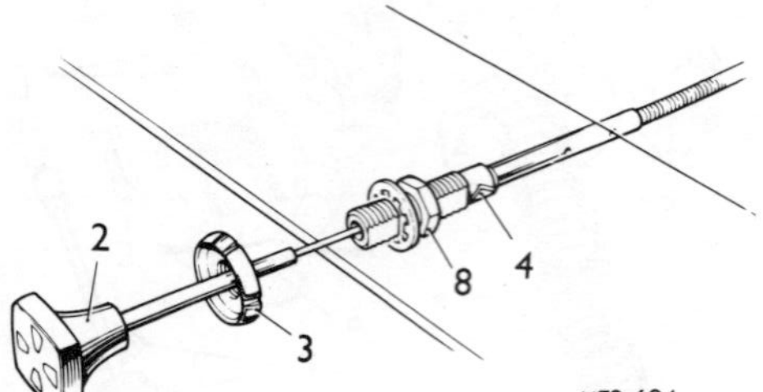

FUEL MAIN FILTER (specified markets only) 19.25.02

— Remove and refit

Removing

1. Open the luggage compartment lid.
2. Remove three top screws securing the tank trim pad to the body.
3. Ease forward the pad.
4. Disconnect the fuel feed pipes.
CAUTION: Plug the pipe ends to prevent loss of fuel and ingress of dirt.
5. Withdraw filter.

Refitting

6. Reverse instructions 1 to 5, ensuring the filter is inserted into piping with the side marked 'IN' uppermost.

NOTE: On some earlier cars this filter (where specified) is positioned near the fuel pump in the engine compartment, and is secured by a bolt on bracket. When replacing the filter ensure that it is inserted into the piping with the side marked 'IN' correctly located.

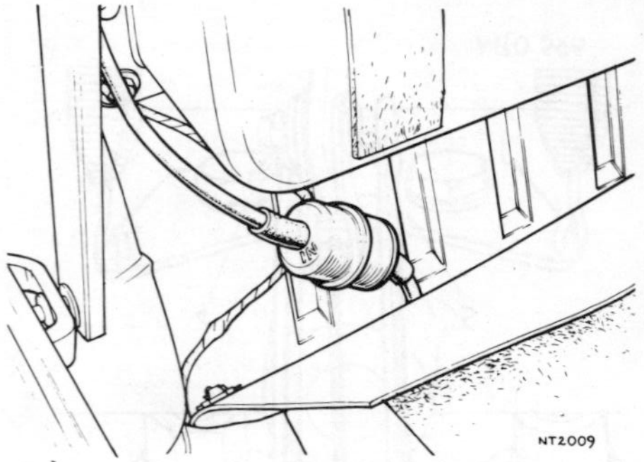

FUEL PIPE – TANK END 19.40.02

— Remove and refit

Removing

1. Disconnect the pipe at the tank end and blank off the connector to prevent syphoning of fuel.
2. Disconnect the pipe at the pump end.
3. Pull the pipe away from the clips.

Refitting

4. Reverse instructions 1 to 3, ensuring that the pipe does not chafe or foul the body or other components.

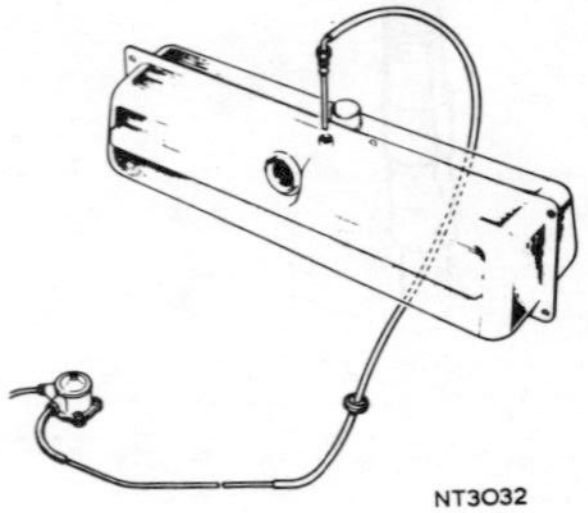

FUEL PIPE – ENGINE END 19.40.04

— Remove and refit

Removing

1. Unscrew the union from the fuel pump.
2. Remove the bolt securing the pipe retaining clip from the thermostat housing.
3. Disconnect the pipe from the rubber connector at the carburetter end.
4. Detach the clip securing the vacuum pipe to the fuel pipe.
5. Remove the fuel pipe.

Refitting

6. Reverse instructions 1 to 5.

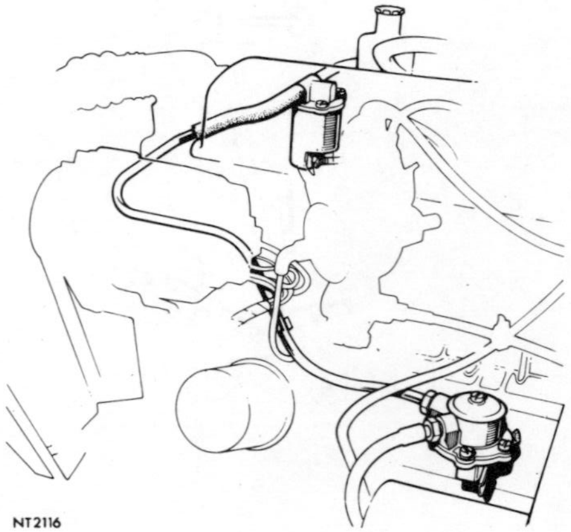

FUEL SYSTEM — TC

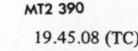

HOSE – FILLER TO TANK

— Remove and refit
19.40.19

Removing
1. Remove the rear squab trim pad – six screws.
2. Slacken the two clips securing the hose to the tank and filler cap.
3. Remove the filler cap.
4. Detach the hose.

Refitting
5. Reverse instructions 1 to 4, using sealing compound as necessary to prevent leakage at the hose connections.

FUEL PUMP

— Test on vehicle
19.45.01

1. Connect a pressure gauge into the pump to carburetter fuel line.
2. Start the engine, and observe the pressure which should be 2·5 to 3·5 lbf/in² (0·029 to 0·040 kgf/m.)
3. Remove the pressure gauge.

NOTE: Where pressure is high, it may be reduced by fitting extra paper washers between the pump and cylinder block. Where pressure is too low, overhaul the pump, 19.45.15, or renew, 19.45.08.

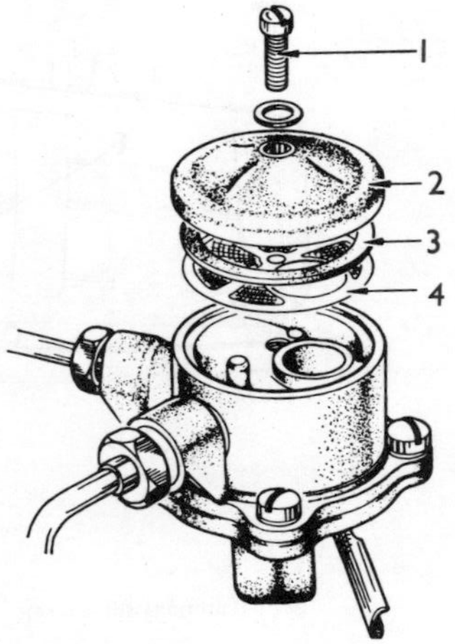

FUEL PUMP

— Clean filter
19.45.05

Upper illustration – early models.
Lower illustration – later models.

1. Remove the screw in the top of the pump.
2. Lift off the dome cover.
3. Lift off the cover sealing ring.
4. Lift out the filter.
5. Use clean lint-free cloth and soak up the fuel in the pump.
6. Clean sediment from the pump and blow out the filter.
7. Examine the dome seal, renew if necessary.
8. Fit the filter and dome, tighten the retaining screw.

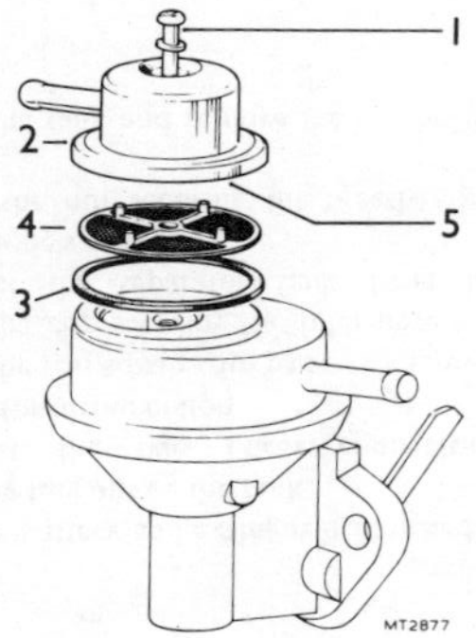

FUEL PUMP

— Remove and refit
19.45.08

Removing
1. Unscrew the pipe unions from the pump, plug the pipes and pump to prevent dirt entering the system.
2. Remove one plain and one special nut securing the pump to the cylinder block.
3. Remove the pump and gasket.

Refitting
4. Reverse instructions 1 to 3.

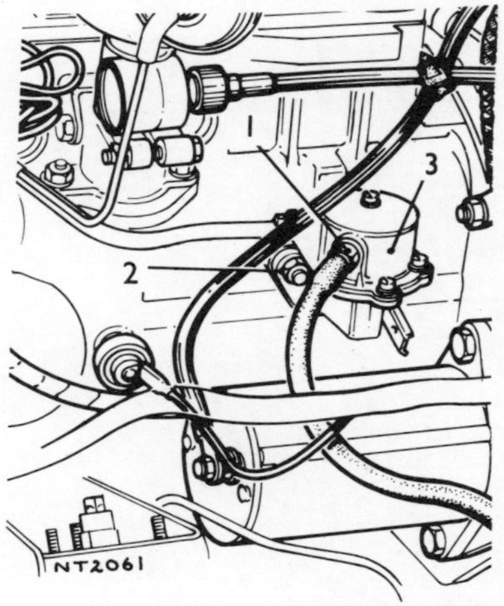

FUEL PUMP

— Overhaul
19.45.15

NOTE: This operation does not apply to the alternative fuel pump illustrated for operation 19.45.05. Overhaul of this alternative fuel pump is not recommended.

Dismantling
1. Remove screw complete with plain washer securing dome cover to upper body.
2. Remove dome cover.
3. Remove sealing ring.
4. Lift out filter.
5. Mark for reassembly the relationship between upper and lower body of pump.
6. Remove five screws complete with spring washers securing upper body to lower body.
7. Lift off upper part of body.
8. Mark for reassembly the relationship of diaphragm to lower body.
9. Turn diaphragm clockwise or anti-clockwise until it can be released from lower body.
10. Remove diaphragm spring from diaphragm assembly.
11. Using a screwdriver, prise out the valves, and remove the gaskets.

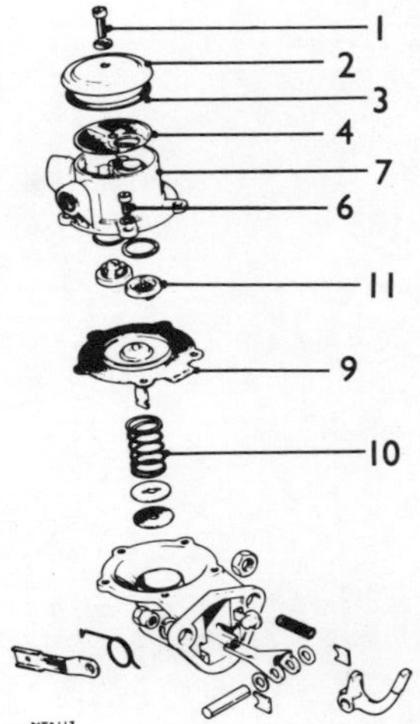

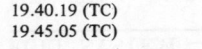

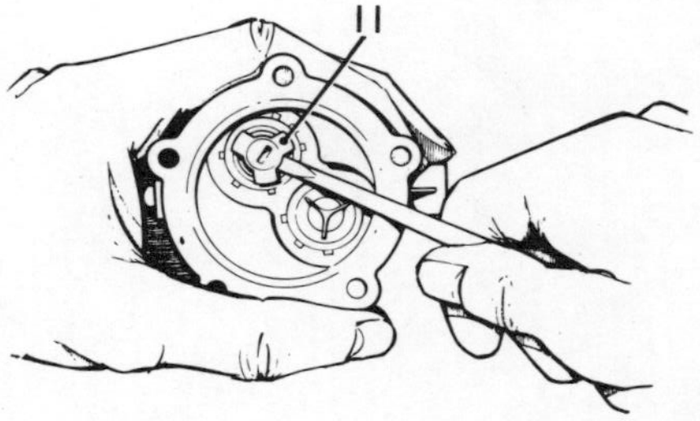

FUEL SYSTEM — TC

FUEL TANK   19.55.01
– Remove and refit

Removing

1. Isolate the battery and extinguish all naked lights.
2. Siphon the fuel out of the tank.
3. Disconnect the two Lucar connectors, noting positions for reconnection.
4. Remove the rear squab trim pad — six screws.
5. Slacken the clip securing the filler hose to the tank.
6. Disconnect the separator tank from the piping (U.S.A. models only).
7. Unscrew the nut securing the breather pipe to the tank.
8. Support the tank and remove the five bolts and plain washers.

Refitting

9. Reverse instructions 1 to 8.

Examination

12. Examine the dismantled components for wear and damage and renew where necessary. Since the valves are damaged during removal, these must be renewed.

Reassembling

13. Renew valves and gaskets. Press valves into casting with a suitable tool (a piece of steel tubing 9/16 in (14·28 mm) inside diameter and ¾ in (19·05 mm) outside diameter. Ensure valves are positioned correctly, i.e.
   a. Inlet to pump valve, press in so raised side faces downwards.
   b. Outlet to engine valve, press in so concave side faces downwards.
14. Stake casting round each valve in six places with a suitable punch.
15. Reverse instructions 1 to 10, renewing all seals and washers.

19.45.15 (TC) Sheet 2
19.55.01 (TC)

Triumph Spitfire Mk IV Manual, Part No. 545254.

FUEL SYSTEM SC

FUEL SYSTEM OPERATIONS (SINGLE CARBURETTER)

Operation	Number
Air cleaner – remove and refit	19.10.01
Air cleaner – renew element	10.10.08
Carburetter – diaphragm – remove and refit	19.15.35
Carburetter – float chamber level – check and adjust	19.15.32
Carburetter – float chamber needle valve – remove and refit	19.15.24
Carburetter – overhaul and adjust	19.15.17
Carburetter – remove and refit	19.15.09
Carburetter – tune and adjust	19.15.02
*Fuel filler cap – remove and refit	19.55.08
*Fuel main filter – remove and refit	19.25.02
*Fuel pump – clean filter	19.45.04
*Fuel pump – overhaul	19.45.16
*Fuel pump – remove and refit	19.45.08
*Fuel pump – test on vehicle	19.45.01
*Fuel tank – remove and refit	19.55.01
*Hose – filler to tank – remove and refit	19.40.19
*Mixture control cable – remove and refit	19.20.13
*Petrol pipe main line – engine end section – remove and refit	19.40.04
*Petrol pipe main line – tank end section – remove and refit	19.40.02
Throttle cable – remove and refit	19.20.06
Throttle linkage – remove and refit	19.20.07
*Throttle pedal – remove and refit	19.20.01

*All operations marked thus are detailed in the twin carburetter section.

Triumph Spitfire Mk IV Manual. Part No. 545254.

19.1 (SC)

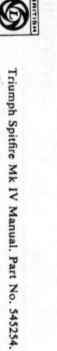

FUEL SYSTEM SC

EMISSION CARBURETTER – FAULT FINDING

NOTE: Before undertaking extensive carburetter servicing it is recommended that other engine factors and components such as cylinder compressions, valve clearance, distributor, sparking plugs, air intake temperature control system, etc., are checked for correctness of operation.

SYMPTOM	CAUSE	ACTION
1. Poor idle quality	a. Air leakage on induction manifold joints.	Remake joints as necessary. Check idle carbon monoxide level with CO meter.
	b. Throttles not synchronized.	Re-balance carburetters and re-set linkage.
	c. Air valve or valves sticking in piston guide-rods.	Clean air valve rods and guides and reassemble. Check piston free movement by hand; unit should move freely and return to carburetter bridge with an audible click.
	d. Partially or fully obstructed float-chamber or diaphragm ventilation holes.	Check that gasket(s) are not causing obstruction or piping obstructed.
	e. Incorrect fuel level caused by maladjusted float assemblies or worn or dirty needle valve.	Reset float heights and clean or replace needle valves worn.
	f. Metering needle incorrectly fitted or wrong type of needle fitted.	Ensure shoulder of needle is flush with face of air valve and that needle bias is correct.
	g. Diaphragm incorrectly located or damaged.	Check location with air valve cover removed, piston depression holes should be in line with and face towards the throttle spindle. Renew diaphragm with correct type if damage is in evidence.
	h. Leakage from ignition advance or retard pipe connections.	Re-make connections and re-check ignition settings.
	i. Temperature compensator faulty.	With engine and carburetter cold, check that compensator cone is seated, and free to move off seat. If any doubt exists, replace unit with new assembly.
	j. After considerable service leakage may occur at throttle spindle or secondary throttle spindles	Replace spindle seals or spindles as required.

continued

Triumph Spitfire Mk IV Manual. Part No. 545254.

19.00.01 Sheet 1

FUEL SYSTEM SC

SYMPTOM	CAUSE	ACTION
	Piston damper inoperative	Check damper oil level and top up with specified oil; re-check damper operation by raising piston by hand, whereupon resistance should be felt.
2. Hesitation or 'flat spot' a, b, c, d, e, f, g and h plus:	Air valve spring missing or wrong part fitted	Check correct grade of spring and refit as required.
	Ignition timing incorrect	Check and reset as required.
	Throttle linkage operation incorrect	Check operation of linkage between carburetters and operation of secondary throttle links; reset or replace parts as required.
3. Heavy fuel consumption 1 and 2 plus:	Leakage from the fuel connections, float-chamber joints or sealing plug 'O' rings	Replace gaskets and 'O' rings as required.
	Faulty by-pass valve	Replace by-pass valve with new unit.
4. Lack of engine braking	Sticking throttles	Check throttle operation and reset as required.
	Ignition retard inoperative	Check ignition setting at idle and ensure correct functioning of retard system.
	Damaged diaphragm	Inspect, and replace if incorrectly fitted or damaged.
5. Lack of engine power	Low fuel flow	Check discharge from fuel pump. Inspect needle valve seating.

NOTE: To ensure compliance with exhaust emission legislative requirements the following items MUST NOT be changed or modified in any way:

The fuel jet assembly; the air valve; the depression cover; the position of the fuel metering needle.

The following items must not be adjusted in service but should be replaced completely by factory-set units.

The temperature compensator; the air valve return spring; the by-pass unit; the starter assembly.

FUEL SYSTEM SC

AIR CLEANER

— Remove and refit 19.10.01
— Renew element 19.10.08

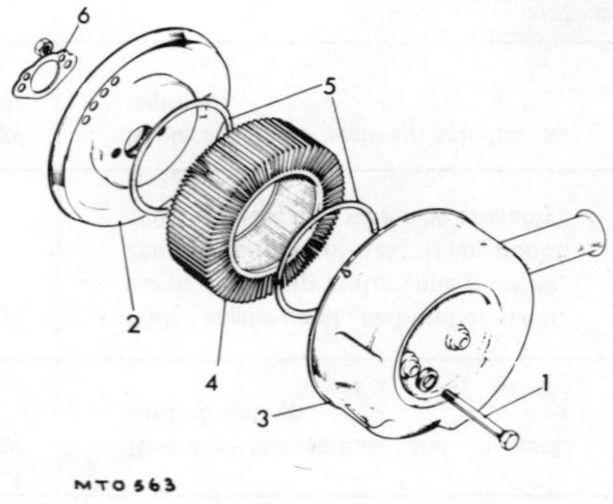

Removing

1. Remove two bolts, plain and rubber washers, securing the air cleaner to the carburetter.
2. Lift off the air cleaner.
3. Separate the components.
4. Remove the gasket from the carburetter.

Refitting

5. Clean or renew the element if required and fit new gasket.
6. Reverse instructions 1 to 3. Do not overtighten air cleaner securing bolts.

FUEL SYSTEM SC

CARBURETTER

— Tune and adjust   19.15.02

Service Tool: S353

NOTE: The following operation assumes all adjustments to be incorrectly set. Omit directions not relavent.

Setting control linkage and idling speed.

1. Remove the air cleaner (two bolts).
2. Slacken the throttle cable abutment nuts right back.
3. Slacken the fast idle screw to obtain maximum cam clearance.
4. Turn the idling screw until the throttle is just closed, then turn screw 1½ turns clockwise to provide a datum setting.
5. Ensure that the mixture control knob is pushed fully 'IN' on the fascia and that the cam is fully back against its stop.
6. Start the engine and attain normal running temperature.
7. Set the engine speed to 800 to 850 rev/min by turning the idling screw, stop engine.
8. Slacken the locknut and set the linkage adjusting screw until the clevis pin is moved to the engine side of the slots in the linkage straps, tighten locknut

NOTE: By moving the throttle spindle bracket independantly it is possible to ascertain the position of the clevis pin in the slot 'B'. Free play is necessary in the linkage to enable a fast idle setting without interfering with the closed position of the throttle.

9. Tighten the throttle cable abutment nuts to to give a cable condition of no tightness no play.

Fast idle adjustment

10. Ensure that the mixture control cable is correctly adjusted with no slackness or tightness.
11. Adjust the gap 'A' between the fast idle screw and the cam to 0·020 to 0·025 in
12. Start engine.
13. Pull the mixture control knob until the cam is turned to a position where the cam pivot, cable clamp screw and fast idle screw are in alignment. Adjust the fast idle speed if necessary to attain an engine speed of 1100 to 1300 rev/min, tighten the locknut.
14. Push the mixture control knob fully 'IN' at fascia.
15. Carry out C.O. level check.

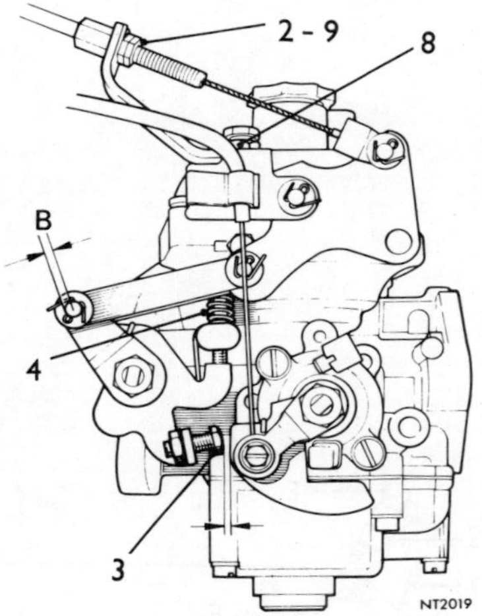

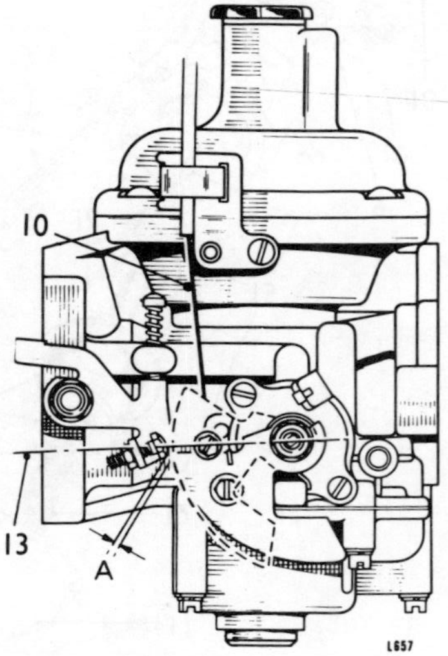

Where necessary adjust mixture as follows:

16. Remove carburetter damper.
17. Slowly insert tool S353 into the dashpot until the outer tool engages in the air valve and the inner tool engages the hexagon in the needle adjuster plug.
18. Hold the tool firmly and turn the inner tool clockwise to enrich the mixture anti-clockwise to weaken.
19. Check as in 15 and repeat as necessary.
20. Top up the dashpot (see maintenance item 7), replace the damper.
21. Fit the air cleaner.
22. Check and if necessary adjust idling speed to 800 to 850 rev/min.
23. Switch off engine.

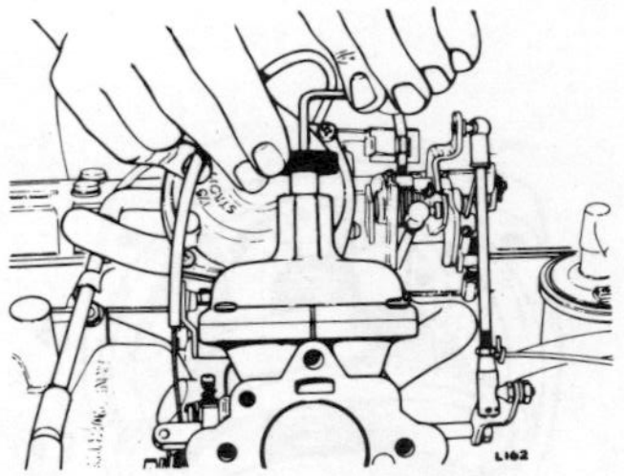

CARBURETTER

— Remove and refit   19.15.09

Removing

1. Remove the air cleaner (two bolts).
2. Disconnect the fuel feed pipe.
3. Disconnect the pipe to rocker cover.
4. Release the throttle return spring.
5. Remove the split pin, clevis pin and washers, slacken the abutment nuts and disconnect the throttle cable.
6. Release the mixture control cable by slackening the clamp screw and prising off the abutment clip.
7. Disconnect the ignition vacuum pipe.
8. Remove the two nuts securing the carburetter.
9. Lift off the carburetter.

Refitting

10. Renew carburetter and air cleaner gaskets.
11. Reverse instructions 1 to 9 and check settings.

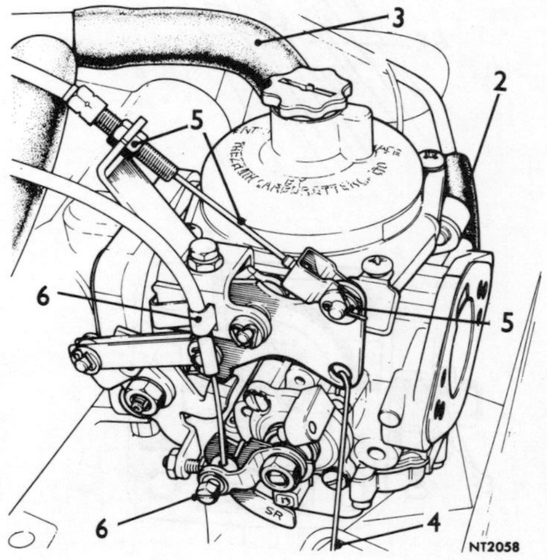

FUEL SYSTEM SC

CARBURETTER

— Overhaul and adjust   19.15.17

Service tool S353

1. Remove carburetter. 19.15.09
2. Remove damper.
3. Remove bottom plug.
4. Drain carburetter of oil and fuel.
5. Remove 'O' ring from plug.
6. Remove six screws securing float-chamber.
7. Remove float-chamber.
8. Remove float assembly by gently prising spindle from clip each end.
9. Remove needle valve.
10. Remove four screws securing top cover to body.
11. Remove top cover.
12. Remove spring.
13. Remove air valve assembly.
14. Remove four screws securing diaphragm and retaining ring to air valve assembly.
15. Remove diaphragm and retaining ring.
16. Slacken grubscrew in side of air valve.
17. Insert tool S353 in stem of air valve, turn anticlockwise approximately two turns, withdraw needle and housing by pulling firmly and straight with the fingers.
18. Remove two screws securing starter box to body.
19. Remove starter box.
20. Remove two screws securing the temperature compensator to body.
21. Remove the temperature compensator and two rubber washers of different diameters.
22. Remove three (slotted) screws securing the by-pass valve to body.
23. Remove the by-pass valve and gasket.
24. Remove two screws securing butterfly to spindle.
25. Turn spindle, remove butterfly.
26. Release spindle return spring.
27. Withdraw spindle and spring.
28. Remove spindle seals from body by hooking out with small screwdriver.
29. Wash all components in clean fuel, allow to drain dry or use compressed air. Place all components on a clean surface. Discard all seals and gaskets.
30. Examine the condition of all components for wear, paying special attention to needle and seat, air valve and diaphragm which should be renewed unless in exceptionally good condition.
31. Use clean compressed air to blow through all ports, needle valve and starter box.

continued

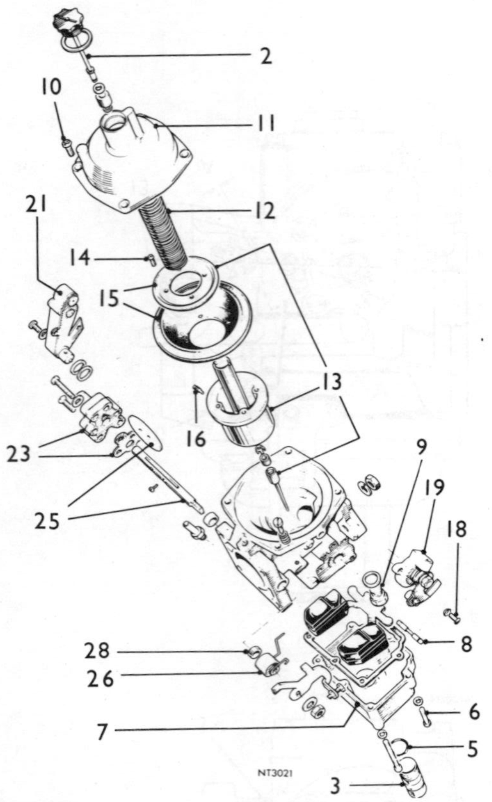

32. Fit spindle seals to body, tapping gently into position, with metal casing of seals flush with body of carburetter.
33. Insert spindle, loading and locating spindle return spring whilst so doing.
34. Insert butterfly with two protruding spots, outboard and below spindle, tighten screws.
35. Fit starter box, tighten screws. 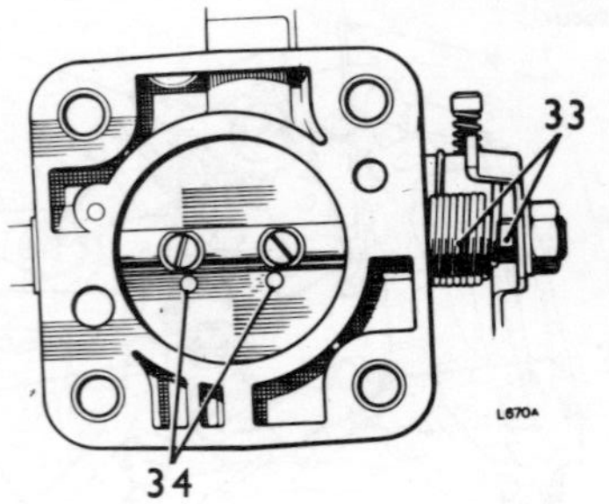
36. Fit by-pass valve and gasket, tighten screws.
37. Fit temperature compensator, tighten screws.
38. Insert needle housing assembly into the bottom of the air valve.
39. Fit tool S353, turning clockwise to engage threads of needle valve assembly with adjusting screw; continue turning until slot in needle housing is aligned with grub screw.
40. Tighten grub screw.

NOTE: The grub screw does not tighten on the needle housing but locates into the slot. This ensures that, during adjustment, the needle will remain in its operating position, i.e. biased, by a spring in the needle housing, towards the air cleaner side of the carburetter.

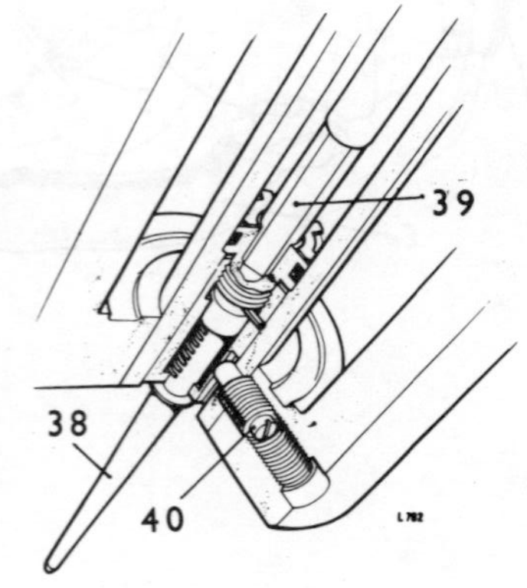

41. Fit diaphragm, locating inner tag into recess in air valve.
42. Fit diaphragm retaining ring; secure with four screws.
43. Fit air valve assembly, locating outer tag and rim of diaphragm in complementary recesses in carburetter body.
44. Fit carburetter top cover with bulge on housing neck towards air intake.
45. Fit and evenly tighten top cover screws.

continued

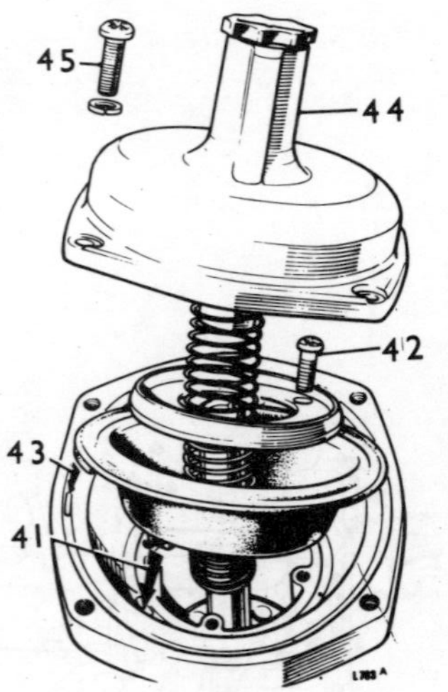

FUEL SYSTEM SC

46. Fit needle valve and sealing washers; tighten.
47. Fit float assembly by levering pivot pin gently into position.
48. Check float height by measuring the distance between the carburetter gasket face and the highest point of the floats.

NOTE: The float heights must be equal and set to 16 to 17 mm (0·625 to 0·672 in). Adjust by bending tabs ensuring that tab sits on needle valve at right angles.

49. Fit float-chamber gasket.
50. Fit float-chamber, secure with six screws.
51. Fit 'O' ring to bottom plug.
52. Fit bottom plug. 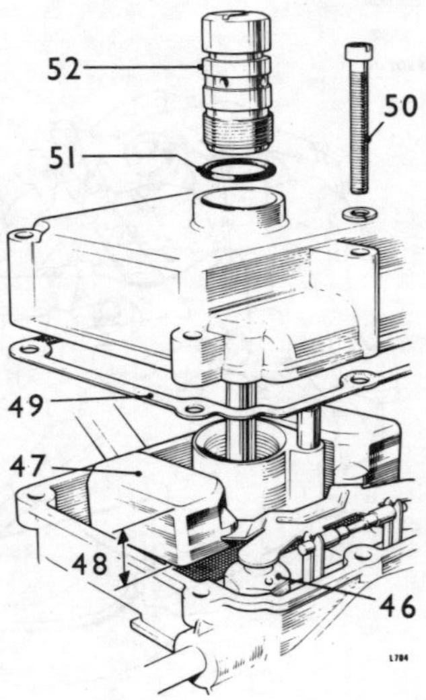
53. Fit carburetter, 17.15.09.
54. Fill carburetter damper dashpot with seasonal grade of engine oil until, using the damper as a dipstick, the threaded plug is 6 mm (0·25 in) above the dashpot when resistance is felt.
55. Fit damper.
56. Tune carburetter, 19.15.01.

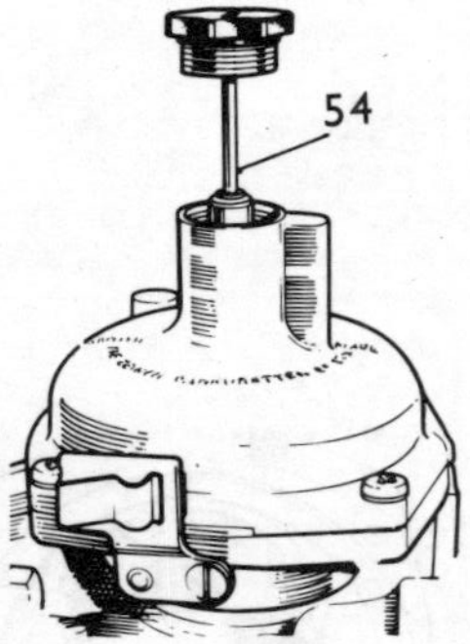

FLOAT-CHAMBER NEEDLE VALVE 19.15.24

—Remove and refit

Removing
1. Remove carburetter, 19.15.09.
2. Remove six screws securing float-chamber to body.
3. Remove float chamber.
4. Remove gasket.
5. Remove float assembly by gently prising spindle from clip each end.
6. Remove needle valve.

Refitting
7. Reverse instructions 1 to 6—renew gasket.

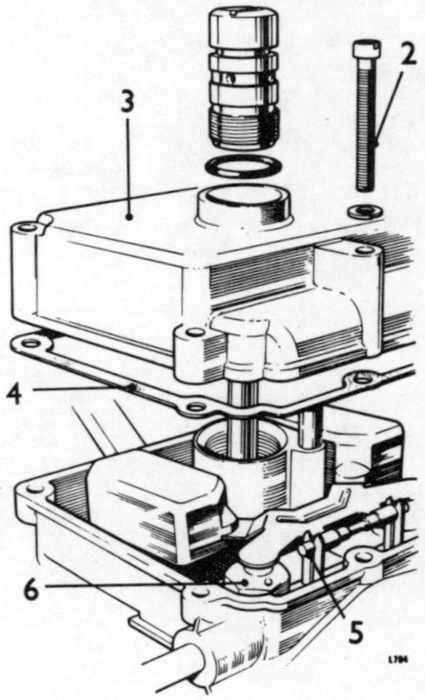

FLOAT-CHAMBER LEVELS 19.15.32

—Check and adjust
1. Remove carburetter, 19.15.09.
2. Remove six screws securing float-chamber to body.
3. Remove float chamber.
4. Remove gasket.
5. Check distance between gasket face on carburetter body to highest point of each float.

NOTE: The height of each float must be equal and correct to datum setting which is 16 to 17 mm (0·625 to 0·672 in).

To adjust
6. Bend tab over to obtain correct setting ensuring that the tab sits on needle valve at right angles.
7. Fit new gasket, reverse instructions 1 to 3.

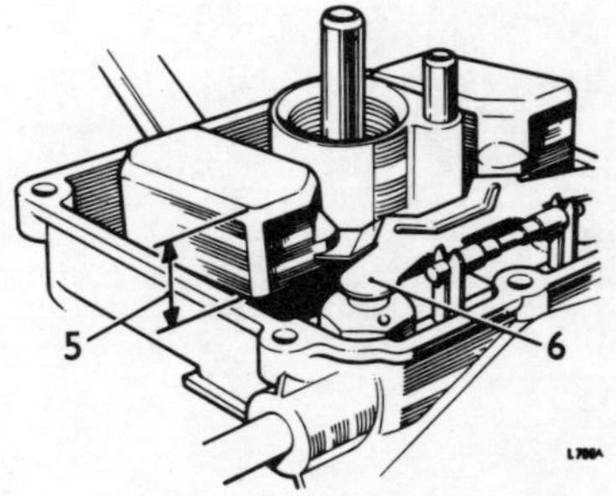

19.15.17 (SC) Sheet 3

Triumph Spitfire Mk IV Manual, Part No. 545254.

19.15.24
19.15.32 (SC)

FUEL SYSTEM SC

DIAPHRAGM

—Remove and refit   19.15.35

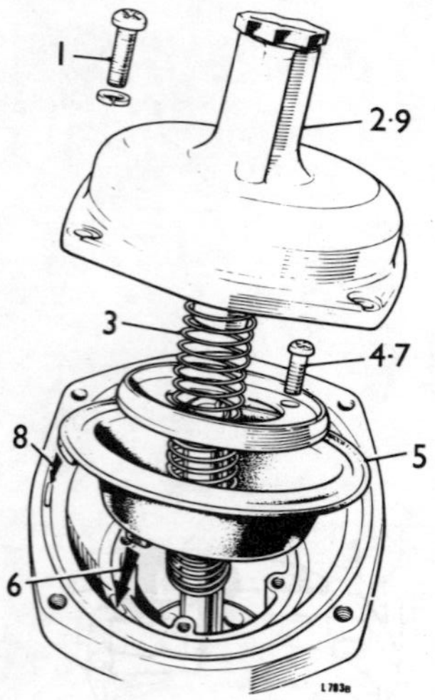

Removing

1. Remove four screws securing top cover to carburetter body.
2. Lift off top cover.
3. Remove spring.
4. Remove diaphragm retaining plate (four screws).
5. Remove diaphragm.

Refitting

6. Fit diaphragm, locating inner tag in air valve recess.
7. Fit retaining plate, ensure correct diaphragm seating, tighten screws.
8. Locate diaphragm outer tag in recess in carburetter body, and rim bead in annular groove.
9. Fit top cover, evenly tighten securing screws.

THROTTLE LINKAGE

Remove and refit   19.20.07

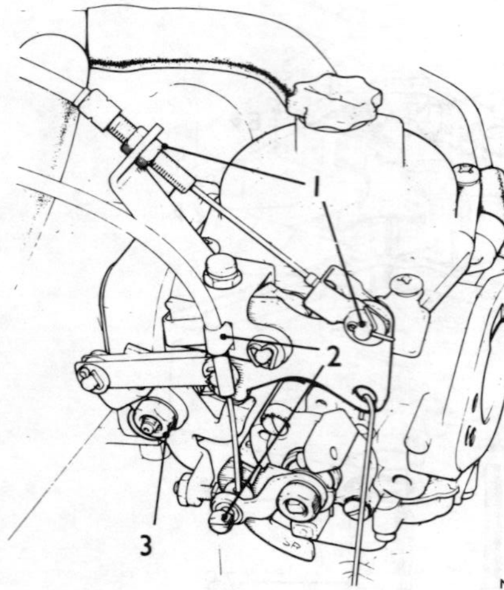

Removing

1. Remove the split pin, washer and clevis pin, slacken the abutment nuts and disconnect the throttle cable.
2. Release the mixture control cable by slackening the clamp screw and prising off the abutment clip.
3. Remove the nut on throttle spindle.
4. De-tab and remove the two screws securing the upper abutment bracket to carburetter.
5. Lift off linkage.

Refitting

6. Ensure that all linkage joints actuate freely and are not worn, lightly oil and reverse instructions 1 to 5.

NOTE: Free play is built into the linkage at point 'A' and should not be confused with wear nor should any attempt be made to adjust it out.

19.15.35
19.20.07 (SC)

Triumph Spitfire Mk IV Manual. Part No. 545254.

COOLING SYSTEM

COOLING OPERATIONS

Coolant – drain and refill	26.10.01
Cooling system – pressure test	26.10.07
Fan – remove and refit	26.25.06
Fan belt – remove and refit	26.20.07
Hoses – remove and refit	
– cylinder head to heater valve	26.30.39
– heater to water pump pipe	26.30.18
– heater valve to heater	26.30.40
– inlet manifold to water pump pipe	26.30.17
– radiator top hose	26.30.01
– radiator bottom hose	26.30.07
– thermostat to inlet manifold	26.30.46
Radiator – remove and refit	26.40.01
Thermostat – remove and refit	26.45.01
– test	26.45.09
Thermostat and water pump housing	26.45.10
Water pump – remove and refit	26.50.01

COOLANT

– Drain and refill   26.10.01

Draining

1. Set the heater control to 'HOT' position.
2. Remove the radiator filler cap. **CAUTION:** If the engine is hot, exercise care. Turn the cap slowly and allow any pressure in the system to release completely before removing the cap.
3. Open the drain tap (if fitted) at the rear right hand rear of the cylinder block.
4. Open the radiator drain tap (if fitted). If the radiator is not fitted with a drain tap release the bottom hose at the radiator.

Refitting

5. Close the drain tap on the cylinder block (if fitted).
6. Close the radiator drain tap or refit the bottom hose to the radiator.
7. Fill the cooling system with clean soft water.
8. Fit the radiator filler cap and run the engine at a fast idling speed for approximately 1 to 2 minutes.
9. Remove the radiator cap and top up as necessary.
10. Replace the radiator filler cap and inspect the cooling system for leaks.
11. Top up the overflow reservoir as necessary.

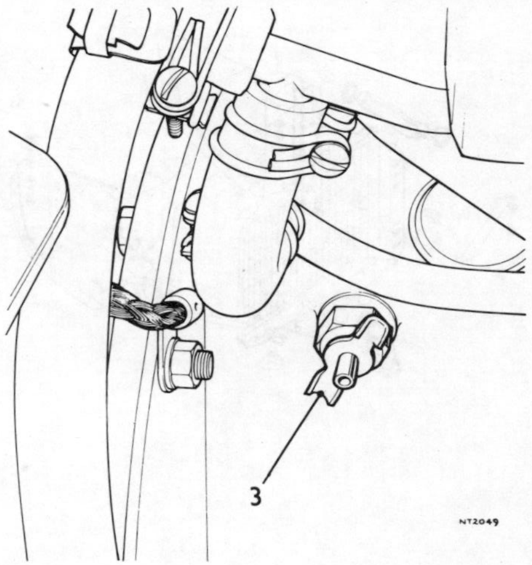

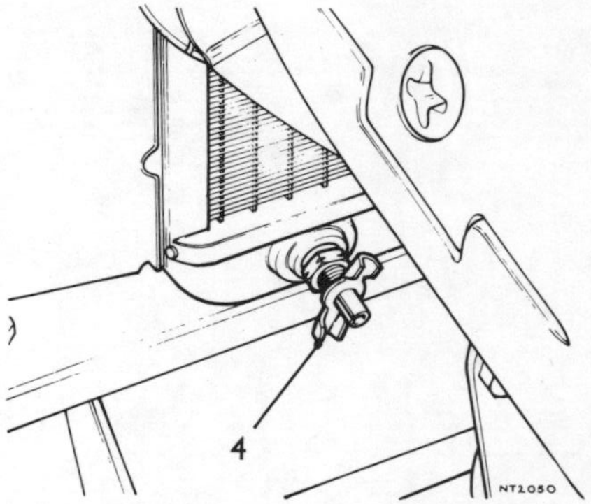

COOLING SYSTEM

– Pressure test   26.10.07

Radiator

1. Rinse radiator filler cap in clean water.
2. Remove the radiator filler cap.
3. Whilst still wet fit the cap to the pressure tester. Pump up pressure until the gauge pointer ceases to rise. Reject the filler cap if it will not register and maintain a pressure of 1 lb in² (0·06 kg/cm²) below the figure stamped on the filler cap for a period of at least ten seconds without additional pumping.

Radiator

4. Warm the engine.
5. Remove the radiator filler cap.
6. Top up the cooling system of required.
7. Fit the pressure tester to the radiator.
8. Pump up to 13 p.s.i. (0·78 kg/cm²).
9. Check that pressure will hold for approximately ten seconds without further pumping.
10. Check for leaks whilst system is pressurised.
11. If pressure falls within ten seconds and no leaks are visible, internal leakage is indicated.

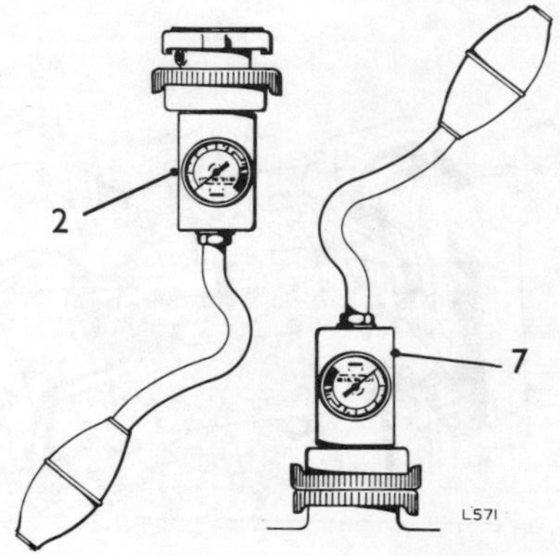

COOLING SYSTEM

FAN BELT

— Remove and refit   26.20.07

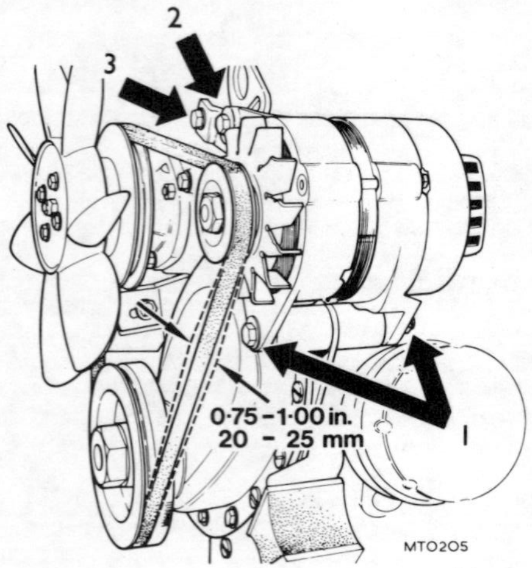

Removing

1. Slacken the pivot bolt and nut on the underside of the alternator.
2. Slacken the bolt securing the alternator to the adjusting plate.
3. Slacken the bolt securing the adjusting plate to the water pump.
4. Pivot the alternator towards the engine to release tension from the fan belt.
5. Release the fan belt from the alternator, water pump and engine crankshaft pulleys.

Refitting

6. Locate the fan belt on the engine crankshaft, water pump and alternator pulleys.
7. Adjust fan belt tension and tighten bolts 1, 2, and 3.

FAN

— Remove and refit   26.25.06

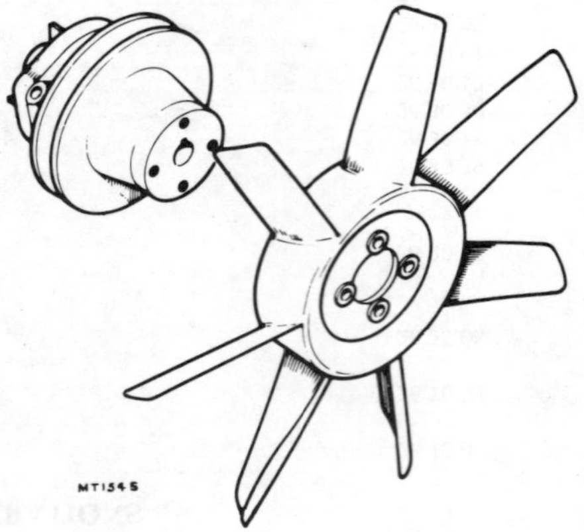

Remove

1. Drain the cooling system and remove the radiator 26.40.01.
2. Remove the four bolts securing the fan to the water pump pulley and withdraw the fan.

Refitting

3. Reverse instructions 1 and 2.

26.20.07
26.25.06

Triumph Spitfire Mk IV Manual. Part No. 545254.

HOSES

— Remove and refit

Cylinder head to heater valve	26.30.39
Heater to water pump pipe	26.30.18
Heater valve to heater	26.30.40
Inlet manifold to water pump pipe	26.30.17
Radiator bottom hose	26.30.07
Radiator top hose	26.30.01
Thermostat to inlet manifold	26.30.46

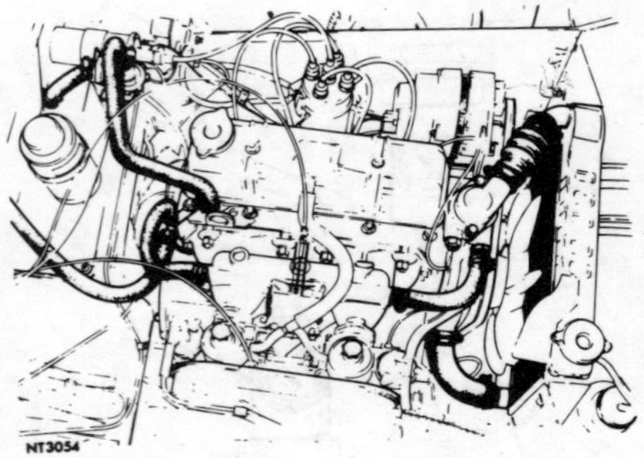

Removing

1. Drain the cooling system.
2. Slacken the hose clips.
3. Remove the hose.

Refitting

4. Reverse instructions 1 to 3.

RADIATOR

— Remove and refit   26.40.01

Removing

1. Remove the radiator filler cap and drain cooling system.
2. Disconnect radiator bottom hose. (If not already disconnected to drain system. Models without radiator drain taps only).
3. Disconnect radiator top hose.
4. Disconnect overflow bottle plastic hose from radiator.
5. Remove four bolts and nuts (2 either side) securing radiator to mounting bracket.
6. Withdraw the radiator.

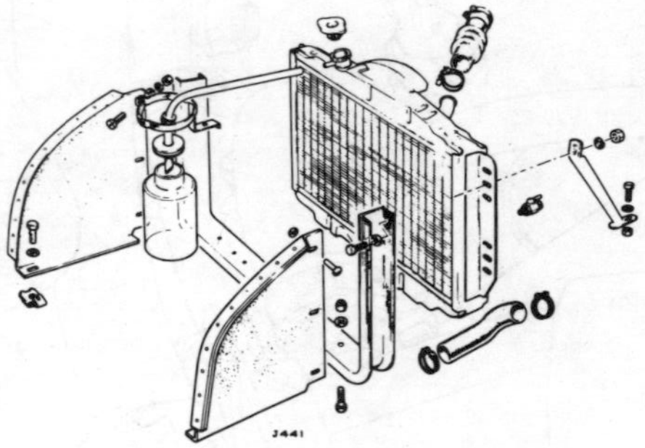

Refitting

7. Reverse instructions 2 to 6.
8. Fill the cooling system.

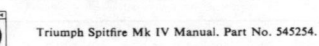

26.30.39/46
26.40.01

Triumph Spitfire Mk IV Manual. Part No. 545254.

COOLING SYSTEM

THERMOSTAT

— Remove and refit 26.45.01

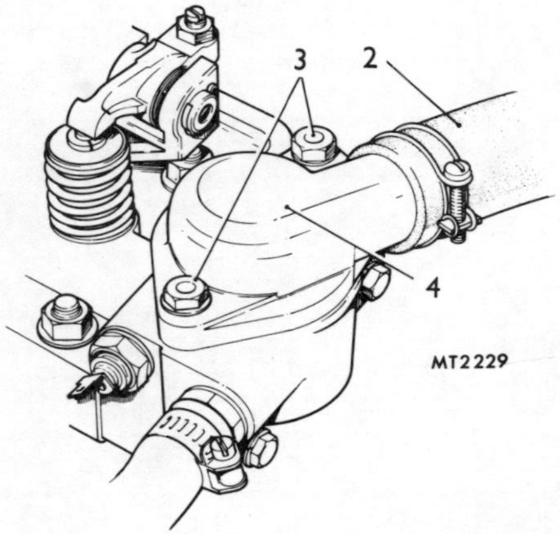

Removing

1. Drain the cooling system.
2. Remove the radiator top hose.
3. Remove the two bolts and spring washers securing the thermostat elbow to the water pump housing.
4. Lift off the thermostat elbow.
5. Lift out the thermostat.

Refitting

6. Clean the mating faces of the thermostat elbow and the water pump housing.
7. Place the thermostat in the water pump housing.
8. Fit a new gasket and the thermostat elbow. Fit and tighten the two securing bolts and spring washers.
9. Fit the radiator top hose.
10. Top up the cooling system.

THERMOSTAT

— Test 26.45.09

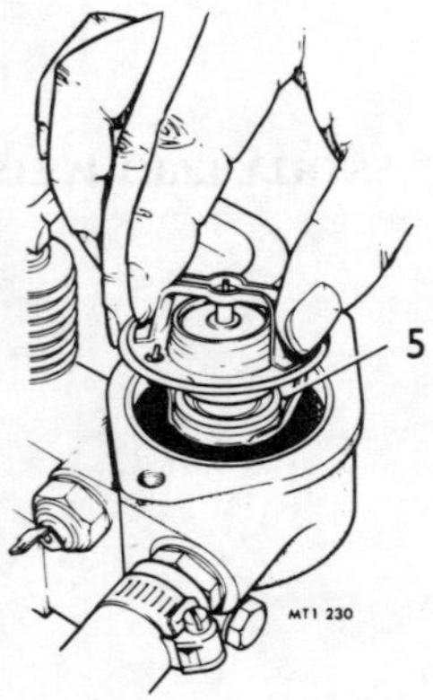

1. Determine the opening temperature of the thermostat stamped on the flange or base.
2. Immerse the thermostat in water heated to the opening temperature of the thermostat. Renew the thermostat if it fails to open.

THERMOSTAT AND WATER PUMP HOUSING

— Remove and refit 26.45.10

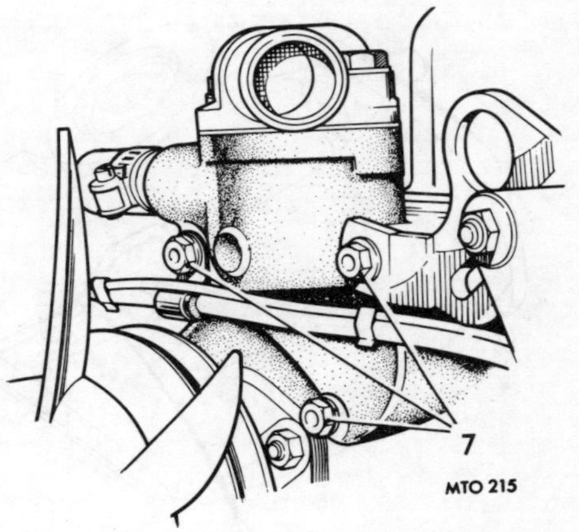

Removing

1. Drain the cooling system and remove the radiator. 26.40.01.
2. Remove the fan belt.
3. Disconnect the induction manifold hose at the thermostat outlet.
4. Disconnect the petrol feed hose to the carburetter.
5. Disconnect the temperature transmitter.
6. Disconnect the return water pipe union at the rear of the thermostat and water pump housing.
7. Remove the three bolts securing the thermostat and water pump housing to the cylinder head. Note the length and position of each bolt.
8. Withdraw the thermostat and water pump housing.
9. Remove the three nuts and spring washers securing the water pump to the housing and withdraw the water pump and fan.
10. Remove the temperature transmitter.

Refitting

11. Reverse instructions 1 to 10. Use new gaskets when fitting the water pump to the housing and the housing to the cylinder head.
12. Fill the cooling system.

WATER PUMP

— Remove and refit 26.50.01

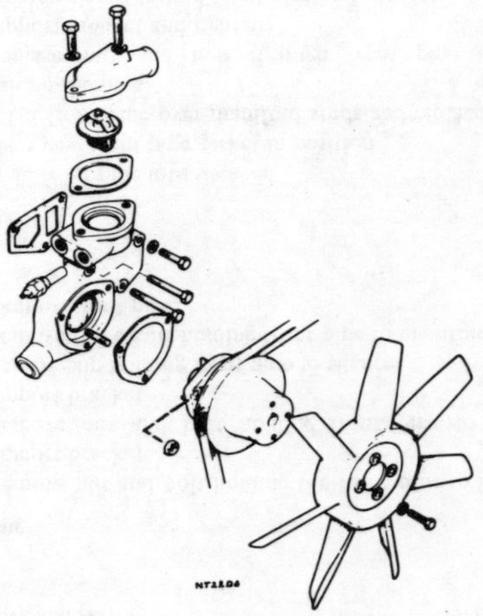

Removing

1. Remove the radiator cap and drain the cooling system.
2. Remove the radiator 26.40.01.
3. Remove the fan belt.
4. Remove the three nuts and spring washers securing the water pump flange to the thermostat and water pump housing.
5. Withdraw the water pump.
6. Remove the fan.

Refitting

7. Ensure that the mating faces of the water pump flanges and the thermostat and water pump housing are clean and free of burrs.
8. Using a new gasket fit the water pump and evenly tighten the three securing nuts.
9. Fit the fan.
10. Reverse instructions 1 to 3.
11. Fill the cooling system.

MANIFOLD AND EXHAUST SYSTEM

MANIFOLD AND EXHAUST SYSTEM OPERATIONS

Exhaust system complete – remove and refit	30.10.01
Front pipe – single or left-hand – remove and refit	30.10.09
Tail pipe or silencer – remove and refit	30.10.22
Down-pipe flange packing – remove and refit	30.10.26
Exhaust manifold – remove and refit	30.15.01

MANIFOLD AND EXHAUST SYSTEM

EXHAUST SYSTEM COMPLETE 30.10.01
– Remove and refit

Removing
1. Remove front pipe 30.10.09.
2. Remove silencer assembly 30.10.22.
3. Remove exhaust manifold 35.15.01.

Refitting
4. Refit exhaust manifold 35.15.01.
5. Refit silencer assembly 30.10.22.
6. Refit front pipe 30.10.09.

FRONT PIPE 30.10.09
– Remove and refit

Removing
1. Remove nut and bolt holding the front pipe to front support bracket.
2. Remove nut and bolt holding front pipe to rear support bracket.
3. Release clip holding front pipe to silencer.
4. Remove three nuts holding front pipe to manifold.
5. Remove front pipe.

Refitting
6. Slide front pipe into silencer.
7. Place new front pipe gasket in position.
8. Align front pipe over manifold studs and replace and tighten the nuts.
9. Replace nut and bolt through front pipe front support bracket and tighten.
10. Tighten clamp around front pipe and silencer.

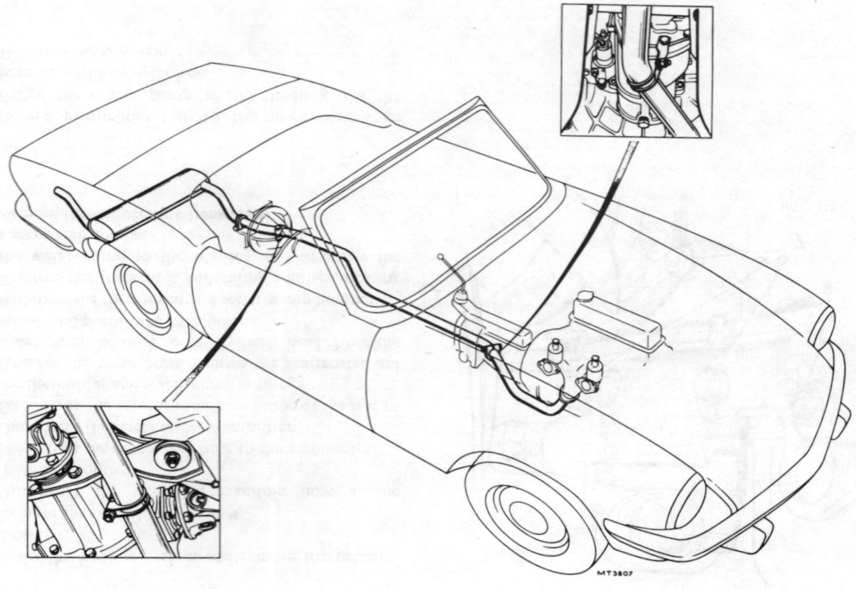

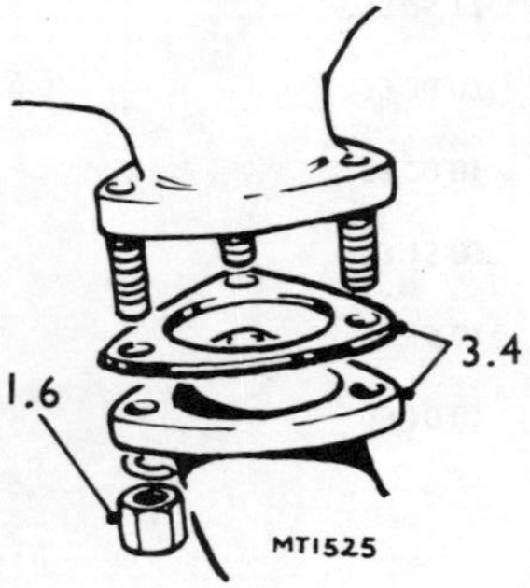

MANIFOLD AND EXHAUST SYSTEM

TAIL PIPE OR SILENCER
— Remove and refit   30.10.22

Removing
1. Release clip holding silencer to front pipe.
2. Remove two nuts and bolts holding silencer to the rubber straps.
3. Remove the silencer.

Refitting
4. Align and slide the silencer over the front pipe.
5. Replace the tail pipe mounting rubber straps.
6. Tighten the clip around the tail pipe and front pipe.

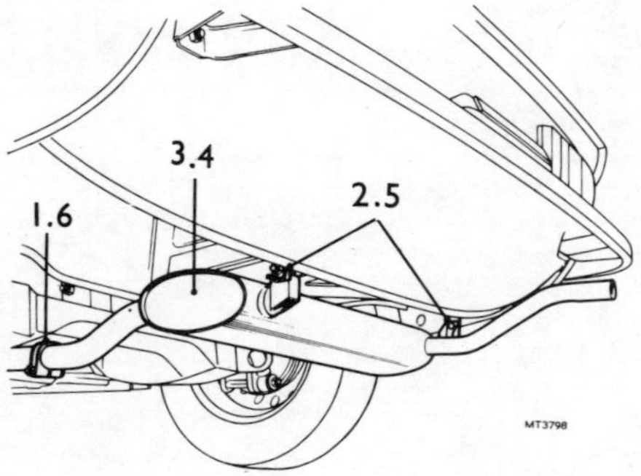

DOWN PIPE FLANGE PACKING
— Remove and refit   30.10.26

Removing
1. Remove three nuts holding the front pipe to manifold.
2. Remove nut and bolt holding front pipe to support bracket.
3. Pull down front pipe and remove flange packing.

Refitting
4. Pull front pipe down and replace packing.
5. Refit front pipe and tighten manifold stud nuts.
6. Refit nut and bolt in front pipe mounting bracket.

EXHAUST MANIFOLD
— Remove and refit   30.15.01

Removing
1. Remove carburetter and inlet manifold as in operation 19.15.11.
2. Remove three nuts on down-pipe flange and pull clear.
3. Remove down-pipe flange packing.
4. Remove two nuts holding exhaust manifold to cylinder head.
5. Pull manifold clear of studs and remove from engine.
6. Remove induction and exhaust manifold gasket.

Refitting
7. Renew and refit the manifold gasket up to cylinder head.
8. Refit the manifold onto the head studs.
9. Tighten nuts holding manifold to head.
10. Renew down-pipe flange packing and fit over studs.
11. Replace and tighten three nuts holding front pipe in position.
12. Refit carburetter and inlet manifold as in operation 19.15.11.

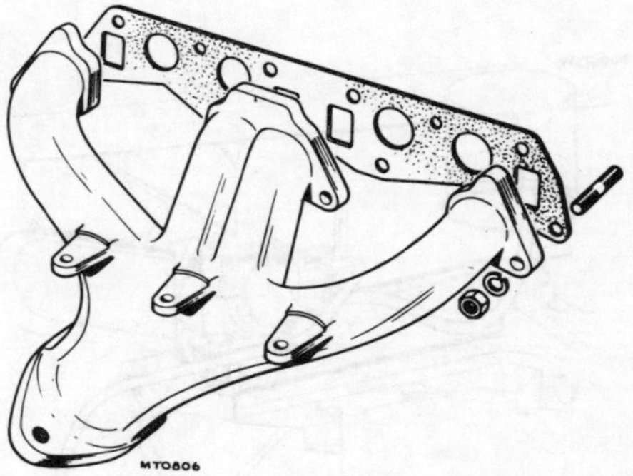

CLUTCH

CLUTCH OPERATIONS

Clutch assembly – remove and refit	33.10.01
Hydraulic system – bleed	33.15.01
Fluid pipe – remove and refit	33.15.09
Master cylinder – remove and refit	33.20.01
Master cylinder – overhaul	33.20.07
Release bearing assembly – remove and refit	33.25.12
Bearing assembly – overhaul	33.25.17
Clutch pedal – remove and refit	33.30.02
Clutch pedal – overhaul	33.30.06
Clutch pedal return spring – remove and refit	33.30.03
Slave cylinder – remove and refit	33.35.01
Slave cylinder – overhaul	33.35.07

Triumph Spitfire Mk IV Manual. Part No. 545254.

33.1

CLUTCH ASSEMBLY

– Remove and refit   33.10.01

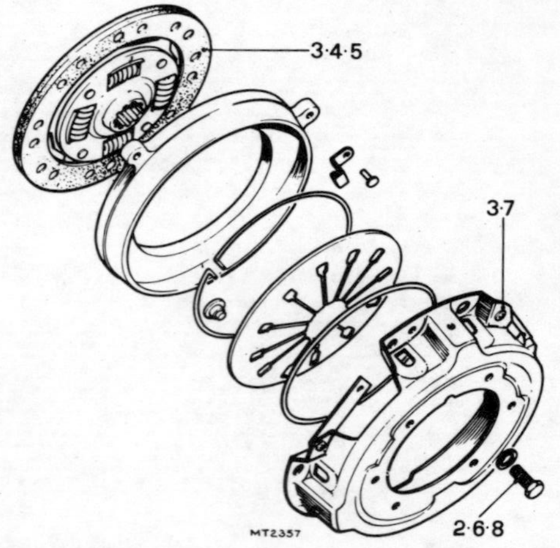

Removing

1. Remove the gearbox 37.20.01.
2. **Working from inside the car, remove six bolts – earlier models or screws – later models, holding clutch to flywheel. **
3. Remove the clutch driven plate and pressure plate.

Refitting

4. With the longer boss of the splined hub towards the gearbox, offer up the driven plate to the flywheel.
5. Centralise the driven plate with the bush at the rear of the crankshaft.
6. **Insert the six bolts – earlier models, or screws – later models, holding the clutch to the flywheel. **
7. Ensure that the pressure plate locates correctly on the dowels on the flywheel.
8. Tighten the six bolts holding the pressure plate to the flywheel.
9. Refit the gearbox 37.20.01.

HYDRAULIC SYSTEM

– Bleed   33.15.01

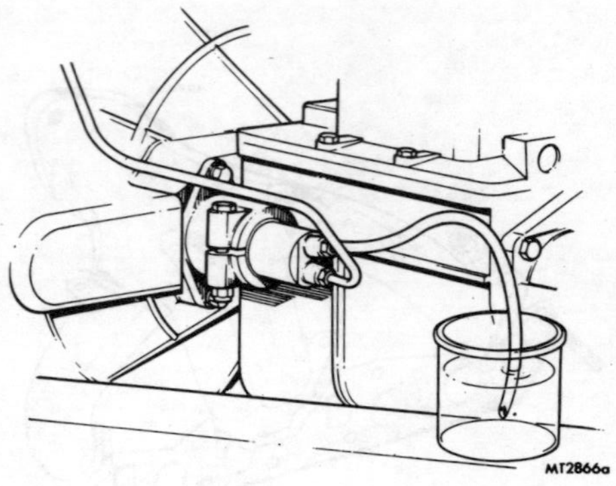

1. Ensure that the reservoir is topped up to ¼in from the top.
2. Remove the gearbox cover 76.25.07.
3. Wipe the bleed nipple clean.
4. Attach a piece of small bore tubing to the nipple and let it hang in a container partially filled with hydraulic fluid.
5. Unscrew the bleed nipple one complete turn.

NOTE: During bleeding, care should be taken to ensure that the reservoir does not become empty, resulting in air being drawn into the system. Ensure that fluid used is clean or air-free.

6. Depress the clutch pedal fully and let it return without assistance.
7. Repeat this operation with a slight pause between each depression of the pedal.
8. Observe the fluid being discharged from the pipe.
9. When it is air free, hold the pedal in the depressed position.
10. Securely tighten the bleed screw.
11. Remove the pipe from the slave cylinder.
12. Refit the gearbox cover 76.25.07.

Triumph Spitfire Mk IV Manual Part No. 545254

33.10.01
33.15.01

CLUTCH

FLUID PIPE

– Remove and refit   33.15.09

Removing

1. Drain the hydraulic system.
2. Unscrew the pipe from slave cylinder.
3. Unscrew pipe from master cylinder.
4. Remove pipe from car.

Refitting

5. Align new pipe in approximate position in car.
6. Screw pipe into the master cylinder.
7. Screw pipe into the slave cylinder.
8. Top up master cylinder with new brake fluid.
9. Bleed hydraulic system 33.15.01.

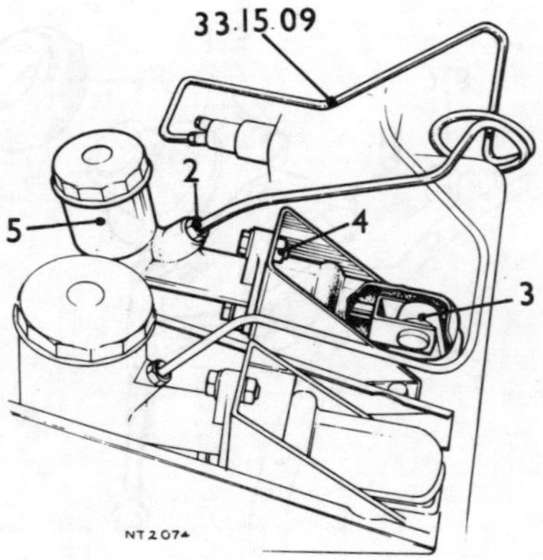

MASTER CYLINDER

– Remove and refit   33.20.01

Removing

1. Drain the fluid system.
2. Disconnect the fluid pipe at the master cylinder; plug open ends.
3. Lift the rubber boot, remove split pin and cotter pin from top of pedal.
4. Remove two bolts securing master cylinder to bracket.
5. Remove master cylinder from car.

Refitting

6. Hold master cylinder in place in engine compartment.
7. Renew two bolts securing master cylinder to bracket and fit.
8. Refit cotter pin, renew split pin, refit boot.
9. Connect the fluid pipe to the master cylinder.
10. Bleed the system 33.15.01.

MASTER CYLINDER

– Overhaul   33.20.07

1. Drain the fluid reservoir.
2. Remove the master cylinder from the car 33.20.01.
3. Slide the rubber along the push rod.
4. Remove the circlip from the end of the master cylinder and withdraw the push rod and washer.
5. Withdraw the piston spring and seal assembly from the master cylinder. Withdrawal may be facilitated by applying a compressed air line to the fluid outlet union.
6. Straighten the prong of the spring thimble and remove the thimble and spring from the piston.
7. Release the valve stem from the key hole slot in the thimble.
8. Slide the valve seal spacer along the valve stem.
9. Remove the valve seal from the valve stem and fit a new seal.
10. Assemble the spacer, spring and thimble to the valve stem.
11. Remove the seal from the piston and fit a new seal (seal lip towards the spring).
12. Engage the spring thimble on the piston and carefully depress the thimble prong.
13. Lubricate the bore of the master cylinder with clean brake fluid and insert the seal assembly spring and piston.
14. Fit a new rubber to the push rod.
15. Fit the push rod and washer to the master cylinder and secure with the clip.
16. Slide the rubber into position on the master cylinder.
17. Refit the master cylinder to the car 33.20.01.
18. Bleed the cylinder.

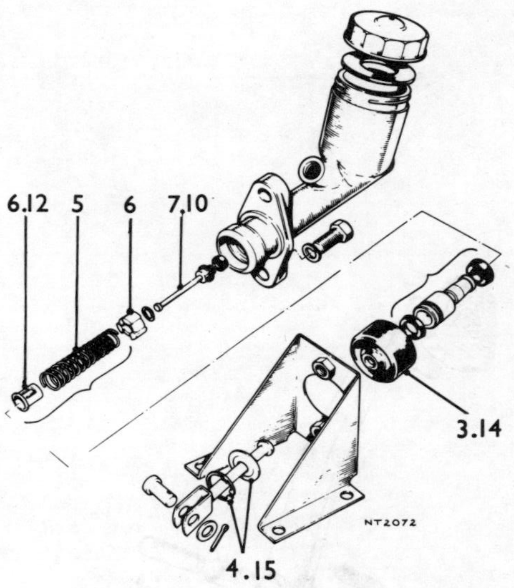

Triumph Spitfire Mk IV Manual. Part No. 545234.

33.15.09
33.20.01

33.20.07

CLUTCH

RELEASE BEARING ASSEMBLY

— Remove and refit   33.25.12

Removing

1. Remove the gearbox 37.20.01.
2. Drive the pin from the clutch housing.
3. Remove the operating lever from the housing.
4. Press out mills pin and release bearing sleeve by extracting plugs.
5. Withdraw the bearing from the sleeve.

Refitting

6. Reverse procedure 1 to 5.

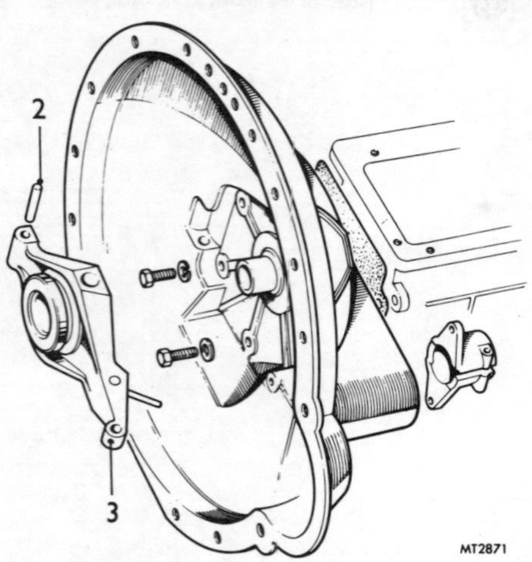

BEARING ASSEMBLY

— Overhaul   33.25.17

1. Remove the gearbox 37.20.01.
2. Remove operating lever assembly.
3. Remove bearing sleeve.
4. Remove bearing.
5. Renew bearing sleeve.
6. Renew bearing.
7. Grease bearing and sleeve.
8. Replace and refit operating lever.
9. Refit gearbox 37.20.01.

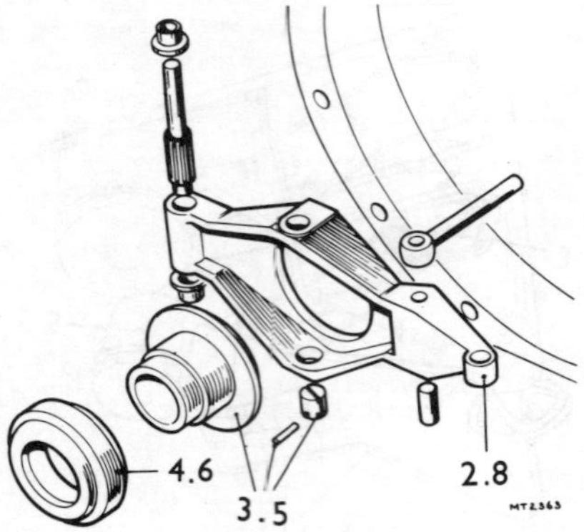

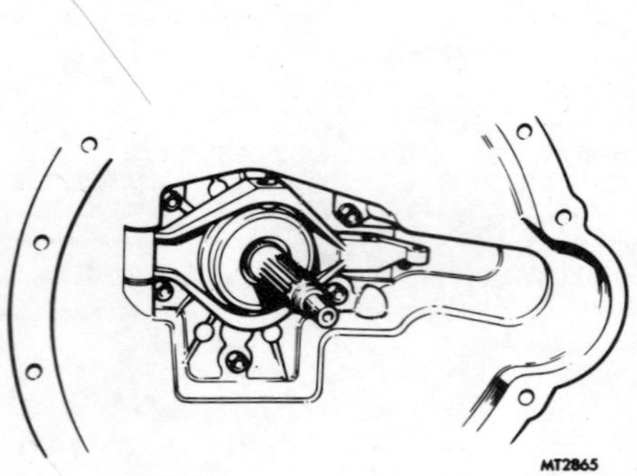

CLUTCH PEDAL

— Remove and refit   33.30.02

Removing

1. Remove split pin, washer and clevis pin.
2. Remove return spring.
3. Remove eight bolts holding clutch pedal bracket to body.
4. Remove bracket and pedal from car.
5. Remove one circlip from the pivot pin.
6. Push pivot pin clear of pedal.
7. Push bush out of pedal.
8. Remove pedal from bracket.

Refitting

9. Reposition pedal in bracket.
10. Push bush through pedal.
11. Push lubricated pivot pin through bush.
12. Replace circlip and ensure it locates properly in the groove.
13. Reposition bracket in the car.
14. Refit eight screws in position and tighten.
15. Refit clevis pin and washer.
16. Renew split pin and fit.
17. Refit return spring.

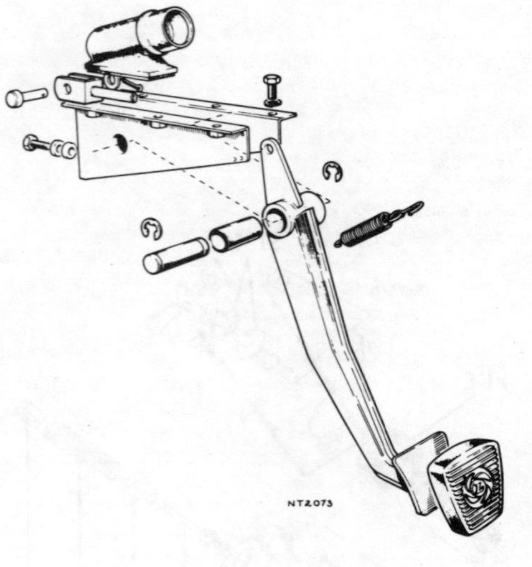

CLUTCH PEDAL RETURN SPRING

— Remove and refit   33.30.03

Removing

1. Lever spring from hole in pedal.
2. Remove spring from bracket.

Refitting

3. Fit new return spring to bracket.
4. Spread spring and position it through hole in pedal.

CLUTCH PEDAL

— Overhaul   33.30.09

1. Remove clutch pedal 33.30.02.
2. Remove bush from pedal.
3. Remove pedal rubbers.
4. Fit new bushes and lubricate.
5. Renew pedal rubber and fit.
6. Refit clutch pedal 33.30.02.

Triumph Spitfire Mk IV Manual. Part No. 545254.

33.25.12
33.25.17
33.30.02
33.30.09

CLUTCH

SLAVE CYLINDER

— Remove and refit 33.35.01

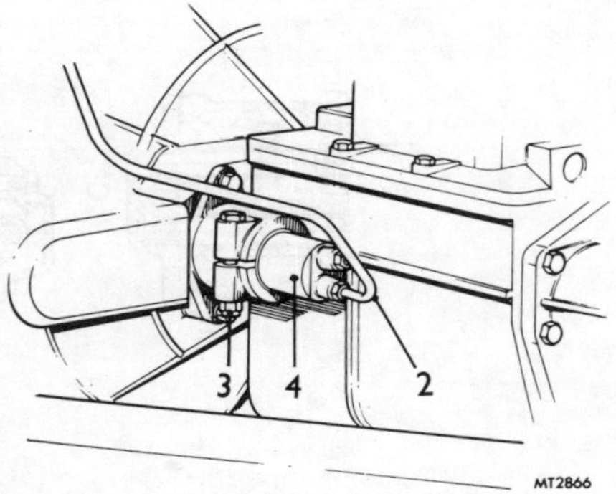

Removing
1. Drain the clutch system.
2. Disconnect hydraulic pipe and push clear of slave cylinder.
3. Remove locating bolt, nut and washer.
4. Pull slave cylinder clear of housing.

Refitting
5. Centralise push rod in housing.
6. Push slave cylinder into housing.
7. Line up groove with hole and place bolt in through hole and tighten nut.
8. Line up hydraulic pipe and tighten nut up in slave cylinder.
9. Bleed the system 35.15.01.

SLAVE CYLINDER

— Overhaul 33.35.07

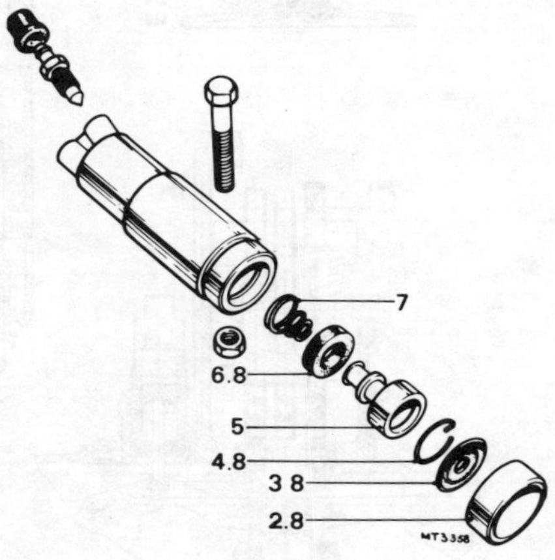

1. Remove slave cylinder from car 33.35.01.
2. Remove dust cover retainer.
3. Remove dust cover.
4. Remove circlip.
5. Remove plunger.
6. Remove the seal.
7. Remove the spring.
8. Fit new seal, spring circlip, dust cover and retainer and lubricate.
9. Refit slave cylinder to car 33.35.01.

33.35.01
33.35.07

Triumph Spitfire Mk IV Manual. Part No. 545254.

SYNCHROMESH GEARBOX

SYNCHROMESH GEARBOX OPERATIONS

Bell housing — remove and refit	37.12.07
Constant pinion — overhaul	37.20.34
Drive flange — remove and refit	37.10.01
Gearbox assembly	
— overhaul	37.20.04
— remove and refit	37.20.01
Gearchange lever	
— check and adjust	37.16.01
— overhaul	37.16.10
— remove and refit	37.16.04
Gearchange lever draught excluder — remove and refit	37.16.05
Layshaft cluster assembly — overhaul	37.20.29
Rear extension	
— overhaul	37.12.04
— remove and refit	37.12.01
Rear oil seal — remove and refit	37.23.01
Speedometer drive gear pinion — remove and refit	37.25.01
Speedometer drive gear pinion — remove and refit	37.25.05
Synchroniser assemblies — overhaul	37.20.08
Top cover	
— overhaul	37.12.16
— remove and refit	37.12.19
Top cover extension	
— overhaul	37.12.13
— remove and refit	37.12.10

Triumph Spitfire Mk IV Manual. Part No. 545254.

37-1

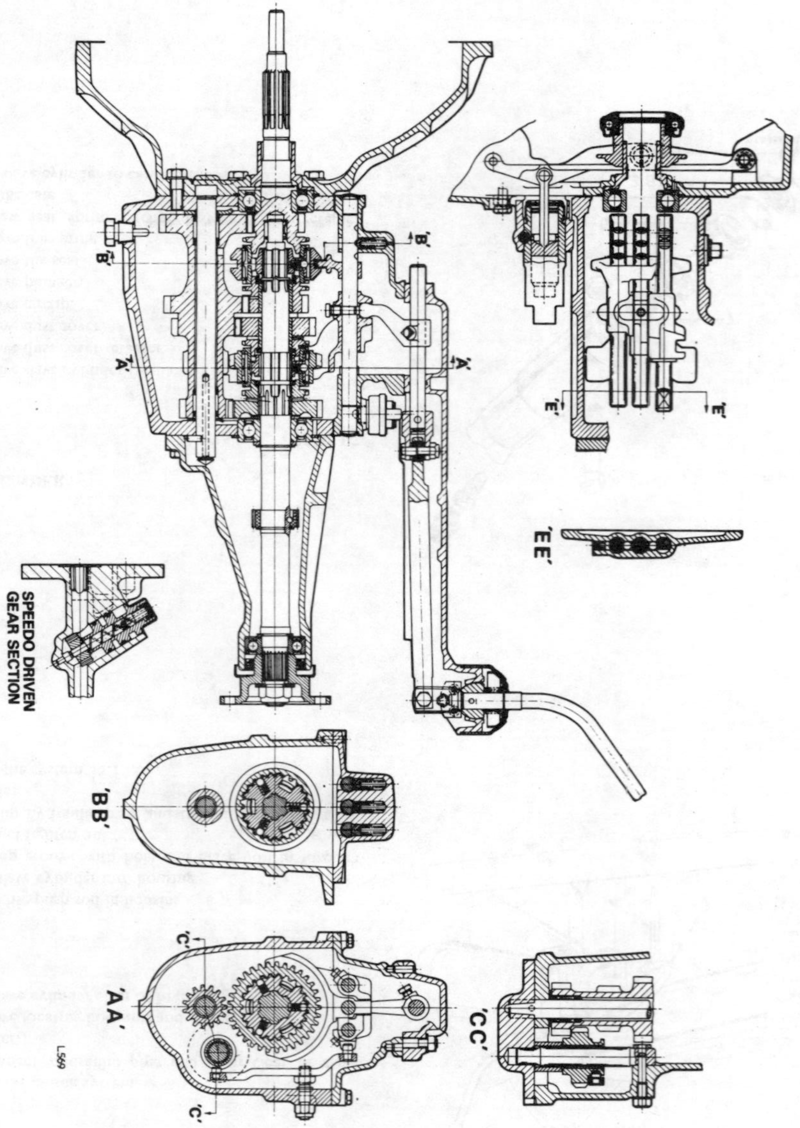

SYNCHROMESH GEARBOX

DRIVE FLANGE
— Remove and refit
37.10.01

Removing
1. Drive the vehicle onto a ramp and raise the ramp.
2. Disconnect the propeller shaft from the gearbox drive flange.
3. Select first gear.
4. Remove split pin.
5. Unscrew the flange nut and remove the washer.
6. Carefully remove the flange.

Refitting
7. Locate the flange in position.
8. Fit and tighten the nut and washer.
9. Refit the split pin.
10. Attach the propeller shaft to the drive flange.
11. Lower the ramp.

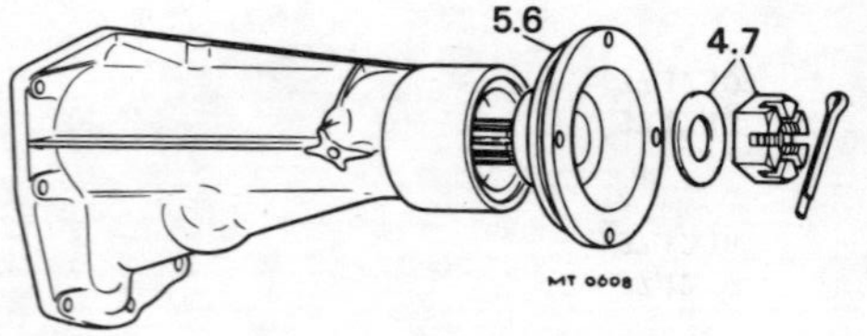

REAR EXTENSION
— Remove and refit
37.12.01

Removing
1. Drive the vehicle onto a ramp. Raise the ramp and drain the gearbox oil.
2. Remove the propeller shaft assembly.
3. Remove splitpin, nut and washer.
4. Remove the drive flange.
5. Support the engine under the sump, using a ramp jack (interpose a piece of wood between the jack head and sump to spread the load).
6. Disconnect the exhuast support bracket from the front pipe.
7. Remove the gearbox mounting assembly.
8. Disconnect the speedometer cable from the rear extension.
9. Remove the bolts and spring washers.
10. Withdraw the rear extension assembly joint washer and mainshaft washer.

Refitting
11. Locate the washer on the end of the mainshaft.
12. Refit the rear extension and a new joint washer.
13. Fit and tighten the bolts and spring washers.
14. Reconnect the speedometer drive cable.
15. Refit the gearbox mounting assembly and remove the ramp jack.
16. Attach the exhaust front pipe to the support bracket.
17. Refit the drive flange.
18. Fit washer and nut, tighten, fit splitpin.
19. Refit the propeller shaft assembly.
20. Refill the gearbox with oil.

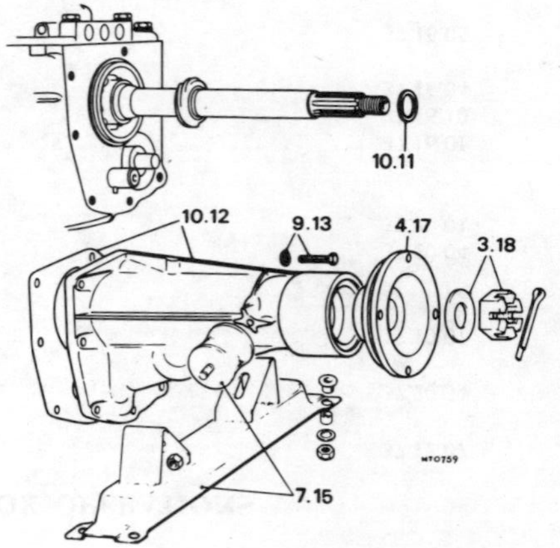

Section through gearbox assembly

SYNCHROMESH GEARBOX

REAR EXTENSION 37.12.04

— Overhaul

1. Remove the rear extension 37.12.01 or 37.20.04.

Dismantling

2. Unscrew and remove the peg bolt and washer.
3. Withdraw the speedometer driven gear and housing assembly.
4. Extract the seal.
5. Drive out the bearing.

Reassembling

6. Press the bearing into the extension.
7. Press a new seal into the housing.
8. Refit the speedometer driven gear and housing assembly.
9. Fit and tighten the peg bolt and washer.
10. Refit the rear extension 37.12.01 or 37.20.04.

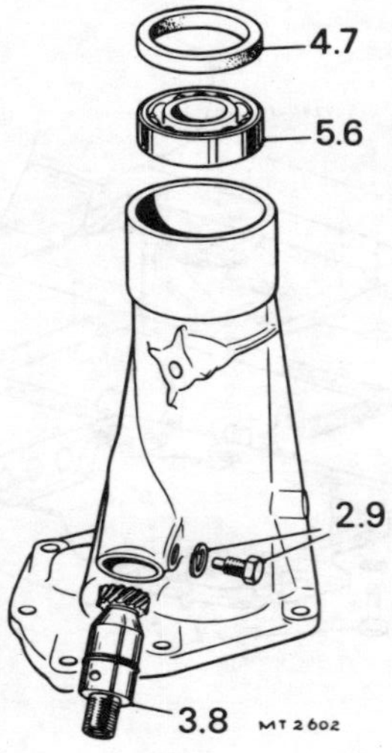

CLUTCH HOUSING 37.12.07

— Remove and refit

1. Remove the gearbox assembly 37.20.01.

Removing

2. Remove the clutch release mechanism 33.35.12.
3. Unscrew and remove the five bolts.
4. Remove the clutch housing and joint washer.

Refitting

5. Replace the clutch housing and a new joint washer.
6. Fit and tighten the five bolts' ensure that the copper washer and bolt with plain shank is fitted at the bottom.
7. Refit the clutch release mechanism 33.35.12 operation 2.
8. Refit the gearbox assembly 37.20.01.

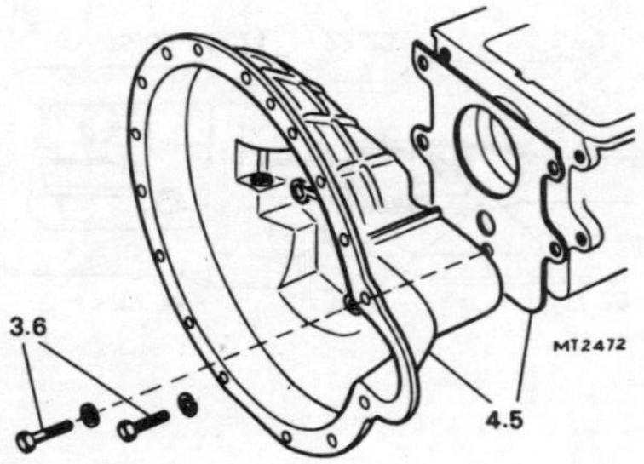

TOP COVER EXTENSION 37.12.10

— Remove and refit

Removing

1. Remove the gear change lever 37.16.04.
2. Working inside the car, unscrew the nuts and washers securing the extension to the top cover.
3. Lift off the extension and remove the joint washer.

Refitting

4. Fit the extension and a new joint washer on to the top cover.
5. Fit and tighten the nuts and washers.
6. Refit the gearchange lever 37.16.04.

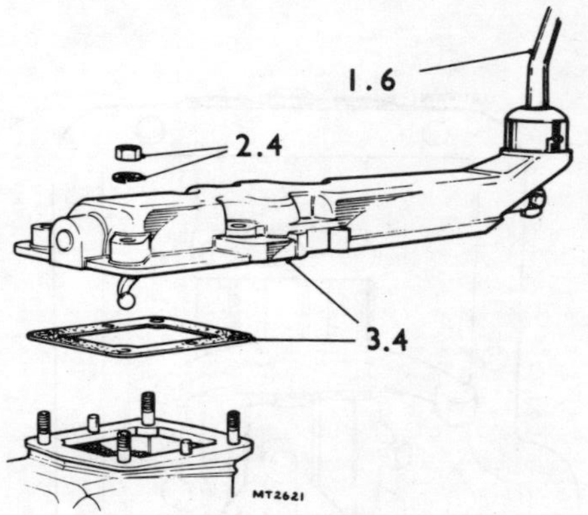

TOP COVER EXTENSION 37.12.13

— Overhaul

Dismantling

1. Remove the top cover extension 37.12.10.
2. Remove the cap.
3. Lift off the steel and nylon cups.
4. Remove the spring.
5. Release the lever from the operating shaft.
6. Withdraw the lever.
7. Remove the circlip.
8. Take off the spring.
9. Remove the nylon sphere.
10. Unscrew the stop-bolt and locknut.
11. Drill out the two rivets.
12. Remove the reverse stop plate.
13. Unscrew the taper locking pin.
14. Withdraw the shaft assembly.
15. Remove the actuator.
16. Remove the 'O' rings from the extension housing bores.
17. Unscrew and remove the nut.
18. Withdraw the bolt.
19. Separate the shafts and remove the washers.
20. Press out the bush.
21. Drive out the Mills pin.
22. Remove the fork end.

continued

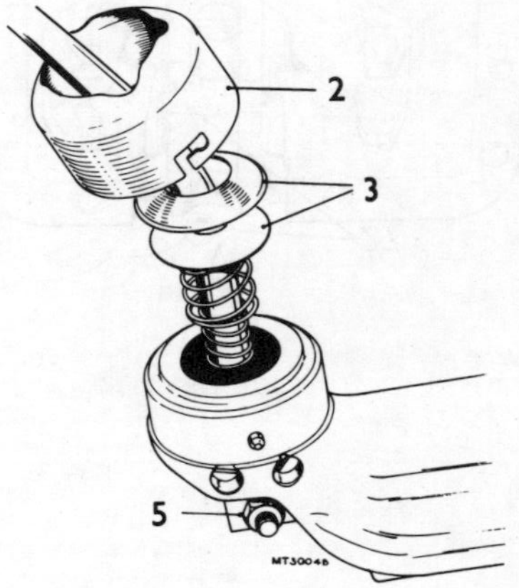

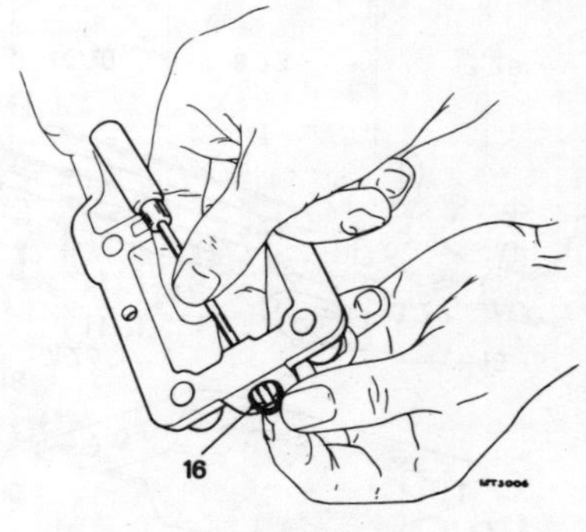

37.12.10
37.12.13 Sheet 1

SYNCHROMESH GEARBOX

Reassembling

23. Fit the fork end onto the actuator shaft.
24. Refit the Mills pin.
25. Press the bush into the primary shaft.
26. Fit the 'O' ring to the extension housing bore.
27. Fit washers on both sides of the bush.
28. Assemble the shafts and fit the bolt from the underside.
29. Fit and tighten the nut to a torque loading of 8 to 10 lbf ft (1·1 to 1·4 kgf m).
30. Fit the 'O' ring to the extension housing bores.
31. Place the reverse stop plate in position.
32. Secure the stop plate with pop rivets.
33. Fit the actuator shaft through the rear bore of the extension housing.
34. Locate the actuator onto the shaft.
35. Push the shaft into position and align the taper pin holes in the actuator and shaft. Fit the taper locking pin.
36. Loosely fit the stop-bolt and locknut to the lever.
37. Fit the nylon sphere to the lever.
38. Fit the reverse baulk spring.
39. Secure the circlip.
40. Fit the lever assembly into the extension.
41. Secure the lever to the shaft.
42. Fit the spring.
43. Refit the nylon and steel cups.
44. Refit the cap.
45. Refit the top cover extension and adjust the reverse stop bolt 37.12.13 and 37.16.01.

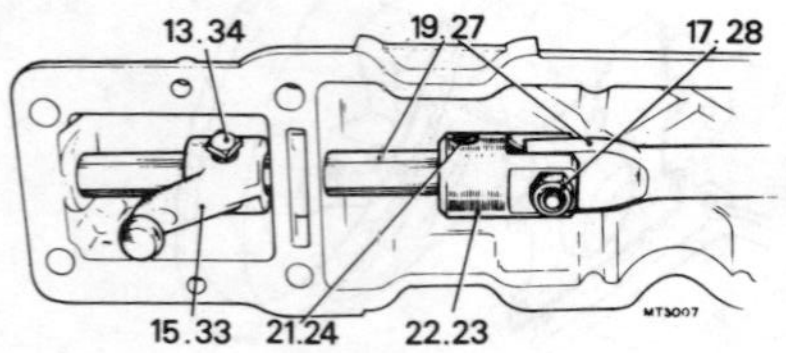

TOP COVER
— Remove and refit   37.12.16

Removing
1. Select first gear.
2. Remove the top cover extension 37.12.13.
3. Working from inside the car, unscrew and remove the bolts and washers.
4. Remove the top cover and joint washer.

Refitting
5. Ensure that the first gear position is selected.
6. Fit the top cover and a new joint washer.
7. Fit and tighten the bolts and washers.
8. Refit the top cover extension 37.12.13.
9. Check that each gear position may be selected.

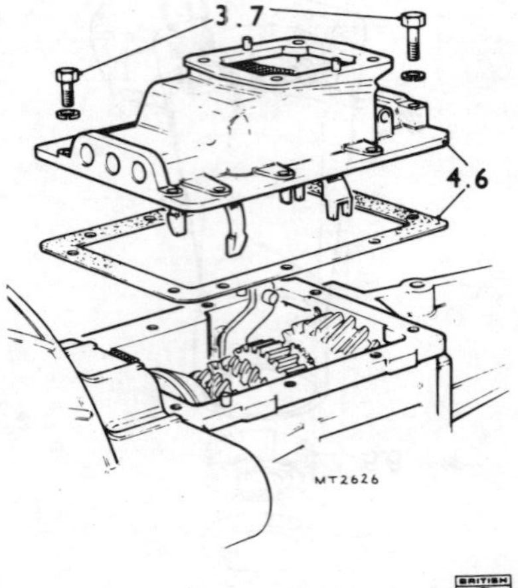

37.12.13 Sheet 2
37.12.16

SYNCHROMESH GEARBOX

TOP COVER
— Overhaul   37.12.19

Dismantling
1. Remove the top cover 37.12.16.
2. Using a 0·125 in (30 mm) dia pin punch, drive out the selector shaft welch plugs.
3. Unscrew the taper locking pins.
4. Drive out the 1st/2nd selector shaft towards the rear of the top cover.
5. Remove the 1st/2nd selector fork.
6. Remove the sleeve fitted on earlier models.
7. Remove the detent plunger and spring.
8. Remove the interlock plunger from the shaft.
9. Shake out the interlock balls.
10. Drive out the 3rd/top selector shaft towards the rear of the top cover.
11. Remove the detent plunger and spring.
12. Remove the 3rd/top selector fork.
13. Drive out the reverse selector fork.
14. Remove the detent plunger and spring.
15. Remove the reverse actuator.

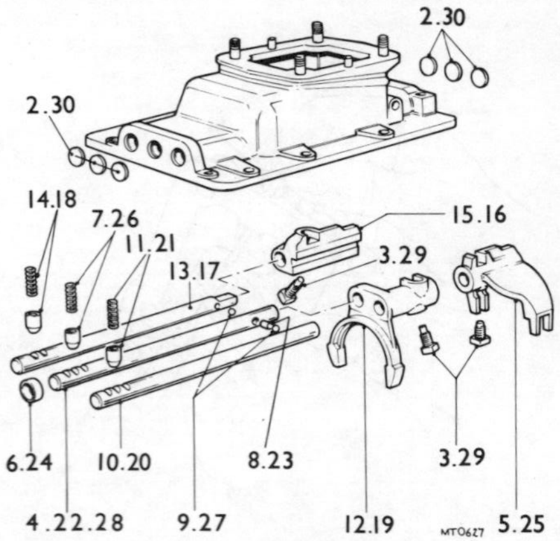

Reassembling
16. Invert the top cover and place the reverse actuator inside.
17. Slide the reverse selector shaft through the rear end of the top cover and through the reverse actuator.
18. Fit the spring and detent plunger into the top cover and push the selector shaft into the neutral position (2nd detent).
19. Place the 3rd/top selector fork into the top cover.
20. Slide the 3rd/top selector shaft through the rear end of the top cover and through the 3rd/top fork.
21. Fit the spring and detent plunger into the top cover and push the shaft into the neutral position (middle detent).
22. Slide the 1st/2nd selector shaft through the rear end of the top cover.
23. Fit the interlock plunger into the shaft.
24. Fit the sleeve over the shaft.
25. Fit the 1st/2nd selector fork in position and slide the shaft through both selector forks.
26. Fit the spring and detent plunger into the top cover and push the shaft through until it just protrudes through the front end of the cover.
27. Locate the interlock balls in the top cover.
28. Push the 1st/2nd selector shaft rearwards until it locates in the neutral (middle detent) position.
29. Fit and tighten the three taper locking pins.
30. Apply sealing compound to the edges of six new welch plugs and fit them into the top cover.
31. Refit the top cover 37.12.16.

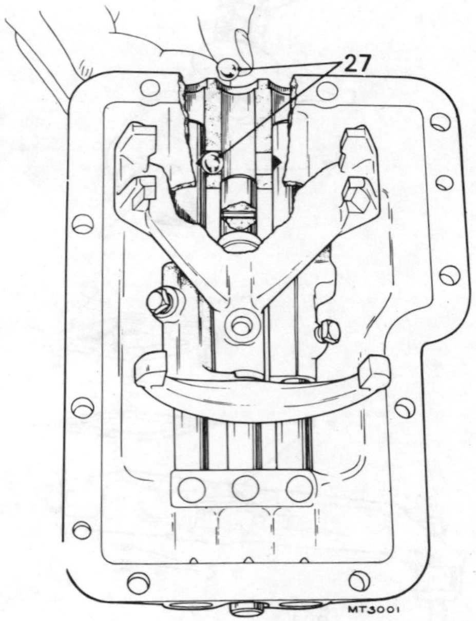

37.12.19

SYNCHROMESH GEARBOX

GEARCHANGE LEVER 37.16.01

— Check and adjust

1. Drive the vehicle onto a ramp and raise the ramp.
2. Slacken the locknut.
3. Place the gear lever in the neutral position of the 1st/2nd gate.
4. Adjust the stop bolt to prevent inadvertent selection of the reverse gate without depressing the lever. Check that the reverse gate can be selected by depressing the lever.
NOTE: Failure to obtain the required adjustment will necessitate the renewal of the reverse stop bolt and reverse stop plate.
5. Tighten the locknut.

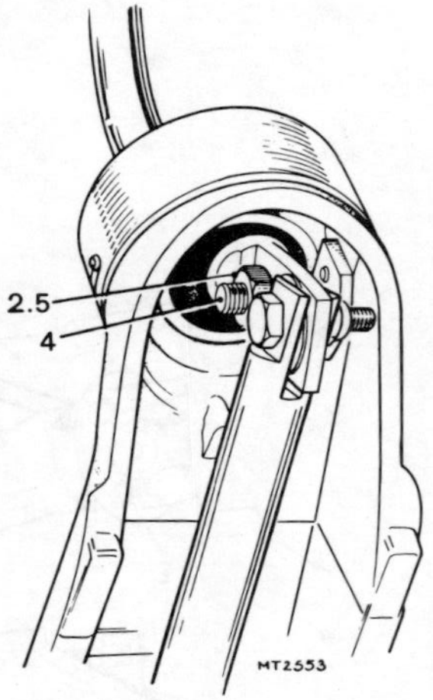

GEARCHANGE LEVER 37.16.04

— Remove and refit

Removing

1. Drive the vehicle onto a ramp.
2. Remove the gear lever grommet 37.16.05.
3. Unscrew the nut and bolt and remove the bottle washer.
4. Remove the bushes, washers, pinch sleeve.
5. Release the cap.
6. Remove the steel and nylon cups.
7. Remove the spring.
8. Withdraw the gear change lever.

Refitting

9. Fit the gear change lever into the extension.
10. Replace the spring.
11. Replace the nylon and steel cups.
12. Refit the cap.
13. Refit the bushes, washers and pinch sleeve.
14. Assemble the lever, to the selector shaft and fit the bolt and washer.
15. Fit and tighten the nut to a torque loading of 6 to 8 lbf. ft (0·8 to 1·1 kgf. m).
16. Adjust the reverse stop bolt 37.16.01.
17. Refit the fabric washer.
18. Refit the gear lever grommet 37.16.05.

37.16.01
37.16.04

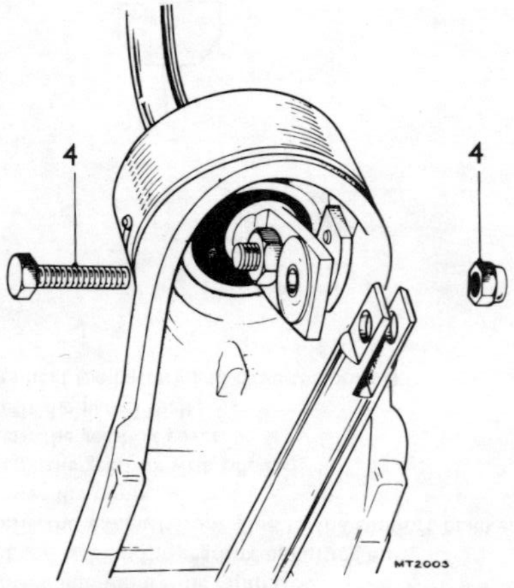

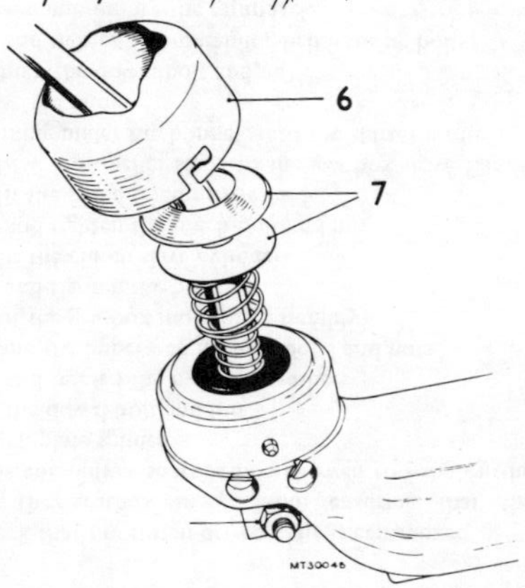

GEARLEVER DRAUGHT EXCLUDER 37.16.05

— Remove and refit

Removing

1. Remove gearlever knob.
2. Remove gearbox trim pads.
3. Remove facia support bracket 76.46.09.
4. Remove gearbox cover carpet 76.49.01.
5. Remove four screws holding draught excluder to gearbox cover.
6. Remove draught excluder.

Refitting

7. Replace draught excluder and refit.
8. Reposition metal ring and refit four screws.
9. Refit gearbox cover carpet 76.49.01.
10. Refit facia support bracket 76.46.09.
11. Refit gearbox trim pads.
12. Refit gearlever knob.

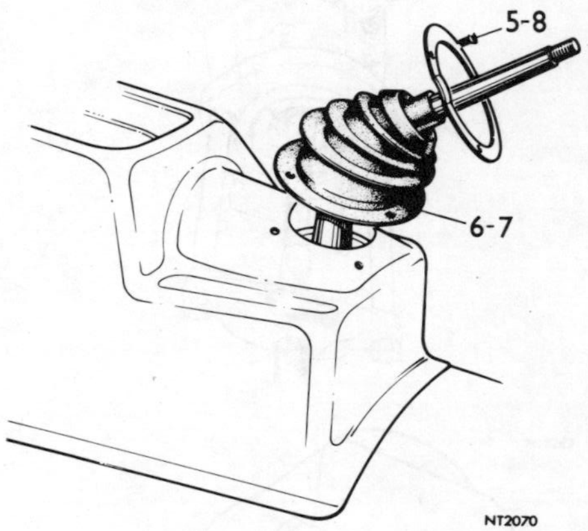

GEARCHANGE LEVER 37.16.10

— Overhaul

Dismantling

1. Remove the gear-change lever 37.16.04.
2. Take out the pinch sleeve.
3. Remove the bushes and washers.
4. Slacken and remove the locknut and unscrew the stop bolt.
5. Remove the snap-ring.
6. Take off the spring.
7. Remove the nylon sphere.

Reassembling

8. Fit a new nylon sphere to the lever.
9. Fit a new spring.
10. Fit a new snap-ring.
11. Screw a new reverse stop bolt into the lever.
12. Refit the locknut.
13. Assemble new bushes and the washers to the lever.
14. Refit the pinch sleeve.
15. Refit the gear-change lever assembly 37.16.04.

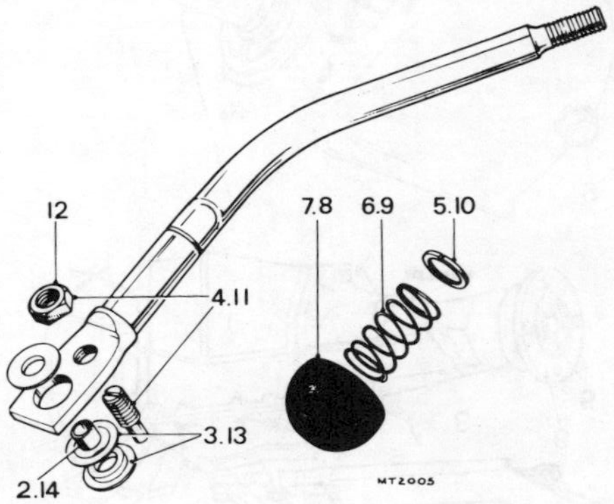

37.16.05
37.16.10

SYNCHROMESH GEARBOX

GEARBOX ASSEMBLY

— Remove and refit   37.20.01

Removing

1. Drive the vehicle onto a ramp and disconnect the battery.
2. Take out the gearbox cover 76.25.07.
3. Disconnect the propeller shaft from the gearbox drive flange.
4. Disconnect the speedometer cable from the gearbox.
5. Take out the pinch-bolt and withdraw the clutch slave cylinder.
6. Raise the ramp, drain the gearbox oil and support the sump with a ramp jack.
7. Disconnect the exhaust pipe from the support bracket.
8. Remove the gearbox mounting nuts and washers.
9. Take out the bell housing bolts accessible from below.
10. Lower the ramp and open the bonnet.
11. Take out the starter motor attachment bolts.
12. Working inside the vehicle, remove the top cover extension nuts.
13. Detach the gearbox mounting.
14. Remove the remaining bell housing bolts and nuts.
15. Carefully withdraw the gearbox assembly and remove it from the vehicle.

Refitting

16. Check that the clutch driven plate is centralized.
17. Fit the gearbox in position, ensuring that the constant pinion shaft is not allowed to hang on the clutch plate splines.
18. Fit the dowel bolt and nut.
19. Fit and tighten the nuts and washers.
20. Secure the upper bell housing bolts and nuts.
21. Refit the gearbox mounting assembly.
22. Fit and tighten the bolts.
23. Refit the clutch slave cylinder.
24. Fit and tighten the pinch-bolt and nut.
25. Refit the speedometer drive cable.
26. Refit the propeller shaft to the gearbox drive flange.
27. Working under the bonnet, refit the starter motor.
28. Raise the ramp.
29. Tighten the dowel bolt and nut.
30. Fit and tighten the remaining bell housing bolts.
31. Lower and remove the ramp jack.
32. Refit the exhaust front pipe to the support bracket.
33. Fit and tighten the gearbox mounting nut.
34. Lower the ramp.
35. Refill the gearbox with oil.
36. Refit the gearbox cover.
37. Refit the parcel shelf.
38. Connect the battery and close the bonnet.

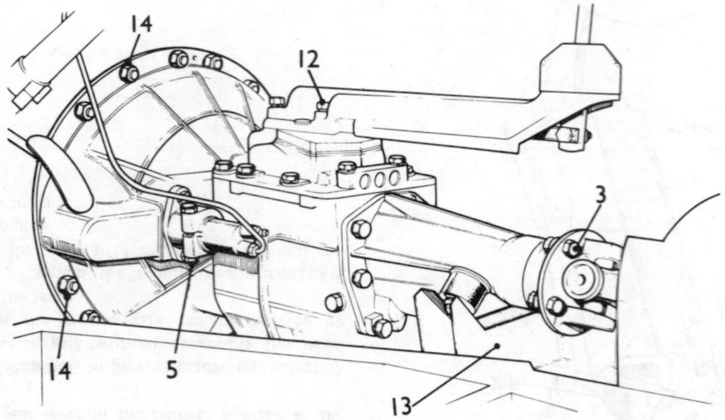

GEARBOX ASSEMBLY

— Overhaul   37.20.04

Service tools: RG 421, S4235A, S4235A-2, S4221A, S4221A-19/3, S144, A145, S314/1, Needle-roller retaining tube.

Dismantling

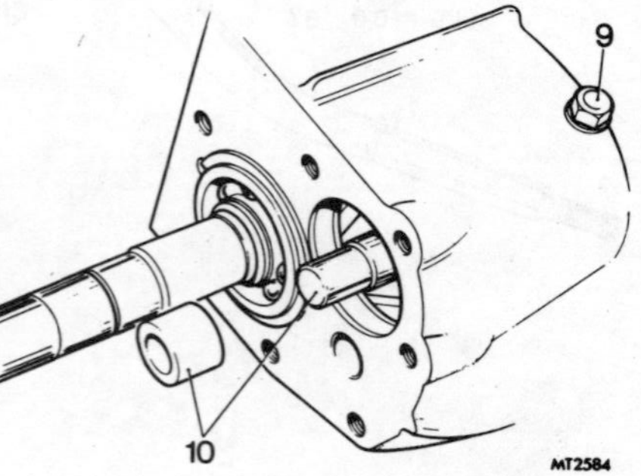

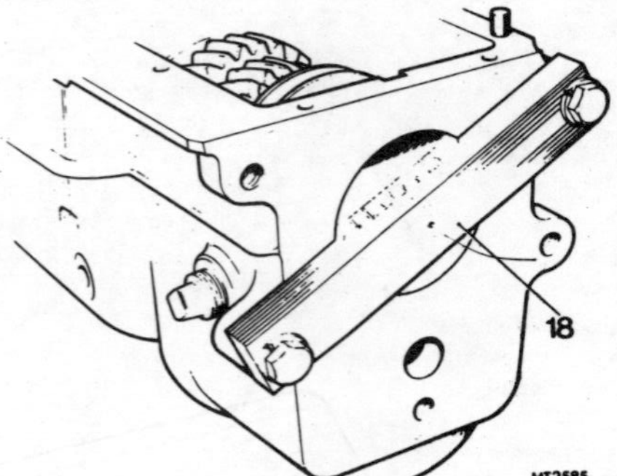

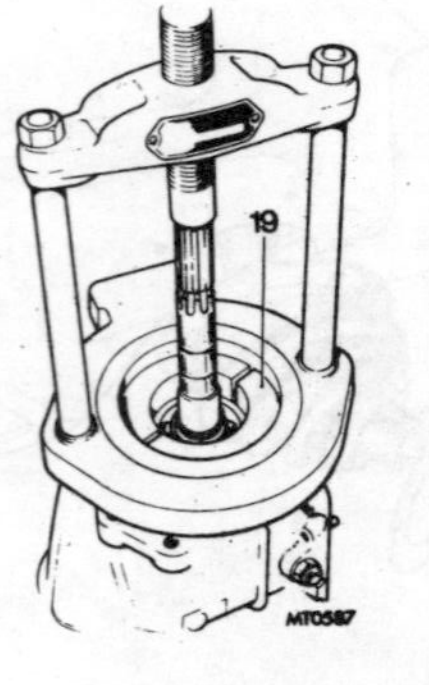

1. Remove the gearbox 37.20.01.
2. Remove the bell housing 37.12.07.
3. Take out the bolts.
4. Lift off the top cover and extension and the washer.
5. Using Tool RG 421 unscrew the flange nut and remove the washer.**
6. Withdraw the flange.
7. Unscrew the bolts.
8. Withdraw the rear extension and joint washer.
9. Unscrew the retaining bolt.
10. Withdraw the reverse idler spindle and distance tube.
11. Insert the needle-roller retaining tube (corresponding to the dimensions given) and eject the layshaft spindle to the rear. Allow the layshaft cluster to drop to the bottom of the gearbox.
12. Using Tool No. S4235A-2, withdraw the constant pinion assembly.
13. Remove the top gear baulk ring.
14. Remove the circlip retaining the speedometer drive gear.
15. Remove the speedometer drive gear and ball.
16. Remove the snap-ring from the mainshaft ballrace.
17. Remove the circlip from the mainshaft ballrace.
18. Fit the abutment plate, Tool No. S4221A-19.
19. Fit Tool No. S4221A and adaptor S4221A-19/1, to the annular groove in the mainshaft centre ballrace.
20. Withdraw the ballrace.

continued

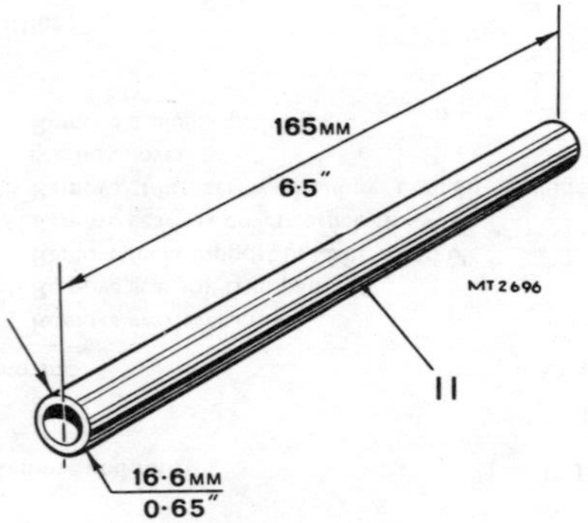

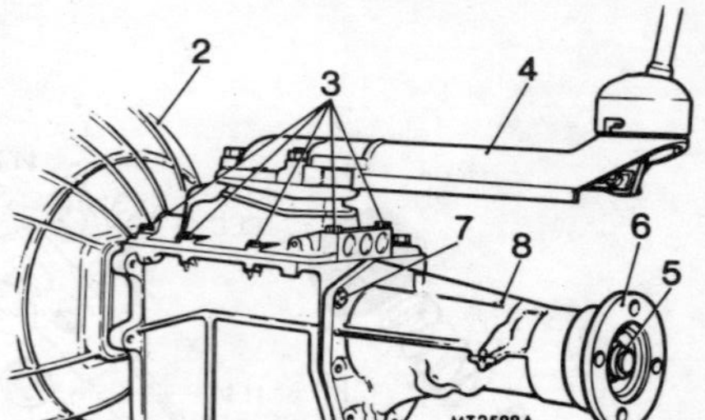

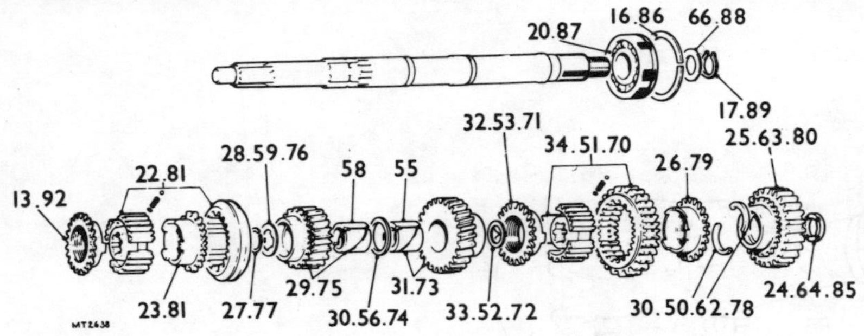

SYNCHROMESH GEARBOX

21. Tilt the mainshaft and remove it from the gearbox.
22. Remove the 3rd/top synchro unit.
23. Remove the 3rd gear baulk ring.
24. From the rear of the mainshaft, remove the thrust washer.
25. Remove the 1st speed gear.
26. Remove the 1st gear baulk ring.
27. Remove the circlip. Where the third gear mainshaft thrust washer has three lugs use Tool S.144. Where the washer has six lugs use Tool S.14A.**
28. Withdraw the washer.
29. Remove the 3rd speed gear and bush.
30. Remove the thrust washer.
31. Remove the 2nd speed gear and bush.
32. Remove the 2nd gear baulk ring.
33. Remove the thrust washer.
34. Remove the 1st/2nd synchro unit.
35. Remove the split collars.
36. Lift out the layshaft thrust washers.
37. Take out the layshaft cluster.
38. Remove the reverse idler gear.
39. Unscrew the nut.
40. Remove the reverse actuator and pivot pin.

Reassembling

41. Screw the pivot pin into the reverse actuator until one full thread protrudes through the lever boss.
42. Fit the actuator and pivot pin into the gear casing.
43. Fit the plain washer and tighten the nut.
44. Smear the front face of the layshaft front thrust washer with grease and stick it in position in the gear casing. Insert one end of the layshaft spindle through the casing to centralize the washer.
45. Lower the layshaft cluster assembly into the gearbox.
46. Fit the rear thrust washer in position.
47. Insert the layshaft spindle and eject the needle-roller retaining tube.
48. Measure the layshaft cluster end-float. Adjust the layshaft end-float to 0·007 to 0·013 in (0·18 to 0·33 mm), by selective use of thrust washers, repeating 44 to 48 as necessary. Do not remove metal from the bronze face of the thrust washers.
49. Insert the needle-roller retaining tube, eject the layshaft spindle and allow the cluster to drop to the bottom of the gearbox.

continued

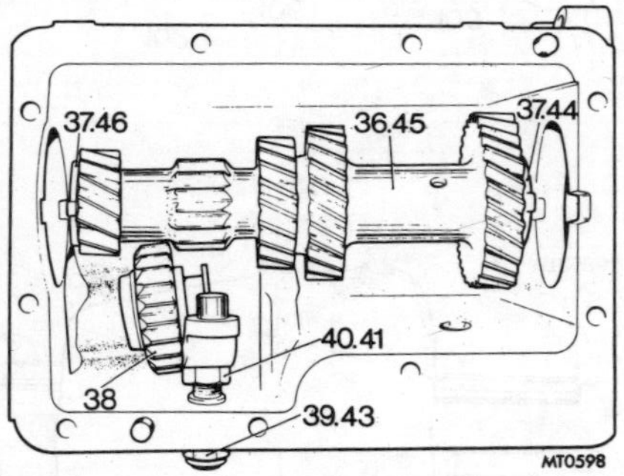

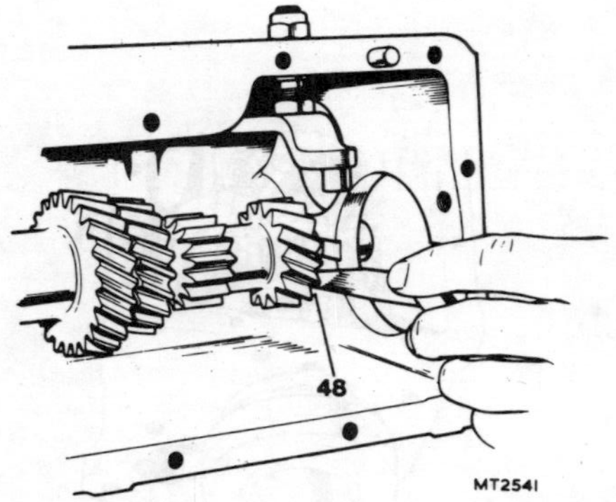

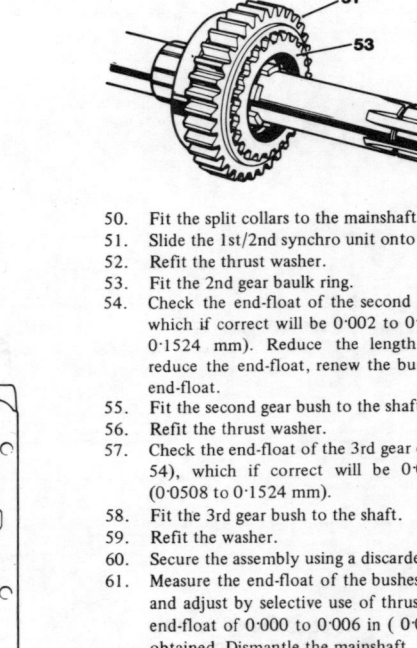

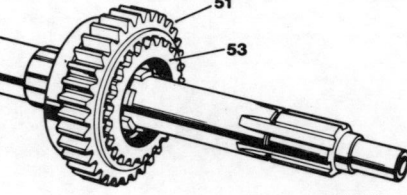

37.20.04 Sheet 2

50. Fit the split collars to the mainshaft.
51. Slide the 1st/2nd synchro unit onto the shaft.
52. Refit the thrust washer.
53. Fit the 2nd gear baulk ring.
54. Check the end-float of the second gear on the bush, which if correct will be 0·002 to 0·006 in (0·0508 to 0·1524 mm). Reduce the length of the bush to reduce the end-float, renew the bush to increase the end-float.
55. Refit the thrust washer.
56. Refit the second gear and bush.
57. Check the end-float of the 3rd gear on the bush, (Ref. 54), which if correct will be 0·002 to 0·006 in (0·0508 to 0·1524 mm).
58. Fit the 3rd gear bush to the shaft.
59. Refit the washer.
60. Secure the assembly using a discarded half circlip.
61. Measure the end-float of the bushes on the mainshaft and adjust by selective use of thrust washers until an end-float of 0·000 to 0·006 in (0·000 to 0·15 mm) is obtained. Dismantle the mainshaft.
62. Fit the split collars to the mainshaft.
63. Fit the 1st speed gear.
64. Fit the thrust washer.
65. Fit a discarded bearing inner race to distance tube 0·784 to 0·750 in (18·99 to 19·05 mm) long.
66. Measure the thickness of the circlip washer and assemble to the shaft.
67. Fit a discarded half circlip.
68. Measure the 1st speed gear end-float and determine the thickness of the circlip washer required to provide an end-float of 0·000 to 0·002 in (0·00 to 0·05 mm).
69. Dismantle the mainshaft.
70. Assemble components to the mainshaft as follows:
71. First/second synchro unit.
72. Second gear baulk ring.
73. Thrust washer.
74. Second speed gear and bush.
75. Third speed gear and bush.
76. Washer.
77. Circlip, offset outermost (locate lip of clip in recess of tool No. S145)
78. Split collars.
79. First gear baulk ring.
80. First speed gear.
81. Third/top synchro unit.
82. Position the reverse idler gear in the casing.
83. Place the mainshaft assembly in the gearbox.

continued

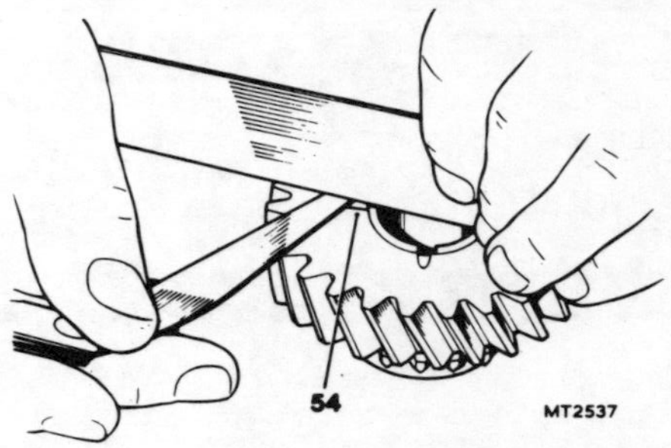

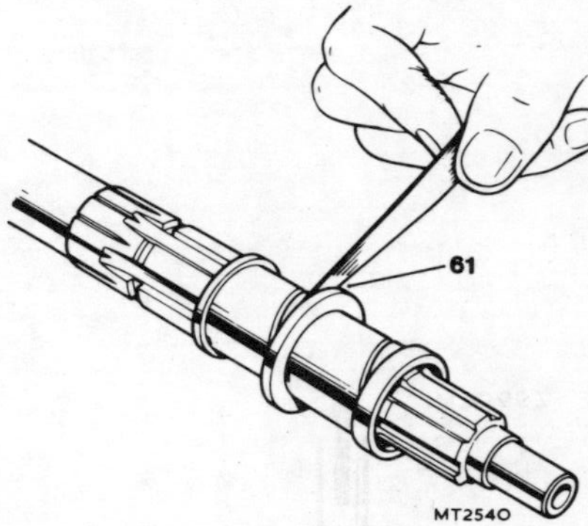

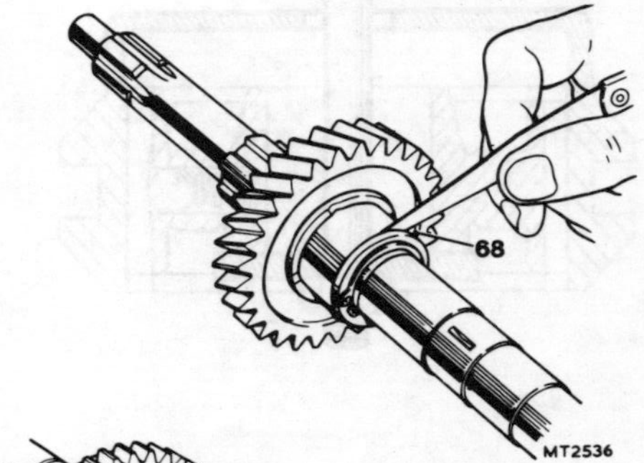

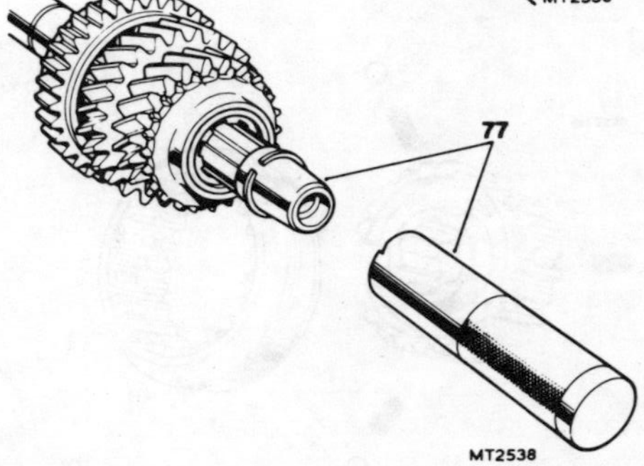

37.20.04 Sheet 3

SYNCHROMESH GEARBOX

84. Fit the abutment plate to the gearbox and mount in a vice.
85. Fit the thrust washer over the mainshaft.
86. Assemble the snap-ring to the ball race.
87. Place the ball race over the mainshaft and drive into position using Tool No. S314/1 and adaptor S4221A-19/3½.
88. Fit the circlip washer selected (Ref. 68).
89. Fit a new circlip.
90. Refit the speedometer drive gear, ball and circlip.
91. Remove the gearbox from the vice and take off the abutment plate.
92. Place the top gear baulk ring in the 3rd/top synchro unit.
93. Refit the constant pinion assembly using Tool No. S314/1 and adaptor S4221A-19/3, ensuring that the top gear baulk ring is correctly located.
94. Invert the gearbox and align the layshaft cluster and thrust washers.
95. Insert the layshaft spindle from the gear and eject the needle-roller retaining tube.
96. Position the reverse idler gear and fit the spindle and distance tube. Fit the locating bolt.
97. Locate the washer on the end of the mainshaft.
98. Refit the rear extension assembly and a new joint washer.
99. Fit the bolts and washers.
100. Replace the drive flange.
101. Fit and tighten the nut and washer and secure with splitpin.
102. Refit the bell housing assembly and a new joit washer 37.12.07.
103. Fit and tighten the bottom bolt and copper washer.
104. Select 1st gear on the top cover and the gearbox.
105. Fit the top cover and a new joint washer.
106. Fit and tighten the bolts and washers.

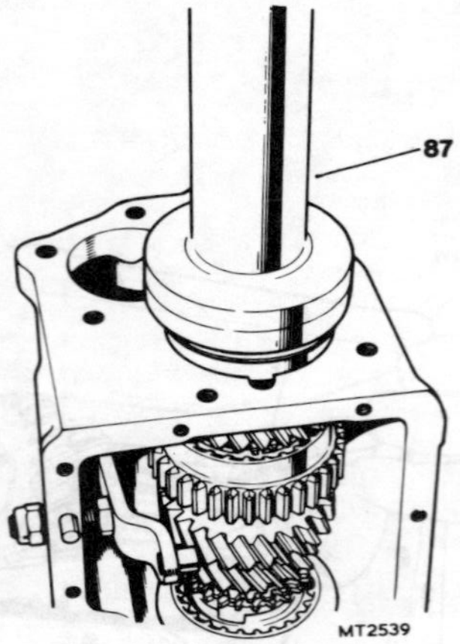

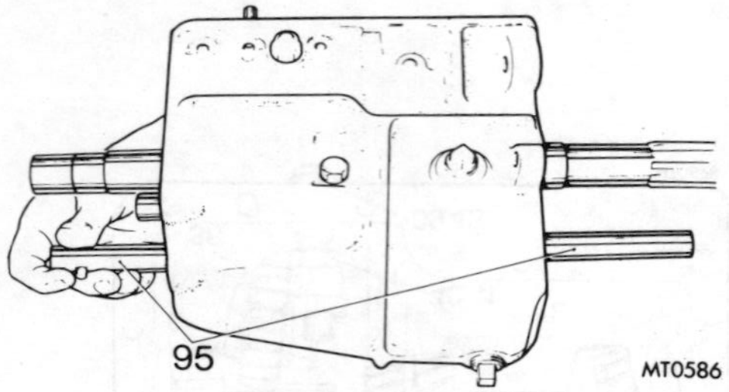

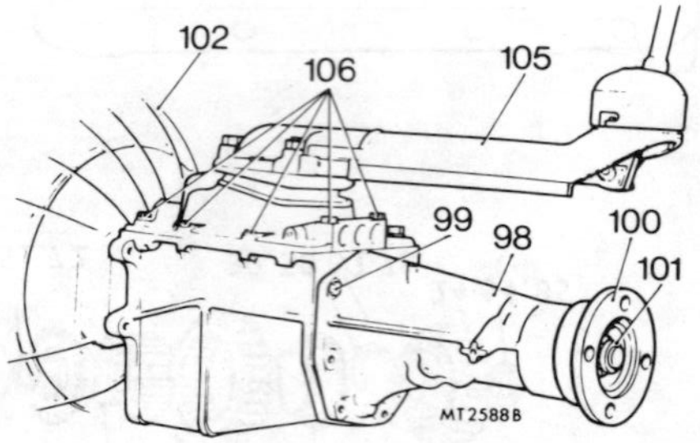

37.20.04 Sheet 4

Triumph Spitfire Mk IV Manual, Part No. 545254.

SYNCHROMESH GEARBOX

SYNCHRONIZER ASSEMBLIES 37.20.08

— Overhaul

Service tools: spring balance and adaptor.

1. Remove the gearbox assembly 37.20.01.
2. Dismantle the gearbox 37.20.04.

Dismantling

3. Place the assembly in a small box to prevent losing the spring loaded balls, and press the hub through the sleeve.

Reassembling

4. Assemble the synchro springs and balls to the synchro hub and retain them in position with petroleum jelly.
5. Carefully press the sleeve onto the hub.
6. Using the spring balance and adaptor, check the axial release loads, which should be:
   - 1st/2nd .. .. .. 19 to 21 lb (8·6 to 9·5 kg).
   - 3rd/top .. .. .. 19 to 21 lb (8·6 to 9·5 kg).
   If the release loads differ from the specified figures, fit new springs and/or add shims under the springs until the correct loading is achieved.
7. Reassemble the gearbox 37.20.04.
8. Refit the gearbox 37.20.01.

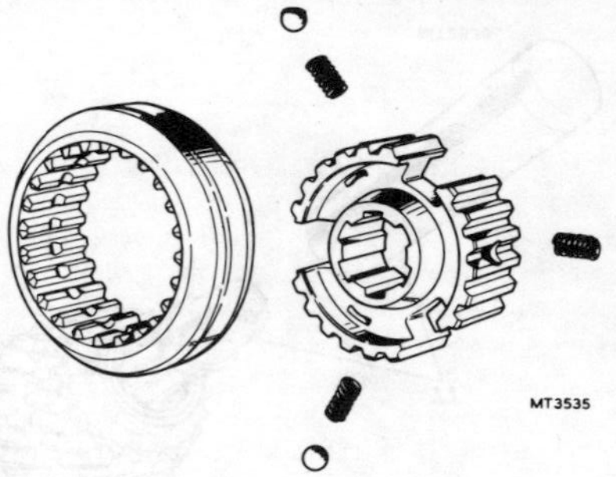

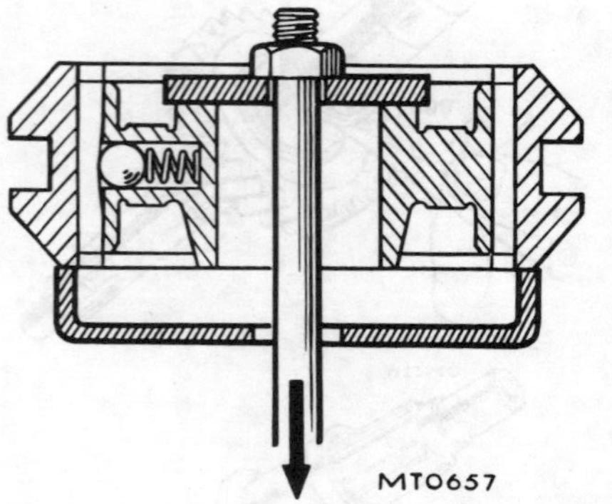

Triumph Spitfire Mk IV Manual, Part No. 545254.

37.20.08

SYNCHROMESH GEARBOX

LAYSHAFT CLUSTER
— Overhaul
37.20.29

1. Remove the gearbox 37.20.01.
2. Remove the layshaft cluster 37.20.04.

Dismantling
3. Withdraw the needle-roller retaining tube.
4. Shake out the needle-rollers.
5. Prise out the retaining rings.

Reassembling
6. Using a shouldered mandrel, drive the retaining rings into the end bores of the layshaft cluster to the depth shown.
7. Using heavy grease to retain them, refit the needle-rollers.
8. Insert the needle-roller retaining tube.
9. Refit the layshaft cluster 37.20.04.
10. Refit the gearbox 37.20.01.

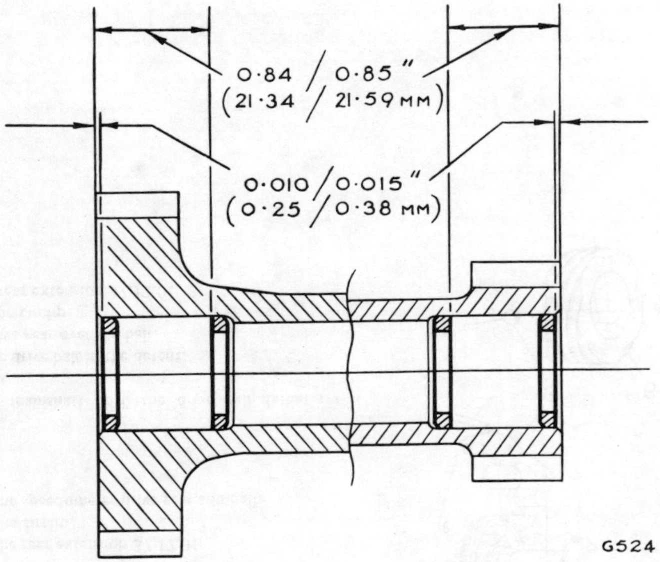

Dimensions shown: 0.84/0.85" (21.34/21.59 mm); 0.010/0.015" (0.25/0.38 mm)

SYNCHROMESH GEARBOX

CONSTANT PINION
— Overhaul
37.20.34

Service tools S4221A, S4221A-19/1

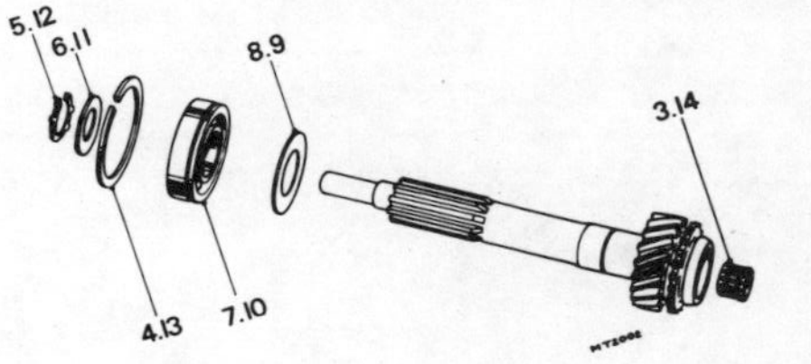

1. Remove the gearbox 37.20.01.
2. Remove the constant pinion 27.20.04 operation 12.

Dismantling
3. Remove the roller bearing.
4. Remove the snap ring.
5. Extract the circlip.
6. Remove the washer.
7. Utilizing Tool No. S4221A and adaptor S4221A-19/1, withdraw the bearing.
8. Remove the oil thrower.

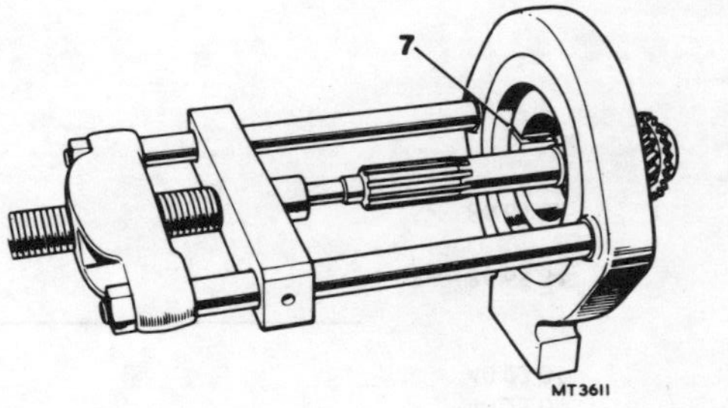

Reassembling
9. Refit the oil thrower.
10. Utilizing Tool No. S4221A and adaptor S4221A-19/1, draw the bearing onto the pinion ensuring that the oil thrower is correctly located.
11. Replace the washer.
12. Refit the circlip.
13. Refit the snapring.
14. Replace the roller bearing.
15. Refit the constant pinion 37.20.04 operation 93.
16. Refit the gearbox 37.20.01.

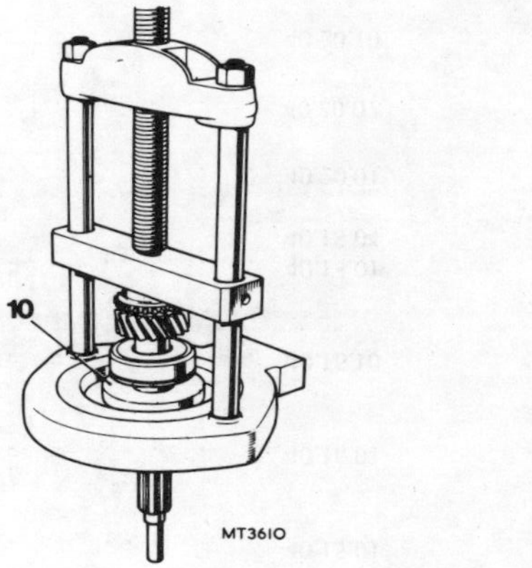

REAR OIL SEAL
— Remove and refit
37.23.01

Removing
1. Remove the propeller shaft assembly.
2. Remove the gearbox drive flange 37.10.01.
3. Prise out the seal.

Refitting
4. Drive a new seal into the rear extension.
5. Refit the gearbox drive flange 37.10.01.
6. Refit the propeller shaft.

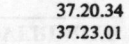

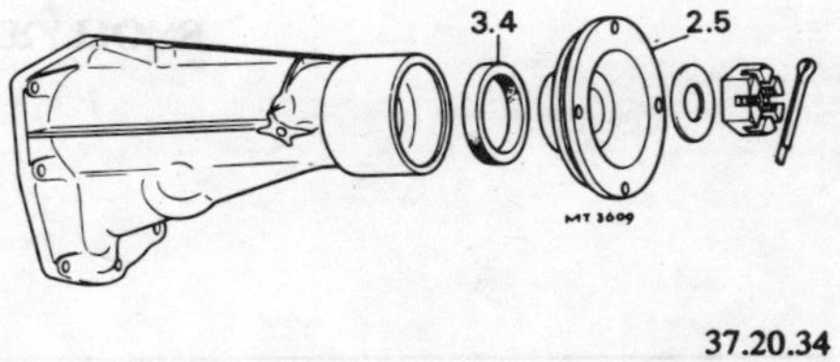

SYNCHROMESH GEARBOX

SPEEDOMETER DRIVE GEAR

— Remove and refit   37.25.01

Removing

1. Remove the rear extension 37.12.01
2. Remove the circlip.
3. Remove the speedometer drive gear and ball.

Refitting

4. Turn the mainshaft until the drive ball detent is uppermost.
5. Locate the drive ball in the detent.
6. Fit the drive gear over the ball.
7. Replace the circlip.
8. Refit the rear extension 37.12.01.

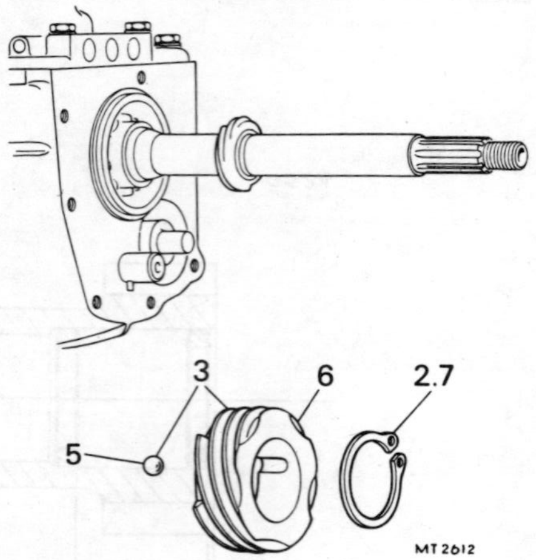

SPEEDOMETER DRIVE GEAR PINION

— Remove and refit   37.25.05

Removing

1. Remove gearbox tunnel cover 76.25.07.
2. Disconnect the speedometer cable from the gearbox.
3. Unscrew and remove the peg bolt and washer.
4. Withdraw the speedometer pinion and housing.
5. Withdraw the pinion from the housing.
6. Remove the 'O' ring.
7. Prise out the seal.

Refitting

8. Fit a new seal into the housing.
9. Fit a new 'O' ring.
10. Fit the pinion into the housing.
11. Refit the assembly to the gearbox.
12. Fit and tighten the peg bolt and washer.
13. Reconnect the speedometer cable.
14. Refit gearbox tunnel cover 76.25.07.

37.25.01
37.25.05

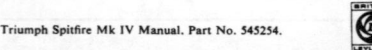

Triumph Spitfire Mk IV Manual, Part No. 545234.

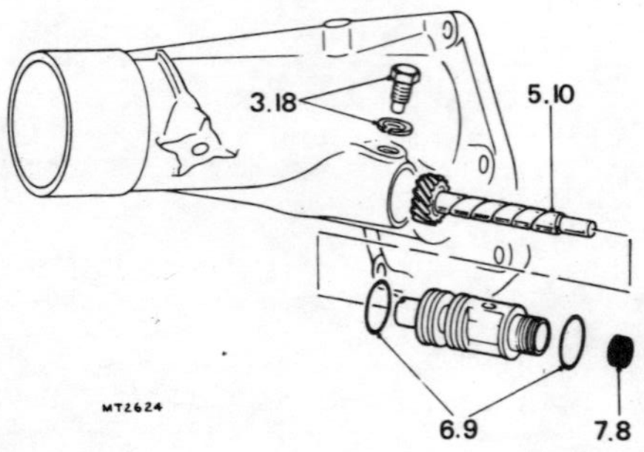

OVERDRIVE OPERATIONS

Working Principles	40.00.01
Fault Finding D types	40.00.02
Filter — remove and refit	40.10.01
Oil seals — rear — remove and refit	40.15.01
Operating valve — remove and refit	40.16.01
Non return valve — remove and refit	40.16.10
Oil pump — remove and refit	40.18.01
— overhaul	40.18.04
Overdrive assembly — hydraulic press test	40.20.01
Overdrive assembly — remove and refit	40.20.07
Overdrive assembly — overhaul	40.20.10
Solenoid — test and adjust	40.22.01
— remove and refit	40.22.04
— remove, refit and adjust lever	40.22.05
Overdrive gearlever switch — remove and refit	See 86.65.33
Overdrive gearbox switch — remove and refit	See 86.65.34

OVERDRIVE

40-1

Triumph Spitfire Mk IV Manual, Part No. 545234.

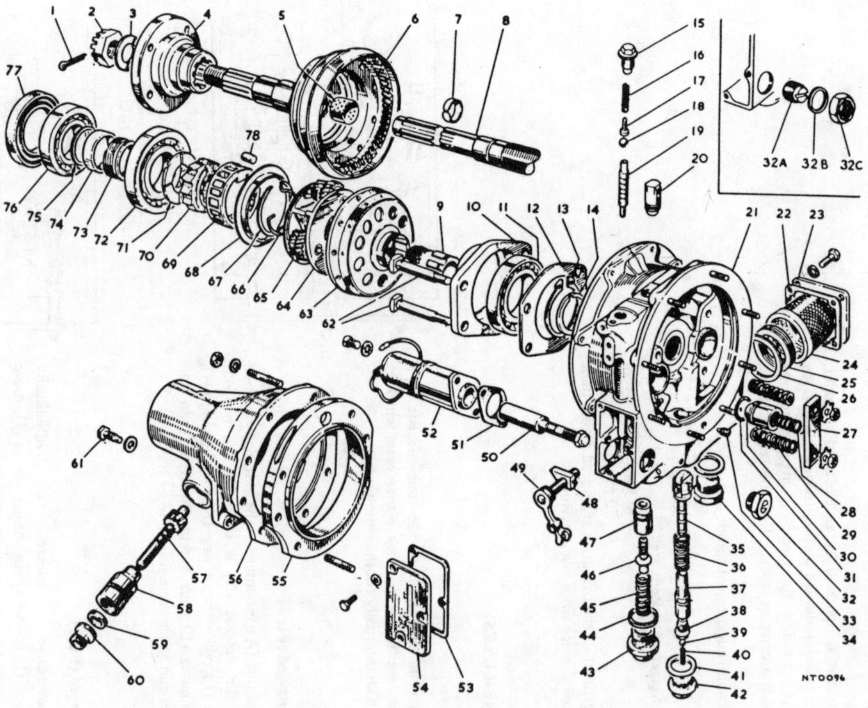

OVERDRIVE

KEY

1	Split pin	22	Gasket	40	Spring	61	Locating screw
2	Nut	23	Cover plate	41	Washer	62	Bolts
3	Washer	24	Filter	42	Plug	63	Cone clutch
4	Coupling flange	25	Magnetic rings	43	Plug	64	Planet carrier assembly
5	Bush	26	Rubber/Steel washer	44	Washer	65	Planet gear
6	Annulus	27	Bridge piece	45	Spring	66	Spring
7	Spring	28	Bias spring	46	Relief valve plunger	67	Circlip
8	Main shaft	29	Clutch return spring	47	Relief valve body	68	Oil thrower
9	Sungear	30	Piston	48	Cam	69	Cage
10	Thrust ring	31	Piston 'O' ring	49	Operating lever	70	Inner member
11	Thrust bearing	32	Plug	50	Solenoid plunger	71	Thrust washer
12	Retaining plate	32A	Adjuster screw ⎫ These items	51	Gasket	72	Front bearing
13	Circlip	32B	Locknut ⎬ replace items 52	52	Solenoid	73	Speedometer drive gear
14	Circlip	32C	Fibre washer ⎭ 32 on later units	53	Gasket	74	Distance piece
15	Plug	33	Pump locating screw	54	Cover plate	75	Spacer
16	Spring	34	Plug	55	Brake ring	76	Rear bearing
17	Plunger	35	Pump plunger	56	Rear casing	77	Oil seal
18	Ball	36	Return spring	57	Speedometer pinion	78	Roller
19	Operating valve	37	Pump body	58	Speedometer pinion bush	79	Woodruff key
20	Lubrication bush	38	Non-return valve body	59	Seal	80	Ring spring
21	Front casing	39	Ball	60	Screwed end	81	Cam

Triumph Spitfire Mk IV Manual. Part No. 545254.

40.00.01

40.00.02

OVERDRIVE

LAYCOCK DE NORMANVILLE OVERDRIVE

The overdrive is an additional gear unit, mounted on the rear face of the gearbox in place of the normal extension. When in operation, the unit provides a higher overall gear ratio than is available with the standard transmission. Reduced engine speed, resulting from the higher ratio, will reduce fuel consumption, increase engine life, and ensure greater driving comfort, providing the unit is used correctly.

The overdrive is operated by an electrical solenoid, controlled by a switch mounted on the steering column. An inhibitor switch, fitted in the electrical circuit, prevents engagement of overdrive in reverse, first and second gears.

Suggested minimum engagement speeds are:

Top gear . . . . 40 m.p.h.
Third gear . . . . 30 m.p.h.

Maximum disengagement speeds are:

Top gear . . . . At driver's discretion
Third gear . . . . 70 m.p.h.

Disengagement of the overdrive at a speed higher than stated may cause damage from 'over-revving'.

WORKING PRINCIPLES

Overdrive gears

The epicyclic gear train of the unit consists of a central sungear, meshing with three planet gears which in turn mesh with an internally toothed annulus.

Overdrive disengaged (Fig 1)

A cone clutch (A), mounted on the externally splined extension of the sungear (G) is spring-loaded, by four clutch springs (L), via a thrust ring (K) and bearing (M), against the annulus (E) thus locking the gear train and permitting over-run and reverse torque to be transmitted.

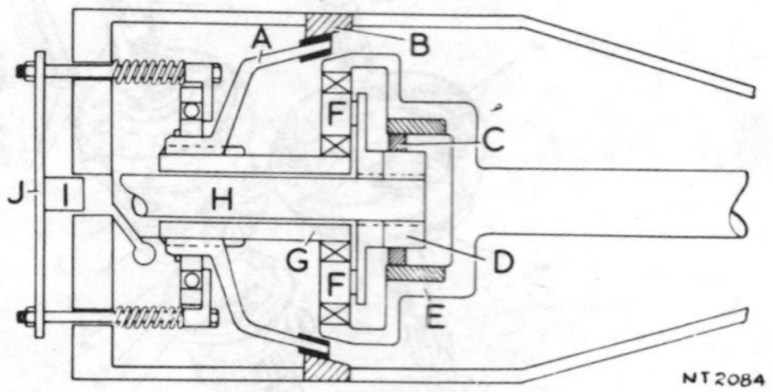

Overdrive engaged (Fig 2)

When overdrive is selected, two hydraulically operated pistons (1) acting against bridge pieces (J), move forward and, overcoming the spring pressure, cause the cone clutch (A) to engage the brake ring (B) with sufficient load to hold the sungear (G) at rest. The planet carrier (D) can now rotate about its own axis to drive the annulus gears (F) to rotate with the input shaft (H) causing the planet at a faster speed than the input shaft, this being allowed by the free-wheeling action of the uni-directional clutch (C).

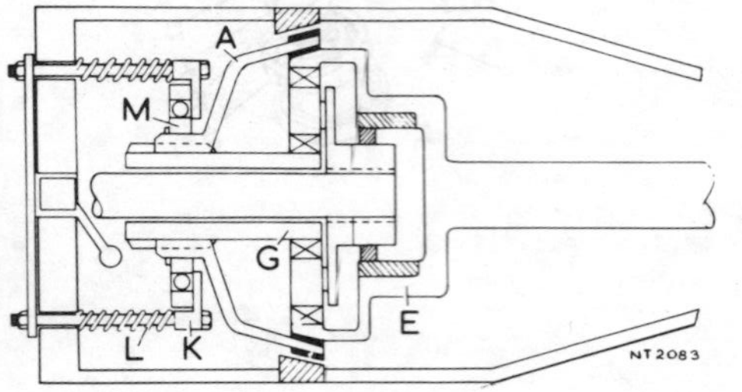

HYDRAULIC SYSTEM

Hydraulic pressure is developed by a plunger pump, cam operated, from the input shaft. The pump draws oil through a wire mesh filter and delivers it to the operating valve. A relief valve, incorporated in the system, controls the working pressure.

Operating valve (Fig 3)

In direct drive position, the ball valve (G) is seated in the casing thereby isolating the supply (B) from the operating cylinders (F).

When overdrive is selected, a solenoid causes cam (D) to rotate lifting the ball from its seat in the casing, and sealing the 'top' of the valve, thus directing oil under pressure from port (B) to the operating cylinders (F).

When the valve is returned to the direct drive position, oil from the operating cylinders is exhausted down the hollow valve stem through the restrictor (E).

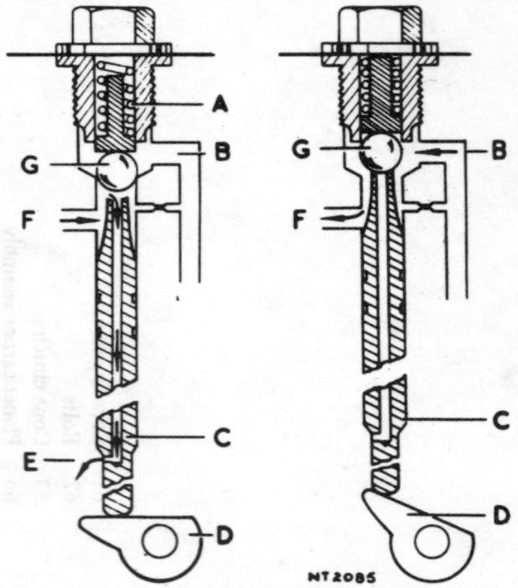

LUBRICATION

Being interconnected, the gearbox and overdrive units have a common oil level, indicated by a plug on the side of the gearbox. When draining the oil, remove the overdrive unit drain plug and gearbox drain plug. Access to the gauze filter, which must be removed and cleaned prior to refilling with oil, is effected by removing plate (1) (Fig 4) retained by four setscrews.

Spill oil, from the relief valve, is diverted through drilled passages to a bush in the front casing, then into the mainshaft and along a central drilling to the rear bearing. From the bearing, oil is passed, due to centrifugal force, through the uni-directional clutch to an oil thrower, from which it is picked up by a catcher on the planet carrier and then to the planet gears via the hollow bearing pins.

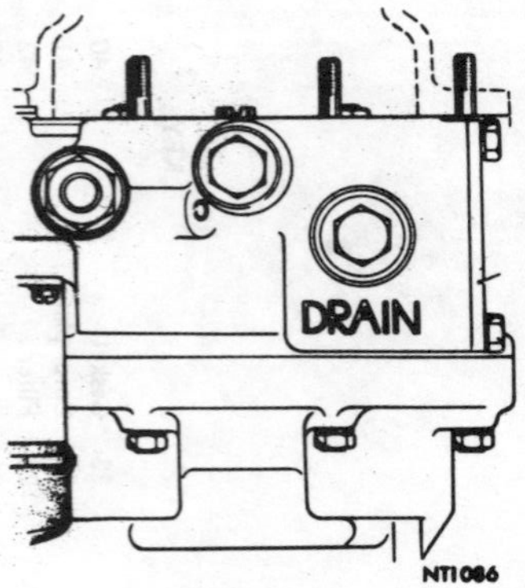

NOTE: All gearbox and overdrive units fitted to new cars are filled with a special oil, formulated to give all necessary protection to new gears. Under normal circumstances, this oil should not be changed, but may be topped up with any of the approved oils. If a new unit is fitted, or parts of an existing unit renewed, the unit should be replenished with new special oil, supplied with a new unit, or ordered separately from the Spares Division.

Should difficulty be experienced in obtaining the special oil, use one of the approved lubricants. ON NO ACCOUNT SHOULD ANTI-FRICTION ADDITIVES BE PUT INTO THE OIL.

After refilling the gearbox and running the car for a short distance, re-check and top up the oil level to replace the oil which has been distributed around the hydraulic system. Always use clean oil and take great care to prevent the entry of foreign matter when any part of the casing is opened.

OVERDRIVE

FAULT FINDING 'D' TYPES

SYMPTOM	POSSIBLE CAUSE
Overdrive does not engage	1. Insufficient oil in gearbox. 2. Electrical system not working. 3. Solenoid operating lever out of adjustment. 4. Insufficient hydraulic pressure due to pump non-return valve incorrectly seating (probably dirt on seat). 5. Insufficient hydraulic pressure due to sticking or worn relief valves. 6. Pump not working due to choked filter. 7. Pump not working due to damaged pump roller or cam. 8. Leaking operating valve due to dirt on ball seat. 9. Damaged parts within the unit requiring removal and inspection.
Overdrive does not disengage	NOTE: IF OVERDRIVE DOES NOT DISENGAGE DO NOT REVERSE THE CAR OTHERWISE EXTENSIVE DAMAGE MAY RESULT. 1. Fault in electrical control system. 2. Solenoid sticking. 3. Blocked restrictor jet in operating valve. 4. Solenoid operating lever incorrectly adjusted. 5. Sticking clutch. 6. Damaged gears, bearings, or sliding parts within the unit.
Clutch slip in overdrive	1. Insufficient oil in gearbox. 2. Solenoid lever out of adjustment. 3. Insufficient hydraulic pressure due to pump non-return valve incorrect seating. (Probably dirt on seat). 4. Insufficient hydraulic pressure due to sticking or worn relief valve. 5. Operating valve incorrectly seated. 6. Worn or glazed clutch lining.
Clutch slip in reverse or free wheel condition on over-run	1. Solenoid operating lever out of adjustment. 2. Partially blocked restrictor jet in operating valve. 3. Worn or burnt inner clutch lining. NOTE: Before removing any of the valve plugs it is essential to operate the solenoid several times in order to release all hydraulic pressure from the system. To do this, engage top gear, switch on the ignition and operate the overdrive control switch several times.

40.00.05

OIL FILTER
—Remove and refit

40.10.01

Removing
1. Remove four screws.
2. Remove the cover plate.
3. Carefully remove the cork filter.
4. Lift out copper gauze filter.
5. Remove three small rubber/steel bonded sealing washers.
6. Remove one large rubber/steel bonded sealing washer.

Refitting
7. Clean filter.
8. Place large rubber/steel bonded sealing washer in filter housing.
9. Place small washers in filter and place in housing.
10. Place cork gasket on filter housing.
11. Place plate back on housing.
12. Replace four screws and star washers and tighten.

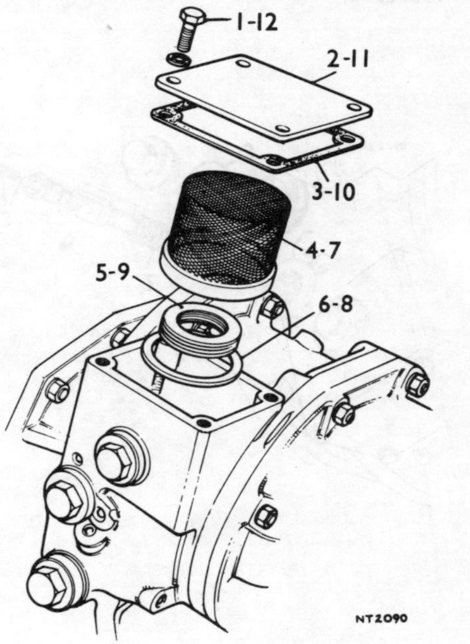

OIL SEAL
—Remove and refit

40.15.01

Removing
1. Remove the cotter pin.
2. Remove the nut.
3. Remove the washer.
4. Remove drive flange.
5. Prise out rear oil seal with a driver or similar tool.

Refitting
6. With the use of a large socket tap a new seal into place.
7. Refit the driver flange.
8. Refit the washer.
9. Refit the nut.
10. Replace and fit a new cotter pin.

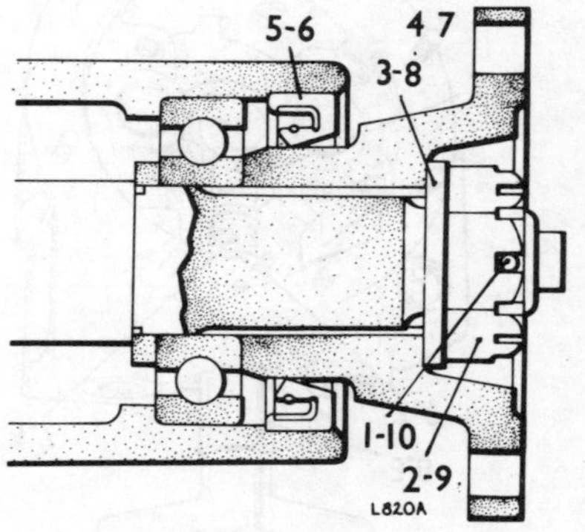

40.10.01
40.15.01

OVERDRIVE

OPERATING VALVE

—Remove and refit 40.16.01

Removing

1. Operate the solenoid several times to release the hydraulic pressure.
2. Unscrew the valve plug.
3. Remove the spring, plunger and ball with a magnet taking care to avoid damage to the valve seat.
4. Remove the operating valve by inserting a length of stiff wire down the centre and drawing it up.
5. Ensure that the small hole at the bottom of the valve is clear, the hole provides a passage for oil exhausted from the operating cylinders when the valve is moved to the direct drive position.

Refitting

6. Reverse operations 1 to 5.
   If the ball does not seat properly:—
7. Place the ball on a block of wood.
8. Position the valve on the ball and give the valve a sharp gentle tap.
9. Clean the valve seat in the casing.
10. Locate the ball on its seat and very gently tap the ball. TAPPING THE BALL TOO HARD WILL CLOSE THE MOUTH OF THE VALVE SEAT AND PREVENT VALVE REASSEMBLY.

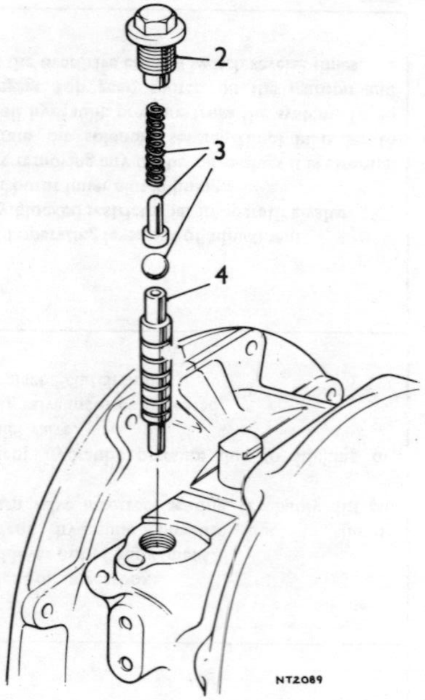

NON RETURN VALVE

—Remove and refit 40.16.10

Removing

1. Remove the pump plug.
2. Remove the non return valve spring.
3. Remove the ball.
4. Unscrew the non return valve body using tool L213.

Refitting

5. Refit the non return valve body using tool L213.
6. Re-position the ball.
7. Re-position the non return valve spring.
8. Refit the pump plug ensuring that the spring locates correctly in the plug recess.

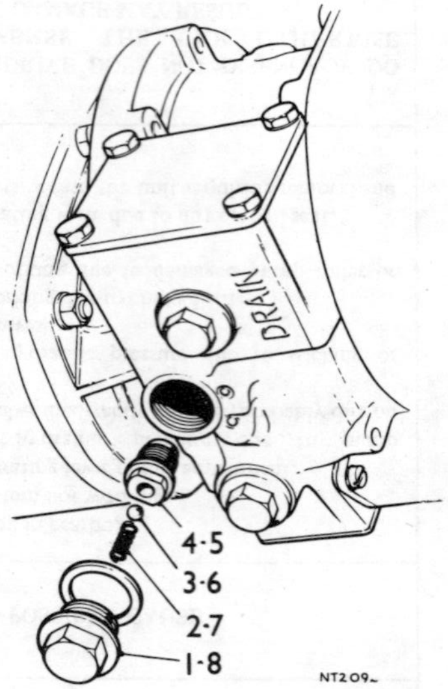

40.16.01
40.16.10

OIL PUMP

—Remove and refit 40.18.01

Removing

1. Remove the non return valve body 40.16.10
2. Remove the grub screw from housing.
3. Using tools L183A and adaptor L183A-2A, remove the pump body using tool L213, by screwing the spindle into the pump body, positioning the adaptor against the casing and screwing the wing nut down which will remove the body.
4. Remove the spring.
5. Remove the pump plunger.

Refitting

6. Refit the pump plunger.
7. Refit the spring.
8. Refit the pump body by locating the assembly within the orifice in the front casing locating the flat of the plunger roller fork against the thrust button situated below the centre bush. Press the pump home using tool L206A until the annular groove in the pump body is in alignment with the locating screw orifice.
9. Insert the dowelled locating screw and tighten, ensuring that the dowel locates in the groove.
10. Refit the non return valve body 40.16.10.

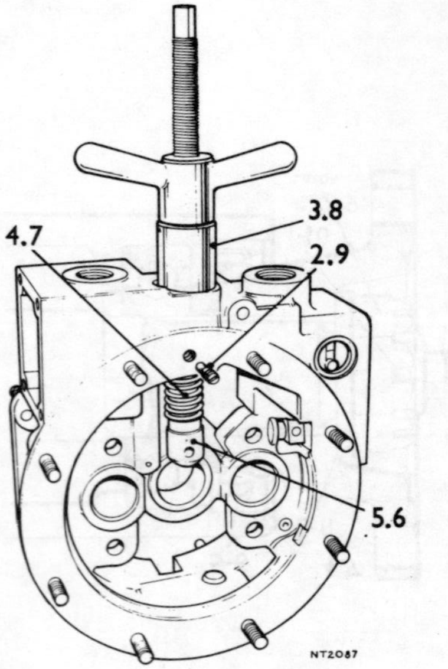

OIL PUMP

—Overhaul 40.18.04

1. Remove the oil pump 40.18.01
2. Replace the spring which fits over the pump plunger.
3. Replace the spring, ball and copper seal in the non return valve.
4. Refit the pump plug.
5. To check the pump is working, jack up the rear wheels of the car securely and remove the operating valve plug.
6. Start the engine.
7. Engage top gear.
8. Run the engine slowly.
9. Watch for oil being pumped into the valve chamber.
10. If none appears the pump is not functioning.
11. In this case the valve should be cleaned and reseated.
12. To reseat remove the valve body using tool L213.
13. Clean the valve body.
14. Tap the ball sharply onto its seal.
15. A flow of oil does not necessarily indicate that the hydraulic pressure is correct.

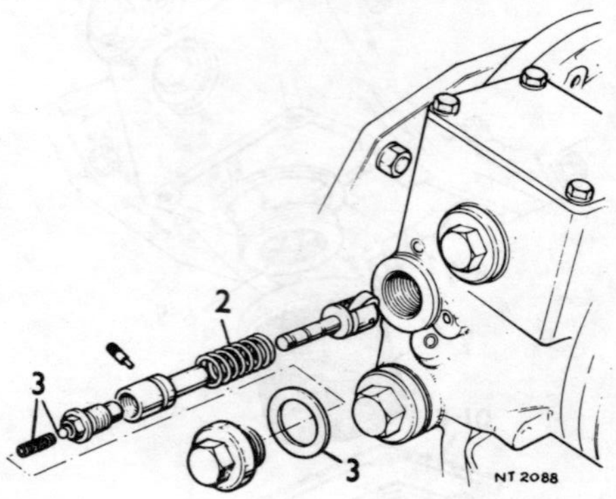

40.18.01
40.18.04

OVERDRIVE

OVERDRIVE ASSEMBLY

Hydraulic pressure test   40.20.01

1. Release the hydraulic pressure by switching on the ignition, engaging third or top gear and operating the overdrive switch several times.
2. Remove the operating valve plug.
3. Replace the valve plug with the hydraulic test equipment (churchill tool L188).
4. Jack up the rear wheels of the car securely.
5. Start the engine and run up to at least 20 m.p.h. on the speedometer.
6. Check the hydraulic pressure in the overdrive which should be 540 – 560 lb/sq. in. (37·962 – 39·368 kg/cm).
7. Lack of pressure when overdrive is selected may indicate the pump return valve requires cleaning and reseating and/or the relief valve and filter cleaning.

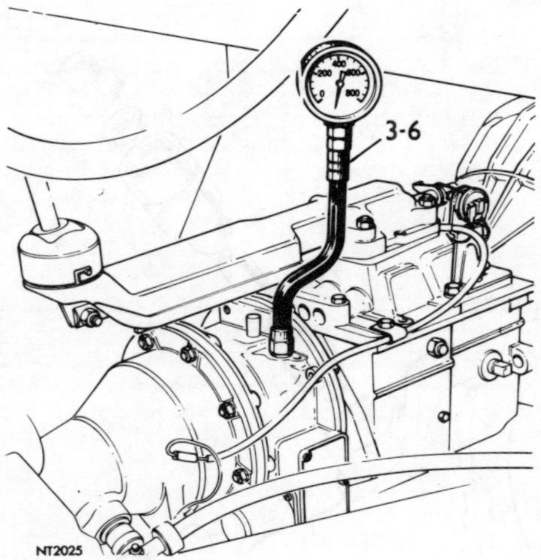

OVERDRIVE ASSEMBLY
–Remove and refit   40.20.07

Removing

NOTE: If possible it is advantageous to jack the rear wheels of the car off the ground and run in an overdrive condition before removing the overdrive, this eases removal from gearbox.

1. Disconnect the connectors from the gearbox overdrive switch and solenoid.
2. Remove the gearbox, operation No. 37.20.01.
3. Remove the nuts and spring washers securing the overdrive to the adaptor flange.
4. Carefully remove the overdrive.

Refitting

5. Line up the splines of the planet carrier and the uni-directional clutch by turning the lower set of splines anti-clockwise. Check the final alignment with a dummy drive shaft (churchill tool L201), if available.
6. Turn the shaft to position the cam with its highest point uppermost. The lowest point will then coincide with the overdrive pump roller. Carefully fit overdrive. If the overdrive fails to meet the adaptor plate face by approximately 5/8" it means that the planet carrier and uni-directional clutch splines have become mis-aligned. In this case remove the unit and re-align the splines.

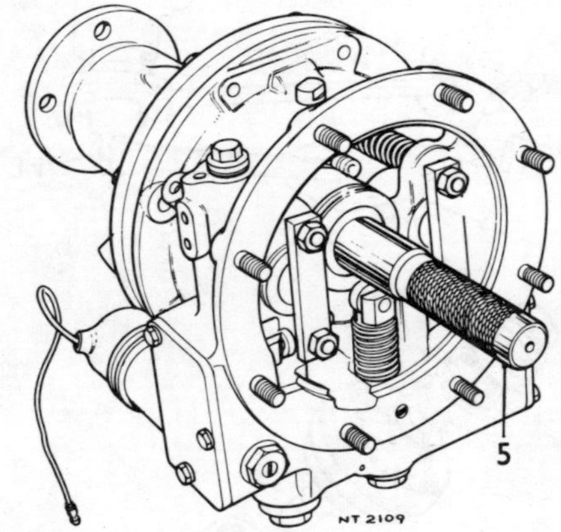

40.20.01
40.20.07

OVERDRIVE ASSEMBLY
–Overhaul   40.20.10.

Special Tools: RG 421 or S337,
L.206A, L178

1. Remove gearbox from car 30.20.01.
2. Remove overdrive from gearbox 40.20.07.
3. To prevent damage or faulty operation resulting from foreign matter, scrupulous cleanliness must be observed during all service operations.
4. Prepare a clean area in which to lay out the dismantled unit, and clean containers to receive the smaller parts.
5. With the front casing uppermost, secure the unit in suitably protected vice jaws.
6. Release the four bridge retaining nuts and washers.
7. Remove the piston springs.
8. Loosen the two solenoid cover securing screws to prevent the rubber solenoid cover fouling during front casing removal.
9. Progressively loosen the eight nuts securing the front casing, this ensures the gradual release of the clutch spring loading.
10. If the brake ring remains with the rear casing tap gently to remove.
11. Remove the four clutch return springs.
12. Withdraw the clutch sliding member complete with thrust bearing, thrust ring retaining plate and sungear.
13. Remove the operating valve 40.16.01.
14. Remove the relief valve by removing the plug at the bottom of the front casing adjacent to the solenoid housing cover plate. 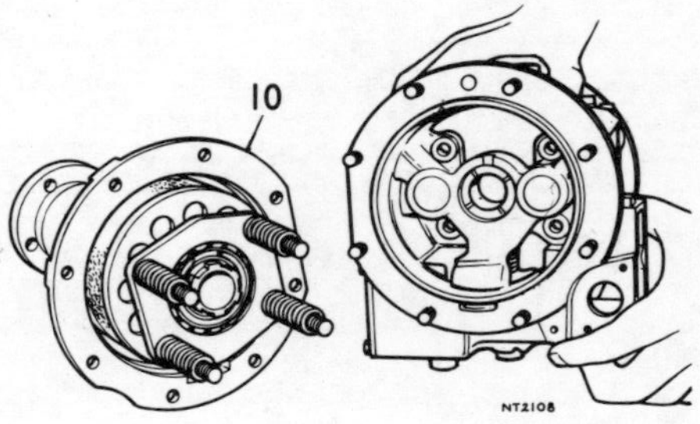 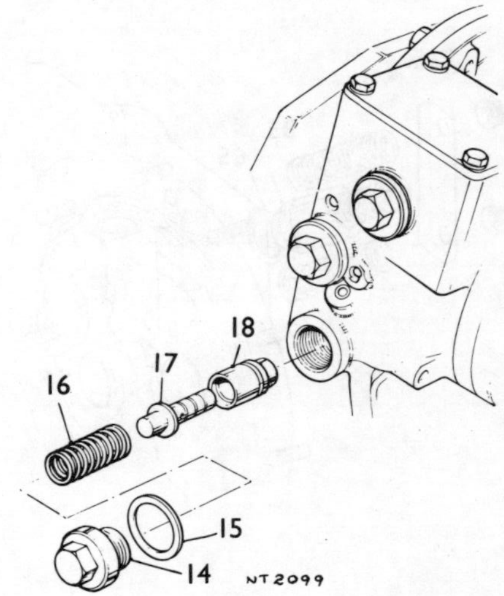
15. Remove the washer.
16. Remove the spring.
17. Remove the relief valve plunger.
18. Remove the relief valve body, this can be withdrawn using a piece of stiff wire shaped into a hook form, into the hole in the side of the body and pulling out.
19. Remove the pump 40.18.01.
20. Remove the filter 40.16.01.
21. Remove the operating pistons from their respective housings.
22. Remove the sungear retaining clip from its groove in the sungear extension.

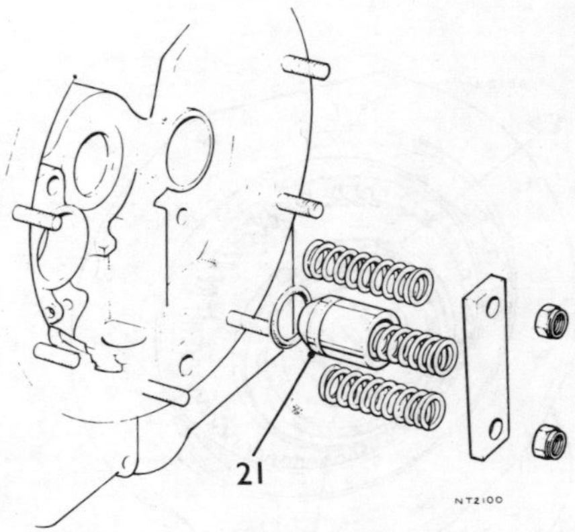

40.20.01
40.20.10 sheet 1

OVERDRIVE

23. Withdraw the sungear.
24. Remove the thrust bearing retaining plate.
25. Remove the bearing circlip from its groove on the cone clutch hub.
26. Press the hub from the bearing and thrust ring.
27. Extract the bearing from the thrust ring.
28. Remove the thrust ring MUST be replaced, if this is necessary.
29. Remove the solenoid 40.22.04.
30. Inspect the gear teeth on the planet carrier assembly for damage and wear and check for excessive movement indicating needle bearing or retaining pin wear.
31. If necessary renew the complete carrier assembly.
32. Remove the speedometer bush locating screw.
33. Remove the pinion from the rear casing.
34. Remove the split pin.
35. Remove the nut holding the flange with tool RG 421 or S337.
36. Remove the washer.
37. Remove the flange.
38. Press the annulus forward out of the rear case.
39. The rear bearing oil seal will remain in situ.
40. Remove the front bearing.
41. Remove the speedo drive gear.
42. Remove the distance piece.
43. Remove the spacer.

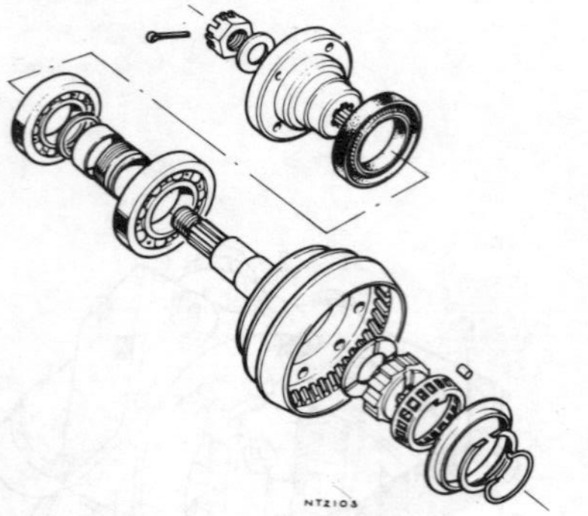

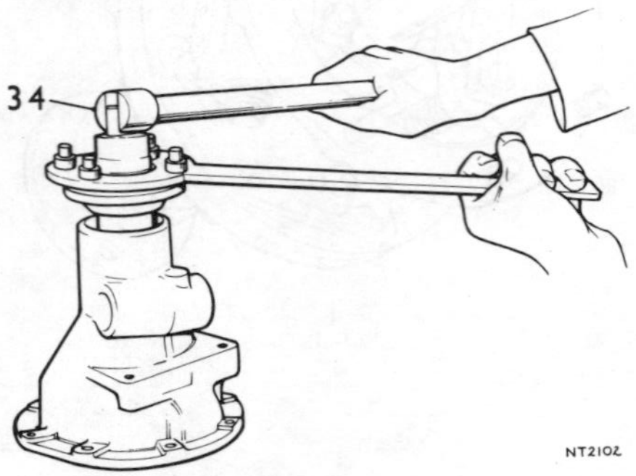

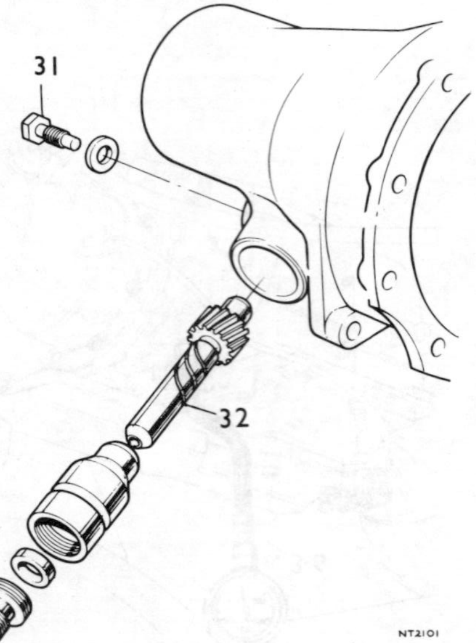

43. Remove the circlip.
44. Remove the brass oil thrower ring.
45. Withdraw the uni-directional clutch from the annulus.
46. Remove the bush from the annulus.
47. Remove oil seal.
48. Remove rear bearing with tool L206A.
49. Clean all components ready for reassembly.

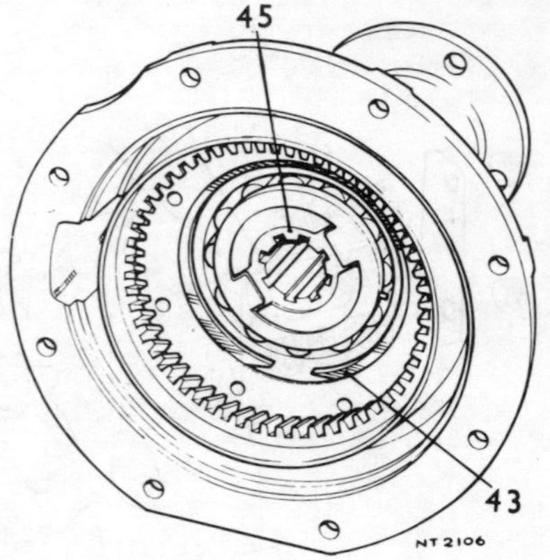

50. Inspect and renew all faulty gaskets, seals and tab washers.
51. Refit operating valve 40.16.01.
52. Insert the relief valve plunger in the relief valve body.
53. Locate the assembly within its orifice at the base of the front casing.
54. Insert the spring locate it on the boss of the plunger.
55. Secure the assembly with the relief valve blanking plug.
56. Reassemble and fit oil pump 40.18.01.
57. Reassemble and fit oil filter 40.10.01.
58. Replace the operating pistons with the open end of the piston bore facing forward.
59. Carefully ease the sealing rings into the bores during this operation.

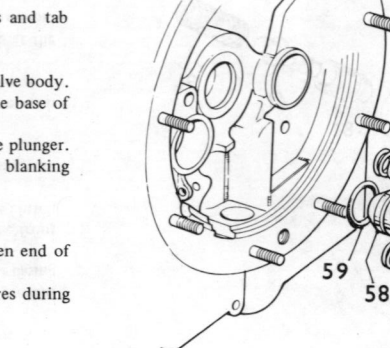

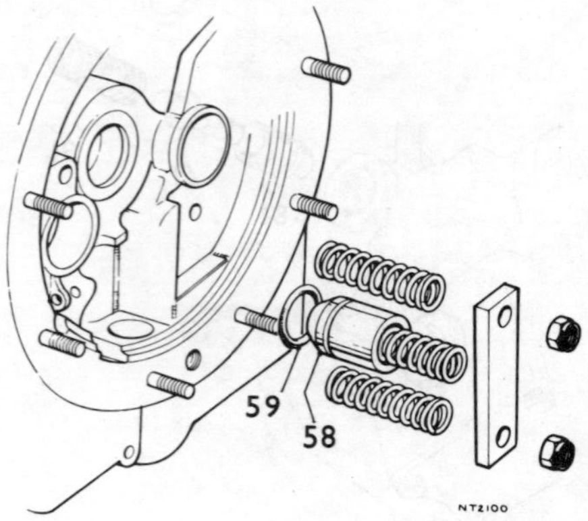

OVERDRIVE

60. Locate the front bearing over the annulus tail shaft.
61. Press into position against the locating shoulder at the reat of the annulus.
62. Position the distance piece.
63. Position the speedometer drive gear.
64. Position if fitted the spacing washer on the tail shaft.
65. Fit assembly to rear casing.

NOTE: Where new parts have been fitted, make a dimensional check between the distance piece and the abutment shoulder at the rear bearing.

66. Fit spacing washers as required to give a ·005 in - ·010 in (·1270 - ·254 mm) end float between the rear bearing and the casing.
67. Press the rear bearing onto the rail shaft and into the rear casing simultaneously.
68. Fit the oil seal.
69. Press the rear coupling flange onto the tailshaft.
70. Fit washer.
71. Refit and tighten the castellated nut to (70 – 80 lbs. ft).
72. Line up the castellations with the hole in the tailshaft.
73. Fit split pin.
74. Insert the speedometer drive pinion.
75. Insert the bush.
76. Rotate the annulus to engage the gear.
77. Align the bush and casing holes.
78. Fit the dowelled locating screw.
79. Insert the bush in the centre of the annulus.
80. Fit the spring in the roller cage of the uni-directional clutch engaging one end of the cage.
81. Insert the inner member.
82. Engage the opposite end of the spring on the hole provided.
83. Ensure that the slots of the inner member engage the tongues of the cage.
84. Place the assembly front face down in the assembly tool L178.
85. Fit the rollers.
86. Check that the spring rotates the cage to drive the rollers up the inclined faces of the inner member.
87. Refit the thrust washer.
88. Refit the uni-directional clutch, transferring the clutch direct from the assembly tool.
89. Fit the brass oil thrower ring.
90. Secure the thrower ring with the circlip.
91. Rotate the gears until the etched lines on the gear and carrier coincide.

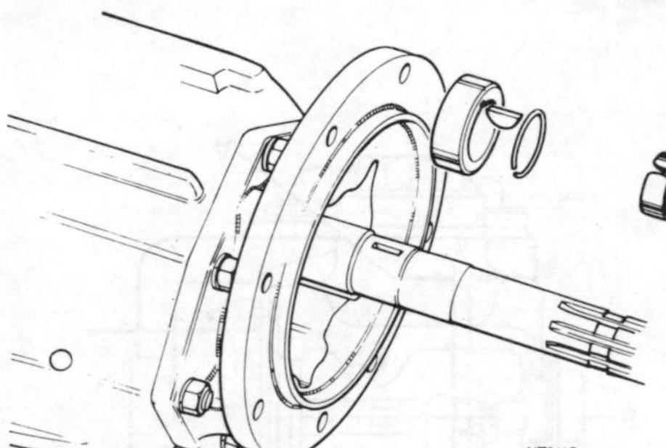

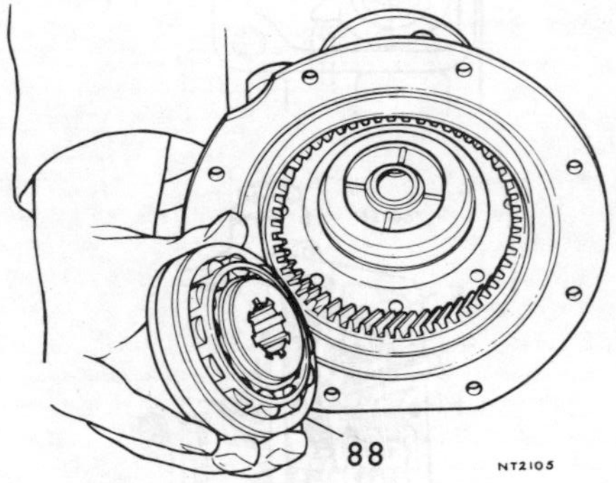

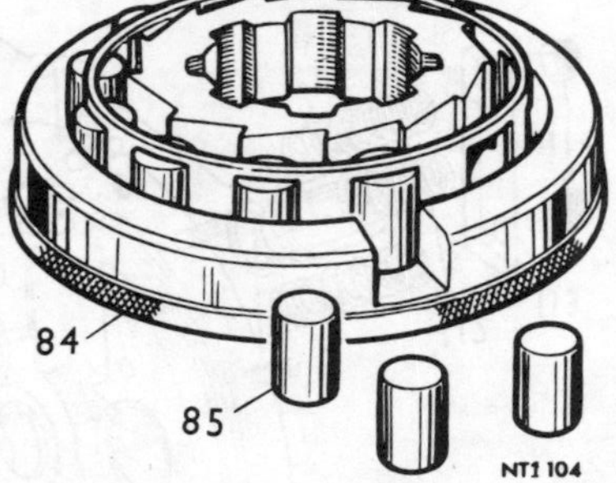

40.20.10 sheet 4   Triumph Spitfire Mk IV Manual. Part No. 545254.

NOTE: On one of the three gears the etched line occurs on the same tooth as the centre pop mark. Two gears have etched lines but all three have centre pop marks. Align the etched lines on the two gear teeth with the corresponding lines on the carrier. Align the centre pop mark on the remaining unetched gear with the corresponding line on the carrier.

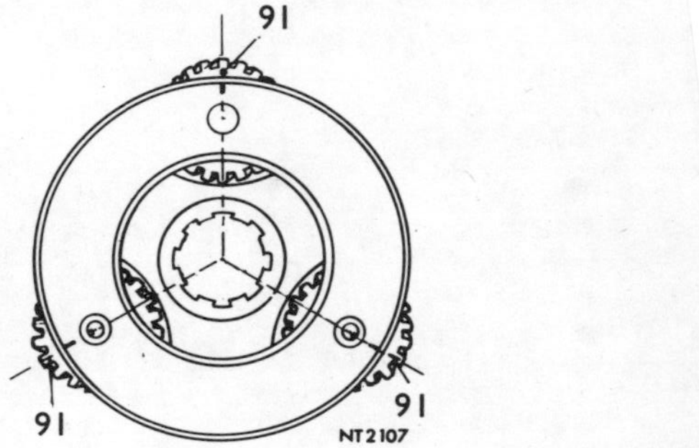

92. Insert the sungear.
93. Re-check the etched lines for alignment.
94. Position the assembly within the annulus.
95. Remove the sungear.
96. Press the thrust bearing into the thrust ring.
97. Fit the four bolts ensuring the heads are correctly positioned.
98. Press the assembly on the cone clutch hub.
99. Secure with a circlip.
100. Fit the retaining plate.
101. Insert the sungear in the splined bore of the cone clutch.
102. Secure with circlip.
103. Locate the assembly within the annulus.
104. Fit the four clutch return springs.
105. Coat both faces of the brake ring with suitable jointing compound.
106. Position the brake ring on the rear face of the front case.
107. Ensure the kidney shaped slot in the brake ring is located at the bottom.
108. Fit the front casing to the rear casing.
109. Clutch spring pressure will now be felt and it will now be necessary to exert a slight pressure to bring the two casings together sufficiently to start the nuts.
110. Ensure that the spring washers are under the nuts before tightening.

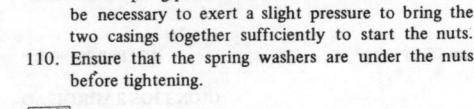

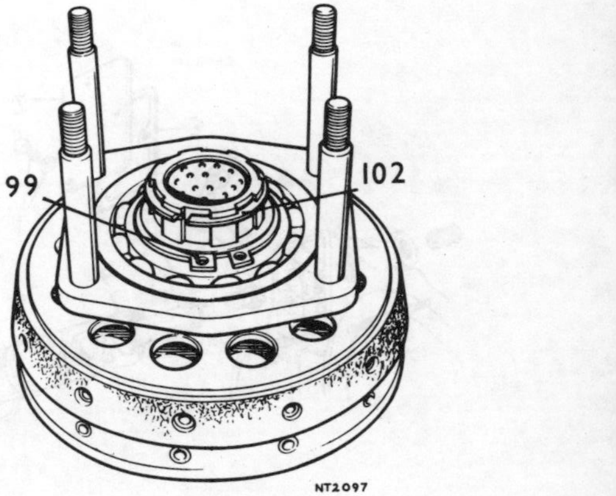

40.20.10 sheet 5   Triumph Spitfire Mk IV Manual. Part No. 545254.

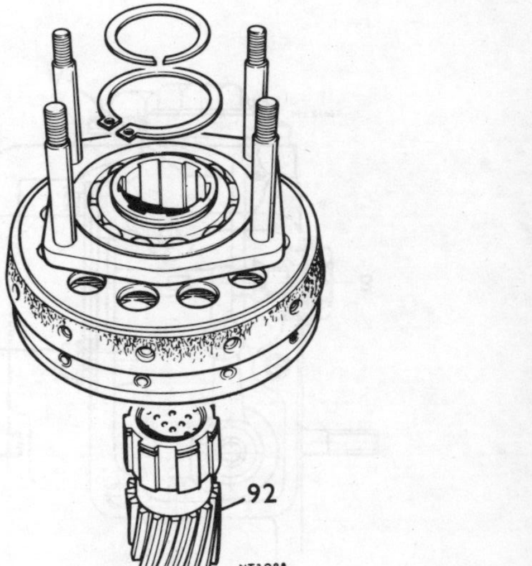

OVERDRIVE

111. Tighten diametrically opposed nuts until the two faces meet.
112. Locate the piston springs with the piston bores.
113. Fit the bridge pieces.
114. Tighten the lock nuts.
115. Position the solenoid plunger in the fork of the operating lever.
116. Screw on the adjusting nut.
117. Fit solenoid 40.22.04.
118. Adjust and test solenoid 40.22.04.
119. Refit overdrive to gearbox 40.20.07.
120. Refit the gearbox to the car 37.20.01.
121. Connect gearbox overdrive switch.
122. Connect the solenoid.

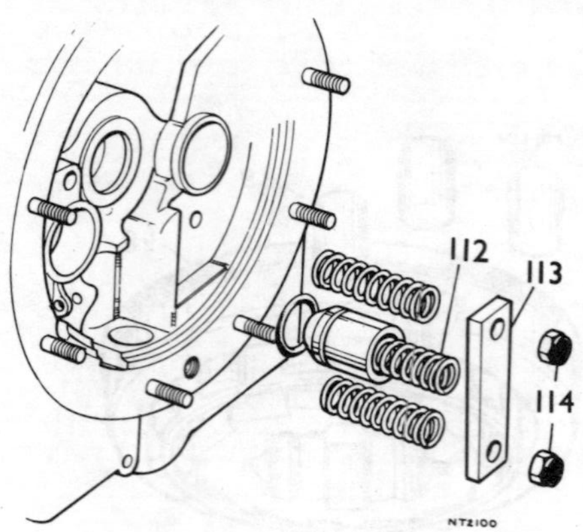

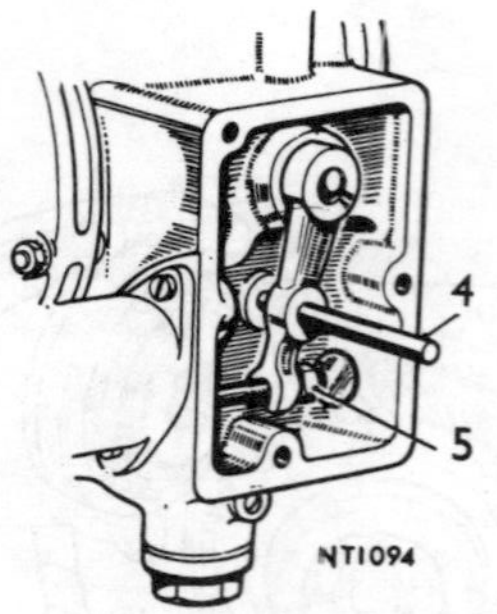

OVERDRIVE SOLENOID
—Test and adjust   40.22.01

1. Remove the three screws and star washers.
2. Remove the cover plate.
3. Remove the gasket.
4. Move the operating lever until a 3/16 in (4·762 mm) setting pin pushed through the hole in the lever aligns with the hole in the casing.
5. With the solenoid energised screw the adjusting nut until it just contacts the operating lever.
6. Remove the setting pin.
7. De-energise the solenoid.
8. Energise the solenoid.
9. Re-check the alignment of the holes.
10. Check the current consumption is approximately 2 amps.
11. A reading of 20 amps indicates the solenoid plunger is not moving far enough to switch from the solenoid operating coil to the holding coil of the solenoid. If this is the case the operating lever must be readjusted (operations 5 to 9).
12. Continuous high current will cause premature solenoid failure.

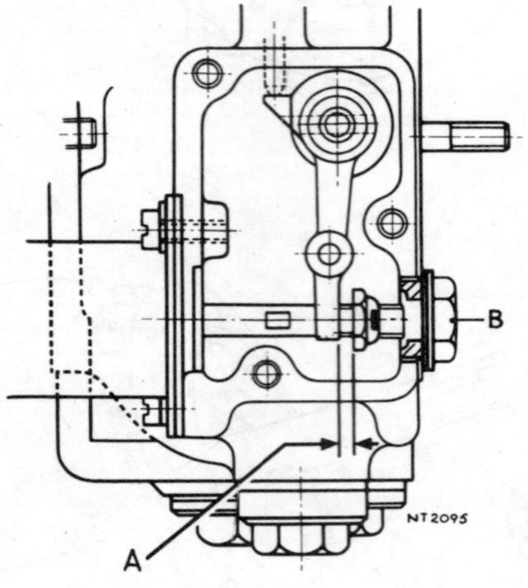

NOTE: When the solenoid is not energised ensure a clearance exists at A, this can be adjusted at B.

40.20.10 sheet 6
40.22.01

Triumph Spitfire Mk IV Manual. Part No. 545254.

OVERDRIVE

OVERDRIVE SOLENOID
—Remove and refit   40.22.04

Removing
1. Remove three screws and star washers.
2. Remove cover plate.
3. Remove gasket.
4. Unscrew the two solenoid retaining screws.
5. Remove the solenoid.
6. Remove the joint washer.
7. Remove the plunger.

Refitting
8. Reverse instructions 1 to 7 ensuring that the solenoid is tested and adjusted operation No. 40.22.01.

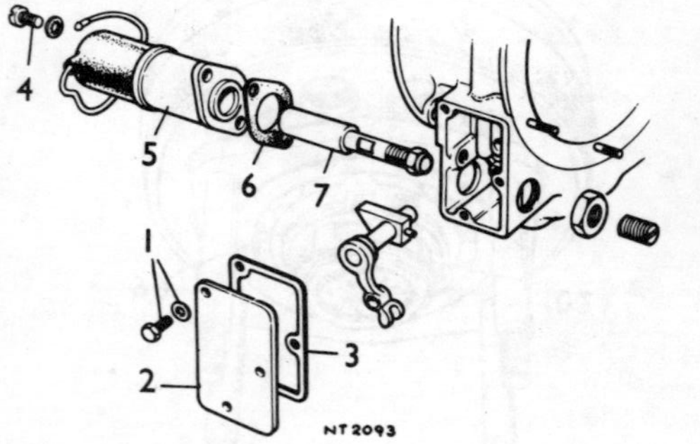

OVERDRIVE SOLENOID
—Remove, refit, test and adjust   40.22.05

1. Remove and refit, operation No. 40.22.04.
2. Test and adjust, operation No. 40.22.01.

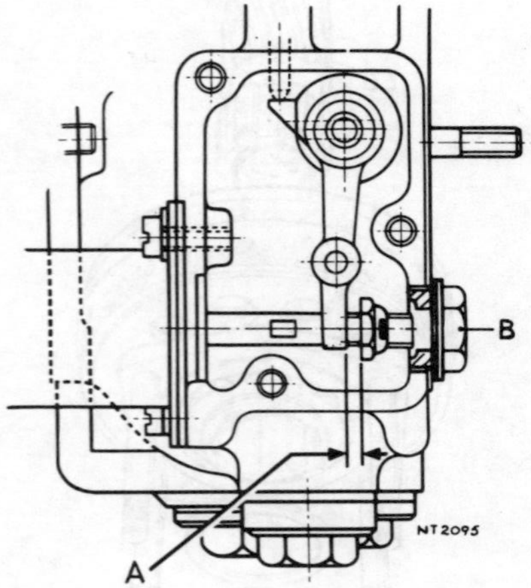

40.22.04
40.22.05

Triumph Spitfire Mk IV Manual. Part No. 545254.

OVERDRIVE — J TYPE

LIST OF OPERATIONS

Control orifice — clean	40.16.19
Oil pump — overhaul	40.18.04
— remove and refit	40.18.01
Oil seal — rear — remove and refit	40.15.01
Operating pistons — overhaul	40.16.29
— remove and refit	40.16.24
Overdrive assembly — hydraulic pressure test	40.20.01
— overhaul or dismantle	40.20.10
— remove and refit	40.20.07
Pressure filter — remove and refit	40.10.08
Pump non-return valve — overhaul	40.16.14
— remove and refit	40.16.10
Relief valve and dashpot assembly — overhaul	40.16.07
— remove and refit	40.16.04
Solenoid and operating valve — overhaul	40.22.13
— remove and refit	40.22.04
— test	40.22.01
Speedo drive gear — remove and refit	40.25.01
Sump filter — remove and refit	40.10.01

OVERDRIVE — J TYPE

J TYPE OVERDRIVE COMPONENTS

1. Locknut
2. Washer
3. Drive flange
4. Oil seal
5. Annulus rear ball race
6. Rear case
7. Spacer
8. Speedometer driving gear
9. Annulus front ball race
10. Clutch sliding member
11. Sun wheel
12. Planet carrier assembly
13. Circlip
14. Oil thrower
15. Unidirectional clutch cage
16. Bolt
17. Star washer
18. Speedometer retaining clamp
19. Oil seal
20. Speedo driven gear housing
21. 'O' ring
22. Speedometer driven gear
23. Unidirectional clutch rollers
24. Unidirectional clutch roller track
25. Thrust washer
26. Mainshaft bush
27. Annulus
28. Unidirectional clutch spring
29. Unidirectional clutch spring
30. Thrust pin
31. Thrust ring
32. Clutch return springs
33. Thrust ball race
34. Retaining circlip
35. Circlip for sliding member
36. Circlip for sun wheel

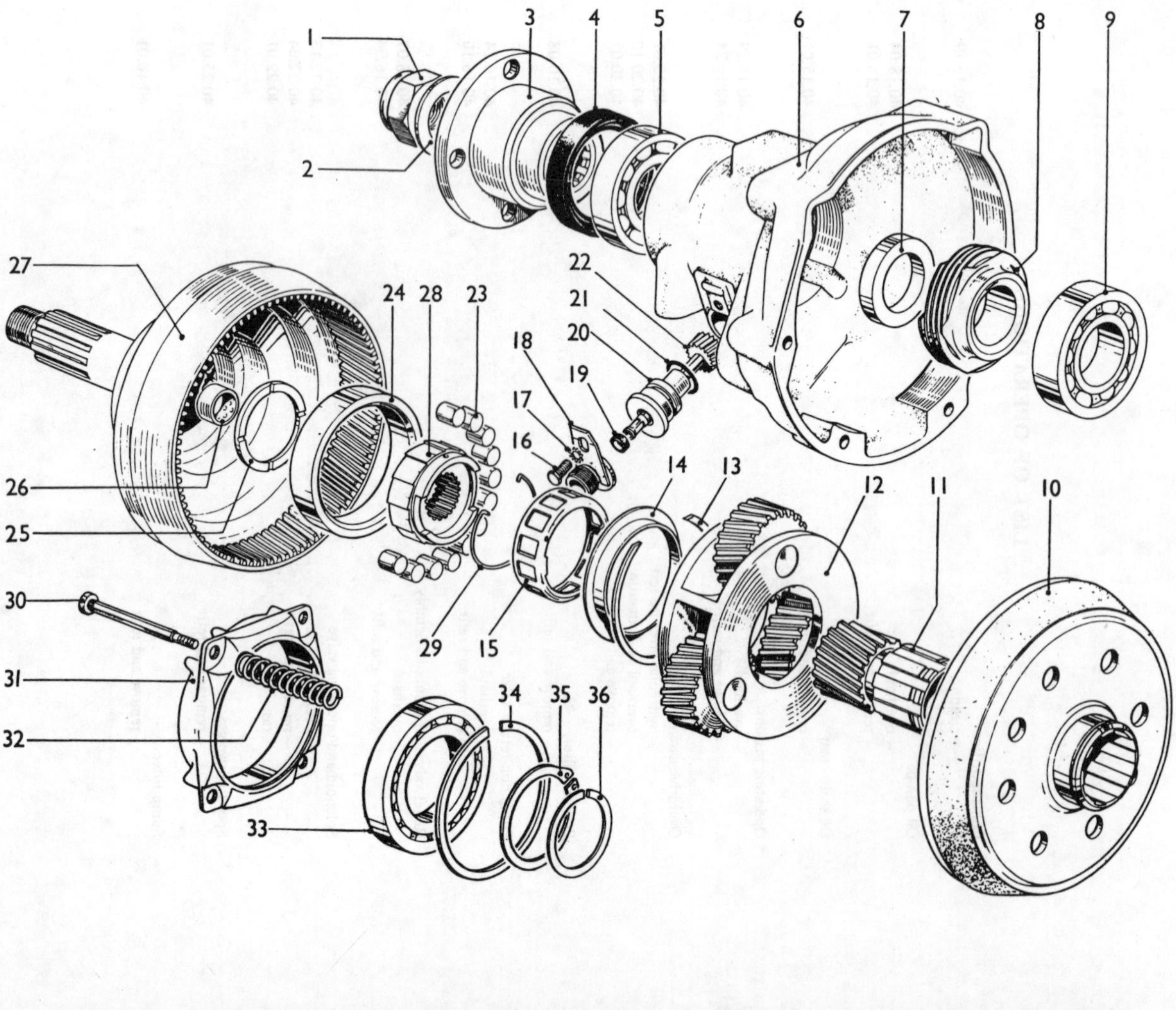

OVERDRIVE — J TYPE

J TYPE OVERDRIVE COMPONENTS

1. Gasket
2. Locknut
3. Bridge piece
4. Operating piston
5. 'O' ring
6. Stud
7. Main case
8. Washer (copper)
9. Gasket
10. Pressure tapping plug
11. Brake ring
12. Gasket
13. Clutch return spring
14. Thrust ring
15. Thrust pin
16. Thrust ball race
17. Retaining circlip
18. Circlip for sliding member
19. Circlip for sun wheel
20. Dashpot sleeve
21. Relief valve assembly
22. Double dashpot spring
23. Dashpot piston assembly
24. Dashpot plug
25. 'O' ring
26. Sump filter
27. Sump gasket
28. Sump
29. Star washer
30. Bolt
31. Pump plug
32. Non-return valve spring
33. Steel ball
34. Non-return valve seat
35. 'O' ring
36. Pump body
37. Pressure filter plug
38. Pressure filter washer
39. Pump plunger
40. Pressure filter
41. 'O' ring
42. Relief valve body
43. 'O' ring
44. Stud
45. Steel ball
46. Lubrication relief valve spring
47. Lubrication relief valve plug
48. Pump strap
49. Pump pin
50. Cam
51. Woodruff key

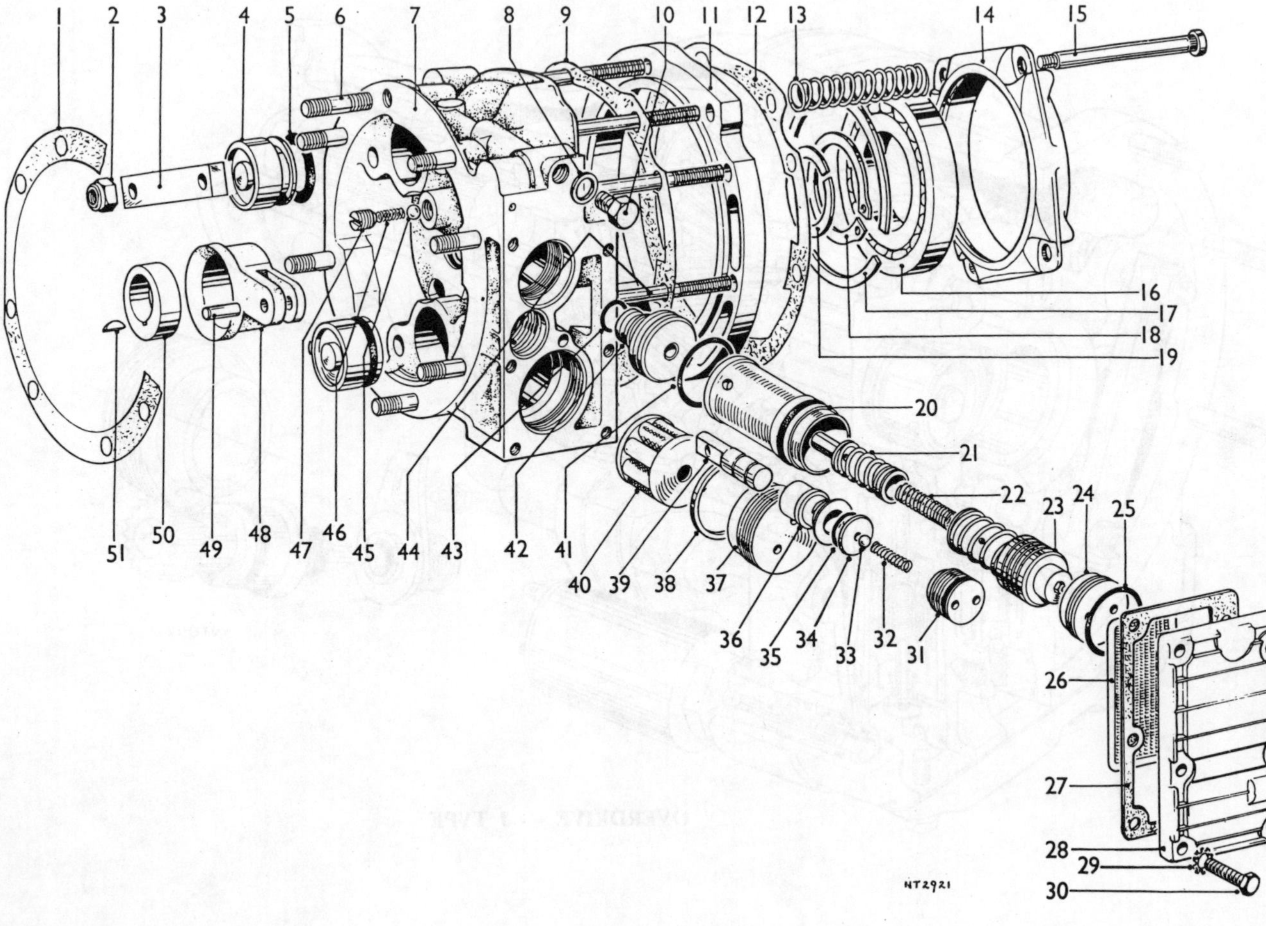

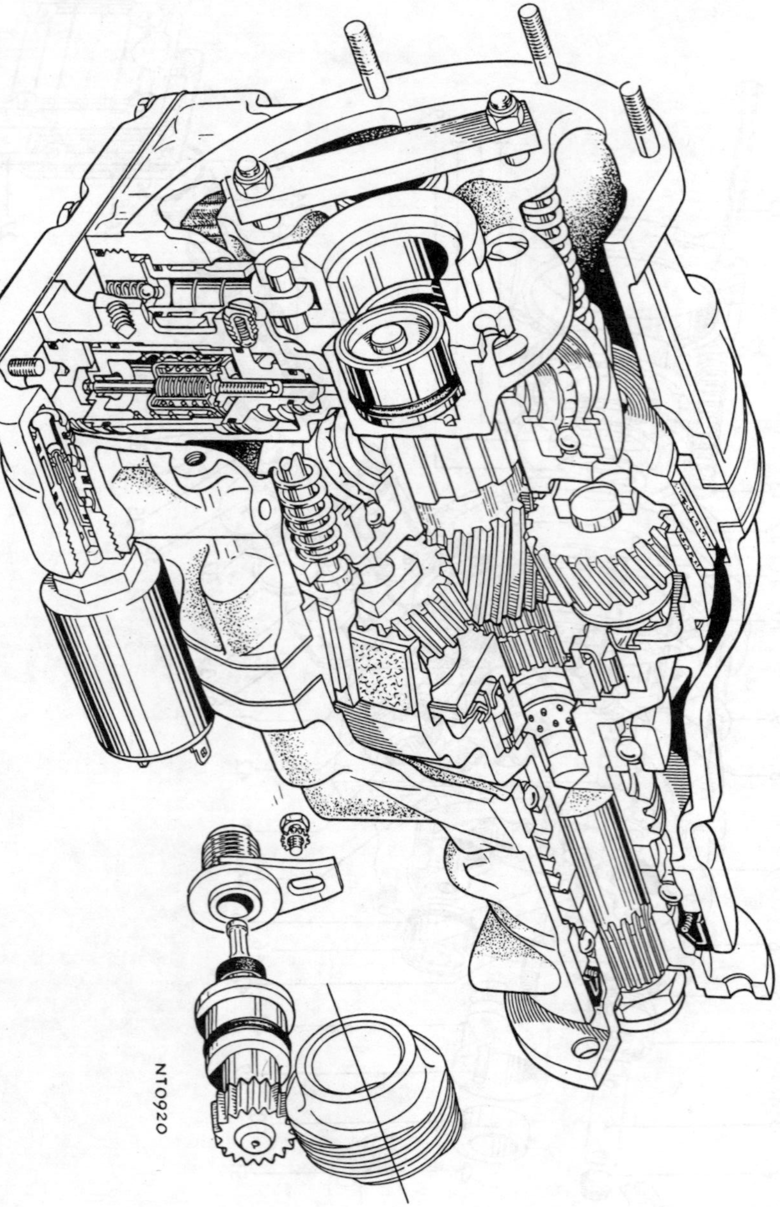

OVERDRIVE — J TYPE

INTRODUCTION

The overdrive is an additional gear unit between the gearbox and propeller shaft. When in operation it provides a higher overall gear ratio than that given by the final drive.

The primary object of an overdrive is to provide open road cruising at an engine speed lower than it would be in normal top gear. This reduced engine speed gives a considerable reduction in petrol consumption and increase in engine life. Overdrive may also be used on the indirect gears to enhance performance or to provide easy and clutchless gear-changing, for example in town traffic.

The overdrive is operated by an electric solenoid controlled by a switch, fitted in the gear-lever knob. An inhibitor switch is fitted in the electrical circuit to prevent engagement of overdrive in reverse, and some or all of the indirect gears.

Overdrive can be engaged or disengaged at will at any speed, but usually above 30 m.p.h. in top gear. It should be operated without using the clutch pedal and at any throttle opening because the unit is designed to be engaged and disengaged when transmitting full power. The only precaution necessary is to avoid disengaging overdrive at too high a road speed, particularly when using it in an indirect gear, since this would cause excessive engine revolutions.

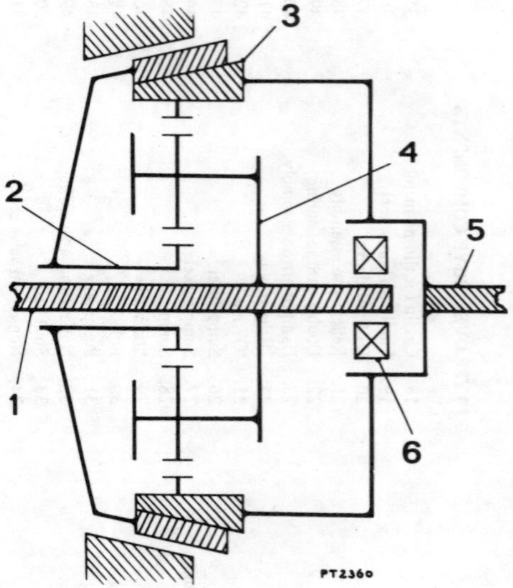

OVERDRIVE — J TYPE

KEY

1. Input shaft connected to planet carrier
2. Sun gear
3. Annulus
4. Planet carrier
5. Output shaft connected to annulus
6. Roller clutch **

OVERDRIVE — J TYPE

**WORKING PRINCIPLES

The overdrive gears are epicyclic and consist of a central sun wheel meshing with three planet gears which in turn mesh with an internally toothed annulus. All gears are in constant mesh. The planet carrier is attached to the input shaft and the annulus is integral with the output shaft.

The unit is shown diagrammatically below.

An extension of the gearbox mainshaft forms the overdrive input shaft. Forward direct drive power is transmitted from this shaft to the inner member of the unidirectional clutch and then to the outer member of this clutch through rollers which are driven up inclined faces and wedge between the inner and outer members. The outer member forms part of the combined annulus and output shaft.

The gear train is inoperative. A cone clutch is mounted on the externally splined extension of the sun wheel and is loaded in contact with the annulus by a number of springs which have their reaction against the casing of the overdrive unit. The spring load is transmitted to the clutch member through a thrust ring and ball bearing. This arrangement causes the inner friction lining of the cone clutch to contact the outer cone of the annulus and rotate with the annulus, whilst the springs and thrust ring remain stationary. Since the sun wheel is splined to the clutch member the whole gear train is locked, permitting over-run and reverse torque to be transmitted by the cone clutch, without which the uni-directional clutch would give a free-wheel condition. Additional load is imparted to the clutch member, during over-run and reverse, by the sun wheel which, due to the helix angle of its gear teeth, thrusts rearward and has for its reaction member the cone clutch.

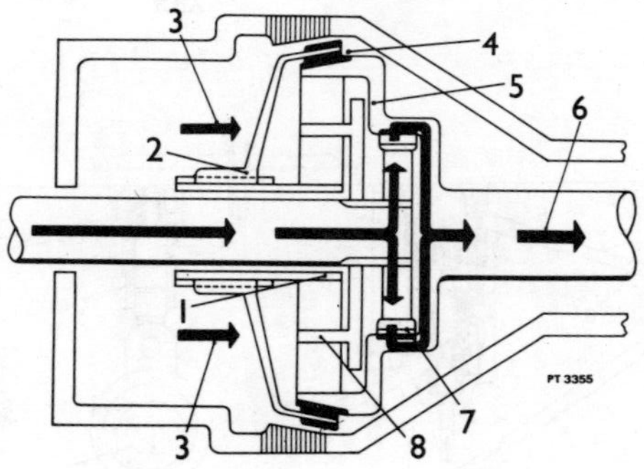

IN DIRECT DRIVE

KEY

1. Sun wheel
2. Sliding cone clutch
3. Spring pressure
4. Annulus and sun wheel locked
5. Annulus
6. To propeller shaft
7. Uni-directional roller clutch
8. Planet wheels**

** The diagram below shows the position of the cone clutch when overdrive is engaged.

It will be seen that it is no longer in contact with the annulus but has moved forward so that its outer friction lining is in contact with a brake ring forming part of the overdrive casing. The sun wheel to which the clutch is attached is therefore held stationary. The output shaft and annulus continue to rotate at the same speed, so the planet wheels rotate on their axes around the stationary sun wheel, reducing the planet carrier and input shaft speed. The uni-directional clutch permits the outer member to over-run the inner member.

This condition give a lower engine speed for a given road speed.

Movement of the cone clutch in a forward direction is effected by means of hydraulic pressure which acts upon two pistons when a valve is opened, by operating the driver-controlled selector switch. This hydraulic pressure overcomes the springs which load the clutch member on to the annulus and causes the clutch to engage the brake ring with sufficient load to hold the sun wheel at rest. Additional load is imparted to the clutch in a forward direction due to the helix angle of the gear teeth.

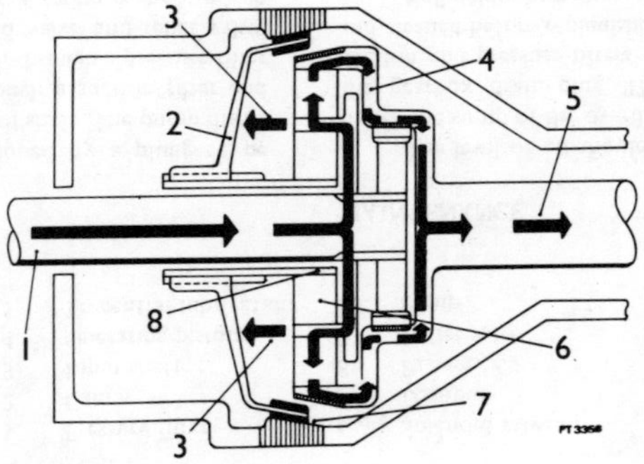

IN OVERDRIVE

KEY

1. From gearbox
2. Sliding cone clutch
3. Hydraulic pressure
4. Annulus driven by planet gears
5. To propeller shaft
6. Planet wheels
7. Locked cone clutch holds sun wheel
8. Sun wheel**

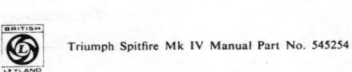

OVERDRIVE — J TYPE

SOLENOID AND OPERATING VALVE

The solenoid and operating valve is a self-contained factory sealed unit, situated on the main case of the overdrive.

The solenoid has a single coil, encapsulated and completely waterproof, with a continuous current consumption of approximately 2 amperes. There are no electrical contacts in the solenoid.

Energizing

When the solenoid is energized, its valve opens and oil which is at residual pressure is directed via passage 'Z' to the bottom of the dashpot piston. This causes the dashpot piston to rise and compress the dashpot spring, causing a progressive increase in hydraulic pressure until the piston reaches its stop, by which time the relief valve spring has been compressed to its working length, thus giving full operating pressure. This pressure causes the operating pistons to move forward, overcoming the clutch springs, and engages the cone clutch in the brake ring.

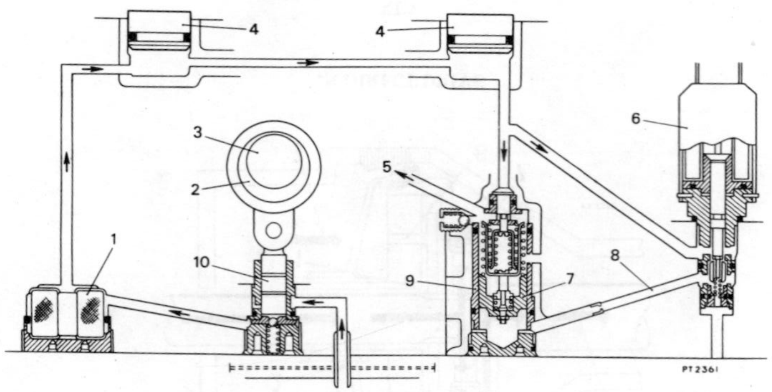

In direct drive a residual pressure of approximately 20 lb/in² maintains the system in primed condition and provides lubrication. This is achieved by the relief valve piston reacting on the residual pressure spring. When the overdrive is engaged, pressure increases to a pre-determined operating pressure of 320/350 lb/in².

KEY

1. Pressure filter
2. Cam
3. Input shaft
4. Operating pistons
5. To central lubrication
6. Solenoid valve
7. Dashpot
8. Passage 'Z'
9. Relief valve
10. Pump **

De-energizing

When the solenoid is de-energized its valve is closed by a spring, cutting off the oil supply from the pump to the dashpot. Oil is now exhausted via the control orifice in passage 'Z' which allows the relief valve spring to relax to its direct drive position. The dashpot spring moves the dashpot piston to its stop, allowing the system pressure to progressively drop which enables the clutch springs to move the cone clutch gently into contact with the annulus. The residual pressure of approximately 20 lb/in² is now maintained in direct drive.

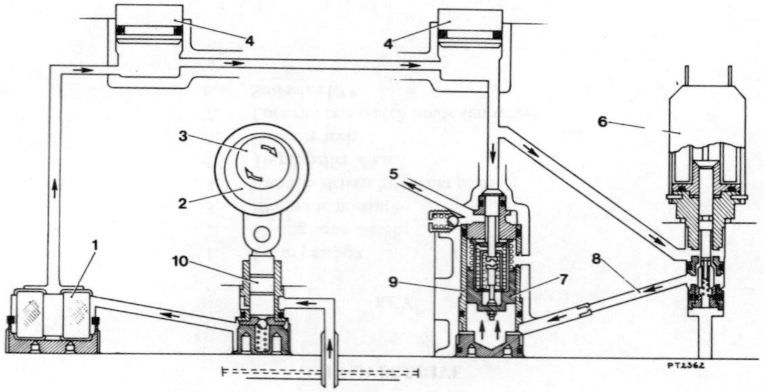

KEY

1. Pressure filter
2. Cam
3. Input shaft
4. Operating pistons
5. To central lubrication
6. Solenoid valve
7. Dashpot
8. Passage 'Z'
9. Relief valve
10. Pump

HYDRAULIC SYSTEM

Hydraulic pressure is developed by a plunger-type pump, cam-operated from the input shaft. The pump draws oil from an air-cooled sump through a suction filter and delivers it via the non-return valve, through a pressure filter to the operating pistons, solenoid valve and relief valve. Incorporated in the relief valve is a spring dashpot which ensures smooth overdrive engagement and disengagement under varying conditions.

LUBRICATION SYSTEM

Oil is discharged through the relief valve direct to an annular channel in the centre of the main casing and then through drillings in the mainshaft to the annulus spigot bearing. Immediately in front of the spigot bearing a radial drilling passes oil through the uni-directional clutch; from here it is directed by an oil thrower into a catcher disc on the planet carrier and to the planet bearings via the hollow planet bearing pins.

The pressure in the lubrication passage is controlled by the lubrication relief valve.

MAINTENANCE

The level of oil should be checked at the gearbox. To drain, the sump of the overdrive must be removed as well as the gearbox drain plug. This will provide access to the suction and pressure filters, which should also be removed and cleaned before replenishing with new oil.

Following complete draining and refilling, run the transmission for a short period, then re-check the oil level.

It is essential that only the approved lubricant is used for topping-up and refilling. ON NO ACCOUNT SHOULD ANY ANTI-FRICTION ADDITIVES BE USED.

CLEANLINESS

Scrupulous cleanliness must be maintained throughout all servicing operations. Even minute particles of dust, dirt or lint from cleaning cloths may cause malfunction. When the overdrive and gearbox have a common oil supply, it is naturally as important that the same high standards of cleanliness must be maintained when servicing the gearbox.

Great care must be taken to avoid the entry of dirt when topping-up or refilling.

For cleaning, use petrol or paraffin ONLY, and on no account should water be used. **

OVERDRIVE — J TYPE

FAULT DIAGNOSIS AND RECTIFICATION

Fault	Possible Cause	Remedy
OVERDRIVE DOES NOT ENGAGE	a. Insufficient oil in unit.	Top up gearbox/overdrive.
	b. Solenoid not energizing.	Check electrical circuit.
	c. Solenoid energizing but not operating	Remove solenoid and check operation of solenoid valve.
	d. Insufficient hydraulic pressure.	Fit pressure gauge and check operating pressure. Clean filters. Re-seat pump non-return valve if necessary. Check relief valve operation.
	e. Pump damaged.	Clean control orifice. DO NOT PROBE WITH WIRE. DO NOT
	f. Internal damage.	Remove and check. Remove and examine overdrive.
*OVERDRIVE DOES NOT RELEASE	* THIS CALLS FOR IMMEDIATE ATTENTION. DO NOT REVERSE THE CAR, OR EXTENSIVE DAMAGE MAY BE CAUSED.	
	a. Fault in electrical control circuit	Check electrical system for closed circuit.
	b. Sticking solenoid valve.	Remove solenoid and check valve.
	c. Residual pressure too high.	Fit pressure gauge and check residual pressure. If pressure is too high, check for sticking relief valve.
	d. Control orifice blocked.	Check and blow through with compressed air. DO NOT PROBE WITH WIRE.
	e. Cone clutch sticking.	Tap the brake ring several times with a hide mallet.
	f. Internal damage.	Remove and examine overdrive.
CLUTCH SLIP IN OVERDRIVE	a. Insufficient oil in unit.	Top up gearbox/overdrive.
	b. Operating pressure too low.	Fit the pressure gauge and check the pressure. Check the filters, pump non-return ball valve and relief valve.
	c. Sticking solenoid valve.	Check that the control orifice is clear. Remove solenoid and check operation of solenoid valve.
	d. Worn or glazed clutch linings.	Remove overdrive and examine the linings for mechanical obstruction to movement of cone clutch.
SLOW DISENGAGEMENT OF OVERDRIVE, FREE-WHEELING ON OVER-RUN, SLIP IN REVERSE GEAR	(THESE SYMPTOMS MAY OCCUR TOGETHER OR SEPARATELY)	
	a. Sticking relief valve.	Check for sticking relief valve.
	b. Sticking or partially blocked control valve.	Remove solenoid and check.
	c. Control orifice blocked.	Check to ensure the orifice is clear.
	d. Internal damage.	Remove and examine overdrive.

40.00.11J

DIMENSIONS AND CLEARANCES FOR PARTS WHEN NEW

	Dimensions New	Clearances New
CAM		
Outside diameter of cam	1·4590 in/1·4600 in	0·0010 in/0·0030 in
Inside diameter of pump strap	1·4610 in/1·4620 in	
GEARBOX MAINSHAFT		
Diameter of oil transfer	0·9640 in/0·9650 in	0·0010 in/0·0030 in
Inside diameter of main case at oil transfer	0·9660 in/0·9670 in	
Diameter of sun wheel	0·9410 in/0·9430 in	0·0040 in/0·0080 in
Inside diameter of sun wheel bush (where fitted)	0·9470 in/0·0490 in	
Diameter at mainshaft spigot	0·5620 in/0·5625 in	0·0003 in/0·0018 in
Inside diameter at spigot bearing	0·5628 in/0·5638 in	
OPERATING PISTONS		
Operating piston diameter	1·2492 in/1·2497 in	0·0003 in/0·0020 in
Operating piston bore diameter	1·2500 in/1·2512 in	
RELIEF VALVE PUMP		
Pump plunger diameter	0·4996 in/0·5000 in	0·0003 in/0·0013 in
Pump body bore	0·5003 in/0·5009 in	
RELIEF VALVE		
Outside diameter of relief valve piston	0·2496 in/0·2498 in	0·0002 in/0·0009 in
Inside diameter of relief valve body	0·2500 in/0·2505 in	
Outside diameter of dashpot piston	0·9370 in/0·9373 in	0·0002 in/0·0015 in
Inside diameter of dashpot sleeve	0·9375 in/0·9385 in	
SPEEDOMETER PINION		
Outside diameter of speedometer pinion	0·3105 in/0·3110 in	0·00010 in/0·0030 in
Inside diameter of speedometer bearing	0·3120 in/0·3135 in	
MISCELLANEOUS		
Sliding member travel from direct drive to overdrive (measured at bridge pieces)	0·090 in/0·115 in	

40.00.12J

OVERDRIVE — J TYPE

SUMP FILTER

— Remove and refit   40.10.01

Removing

1. Remove the six bolts and star washers holding the sump on.
2. Remove the sump.
3. Remove the sump gasket.
4. Pull the filter out.
5. Clean the filter in either paraffin or petrol.

Refitting

6. Push the filter back into position.
7. Refit the sump and gasket.
8. Refit the bolts and star washers and tighten to a torque of 6 lbf ft (0·8 kgf m).

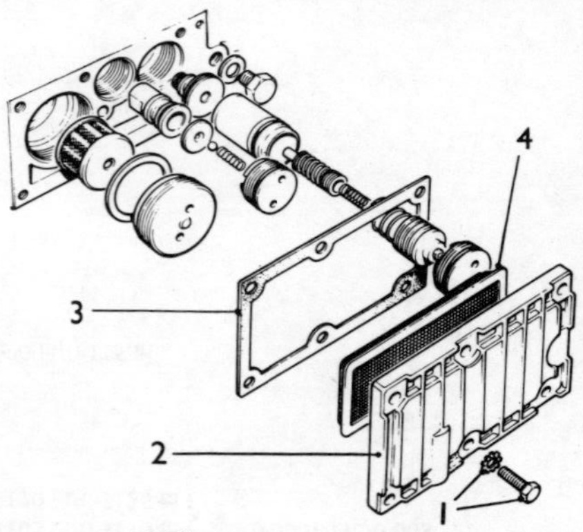

PRESSURE FILTER

— Remove and refit   40.10.08

Removing

1. Remove the sump and suction filter.
2. Remove the pressure filter base plug (largest plug), using tool L354, the filter element will come away with the plug.
3. Remove the aluminium washer which locates on the shoulder in the filter bore.
4. Remove foreign matter and wash the element in petrol or paraffin.
5. Renew the aluminium washer if there are any signs of damage or scoring.
6. Refit the filter and pressure filter base plug, using tool L354.
7. Tighten up until the plug is flush with the base, a torque loading of 16 lbf ft (2·2 kgf m).

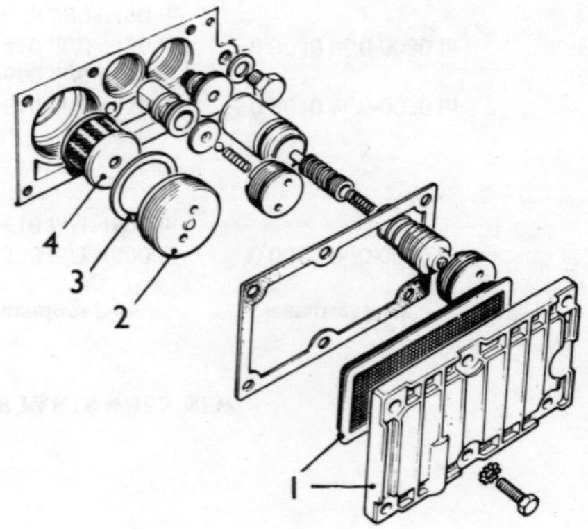

OVERDRIVE — J TYPE

OIL SEAL — REAR

— Remove and refit 40.15.01

Removing
1. Remove the nut.
2. Remove the washer.
3. Remove the drive flange.
4. Remove the rear oil seal, using special tool L176A with 7657.

Refitting
5. Fit the oil seal using special tool L177 with 550.
6. Refit the drive flange.
7. Refit the washer.
8. Fit a new self-locking nut and tighten to a torque of 80 to 130 lbf ft (11·1 to 18·0 kgf m).

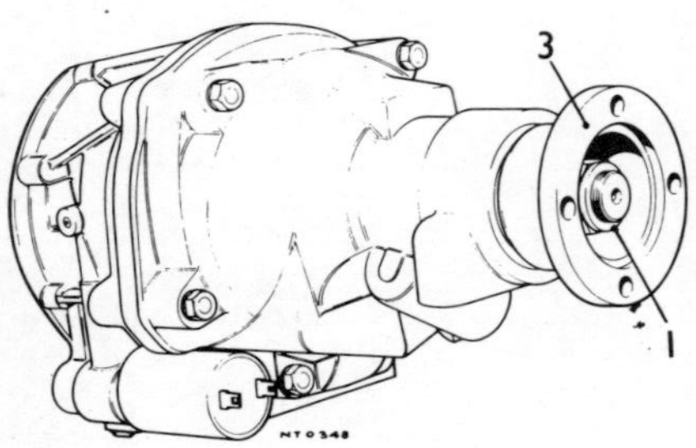

RELIEF VALVE AND DASHPOT ASSEMBLY

— Remove and refit 40.16.04

NOTE: If the vehicle has been in recent use, care should be taken to avoid hot oil burning the skin.

1. Remove six bolts and star washers securing the sump to the main case.
2. Remove the gasket.
3. Remove the gauze filter.
4. Using Churchill tool L354, remove the relief valve plug.
5. Withdraw the dashpot piston complete with its component springs and cup.
6. Remove the residual pressure spring.

NOTE: This is the only loose spring in the general assembly.

continued

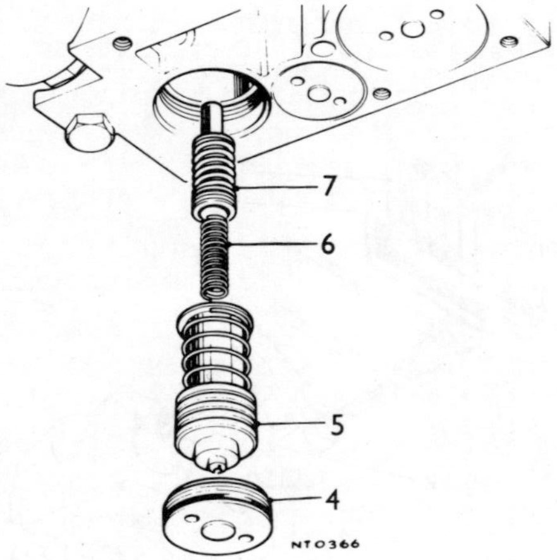

7. The relief valve piston assembly can now be withdrawn by carefully pulling down with a pair of pliers.
8. Insert tool L401 into the now exposed relief valve bore (taking care not to damage this) and withdraw the relief valve together with the dashpot sleeve.

NOTE: Do not dismantle the dashpot and relief valve piston assemblies otherwise the predetermined spring pressures will be disturbed.

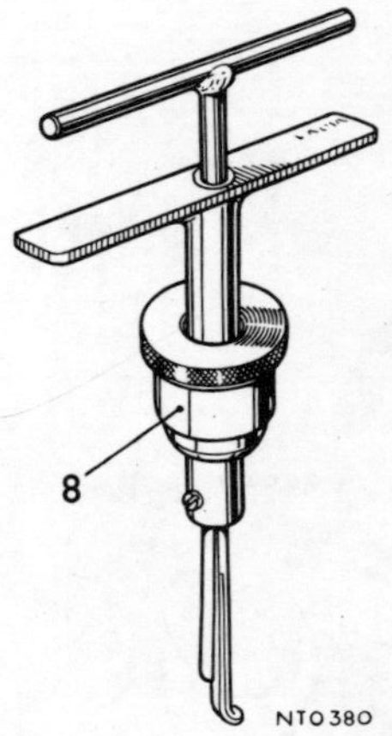

Refitting
9. Ensure that before assembly all the components are clean and lightly oiled.
10. Insert the relief body in the bore and, using the relief valve outer sleeve, push fully home.

NOTE: The end with the 'O' ring is nearest to the outside of the casing.

11. Position the relief valve spring and piston assembly into the dashpot cup, ensuring that both ends of the residual pressure spring are correctly located.
12. Carefully position these components in the relief valve outer sleeve, at the same time engaging the relief valve piston in its housing.
13. Fit the base plug and tighten it flush with the casing to a torque loading of 16 lbf ft (2·2 kgf m).

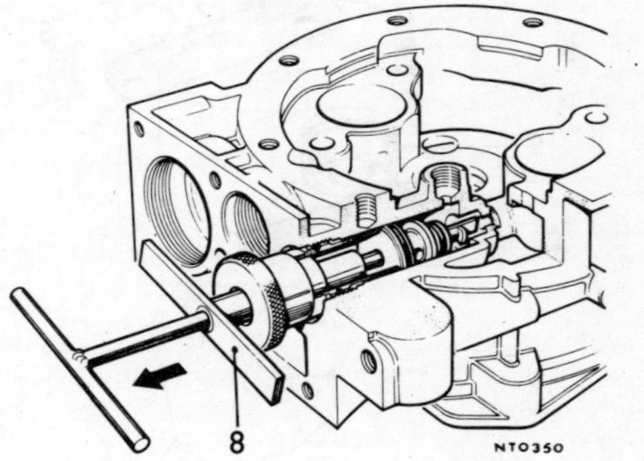

RELIEF VALVE AND DASHPOT ASSEMBLY

— Overhaul 40.16.07

1. Remove the relief valve and dashpot assembly. 40.16.04.
2. Inspect the pistons and ensure that they move freely in their respective housings.
3. Inspect the 'O' rings and ensure that they are in good condition.
4. If they are damaged at all, the 'O' ring should be renewed.
5. Refit the relief valve and dashpot assembly. 40.16.04.

OVERDRIVE — J TYPE

PUMP NON-RETURN VALVE

— Remove and refit 40.16.10

Removing
1. Remove the overdrive sump.
2. Remove the suction filter.
3. With Churchill tool L354, remove the pump plug (centre plug) taking care not to lose the non-return valve spring and ball.
4. Remove the non-return valve seat.

Refitting
5. Place the spring in the non-return valve plug.
6. Position the ball on the spring.
7. Locate the non-return seat on the ball.
8. Screw the complete assembly into the maincase, using tool L354.
9. Screw up flush with the case to a torque loading of 16 lbf ft (2·2 kgf m).

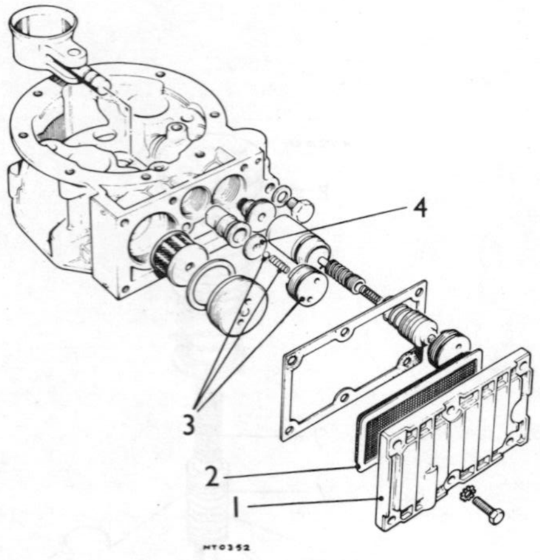

PUMP NON-RETURN VALVE

— Overhaul 40.16.14

1. Remove the pump non-return valve. 40.16.10.
2. Carefully inspect the non-return valve ball and valve seat. If necessary, reseat the ball on the seat by tapping gently with a copper drift.
3. Ensure that the 'O' ring is undamaged.
4. If the 'O' ring is damaged, renew it.
5. Refit the 'O' ring after smearing with petroleum jelly.
6. Refit the pump non-return valve. 40.16.10.

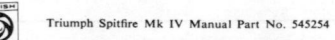

CONTROL ORIFICE

— Clean 40.16.19

The control orifice is situated in the angled drilling between the relief valve and the solenoid control valve.

1. To gain access, remove the solenoid control valve. 40.22.04.
2. Remove the relief valve and outer sleeve. 40.16.04.
3. Clean the orifice with a high pressure air-line.
   NOTE: Do not attempt to clean the orifice with wire or its calibration may be impaired.
4. Refit the relief valve and outer sleeve. 40.16.04.
5. Refit the solenoid control valve. 40.22.04.

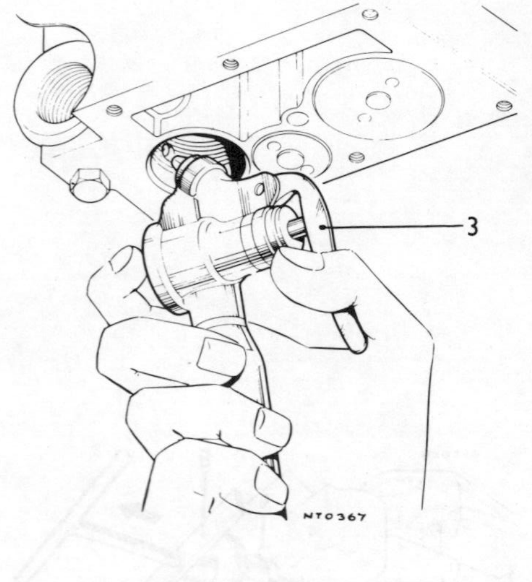

OPERATING PISTONS

— Remove and refit 40.16.24

Removing
1. Remove the gearbox and overdrive from the car. 37.20.01.
2. Remove the overdrive from the gearbox. 40.20.07.
3. Remove four nuts.
4. Remove two bridge pieces.
5. With a pair of pliers, remove the operating pistons, identifying them with their respective cylinders.

Refitting
6. Lightly oil the operating pistons.
7. Push the pistons into the housings.
8. Fit the two bridge pieces.
9. Fit and tighten the four new nuts to a torque of 6 to 8 lbf ft (0·8 to 1·1 kgf m).
10. Refit the overdrive to the gearbox. 40.20.07.
11. Refit the gearbox and overdrive to the car. 37.20.01.

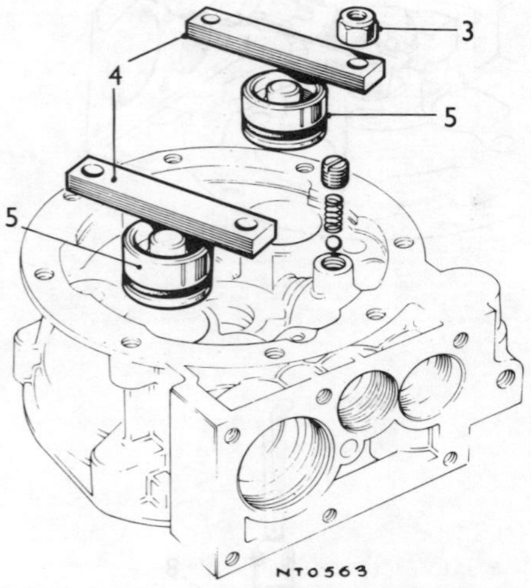

OPERATING PISTONS

— Overhaul 40.16.29

1. Remove the operating pistons. 40.16.24.
2. Inspect each of the 'O' rings for any damage or wear.
3. If any damage is found the ring must be replaced and smeared with petroleum jelly.
4. Refit the operating pistons. 40.16.24.

OVERDRIVE — J TYPE

OIL PUMP
— Remove and refit   40.18.01

Removing
1. Remove the overdrive from the car. 40.20.07.
2. Remove the sump and filter. 40.10.01.
3. Remove the pump plug, using tool L354A.
4. Remove the non-return valve spring.
5. Remove the steel ball.
6. Remove the non-return valve seat.
7. Work the pump body out of the main casing.
8. Remove the pump plunger assembly.

Refitting
9. Position the pump plunger assembly in the main case.
10. Fit the pump body in the main casing, ensuring that the flat on the body faces towards the pressure filter housing.
11. Fit the non-return valve seat.
12. Fit the steel ball.
13. Fit the non-return valve spring into the pump plug.
14. Fit the plug and tighten to a torque of 16 lbf ft (2.2 kgf m).
15. Clean the sump filter and replace.
16. Fit the sump with a new joint.
17. Tighten the sump bolts to a torque of 6 lbf ft (0·8 kgf m).
18. Refit the overdrive to the car. 40.20.07.

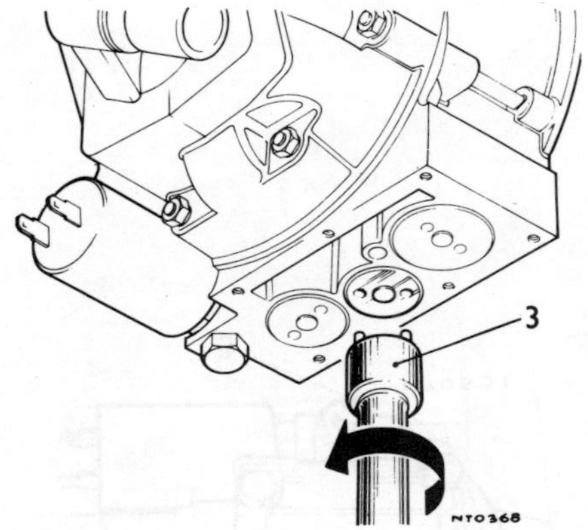

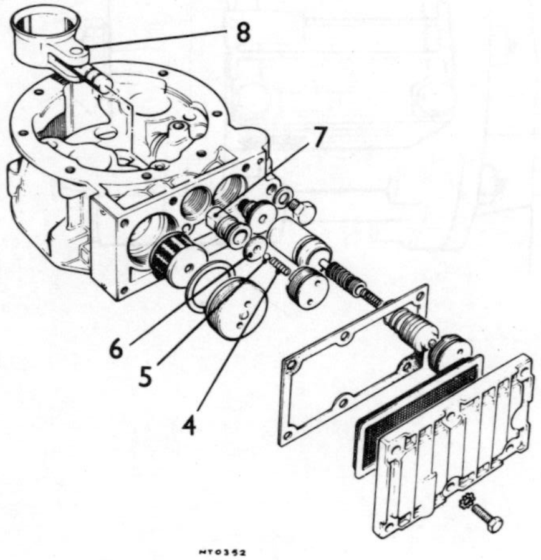

OIL PUMP
— Overhaul   40.18.04

1. Remove the pump plunger assembly. 40.18.01.
2. Check that the strap is a good fit on the mainshaft cam.
3. Check that there is no excess play between the strap and the plunger.
4. If the pump plunger assembly is worn or damaged, this must be replaced as a complete assembly.
5. Check that the 'O' rings on the pump body and the plug are perfect, if not, these must be replaced.
6. Refit the pump plunger assembly. 40.18.01.

40.18.01J
40.18.04J

OVERDRIVE — J TYPE

— Hydraulic pressure test   40.20.01

1. Check that the oil level in the gearbox is correct.
2. Remove the plug adjacent to the solenoid and fit a hydraulic pressure gauge (special tool L188) together with adaptor (L188–2).
3. Jack the car up and run the transmission at approximately 25 m.p.h. (40 km/h).
   In direct drive the residual pressure should register on the gauge to approximately 20 lbf/in² (2·8 kgf/cm²).
4. Engage the overdrive, a pressure of 320 to 350 lb/in² (44 to 49 kgf/cm²) should be recorded.
5. Disengage the overdrive and the gauge should return to show the residual pressure.

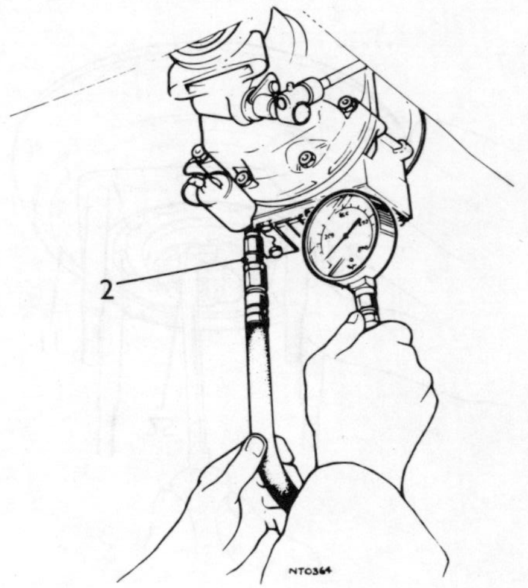

40.20.01J

OVERDRIVE — J TYPE

OVERDRIVE ASSEMBLY

— Remove and refit 40.20.07

Removing

NOTE: Before commencing overdrive removal it is advisable to raise the rear wheels and run the transmission. Engage overdrive, then disengage with the clutch depressed leaving the overdrive ready for removal. This will release the spline loading between the planet carrier and the uni-directional roller clutch which could make removal difficult.

1. Remove the gearbox and overdrive from the car as operation number 37.20.01.
2. Remove the eight ½ in U.N.F. nuts securing the unit to the adaptor plate.
3. Remove the overdrive over the mainshaft, leaving the adaptor plate in position on the gearbox.
   If difficulty is experienced in separating the overdrive from the gearbox, use the following procedure: Remove the hexagon plug adjacent to the solenoid, and screw in and tighten tool L402. Energize the solenoid, then pressurize the unit by pumping clean oil through the nipple on the tool with a lubrication gun. This will release the spline loading on the mainshaft and permit easy removal. De-energize the solenoid when the overdrive has separated by about ¾ in (19 mm).
4. Use a screwdriver of suitable length to rotate the inner member of the uni-directional roller clutch (this is the innermost set of splines), in an anti-clockwise direction until the splines of this member are in line with the splines in the planet carrier.
5. Ensure that the pump cam and sun gear spring ring are correctly located on the mainshaft.
6. Rotate the gearbox mainshaft so that the peak of the pump cam is at the bottom to assist engagement with the pump strap.
7. Engage the bottom gear in the gearbox.
8. Fit a new joint to the front face of the overdrive.
9. Offer up the overdrive to the gearbox.
10. Rotate the output shaft of the unit in a clockwise direction.
11. At the same time apply slight pressure until the splines are engaged.
12. Ensure that the pump strap assembly rides smoothly onto the cam and that the overdrive pushes home to the adaptor plate face without excessive force.
13. Fit and tighten the eight nuts which secure the unit.
14. If the overdrive fails to meet the adaptor plate face by approximately 5/8 in (16 mm) it means that the planet carrier and the uni-directional roller splines have become mis-aligned. In this case remove the unit and re-align the splines.

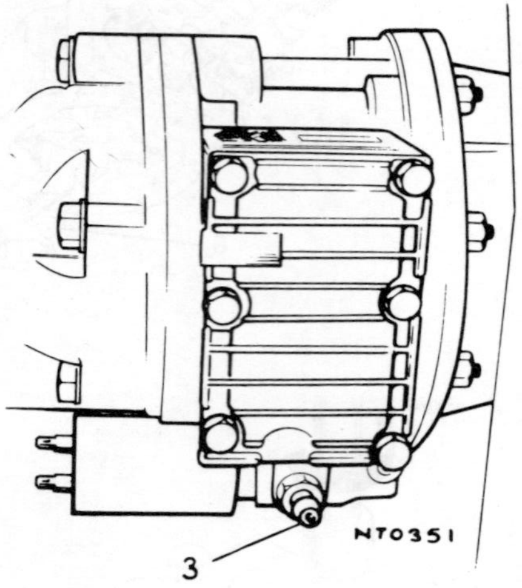

OVERDRIVE ASSEMBLY

— Overhaul or dismantle 40.20.10

1. Remove the gearbox and overdrive from the car. 37.20.01.
2. Remove the overdrive from the gearbox. 40.20.07.
3. Before starting to dismantle the overdrive assembly, the exterior of the casings must be thoroughly cleaned.
4. Mount the unit vertically in a vice with the use of 'soft' jaws.
5. Remove the four nuts securing the bridge pieces.
6. Remove the bridge pieces.
7. Progressively release the six nuts around the main casing to release the clutch return spring pressure.
8. Note the position of the two copper washers which fit on the two studs at the top of the casing.
9. Remove all the washers from the casing.
10. Separate the main casing complete with the brake ring from the rear case.
11. Lift out the sliding member assembly complete with the sun wheel.
12. Lift out the planet carrier assembly, taking care not to damage the oil catcher which is attached to the underside of the carrier.
13. Tap the brake ring from its spigot in the main casing with a suitable drift.
14. Using a pair of pliers, withdraw the operating pistons.
15. Remove the oil pump assembly. 40.10.08.
16. Remove the relief valve assembly. 40.16.04.
17. Remove the pump non-return valve assembly. 40.16.10.
18. Remove the oil pump assembly. 40.10.08.
19. Remove the sump and suction filter. 40.10.01.
20. Remove the solenoid control valve. 40.22.09.
21. Inspect the main casing for cracks.
22. Examine the operating cylinder bores for scores or wear.
23. Check the operating pistons for wear.
24. Replace the sealing rings if there is any sign of damage.
25. Remove the circlip from the sun wheel.
26. Take out the sun wheel.
27. Remove the circlip from its groove on the cone clutch hub.
28. Tap out the clutch from the thrust ring bearing, using a hide mallet.
29. Extract the large circlip.
30. Press the bearing from its housing.
31. Examine the clutch linings on the sliding member for any signs of excessive wear or charring.
32. If there is any sign of this condition, the sliding member complete must be replaced.

NOTE: It is not possible to fit new linings as these are precision machined after they are bonded.

continued

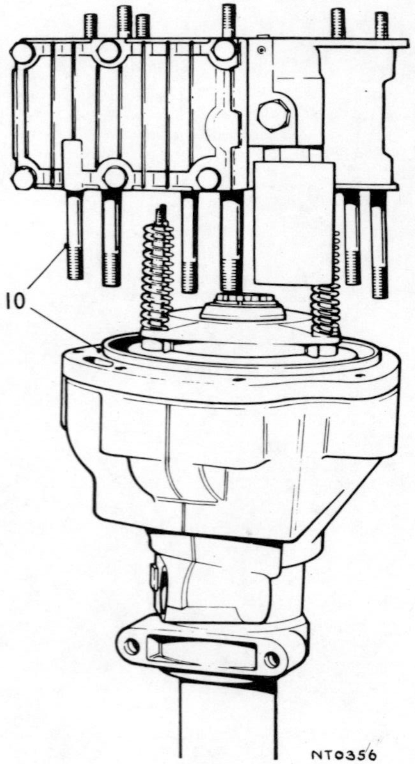

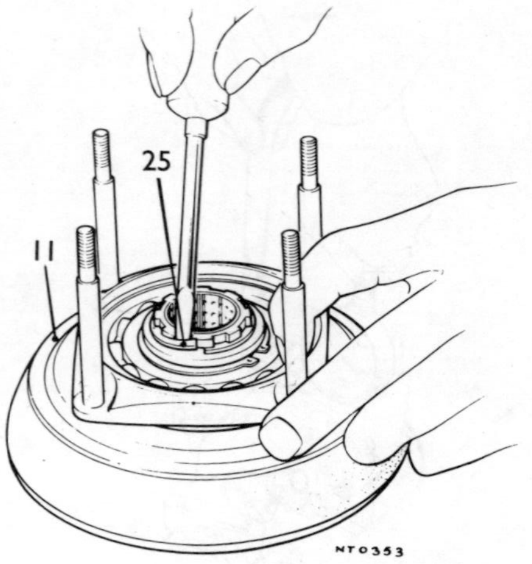

OVERDRIVE — J TYPE

33. Check the ball race and ensure that it rotates smoothly as this can be a source of noise when running in direct drive.
34. Examine the clutch return springs for any signs of distortion or collapse.
35. Inspect the sun wheel teeth for wear or damage.
36. Inspect the planet gears for damage or wear.
37. Check the planet gear bearings for any excessive clearance.
38. Examine the oil thrower for damage.
39. Using a screwdriver blade, remove the circlip.
40. Lift out the oil thrower.
41. Place tool L178 over the exposed uni-directional roller clutch.
42. Lift the inner member complete with rollers into the special tool.
43. Remove the bronze thrust washer.
44. Remove the speedometer drive bolt.
45. Remove the speedometer driven gear clamp.
46. Pull the speedometer driven gear out with a pair of pliers, this will also remove the speedometer bush.

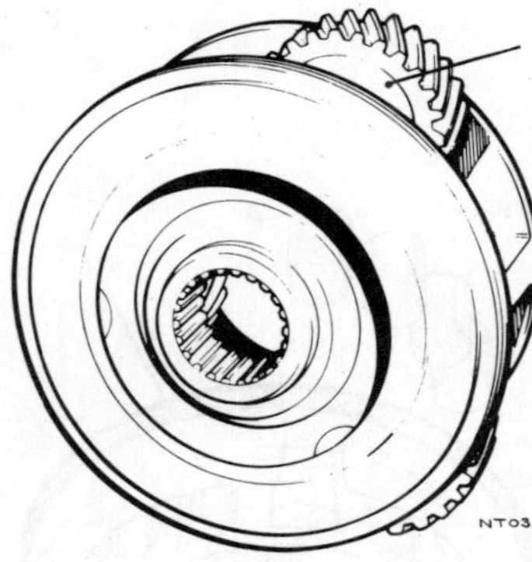

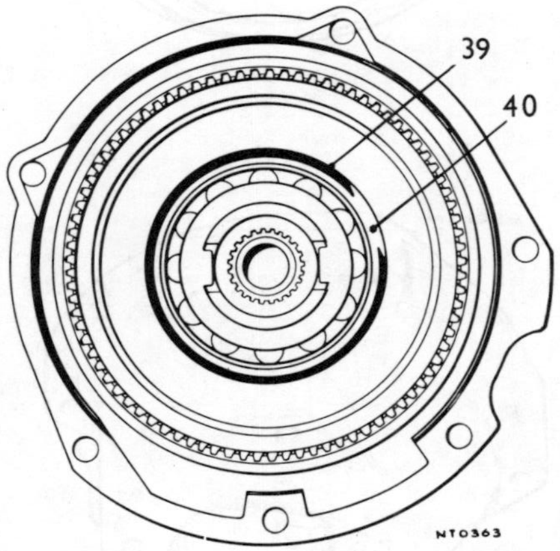

continued

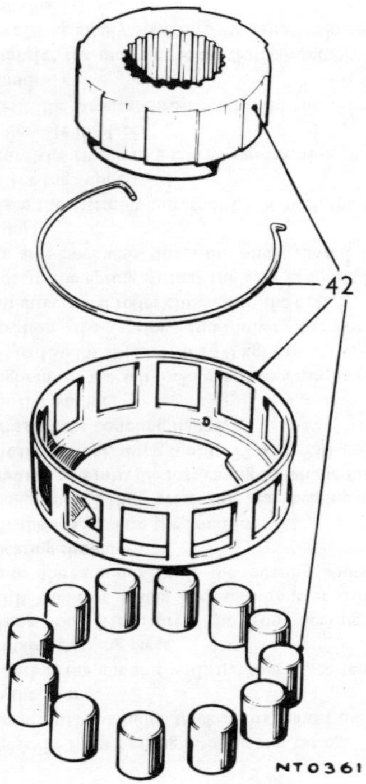

47. Separate the bush from the driven gear.
48. Remove the coupling flange nut and washer.
49. Withdraw the flange, using a suitable extractor.
50. Drift out the annulus, using a hide mallet applied to the end of the tail shaft.
51. The front bearing, speedometer drive gear and spacer will be withdrawn together with the annulus.
52. Remove the oil seal.
53. Drive out the rear bearing.
54. Check, and renew if necessary, all the 'O' rings.
55. Inspect the teeth and the cone surface of the annulus for wear.
56. Check that the uni-directional clutch rollers are not chipped.
57. Check that the inner and outer members are not damaged.
58. Examine the spring and cage for distortion.
59. The oil seal must be replaced.
60. Examine the speedometer drive and driven gears for wear and chafing, in either case they must be replaced.
61. Position the speedometer drive gear in the rear casing with its plain boss facing the front bearing.
    NOTE: The speedometer drive gear cannot be fitted from the rear of the casing.

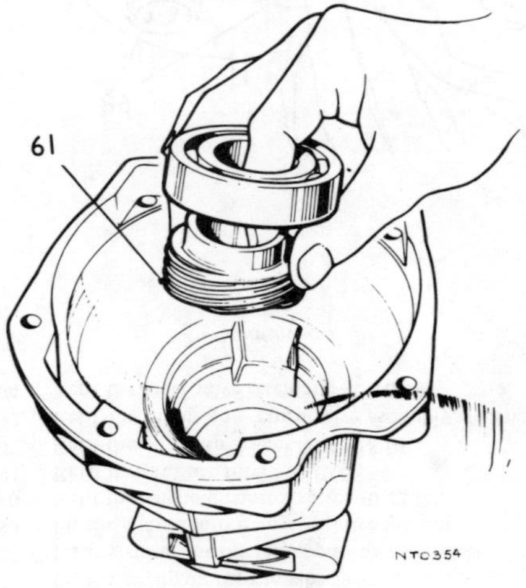

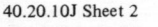

continued

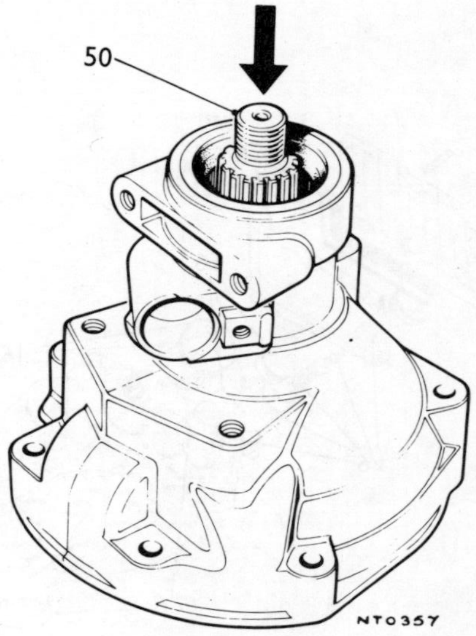

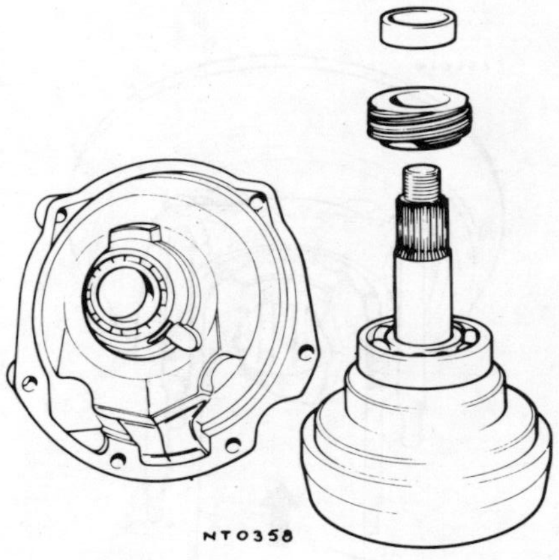

OVERDRIVE — J TYPE

62. Press the front bearing into the rear casing.
63. Ensure that its outer track abuts against the shoulder in the casing.
64. Position the annulus with the inner face resting on a suitable packing piece.
65. Using tool L186, press the front bearing together with the rear casing and speedometer driving gear onto the annulus until the bearing abuts on the locating shoulder.
66. Fit the spacer onto the annulus.
67. Using tool L186, press the rear bearing onto the annulus and into the rear casing simultaneously.
68. Fit the oil seal, using tool L177 with 550.
69. Press on the coupling flange.
70. Fit the washer.
71. Tighten up the self-locking nut to a torque loading of 80 to 130 lbf ft (11·1 to 18·0 kgf m).
72. Position the spring and inner member of the uni-directional roller clutch into the cage.
73. Locate the spring so that the cage is spring loaded in an anti-clockwise direction when viewed from the front.
74. Place the assembly into tool L178, with the open side of the cage uppermost.
75. Move the clutch in a clockwise direction until all the rollers are in place.
76. Refit the bronze thrust washer in the recess in the annulus.
77. Transfer the uni-directional clutch assembly from the special assembly tool into its outer member up the annulus.
78. Position the oil thrower.
79. Secure with the circlip.
80. Check that the clutch rotates in an anti-clockwise direction only.

continued

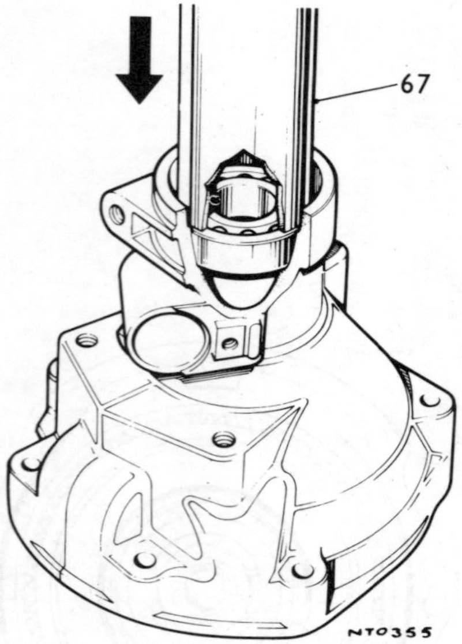

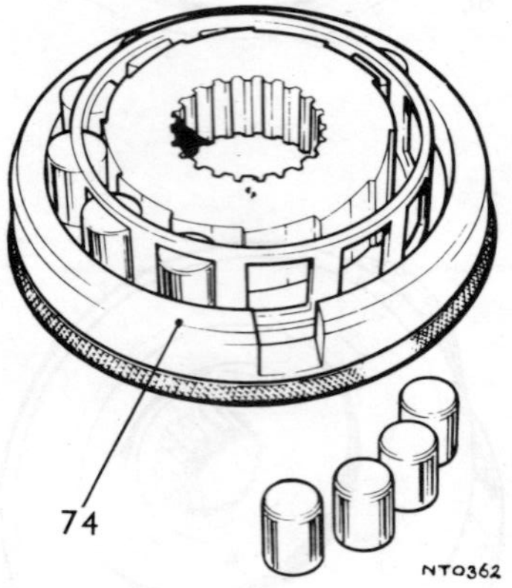

OVERDRIVE — J TYPE

81. Fit the ball race into its housing.
82. Secure the ball race with the large circlip.
83. Position this assembly onto the hub of the cone clutch.
84. Secure with a circlip.
85. Ensure that the circlip locates properly in the groove.
86. Insert the sun wheel into the hub.
87. Fit the circlip on the sun wheel extension.
88. Lightly smear the operating pistons with oil.
89. Fit the pistons into their respective housings.
90. Refit the solenoid control valve. 40.10.08.
91. Refit the pressure filter. 40.22.09.
92. Refit the oil pump assembly. 40.18.01.
93. Refit the pump non-return valve assembly. 40.16.10.
94. Refit the relief valve assembly. 40.16.04.

continued

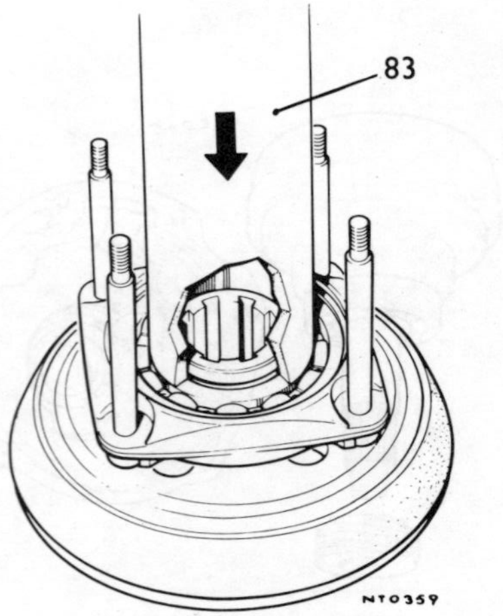

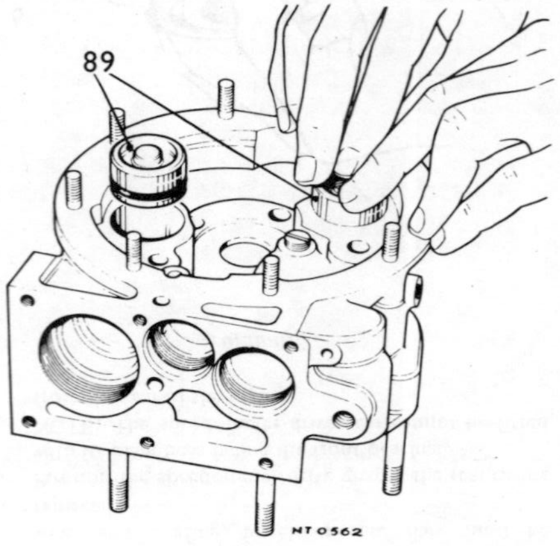

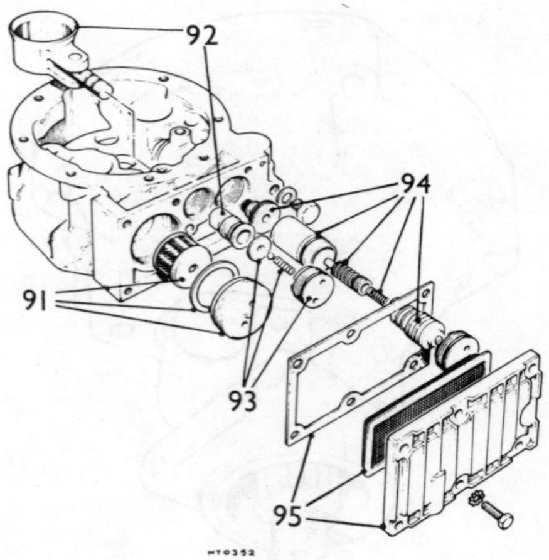

OVERDRIVE — J TYPE

95. Refit the sump and suction filter. 40.10.01.
96. Mount the rear casing assembly vertically in a vice.
97. Insert the planet carrier assembly.
    NOTE: The gears can be meshed in any postion.
98. Place the sliding member assembly complete with the clutch return springs onto the cone of the annulus.
99. Engage the sun wheel with the planet gears.
100. Apply Wellseal to new gaskets either side of the brake ring.
     NOTE: These gaskets are different.
101. Fit the brake ring onto its spigot in the tail casing, aligning the stud holes.
102. Position the main casing assembly over the thrust housing pins, at the same time entering the studs in the brake ring.
103. Fit and progressively tighten the six nuts securing the rear and main case assemblies to a torque setting of 13 to 15 lbf ft (1·8 to 2·1 kgf m).
104. Apply Wellseal to the two copper washers and threads of the two top studs.
105. Secure the earth lead to the stud above the solenoid aperture.
106. The clutch return spring pressure will be felt as the two casings go together.
107. Fit the two bridge pieces.
108. Secure with four new self-locking nuts to a torque setting of 6 to 8 lbf ft (0·8 to 1·1 kgf m).

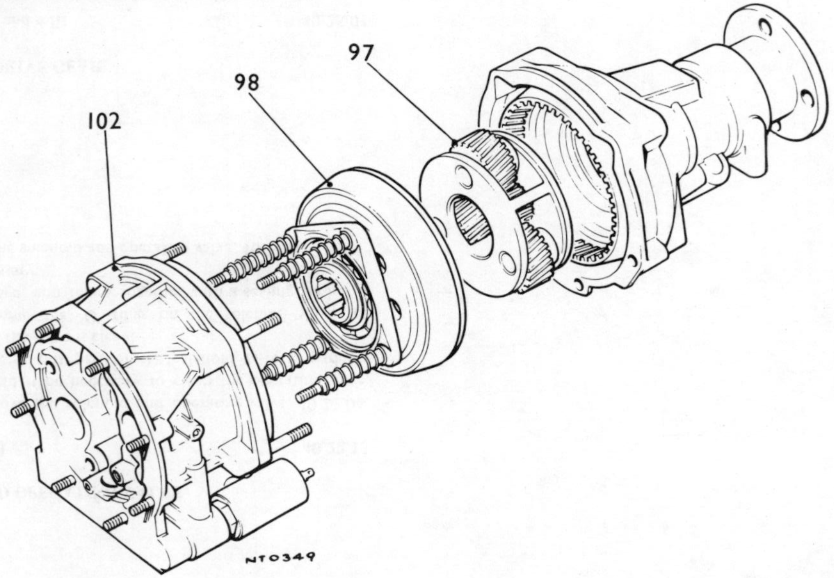

40.20.10J Sheet 6

SOLENOID

— Test 40.22.01

1. Connect the solenoid in series with a 12-volt battery and ammeter.
2. The solenoid should draw approximately 2 amps.
3. Check that the plunger in the valve moves forward when the solenoid is energized.
4. Check that the plunger in the valve returns to its direct drive position by spring pressure when the solenoid is de-energized.
   NOTE: The solenoid does not operate with a loud click as the other types of overdrive.
5. If the solenoid is still faulty, the complete unit must be renewed.

SOLENOID OPERATING VALVE

— Remove and refit 40.22.04

Removing

1. Disconnect the negative battery lead.
2. Disconnect the two Lucar connectors from the solenoid.
3. Using a 1 in (25 mm) A.F. open-ended spanner on the hexagon, loosen and unscrew the solenoid.
   NOTE: Do not attempt to remove the solenoid by gripping the cylindrical body as this is very easily damaged.

Refitting

4. Screw the solenoid into the casing.
5. Tighten with a spanner.
6. Connect Lucar connectors to the terminals, these can be connected either way round.
7. Connect the negative lead of the battery.

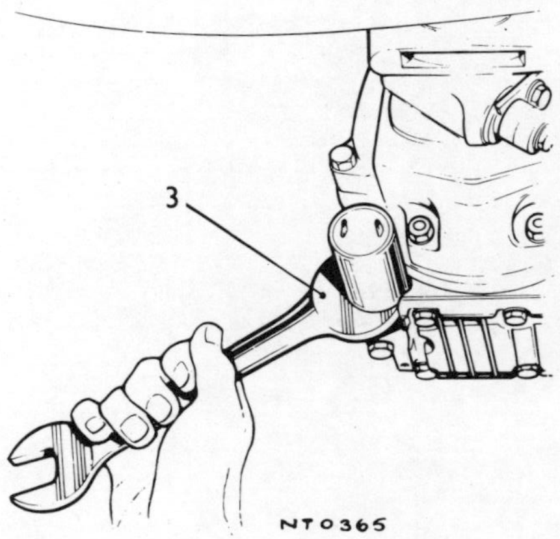

40.22.01J
40.22.04J

OVERDRIVE — J TYPE

SOLENOID OPERATING VALVE

— Overhaul   40.22.13

1. Remove the solenoid and operating valve. 40.22.04.
2. Should it be necessary to clean the operating valve, immerse this part of the solenoid valve in paraffin until the valve is clean.
3. Examine the 'O' rings on the solenoid valve for damage, and renew together with a sealing washer if necessary.
4. Fit the solenoid and operating valve. 40.22.04

SPEEDO DRIVE GEAR

— Remove and refit   40.25.01

Removing
1. Working from under the car, remove the locking plate screw.
2. Remove the drive pinion and holder.

Refitting
3. Refit the drive gear, ensuring that the drive gear meshes with the driven gear.
4. Refit the locking plate and screw.
5. Top up any oil lost.

40.22.13J
40.25.01J

Triumph Spitfire Mk IV Manual Part No. 545254

PROPELLER AND DRIVE SHAFT

PROPELLER AND DRIVE SHAFT OPERATIONS

Propeller shaft — remove and refit	47.15.01
Rear drive shaft — remove and refit	47.10.01
Rear drive shaft and hub bearings — remove and refit	47.10.18
Rear drive shaft trunnion bushes — remove and refit	47.10.19
Universal joint — overhaul	47.15.18

REAR DRIVE SHAFT

— Remove and refit   **47.10.01**

Rear drive shaft and hub bearings — remove and refit   **47.10.18**

Special tools S109C, S4221A, S4221A-14, S300A.

Removing

1. Jack up the rear of the car, support it on chassis stands and remove the road wheel.
2. Disconnect the flexible brake hose from the chassis bracket and pipe union and wheel cylinder.
3. Disconnect the hand brake cable from the brake back plate lever and release the return spring.
4. Using a jack under the vertical link to relieve the damper load, remove the bolt securing the radius arm to the vertical link bracket. 64.35.28. 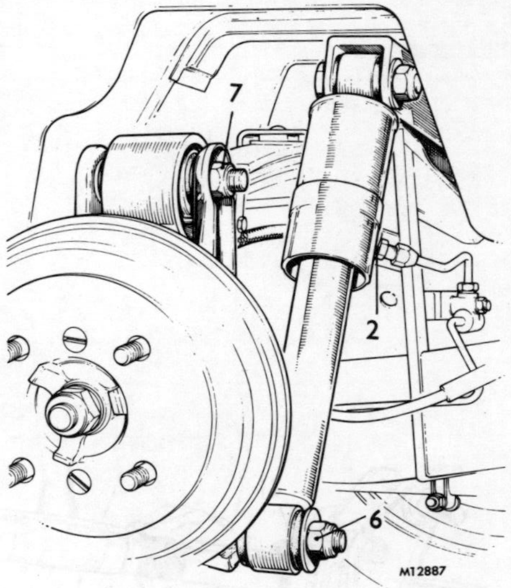
5. Remove the four bolts and nyloc nuts securing the drive shaft universal joint to the inner drive shaft flange.
6. Remove the nyloc nut and washer securing the damper lower attachment to the vertical link and pull the damper clear of its mounting pin.
7. Remove the jack from beneath the vertical link and whilst supporting the brake drum by hand, remove the nut and bolt securing the road spring to the vertical link.
8. Withdraw the drive shaft from the chassis together with the brake, hub and vertical link assembly.

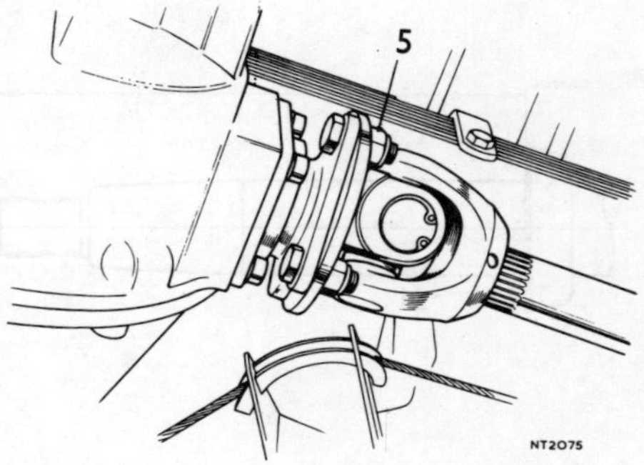

PROPELLER AND DRIVE SHAFT

9. Hold the assembly in a vice and remove the brake drum and the hub nut.
10. Using special tool S109C withdraw the hub and key.
11. Remove the nyloc nut and withdraw the bolt securing the trunnion to the vertical link assembly and separate the trunnion from the vertical link.
12. Bend back the lock tabs and remove the four bolts securing the grease trap and brake back plate to the hub bearing housing and remove:
    a. The grease trap.
    b. The back plate.
    c. The seal housing complete with seal.
    d. The joint washer.
13. Using special tool S4221A with adaptor S4221A-14, press the drive shaft from the hub bearing housing. The flinger may be left in position if it is not damaged and is a satisfactory tight fit on the shaft.
14. From the hub bearing housing press or drift out the inner oil seal and needle roller bearing.

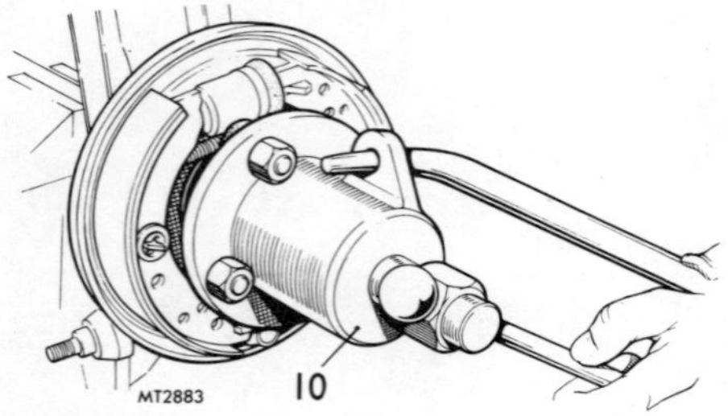

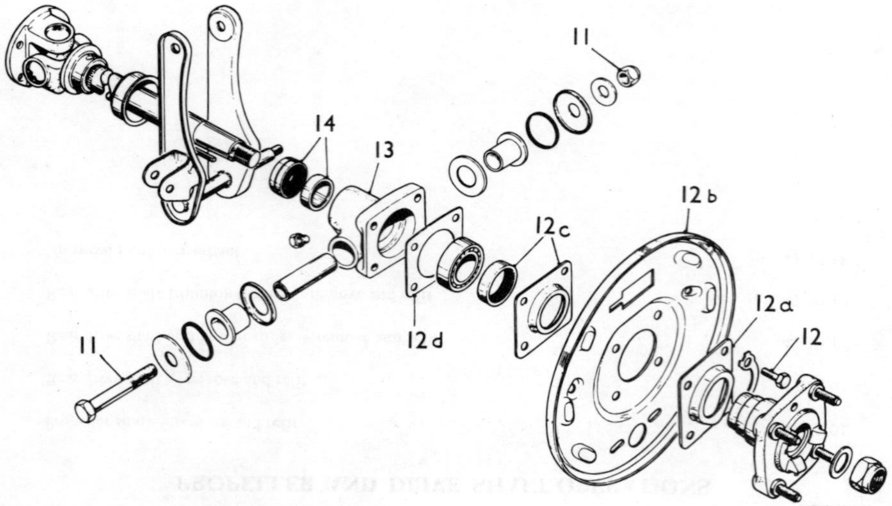

PROPELLER AND DRIVE SHAFT

Refitting

15. Press the needle roller bearing (lettered end trailing) into the hub bearing housing to a depth of 0·5 in (12·7 mm) from the housing face using special tool No. S300A.
16. Drift the inner oil seal into the housing with the sealing lips trailing. 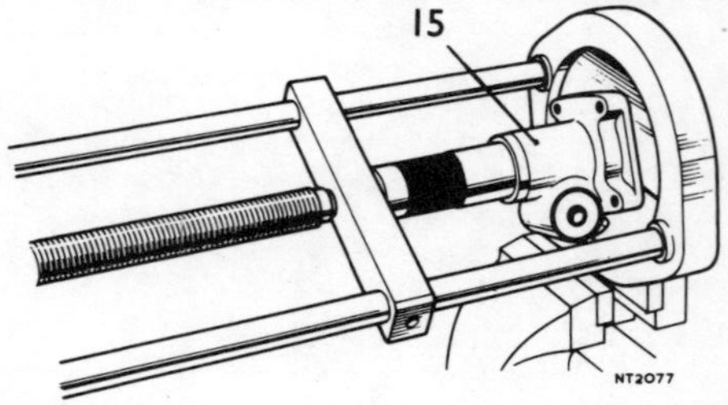
17. If previously removed, drive the flinger on to the axle shaft with a suitable tool to a position 5·740 to 5·760 in (145·8 to 146·3 mm) from the end of the shaft indicated by dimension A.
18. Pack the needle rollers with grease and fit the housing to the axle shaft taking care not to damage the oil seal and needle rollers. 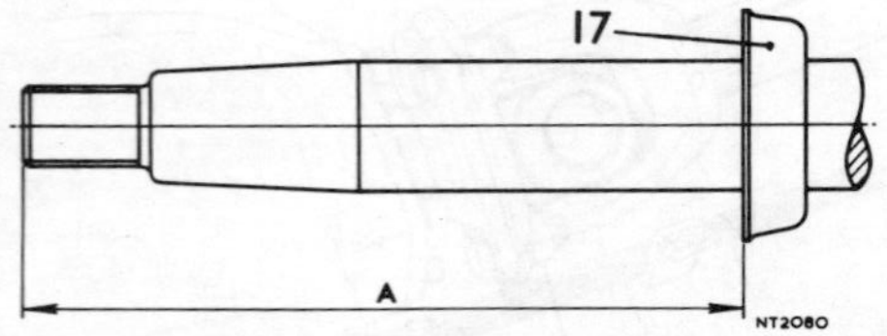
19. Hold the axle shaft in the soft jaws of a vice, pack the bearing housing and ball race with grease and drift the ball race on to the shaft, using special tool No. S304.

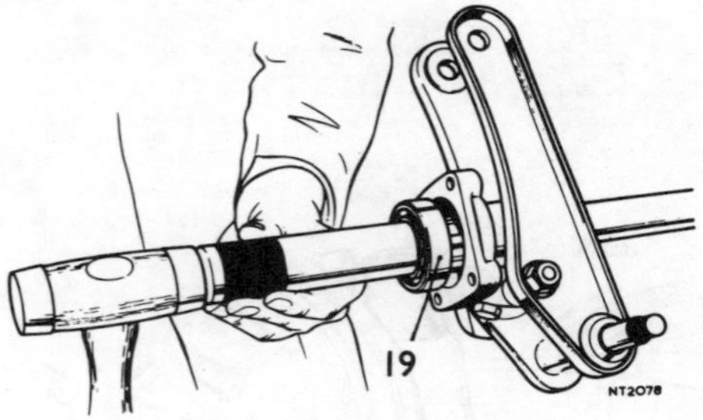

PROPELLER AND DRIVE SHAFT

20. Press the outer oil seal into the seal housing with the sealing lip trailing i.e. lip facing towards the bearing.
21. Smear a new paper joint with grease and place it in position on the bearing housing face.
22. Assemble tie seal housing together with the brake back plate and grease trap and secure to the bearing housing with new lock plates and the four bolts. Ensure that the following is observed:
    a. The back plate is fitted with the wheel cylinder at the top.
    b. The grease trap is fitted with the duct at the bottom.
23. Insert the key into the key-way and check that the taper on the axle shaft and in the hub is clean and free from burrs. Fit the hub and secure with a plain washer and a new nyloc nut and tighten to 90 to 120 lb ft. (12·4 to 16·6 kgf m).
24. Offer up the vertical link and drive shaft assembly with the special trunnion and drive shaft assembly with the special bolt and a new nyloc nut tightening to 38 to 48 lbf ft. (5·2 to 6·6 kgf m). (Nut to the rear).
25. Fit the vertical link and drive shaft assembly to the road spring eye leaving the securing nyloc nut and bolt slack at this stage (nut to the rear).
26. Jack up the assembly under the vertical link and secure the damper to its lower attachment pin with a new nyloc nut and tighten to 28 to 38 lbf. ft (3·9 to 5·2 kgf. m).
27. Attach the radius arm to the vertical link and tighten to 24 to 32 lbf. ft (3·3 to 4·4 kgf m), 64.35.28.
28. Fit the axle shaft universal coupling to the final drive inner axle shaft flange and secure with bolts and new nyloc nuts. Remove the supporting jack.
29. Fit the handbrake cable to the brake back plate lever and reconnect the return spring.
30. Fit the brake drum and reconnect the flexible hose to the chassis bracket and pipe union and to the wheel cylinder.
31. Bleed the hydraulic brake system 70.25.02.
32. Fit the road wheel and remove the car from the chassis stand.
33. Roll the car to settle the suspension and finally tighten the spring eye bolt to 38 to 48 lbf. ft (5·2 to 6·6 kgf. m).

47.10.01 Sheet 4
47.10.18 Sheet 4

PROPELLER AND DRIVE SHAFT

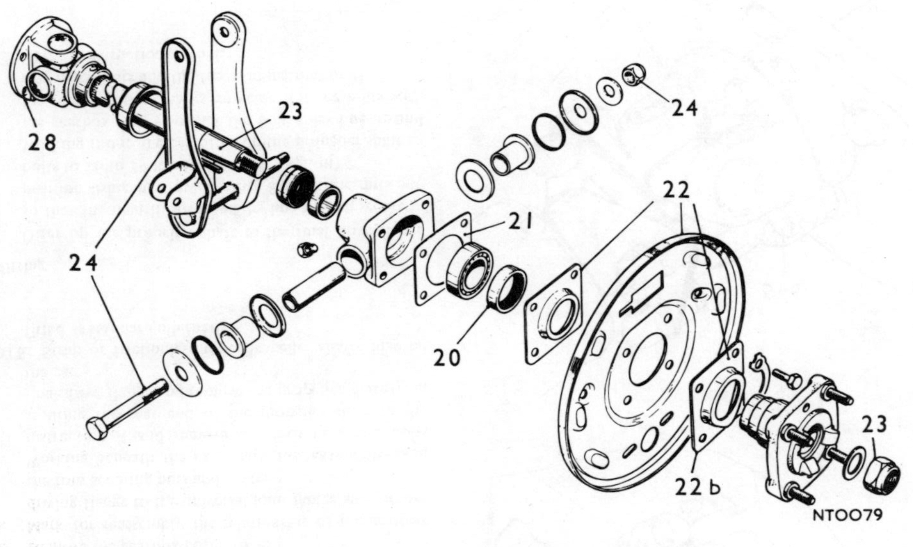

REAR DRIVE SHAFT TRUNNION BUSHES 47.10.19

— Remove and refit

Removing

1. Jack up the rear of the car and remove the road wheel.
2. Jack up under the vertical link to relieve the damper load and disconnect the damper from its lower attachment.
3. Disconnect the radius rod from the vertical link.
4. Lower the jack under the vertical link.
5. Remove the special trunnion nut and bolt.
6. Push the vertical link assembly towards the final drive unit to expose the trunnion and remove the following:
    a. two outer shims
    b. two rubber seals
    c. one distance tube
    d. two nylon bushes
    e. two inner shims

Refitting

7. Assemble the components to the trunnion in the following order:
    a. Fit the two inner shims (smaller diameter)
    b. Press in the two nylon bushes
    c. Fill the space between the two nylon bushes with grease
    d. Fit the rubber seals
    e. Fit the distance tube
    f. Fit the outer shims (larger diameter)
8. Pull the vertical link assembly back into its correct position and secure the trunnion assembly to the vertical link with the special bolt and nyloc nut.
9. Jack up under the vertical link and reconnect the damper to its lower attachment pin on the vertical link.
10. Reconnect the radius rod to the vertical link and lower the jack under the vertical link.
11. Refit the road wheel and lower the jack.
12. Remove the lubrication plug and grease the hub — see maintenance section.

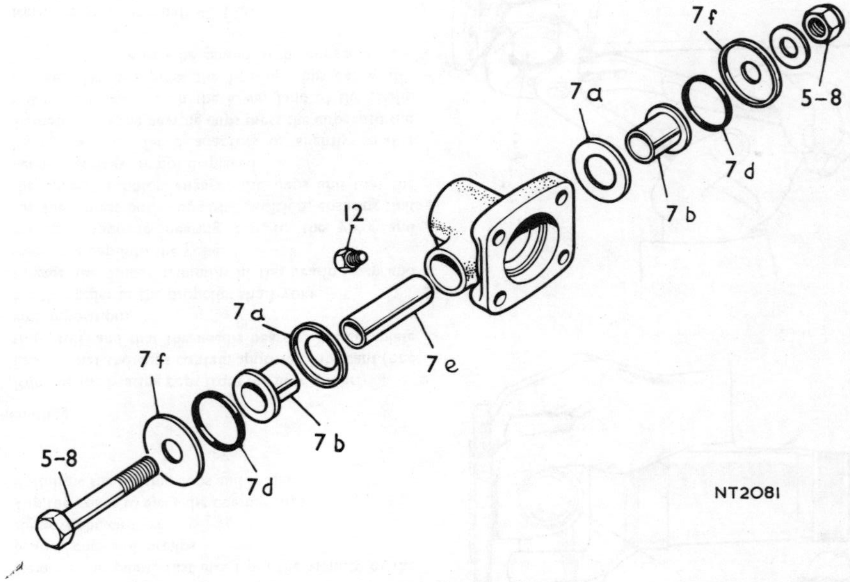

47.10.19

PROPELLER AND DRIVE SHAFT

PROPELLER SHAFT 47.15.01

— Remove and refit

Removing

1. Place the car on a ramp or over a pit.
2. Remove the fascia support bracket 76.46.09.
3. Remove the gearbox cover 76.25.07.
4. Mark for reassembly the relationship of the gearbox driving flange to the universal joint flange and remove the four securing nuts and bolts.
5. Working beneath the car, mark for reassembly as in instruction 4 and remove the four nuts and bolts securing the rear end of the propeller shaft to the final drive flange and remove the propeller shaft from the car.

NOTE: Strap or frictionless type propeller shafts may be fitted as standard alternatives.

Refitting

6. Offer up the propeller shaft to the final drive flange so that the identification marks line up and secure in position using new nyloc nuts. Tighten the nuts and bolts to 26 to 34 lbf. ft (3·6 to 4·7 kgf. m).
7. Working inside the car offer up the propeller shaft to the gearbox flange so that the bolt holes line up and the identification marks coincide. Fit the bolts with new nyloc nuts and tighten as in instruction 6.
8. Reverse instructions 1 to 3.

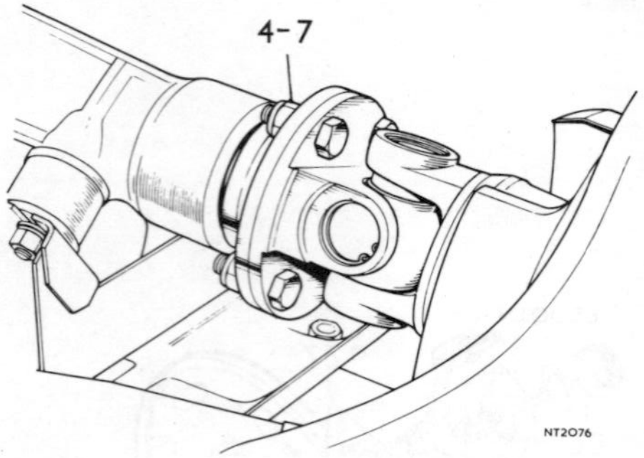

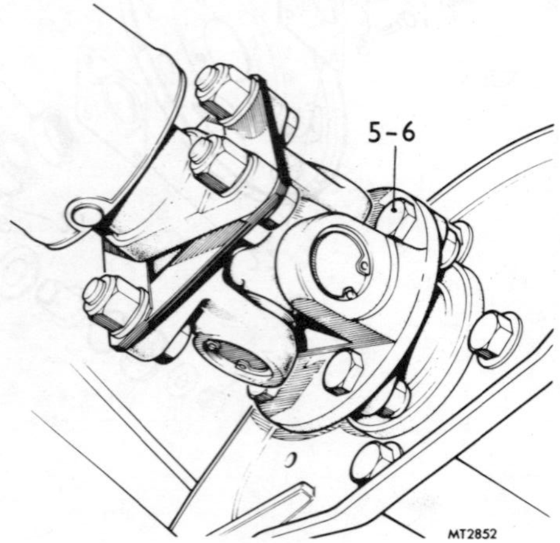

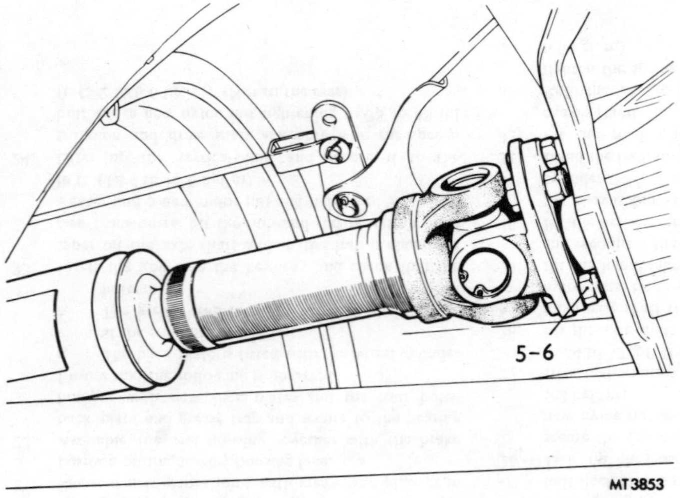

UNIVERSAL JOINT 47.15.18

— Overhaul

Dismantling

1. Remove the propeller shaft 47.15.01.
2. Remove the paint, rust etc. from the vicinity of the bearing cups and circlips.
3. Remove the circlips.
4. Tap the yokes to eject the bearing cups.
5. Withdraw the bearing cups and spider.

Reassembling

6. Remove the bearing cups from the new spider.
7. Ensure that the cups contain approved lubricant (one third full) and that the needle bearings are complete and in position.
8. Fit the spider to the propeller shaft yoke.
9. Engage the spider trunnion in the bearing cup and insert the cup into the yoke.
10. Fit the opposite bearing cup to the yoke and carefully press both cups into position, ensuring that the spider trunnion engages the cups and that the needle bearings are not displaced.
11. Using two flat faced adaptors of slightly smaller diameter than the bearing cups press the cups into the yokes until they reach the lower land of the circlip grooves. Do not press the bearing cups below this point or damage may be caused to the cups and seals.
12. Fit the circlips.
13. Refit the propeller shaft 47.15.01.

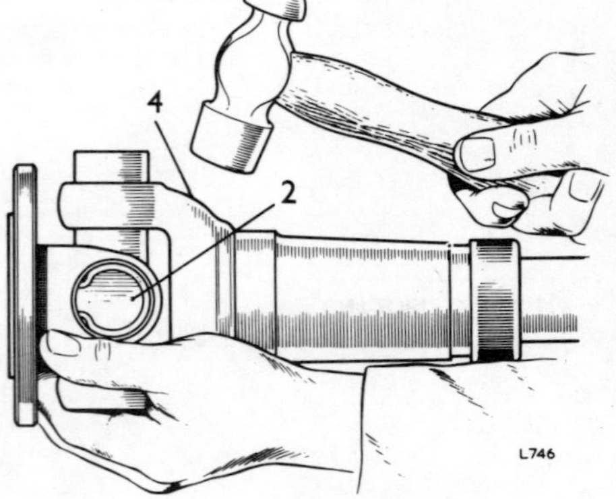

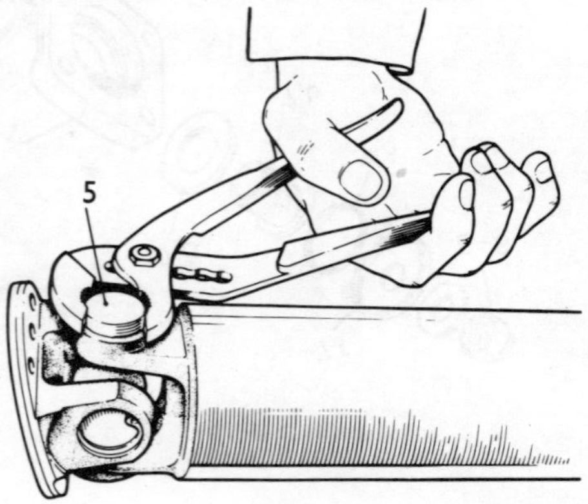

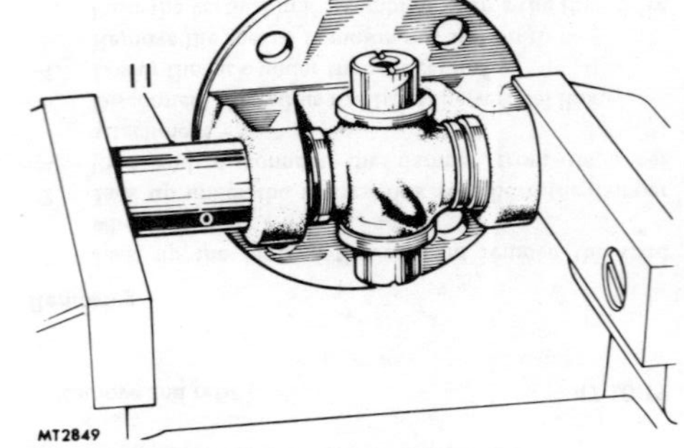

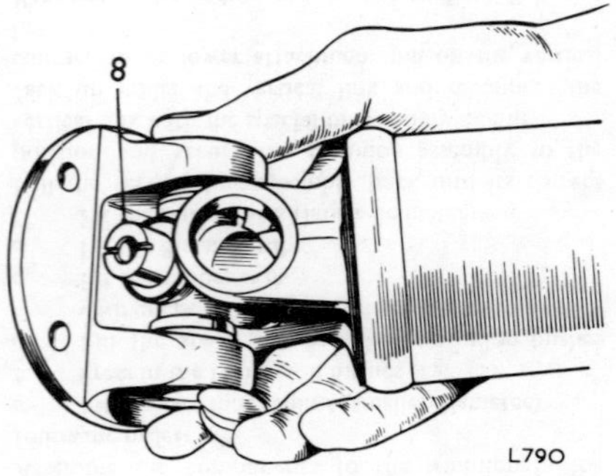

FINAL DRIVE OPERATIONS

Differential assembly – remove and refit	51.15.01
Differential assembly – overhaul	51.15.07
Final drive mounting plate rubbers – remove and refit	51.25.34
Final drive mounting plate – remove and refit	51.25.33
Final drive unit – remove and refit	51.25.13
Inner drive shaft bearing – remove and refit	51.10.04
Inner drive shaft oil seal – remove and refit	51.10.05
Pinion oil seal – remove and refit	51.20.01

FINAL DRIVE

INNER DRIVE SHAFT BEARING

— Remove and refit 51.10.04
Inner drive shaft oil seal – remove and refit 51.10.05

Special tools S4221A and adaptor set S4221A-7B.

Removing

1. Remove the rear drive shaft assembly – instructions 1 to 8, 47.10.01.
2. Using a hexigon socket key remove the four socket headed screws securing the seal housing plate to the final drive casing. **NOTE**: if both shafts are being removed identify for reassembly.
3. Place a suitable receptacle under the drive shaft to catch the oil and withdraw the inner drive shaft complete with bearing and oil seal housing plate.
4. Remove the circlip locating the bearing.

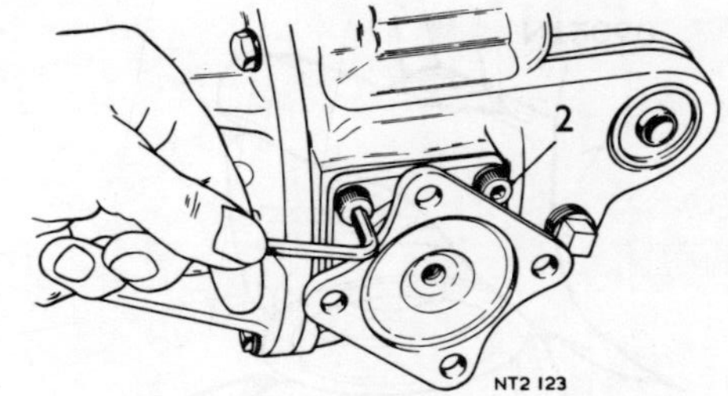

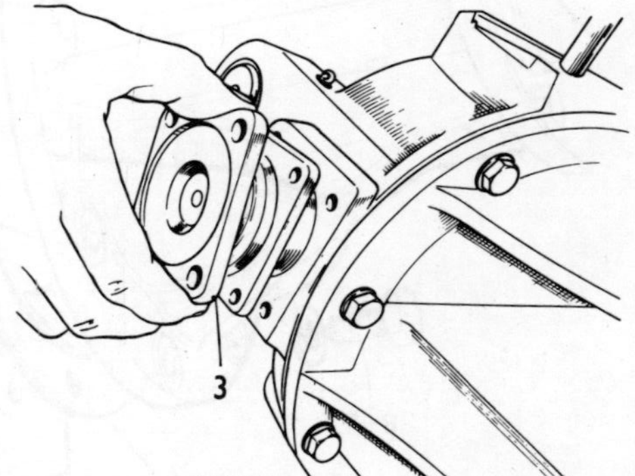

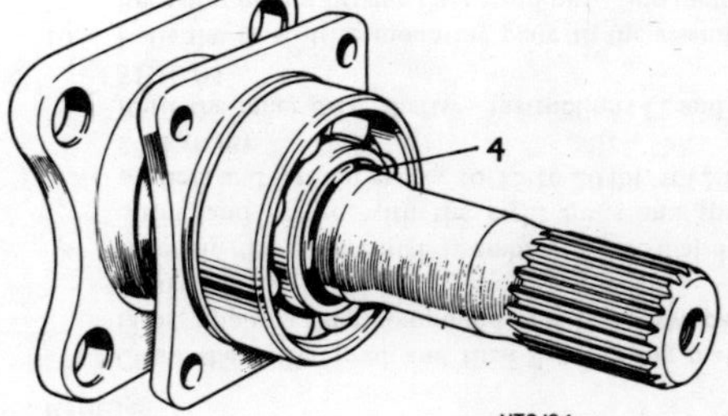

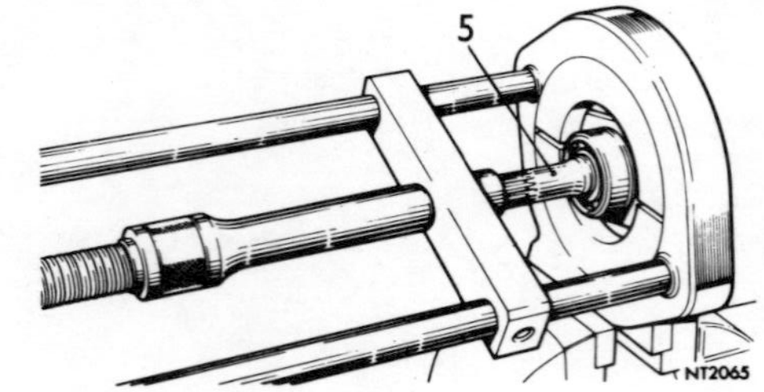

FINAL DRIVE

5. Using special tool S4221A and S4221A-7B remover, press the inner drive shaft from the bearing.
6. Remove the oil seal housing plate and drift out the oil seal.

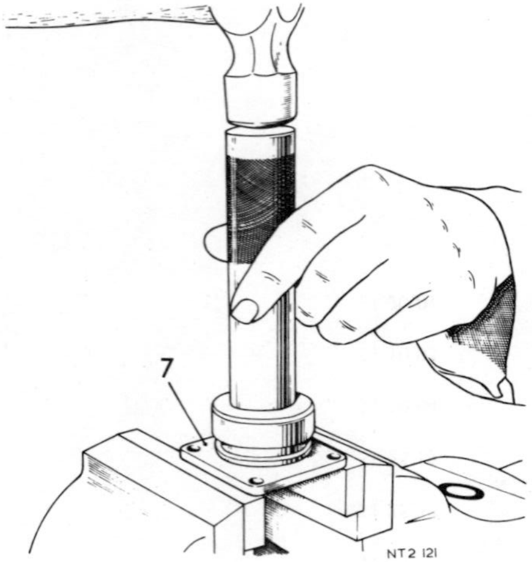

Refitting

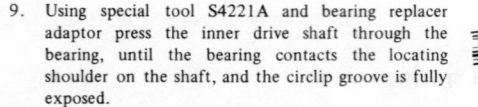

7. With the lip of the oil seal leading press or drift a seal into the housing plate.
8. With the sealing lip trailing assemble the housing plate to the inner drive shaft taking care not to damage the seal when passing it over the splines. 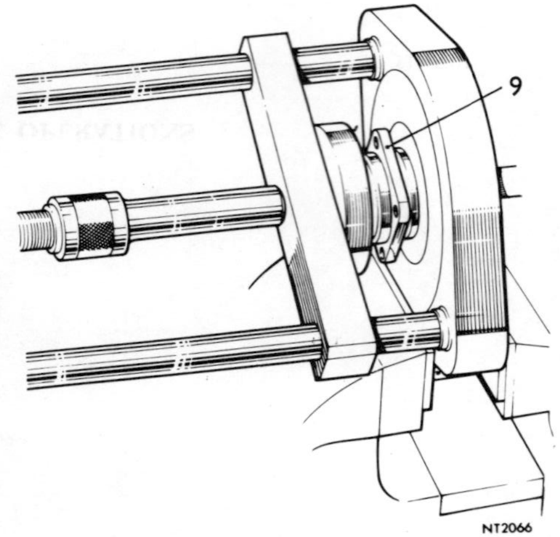
9. Using special tool S4221A and bearing replacer adaptor press the inner drive shaft through the bearing, until the bearing contacts the locating shoulder on the shaft, and the circlip groove is fully exposed.
10. Fit the circlip ensuring that it is properly located in the groove around its entire circumference.
11. Clean the housing plate mating faces and apply a sealing compound, clean and lubricate the shaft splines and insert the assembly into the final drive casing. Oscillate the drive shaft to enable the splines to locate in the internal splines of the sun gear before finally pushing the assembly home.
12. Secure the assembly to the final drive casing with four socket headed screws and washers.
13. Refit the rear drive shaft assembly 47.10.01.
14. Refil the final drive unit with a recommended E.P. oil — see maintenance.

51.10.04 Sheet 2
51.10.05 Sheet 2

FINAL DRIVE

DIFFERENTIAL ASSEMBLY

— Remove and refit   51.15.01

Removing

1. Remove the final drive unit from the car 51.25.13.
2. Clean and degrease the unit.
3. Identify for reassembly and remove the inner drive shafts — instructions 2 and 3, 51.10.04.
4. Remove the pinion nut and driving flange — instructions 4 and 5, 51.20.01.
5. Remove the four drive mounting plate to the differential housing and remove the plate 51.25.33
6. Remove the eight bolts and spring washers securing the differential housing to the final drive casing and withdraw the differential assembly.

Refitting

7. Clean the differential and final drive casing mating faces, apply sealing compound and fit a new paper gasket.
8. Offer up the differential assembly to the final drive casing and secure with the eight bolts and spring washers and tighten evenly to 15 to 20 lbf. ft (2·1 to 2·8 kgf. m).
9. Refit the inner drive shafts — instructions 12 and 13, 51.10.04.
10. Refit the final drive mounting plate to the assembly, 51.10.04.
11. Refit the pinion driving flange and nut — instructions 8 and 9, 51.20.01.
12. Fit the final drive unit to the car — 51.15.01 and refil the unit with a recommended grade of E.P. oil.

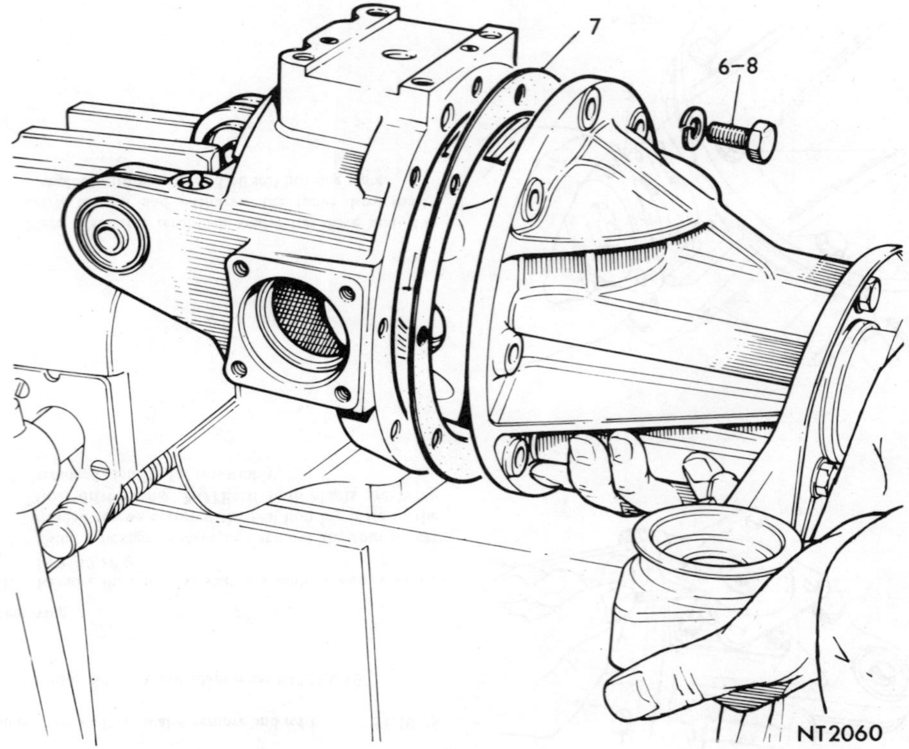

51.15.01 Sheet 1

FINAL DRIVE

DIFFERENTIAL ASSEMBLY

— Overhaul

51.15.07

Service tools: S101, S101-1, S4221A, S4221A-8C, S4221A-17, S337 (or RG 421), 18G 134, 18G 134 DH, 18G 191, 18G 191 M.

Dismantling

1. Remove the differential assembly, 51.15.01.
2. Place the unit upright in a vice and mark one bearing cap and adjacent side of the differential carrier to ensure the bearing caps are refitted in their original positions.
3. Remove the bearing cap retaining bolts and spring washers and remove the bearing caps. 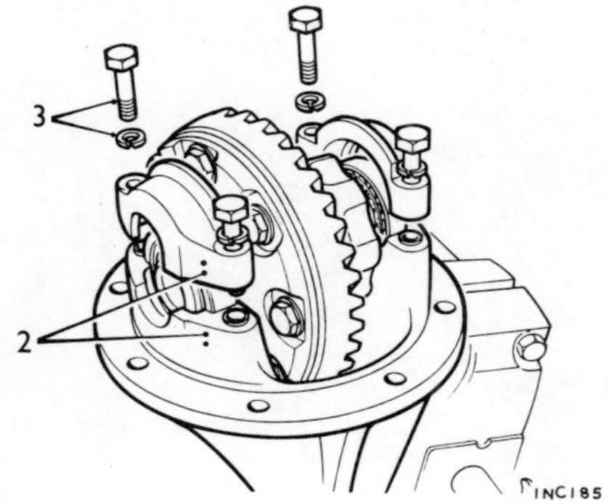
4. Assemble the spreader S101 and adaptor S101-1 to the casing.
5. Stretch the unit case by tightening the turnbuckle three to four flats until the differential carrier can be levered out and the bearing shims and caps removed.

   IMPORTANT: To avoid damaging the case, do not spread any more than is necessary. Each flat on the turnbuckle is numbered to provide a check on the amount turned. The maximum stretch is 0·008 in (0·20 mm). Do not lever against the stretcher.

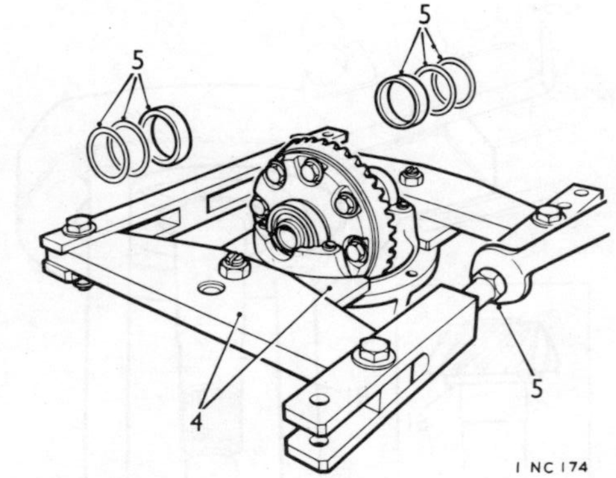

6. Remove the gear carrier bearing cups, using 18G 47 C and 18G 47 BD.

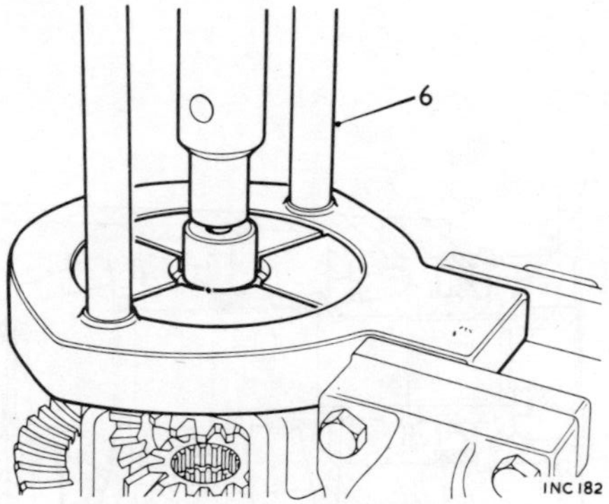

continued

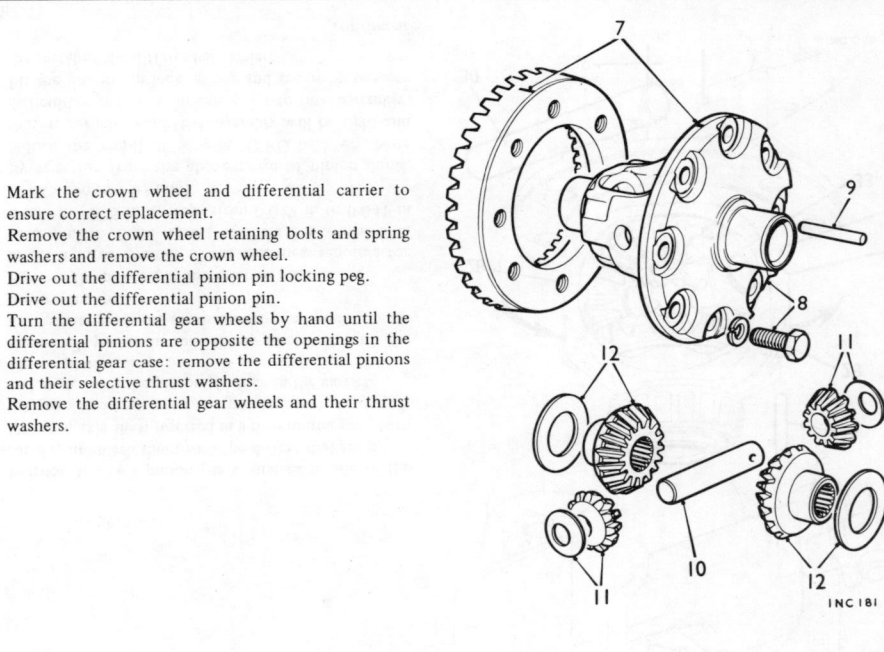

7. Mark the crown wheel and differential carrier to ensure correct replacement.
8. Remove the crown wheel retaining bolts and spring washers and remove the crown wheel.
9. Drive out the differential pinion pin locking peg.
10. Drive out the differential pinion pin.
11. Turn the differential gear wheels by hand until the differential pinions are opposite the openings in the differential gear case: remove the differential pinions and their selective thrust washers.
12. Remove the differential gear wheels and their thrust washers.
13. Remove the drive flange nut split pin.
14. Restrain the drive flange, using RG421 or S337, and remove the drive flange nut.
15. Remove the drive flange.

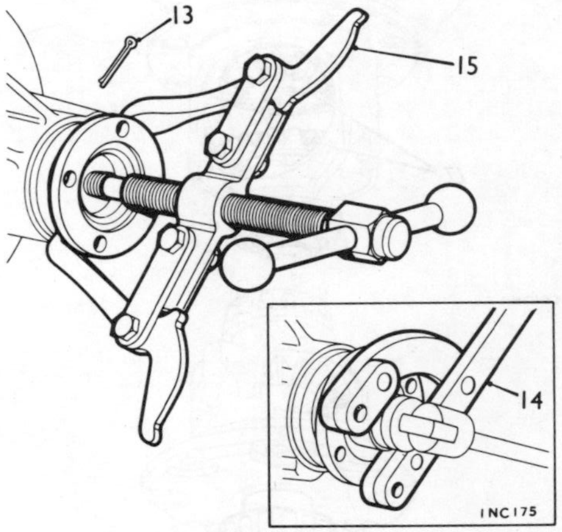

FINAL DRIVE

16. Press out the pinion.
17. Remove the pinion bearing shims and pinion bearing spacer.
18. Using S4221A and adaptor S4221A-17, remove the inner bearing from the pinion.
19. Remove the pinion head washer.
20. Drift out the pinion outer bearing cup, bearing and oil seal.
21. Drift out the pinion inner bearing cup.

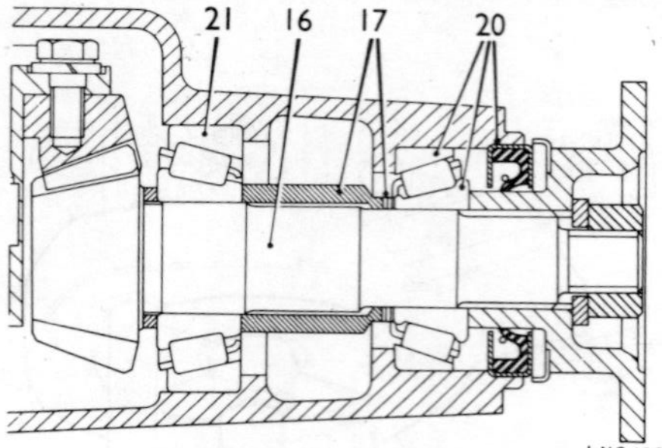

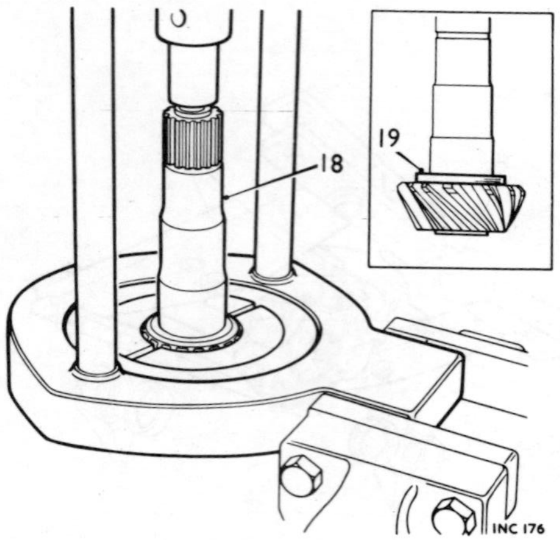

Inspection

22. Clean all components.
23. Renew all worn or damaged parts.
24. The crown wheel and pinion must only be replaced as a matched pair. The pair number is etched on the outer face of the crown wheel and the forward face of the pinion.
25. If one differential bearing is defective replace both differential bearings. If one pinion bearing is defective replace both pinion bearings.

continued

51.15.07 Sheet 3

Triumph Spitfire Mk IV Manual, Part No. 545254.

FINAL DRIVE

Reassembling

Setting the crown wheel position

26. Fit the differential bearing cones to the gear carrier, using 18G 134 and adaptor 18G 134 DH.
27. Fit the two differential gears to the carrier, ensuring each thrust washer is correctly positioned. 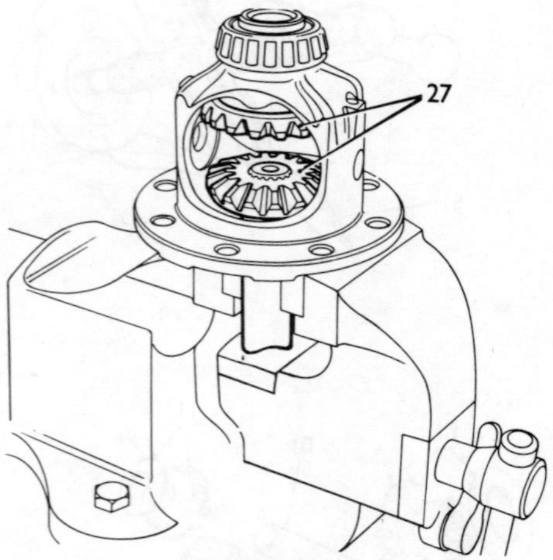
28. Position the two pinion gears, one each side of the carrier, and mesh them with the differential gears.
29. Using an axle shaft inserted in a differential gear, turn the gears and ensure the two pinions rotate into mesh and align awith the pinion pin hole in the carrier.
30. Fit the pinion pin.
31. Press each pinion in turn firmly into mesh with the differential gears and assess the required pinion thrust washer thickness.
32. Remove the pinion pin and the two pinions.
33. Select a thrust washer of the thickness required for each pinion. Eight thrust washers are available in 0·002 in (0·05 mm) steps from 0·027 in to 0·041 in (0·685 mm to 1·03 mm).
34. By selection from the above range of pinion shims, reduce the end-float to give ZERO backlash. Note that at zero backlash the assembly will be tight and difficult to rotate. Lubricate prior to final assembly.
35. Fit the pinion pin locking peg and secure by peening the metal of the differential carrier.

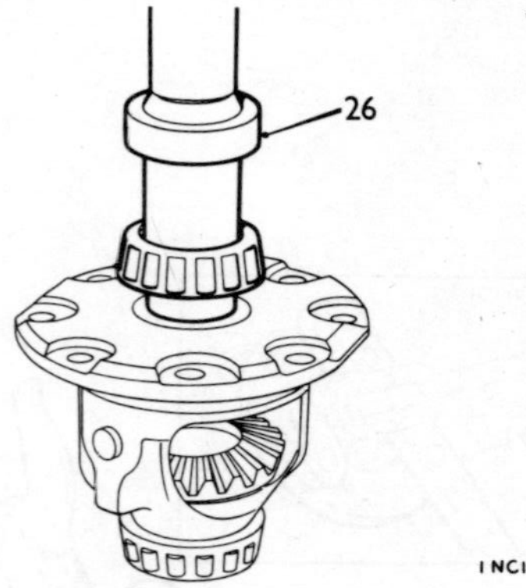

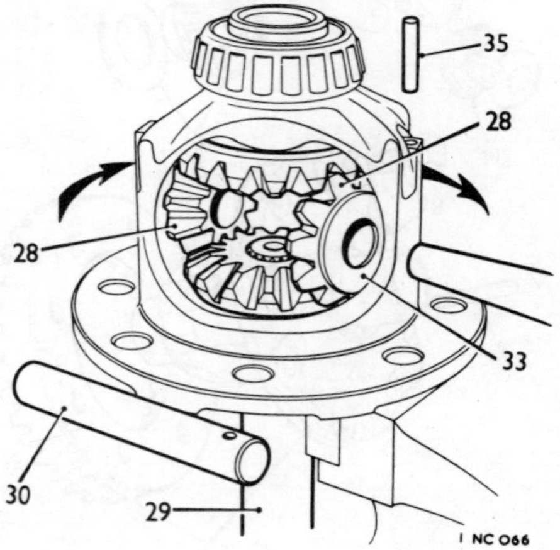

continued

51.15.07 Sheet 4

FINAL DRIVE

36. Clean the crown wheel mounting and gear carrier face and fit the crown wheel. Treat the bolts with loctite compound and fit bolts, together with spring washers.
37. Tighten the bolts.
38. Assemble the carrier bearing cups to the bearings and position the assembly in the case; do not fit the bearing shims.
39. Fit and secure the bearing caps as originally marked.
40. Using 18G 191 mounted on the axle spreader adaptor plate S101-1 with the plunger operating squarely on the rear of the crown wheel. Rotate the carrier and check the 'run-out'. Maximum 'run-out' must not exceed 0·003 in (0·076 mm).
41. Remove the bearing caps.
42. Press the differential bearings cups onto the bearings and move the carrier assembly to one side of the case. Zero the dial gauge and move the carrier assembly fully in the opposite direction. The indicated movement, which should be noted, is the **Total side-float** and is referred to as **Dimension 'A'**.
43. Remove the differential assembly from the case.

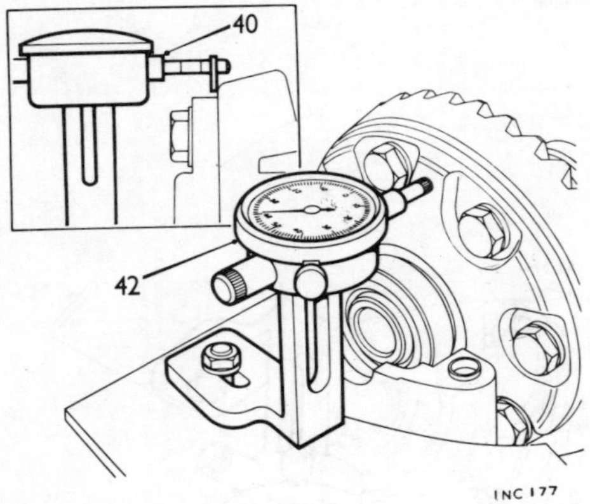

Setting the pinion position

44. Drift the pinion inner and outer bearing cups into the casing.
45. Fit the pinion inner bearing to the dummy pinion 18G 191 M.
 The standard pinion head spacer 0·077 in (1·95 mm) is incorporated in the dummy pinion.
46. Oil the bearings and fit the dummy pinion, outer bearing, tool spacer, washer and nut.

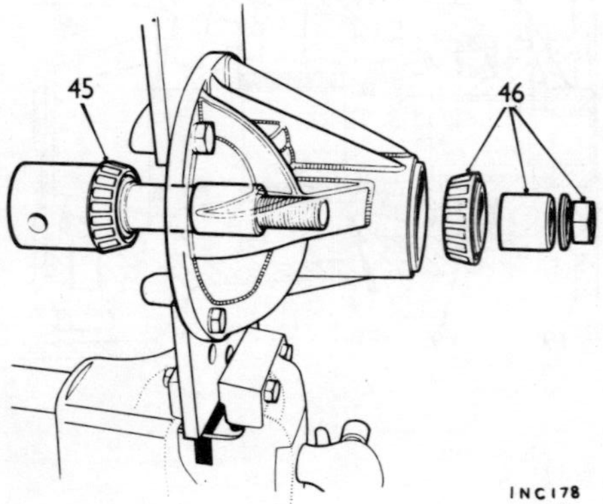

47. Tighten the nut gradually until a bearing pre-load of 15 to 18 lbf. in (0·17 to 0·21 kgf. m) is obtained. This can be measured using a lbf. in (kgf. m) scale torque wrench and suitable size socket.
48. Clean the dummy pinion head. Position the dial gauge foot of 18G 191 on the dummy head and zero the gauge onto the head.
49. Move the gauge foot over the centre of one differential bearing bore. Note the indicated measurement. Repeat for the opposite bearing bore.
 Add the two measurements figures and divide by two.
51. Twenty-two **pinion head washers** are available ranging in size from 0·075 to 0·096 in (1·91 to 2·44 mm).
52. Remove the dummy pinion 18G 191 M
53. Remove the inner bearing from the dummy pinion.

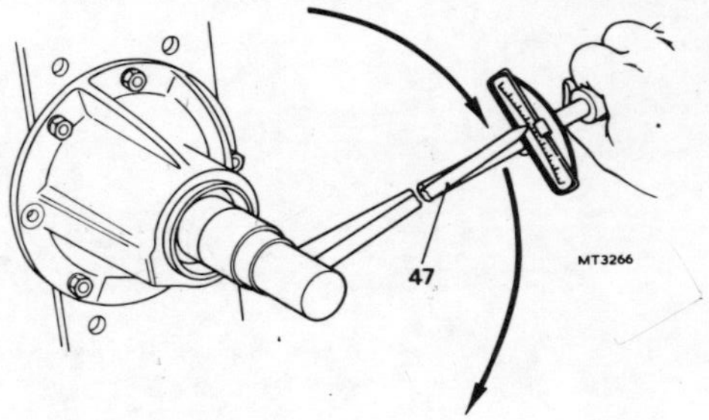

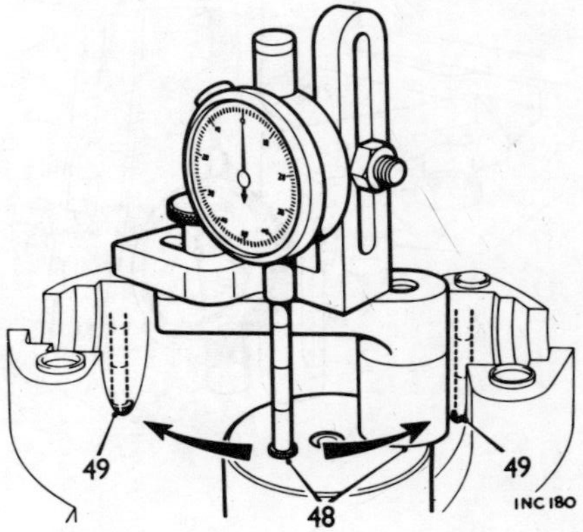

Calculating pinion head washer size

Example

Sum of each bore measurement divided by two	0·002 in	(0·05 mm)
Plus dummy pinion washer allowance from 18G 191 M	0·077 in	(1·95 mm)
Required size of pinion head washer	0.79 in	(2·00 mm)

NOTE: Whilst etched +, −, or 'N' markings will be found on the pinion face these should be ignored since they are taken into consideration in the design and method of using the dummy pinion.

FINAL DRIVE

Setting the pinion bearing pre-load

54. Fit the correct **pinion head washer** to the pinion.
55. Fit the inner bearing, using S4221A and adaptor S4221A-17.
56. Oil the bearing and fit the pinion to the casing.
57. Fit the bearing spacer, chamfered end towards the drive flange.
58. Fit the shims; oil and fit the outer bearing.
59. Fit the drive flange washer and nut.
60. Gradually tighten the nut, **do not exceed** 90 lbf. ft (12·4 kgf. m), checking the bearing pre-load during tightening operations.
61. Rotate the flange to settle the bearings, and check the pre-load using S98A. Pre-load should be set at 15 to 18 lbf. in (0·17 to 0·21 kgf. m) at 90 lbf. ft (12·4 kgf. m) torque on the flange nut.
    If the pre-load is high, decrease shim thickness.
    If the pre-load is low, increase shim thickness.
62. Four shims are available ranging in size from 0·003 to 0·030 in (0·076 to 0·762 mm). Note: 0·001 shim thickness equals approximately 4 lbf. in (0·046 kgf. m) pre-load.
63. Remove the drive flange nut washer and flange nut.
64. Soak the new oil seal in oil for **one hour** and fit the seal.
65. Fit the drive flange, washer and flange nut.
66. Tighten the drive flange nut to 90 lbf. ft (12·4 kgf. m) using RG421 or S337 to retain the flange.
67. Lock the nut, using a new split pin.

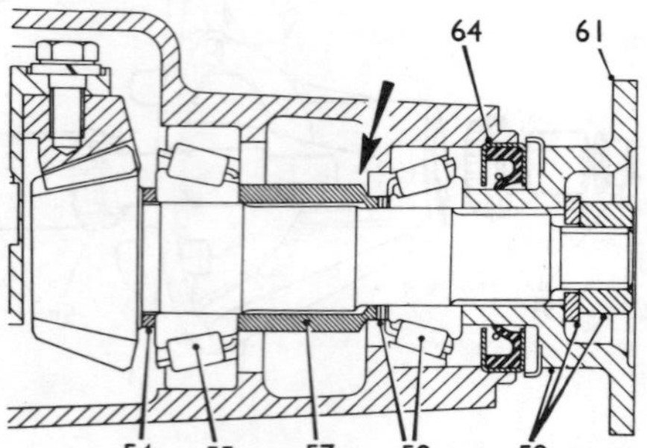

Setting the backlash

68. Place the bearing cups on the differential bearings and fit the differential carrier in the case.
69. Position dial gauge 18G 191 on the axle spreader adaptor plate S101-1, crown wheel side.
70. Move the crown wheel fully into mesh with the pinion and zero the gauge on the rear of the crown wheel.
71. Move the crown wheel and carrier in the opposite direction until the bearing crown-wheel-side is butted in its housing. The indicated measurement, which should be noted, is the 'IN-OUT' of mesh clearance.

continued

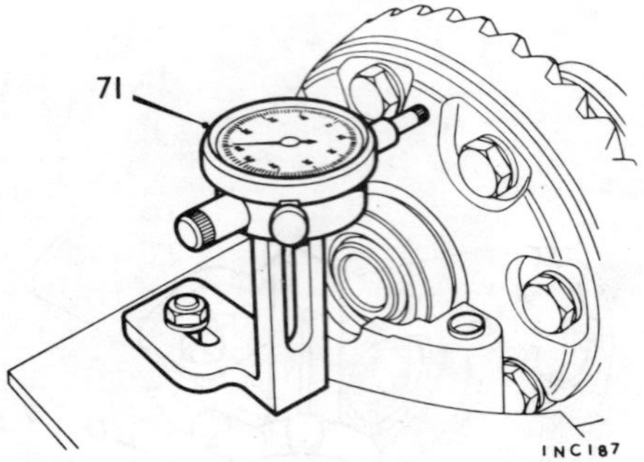

Setting the crown wheel backlash

In-Out of mesh clearance (from operation 71)	0·025 in	(0·63 mm)
Minus backlash (see DATA)	0·005 in	(0·13 mm)
Required crown wheel side shim pack	**0·020 in**	**(0·50 mm)**

Total side-float (dimension 'A', operation 42)	0·060 in	(1·52 mm)
Minus crown wheel side shim pack	0·020 in	(0·50 mm)
Required shim pack opposite crown wheel	**0·040 in**	**(1·02 mm)**

* Pre-load: add **0·002 in (0·051 mm)** to each shim pack calculated above.

72. Fit S101 and S101-1, and stretch the unit case by tightening the turnbuckle three or four flats.
73. From the calculations made in 76 and 77, select the required shim pack from those available: 0·003 in (0·0762 mm), 0·005 in (0·127 mm), 0·010 in (0·25 mm), 0·20 in (0·50 mm).
74. Fit the differential assembly to the case and fit the shim packs. Slacken S101 and remove.
75. Refit the bearing caps as originally marked, and secure using the bolts and spring washers.
76. Rotate the pinion to settle the differential bearings. Position dial gauge service tool 18G 191 on the adaptor plate and position the foot on the crown wheel gear. Measure the total backlash at several positions, which must be 0·004 to 0·006 in (0·10 to 0·15 mm).
NOTE: A movement of 0·002 in (0·05 mm) shim thickness from one differential bearing to the other will vary the backlash by approximately 0·002 in (0·05 mm).
77. Tighten the bearing cap bolts.
78. Remove S101-1.
79. Refit the differential assembly - 51.15.01.

continued

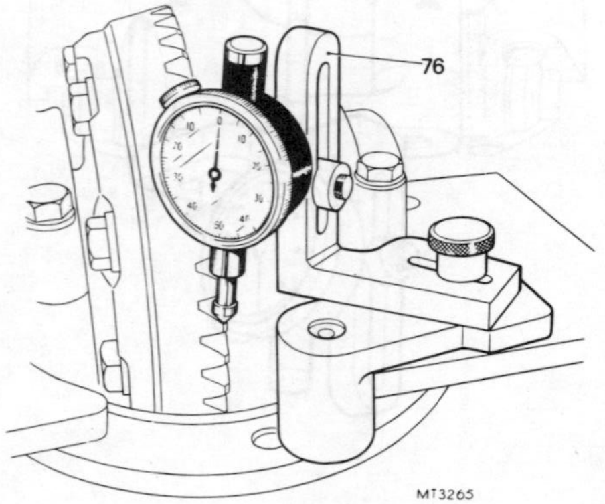

FINAL DRIVE

DATA

Differential bearing shims . . . . . . 0·003 in (0·076 mm)
0·005 in (0·127 mm)
0·010 in (0·254 mm)
0·020 in (0·508 mm)

Differential case, maximum stretch . . . 0·008 in (0·20 mm)

Differential pinion gears thrust washer Sizes . . . . 8, in 0·002 in (0·05 mm) steps

0·035 in (0·889 mm)
0·027 in (0·685 mm)
0·029 in (0·737 mm)
0·031 om (0·787 mm)
0·033 in (0·838 mm)

Crown wheel run-out . . . . . . Max. 0·003 in (0·076 mm) 0·004 to 0·006 in (0·102 to
0·152 mm)

Optimum setting . . . . 0·005 in (0·127 mm)

Pinion bearing pre-load . . . . . 15 to 18 lbf. in (0·17 to 0·21 kgf. m)

Pinion head washer sizes:
STD: . . . . 0·077 in (1·956 mm)

Alternatives:
0·075 in (1·905 mm)
0·0765 in (1·930 mm)
0·078 in (1·981 mm)
0·079 in (2·007 mm)
0·0795 in (2·019 mm)
0·080 in (2·032 mm)
0·081 in (2·057 mm)

Pinion bearing shims sizes . . . . 0·082 in (2·083 mm)
0·0825 in (2·095 mm)
0·083 in (2·108 mm)
0·084 in (2·134 mm)
0·085 in (2·159 mm)
0·0855 in (2·171 mm)
0·086 in (2·184 mm)

0·087 in (2·210 mm)
0·0885 in (2·247 ,,)
0·090 in (2·286 mm)
0·0915 in (2·323 mm)
0·0935 in (2·337 mm)
0·0945 in (2·400 mm)
0·096 in (2·438 mm)

51.15.07 Sheet 9

Triumph Spitfire Mk IV Manual. Part No. 545254.

FINAL DRIVE

PINION OIL SEAL

— Remove and refit   51.20.01

Special tool S337 or RG421

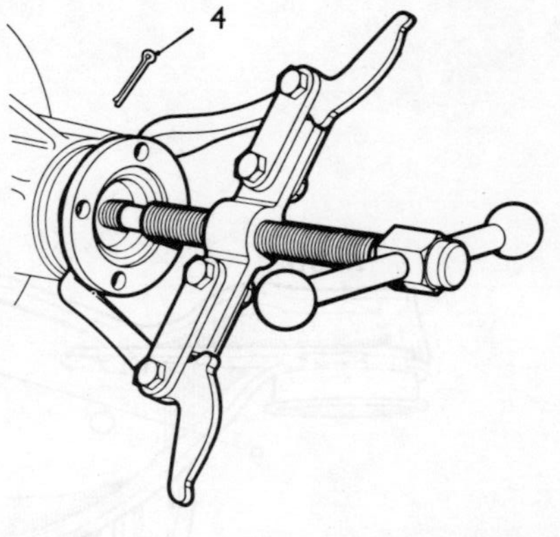

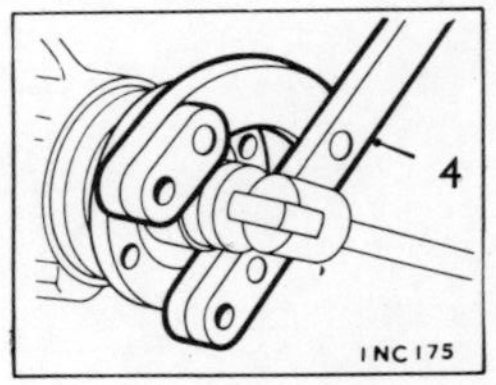

Removing

1. Place the car on a ramp or over a pit.
2. Disconnect the exhaust pipe at its rear mounting and the silencer at the two attachment points.
3. Disconnect the rear end of the propeller shaft from the pinion driving flange — instruction 5, 47.15.01.
4. Withdraw the split pin from the pinion securing nut and remove the nut, using special flange holder tool S337 or RG421.
5. Place a receptacle under the drive flange to collect oil and remove the flange — instruction 15, 51.15.07.
6. Lever out the old oil seal.

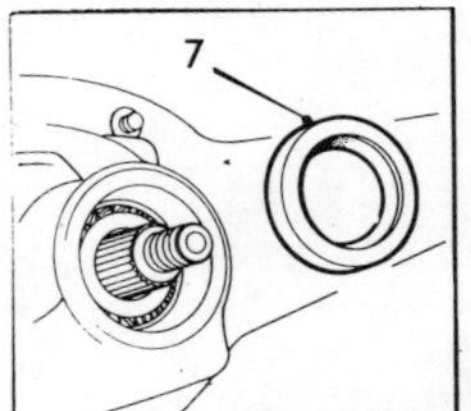

Refitting

7. Immerse a new seal in light oil for one hour before fitting.
8. With the sealing lip leading, drive in the seal.
9. Refit the driving flange and secure with the pinion nut and tighten to 90 to 120 lbf. ft (12·4 to 16·6 kgf. m).
10. Fit a new split pin.
11. Reconnect the rear end of the propeller shaft to the driving flange — instruction 6, 47.15.01.
12. Reverse instructions 1 and 2.
13. Recharge the final drive unit with a recommended E.P. oil.

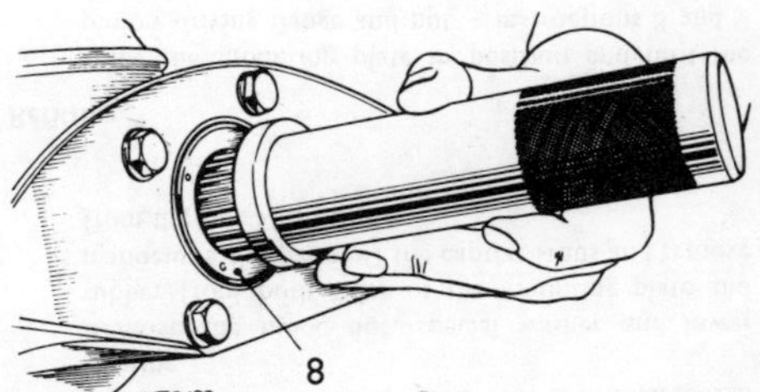

Triumph Spitfire Mk IV Manual. Part No. 545254.

51.20.01

FINAL DRIVE

FINAL DRIVE UNIT

— Remove and refit   51.25.13

1. Place the car on a ramp or over a pit.
2. Jack up the car on both sides under the rear body jacking points.
3. Disconnect the exhaust pipe at its rear mounting and remove the silencer.
4. Disconnect the propeller shaft from the pinion driving flange, 47.15.01.
5. Disconnect the two rear drive shaft universal joint couplings from the inner drive shafts 47.10.01.
6. Lower the ramp and remove the rear trim panel and rear spring access cover.
7. Remove the four nuts and studs securing the rear spring to the final drive assembly.
8. Raise the ramp and remove the final drive rear mounting nut and special bolt.
9. Whilst supporting the final drive unit remove the two nyloc nuts securing the final drive front mounting plate to the chassis, 51.25.34.
10. Manoeuvre the final drive unit clear of the chassis taking care to keep the unit upright to avoid oil spillage from the stud holes.

Refitting

11. Offer up the final drive unit to its rear mounting location ensuring that the two rubber washers are positioned correctly on the outside of the mounting lugs. Secure the rear mounting with the special bolt and nyloc nut.
12. Connect the final drive front mountings, ensuring the rubbers are correctly positioned i.e. the upper rubber with the stepped end facing downwards. Fit the lower rubber and special washer and secure with the nyloc nuts. Tighten to 26 to 34 lbf. ft (3.6 to 4.7 kgf. m). It should be possible to revolve the lower rubbers with the fingers when the nuts are tightened to this torque figure, 51.25.34.
13. Reconnect the rear drive shaft couplings to the inner drive shafts.
14. Reconnect the propeller shaft to the pinion flange.
15. Reconnect the exhaust pipe to its rear mounting and fit the silencer.
16. Lower the ramp and position the spring so that the dowel on the bottom leaf locates in the hole in the final drive spring platform. Refit the studs and secure with the nyloc nuts and plain washers and tighten to 26 to 34 lbf. ft (3.6 to 4.7 kgf. m).
17. Lower the body jacks fit the rear spring access cover plate and rear trim panel.
18. Check the final drive oil level — see maintenance and if necessary top up with a recommended E.P. oil.
19. Remove the car from the ramp.

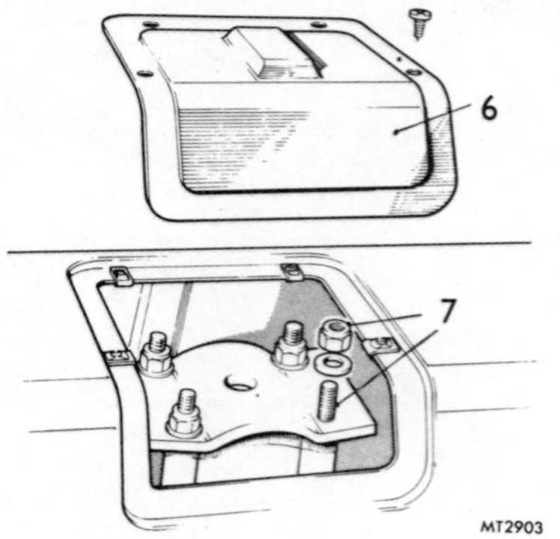

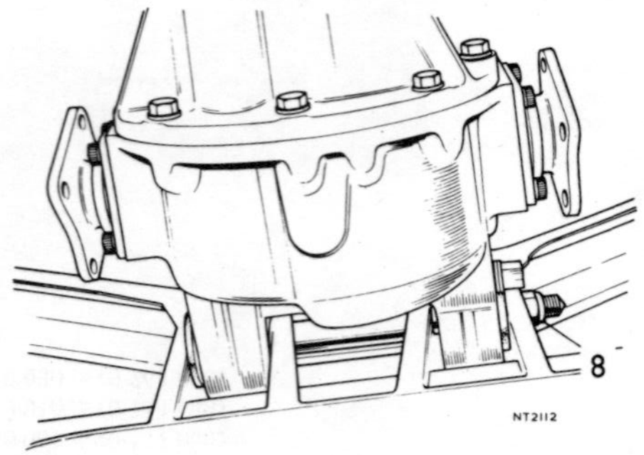

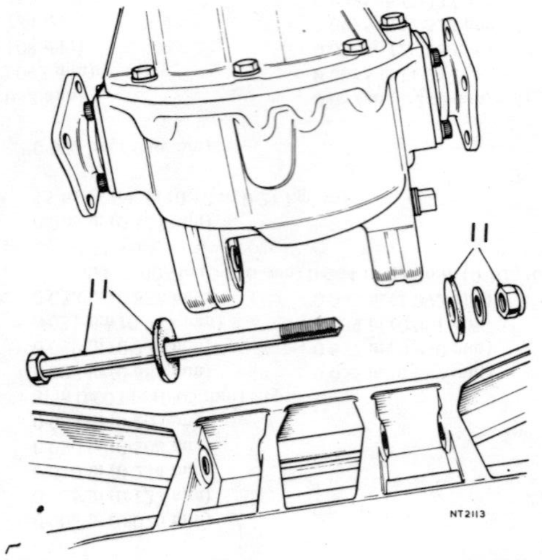

FINAL DRIVE UNIT MOUNTING PLATE

— Remove and refit   51.25.33

Removing

1. Place the car on a ramp or over a pit.
2. Jack up the rear of the car at the two rear jacking points until the wheels are clear of the ramp or ground.
3. Disconnect the exhaust pipe at its rear mounting and the silencer at its two attachment points.
4. Mark for reassembly and disconnect the rear end of the propeller shaft from the pinion flange, 47.15.01.
5. Remove the pinion nut and flange — instructions 4 and 5, 51.20.01.
6. Remove the four bolts and shakeproof washers securing the mounting plate to the differential housing.
7. Remove the nyloc nut, special washer and lower rubber from both sides of the mounting plate and manoeuvre the plate off the captive studs and remove from the car, 51.25.34.

Refitting

8. Place the mounting plate in position and refit the pinion, driving flange and nut — instructions 8 and 9, 51.20.01.
9. Refit the mounting plate and rubbers to the chassis — instructions 8 to 12, 51.25.34.
10. Reconnect the exhaust pipe and silencer.
11. Remove the car from the ramp.

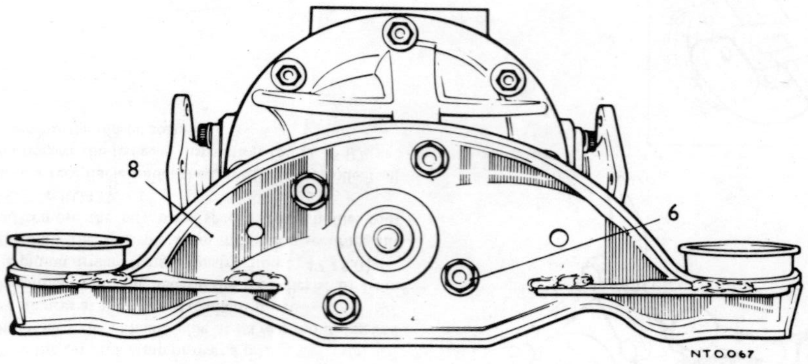

FINAL DRIVE

FINAL DRIVE UNIT MOUNTING PLATE RUBBERS
51.25.34

— Remove and refit

Removing

1. Place the car on a ramp or over a pit.
2. Disconnect the exhaust pipe at its rear mounting and the silencer at its two attachment points.
3. Jack up the rear of the car under both sides of the chassis until the rear wheels are clear of the ramp or ground.
4. Mark for reassembly and disconnect the rear end of the propeller shaft from the pinion flange.
5. Remove the four bolts and shakeproof washers securing the final drive mounting plate to the differential casing, 51.25.33.
6. Remove the two nyloc nuts (one each side) securing the mounting to the chassis, together with the special washer and lower rubber.
7. Using a suitable lever prise the mounting plate downwards until the upper mounting rubber can be removed from the captive stud. Repeat instructions on the other side.

Refitting

8. Prise the mounting plate downwards as in instruction 7 sufficiently to enable the replacement upper rubber to be fitted over the captive stud. Ensure that the stepped end of the rubber is facing downwards and locates squarely in the mounting plate cup. Repeat this instruction on the opposite side.
9. Fit the lower rubber and special washer and loosely secure — at this stage — with the nyloc nut. Repeat this instruction on the other side.
10. Secure the mounting plate to the differential casing with the four bolts and shakeproof washers.
11. Reconnect the rear end of the propeller shaft to the pinion flange ensuring that the assembly marks line up.
12. Lower the jack and finally tighten the two nyloc mounting nuts to 26 to 34 lbf. ft (3·6 to 4·7 kgf. m). It should be possible to revolve the lower mounting rubbers with the fingers when the nuts are tightened to this torque figure.
13. Reverse instructions 1 and 2.

STEERING OPERATIONS

Camber angle — check and adjust	57.65.05
Front wheel alignment — check and adjust	57.60.01
Steering column	
— flexible coupling — remove and refit	57.40.25
— lock/ignition switch — remove and refit	57.40.31
— overhaul	57.40.10
— remove and refit	57.40.01
— safety clamp — remove and refit	57.40.07
Steering geometry — check	57.65.02
Steering rack	
— damper — remove and refit	57.35.10
— gaiters — remove and refit	57.25.02
— overhaul	57.25.07
— remove and refit	57.25.01
Steering wheel	
— hub — remove and refit	57.60.02
— remove and refit	57.60.01
Tie rod ball joint	
— inner — remove and refit	57.55.03
— outer — remove and refit	57.55.02

STEERING RACK AND PINION

— Remove and refit   57.25.01

Service Tool S.341

Removing

1. Remove the nyloc nut and plain washer securing the outer tie rod to left and right hand steering arms.
2. Release both outer tie rod ends from the steering arms.
3. Remove the pinch bolt clamping the steering rack pinion to the lower end of the flexible coupling.
4. Remove the four nyloc nuts and plain washers securing the steering rack 'U' bolts to the chassis. Withdraw the two reinforcement plates.
5. Remove the 'U' bolts complete with the rack clamp brackets.
6. Slide rack forward to disengage the rack pinion splines from the flexible coupling.
7. Withdraw the steering rack.

Refitting

8. Remove the centre plug from rack plunger and align dimple in the rack shaft with plug aperture. In this position the rack shaft is centralised.
9. Fit plug to plunger ensuring bonding strap is not omitted.
10. Carefully slide rack into position in car taking care not to disturb position of rack shaft.
11. With steering wheel held in straight ahead position engage rack pinion shaft splines in the flexible coupling and fit and tighten the pinch bolt in the flexible coupling.
12. Ensure the rack mounting rubbers are correctly positioned on inboard side of rack flanges with lip under the straight face on the flange. — (Tool S341).
13. Fit 'U' bolts and clamp brackets.
14. Fit the reinforcement plates to the 'U' bolts ensuring angled lips are inboard with lip projecting downward.
15. Fit the plain washers and nyloc nuts to 'U' bolts taking care not to omit the bonding strap at the pinion end of rack.
16. With angled lips of the reinforcement plates in contact with the inboard edges of the chassis brackets and the mounting rubbers compressed tighten the 'U' bolt securing nuts.
17. Fit tie rod outer ends to steering arms.

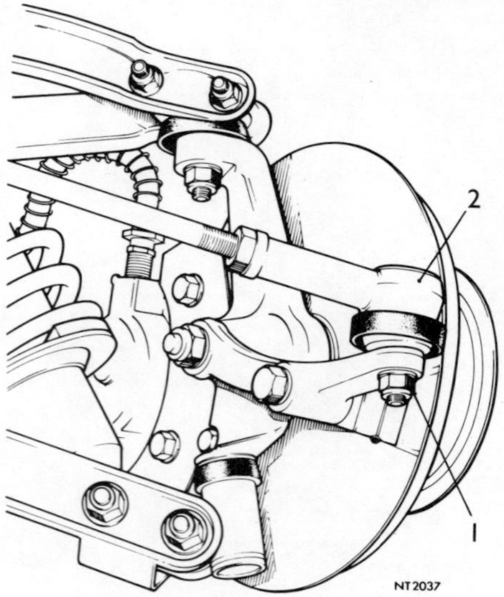

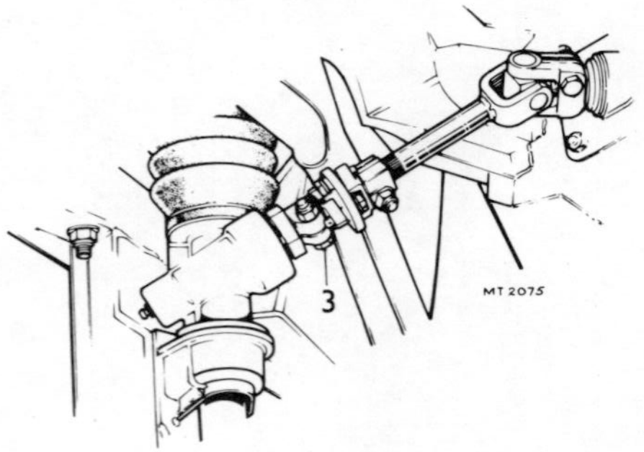

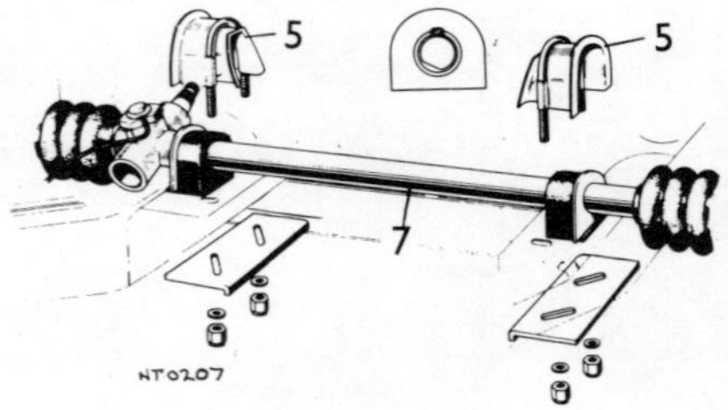

STEERING

STEERING RACK GAITERS

— Remove and refit   57.25.02

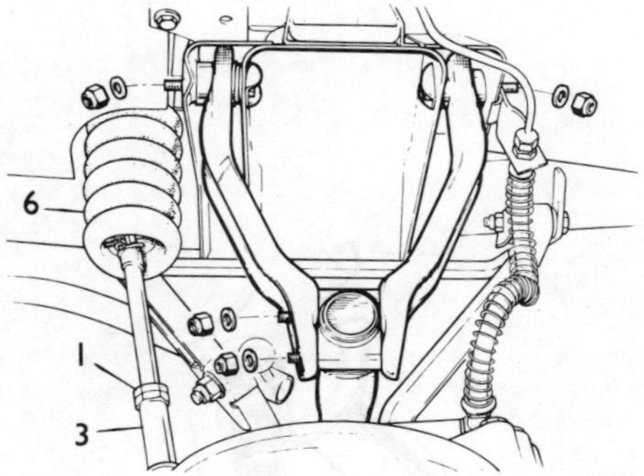

Removing

1. Slacken the locknut securing tie rod outer ball joint.
2. Remove the nut and washer securing the tie rod outer ball joint to the steering arm.
3. Release the outer ball joint from the steering arm.
4. Unscrew the outer ball joint and locknut from the tie rod.
5. Remove the inner and outer ball clips retaining the gaiter to the rack and tie rod respectively.
6. Withdraw the gaiters.
7. Repeat above instructions on opposite tie rod.

Refitting

8. Lubricate the tie rod inner ball joints with fresh grease.
9. Slide the new gaiters along the tie rods into position on the rack and secure with clip.
10. Screw locknut and tie rod outer ball joint assembly on tie rod and locate them as near as possible to original locations.
11. Connect outer ball joint to steering arm and fit plain washer and nut.
12. Repeat instructions 8 to 11 on opposite tie rod.
13. Check front wheel toe-in and adjust as necessary, ensuring tie rods are equally adjusted.
14. Secure the outer ball joint assemblies with their respective locknuts.
15. Adjust the outer end of both gaiters so that they are capable of accommodating movement of the tie rods when moving from lock to lock.

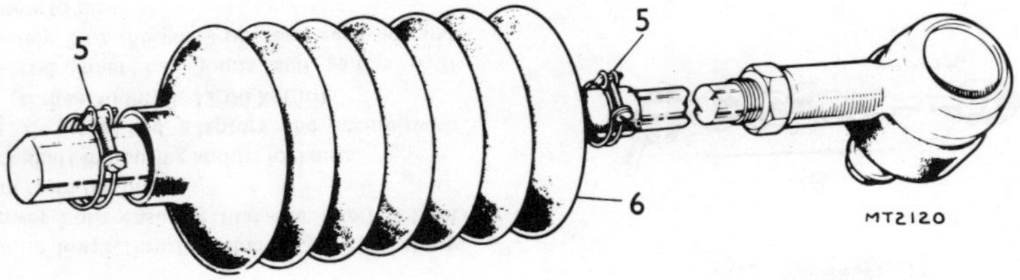

STEERING RACK AND PINION

— Overhaul   57.25.07

1. Remove the rack from the car 57.25.01.

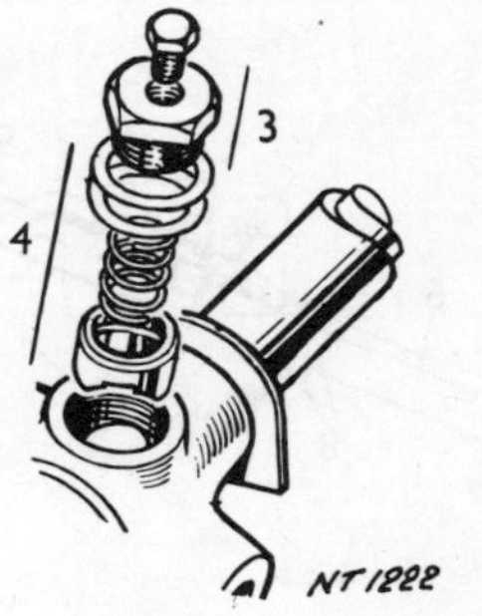

Dismantling

Rack plunger

2. Slacken the plug securing the rack plunger to the rack housing.
3. Remove the plug and shim pack.
4. Withdraw the spring, washer and plunger.

Pinion

5. Remove the circlip retaining the pinion to the rack housing.
6. Withdraw pinion complete with plug-end, locating pin, shims, bush and upper thrust washer.

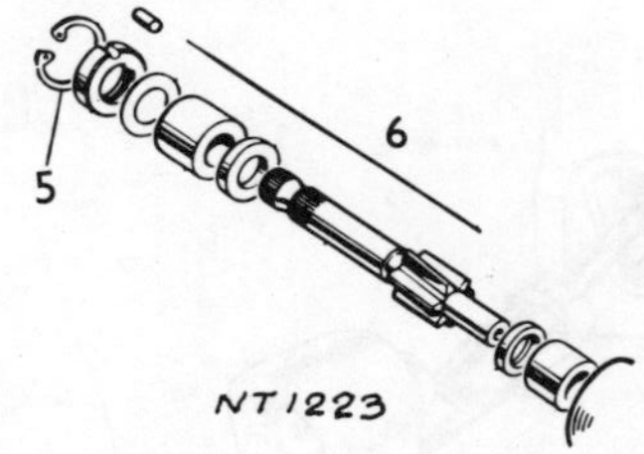

Tie rods and rack shaft

7. Release the clips securing the gaiters to the rack housing and tie rods and slide the gaiters clear of the rack.
8. Slacken the locknuts securing inner ball joint adaptors to the rack shaft.
9. Unscrew and remove the inner ball joint adaptors and tie rods.
10. Remove the locknuts and withdraw the rack shaft.

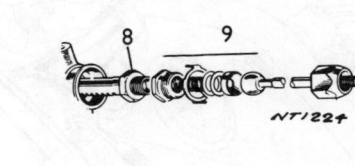

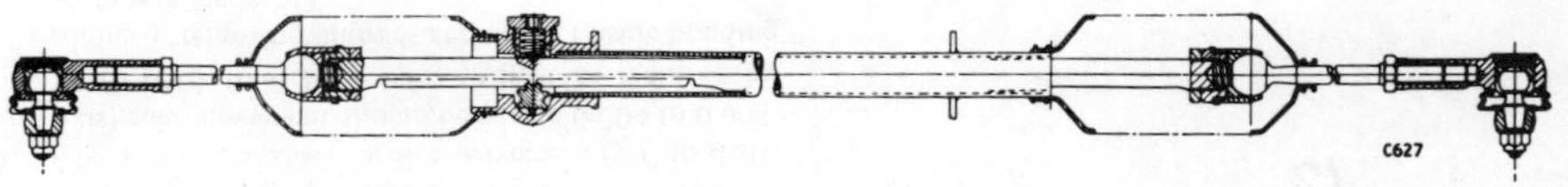

Rack housing bush

11. Remove the bush from the rack housing.

Pinion housing

12. Extract the pinion lower thrust washer.
13. Drive or press out the pinion end cover and the lower bush.

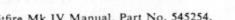

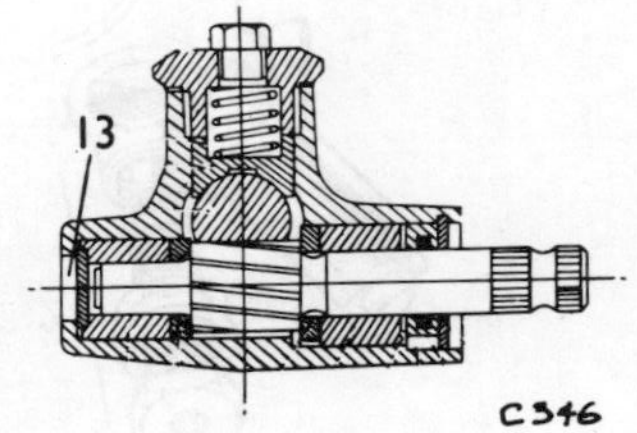

STEERING

Assembling

Rack housing bush
14. Fit a new bush to the rack housing.

Pinion housing
15. Fit the end cover and lower bush to the pinion housing ensuring that the recessed end of the bush is adjacent to the end cover.

Rack shaft and tie rods
16. Insert pinion lower thrust washer in position above pinion lower bush ensuring that the internal fillet faces away from the bush.
17. Insert rack shaft in housing and fit locknuts.
18. Fit both tie rods and adaptors and secure with locknuts. (torque 80 lbf/ft. 11·06 kgf/m).
19. Pack tie rod inner ball joints and gaiters with approximately 2 oz (56 gms.) of grease each side and secure gaiters to rack.

Pinion
20. Rotate rack shaft until teeth will permit pinion engagement.
21. Fit pinion to pinion housing.
22. Fit upper thrust washer, bush and shims.
23. Fit a new internal 'O' ring to the plug-end.
24. Fit circlip and check pinion end movement. End movement must not exceed 0·010 in (0·254 mm). Adjust shim pack as necessary.

Rack plunger
25. Fit plunger.
26. Fit the damper plug, shims and spring.
27. Check the rack shaft for side movement (90° to shaft axis). Side movement should be within 0·004 to 0·008 in (0·1016 to 0·2032 mm). Adjust as required by adding or removing shims as necessary.

57.25.07 Sheet 2

Triumph Spitfire Mk IV Manual. Part No. 545254.

STEERING

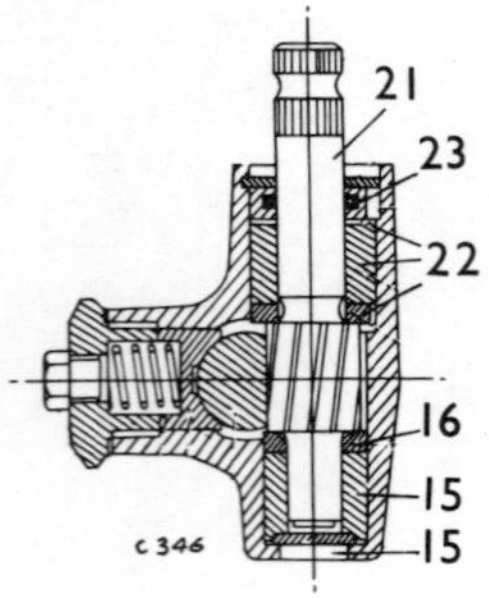

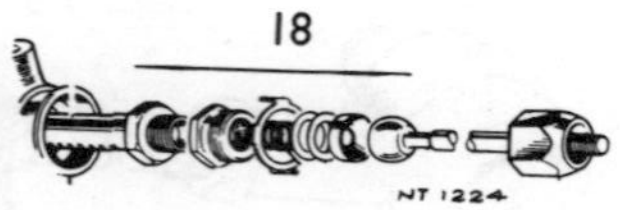

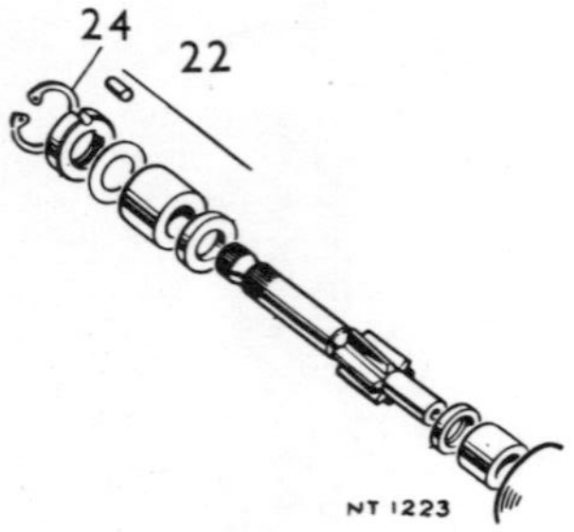

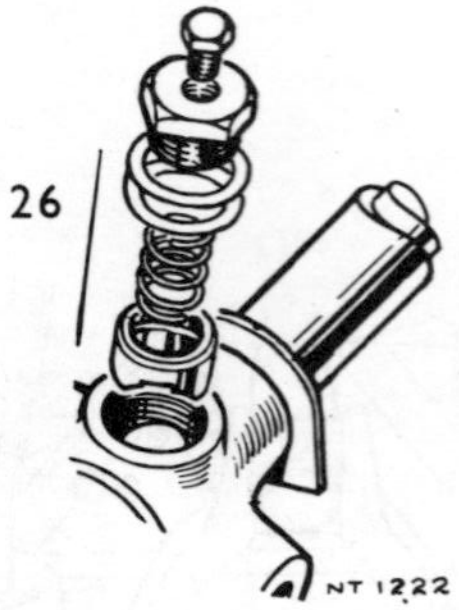

STEERING RACK DAMPER
— Remove and refit   57.35.10

Removing
1. Disconnect the bonding strap at the damper plug.
2. Unscrew the damper plug and remove plug, shims, spring washer and plunger.

Refitting
3. Fit plunger and washer.
4. Fit the damper plug, shims and spring.
5. Check the rack shaft for side movement (90° to shaft axis) side movement should be within 0·004 to 0·008 in (0·1016 to 0·2032 mm). Adjust as required by adding or removing shims as necessary. Ensure bonding strap is reconnected.

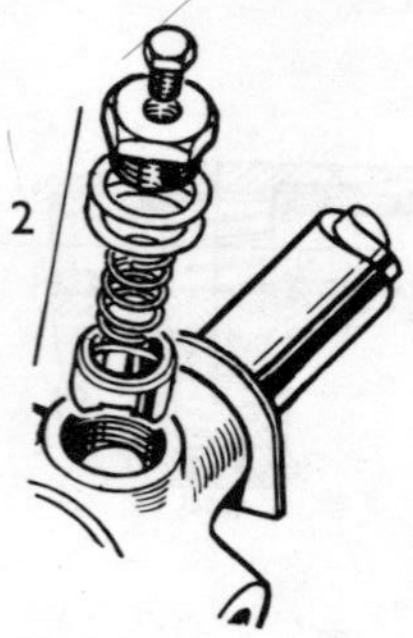

STEERING COLUMN ASSEMBLY
— Remove and refit   57.40.01

Removing
1. Disconnect the battery.
2. Remove the driver's parcel shelf.
3. Remove the pinch bolt securing the steering mast to the flexible coupling.
4. Remove the nuts, spring and plain washers from the two bolts securing the steering column forward bracket.
5. Withdraw forward support housing and felt liner.
6. Disconnect connections for horn, trafficators and lights.
7. Disconnect electrical plug from steering column lock.
8. Remove the two cap screws securing the steering column rear bracket and withdraw both clamp halves and upper screwed plate.
9. Withdraw steering column complete with tie-bar.

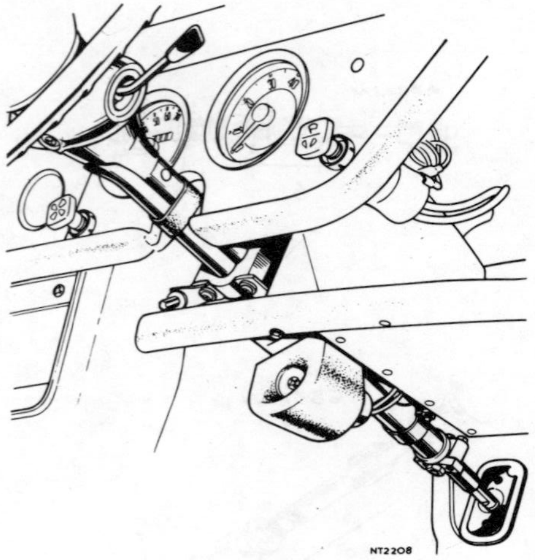

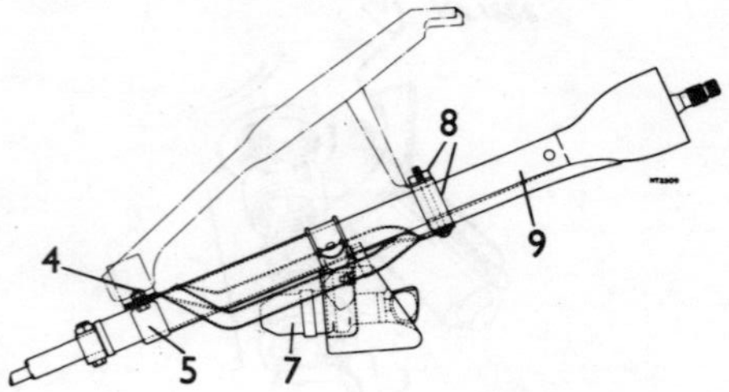

57.35.10
57.40.01 Sheet 1

Triumph Spitfire Mk IV Manual. Part No. 545254.

STEERING

Refitting

10. Locate road wheels in straight ahead position.
11. Hold steering wheel with two spokes horizontal and the third spoke towards drivers seat and engage lower end of steering mast in splines of flexible coupling.
12. Fit and tighten pinchbolt in flexible coupling.
13. Slide cardboard tube rearwards and fit felt over steering mast housing ensuring ends of felt are below mast housing.
14. Engage forward ends of tie-bar in forward mounting bolts.
15. Fit felt housing and engage forward mounting bolts.
16. Fit plain and spring washers and nuts to mounting bolts.
17. Ensure spring clip is fitted on mast housing to align with rear clamp bracket.
18. Fit upper and lower clamp halves to mast housing.
19. Place screwed plate in bracket above clamp halves.
20. Enter cap bolts through tie bar, upper and lower clamp halves, and mounting bracket and engage screwed plate. Tighten cap bolts.
21. Tighten bolts and nuts securing forward bracket.
22. Make good connections to horn, lights, trafficators and steering lock.
23. Fit drivers parcel tray.
24. Connect battery.

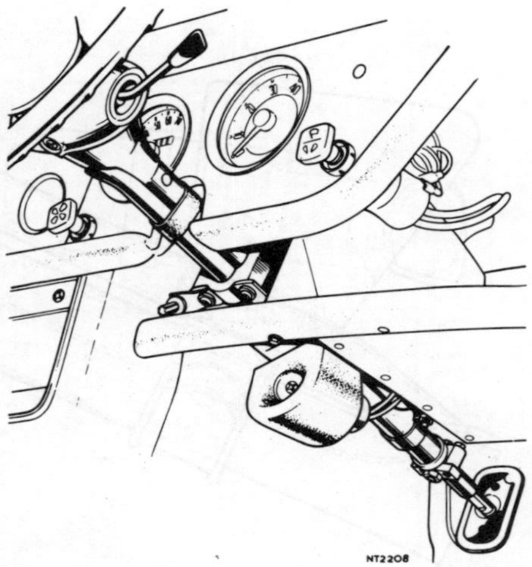

STEERING COLUMN SAFETY CLAMP

— Remove and refit 57.40.07

Removing

1. Slacken and remove the two bolts and spring washers securing clamp halves to steering mast.
2. Withdraw clamp.
3. Slacken locknut and pinch screw.

Refitting

4. Offer up clamp halves to steering mast ensuring the straight member sits across the flat on the steering mast.
5. Engage bolts complete with spring washers.
6. Slide clamp rearwards until it is against the steering mast housing. Ensure plastic thrust washer is located between clamp bracket and mast housing.
7. Tighten clamp bolts to 6 to 9 lbf/ft (0·8 to 1·2 kgf/m).
8. Tighten grubscrew to 18 to 20 lbf/ft (2·5 to 2·8 kgf/m).
9. Tighten locknut.

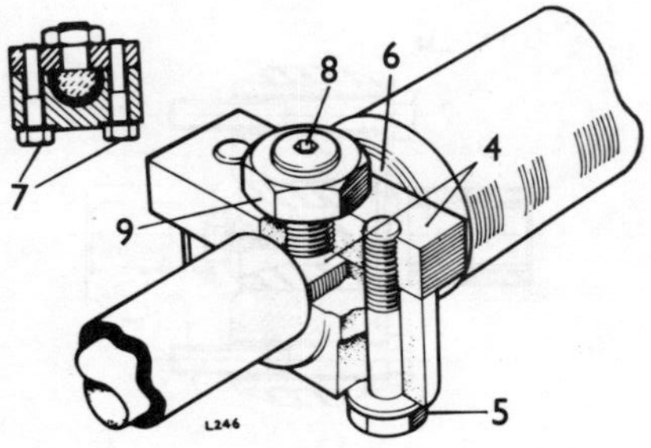

57.40.01 Sheet 2
57.40.07

Triumph Spitfire Mk IV Manual. Part No. 545254.

STEERING

STEERING COLUMN UNIT

— Overhaul 57.40.10

1. Remove the steering column from the car 57.40.01

Dismantling

2. Remove the steering wheel 57.60.01
3. Remove the lights and trafficator switches, 86.55.54, 86.65.17.
4. Unlock the steering column lock.
5. Remove the two set bolts and spring washers securing the safety clamp and remove the safety clamp and thrust washer.
6. Withdraw the lower steering mast.
7. Withdraw the cap from the lower end of the steering column tube and remove the tubular cardboard distance piece.
8. Move the upper steering mast axially towards the upper end of the column tube, and remove the trafficator cam.
9. Move the steering mast axially towards the lower end of the column tube until the column is felt to butt against the column tube lower bush.
10. Depress the rubber locating buttons on the column lower bush and withdraw the steering mast and the lower bush.
11. Remove the lower bush from the mast.
12. Remove the upper bush from the column tube.

Assembling

13. Fit a new upper bush to the column tube ensuring that it is entered with the rubber dots on the end face of the bush leading. That is with the rubber dots towards the bottom of the column tube.
14. Enter the steering mast from the bottom of the column tube ensuring that the upper bush is not displaced and that the rubber locating dowels remain aligned with the holes in the column tube.
15. Enter the lower bush in the column tube ensuring that the rubber dots on the end face of the bush are trailing (dots to bottom of tube) and that the rubber locating dowels engage the holes in the column tube.
16. Fit the trafficator cam.
17. Fit the end cap to the column tube.
18. Fit the lower steering mast.
19. Align the flat on the lower mast with the slot on the upper mast and fit the thrust washer and safety clamp. Do not tighten the safety clamp at this stage. The safety clamp must be tightened after the column is installed in the car and the position of the lower column determined. (Instructions 6 and 7, 57.40.25).
20. Fit the lights and trafficator switches.
21. Fit the steering wheel.

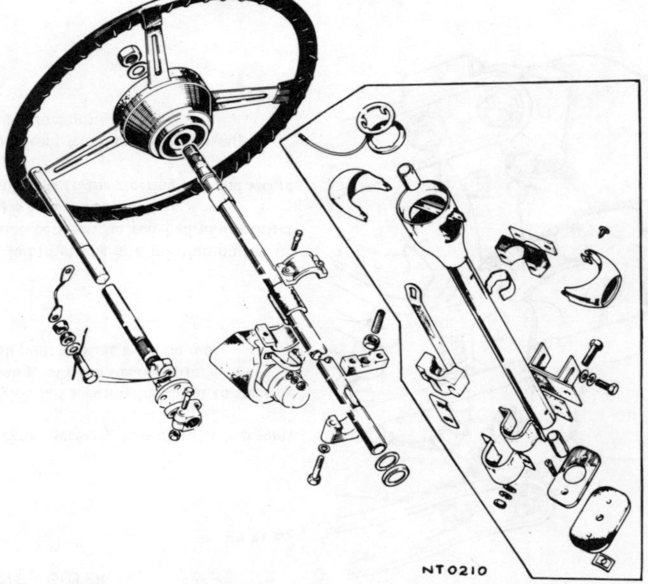

57.40.10

Triumph Spitfire Mk IV Manual. Part No. 545254.

STEERING

STEERING COLUMN FLEXIBLE COUPLING

— Remove and refit 57.40.25

Removing

1. Slacken the two bolts on the steering column safety clamp.
2. Remove the pinchbolts securing the flexible coupling to the steering column lower shaft and the rack pinion shaft.
3. Slide lower steering column shaft clear of flexible coupling.
4. Withdraw flexible coupling from pinion shaft.

Refitting

5. Engage flexible coupling on pinion shaft and fit and tighten the pinchbolt.
6. With front wheels in straight ahead position and steering wheel in central position engage the lower steering column shaft in flexible coupling. Fit and tighten pinchbolt.
7. Slide safety clamp upwards until it abuts against the steering column housing. Tighten the safety clamp bolts, Torque 6 to 9 lbf/ft (0·8 to 1·2 kgf/m).

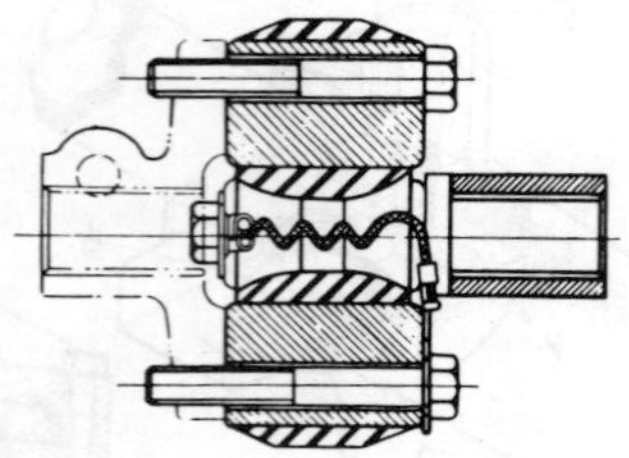

STEERING COLUMN LOCK/IGNITION SWITCH

— Remove and refit 57.40.31

Removing

1. Remove steering column assembly 57.40.01.
2. Remove the two nuts and washers securing steering lock shroud and withdraw shroud and steering column tie-bar.
3. With a centre punch mark the centre of the two shear bolt heads securing the steering lock clamp bracket.
4. Using a small chisel unscrew the shear head bolts.

or

4a. If instruction 4 proves unsuccessful drill into the shear bolt heads where previously marked by centre punch and using an Easiout extractor unscrew the shear-heads bolts.
5. Remove the steering lock.

Refitting

6. Offer up steering column lock to steering column and locate the dowel in the column drilling.
7. Fit steering lock clamp and secure with two new shear bolts.
8. Evenly tighten shear bolts until heads shear.
9. Install steering column assembly in car 57.40.01.

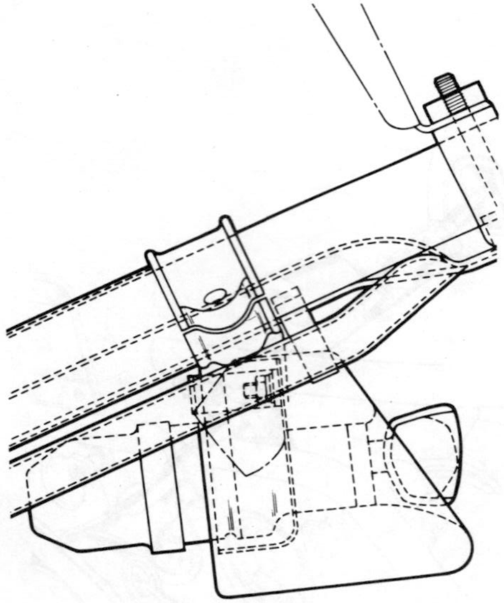

57.40.18
57.40.31

STEERING

TIE ROD BALL JOINT — OUTER

— Remove and refit 57.55.02

Removing

1. Slacken the locknut securing tie rod outer ball joint to tie rod.
2. Remove the nyloc nut securing ball joint to steering arm. Detach ball joint from steering arm.
3. Unscrew the ball joint housing from tie rod.

Refitting

4. Screw the ball joint housing into position on the tie rod. The distance between tie rod ball joint centres (inner to outer) is 8·72 in (221·5 mm).
5. Connect the ball joint to the steering arm and secure with the nyloc nut.
6. Check and adjust front wheel track as necessary.
7. Tighten the tie rod locknut.

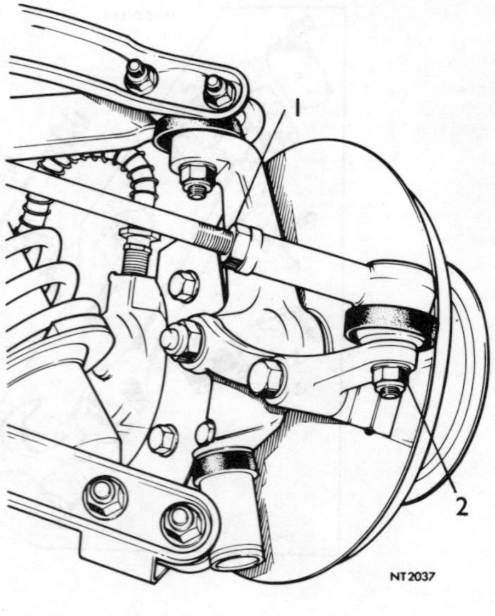

57.55.02

STEERING

TIE ROD BALL JOINT – INNER

57.55.03

– Remove and refit

Removing

1. Remove the tie rod outer ball joint and housing.
2. Release the gaiter clips and remove the gaiter.
3. Wipe the grease from the inner ball joint.
4. Slacken the locknut securing inner ball joint adaptor to the steering rack. To prevent stress being transmitted to the pinion the opposite adaptor should be held with a spanner.
5. Unscrew the inner ball joint adaptor from the rack shaft observing the precaution mentioned in 4.
6. Straighten the lock tabs on the adaptor/ball housing washer.
7. Unscrew the adaptor from the ball housing and withdraw spring, shims, ball seat and tie rod from housing.

Refitting

8. Lubricate the ball housing and insert the tie rod.
9. Fit the ball seat, shim(s), new tab washer and adaptor.
10. Tighten the adaptor, torque 80 lbf/ft. (11.06 kgf/m), and check the tie rod for end-float and articulation. End-float should be within 0·0005 to 0·003 in (0·0127 to 0·0762 mm), there must be no tight spots in articulation. Adjust by adding or removing shims as necessary. Shims available are 0·002,0·004 and 0·010 in (0·0508, 0·1016 and 0·254 mm).
11. Bend over lock washer tabs.
12. Slide the spring into the adaptor.
13. Fit the locknut to the rack shaft.
14. Fit and tighten the adaptor to the rack shaft and secure with the locknut. When tightening the adaptor and locknut employ a spanner at the opposite adaptor to prevent stress to the pinion. Locknut torque should be 80 lbf/ft (11.06 kgf/m).
15. Cover the adaptor with fresh grease.
16. Fit the gaiter and clips.
17. Fit the tie rod outer end.
18. Check and adjust front wheel toe-in as necessary.

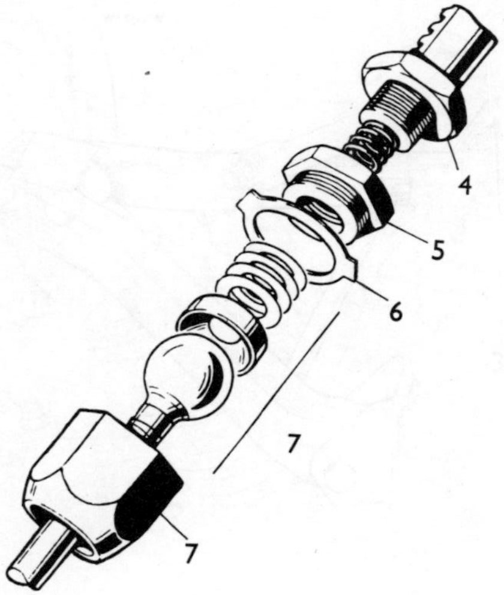

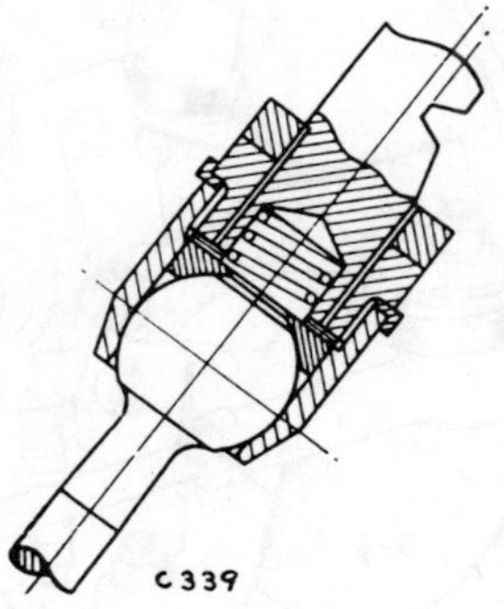

STEERING WHEEL

57.60.01

– Remove and refit

Removing

1. Prise off steering wheel pad.
2. Prise out horn push.
3. Withdraw the horn brush connection.
4. Remove the nut and washer securing steering wheel hub to steering mast.
5. To ensure that the steering wheel hub will be replaced in its original spline location scribe both hub centre and top of steering mast.
6. Using a suitable extractor withdraw the steering wheel.

Refitting

7. Fit steering wheel and hub to steering mast. If the steering wheel was withdrawn without spline location being marked, set the front wheels to the straight ahead position and centralise the steering wheel.
8. Reverse instructions 1 to 4.

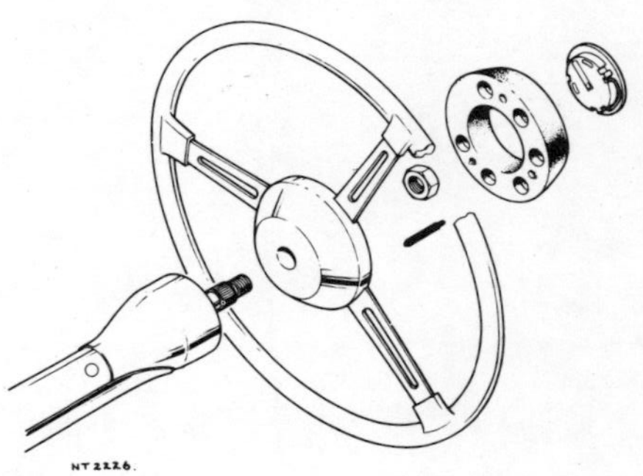

STEERING WHEEL HUB

57.60.02

– Remove and refit

Removing

1. Remove steering wheel and hub from car 57.60.01.
2. Remove the six bolts and washers securing the steering wheel spokes to the hub.

Refitting

3. Reverse instructions 1 and 2.

STEERING

STEERING GEOMETRY 57.65.00

Only two adjustments are possible: Front wheel alignment and Camber angle.

DATA

	Kerb condition	Laden condition (2 up)
Camber	3° Positive ±1°	2° Positive ±1°
Castor	4°±1°	4½° ±½°
King pin inclination	5¾°±1°	6¼° ±¾°
Wheel alignment	1/16 to 1/8 in Toe-in (1·59 - 3·18 mm)	0 - 1/16 in Toe-in (0 - 1·59 mm)

FRONT WHEEL ALIGNMENT
— Check and adjust 57.65.01

Checking

1. Locate the car on level ground and position the front wheels in straight ahead position.
2. Using wheel alignment equipment check the front wheels for toe-in. Front wheel toe-in should be within 1/16 to 1/8 in (1.59 to 3.18 mm).

Adjusting

3. Slacken the outer clips on the rack gaiter.
4. Slacken the locknuts at the tie rod outer ends.
5. Shorten or extend both the rods an equal amount to obtain the required toe-in of 1/16 to 1/8 in (1·59 to 3·18 mm).
6. Tighten the locknuts at the tie rod outer ends.
7. Tighten the gaiter clips.

NOTE: that both tie rods should be adjusted equally. Differences in tie rod lengths will result in incorrect wheel angles on turns.

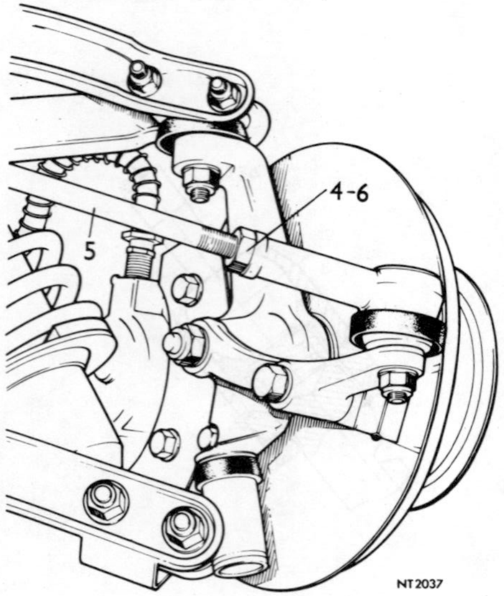

CAMBER ANGLE
— Check and adjust 57.65.05

Front wheel camber should be within the following limits:
Kerb condition 3° Positive ±1°
Laden condition (2 up) 2° Positive ±½°

Adjusting 57.65.05

1. Jack up the car and support chassis on stands.
2. Slacken the two nuts securing the lower wishbone bracket studs to the inner side of the chassis.
3. Remove or add shims equally to both lower wishbone brackets as necessary. Add shim(s) to go negative: remove shim(s) to go positive. One shim equals approximately 1°. Repeat as necessary on opposite wishbone.
4. Tighten the nuts securing the lower wishbone mounting bracket studs. 57.65.01
5. Remove the chassis stands. 57.65.05

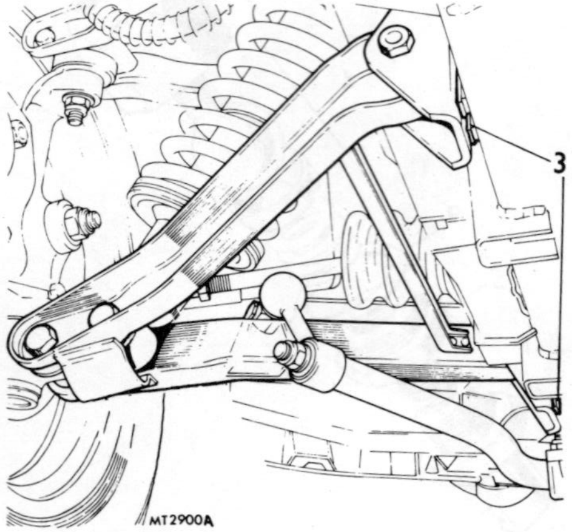

FRONT SUSPENSION

FRONT SUSPENSION OPERATIONS

Anti-roll bar	
– link – remove and refit	60.10.02
– remove and refit	60.10.01
– rubbers – remove and refit	60.10.04
Ball joint – remove and refit	60.15.02
Front damper	
– bushes – remove and refit	60.30.07
– remove and refit	60.30.02
Front hub	
– bearing end-float – check and adjust	60.25.13
– bearings – remove and refit	60.25.14
– oil seal – remove and refit	60.25.15
– overhaul	60.25.07/08
– remove and refit	60.25.01/02
– stub axle – remove and refit	60.25.22
– wheel studs – remove and refit	60.25.29
Front road spring – remove and refit	60.20.01
Trunnion	
– overhaul	60.15.13
– remove and refit	60.15.03
Vertical link – remove and refit	60.25.23
Wishbone	
– lower – remove and refit	60.35.03
– upper – remove and refit	60.35.01

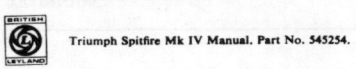

FRONT SUSPENSION

ANTI-ROLL BAR

– Remove and refit   60.10.01

Removing

1. Remove nyloc nut and plain washer securing anti-roll bar link to left and right hand lower wishbones.
2. Release anti-roll bar links from wishbones.
3. Remove the nyloc nuts and plain washers securing anti-roll bar 'U' bolts to left and right hand chassis brackets.
4. Withdraw 'U' bolts and bush housing bottom halves.
5. Withdraw anti-roll bar.

Refitting

6. Reverse instructions 1 to 5.

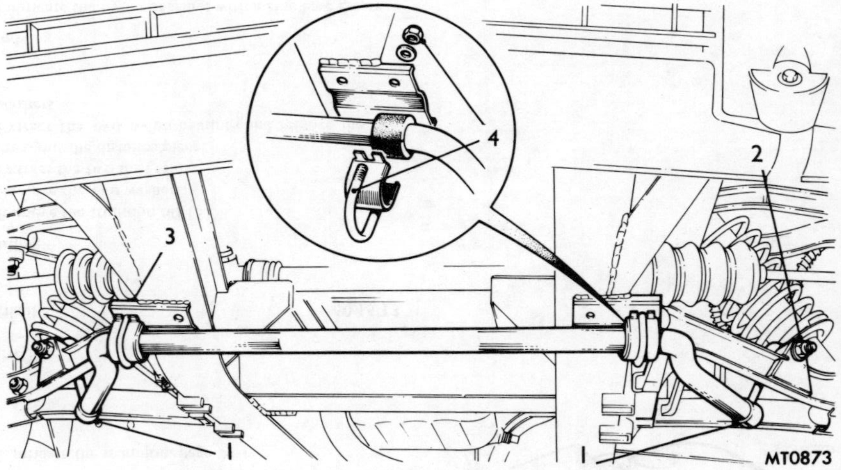

ANTI-ROLL BAR LINK

– Remove and refit   60.10.02

Removing

1. Remove the nyloc nut and plain washer securing the anti-roll bar link to the lower wishbone.
2. Withdraw the anti-roll bar link from the lower wishbone.
3. Remove the nyloc nut and plain washer securing the lower end of link to the anti-roll bar.
4. Withdraw the anti-roll bar link.

Refitting

5. Reverse instructions 1 to 4.

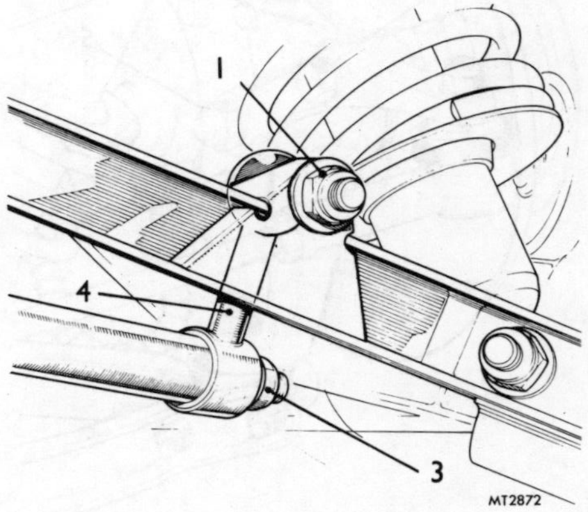

FRONT SUSPENSION

ANTI-ROLL BAR RUBBERS 60.10.04

— Remove and refit

Removing
1. Remove anti-roll bar 60.10.01.
2. Remove the anti-roll bar links from anti-roll bar.
3. Slide off anti-roll bar bushes.

Refitting
4. Slide new bushes into position on anti-roll bar.
5. Fit the anti-roll bar links to the anti-roll bar.
6. Connect the anti-roll bar link to the lower wishbone.
7. Offer up the anti-roll bar to its mounting brackets and align the rubber bushes.
8. Fit the bush housings and 'U' bolts.
9. Secure the 'U' bolts with nyloc nuts and plain washers.

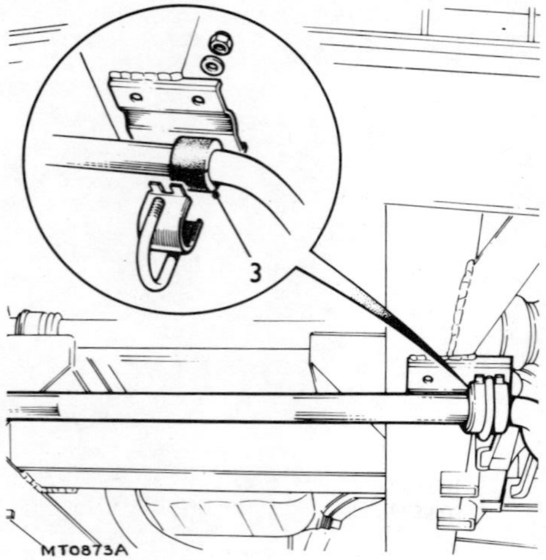

BALL JOINT 60.15.02

— Remove and refit

Removing
1. Jack up car and support chassis on stand(s).
2. Remove road wheel.
3. Remove nyloc nut and plain washer securing ball joint shank to vertical links.
4. Release ball joint shank from vertical link.
5. Remove the two bolts and nuts securing ball joint to upper wishbone.
6. Withdraw ball joint.

Refitting
7. Reverse instructions 1 to 6.

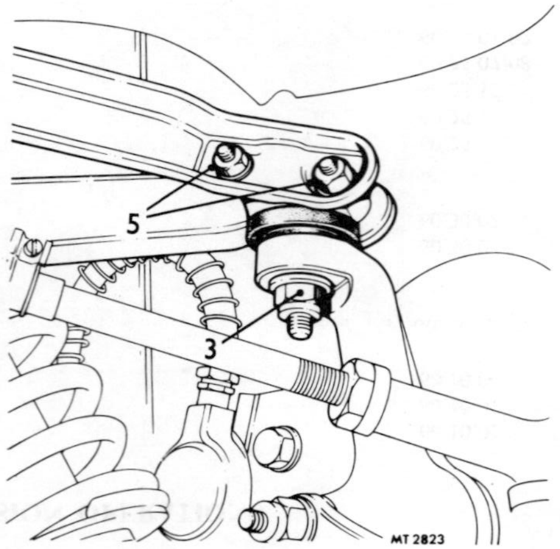

TRUNNION 60.15.03

— Remove and refit

Removing
1. Jack up the car and support the chassis on stand(s).
2. Remove the road wheel.
3. Remove the hub 60.25.01/02.
4. Remove the bolt securing the steering arm and disc shield to the vertical link.
5. Slacken the nut and lift off the disc shield.
6. Remove the nut and bolt securing the trunnion to the lower wishbone.
7. Slacken the nut and bolt securing the shock absorber to the lower wishbone.
8. Detach the trunnion from the lower wishbone and unscrew the trunnion.

Refitting
9. Reverse instructions 1 to 8, ensure that the trunnion outer washers and dust seals are correctly positioned.
10. Lubricate the trunnion, page 09-1.

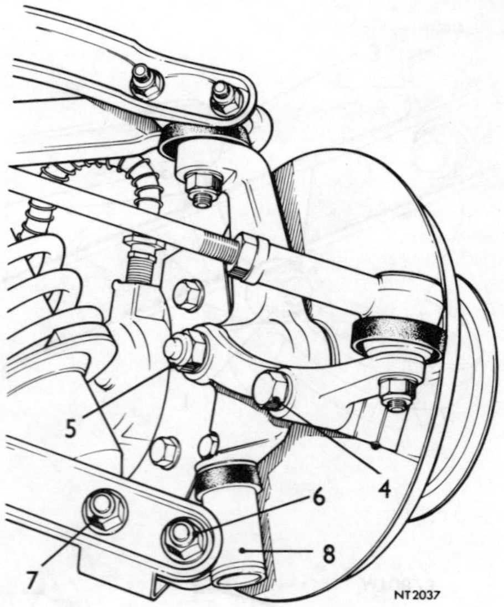

TRUNNION 60.15.13

— Overhaul

Dismantling
1. Remove the trunnion 60.15.03.
2. Remove the two washers.
3. Extract the two dust seals.
4. Press out the distance piece.
5. Extract the two nylon bearings and remove the two washers.

Reassembling
6. Lubricate the nylon bearings with a zinc base grease.
7. Reverse instructions 1 to 5.

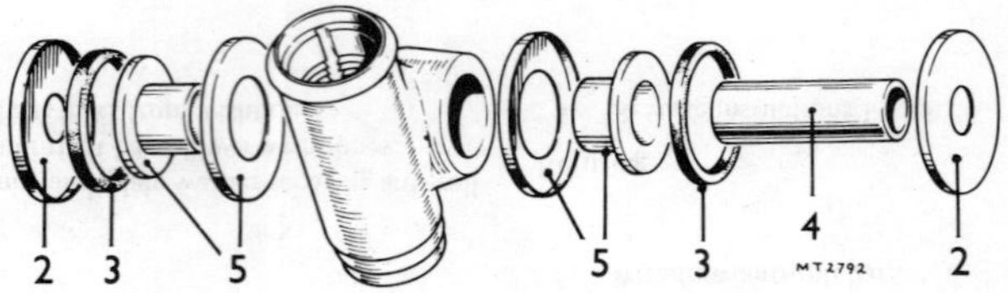

FRONT SUSPENSION

FRONT ROAD SPRING

— Remove and refit

60.20.01

Service Tools: S4221A, S4221A-5, S4221A-18.

Removing

1. Jack up the car and support chassis on stand(s).
2. Remove front wheel.
3. Slacken the bolt and nut securing the steering trunnion to lower wishbone.
4. Remove the bolt, nut and washer securing bottom of damper to lower wishbone.
5. Remove three nyloc nuts and washers securing road spring pad to bracket.
6. Release damper from lower wishbone and withdraw damper and spring assembly complete.
7. Using Tool S4221A and adaptor S4221A-5 and S4221A-18 compress the road spring until the upper mounting flange is released of spring loading.
8. Remove locknut and nut securing damper rod to mounting flange.
9. Withdraw mounting rubbers, mounting rubber seats and mounting flange from damper rod.
10. Release spring tension and remove tool.
11. Remove spring from damper.

Refitting

12. Fully extend damper rod and locate road spring on damper flange.
13. Using Tool S4221A and adaptors 5 to 18, compress road spring until the free end of the spring is below the damper rod end.
14. Fit the mounting rubbers, mounting rubber seats and mounting flange.
15. Fit and tighten nut and locknut.
16. Remove spring and damper from the tool.
17. Offer up spring and damper assembly to vehicle and engage mounting flange studs in upper bracket.
18. Fit plain washers and nyloc nuts to mounting flange studs. Tighten nuts.
19. Engage bottom end of damper in lower wishbone and secure with bolt, washer and nut.
20. Tighten bolt and nut securing lower swivel to wishbone.
21. Fit road wheel and remove jack.

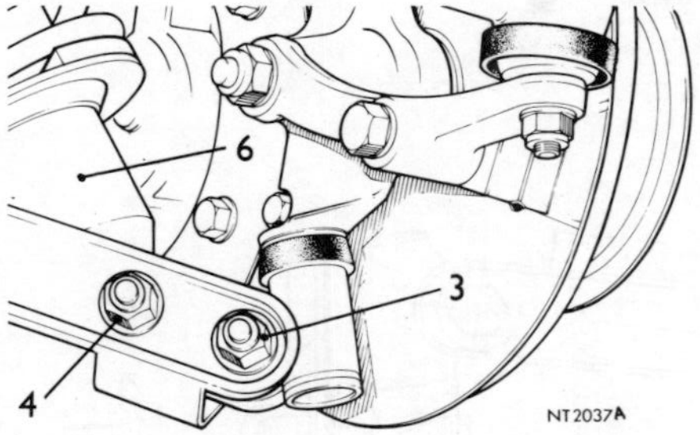

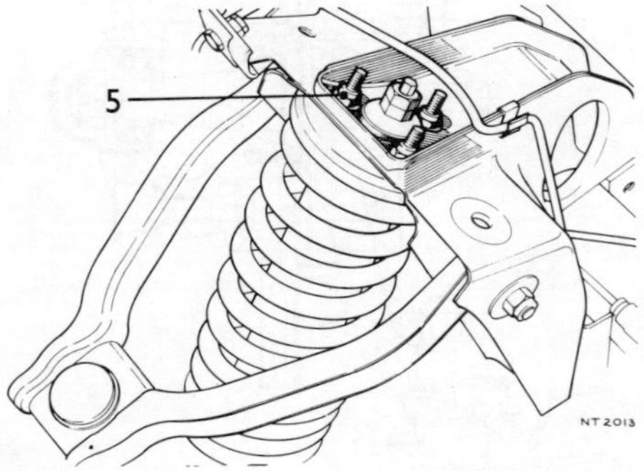

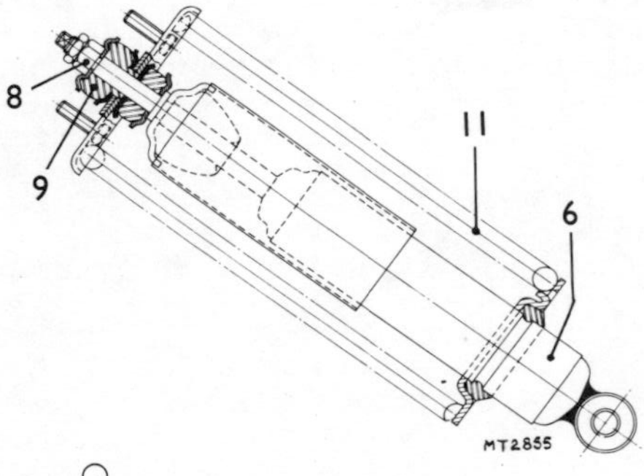

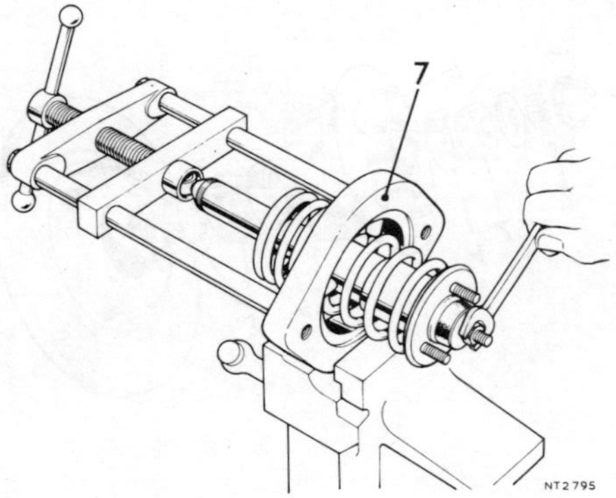

FRONT HUB

— Remove and refit

60.25.01/02

Removing

1. Jack up car and support chassis on stand(s).
2. Remove front wheel 74.20.01.
3. Remove the two bolts and spring washers securing brake caliper to vertical link.
4. Remove caliper shield and withdraw caliper from vertical link and disc. Ensure that weight of caliper is not supported by brake hose.
5. Remove hub cap.
6. Remove split pin, slotted nut and washer from stub axle.
7. Withdraw front hub complete with bearings and oil seal.

Refitting

8. Partially pack hub with fresh grease.
9. Locate the oil seal in the hub and enter the hub and bearings on the stub axle.
10. Fit the washer and slotted nut to the stub axle.
11. Tighten the slotted nut to obtain hub end-float of 0·002 to 0·005 in (0·0508 to 0·1270 mm).
12. Secure the slotted nut with a new split pin.
13. Partially fill the hub cap with fresh grease and fit the cap to the hub.
14. Fit the caliper and shield to the vertical link and secure with two bolts and spring washers.
15. Fit the road wheel and remove the stand(s).

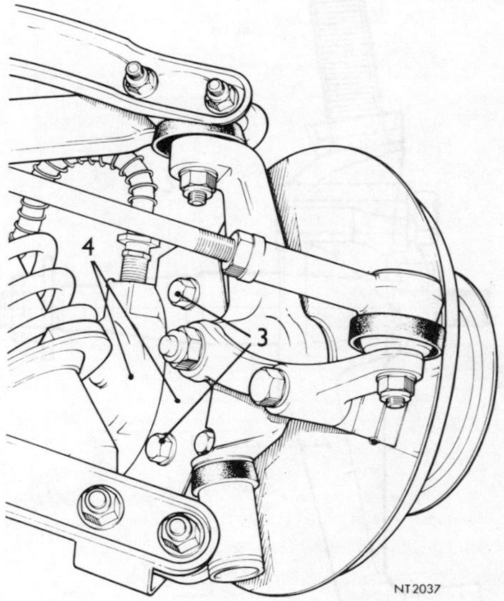

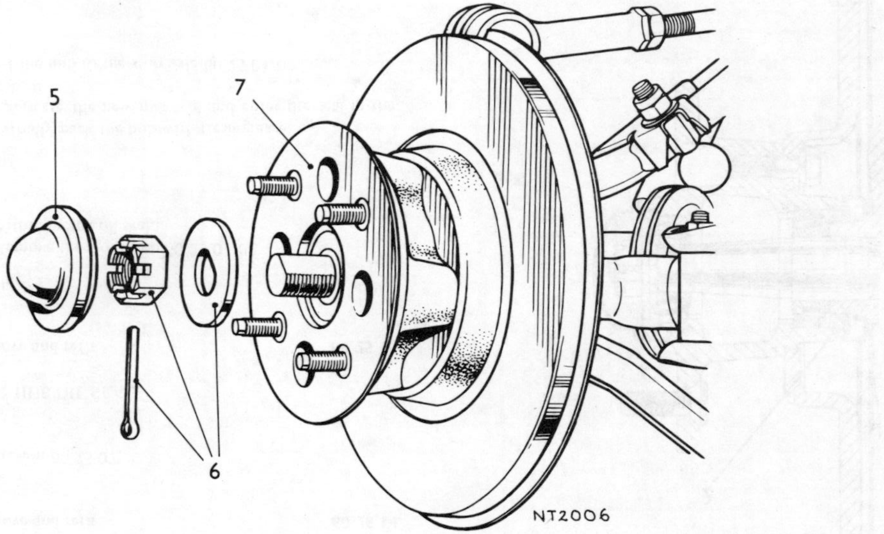

FRONT SUSPENSION

FRONT HUB

— Overhaul
60.25.07/08

Dismantling
1. Remove the front hub 60.25.01/02.
2. Withdraw the outer bearing.
3. Withdraw the oil seal, inner bearing shield and inner bearing.
4. Carefully and evenly extract the inner and outer bearing tracks. The removal of the bearing tracks is not advised unless renewal is intended.
5. Thoroughly clean all components.

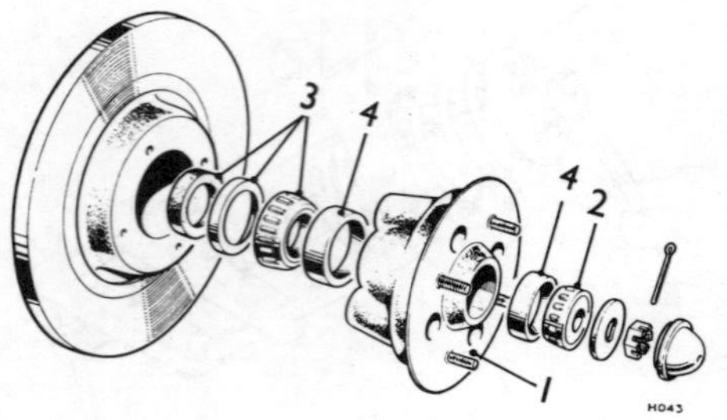

Reassembling
6. Examine all components and renew as necessary.
7. Fit the inner and outer bearing tracks to the hub.
8. Partially fill the hub with fresh grease and fit the inner bearing.
9. Fit the inner bearing shield.
10. Lubricate the new felt seal and enter the seal in the hub.
11. Fit the outer bearing.
12. Install the hub on the stub axle 60.25.01/02.

FRONT HUB BEARING END-FLOAT

— Check and adjust
60.25.13.

Checking
1. Jack up the car and remove the front wheel.
2. Remove the front brake pads.
3. Check hub bearing end-float. A correctly adjusted hub will have end-float within 0·002 to 0·008 in (0·2032 to 0·508 mm). A dial gauge can be used for checking purposes.

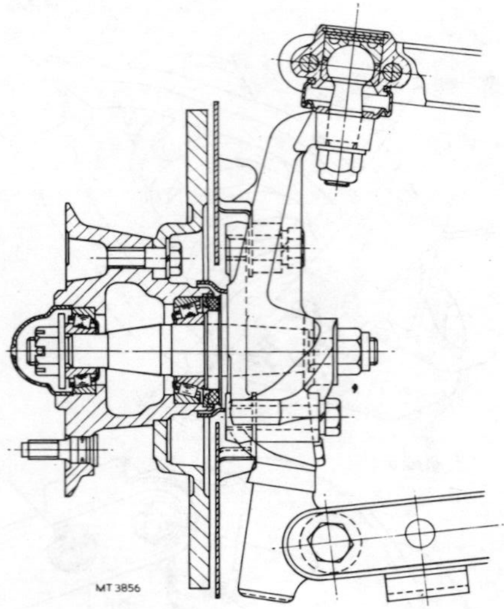

Adjusting
4. Remove the hub cap.
5. Remove the split pin from the slotted nut at the end of the stub axle.
6. Tighten or slacken the slotted nut as necessary to obtain the required end-float (item 3 above.)
7. Fit a new split pin.
8. Clean the hub cap and partially fill with fresh grease.
9. Fit the hub cap.
10. Fit the front brake pads.
11. Fit the front wheel and remove the jack.

FRONT HUB BEARINGS

— Remove and refit
60.25.14

As operation 60.25.07.

FRONT HUB OIL SEAL

— Remove and refit
60.25.15

Removing
1. Remove the front hub 60.25.01/02.
2. Withdraw the oil seal.

Refitting
3. Partially pack the hub with fresh grease.
4. Lubricate the new hub seal and enter the seal in the hub.
5. Fit the hub to the stub axle 60.25.01/02.

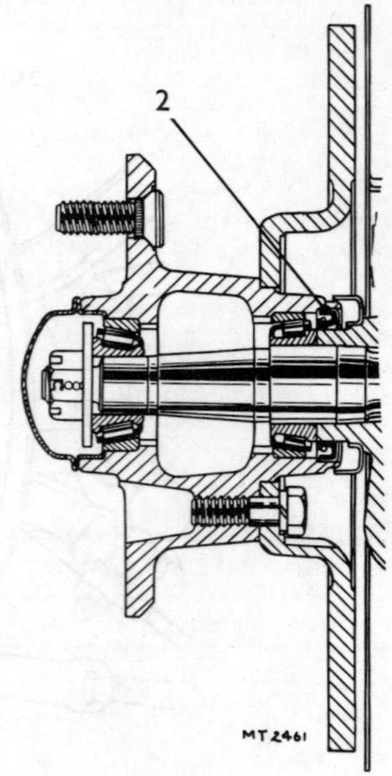

FRONT HUB STUB AXLE

— Remove and refit
60.25.22

Removing
1. Remove the vertical link 60.25.23.
2. Press out the stub axle from the vertical link.

Refitting
3. Reverse instructions 1 and 2.
4. Fit the vertical link and hub assembly 60.25.23.

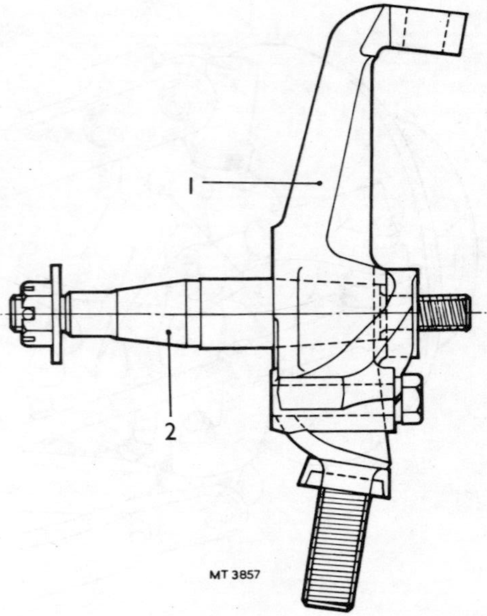

FRONT SUSPENSION

VERTICAL LINK 60.25.23

— Remove and refit

Removing

1. Jack up the car and support chassis on stand(s).
2. Remove front wheel.
3. Remove two bolts and spring washers securing caliper shield and caliper to vertical link and withdraw shield and caliper. Do not permit caliper to hang suspended by brake hose.
4. Remove hub and disc (items 5-7, 60.25.01/02).
5. Remove the bolt and spring washer securing steering arm and disc shield to vertical link.
6. Remove disc shield.
7. Remove the nyloc nut and plain washer securing steering arm to stub axle and withdraw steering arm.
8. Remove the nyloc nut and plain washer securing upper ball joint to vertical link and release ball shank from vertical link.
9. Slacken the nut and bolt securing bottom end of damper to lower wishbone.
10. Remove the nut, washer and bolt securing lower swivel to lower wishbone.
11. Withdraw vertical link.

Refitting

12. Reverse instructions 1 to 11.

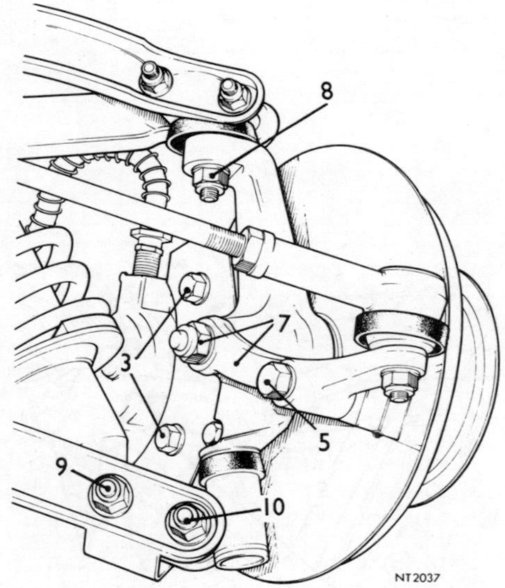

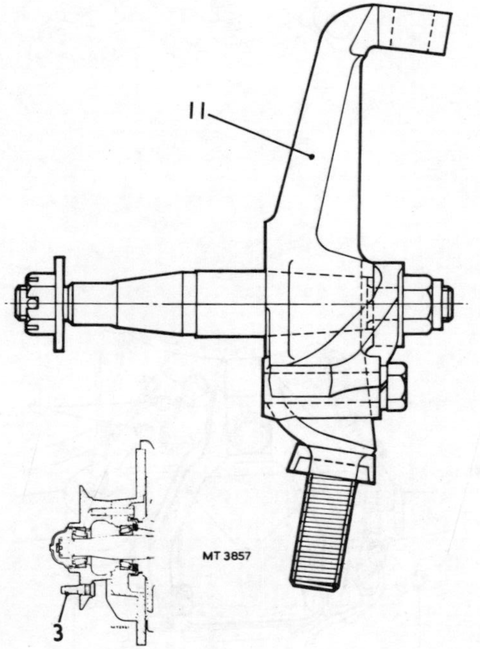

FRONT HUB WHEEL STUDS 60.25.29

— Remove and refit

Removing

1. Jack up the car and remove the front wheel.
2. Tap the wheel stud towards the disc.
3. Withdraw the stud. Wheel studs should not be removed except for purposes of renewal.

Refitting

4. Ensure that the mating countersunk faces of both stud and hub are clean.
5. Enter the wheel stud from the rear of the hub flange.
6. Using suitable packing (e.g. a short length of steel tubing) draw the stud into position.
7. Remove the nut and packing.
8. Fit the road wheel and remove the jack.

FRONT DAMPER 60.30.02

— Remove and refit

As operation 60.20.01.

FRONT DAMPER BUSHES 60.30.07

— Remove and refit

1. Remove damper and road spring assembly from the car (items 1 to 6 operation 60.20.01).

Service Tools: S4221A, S4221A-5, S4221A-18

2. Using above tools, release spring load from damper upper mountings.

Upper mountings — remove and refit.

3. Remove locknut and nut securing damper rod to mounting flange.
4. Withdraw mounting rubbers, mounting rubber seats and mounting flange from damper rod.
5. Fit new mounting rubbers, mounting rubber seats, and mounting flange in order illustrated in operation 60.20.01.
6. Fit and tighten damper rod nut and locknut.
7. Release spring and damper assembly from Service Tool.

Lower bush — remove and refit

8. Press out bush and sleeve from damper eye.
9. Press in new bush and sleeve ensuring both are centralised.
10. Install damper and road spring assembly on car (60.20.01).

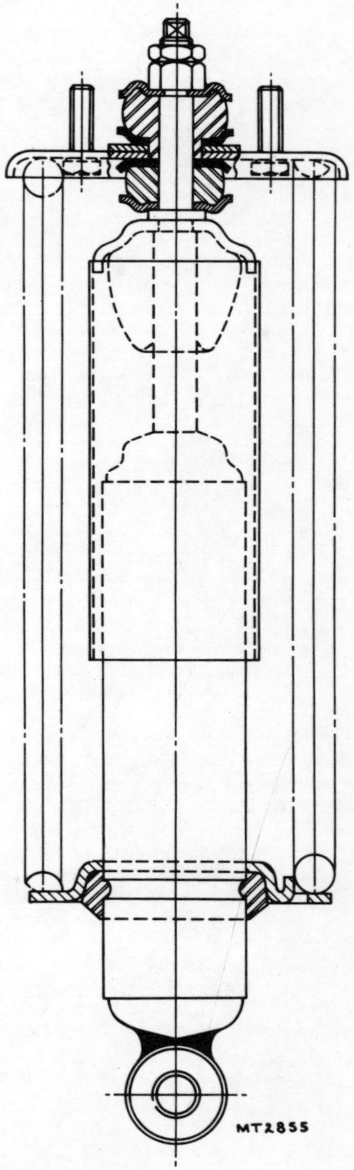

FRONT SUSPENSION

WISHBONE – UPPER

– Remove and refit 60.35.01

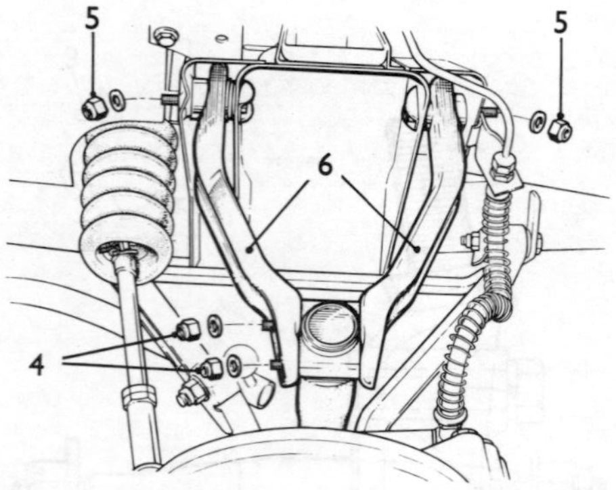

Removing

1. Jack up car and support chassis on stand(s).
2. Remove front wheel.
3. Remove front spring and damper assembly 60.20.01.
4. Remove two nyloc nuts, plain washers and bolts securing upper ball joint to outer end of wishbone.
5. Remove two nyloc nuts, plain washers and bolts securing inner ends of wishbone to bracket.
6. Withdraw upper wishbone.

Refitting

7. Reverse instructions 1 to 6. Do not tighten wishbone inner fulcrum bolts until car is static laden.
8. Fit front wheel and remove stand(s).
9. Tighten wishbone inner fulcrum bolts.

WISHBONE – LOWER

– Remove and refit 60.35.03

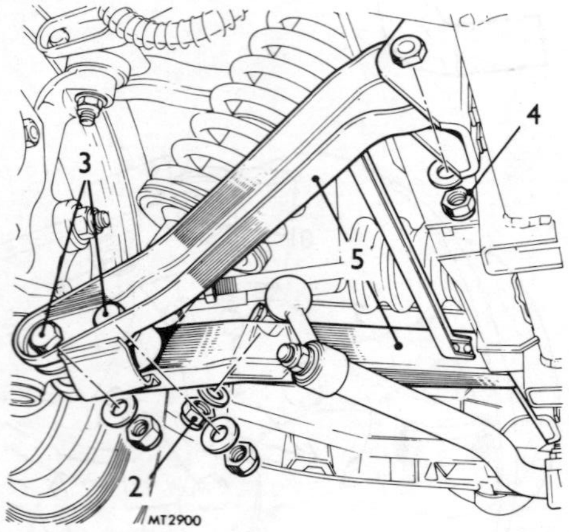

Removing

1. Jack up car and support chassis on stand(s).
2. Disconnect anti-roll bar link from lower wishbone.
3. Remove two bolts and nyloc nuts securing bottom end of damper and lower swivel bearing to outer end of lower wishbone.
4. Remove two nyloc nuts and bolts securing inner ends of wishbone to brackets.
5. Withdraw lower wishbone.

Refitting

6. Reverse instructions 1 to 5. Do not tighten wishbone inner fulcrum bolts until car is static laden.
7. Fit front wheel and remove stand(s).
8. Tighten wishbone inner fulcrum bolts.

REAR SUSPENSION OPERATIONS

Radius rod	
– bushes – remove and refit	64.35.29
– remove and refit	64.35.28
Rear damper – remove and refit	64.30.01
Rear hub	
– remove and refit	64.15.01
– wheel studs – remove and refit	64.15.26
Rear wheel alignment – check and adjust	64.25.17
Road spring	
– overhaul	64.20.04
– remove and refit	64.20.01
Vertical link – remove and refit	64.35.03

REAR HUB

– Remove and refit   64.15.01

Service Tool: S109C

Removing

1. Jack up the car and remove the road wheel.
2. Release the handbrake and remove the brake drum.
3. Remove the nyloc nut and plain washer securing the rear hub to the drive shaft.
4. Using Tool S109C, withdraw the rear hub.

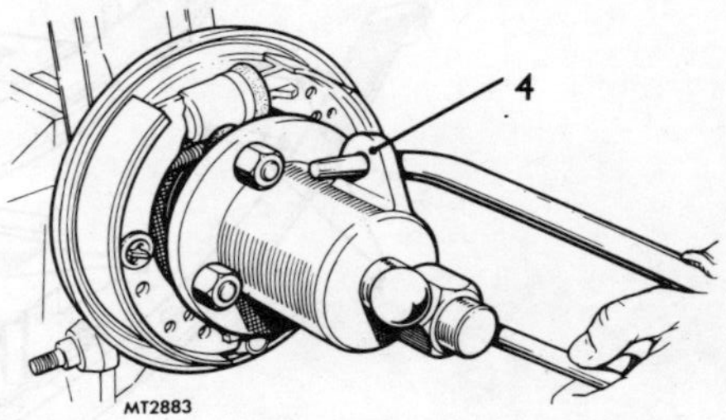

Refitting

5. Ensure that the mating tapered faces, of the drive shaft and hub are clean.
6. Enter hub on drive shaft, engaging the key in the keyway.
7. Fit the plain washer and the nyloc nut. Tighten the nut. Use a tyre lever or similar across the hub studs to apply reverse torque.
8. Fit the brake drum.
9. Fit the road wheel and remove the jack.

REAR HUB WHEEL STUDS

– Remove and refit   64.15.26

Removing

1. Jack up the car and remove the road wheel.
2. Remove the brake drum.
3. Rotate hub until rear face of wheel stud is clear of brake shoe return springs.
4. Tap out wheel stud towards the brake backplate. Wheel studs should not be removed unless renewal is intended.

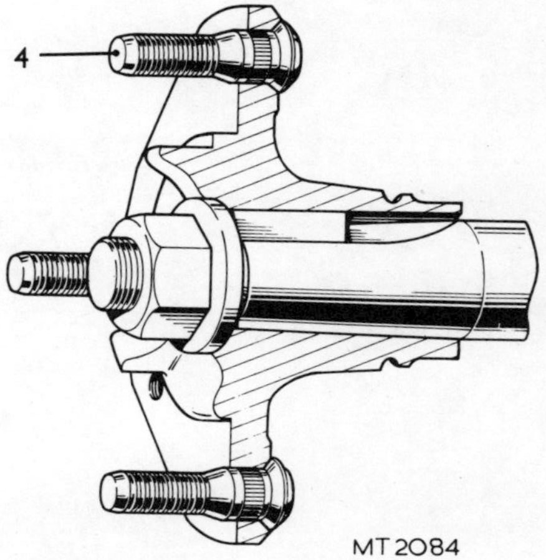

Refitting

5. Enter the stud squarely from the rear of the hub flange ensuring that the tapered faces on both hub and studs are clean.
6. Using suitable packing (e.g. a short length of tubing and washers) inserted over the wheel stud draw the stud into position. If new studs are a loose fit in the hub flange, a new hub should be fitted.
7. Fit the brake drum and road wheel and remove the jack.

REAR SUSPENSION

REAR ROAD SPRING
– Remove and refit   64.20.01

Removing

1. Jack up the car and support the chassis on stands.
2. Remove the road wheels.
3. Remove the two nyloc nuts, plain washers and bolts securing the road spring to the vertical links.
4. Remove the two nyloc nuts and plain washers. Disconnect the lower end of the dampers from the vertical links.
5. Remove the rear squab trim pad – six screws and cup washers.
6. Remove the panel – two bolts.
7. Remove the four nyloc nuts securing the spring bracket to the differential casing.
8. Using two nuts, remove the four studs from the differential casing.
9. Ease the spring ends clear of the vertical links and withdraw the spring from the car.

Refitting

10. Slide the spring into position with the spring clips stamped 'FRONT' facing the front of the car and the ground edge of the main leaf facing rearwards.
11. Locate the spring centre bolt in the recess in the differential casing.
12. Reverse 1 to 8. Do not fully tighten bolts (3) until the car is lowered to the ground.

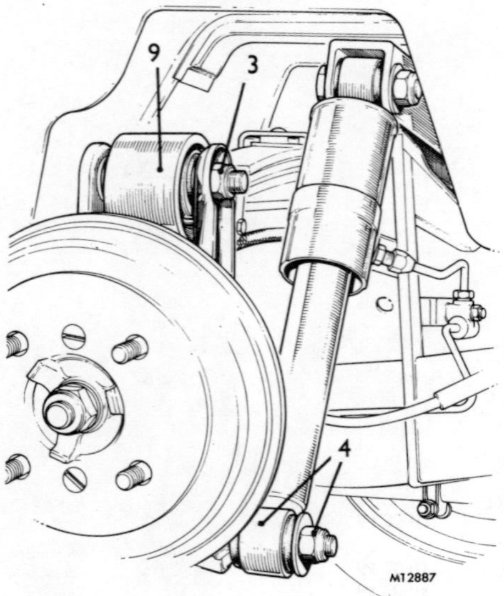

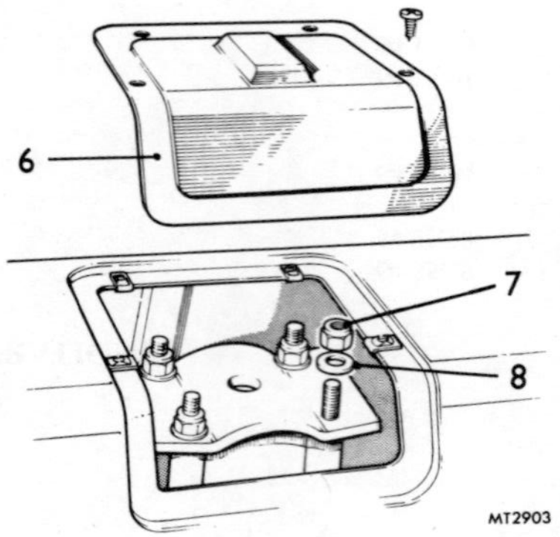

REAR ROAD SPRING
– Overhaul   64.20.04

Dismantling

1. Remove the spring 64.20.01.
2. Withdraw the spring plate.
3. Compress the spring in a vice and remove the spring bracket and rubber pad, one nut, bolt, spring washer and spacer. Release the spring from the vice.
4. Remove the four nuts, bolts and spacers from the spring clips.
5. Lift off the top three leaves.
6. Slightly bend the leg of each spring clip on the safety leaf and withdraw the main leaf.

Reassembling

7. Clean the spring leaves and lubricate with graphite grease.
8. Insert the main leaf into the safety leaf with the ground edge facing the plain, unstamped legs of the spring clips.
9. Reverse 1 to 5, ensuring that all eight rubber buttons are correctly located in the recessed tips of the spring leaves.

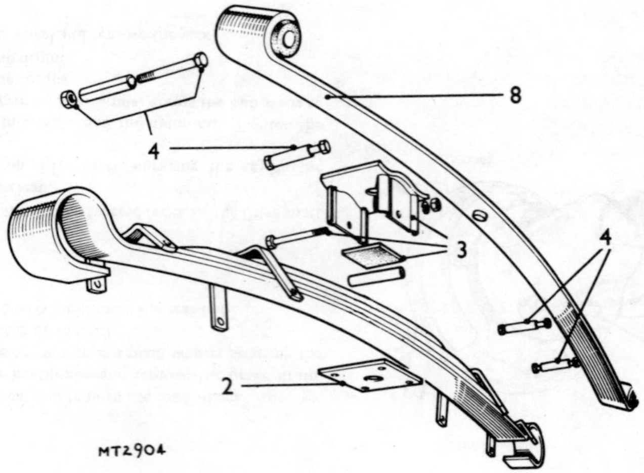

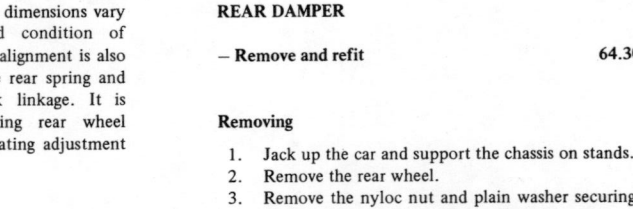

REAR SUSPENSION

REAR WHEEL ALIGNMENT

— Check and adjust 64.25.17

Checking

Toe-in/Toe-out. Rear wheel toe-in/toe-out dimensions vary as given according to the load condition of the vehicle. In addition rear wheel alignment is also influenced by the condition of the rear spring and wear factors in the vertical link linkage. It is important therefore before altering rear wheel alignment, that the causes necessitating adjustment are understood.

Adjusting

1. Locate car on level ground.
2. Using suitable equipment, check for alignment.
3. Adjust as necessary by adding to or removing from the shims fitted between the radius rod front brackets and the body. Add shims to increase toe-out shims to reduce toe-out.

In contrast to front wheel track adjustment where alteration is made equally to both tie rods to maintain balanced steering lock angles, adjustment to rear wheel track is individual to either wheel and is determined with alignment with its respective front wheel to which it has a tolerance of 0 to 1/32 in (0 to 0·79 mm) toe-in – kerb condition or 1/64 in – 3/64 in (0·39 to 1·19 mm) toe-out – laden condition (2 up).

Rear Suspension Data

Kerb condition:
- Camber . . . 1° negative ±1°
- Toe-out . . . 1/32 in – 3/32 in (0·79 – 2·38 mm)

Laden condition (2 up):
- Camber . . . 3·3/4° negative ±1°
- Toe-in . . . 0 in – 1/16 in (0 to 1·59 mm)

Camber. No provision is made for adjustment to camber angle. Camber angles found to be outside the above limits are generally indicative of a weak or incorrectly set spring, or wear in the vertical link bushes.

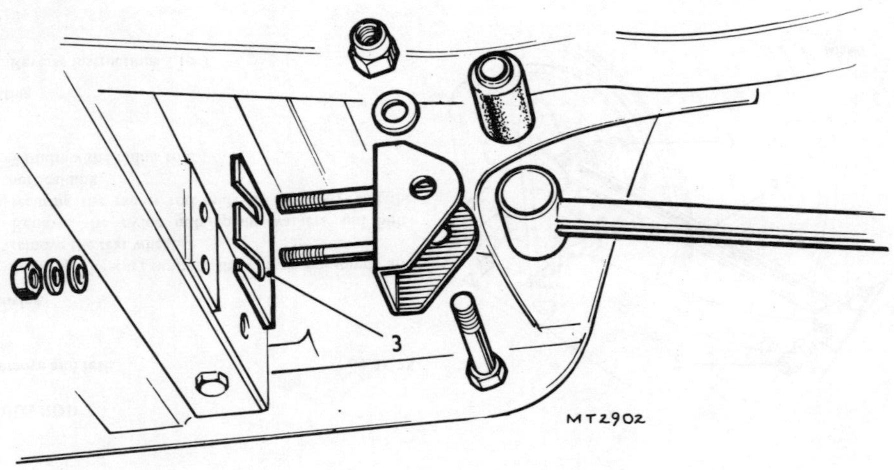

REAR DAMPER

— Remove and refit 64.30.01

Removing

1. Jack up the car and support the chassis on stands.
2. Remove the rear wheel.
3. Remove the nyloc nut and plain washer securing the lower end of damper to the vertical link.
4. Remove the nyloc nut, plain washer and bolt securing the upper end of damper to the chassis.
5. Withdraw the damper.

Refitting

6. Reverse instructions 1 to 5.

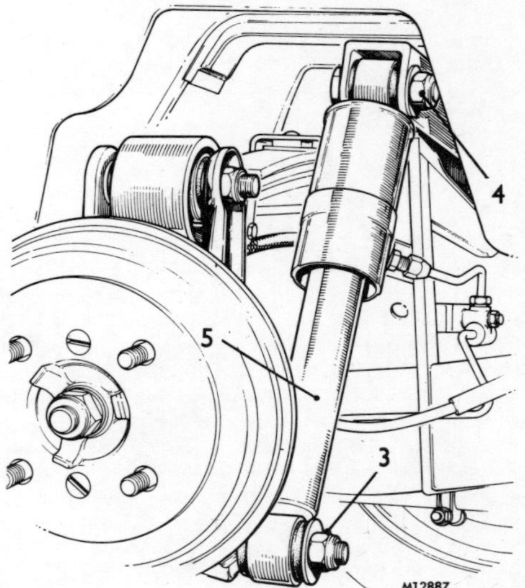

VERTICAL LINK

— Remove and refit 64.35.03

Removing

1. Jack up the car and support the chassis on stands.
2. Remove the rear wheel.
3. Remove the nyloc nut, plain washer and bolt securing the radius rod from the bracket on the vertical link. Detach the radius rod from the vertical link.
4. Remove the nyloc nut and plain washer securing lower end of damper to vertical link. Detach damper.
5. Remove the nyloc nut, plain washer and bolt securing the upper end of the vertical link to the road spring.
6. Remove the nyloc nut, plain washer and bolt securing the vertical link to the inner hub.
7. Remove the vertical link.

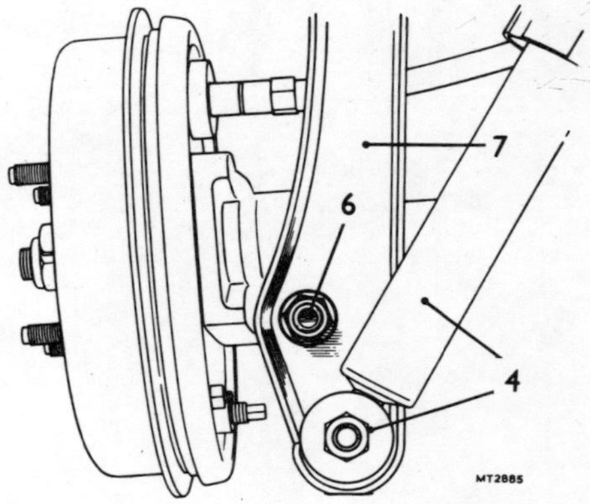

Refitting

8. Offer up the vertical link to the car and engage the lower end of the link in the damper bush.
9. Ensure inner hub pivot bush seals and covers are intact and in position and fit the vertical link to the inner hub. Secure in position with bolt, plain washer and nyloc nut.
10. Fit bolt, plain washer and nyloc nut to upper end of vertical link and road spring.
11. Fit plain washer and nyloc nut to secure the damper to the vertical link.
12. Connect the radius rod to the vertical link bracket and secure with bolt, plain washer and nyloc nut.
13. Fit the road wheel.
14. Remove the chassis stands.

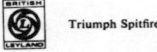

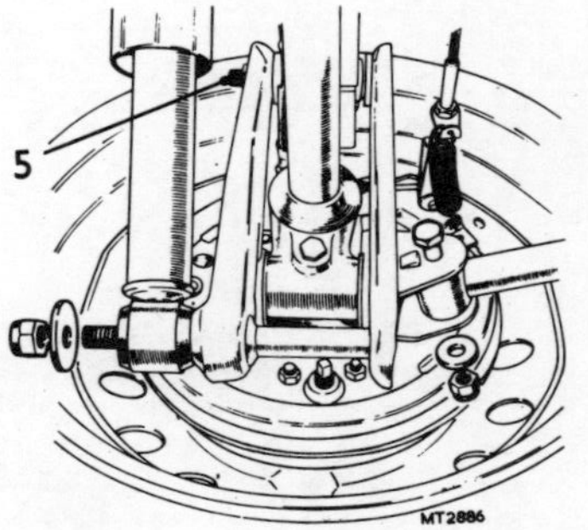

REAR SUSPENSION

RADIUS ROD
— Remove and refit   64.35.28

Removing
1. Jack up the car, support the chassis on stands and remove the rear wheel.
2. Remove the nyloc nuts, plain washers and bolts securing the radius rod ends to the body and the vertical link.
3. Withdraw the radius rod.

Refitting
4. Reverse instructions 1 to 3.

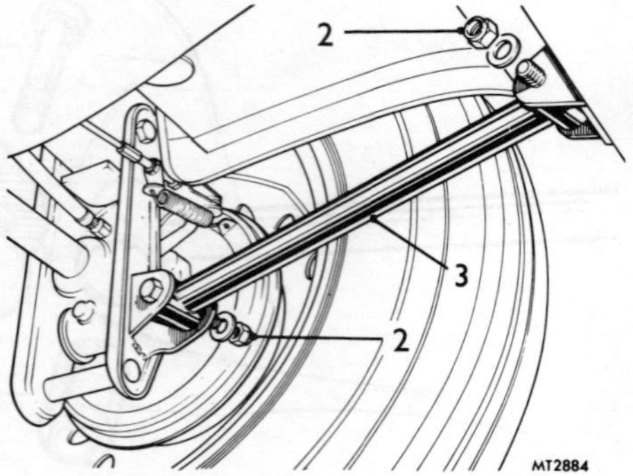

RADIUS ROD BUSHES
— Remove and refit   64.35.29

Removing
1. Remove the radius rod 64.35.28.
2. Press out bushes.

Refitting
3. Press in new bushes.
4. Fit the radius rod to the car.

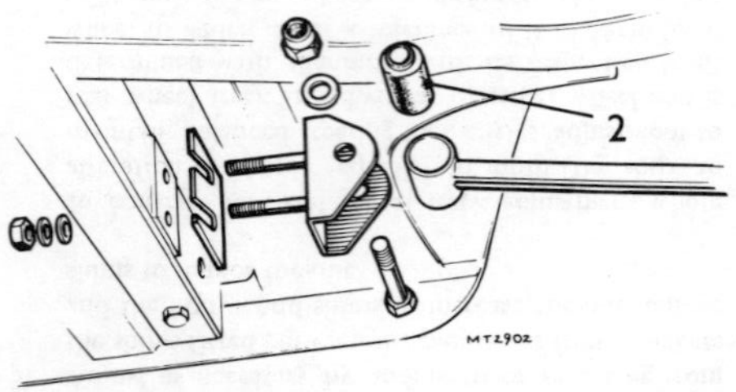

BRAKE OPERATIONS

Brake hose	
– front – remove and refit	70.15.02/03
– rear – remove and refit	70.15.17/18
Brake pedal – remove and refit	70.35.01
Brakes	
– adjust	70.25.03
– bleed	70.25.02
Connectors	
– 2-way – remove and refit	70.15.32
– 3-way – remove and refit	70.15.34
– 4-way – remove and refit	70.15.35
Front brake	
– brake pads – remove and refit	70.40.02
– caliper – remove and refit	70.55.02
– caliper seals – remove and refit	70.55.13
– disc – remove and refit	70.10.10
– disc shield – remove and refit	70.10.18
Handbrake	
– cables – adjust	70.35.10
– cables – remove and refit	70.35.16
– compensator – remove and refit	70.35.11
– lever – remove and refit	70.35.08
– pawl and ratchet – remove and refit	70.35.09
– relay lever – remove and refit	70.35.22
Hydraulic pipes – remove and refit	70.20.01/27
P.D.W.A. unit	
– remove and refit	70.15.36
Rear brake	
– adjust	70.25.03
– backplate – remove and refit	70.40.17
– brake adjuster – remove and refit	70.10.26
– brake drum – remove and refit	70.10.03
– brake shoes – remove and refit	70.40.03
– Wheel cylinder – overhaul	70.60.26
– wheel cylinder – remove and refit	70.60.18
Master cylinder	
– overhaul	70.30.02
– remove and refit	70.30.01
– tandem type – overhaul	70.30.09
– tandem type – remove and refit	70.30.08

REAR BRAKE DRUM   70.10.03

– Remove and refit

Removing

1. Jack up the car and support the chassis on stands.
2. Remove the rear wheel.
3. Remove two countersunk screws securing the rear brake drum to the hub.
4. Release the handbrake.
5. Withdraw the brake drum.

Refitting

5. Reverse instructions 1 to 5.

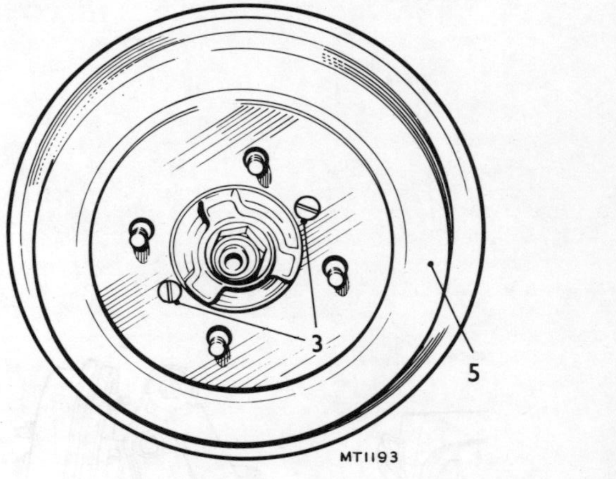

FRONT DISC   70.10.10

– Remove and refit

Removing

1. Jack up the car and support the chassis on stands.
2. Remove the front wheel.
3. Remove two bolts securing the caliper shield and caliper to the vertical link.
4. Withdraw the caliper ensuring that strain is not imposed on the brake hose.
5. Remove the front hub 60.25.01.
6. Remove four bolts and spring washers securing the disc to the front hub.
7. Withdraw the disc.

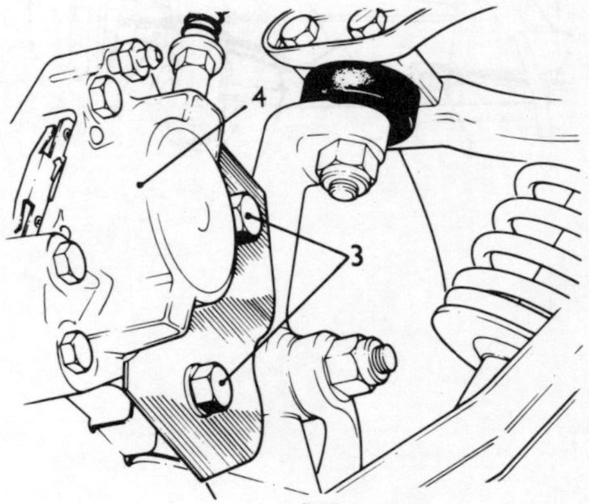

Refitting

8. Offer up the disc to the front hub ensuring that the mating faces are clean.
9. Fit and tighten the four spring washers and bolts.
10. Locate the felt oil seal in the hub.
11. Fit the hub and disc to the stub axle.
12. Fit the caliper and shield to the vertical link.
13. Fit the road wheel and remove the chassis stands.

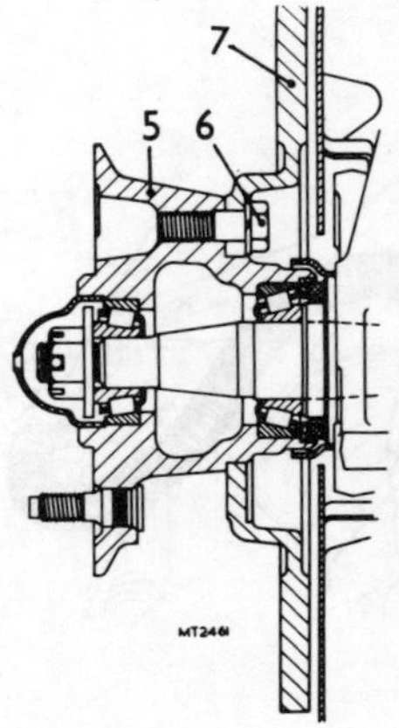

BRAKES

FRONT DISC SHIELD

— Remove and refit

70.10.18

Removing

1. Jack up the car and support the chassis on stands.
2. Remove the front wheel.
3. Remove the brake caliper and the front hub 60.25.01.
4. Slacken the nyloc nut securing the steering arm to the stub axle.
5. Remove the bolt and spring washer securing the steering arm to the vertical link.
6. Withdraw the disc shield.

Refitting

7. Reverse instructions 1 to 6.

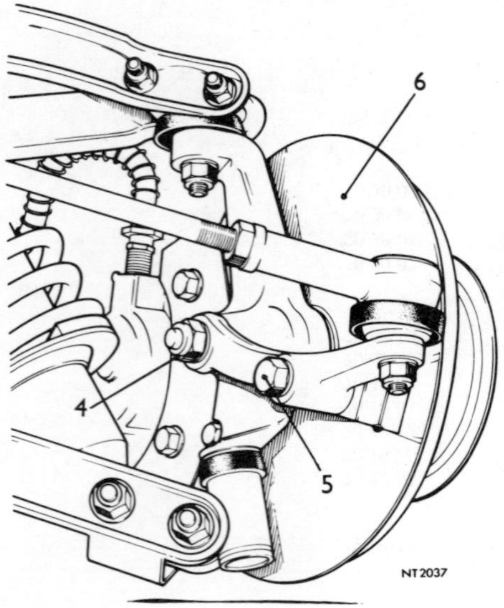

REAR BACKPLATE

— Remove and refit

70.10.26

Removing

1. Jack up the car and support the chassis on stands.
2. Remove the rear wheel.
3. Remove the rear brake drum and hub 64.15.01
4. Detach the handbrake cable return spring from the bracket on the backplate.
5. Remove the clevis pin securing the handbrake lever to the brake shoe operating lever.
6. Remove the rear flexible brake hose.
7. Straighten tabs on locking plates securing the backplate bolts.
8. Remove the backplate securing bolts.
9. Withdraw the backplate and bearing shield.

Refitting

10. Reverse instructions 1 to 9.
11. Bleed the brakes.

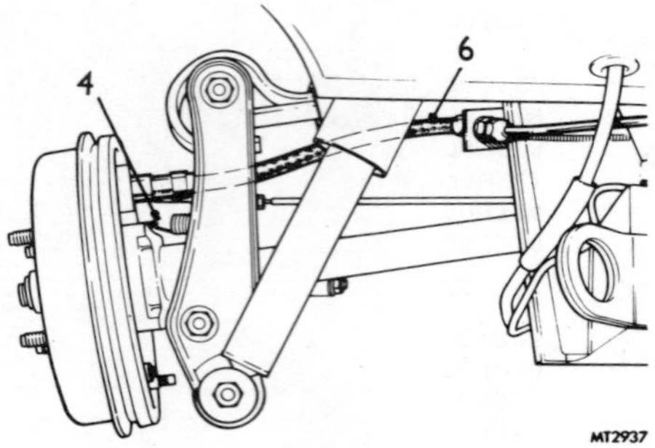

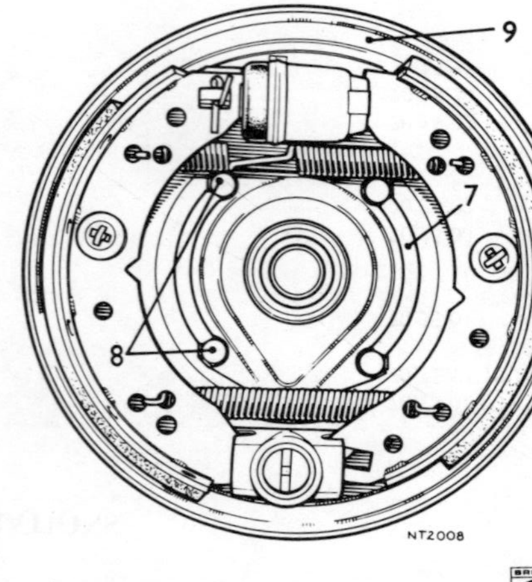

BRAKE HOSE — FRONT

— Remove and refit

Left hand **70.15.02**
Right hand **70.15.03**

Removing

1. Disconnect the brake pipe from the inboard end of the flexible hose.
2. Using two spanners remove the nut and washer securing the inboard end of the flexible hose to the front suspension bracket.
3. Withdraw the inboard end of the flexible hose from the suspension bracket.
4. Unscrew the outboard end of the flexible hose from the brake caliper.

Refitting

5. Reverse instructions 1 to 4, ensure that the hose is neither kinked nor twisted when installed.
6. Bleed the brakes.

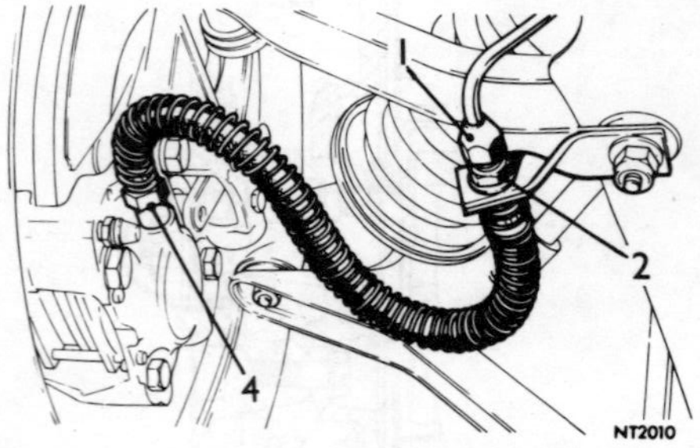

BRAKE HOSE — REAR

— Remove and refit

Left hand **70.15.17**
Right hand **70.15.18**

Removing

1. Disconnect the union and brake pipe from the inboard end of the flexible hose.
2. Using two spanners remove the nut and washer securing the flexible hose to the chassis bracket.
3. Withdraw inboard end of hose from the chassis bracket.
4. Unscrew the outboard end of the hose from the brake backplate.

Refitting

5. Reverse instructions 1 to 4. Ensure that the hose is neither kinked nor twisted when installed.
6. Bleed the brakes.

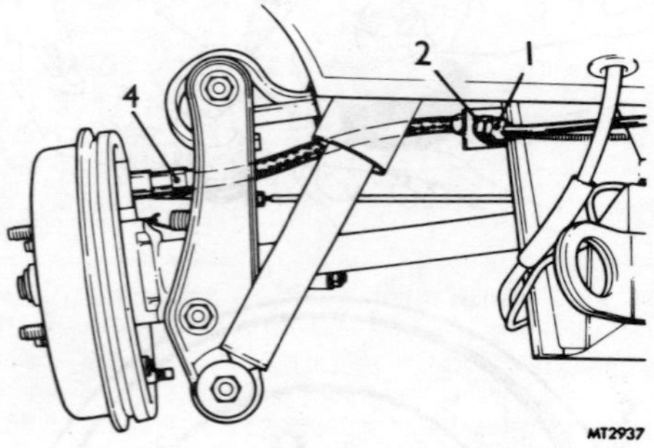

BRAKES

CONNECTOR – 2-WAY
– Remove and refit 70.15.32

Removing
1. Disconnect the unions and brake pipes from he connector.
2. Withdraw the connector.

Refitting
3. Reverse instructions 1 and 2.
4. Bleed the brakes.

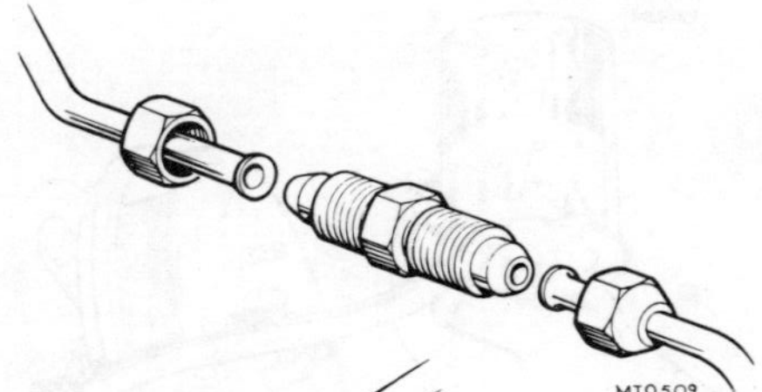

CONNECTOR
– Remove and refit

3-way 70.15.34
4-way 70.15.35

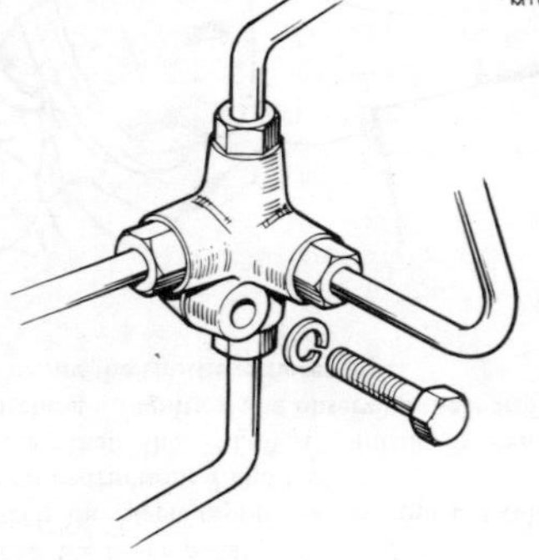

Removing
1. Disconnect the unions and brake pipes from the connector.
2. Remove the nut, spring washer and bolt securing the connector to the chassis.
3. Remove the connector.

Refitting
4. Reverse instructions 1 to 3.
5. Bleed the brakes.

P.D.W.A. UNIT
– Remove and refit 70.15.36

Removing
1. Release the snap connector from P.D.W.A. unit.
2. Disconnect the four brake pipe unions at P.D.W.A. unit.
3. Remove the bolt securing P.D.W.A. unit to car.
4. Withdraw the P.D.W.A. unit.

Refitting
5. Reverse instructions 1 to 4.
6. Bleed the brakes.
7. Check operation of brake circuit warning light and ensure that the P.D.W.A. shuttle is centralised.

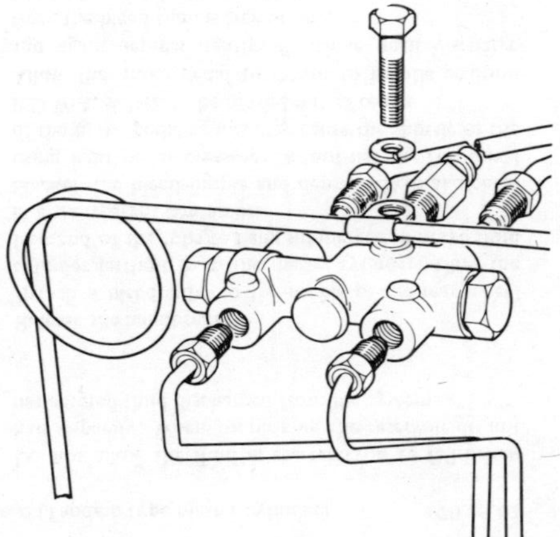

70.15.32
70.15.34/35
70.15.36

BRAKE PIPES
– Remove and refit

Pipe – Master cylinder to 4-way connector	70.20.01
Pipe – 4-way connector to L.H. front hose	70.20.02
Pipe – 4-way connector to R.H. front hose	70.20.03
Pipe – 2-way connector to 3-way connector	70.20.14
Pipe – 3-way connector to L.H. rear hose	70.20.15
Pipe – 3-way connector to R.H. rear hose	70.20.16
Pipe – 4-way connector to 2-way connector	70.20.27

Removing
1. Disconnect unions at both ends of pipe.
2. Release pipe from securing clips (where fitted).

Refitting
3. Reverse instructions 1 and 2.
4. Bleed the brakes.

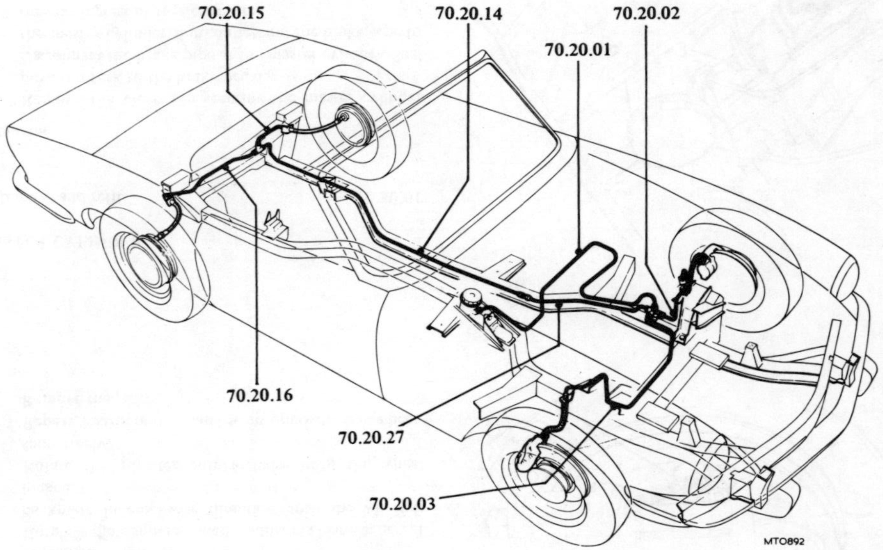

70.20.01
70.20.27

BRAKES

— Bleed 70.25.02

Do not allow the fluid in the reservoir to fall below half capacity. When topping up the reservoir do not use aerated fluid discharged from the system.

1. Release the handbrake.
2. Attach a rubber or plastic tube of suitable bore to the bleed nipple of the front caliper farthest from the master cylinder. Allow the free end of the tube to hang submerged in brake fluid in a transparent container.
3. Slacken the bleed nipple.
4. Depress the brake pedal fully and follow with three rapid strokes. Allow the pedal to return. Repeat until fluid, free from air bubbles issues from the bleed tube.
5. Depress the brake pedal and tighten the bleed nipple.
6. Release the brake pedal and remove the tube and container.
7. Repeat instructions 2 to 6 on opposite front caliper.
8. Bleed both rear wheel cylinders in similar manner commencing with the longest pipe run (i.e. commence with left hand cylinder on right hand steer models and right hand cylinder on left hand steer models).
9. Remove the bleed tube and container.

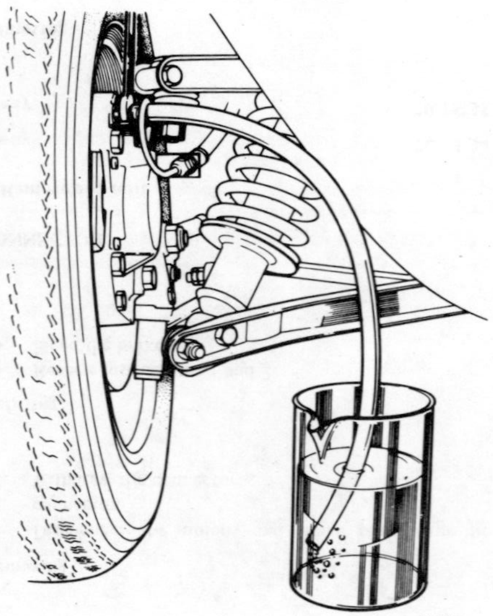

BRAKES

— Bleed (Tandem type master cylinder) 70.25.02

Do not allow the fluid in the reservoir to fall below half capacity. When topping up the reservoir do not use aerated fluid discharged from the system.

1. Release the handbrake.
2. Attach a bleed tube to the nipple of the rear wheel cylinder farthest from the master cylinder. Allow the free end of the tube to hang submerged in brake fluid in a transparent container.
3. Slacken the bleed nipple and depress the brake pedal using light pedal pressure. Do not use the full travel of the pedal as this may cause the shuttle of the P.D.W.A. switch to be moved out of centre. Allow the brake pedal to return to its idle position and again depress lightly. Continue until discharge from the bleed tube is free of air.
4. Hold the pedal depressed, tighten the nipple and remove the bleed tube.
5. Repeat instructions 2 and 3 on the opposite rear wheel cylinder.
6. Attach the bleed tube to the front caliper farthest from the master cylinder.
7. Depress and release the brake pedal until air bubbles cease to issue from the bleed tube.
8. Hold the pedal depressed, tighten the nipple and release the brake pedal.
9. Attach the bleed nipple to the opposite caliper and repeat instructions 7 and 8.
10. Check that the P.D.W.A. shuttle is centred by switching on ignition and observing the warning light. Re-centre the shuttle as necessary.

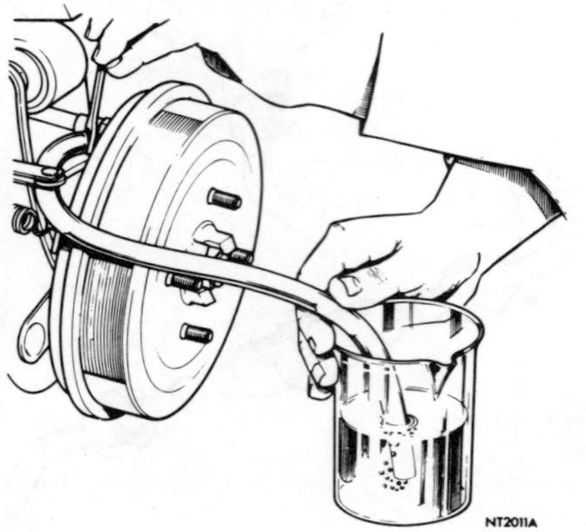

BRAKES

— Adjust 70.25.03

Front

The front disc brakes are self-adjusting.

Rear

1. Release the handbrake and raise the rear wheels clear of ground contact.
2. Rotate the square-ended adjusters on rear of backplate in clockwise direction until the wheel is locked.
3. Rotate the adjuster anti-clockwise until the wheel spins freely.
4. Repeat instructions 3 and 4 on opposite rear wheel.
5. Remove the jack.

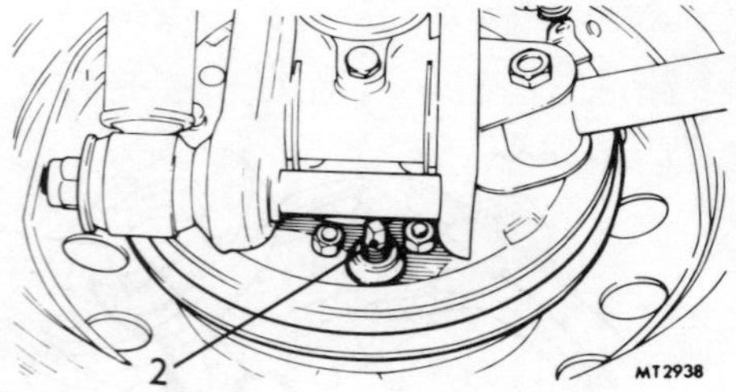

MASTER CYLINDER

— Remove and refit 70.30.01

Removing

1. Remove the clevis pin securing the master cylinder push rod fork to the brake pedal.
2. Disconnect the brake pipe at the master cylinder. Seal the master cylinder fluid outlet and the brake pipe to prevent ingress of foreign matter.
3. Remove the two bolts and spring washers securing the master cylinder to the mounting bracket.
4. Withdraw the master cylinder.

Refitting

5. Reverse instructions 1 to 4.
6. Bleed the brakes.

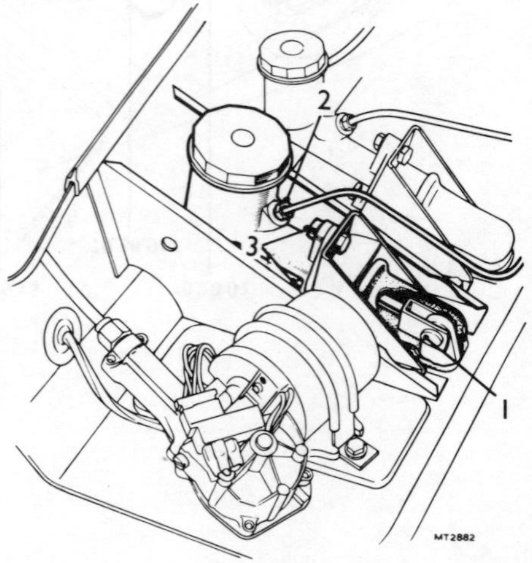

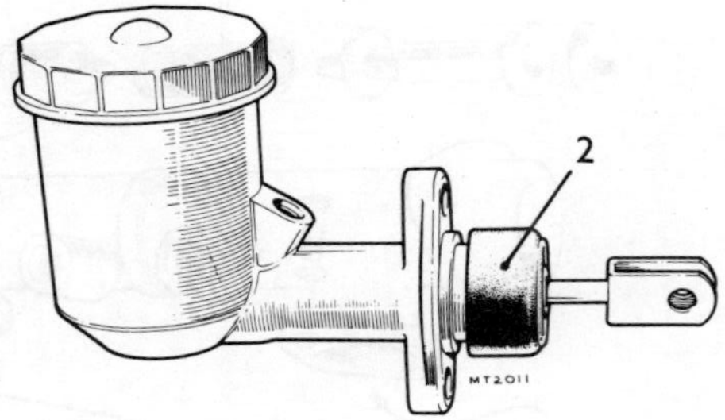

BRAKES

MASTER CYLINDER
— Overhaul
70.30.02

Dismantling

1. Drain the fluid reservoir.
2. Slide the rubber dust cover along the push rod to expose end of master cylinder.
3. Remove the circlip and withdraw the push rod and dished washer.
4. Withdraw the piston and seal assembly.
5. Straighten the prong of the spring thimble and remove the thimble from the piston.
6. Release the valve stem from the keyhole slot in the thimble.
7. Remove the spring and slide the valve seal spacer along the valve stem.
8. Remove the valve seal from the valve stem.
9. Remove the seal from the piston.
10. Clean and examine all components.

Assembling

11. Fit a new seal to the piston.
12. Fit a new seal to the valve stem.
13. Assemble the spacer, spring and thimble to the valve stem.
14. Fit the thimble to the piston and carefully depress the thimble prong.
15. Lubricate the master cylinder bore with clean brake fluid and insert the piston and seal assembly.
16. Fit the push rod and dished washer and secure with the circlip.
17. Fit a new rubber dust cover.

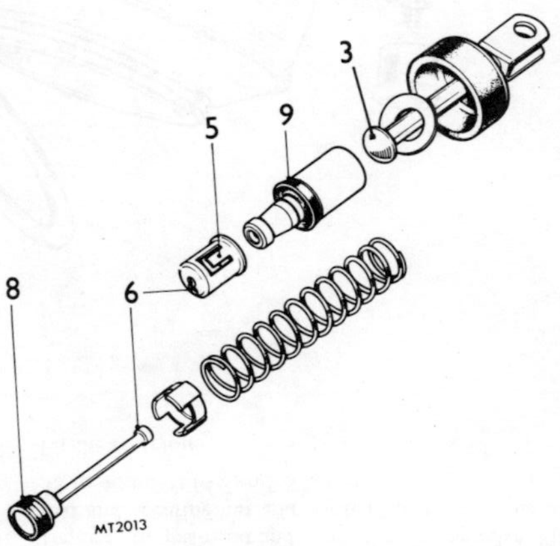

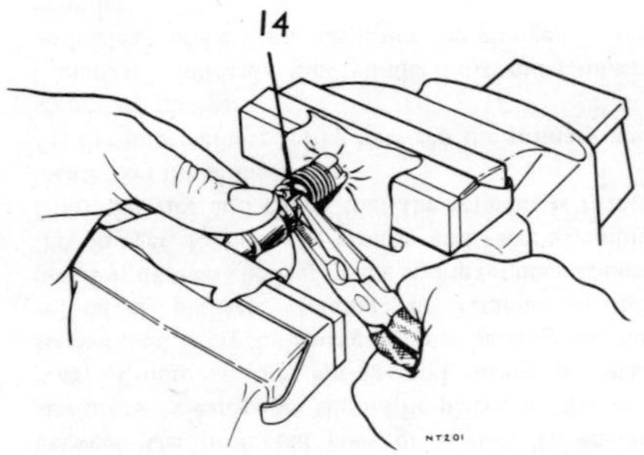

MASTER CYLINDER (TANDEM TYPE)
— Remove and refit
70.30.08

Removing

1. Raise the rubber boot to expose the master cylinder/brake pedal linkage and remove the split pin, plain washer, clevis pin and the rubber boot.
2. Disconnect the brake pipes at the master cylinder. Seal the master cylinder fluid outlets and the brake pipes to prevent ingress of foreign matter.
3. Remove the four bolts and spring washers securing the master cylinder mounting bracket to the scuttle and withdraw the mounting bracket and the master cylinder.
4. Remove the nut, spring washer and the bolt securing the master cylinder flange to the mounting bracket.
5. Remove the bolt and spring washer securing the master cylinder flange to the mounting bracket.

Refitting

6. Reverse instructions 1 to 5.
7. Bleed the brakes.

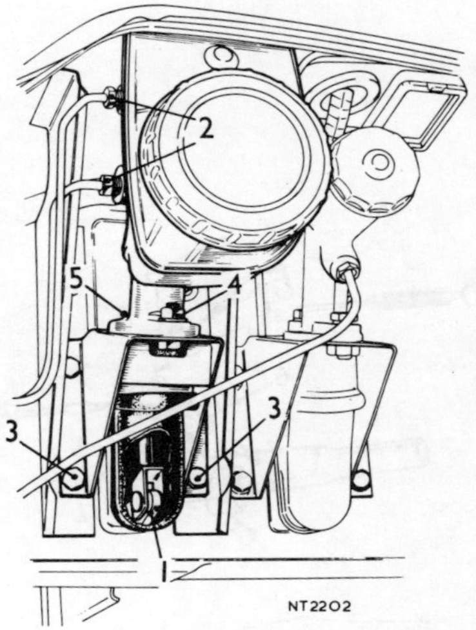

MASTER CYLINDER (TANDEM TYPE)
— Overhaul
70.30.09

Dismantling

1. Remove the master cylinder, detach mounting bracket and drain the brake fluid. 70.30.08.
2. Remove the reservoir (four screws).
3. Remove the internal nut securing the tipping valve to the master cylinder body.
4. Apply slight pressure on the push rod to allow the tipping valve to seat and withdraw the tipping valve.
5. Slide the dust cover clear of the cylinder to expose the circlip retaining the push rod and remove the circlip.

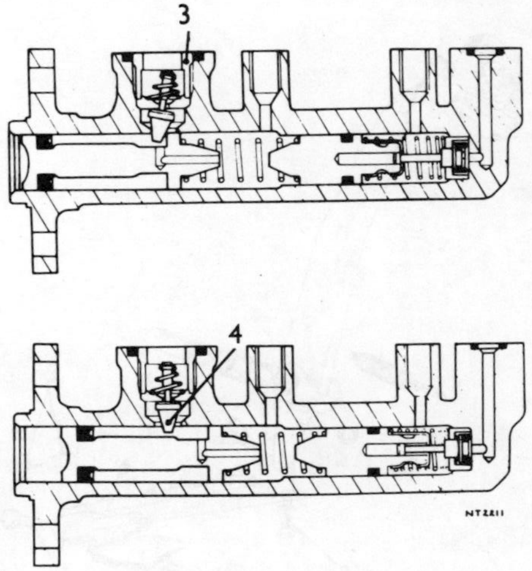

BRAKES

6. Withdraw the push rod.
7. Withdraw the primary and secondary plungers complete with seals and springs.
8. Separate the plungers and the intermediate spring.
9. Prise up the leaf of the spring retainer and remove the spring and centre valve sub-assembly from the secondary plunger.
10. Withdraw the valve spacer, spring washer and valve seal from the valve head.
11. Remove the seals from the primary and secondary plungers.
12. Thoroughly clean all components.
13. Examine the cylinder bore for wear, scoring and corrosion. If damage or wear is evident a new tandem cylinder must be obtained.

Assembling

14. Fit new seals to the primary and secondary plungers.
15. Fit a new valve seal, smaller diameter leading, to the valve head.
16. Place the spring washer on the valve stem ensuring that the convex side of the washer is adjacent to the valve.
17. Fit valve spacer, legs leading.
18. Fit the spring retainer to the valve stem, keyhole leading.
19. Slide the secondary spring over the spring retainer and offer up the secondary plunger.
20. Place the secondary plunger and vale assembly between the protected jaws of a vice. To ensure cleanliness, clean paper should be placed on the vice jaws. Compress the spring and using a small screwdriver, press the spring retainer hard against the secondary plunger. Holding the retainer in this position depress the leaf of the spring retainer against the plunger. Remove the plunger and valve assembly from the vice and check that the retainer is firmly located on the plunger.
21. Fit the intermediate spring between the primary and secondary plungers.
22. Generously lubricate the cylinder bore and plungers with clean brake fluid and insert the plungers in the cylinder.
23. Fit the push rod and the retaining circlip and rubber boot.
24. Depress the push rod and insert the tipping valve. Fit seal and securing nut and tighten nut to a torque of 35 to 40 lbf. ft (4·8 to 5·5 kgf. m).
25. Fit the reservoir.

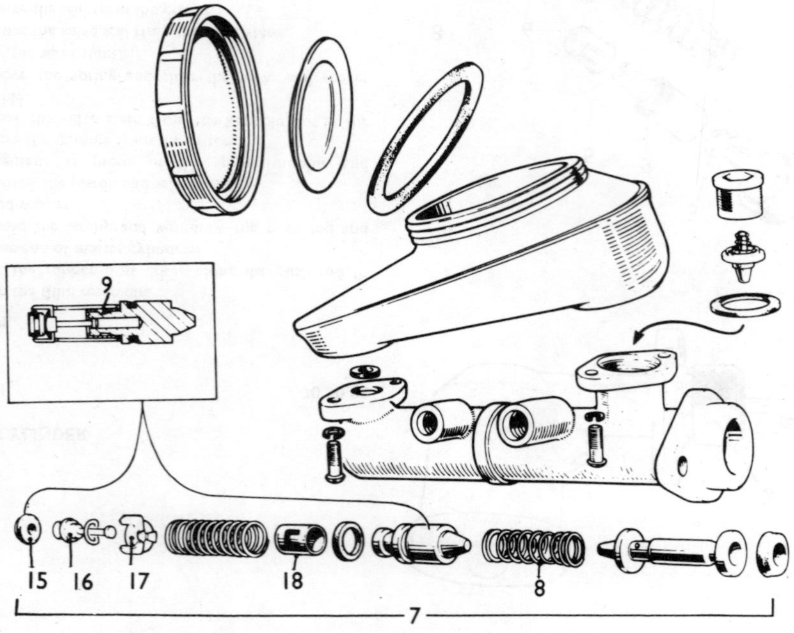

BRAKE PEDAL ASSEMBLY 70.35.01
— Remove and refit

Removing
1. Remove the clevis pin securing master cylinder push rod fork to brake pedal.
2. Remove the terminal connectors from the brake light switch.
3. Remove the bolts, nuts and spring washers securing the brake pedal bracket to the scuttle.
4. Withdraw the brake pedal and bracket assembly.

Refitting
5. Reverse instructions 1 to 4.

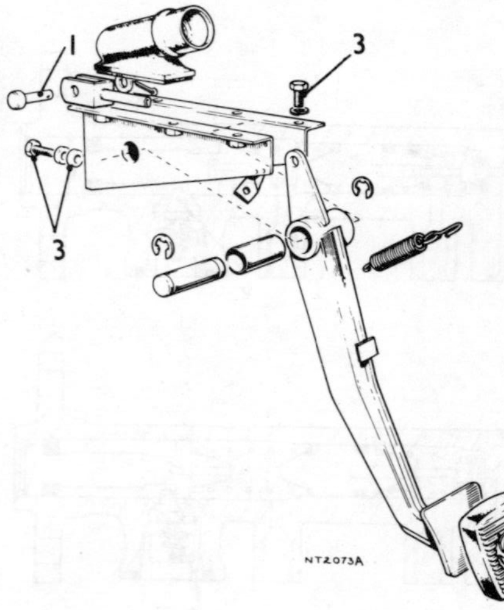

HANDBRAKE LEVER 70.35.08
— Remove and refit

Removing
1. Remove the driver's and passenger's seats complete with runners. 76.70.04/05.
2. Remove the safety belt buckle brackets from tunnel.
3. Remove the safety belt buckles from the floor of car.
4. Remove the carpet.
5. Remove the hand grip from the handbrake lever.
6. Remove the four screws securing the handbrake cover and slide the cover clear of the handbrake.
7. Remove the circlip securing handbrake fulcrum pin to bracket.
8. Remove the fulcrum pin and lift the handbrake clear of the bracket.
9. Remove the split pin and clevis pin securing the handbrake lever to the cable fork and withdraw the handbrake lever.

Refitting
10. Reverse instructions 1 to 9.

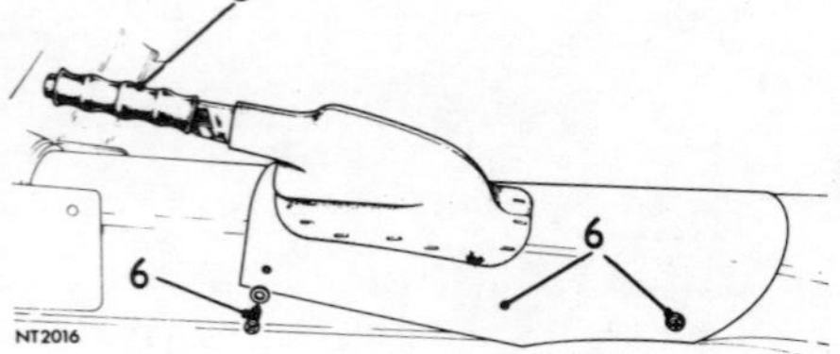

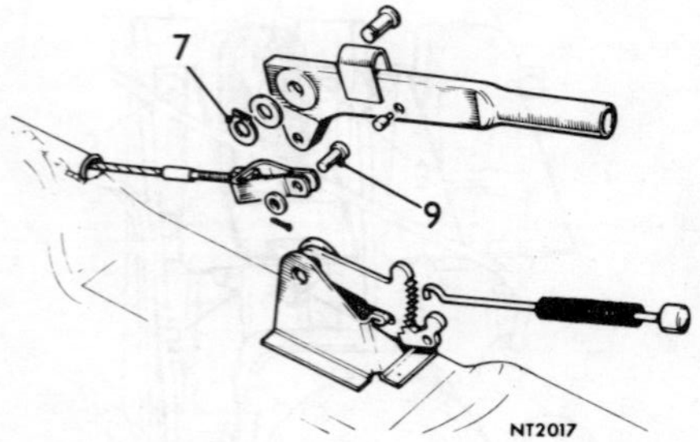

BRAKES

HANDBRAKE PAWL AND RATCHET
– Remove and refit   70.35.09

Removing

1. Remove the handbrake lever, 70.35.08.
2. File the riveted end of the pawl fulcrum pin until the end of the pin is flush with the handbrake lever.
3. Depress the handbrake button and retain in this position with tape.
4. Remove the pawl fulcrum pin and withdraw the pawl and ratchet.

Refitting

5. Insert a new ratchet (hooked end downwards) into the handbrake lever.
6. Insert new pawl (teeth downward, facing teeth on ratchet) into handbrake lever.
7. Fit a new fulcrum pin to pawl and rivet the end of pin ensuring that the pawl pivots freely.
8. Engage hooked end of release lever in the pawl and remove the tape from the release button.
9. Secure the handbrake lever to the handbrake cable fork and fit a new split pin to the clevis pin.
10. Align the ratched hole with the hole in the handbrake lever and fit the lever to the car mounting bracket.
11. Fit the fulcrum pin and secure with the circlip.
12. Refit the handbrake cover, handgrip, carpet and seats. 70.35.08.

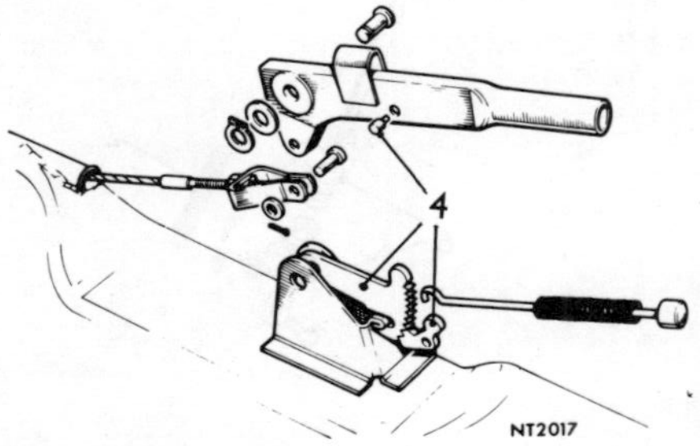

HANDBRAKE CABLES

Adjust   70.35.10

1. Jack up the rear wheels and support the chassis on stands.
2. Release the handbrake.
3. Rotate the rear brake adjusters and lock both rear wheels.
4. Check that the relay lever is positioned as shown. Adjust front and rear cables as necessary to obtain this condition.

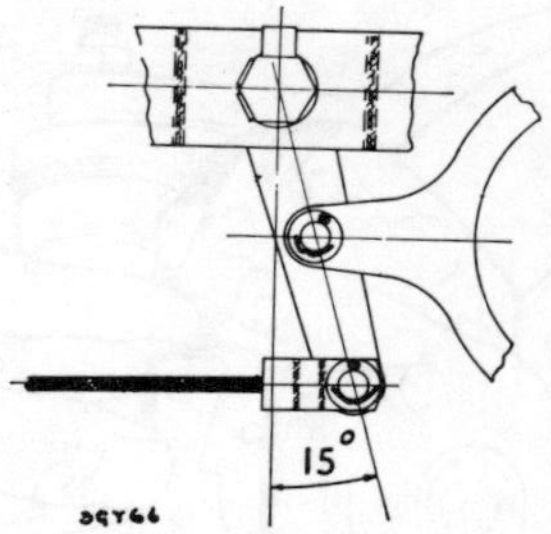

Adjusting the front cable

5. Remove the carpet and handbrake lever cover to expose the handbrake lever 70.35.08.
6. Slacken the cable locknut at the rear of the cable fork and rotate the cable as necessary, clockwise to tighten the cable, anti-clockwise to slacken the cable. Tighten the locknut. Note that it may be necessary to first release the rear cable from the brake backplate.
7. Refit the handbrake lever cover, carpets and seats. 70.35.08.

Adjusting the rear cable

8. Disconnect the cable fork ends from the brake backplate lever.
9. Adjust the cable forks equally at both ends of the cable until with slight strain applied to the cable, the clevis pins can be inserted to secure the cable forks to the backplate levers. Do not force the cables taut to insert the clevis pins.
10. Fit the washers and new split pins to the clevis pins.
11. Tighten the cable fork lock nuts.
12. Slacken the brake adjusters until the wheels spin freely.
13. Remove the chassis stands.

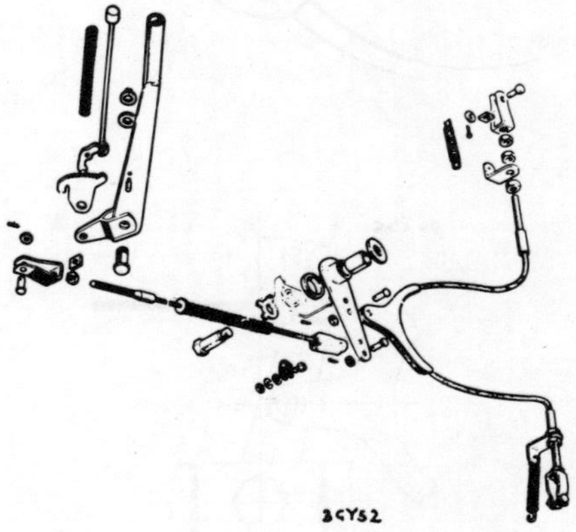

HANDBRAKE COMPENSATOR

Remove and Refit   70.35.11

Removing

1. Release the handbrake.
2. Remove the split pin and plain washer securing the compensator to the relay lever and withdraw the clevis pin.
3. Remove the compensator from the rear cable.

Refitting

4. Reverse instructions 1 to 3.

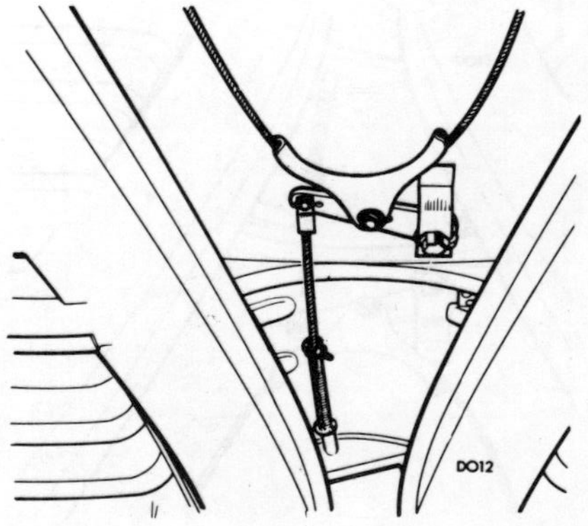

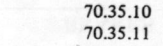

BRAKES

HANDBRAKE CABLES
— Remove and refit   70.35.16

Removing
Front
1. Remove the handbrake lever 70.35.08.
2. Disconnect the cable fork from the handbrake lever.
3. Remove the front cable fork from the cable.
4. Disconnect the cable fork from the relay lever.
5. Withdraw the cable from the car.

Rear
6. Disconnect the compensator from the relay lever.
7. Unhook the cable return springs.
8. Disconnect the cable forks from the backplate levers.
9. Remove the cable forks and spring plates from the cable.
10. Withdraw the cable from the car.

Refitting
Front
11. Fit the cable in position on car.
12. Fit the fork and nuts to the front end of the cables.
13. Connect the front end of the cable to the handbrake lever.
14. Fit the handbrake lever to the car.
15. Set the relay lever as shown and connect the cable rear fork to the left hand inboard hole.
16. With the handbrake lever fully 'OFF' adjust the cable length. Do not alter the position of the relay lever.
17. Check that the cable spring is properly positioned and adjust the spring tension as necessary, by means of the rear pinch clamp.

Rear
18. Thread the cable through the cable guides.
19. Fit the nuts, spring plates and forks to both ends of the cable.
20. With the handbrake lever in the 'OFF' position, attach the cable and compensator to the right hand inboard hole of the relay lever.
21. Jack up the rear wheels and lock the rear brakes by means of the adjusters.
22. With the cable pulled by hand, adjust the fork ends so that the clevis pins will slip into place.
23. Secure fork lock nuts and fit split pins to clevis pins.
24. Attach return springs to the spring plates and backplates.
25. Adjust the position of the spring plates to tension the springs.
26. Slacken the brake adjusters until wheels spin freely.
27. Remove the jack.

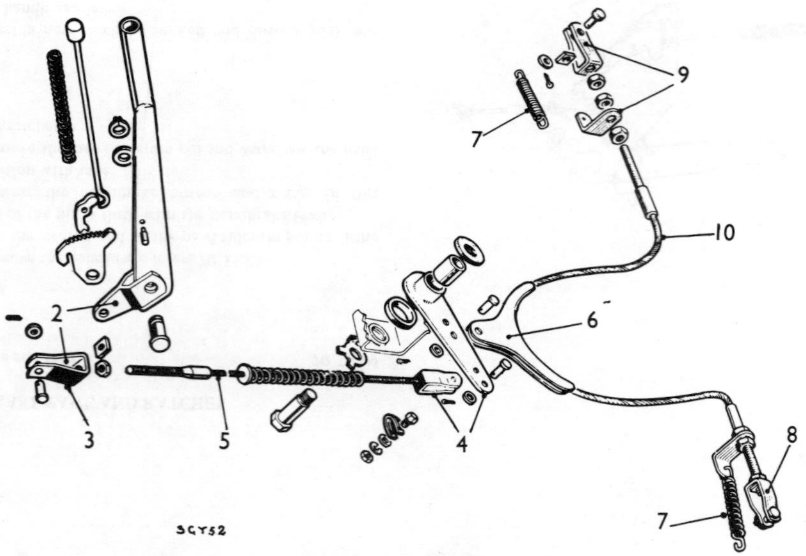

RELAY LEVER
— Remove and refit   70.35.22

Removing
1. Release the handbrake.
2. Disconnect the compensator from the relay lever.
3. Disconnect the front handbrake cable from the relay lever.
4. Straighten the tab washers securing the relay lever fulcrum bolt.
5. Remove the fulcrum bolt.
6. Withdraw the relay lever complete with rubber and felt seals.

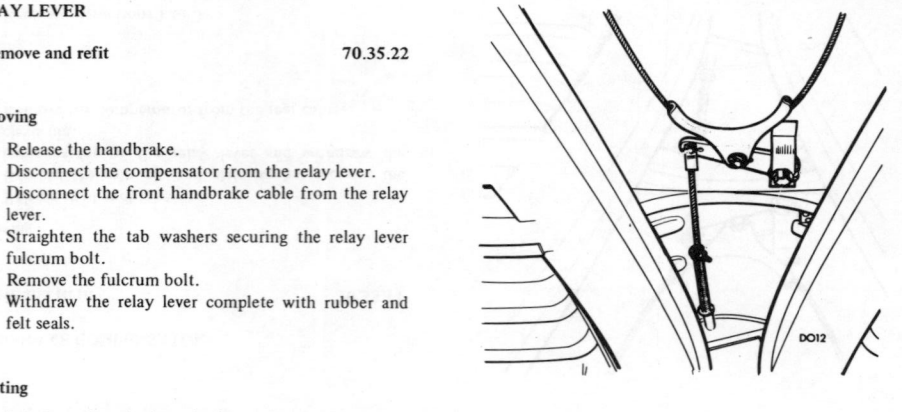

Refitting
7. Lubricate the relay lever bush.
8. With the larger boss of the relay lever downwards position the relay lever and seals in the bracket (felt seal top, rubber seal bottom).
9. Fit the fulcrum bolt and tab washer to the relay lever bracket. Bend the tab washer to retain the bolt.
10. Connect the compensator to the right hand inboard hole in the relay lever.
11. Connect the front brake cable to the left hand inboard hole in the relay lever.

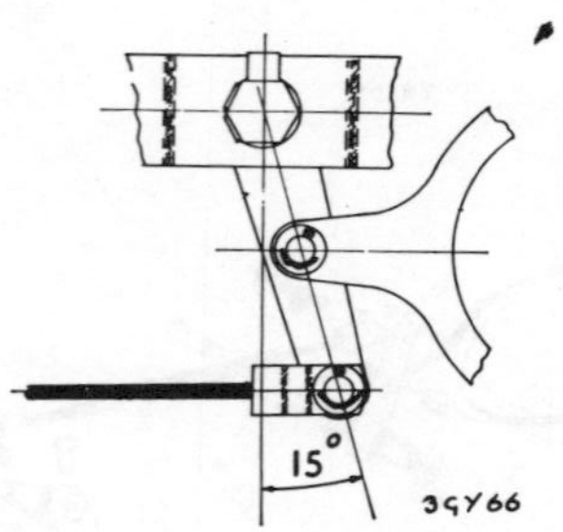

FRONT BRAKE PADS
— Remove and refit   70.40.02

Removing
1. Remove the front wheel.
2. Withdraw the two spring pins from the brake pad retaining pins.
3. Withdraw the brake pad retaining pins.
4. Lift out the brake pads complete with damping shims.

Refitting
5. If new brake pads are being fitted press the caliper pistons into their respective bores.
6. Clean the brake pad locations in the caliper.
7. Fit the brake pads complete with damping shims.
8. Fit the brake pad retaining pins to the caliper and secure with spring pins.
9. Fit the front wheel.

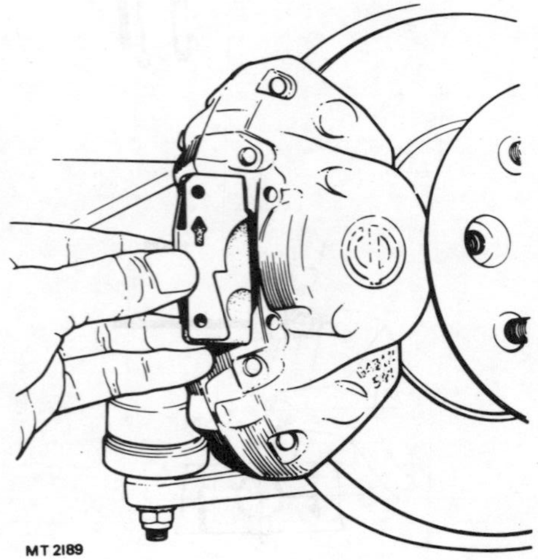

BRAKES

REAR BRAKE SHOES 70.40.03
— Remove and refit

Removing
1. Remove the rear wheel.
2. Remove the brake drum.
3. Remove the split pin from the handbrake lever.
4. Remove the shoe-steady pins, caps and springs.
5. Release the lower end of one shoe from the brake adjuster.
6. Release the upper end of the same shoe from the wheel cylinder.
7. Unhook the brake shoe return springs.
8. Remove the brake shoes.

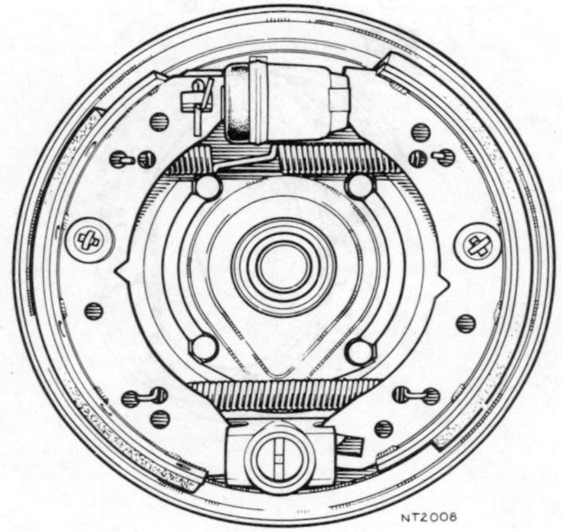

Refitting
9. Reverse instructions 1 to 8. Note that both brake shoe return springs are fitted inboard.

REAR BRAKE ADJUSTER 70.40.17
— Remove and refit

1. Remove the rear wheel.
2. Remove the brake drum.
3. Remove the brake shoes.
4. Remove two bolts and spring washers securing the brake adjuster to the backplate.
5. Withdraw the adjuster.

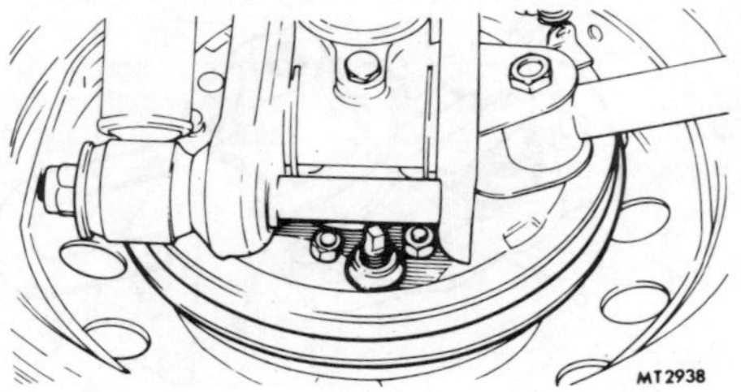

Refitting
6. Reverse instructions 1 to 5.
7. Adjust the brake.

70.40.03
70.40.17

Triumph Spitfire Mk IV Manual. Part No. 545254.

FRONT CALIPER 70.55.02
— Remove and refit

Removing
1. Remove the front wheel.
2. Disconnect the fluid supply pipe to the flexible hose.
3. Remove the nut securing the flexible hose to the front suspension bracket and withdraw the hose from the bracket.
4. Unscrew the flexible hose from the caliper.
5. Remove the two bolts and spring washers securing the caliper shield to the vertical link.
6. Withdraw the caliper shield and caliper.

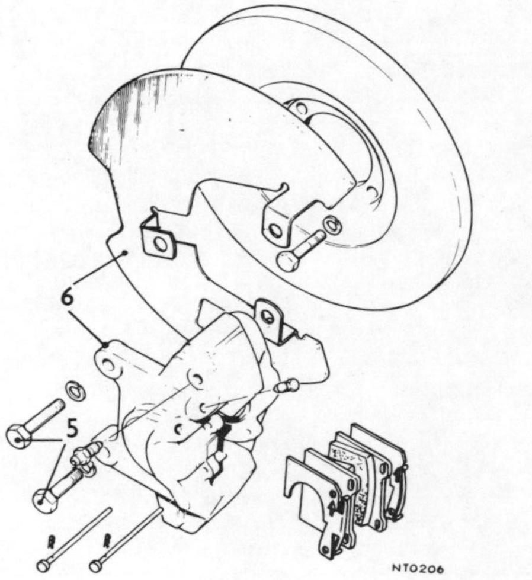

Refitting
7. Reverse instructions 1 to 6.
8. Bleed the brakes.

FRONT CALIPER 70.55.13
— Renew seals

Dismantling
1. Remove the caliper 70.55.02.
2. Remove the spring pins from the brake pad retaining pins.
3. Withdraw the pad retaining pins.
4. Withdraw the brake pads and shims.
5. Remove the circlip retaining the piston dust covers and withdraw the dust covers.
6. Extract the caliper piston. Piston removal may be facilitated using a low pressure air line. Do not interchange the pistons.
7. Prise out the cylinder seals taking care not to damage the cylinder bore.
8. Thoroughly clean the caliper bores and pistons using brake fluid or methylated spirits. If the pistons or the bores are scored or corroded, a new caliper must be obtained.

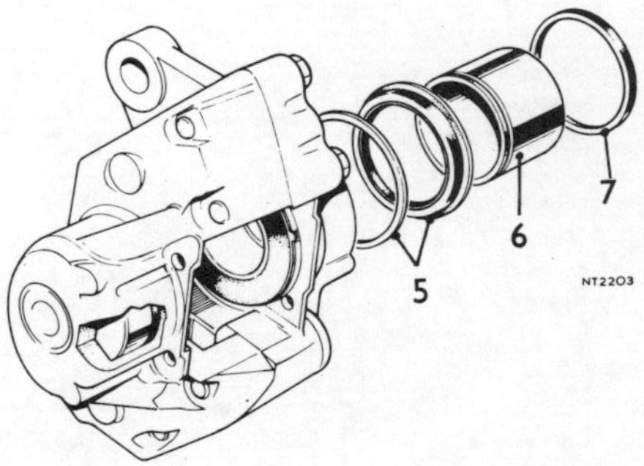

Refitting
9. Carefully install new seals in the cylinder bores.
10. Lubricate the bores with clean brake fluid.
11. Evenly enter the pistons into their original locations in the caliper.
12. Fit new dust covers and circlips.
13. Fit the caliper and caliper shield to the vertical link.
14. Fit the flexible hose.
15. Fit the brake pads and shims.
16. Fit the front wheel.
17. Bleed the brakes.

70.55.02
70.55.13

Triumph Spitfire Mk IV Manual. Part No. 545254.

BRAKES

REAR BRAKE CYLINDER

— Remove and refit   70.60.18

Removing

1. Jack up the car and support the chassis on stands.
2. Remove the rear wheel.
3. Release the handbrake and remove the brake drum.
4. Remove the brake shoes.
5. Disconnect the handbrake cable at the backplate lever.
6. Remove the flexible brake hose.
7. Remove the wheel cylinder rubber shield at the rear of the backplate.
8. Remove the horse-shoe clip and spring plate securing the wheel cylinder to the backplate.
9. Withdraw the wheel cylinder complete with the handbrake operating lever.

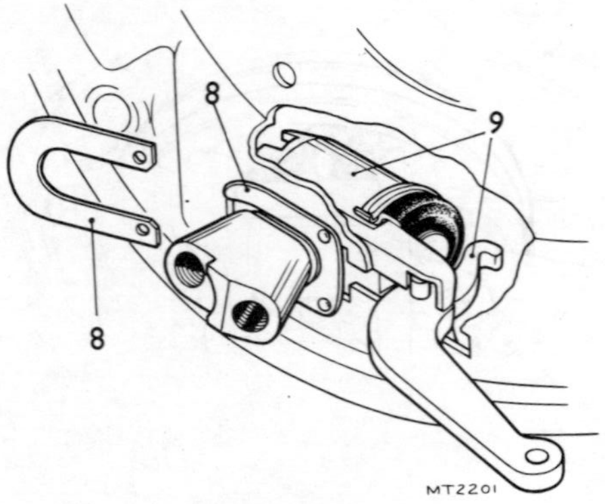

Refitting

10. Ensure that the wheel cylinder mounting face and the backplate are clean.
11. Lightly smear the wheel cylinder mounting face and both sides of the backplate faces with a zinc base grease.
12. Install the handbrake lever in the wheel cylinder.
13. Enter the wheel cylinder and the handbrake lever in the backplate.
14. Install the spring plate at the rear of the wheel cylinder (open end of plate towards rear of car, dimples on plate towards differential).
15. Install the horse-shoe clip (open end of clip towards the front of car). Ensure that the holes in the clip engage the dimples on the spring plate. Check that the wheel cylinder is free to slide on the backplate.
16. Fit the rubber shield.
17. Reverse instructions 1 to 6.
18. Bleed the brakes.

REAR BRAKE CYLINDER

— Overhaul   70.60.26

1. Remove the clip retaining the rubber boot to the cylinder body.
2. Withdraw the piston complete with rubber boot and seal from the cylinder.
3. Remove the boot and seal from the piston.
4. Examine the piston and cylinder bore for signs of corrosion or scoring. If either are damaged a new brake cylinder must be obtained.
5. Fit a new seal to the piston.
6. Fit a new rubber boot to the piston.
7. Lubricate the cylinder bore, seal and piston with clean brake fluid and insert the piston in the cylinder bore.
8. Fit the boot to the cylinder and secure with the clip.

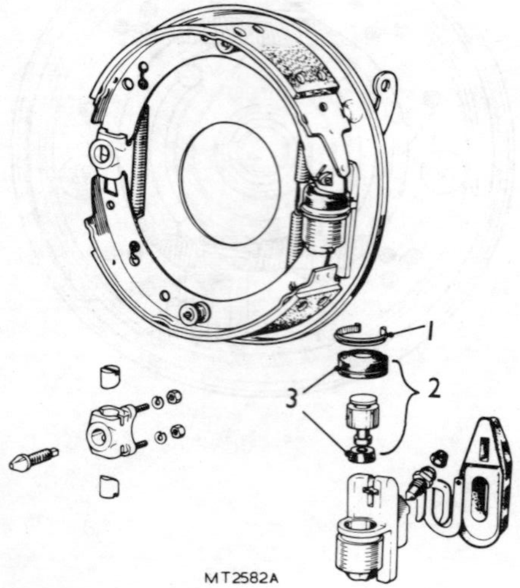

70.60.18
70.60.26

WHEEL AND TYRE OPERATIONS

Tyres general	.. .. 74.10.00
Wheel and Tyre balance	.. .. 74.15.00
Wheels – general	.. .. 74.20.00

WHEEL AND TYRE

TYRES – GENERAL
74.10.00

Type	Size	Load Conditions	Pressures Front lb/in²	Front kg/cm²	Rear lb/in²	Rear kg/cm²
Cross-ply Tubeless	5.20S – 13	All	21	1·476	26	1·828
Radial ply Tubeless	145SR – 13		21	1·476	26	1·828
Radial ply Tubed (Wire Wheels Only)	145SR – 13		21	1·476	26	1·828
Radial Ply Tubed	155 SR – 13		21	1·476	26	1·828
Radial Ply Tubeless.	155 SR – 13		21	1·476	26	1·828

Tyres of the correct type and dimensions, at the correct cold inflation pressures, are an integral part of the vehicle's design and regular maintenance of tyres contributes not only to safety but to the designed functioning of the vehicle. Road-holding, steering and braking are especially vulnerable to incorrectly pressurized, badly fitted or worn tyres.

Tyres of the same size and type but of different make may have widely varying characteristics. It is therefore recommended that tyres of the same make are fitted to all wheels.

Radial and cross-ply tyres

It is both dangerous and, in the U.K. illegal, to use on the public roads a vehicle fitted with unsuitable combinations of tyres. The following recommendations should therefore be observed:

1. Do not mix radial-ply and cross-ply tyres on the same axle.
2. Do not fit radial-ply tyres to the front wheels and cross-ply tyres to the rear wheels.
3. With suitable tyre pressure adjustments it may be possible to obtain acceptable handling with cross-ply tyres on the front wheels and radial-ply tyres on the rear wheels, but this combination is not recommended.

Size, type, pressures

The pressures recommended (see chart) provide optimum ride and handing characteristics for all normal operating conditions. The pressures should be checked, and adjusted if necessary, once per week. Tyre temperatures and pressures increase when running. Bleeding a warm tyre to the recommended pressures will result in under-inflation which may be dangerous. A slight natural pressure loss occurs with time. If this exceeds 2 lb/in² (0·14 kg/cm²) per week, the cause should be investigated and rectified. It should be noted that it is an offence in the U.K. to use a motor vehicle if a tyre is not so inflated as to make it fit for the use to which the vehicle is being put.

The spare wheel tyre should be maintained at the highest pressure quoted in the chart, and adjusted to the correct pressure for its position when fitted for use.

# WHEEL AND TYRE

Wear

All tyres fitted as original equipment include wear indicators in their tread pattern. When the tread has worn to a remaining depth of 0·06 in (1·5 mm) the indicators appear at the surface as bars which connect the tread pattern across the full width of the tyre. It is illegal in the U.K. and certain other countries to continue to use tyres on which the tread is worn to less than 1mm. It should be noted that the properties of many tyres alter progressively with wear. In particular the 'wet grip' and aquaplaning resistance are gradually but substantially reduced. Extra care and speed restriction should therefore be exercised on wet roads as the effective tread depth diminishes. Incorrect wheel alignment will accelerate tyre wear. Fins on the inside or outside edges of the tread pattern are caused by excessive toe-in or toe-out respectively. As fins may also be caused by high cornering speeds or road camber it is better to have the cause ascertained by having the wheel alignment checked (see 'General Specification' for data').

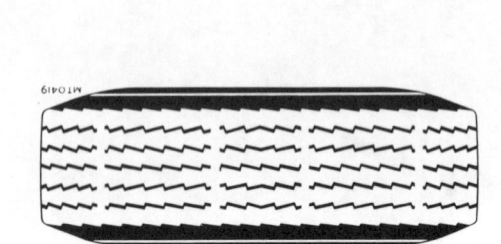

Damage

Excessive local distortion can cause the casing of the tyre to fracture and may lead to premature tyre failure. Tyres should be examined especially for cracked walls, exposed cords, etc. Flints and other sharp objects should be removed from the tyre tread, if neglected they may work through the cover. Any oil or grease which may get onto the tyres should be cleaned off by using fuel sparingly. Do not use paraffin (kerosene) which has a detrimental effect on rubber.

Repairs

Tubeless tyres

A temporary repair can be made to tubeless tyres, using a special kit, provided the puncturing hole is small and confined to the central tread area. The following precautions must, however, be observed.

1. Do not use more than one plug in each hole.
2. Do not use the tyre for high speeds.
3. Ensure that a permanent 'cold patch' or vulcanized repair is made at the earliest opportunity.

Tubes

When repairing tubes, have punctures or injuries vulcanized. Ordinary patches should only be used for emergencies. Vulcanizing is absolutely essential for tubes manufactured from synthetic rubber.

Winter tyres

Winter tyres are designed to give improved traction and braking in mud and snow. Their performance on hard surfaces may, however, be inferior to normal road tyres and extra care is required when using them under normal conditions.

Racing and competition tyres

Should the vehicle be tuned to increase its maximum speed, or be used for racing or competition, consult the respective tyre company regarding the need for tyres of special or racing construction.

Valves

Whenever a new tubeless tyre is fitted, the Schrader snap-in type valve must also be renewed. To facilitate fitting, lubricate the valve with soap solution before using a special tool to snap the valve squarely into an airtight position in the rim hole.

WHEEL AND TYRE BALANCE 74.15.00

Tyre and wheel assemblies should be statically balanced to within 5 oz.f. ins. Balance weights are available in ½oz. increments from ½ to 3 oz.

WHEELS

— General 74.20.00

Pressed Steel Wheels

4½J rims. Wheels are located and retained on hubs by four 3/8 ins. U.N.F. studs and chrome-plated dome nuts tightened to 38 to 48 lbf. ft (5·2 to 6·6. kgf. m). Embellishment is provided by spring-loaded plastic hub covers fitted under the dome nuts.

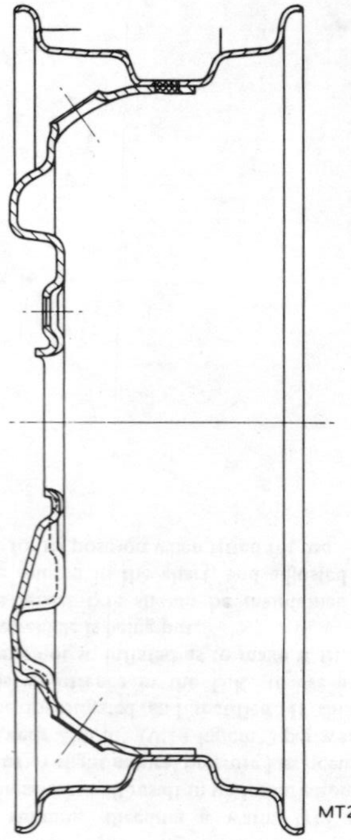

Wire Wheels ** (Earlier models only) **

4½J rims with 16 outer spokes and 32 inner spokes. Wheels are located and retained by four 3/8 in U.N.F. studs and chrome plated dome nuts, tightened to 38 to 48 lbf. ft. (5·2 to 6·6 kgf. m).

It is recommended that the servicing and reconditioning of wire wheels is entrusted to those who are equipped to fulfill this specialist function. It is pointed out that the renewal of a single broken spoke may necessitate extensive re-adjustment to spoke tension throughout the wheel.

The average torque of outer spokes should not be less than 75 lbf. ins (0·86 kgf. m) Average torque of inner spokes should not be less than 60 lbf. ins (0·7 kgf. m). With spokes fully tightened at least two full threads should be visible below the nipple.

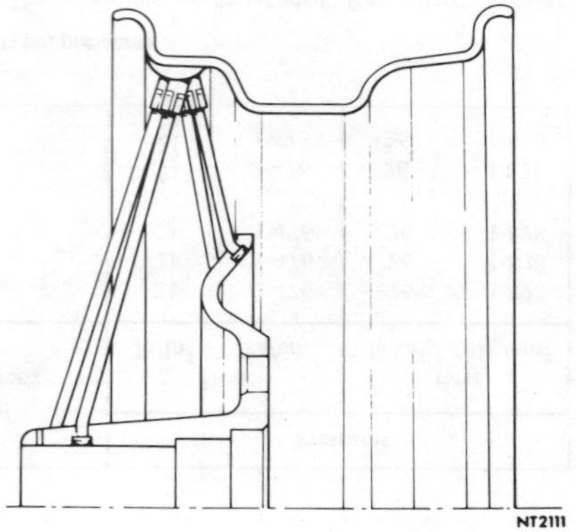

Wheel Tolerances

Wobble

1. Lateral variation measured on the vertical inside face should not exceed 0·050 ins (1·270 mm).

Lift

2. On a truly mounted and revolving wheel the difference between the high and low points measured on either rim ledge should not exceed 0·050 ins (1·270 mm).

BODY

BODY OPERATIONS

Ashtray — front — remove and refit	76.67.13
Bonnet — adjust	76.16.02
Bonnet — remove and refit	76.16.01
Bonnet catch — remove and refit	76.16.34
Bonnet stay — remove and refit	76.16.14
Bonnet — remove and refit	76.46.04
Bumper — front — remove and refit	76.22.08
— over rider remove and refit	76.22.01
Bumper — rear — remove and refit	76.22.15
** — over rider — remove and refit	76.22.02 **
Carpet — front — remove and refit	76.49.02
Carpet — gearbox cover — remove and refit	76.49.01
Carpet — rear — remove and refit	76.49.03
Chassis frame — alignment check	76.10.02
Door check strap — remove and refit	76.40.27
Door — remove and refit	76.28.01
Door glass — remove and refit	76.31.01
Door glass regulator — front — remove and refit	76.31.45
Door handle — remove and refit	76.58.01
Door hinges — remove and refit	76.28.42
Door lock — remove and refit	76.37.12
Door lock remote control — remove and refit	76.37.31
Door lock striker — remove and refit	76.37.23
Door pull	76.58.25

BODY OPERATIONS — continued

Door trim pad — remove and refit	76.34.01
Fascia — centre — remove and refit	76.46.02
— drivers side — remove and refit	76.46.01
— passengers side — remove and refit	76.46.03
Fascia crash pad	76.46.04
Fascia support bracket	76.46.09
Front valance spoiler — remove and refit	76.10.46 **
Gearbox tunnel cover — remove and refit	76.25.07
Glass — windscreen — remove and refit	76.81.01
Grille — front — remove and refit	76.55.03
Hardtop — remove and refit	76.61.01
Hood assembly — remove and refit	76.61.08
Luggage compartment lid — remove and refit	76.19.01
Luggage compartment lid hinges — remove and refit	76.19.07
Luggage compartment lid lock — remove and refit	76.19.11
Luggage compartment lid lock striker — remove and refit	76.19.12
Luggage compartment lid seal — remove and refit	76.19.06
Parcel shelf — drivers side — remove and refit	76.67.04
Parcel shelf — passengers side — remove and refit	76.67.05
Private lock — remove and refit	76.37.39
Rear compartment trim pad — remove and refit	76.13.20
Seat belt — static — remove and refit	76.73.02
** Seat belt — automatic — remove and refit	76.73.10
Seat cushion cover — remove and refit	76.70.02
Seat — driver — remove and refit	76.70.04
Seat — passenger — remove and refit	76.70.05
Seat runners — remove and refit	76.70.21

BODY

BODY OPERATIONS — continued

Seat squab catch – remove and refit	76.70.27
Seat squab cover – remove and refit	76.70.03
Valance – engine L.H. – remove and refit	76.79.07
Valance – engine R.H. – remove and refit	76.79.08
Underriders	76.22.01

BODY

CHASSIS FRAME

– Alignment check 76.10.02

Whilst severe damage to the chassis is readily detected, less serious damage may cause distortion, that is not visually apparent. If steering and suspension checks indicate a fault which cannot be attributed to anything other than chassis distortion, the chassis frame should be checked for twist and squareness.

Checking for Twist

1. Position the vehicle on a clean and level floor.
2. Remove the underriders 76.22.01.
3. Place a jack under each jacking point and remove the road wheels 74.20.01.
4. Adjust the jacks until the following conditions are achieved:
   Points 'A' are 25·29 in (64·23 cm) above the floor.
   Points 'E' are 24·94 in (63·35 cm) above the floor.
   This condition sets the datum 20 in (50·8 cm) above the floor.
   If the height of points 'A' cannot be equalised, the difference in height of points 'A' indicates the amount by which the chassis is twisted.

Checking for squareness

5. Transfer all the lettered points shown to the floor, using a plumb-bob and fine cord.
6. Letter the points on the floor and connect each pair by drawing a line between them.
7. Mark the central point of each line and place a straight edge along these mid-points.
8. Check for squareness.
9. Using a straight edge mark the diagonals as shown.
10. Check for squareness. If the chassis is square then each pair of opposite diagonals must be equal in length and the points of intersection must lie on the same straight line.
11. The extent of lateral chassis distortion is assessed by the amount and direction by which any central point on the transverse line and/or the point of intersection of any pair of diagonals deviates from the centre line.

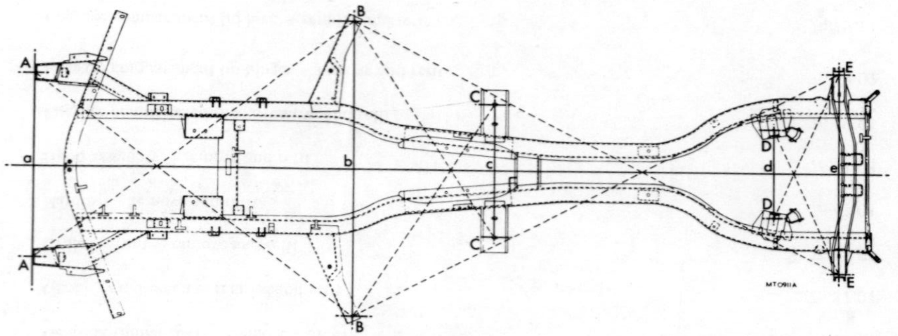

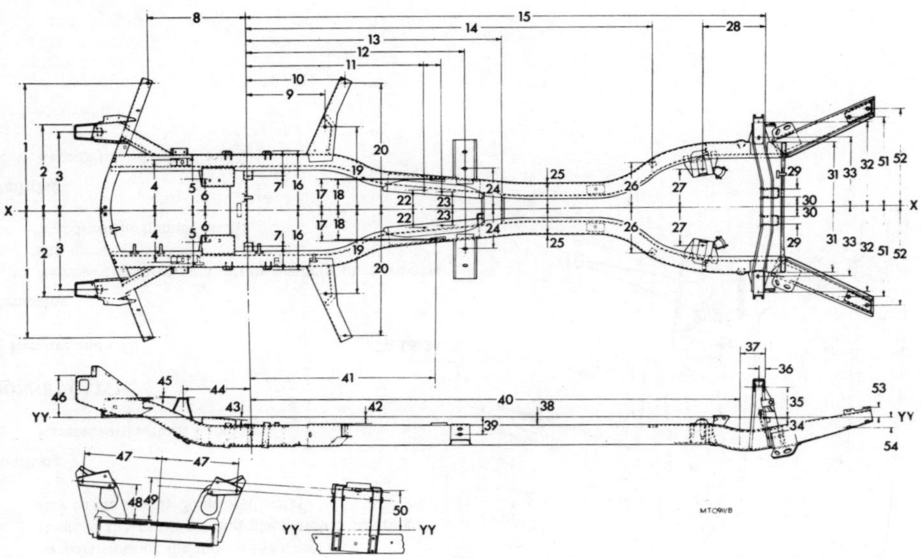

BODY

** SPOILER

— Remove and refit

76.10.46

Removing

1. Remove the outer two screws, spring washers and six spacers.
2. Support the spoiler and remove the inner two screws, spring washers and plain washers securing it to the front crossmember.

Refitting

3. Position the spoiler and loosely fit the outer two screws, spring washers and six spacers.
4. Fit the inner two screws, spring washers and plain washers. Fully tighten the screws to pull the spoiler flush against the crossmember.
5. Fully tighten the outer screws. **

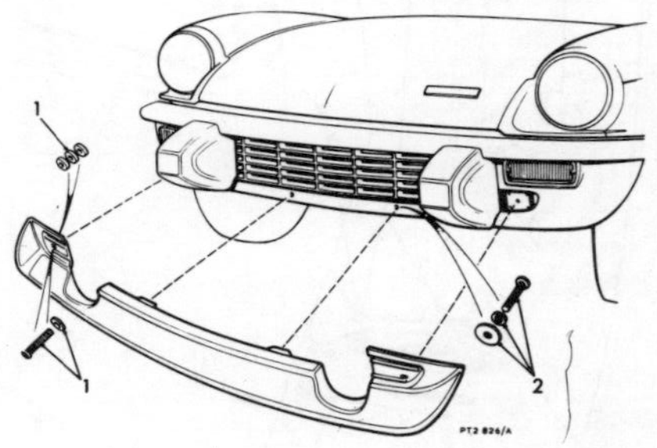

REAR COMPARTMENT TRIM PAD

— Remove and refit

76.13.20

The trim pad is secured to the rear compartment by six screws and cup washers.

BONNET

— Remove and refit

76.16.01

Removing

1. Disconnect the battery.
2. Disconnect the six headlamp leads.
3. Remove the nut, bolt, spring and plain washers securing the bonnet stay.
4. Lower the bonnet and remove the underriders 76.22.01.
5. Remove the two bolts, spring and plain washers.
6. Lift the bonnet away.

Refitting

7. Reverse instructions 1 to 6, ensuring that the distance pieces and thrust washers are correctly located when refitting bolts 5.
8. Adjust the bonnet if necessary 76.16.02.

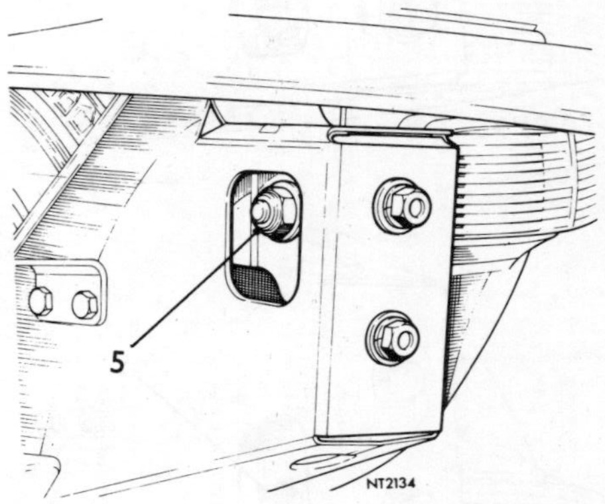

	Inches		Centimetres
1	22.15		59.69
2	22.10		58.42
3	14.56		36.98
4	13.78		35.00
5	13.72		34.85
6	8.64		21.89
7	9.78		24.84
8	9.72		24.69
9 **	5.53		14.04 **
10	5.50		13.97
11	4.32		10.97
12	4.30		10.92
13	17.37		44.12
14	17.29		43.91
15	12.76		32.36
16	12.72		32.31
17	16.09		40.87
18	16.03		40.72
19	29.62		75.13
20	29.50		74.77
21	36.56		92.86
22	36.44		92.56
23	42.19		107.16
24	41.94		104.83
25	68.22		173.28
26	68.10		172.97
27	87.19		221.46
28	86.93		220.80
29	10.32		26.21
30	5.39		13.69
31	5.36		13.61
32	5.23		13.28
33	5.20		13.20
34			
35			
36			
37			

	Inches		Centimetres
38	36.83		
39	36.78		
40	53.39		
41	20.97		53.27
42	3.02		7.67
43	2.98		7.56
44	3.01 **		7.65 **
45	2.99		7.59 **
46	2.91		7.37
47	2.89		7.24
48	7.19		18.26
49	7.13		18.11
50	4.25		10.80
51	7.83		19.86
52	7.80		19.81
53	6.64		16.87
54	6.61		16.79
	10.70		27.18
	10.65		27.05
	1.51		3.83
	1.63		4.14
	1.61		4.09
	11.28		28.65
	11.22		28.50
	14.75		37.46
	12.00		30.48
	0.15		0.38
	5.00		12.70
	4.88		12.40
	1.12		2.87
	1.00		2.54
	4.06		10.31

** 1974 U.S.A. Market only

	Inches	Centimetres
	1.13	2.87
	2.80	7.11
	83.26	211.48
	31.45	79.88
	31.39	77.73
	1.06	2.69
	4½°	4½°
	4½°	4½°
	11.69	29.69
	11.56	29.36
	4½°	4½°
	7.38	18.75
	7.25	18.42 **
	13.06	33.17
	12.94	32.87
	5.91	15.01
	7.31	18.50
	6.29	15.97
	6.17	15.67
	16.22	41.16
	16.09	40.83
	17.61	44.73
	17.49	44.42
	1.93	4.90
	1.81	4.60
	1.515	3.84

76.10.02 Sheet 2 — Triumph Spitfire Mk IV Manual. Part No. 545254

** 76.10.46
76.16.01 **

BODY

BONNET

— Adjust 76.16.02

Adjust the bonnet mountings as follows to achieve a parallel gap of 3/16 in (5 mm) between the bonnet, scuttle and doors:

1. Remove the underriders 76.22.01.
2. Slacken the two bolts and move the bonnet forwards or rearwards as required.
3. Retighten the two bolts.
4. Slacken the four screws and move the stop plates forward or rearwards to ensure correct location of the buffers.
5. Retighten the four screws.
6. Slacken the four bolts and raise or lower the bonnet as required.
7. Retighten the four bolts.
8. Slacken the two locknuts and screw the buffer in or out as required.
9. Retighten the two locknuts.
10. Slacken the four bolts and re-position the catch plates to ensure correct engagement of the bonnet catches.
11. Retighten the four bolts.
12. Refit the underriders 76.22.01.

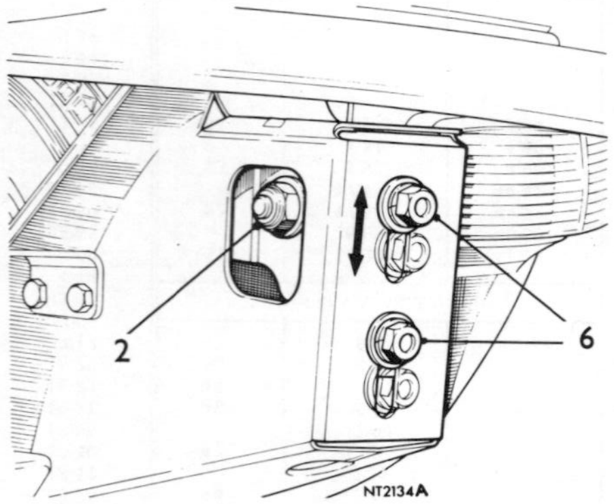

BONNET STAY

— Remove and refit 76.16.14

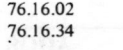

Removing

1. Raise and support the bonnet.
2. Remove the nut, bolt, spring washer and plain washers securing the stay to the wheel arch.
3. Remove the nut, bolt and plain washer securing the stay to the chassis. Remove the stay.

Refitting

4. Reverse instructions 1 to 3.

BONNET CATCH

— Remove and refit 76.16.34

Removing

1. Remove the three nuts, spring washers, plain washers and screws.
2. Withdraw the bonnet catch.

Refitting

3. Reverse instructions 1 and 2.

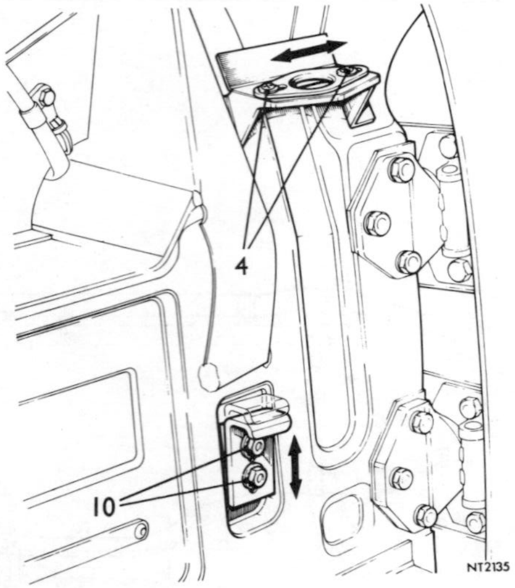

76.16.02
76.16.34

REAR COMPARTMENT TRIM PAD

— Remove and refit 76.13.20

The trim pad is secured to the rear compartment by six screws and cup washers.

BONNET

— Remove and refit 76.16.01

Removing

1. Disconnect the battery.
2. Disconnect the six headlamp leads.
3. Remove the nut, bolt, spring and plain washers securing the bonnet stay.
4. Lower the bonnet and remove the underriders 76.22.01.
5. Remove the two bolts, spring and plain washers.
6. Lift the bonnet away.

Refitting

7. Reverse instructions 1 to 6, ensuring that the distance pieces and thrust washers are correctly located when refitting bolts 5.
8. Adjust the bonnet if necessary 76.16.02

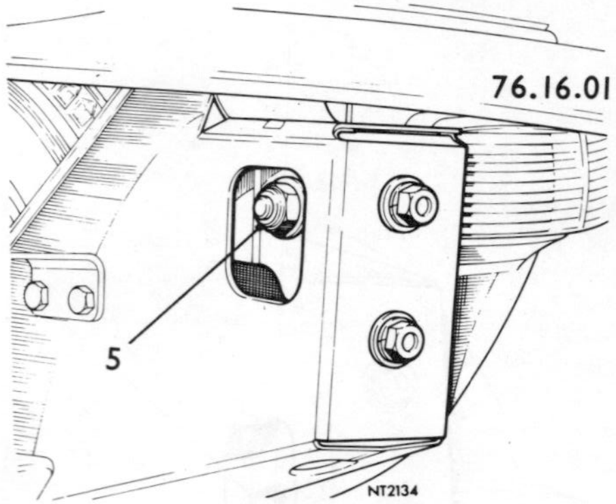

BONNET

— Adjust 76.16.02

Adjust the bonnet mountings as follows to achieve a parallel gap of 3/16 in (5 mm) between the bonnet, scuttle and doors:

1. Remove the underriders 76.22.01
2. Slacken the two bolts and move the bonnet forwards or rearwards as required.
3. Retighten the two bolts.
4. Slacken the four screws and move the stop plates forward or rearwards to ensure correct location of the buffers.
5. Retighten the four screws.
6. Slacken the four bolts and raise or lower the bonnet as required.
7. Retighten the four bolts.
8. Slacken the two locknuts and screw the buffer in or out as required.
9. Retighten the two locknuts.
10. Slacken the four bolts and re-position the catch plates to ensure correct engagement of the bonnet catches.
11. Retighten the four bolts.
12. Refit the underriders 76.22.01.

76.16.02
76.13.20
76.16.02

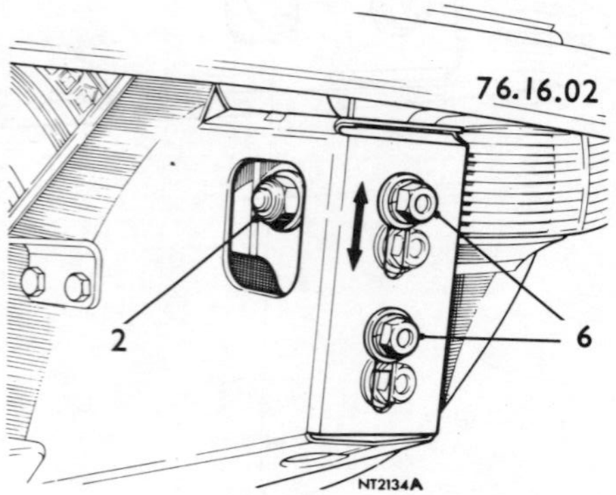

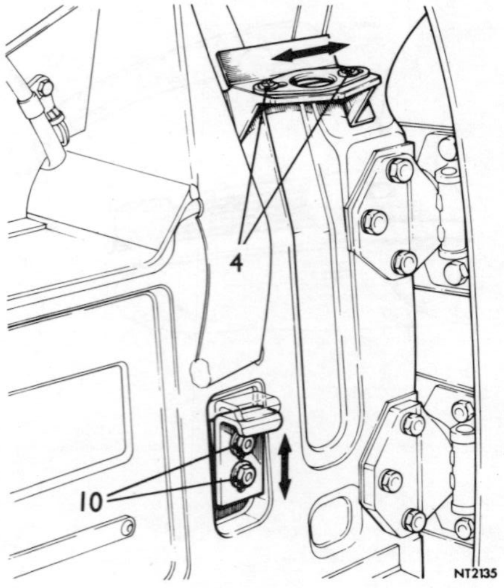

BODY

BONNET STAY
— Remove and refit 76.16.14

Removing
1. Raise and support the bonnet.
2. Remove the nut, bolt, spring washer and plain washers securing the stay to the wheel arch.
3. Remove the nut, bolt and plain washer securing the stay to the chassis. Remove the stay.

Refitting
4. Reverse instructions 1 to 3.

BONNET CATCH
— Remove and refit 76.16.34

Removing
1. Remove the three nuts, spring washers, plain washers and screws.
2. Withdraw the bonnet catch.

Refitting
3. Reverse instructions 1 and 2.

BODY

LUGGAGE COMPARTMENT LID
— Remove and refit 76.19.01

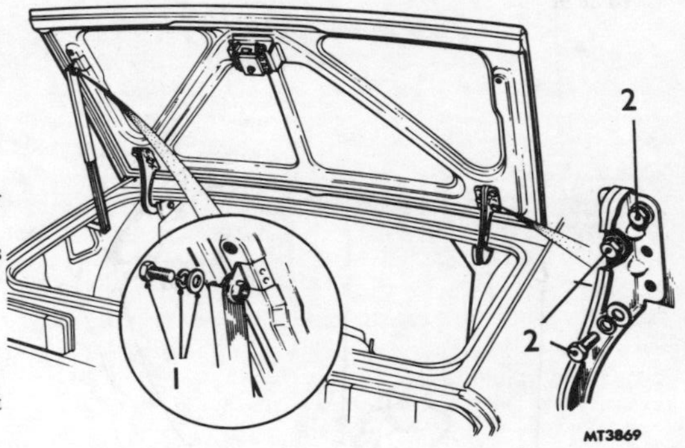

Removing
1. Remove the bolt, spring washer and plain washer securing the support stay to the lid.
2. Remove six bolts, spring washers and plain washers securing the hinges to the lid.

Refitting
3. Reverse instructions 1 and 2, ensuring correct alignment.

LUGGAGE COMPARTMENT LID SEAL
— Remove and refit 76.19.06

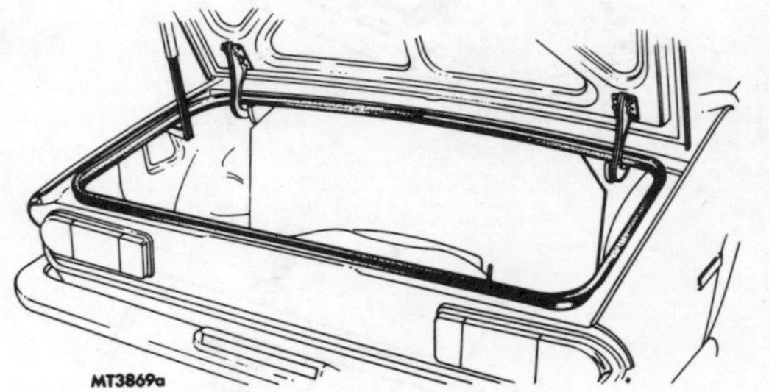

Removing
1. Free the seal from the body, using a suitable blunt tool if necessary.

Refitting
2. Fit the seal, using Seelastik SR51.

LUGGAGE COMPARTMENT LID HINGES
— Remove and refit 76.19.07

Removing
1. Remove the lid 76.19.01.
2. Remove the four nuts, spring washers and plain washers and lift off the hinges.

Refitting
3. Reverse instructions 1 and 2, ensuring correct alignment of the lid.

BODY

LUGGAGE COMPARTMENT LID LOCK 76.19.11

— Remove and refit

Removing
1. Remove the striker sleeve — two screws, spring washers and plain washers.
2. Remove the four screws and shakeproof washers.
3. Remove the screw, spring washer and plain washer and lift off the latch.
4. Withdraw the lock barrel and shaft.
5. Press out the escutcheon and seating washer.

Refitting
6. Reverse instructions 1 to 5, Check lid alignment and adjust striker sleeve if necessary.

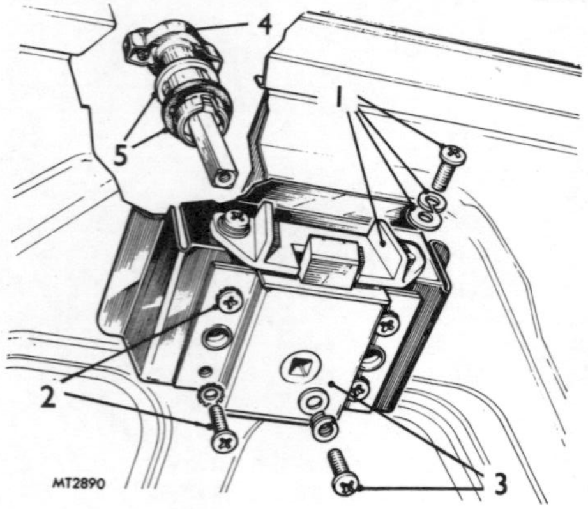

LUGGAGE COMPARTMENT LID LOCK STRIKER 76.19.12

— Remove and refit

Removing
1. Remove the two screws and lift off the striker.

Refitting
2. Reverse instruction 1, ensuring correct lid closing action and alignment.

UNDERRIDERS 76.22.01

— Remove and refit

Removing
1. Remove one screw and plain washer.
2. Remove three bolts, spring washers and plain washers.
3. Lift off underrider together with front grille.
4. Repeat operation 2 to remove the second underrider.

Refitting
5. Reverse instructions 1 to 4.

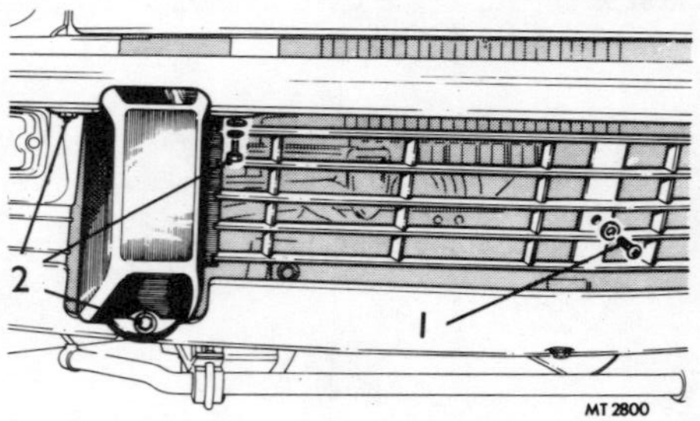

OVERRIDER (U.S.A. Market later models only)

FRONT — Remove and refit 76.22.01

Removing
1. Remove the bolt, spring washer and plain washer from beneath the overrider.
2. Working beneath the overrider remove the bolt, spring washer and plain washer.
3. Raise the bonnet and from inside the engine compartment remove the bolt, spring washer and plain washer.
4. Unclip the overrider from the bumper bracket.

Refitting
5. Reverse the instructions 1 to 4

REAR — Remove and refit 76.22.02

The rear overrider is secured to the bumper bracket by three bolts, spring washers and plain washers.
**

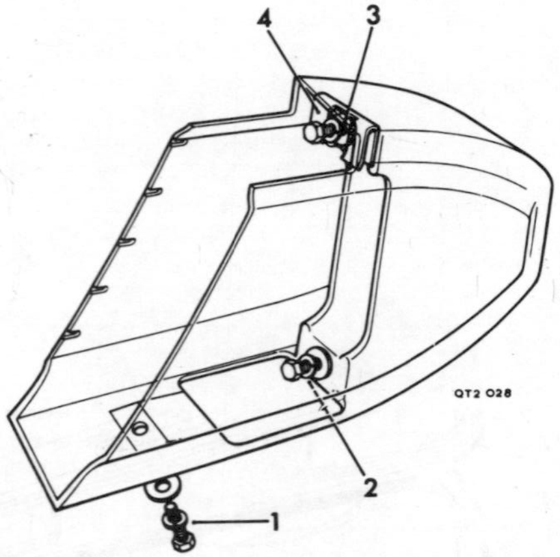

BUMPER — FRONT 76.22.08

— Remove and refit

Removing
1. Remove the four bolts, spring washers and plain washers securing underriders to bumper.
2. Raise the bonnet and remove the four bolts, spring washers and plain washers.
3. Lower the bonnet and lift off the bumper.

Refitting
4. Reverse instructions 1 to 3.

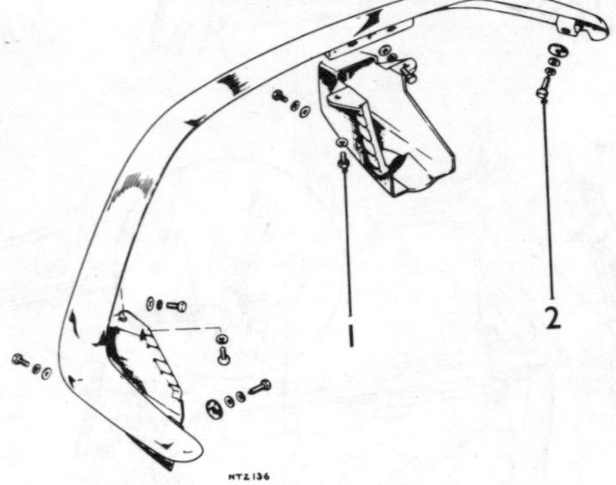

BODY

BUMPER — REAR 76.22.15

Remove and refit

Removing

1. Disconnect the two number plate lamp leads. 86.40.86. Operation 1.
2. Remove the two bolts, spring washers and plain washers.
3. Remove the two nuts, bolts, spring washers and plain washers, and lift off the bumper.

Refitting

4. Reverse instructions 1 to 3.

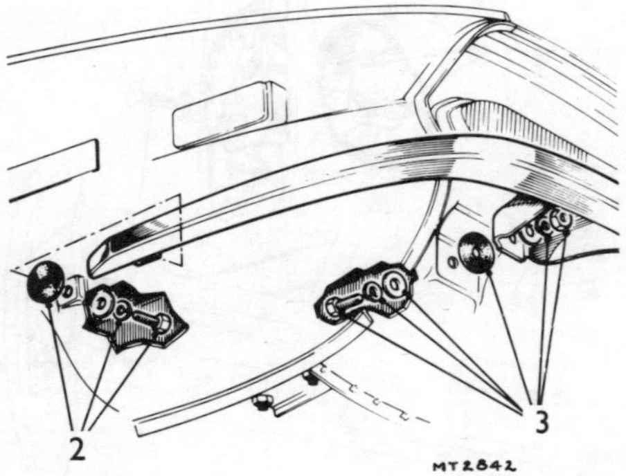

GEARBOX TUNNEL COVER 76.25.07

Remove and refit

Removing

1. Remove gear lever knob.
2. Remove two screws holding trim pads to gearbox.
3. Remove four bolts holding fascia support bracket to floor.
4. Remove two screws holding fascia support bracket to fascia rail.
5. Remove fascia support bracket.
6. Remove carpet.
7. Remove eleven self tapping screws holding gearbox cover to floor.
8. Remove the gearbox cover.

Refitting

9. Reposition gearbox cover.
10. Refit eleven screws holding gearbox cover to floor.
11. Refit carpet.
12. Reposition fascia support bracket.
13. Refit two screws holding fascia support bracket to fascia rail.
14. Refit four bolts holding fascia support bracket to floor.
15. Refit two trim pads and tighten two self tapping screws.
16. Refit gear lever knob.

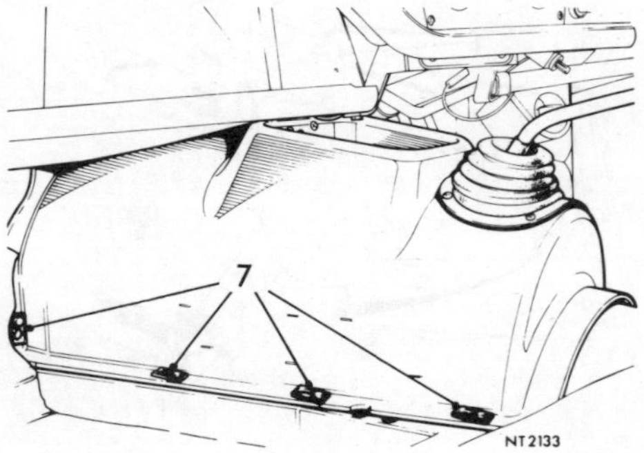

76.22.15
76.25.07

Triumph Spitfire Mk IV Manual. Part No. 545254

BODY

DOOR 76.28.01

— Remove and refit

Removing

1. Isolate the battery.
2. Drill out the rivet securing the check strap.
3. Support the door and remove six bolts, spring washers and plain washers.

Refitting

4. Reverse instructions 1 to 3. Check door closing action and adjust if necessary.

DOOR HINGES 76.28.42

— Remove and refit

Removing

1. Remove the door 76.28.01.
2. Remove hinges — three bolts, spring washers and plain washers.

Refitting

3. Reverse instructions 1 and 2. Check the door closing action and adjust if necessary.

DOOR GLASS 76.31.01

— Remove and refit

Removing

1. Remove the trim pad 76.34.01.
2. Remove the spring.
3. Remove the guide packing pieces — two bolts and spring washers.
4. Prise off the two stud retainers and washers securing the regulator arms to the glass frame.
5. Support the glass and detach the regulator arms from the frame.
6. Lower the glass.
7. Detach the inner and outer door waist seals from the clips.
8. Lift out the glass, taking care to avoid scratching it on the seal clips.

Refitting

9. Reverse instructions 1 to 8.

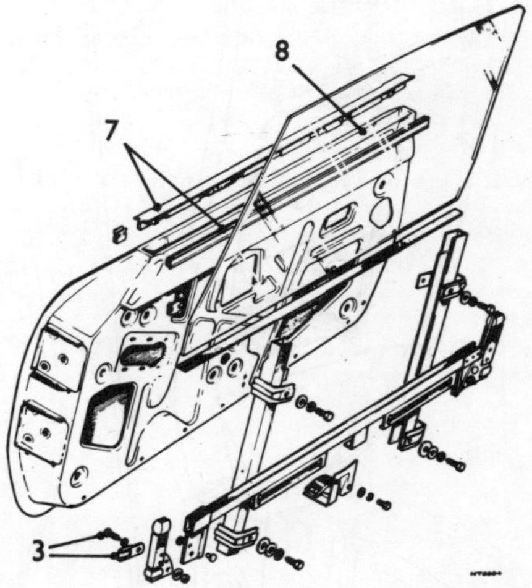

76.28.01
76.31.01

Triumph Spitfire Mk IV Manual. Part No. 545254.

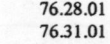

BODY

DOOR GLASS REGULATOR
76.31.45
— Remove and refit

Removing
1. Remove the trim pad 76.34.01.
2. Remove the spring and loosely refit the regulator handle.
3. Raise the door glass and retain it with a small rubber wedge.
4. Detach the regulating arms by prising off the retainer studs.
5. Remove the inter-connecting link and four leather washers.
6. Remove the three bolts, spring washers and plain washers.
7. Remove the four bolts, spring washers and plain washers.
8. Carefully withdraw the regulator assembly.

Refitting
9. Reverse instructions 1 to 8.

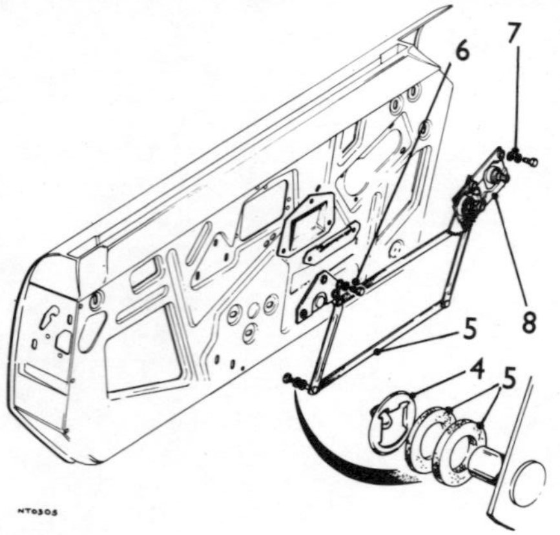

DOOR TRIM PAD
76.34.01
— Remove and refit

Removing
1. Depress the bezel and press out the pin.
2. Remove the handle and bezel.
3. Remove the handle plate — 1 screw.
4. Prise off the trim pad — 21 clips.

Refitting
5. Reverse instructions 1 to 4.

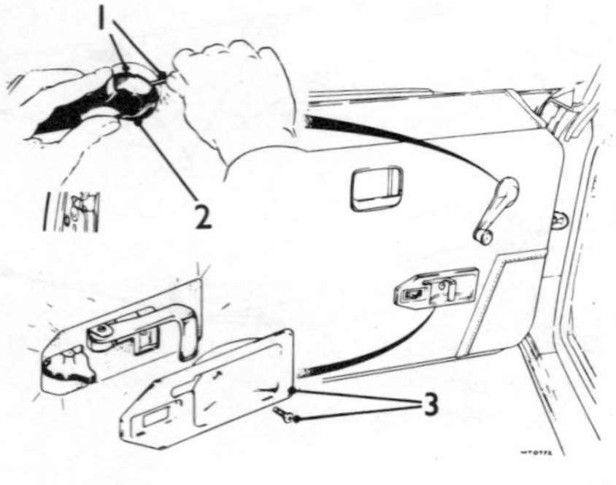

DOOR LOCK
76.37.12
— Remove and refit

Removing
1. Remove the trim pad 76.34.01.
2. Release the two linkages.
3. Remove the three screws.
4. Release the linkage.
5. Remove the door lock.

Refitting
6. Reverse instructions 1 to 5.

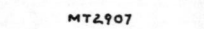

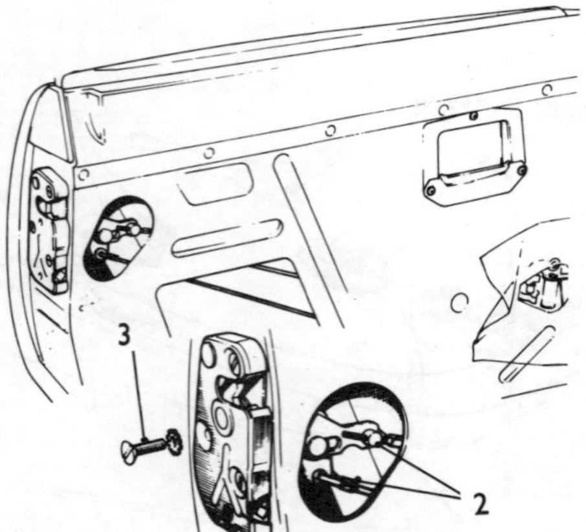

76.31.45
76.37.12

DOOR LOCK STRIKER
76.37.23
— Remove and refit

Removing
1. Remove the three screws and lift off the striker.

Refitting
2. Reverse instruction 1, adjusting if necessary to ensure correct door locking action.

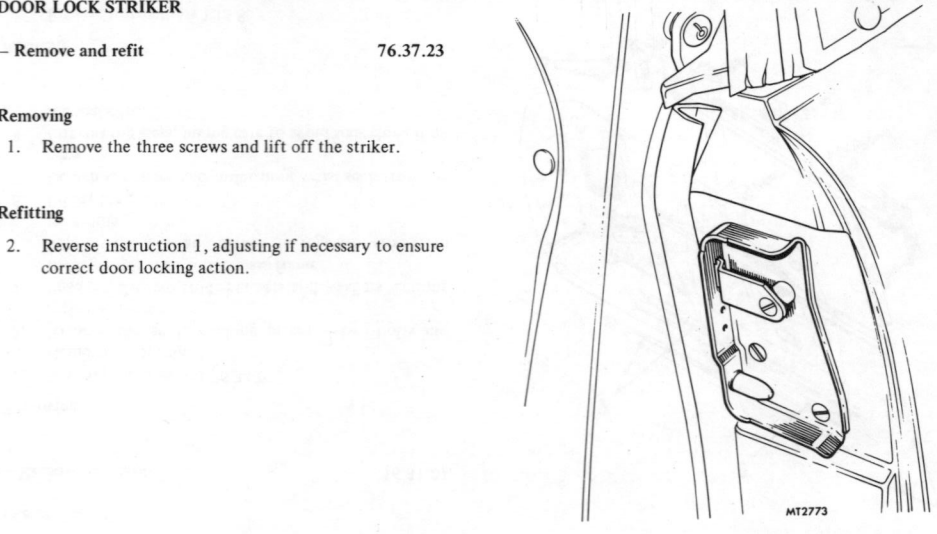

DOOR LOCK REMOTE CONTROL
76.37.31
— Remove and refit

Removing
1. Remove the trim pad 76.34.01.
2. Remove the foam rubber pad.
3. Detach the clip from the control rod.
4. Remove the three bolts, spring washers and plain washers.
5. Disconnect the control rod from the locking lever.
6. Remove the remote control.

Refitting
7. Reverse instructions 1 to 6, adjusting if necessary to ensure correct operation.

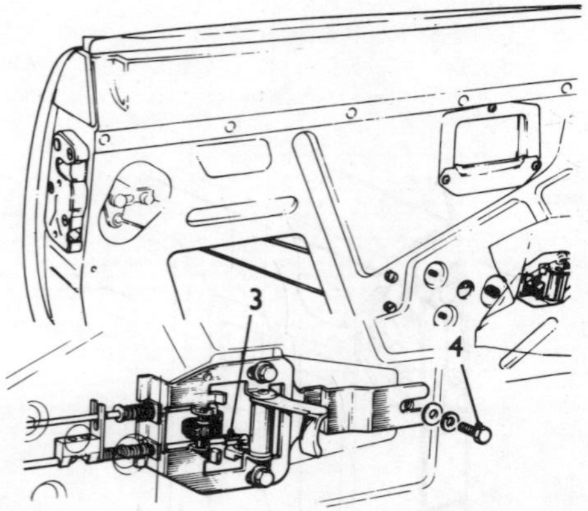

76.37.23
76.37.31

BODY

PRIVATE LOCK

— Remove and refit   76.37.39

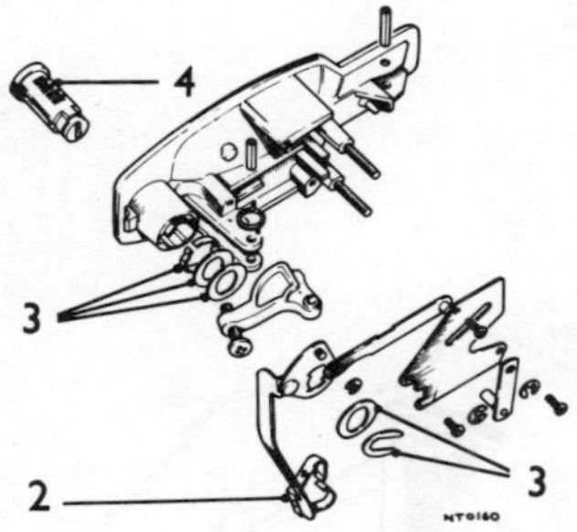

Removing

1. Remove the door handle 76.58.01.
2. Remove the spring clip.
3. Remove the plain washers and waved washer securing the pivot bracket.
4. Push out the lock.

Refitting

5. Reverse instructions 1 to 4.

DOOR CHECK STRAP

— Remove and refit   76.40.27

Removing

1. Isolate the battery.
2. Drill out the rivet.
3. Pull back the dash side carpet and withdraw the check strap.

Refitting

4. Reverse instructions 1 to 3.

FASCIA — DRIVERS SIDE

— Remove and refit   76.46.01

Removing

1. Remove the longer of the two lower padding assemblies — 4 screws and plain washers.
2. Remove the centre fascia 76.46.02.
3. Remove the tachometer 88.30.21.
4. Remove the speedometer 88.30.01.
5. Remove the wiper switch 86.65.38.
6. Remove the mixture control inner cable and bezel 19.20.13, instructions 1 to 3.
7. Remove the hazard switch (if fitted) 86.65.50.
8. Pull out the turn signal bulb holder.
9. Remove the two nuts, spring washers and plain washers from the rear of the fascia.

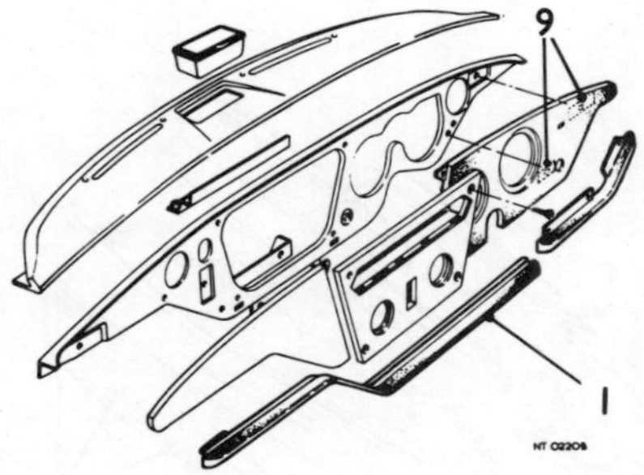

Refitting

10. Reverse instructions 1 to 9.

76.37.39
76.46.01

FASCIA — CENTRE

— Remove and refit   76.46.02

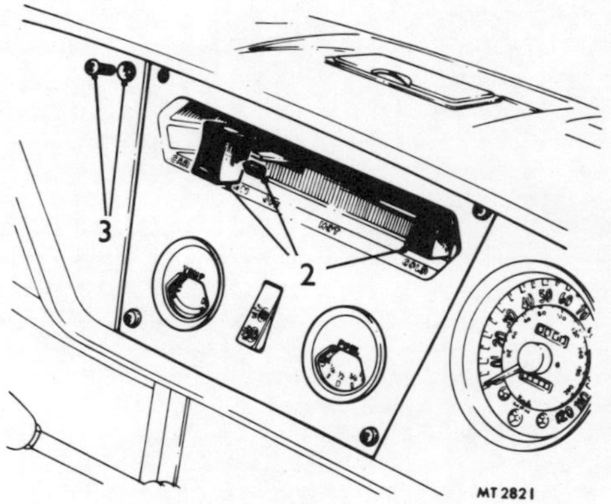

Removing

1. Isolate the battery.
2. Slacken the two grub screws and pull off the heater control knobs.
3. Remove the four screws and cup washers.
4. Lower the fascia centre to the service position.
5. Pull out the two panel light bulb holders.
6. Disconnect the seven Lucar connectors.
7. Remove the fascia centre from the vehicle.
8. Pull out the hazard warning bulb holder if fitted.
9. Pull out the brake warning bulb holder if fitted.

Refitting

10. Reverse instructions 1 to 9.

FASCIA — PASSENGERS SIDE

— Remove and refit   76.46.03

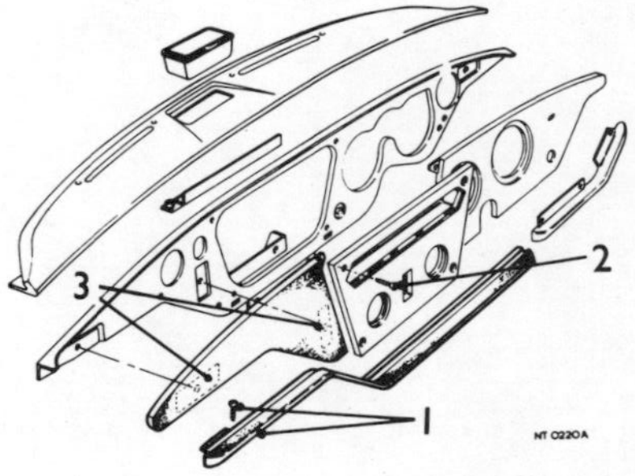

Removing

1. Remove the fascia padding — four screws and plain washers.
2. Remove one screw.
3. Remove the two nuts, spring washers and plain washers from the rear of the fascia.
4. Lift off the fascia.

Refitting

5. Reverse instructions 1 to 4.

76.46.02
76.46.03

BODY

FASCIA CRASH PAD
76.46.04

– Remove and refit

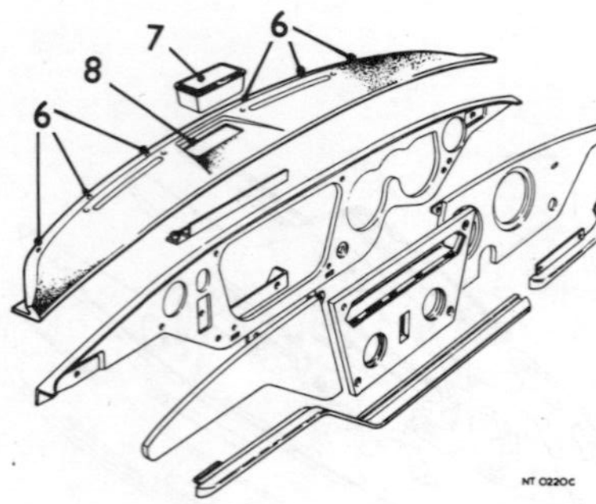

Removing

1. Remove the centre fascia 76.46.02.
2. Remove the driver's side fascia 76.46.01.
3. Remove the passenger's side fascia 76.46.03.
4. Remove the two bolts, spring washers, plain washers and spacers, securing the air flow control to the fascia bracket.
5. Remove the four nuts, plain washers and spring washers securing the demister vents to the body.
6. Remove the demister vents.
7. Remove the six nuts, plain washers and spring washers securing the crash pad to the body.
8. Pull out the ash tray bowl.
9. Straighten the tags securing the ash tray retainer to the body. Lift out the retainer.
10. Carefully raise the crash pad to free the studs from the body. Lift out the crash pad.

Refitting

10. Reverse instructions 1 to 9.

FASCIA SUPPORT BRACKET
76.46.09

– Remove and refit

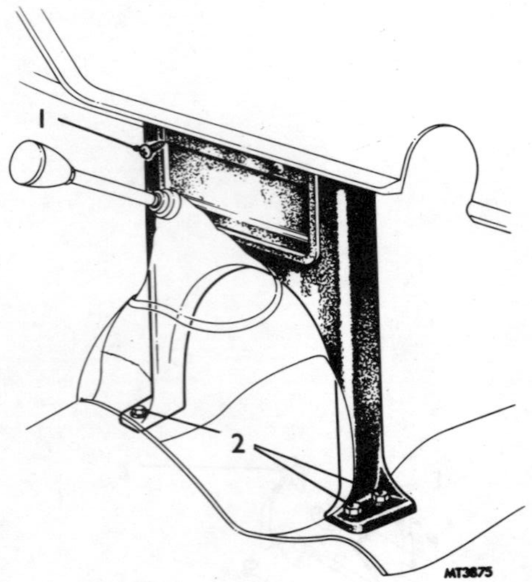

Removing

1. Remove two screws holding support bracket to fascia support rail.
2. Remove four bolts holding fascia support bracket to floor.
3. Remove fascia support bracket.

Refitting

4. Reposition fascia support bracket.
5. Refit four bolts holding fascia support bracket to floor.
6. Refit two screws holding support bracket to fascia support rail.

76.46.04
76.46.09

BODY

GEARBOX COVER CARPET
76.49.01

– Remove and refit

Removing

1. Remove gearlever knob.
2. Remove two screws holding trim pads to gearbox cover.
3. Remove four bolts holding fascia support bracket to floor.
4. Remove two screws holding fascia support bracket to fascia rail.
5. Remove fascia support bracket.
6. Remove carpet.

Refitting

7. Reposition carpet over gearbox cover.
8. Reposition fascia support bracket.
9. Refit two screws holding fascia support bracket to fascia.
10. Refit four bolts holding fascia support bracket to floor.
11. Refit trim pads to gearbox cover.
12. Refit gearlever knob.

FLOOR CARPETS–FRONT
76.49.02

– Remove and refit

Removing

1. Pull R.H. carpet clear of floor pedals.
2. Remove R.H. carpet.
3. Remove L.H. carpet.

Refitting

4. Reposition and fit L.H. carpet.
5. Reposition and fit R.H. carpet.

CARPET – REAR
76.49.03

– Remove and refit

Removing

1. Remove the seats, 76.70.04/76.70.05.
2. Remove the lower seat belt fixings 76.73.02, operations 1 and 2.
3. Disconnect the four fasteners at the front and lift the carpet clear of the handbrake lever.

Refitting

4. Reverse instructions 1 to 3.

76.49.01
76.49.03

BODY

FRONT GRILLE
76.55.03

— Remove and refit

Removing
1. Remove one underrider (either side) 76.22.01.
2. Remove one screw and plain washer.
3. Carefully disengage the grille from the second underrider.

Refitting
4. Reverse instructions 1 to 3.

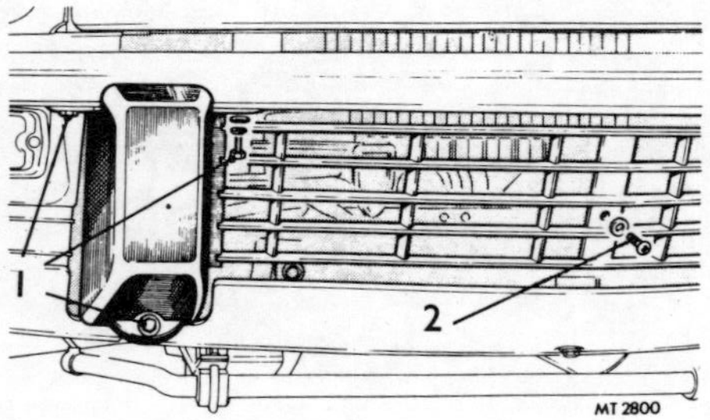

DOOR HANDLE
76.58.01

— Remove and refit

Removing
1. Fully raise the glass.
2. Remove the trim pad. 76.34.01.
3. Remove the spring and the foam pad.
4. Remove the two nuts and plain washers and withdraw the clamping bracket.
5. Disconnect the door lock control rod from the spring clip and carefully withdraw the handle and the seating gasket.

Refitting
6. Reverse instructions 1 to 5.

DOOR PULL
76.58.25

— Remove and refit

Removing
1. Remove the trim pad 76.34.01.
2. Remove the escutcheon — two screws and spring washers.
3. Remove the backing plate — one screw and spring washer.

Refitting
4. Reverse instructions 1 to 3.

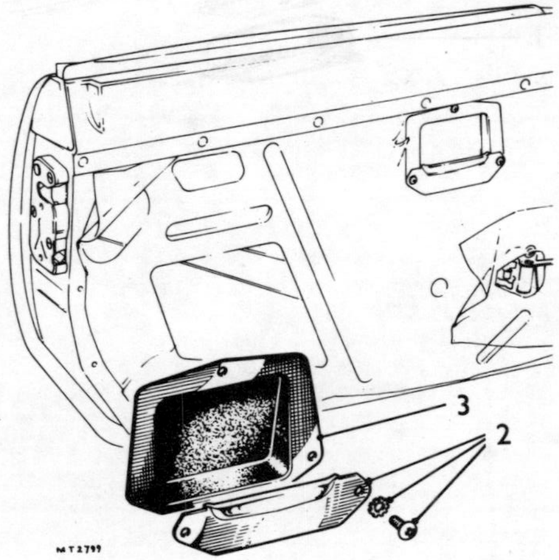

76.55.03
76.58.25

HARDTOP
76.61.01

Remove and refit

Removing
1. Disconnect the three fasteners securing the hood stowage cover to the rear deck.
2. Remove the two domed bolts, spring washers and plain washers.
3. Remove the two domed bolts, spring washers and plain washers.
4. Remove the two bolts and plain washers.
5. With the aid of an assistant, carefully lift the hardtop from the car.

Refitting
6. Reverse instructions 1 to 5. Ensure that the distance tubes are located in the windscreen header rail.

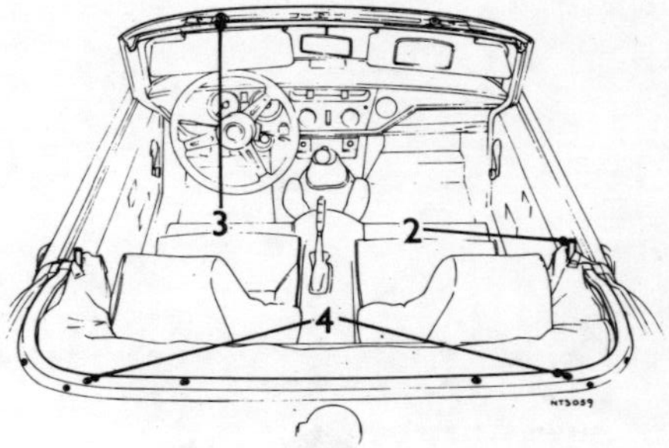

HOOD
76.61.08

— Remove and refit

Removing
1. Disconnect the eight fasteners.
2. Remove the four bolts, spring washers and plain washers.
3. Remove the two caps, bolts, spring washers and plain washers.
4. Remove the four bolts, spring washers and plain washers.
5. Lift off the hood.

Refitting
6. Reverse instructions 1 to 5.

76.61.01
76.61.08

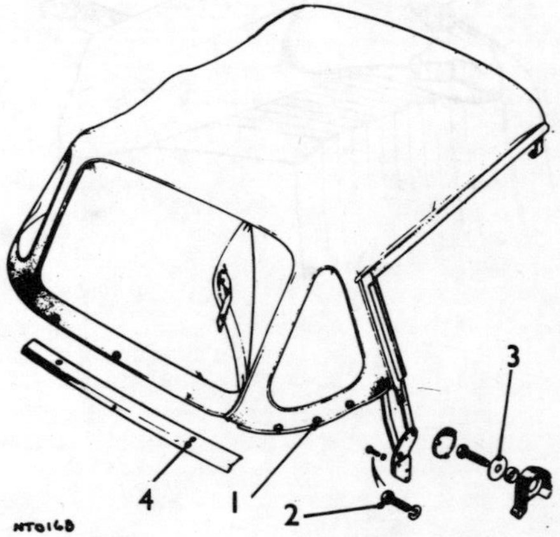

BODY

PARCEL SHELF

— Remove and refit — Drivers side 76.67.04
— Passengers side 76.67.05

Removing
1. Remove the two screws.
2. Remove the two nuts, bolts and plain washers.
3. Lift out the parcel shelf.

Refitting
4. Reverse instructions 1 to 3.

ASHTRAY-FRONT

— Remove and refit 76.67.13

Removing
1. Lever ashtray out of mounting bracket.
2. Straighten legs on mounting bracket and pull bracket clear.

Refitting
3. Place bracket in ashtray aperture.
4. Bend bracket legs to secure mounting bracket in fascia.
5. Pushing securing spring to ashtray, push into mounting bracket.

SEAT CUSHION COVER

— Remove and refit 76.70.02

Removing
1. Remove the seat(s) 76.70.04/76.70.05.
2. Remove the cushion cover — 32 hog rings.

Refitting
3. Reverse instructions 1 and 2.

SEAT SQUAB COVER

— Remove and refit 76.70.03

Removing
1. Remove the seat(s) 76.70.04/76.70.05.
2. Remove the seat squab catch 76.70.27.
3. Remove the squab cover, 11 clips.

Refitting
4. Reverse instructions 1 to 3.

SEATS

— Remove and refit — Drivers seat 76.70.04
— Passengers seat 76.70.05

Removing
1. Move the seat fully forward.
2. Remove the two bolts and spring washers.
3. Move the seat fully rearward.
4. Remove the two bolts and spring washers.
5. Lift out the seat complete with runners.

Refitting
6. Ensure that the packing washers are correctly positioned.
7. Reverse instructions 1 to 5.

SEAT RUNNERS

— Remove and refit 76.70.21

Removing
1. Remove the seat 76.70.04/76.70.05.
2. Detach the runners — two nuts, bolts and four plain washers.

Refitting
3. Reverse instructions 1 and 2.

BODY

SEAT SQUAB CATCH

– Remove and refit   76.70.27

The seat squab catch is secured to the seat frame by two screws, spring washers and plain washers.

SEAT BELTS

– Remove and refit   76.73.02

Removing
1. Remove one bolt and spring washer and lift off the tunnel buckle.
2. Remove the bolt and washer securing the anchor bracket to the floor.
3. Remove the cap, bolt, plain washer, cover and spacer securing the swivel bracket to the wheel arch.
4. Remove the cap, bolt, plain washer, stowage hook and spacer.

Refitting
5. Reverse instructions 1 to 4, ensuring that the swivel bracket is left free to swivel.

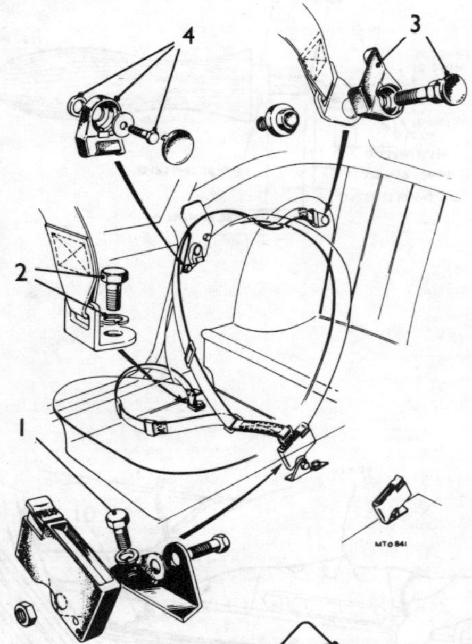

SEAT BELTS – AUTOMATIC (U.S.A. MODELS)

– Remove and refit   76.73.10

Removing
1. Isolate the battery.
2. Remove the buckle unit. 86.65.31/2.
3. Remove the bolt securing the swivel bracket to the floor.
4. Remove the cap, bolt, plain washer, cover and spacer securing the swivel bracket to the wheelarch.
5. Remove the bolt securing the reel to the body.

Refitting
6. Reverse instructions 1 to 5, ensuring that the swivel brackets are left free to swivel. **

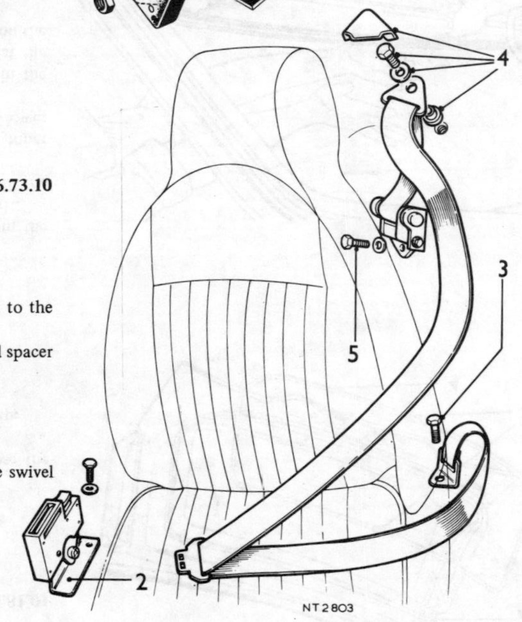

76.70.27
76.73.10

VALANCE – ENGINE

– Remove and refit – L.H.   76.79.07
              – R.H. 2 and 3   76.79.08

Removing
1. Remove one nut, spring washer and plain washer securing the cable harness to the L.H. valance.
2. Remove the two nuts, bolts, spring washers and plain washers.
3. Remove the two nuts, bolts, spring washers and plain washers.

Refitting
4. Reverse instructions 1 to 3.

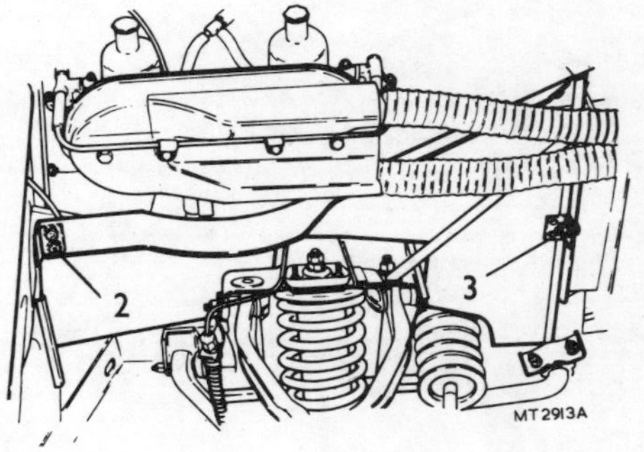

76.79.07
76.79.08

BODY

WINDSCREEN

— Remove and refit   76.81.01

Removing

1. Remove the wiper arms 84.15.01.
2. Remove the interior mirror — two screws.
3. Push the finisher covers to one side to expose the joints, using a suitable piece of wood.
4. Carefully ease the finishers from the weatherstrip.
5. Break the seal, using a suitable blunt tool.
6. Push the glass outwards.

CAUTION: Take care to avoid scratching the glass.

7. Remove the weatherstrip.

Refitting

8. Clean all traces of old sealing compound from the screen aperture flange, using petrol or white spirit.
9. Apply Seelastik SR51 to the glass channel and fit the weatherstrip to the screen.
10. Insert a strong cord into the weatherstrip inner channel allowing the ends to protrude from the lower edge.
11. Have an assistant position the glass centrally in the aperture and maintain a steady pressure whilst the cord ends are pulled to locate the weatherstrip on the body flange.
12. Seal the outer channel of the weatherstrip to the body using Seelastik SR51.
13. Sparingly apply rubber grease or soap/water solution to the weatherstrip finisher recess.
14. Assemble the two finisher covers to the left hand finisher.
15. Fit the finishers using the special tool as follows:
    a. Locate the tool in the recess with open end uppermost and in a vertical position.
    b. Keeping the hook firmly engaged in the recess, draw the tool along to engage the inner flange of the weatherstrip with the finisher.
16. Push the cover finishers centrally over the joins.
17. Fit the interior mirror and wiper arms.

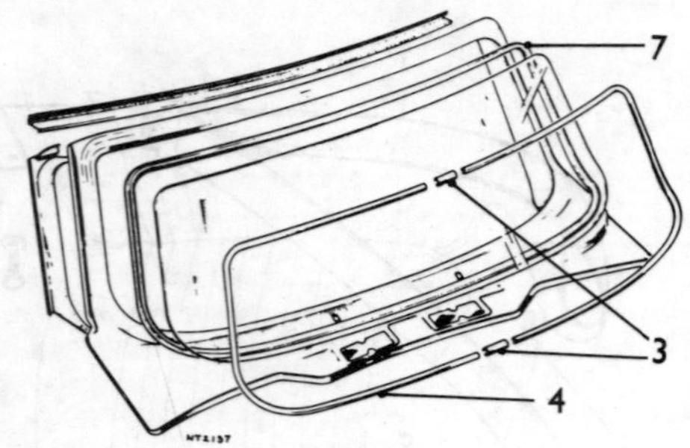

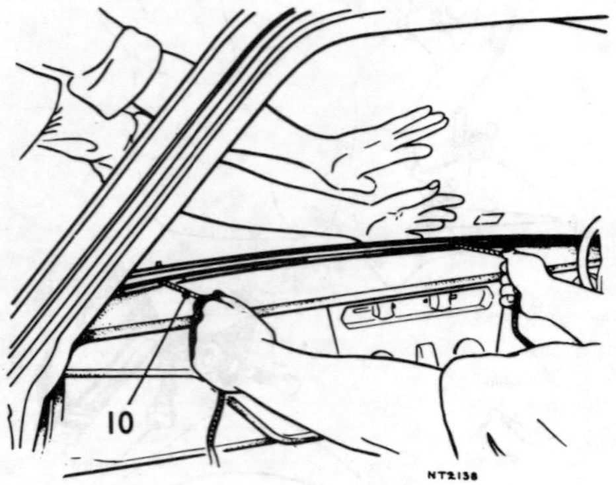

FINISHER STRIP INSERTION TOOL

To fabricate finisher strip insertion tool.

1. Shape a piece of mild steel rod as shown, paying particular attention to the form of the tip. Ensure that the tip is fully rounded and free from burrs.
2. Braze the hook into a metal stock.
3. Fit stock into a file handle and secure with a rivet.

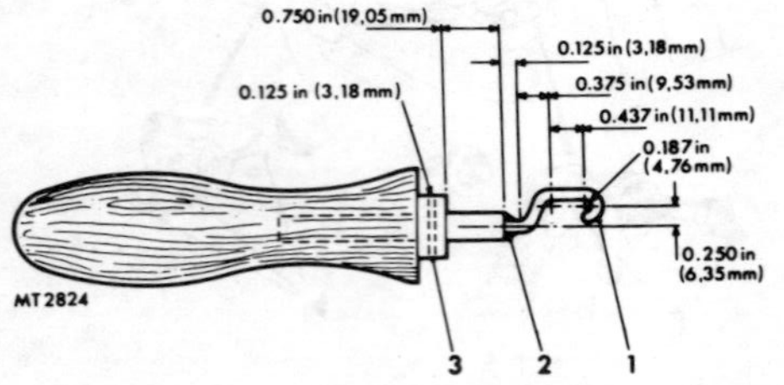

HEATING AND VENTILATION OPERATIONS

Air flow control cable – remove and refit	80.10.06
Air flow control – remove and refit	80.10.09
Fan motor – remove and refit	80.20.15
Heater unit – remove and refit	80.20.01
Water hose	
– cylinder head to water valve (as specified)	
remove and refit	80.25.08
– manifold to water valve (as specified)	
remove and refit	80.25.08
– water valve to heater – remove and refit	80.25.09
– heater to pipe – remove and refit	80.25.07
Water valve	
– control – remove and refit	80.10.10
– control cable – remove and refit	80.10.07
– remove and refit	80.10.16

AIR FLOW CONTROL CABLE
– Remove and refit   80.10.06

Removing
1. Remove the air flow control 80.10.09.
2. Slacken the trunnion bolt and clamp bolt securing the cable to the heater unit. Remove the cable.

Refitting
3. Reverse instructions 1 and 2.

WATER VALVE CONTROL CABLE
– Remove and refit   80.10.07

Removing
1. Remove the water valve control 80.10.10.
2. Slacken the trunnion bolt and clamp bolt securing the cable to the water valve.

Refitting
3. Reverse instructions 1 and 2.

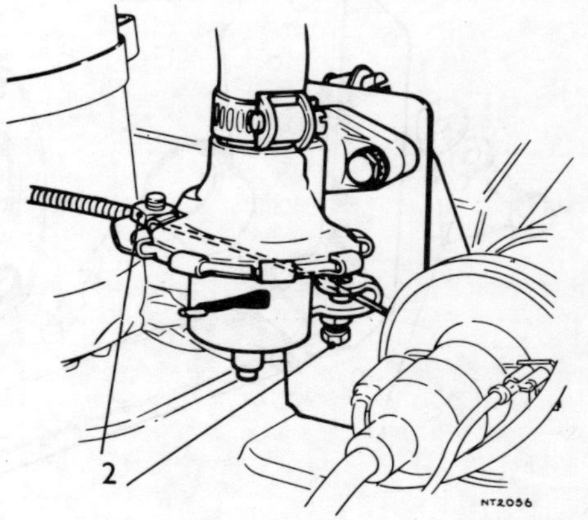

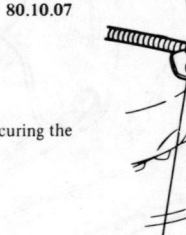

AIR FLOW CONTROL
– Remove and refit   80.10.09

Removing
1. Lower the centre fascia to the service position 76.46.02. Operations 1 to 4.
2. Remove the two bolts, spring washers, plain washers and spacers securing the control to the fascia bracket.
3. Pull out the snap connector and disconnect the Lucar connector from the fan switch.
4. Slacken the trunnion screw and the cable clamp bolt. Detach the cable from the control.

Refitting
5. Ensure that the control cable is positioned to allow full operation of the flap valve.
6. Reverse instructions 1 to 4.

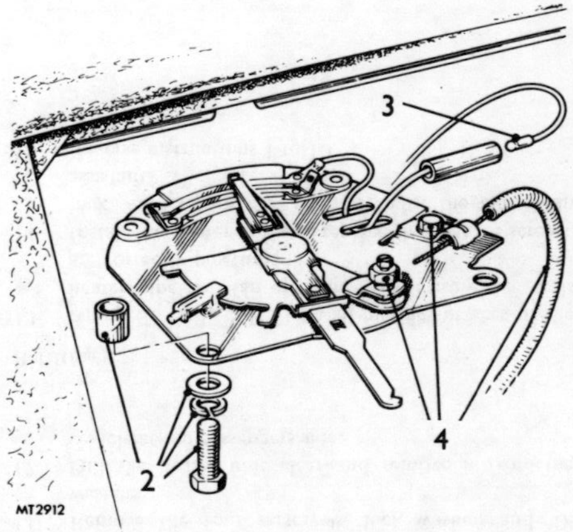

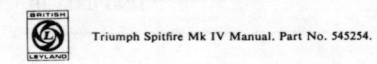

HEATING AND VENTILATION

WATER VALVE CONTROL 80.10.10
— Remove and refit

Removing
1. Lower the centre fascia to the service position 76.46.02. Operations 1 to 4.
2. Remove the two bolts, spring washers, plain washers, and the thick and thin spacers securing the control to the fascia bracket.
3. Slacken the trunnion screw and the cable clamp bolt. Detach the cable from the control.

Refitting
4. Ensure that the control cable is positioned to allow full operation of the water valve.
5. Reverse instructions 1 to 3.

WATER VALVE 80.10.16
— Remove and refit

Removing
1. Drain the cooling system.
2. Slacken the clips and disconnect the two hoses.
3. Slacken the trunnion screw and cable clamp bolt. Detach the control cable.
4. Remove the two nuts, spring washers and plain washers securing the water valve to the bracket.

Refitting
5. Reverse instructions 1 to 4 ensuring that the control cable is positioned to allow full operation of the water valve.

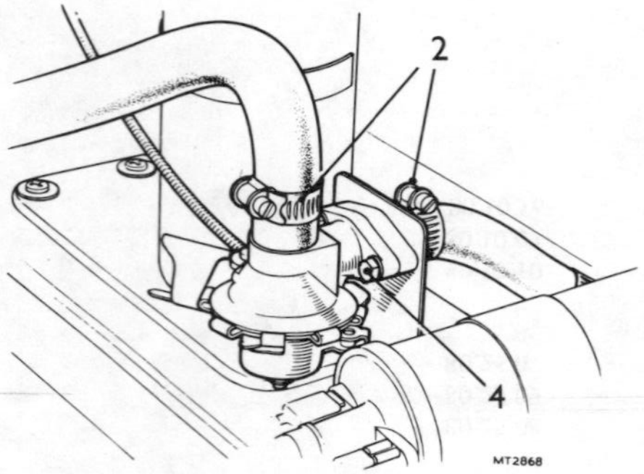

HEATER UNIT 80.20.01
— Remove and refit

Removing
1. Isolate the battery.
2. Drain the cooling system.
3. Slacken the two clips and disconnect the water hoses. Place one hose in a container and blow down the other to clear the coolant from the heater matrix. Remove the hoses.
4. Remove the passengers side parcel shelf 76.67.05.
5. Lower the centre fascia to the service position. 76.46.02, operations 1 to 4.
6. Remove the air flow control, 80.10.09.
7. Remove the air flow control cable, 80.10.06.
8. Remove the passengers side demister hose.
9. Slacken the clip and disconnect the drivers side demister hose from the heater unit.
10. Push the screen washer tubing aside.
11. Remove the four setscrews, lock washers and 'D' washers.
12. Pull the heater unit clear and remove it from the vehicle at the passengers side.

Refitting
13. Apply Seelastik S.R.51 to all mating surfaces of the heater pipe and fan aperture seals. Ensure that seals are correctly positioned.
14. Install the heater unit and replace the four set screws, lock washers and 'D' washers, with the aid of an assistant.
15. Reverse instructions 1 to 10.

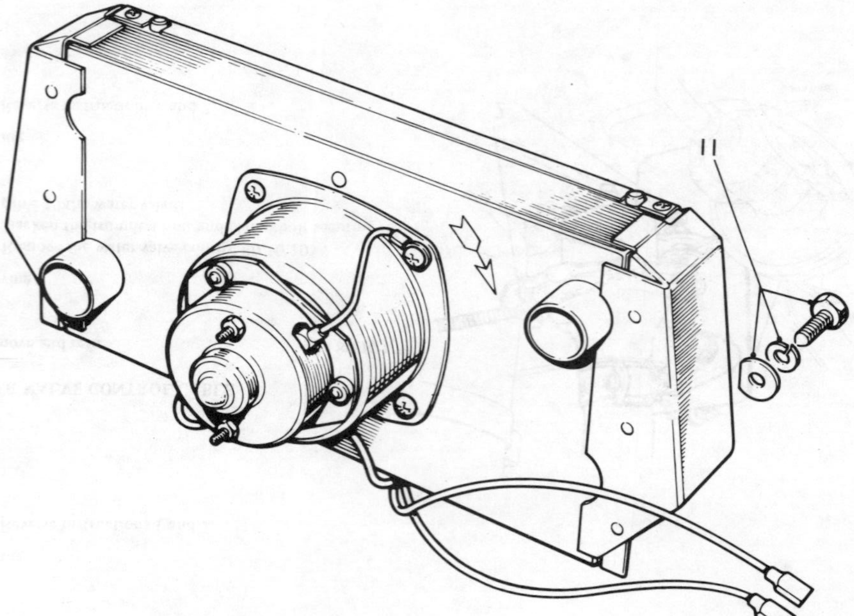

HEATING AND VENTILATION

FAN MOTOR   80.20.15
– Remove and refit

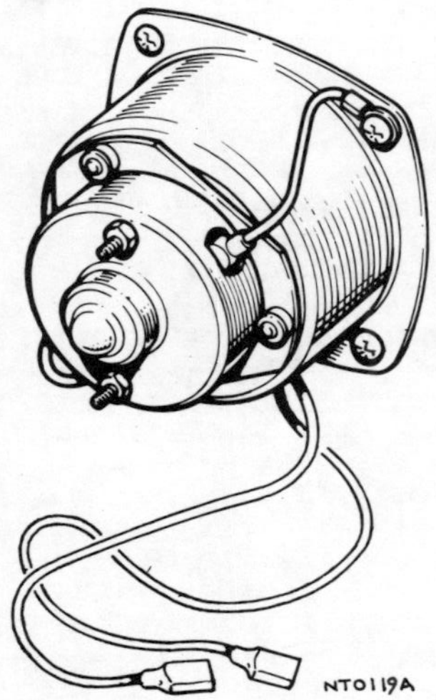

Removing
1. Lower the centre fascia to the service position 76.46.02, operations 1 to 4.
2. Disconnect the Lucar connector and the snap connector.
3. Remove the four screws.
4. Manoeuvre the fan motor clear of the heater unit and remove it from the vehicle on the drivers side.
5. Detach the impellor from the shaft, using a screwdriver to release the retaining clip.

Refitting
6. Refit the impellor, ensuring that ¼ in (6·5 mm) clearance exists between the base of the impellor and the motor.
7. Reverse instructions 1 to 4.

WATER HOSES
– Remove and refit

Hose – cylinder head to water valve (except U.S.A. and Sweden) 80.25.08
– manifold to water valve (U.S.A. and Sweden only) 80.25.08
– heater to water pipe 80.25.07
– water valve to heater 80.25.09

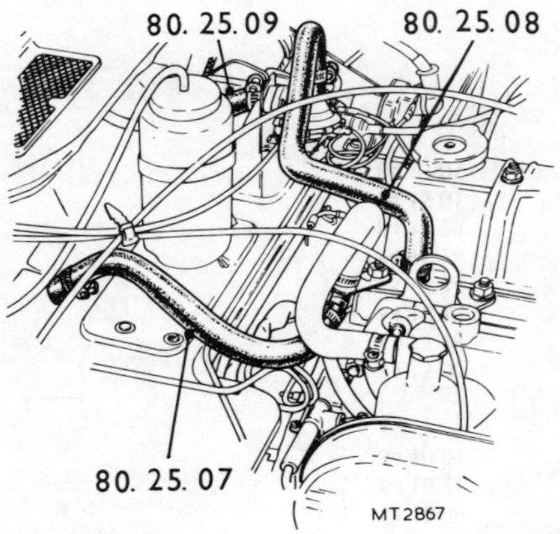

The heater water hoses are each secured by two clips.
Drain the cooling system before removal.

WINDSCREEN WIPERS AND WASHERS OPERATIONS

Windscreen washer system
- jet – remove and refit 84.10.09
- pump – remove and refit 84.10.21
- reservoir – remove and refit 84.10.01

Windscreen wiper system
- data and description 84.15.00
- motor – overhaul 84.15.18
- motor – remove and refit 84.15.12
- rack – remove and refit 84.15.24
- wheelbox – drivers – remove and refit ... 84.15.28
- wheelbox – passengers – remove and refit ... 84.15.29
- wiper arm – remove and refit 84.15.01
- wiper blade – remove and refit ... 84.15.05

NOTE: On U.S.A. models a non return valve is fitted into the windscreen washer system.

It is located between the pipe from the washer pump and the 'T' piece connecting the pipes from the washer jets.

If it is necessary to disturb or replace the non return valve, care must be taken to re-connect it correctly otherwise the washers will fail to function.

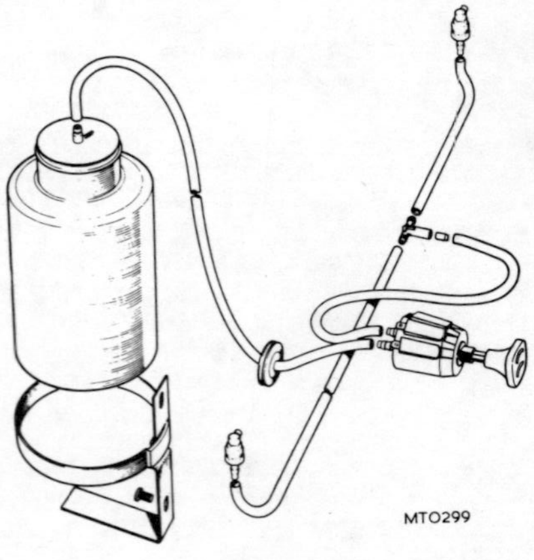

WINDSCREEN WASHER RESERVOIR

— Remove and refit   84.10.01

Removing
1. Unscrew the top and pull off the pipe.
2. Manoeuvre the bottle upwards from the carrier.

Refitting
3. Reverse instructions 1 and 2.

WINDSCREEN WASHER JET

— Remove and refit   84.10.09

Removing
1. Pull the tubing from the jet.
2. Remove the nut and washer.
3. Withdraw the jet.

Refitting
4. Reverse instructions 1 to 3.

WINDSCREEN WASHER PUMP

— Remove and refit   84.10.21

The manual washer pump and electrical wiper switch is a single integral unit. For removing and refitting refer to 86.65.38.

WINDSCREEEN WIPER SYSTEM 84.15.00

— Data and description

Motor:

Manufacturer	Lucas
Type	14W
Lucas part No: motor minus gear assembly	75664
gear assembly — normal	54702581
— U.S.A.	54702582
Stanpart No: motor minus gear assembly	517621
gear assembly	520101
Running current — after 60 seconds from cold with connecting rod removed:	
Normal speed	1.5 amp
High speed	2·0 amp
Running speed — final gear after 60 seconds from cold with connecting rod removed:	
Normal speed	46 to 52 rev/min
High speed	60 to 70 rev/min
Armature end float	0·002 to 0·008 in (0·05 to 0·20 mm)
Brush length — new	0·250 in (6 mm)
renew if less than	0·125 in (3 mm)

Brush spring pressure — when compressed so brush bottom is aligned with brushbox slot end — 5 to 7 0z (140 to 200 g)

Maximum permissible force to move cable rack in tubing — arms and blades removed — 6 lb (3 kg)

For high speed brush this is when narrow section is worn into full width section.

The unit consists of a two speed permanent-magnet motor and a gearbox unit which drives a cable rack mechanism. Rotation of the motor armature is converted to a reciprocating motion of the cable rack by a single stage worm and gear, a connecting rod and a cross-head contained in a guide channel.

Two speed operation is provided by a third brush. When high speed is selected the positive supply is transferred from the normal speed brush to the high speed brush.

A switching feature stops the blades in the park position irrespective of their position when the fascia switch is selected off. This is effected by a two stage limit switch unit attached to the gearbox. The contacts are actuated by a cam on the final gear.

When the fascia switch is selected off, the motor will continue to run until the limit switch first stage contacts open. A momentary period follows during which no contact is made. The second stage contacts then close causing regenerative braking of the armature which maintains constant parking of the blades.

Supply
1. Facia switch

OFF	1 to 2
NORMAL	3 to 2
HIGH	3 to 4

2. Normal speed brush
3. High speed brush
4. Commutator
5. Permanent magnet
6. Earth brush
7. Final gear cam
8. Limit switch unit

WINDSCREEN WIPERS AND WASHERS

WINDSCREEN WIPER ARM

— Remove and refit 84.15.01

Removing

1. Lift the wiper arm and blade from the screen so that it falls into its service position.
2. Position a screwdriver as shown and impart a twisting action to lift the clip from the spindle groove.
3. The assembly may now be removed by hand.

Refitting

4. Ensure that the spindles are in the 'park' position.
5. Hinge the wiper arm against the spring to adopt its service position.
6. Locate the splines for a suitable 'park' position. Push on to engage the clip to the spindle groove.
7. Lower the wiper arm to the screen.

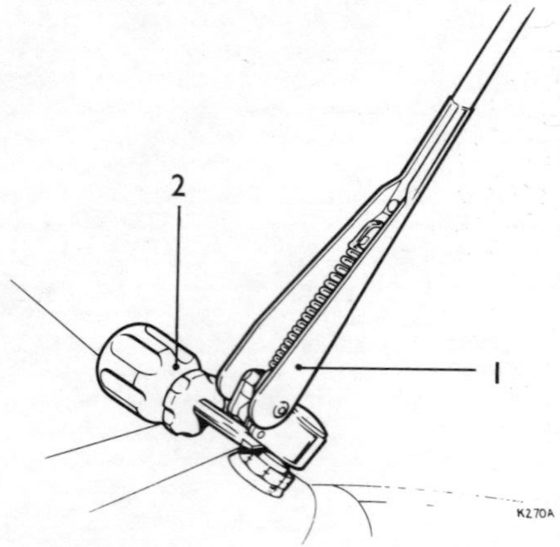

WINDSCREEN WIPER BLADE

— Remove and refit 84.15.05

Removing

1. Lift the wiper arm and blade from the screen so that it falls into its service position.
2. Simultaneously lift the clip 'A', tilt cage 'B' and gently pull the wiper blade from the arm.

Refitting

3. Locate the cage and clip assembly to the wiper arm. Push on to engage 'pip'.
4. Lower the wiper arm to the screen.

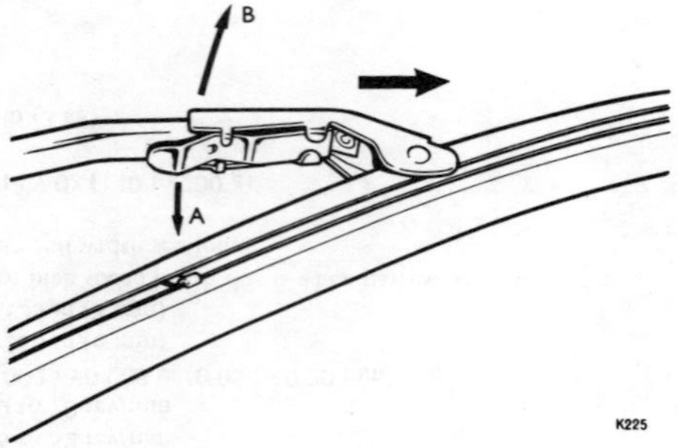

WIPER MOTOR

— Remove and refit 84.15.12

Removing

1. Remove the harness plug.
2. Unscrew the nut securing the tubing to the gear assembly.
3. Remove the strap and sleeve and detach the earth lead. — two bolts, spring washers and plain washers.
4. Lift off the rubber mounting pad.
5. Remove the gearbox cover — four screws.
6. Remove the crank-pin spring clip by withdrawing sideways. Remove the washer.
7. Carefully withdraw the connecting rod and remove the washer.
8. Detach the rack assembly and remove the motor and gear assembly.

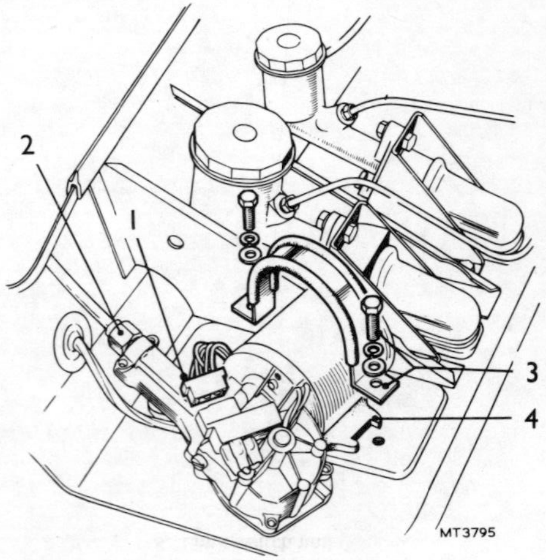

Refitting

9. Lubricate the crankpin with Shell Turbo 41 oil.
10. Lubricate the cross-head end of the connecting rod, including pin with Ragosine Listate grease.
11. Reverse instructions 1 to 8.

WINDSCREEN WIPERS AND WASHERS

WINDSCREEN WIPER SYSTEM

—Motor overhaul   84.15.18

General

If the motor is not operating correctly, first check electrical supply of 12 volts on terminal 5 with normal speed selected and terminal 3 with high speed selected.

If electrical supply is satisfactory, perform the following operations to determine if the fault is in the motor or in the rack, tube and wheelbox assembly, resulting in the motor being required to drive an excessive load.

Running current

1. Remove four screws. Lift off gearbox cover.
2. Remove the crankpin spring clip by withdrawing sideways. Remove washer.
3. Carefully withdraw connecting rod. Remove washer.
4. Connect ammeter suitable for running current (see Data) in supply circuit.
5. Allow motor to run for 60 seconds. Ammeter reading should then be as given in Data for normal speed and high speed respectively.

If the reading is not as stated, a fault in the motor is indicated.

Running speed

1. Remove four screws. Lift off gearbox cover.
2. Remove crankpin spring clip by withdrawing sideways. Remove washer.
3. Carefully withdraw connecting rod. Remove washer.
4. Allow motor to run for 60 seconds. Speed of final gear should then be as given in Data for normal speed and high speed respectively.

If the speed is not as stated, a fault in the motor is indicated.

Force to move rack in tube and wheelbox assembly.

1. Remove four screws. Lift off gearbox cover.
2. Remove crankpin spring clip by withdrawing sideways. Remove washer.
3. Carefully withdraw connecting rod. Remove washer.
4. Remove wiper arms 84.15.02 and 84.15.03.
5. Attach a suitable spring scale to hole in cross-head. Maximum permissible force to move rack is given in Data.

If the required force is greater than stated, a fault in the rack, tube and wheelbox assembly is indicated.

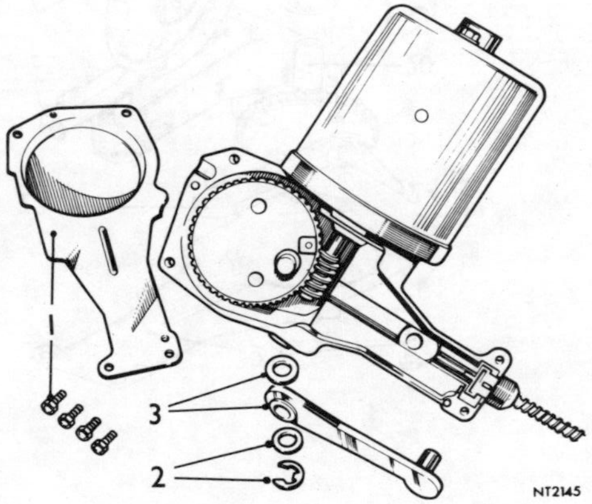

84.15.18 Sheet 1

WINDSCREEN WIPER SYSTEM

—Motor-overhaul   84.15.18

Dismantling

1. Remove four screws. Lift off gearbox cover.
2. Remove crankpin spring clip by withdrawing sideways. Remove washer.
3. Carefully withdraw connecting rod. Remove washer.
4. Remove final gearshaft spring clip by withdrawing sideways. Remove washer.
5. Ensure shaft is burr-free and withdraw. Remove dished washer.
6. Remove thrust screw or thrust screw and lock nut as fitted.
7. Remove through bolts.
8. Carefully withdraw cover and armature about 0·2 in (5 mm). Continue withdrawal, allowing bushes to drop clear of commutator. Ensure three brushes are not contaminated with grease.
9. Pull armature from cover against action of permanent magnet.
10. Remove three screws to release brush assembly. Lift assembly from recess.
11. Lift and slide limit switch out sideways to release spring clip. Remove limit switch and brush assembly joined together by wires.

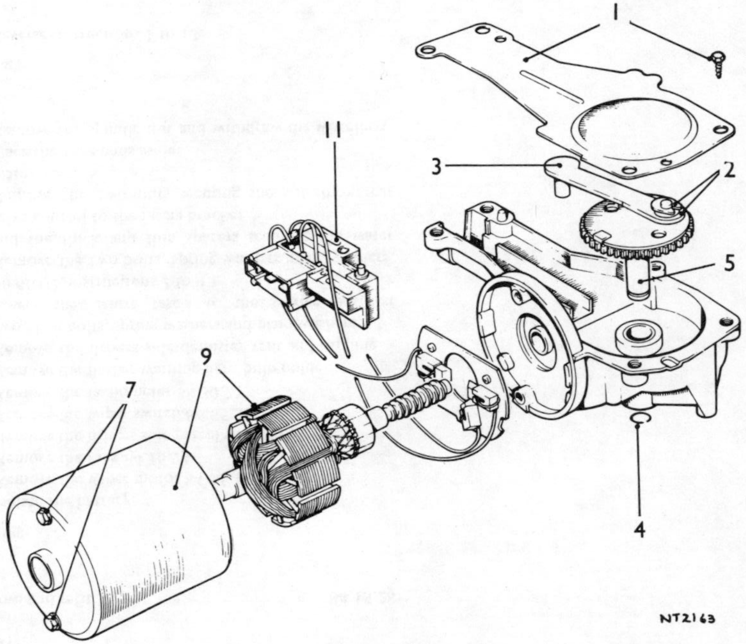

84.15.18 Sheet 2

WINDSCREEN WIPERS AND WASHERS

Reassembling

NOTE: The following lubricants are required during assembly: Shell Turbo 41 oil and Ragosine Listate grease.

12. Slide limit switch in sideways to secure with spring clip.
13. Position brush assembly. Secure with three screws.
14. Lubricate cover bearing and saturate cover bearing felt washer with Shell Turbo 41 oil. Position armature to cover against action of permanent magnet.
15. Lubricate self aligning bearing with Shell Turbo 41 oil. Carefully insert armature shaft through bearing. Ensure that brushes are not contaminated with lubricant. Push three brushes back to clear commutator.
16. Seat cover against gearbox. Turn cover to align marks shown. Fit through bolts.
17. Fit thrust screw or thrust screw and lock nut as fitted.
18. If a non adjustable thrust screw is fitted check armature end float as follows: Position a feeler gauge between armature shaft and thrust screw. Push armature towards cover. End float should be 0·002 – 0·008 in. In the unlikely event of adjustment being required end float may be increased by fitting shim washer/washers under thrust screw head or reduced by mounting thrust screw in lathe and removing metal from underside of head.
19. If an adjustable thrustscrew and lock nut is fitted adjust armature end float and lock nut as follows: Slacken lock nut. Screw thrust screw in until resistance is felt. Screw thrust screw out quarter of a turn – maintain in this position and tighten lock nut.
20. Lubricate final gear bushes with Shell Turbo 41 oil. Fit dished washer with concave surface facing final gear. Insert shaft.
21. Fit washer. Fit spring clip by inserting sideways.
22. Pack Ragosine Listate grease around worm gear, final gear and into cross-head guide channel.
23. Fit washer. Lubricate final gear crankpin with Shell Turbo 41 oil. Lubricate cross-head end of connecting rod, including pin, with Ragosine Listate grease. Carefully insert connecting rod.
24. Fit washer. Fit spring clip by inserting sideways.
25. Position gearbox cover. Secure with four screws.

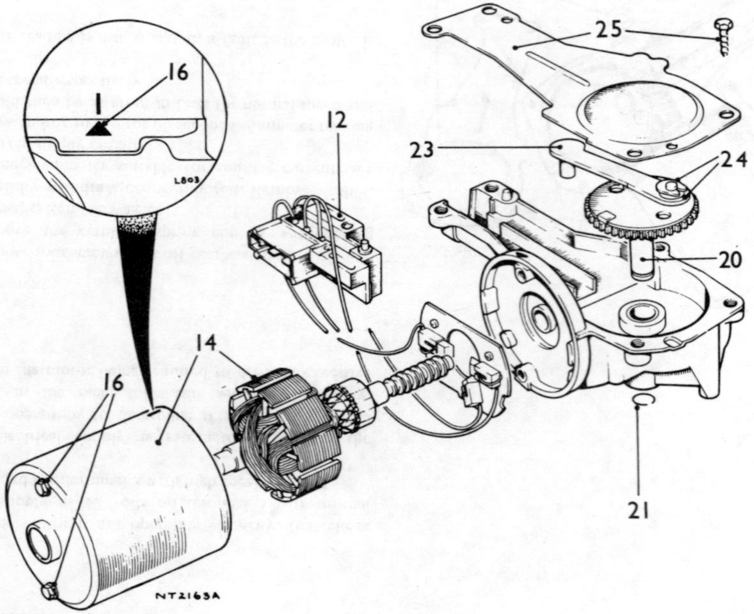

WINDSCREEN WIPER WHEELBOX – DRIVERS (R.H. STEER)

—Remove and refit   84.15.28

Removing
1. Isolate the battery.
2. Remove the wiper motor 84.15.12.
3. Remove the rack 84.15.24.
4. Remove the drivers side parcel shelf 76.67.04.
5. Remove the wiper switch 86.65.38.
6. Remove the tachometer 88.30.21.
7. Remove the flasher warning light bulb holder.
8. Remove the drivers side demister vent and capping – two nuts, bolts, spring washers and plain washers.
9. Lower the centre fascia to the service position 76.46.02, instructions 2 to 4.
10. Remove the two bolts, spring washers, plain washers, and the thick and thin spacers securing the water valve control to the fascia bracket.
11. Remove the two nuts securing the wheelbox rear plate.
12. Place the tube ends aside.
13. Remove the spindle nut and withdraw the wheelbox.

Refitting
14. Reverse instructions 1 to 13.

WINDSCREEN WIPER WHEELBOX – PASSENGERS

—Remove and refit   84.15.29

Removing
1. Remove the wiper motor 84.15.12.
2. Remove the rack 84.15.24.
3. Remove the two nuts securing the wheelbox rear plate.
4. Place the tube ends aside.
5. Remove the spindle nut and withdraw the wheelbox.

Refitting
6. Reverse instructions 1 to 5.

ELECTRICAL OPERATIONS

Alternator
- data and description 86.10.00
- functional check 86.10.01
- overhaul 86.10.08
- remove and refit 86.10.02

Battery — remove and refit 86.15.01

Bulb chart 86.00.01

Buzzers
- description 86.55.00
- remove and refit 86.55.13

Flasher units
- hazard flasher unit — remove and refit 86.55.12
- turn signal flasher unit — remove and refit 86.55.11

Fuse system
- fuse — remove and refit 86.70.02

Ignition coil and ballast resistor
- ballast resistor — remove and refit 86.35.33
- data and description 86.35.00
- ignition coil — remove and refit 86.35.32

Ignition distributor
- contact assembly — remove and refit 86.35.13
- contact gap — adjust 86.35.14
- data and description 86.35.00
- ignition timing — adjust 86.35.15
- lubrication 86.35.18
- overhaul (as specified) 86.35.26
- remove and refit 86.35.20

Key warning system
- buzzer — remove and refit 86.55.13
- description 86.58.00
- diode — remove and refit 86.57.10
- door switch — remove and refit 86.65.14
- key light — remove and refit 86.45.78
- key switch — remove and refit . . . . see 57.40.31

Lamps
- front marker lamp — remove and refit 86.40.59
- front parking and flasher lamp — remove and refit 86.40.26
- headlamp — beam aiming 86.40.17
- headlamp — remove and refit 86.40.02
- plate illumination lamp — remove and refit 86.40.86
- rear marker lamp — remove and refit 86.40.64
- rear tail/stop, flasher and reverse lamp — remove and refit . . 86.40.70
- seat belt warning lamp — remove and refit 86.45.75

continued

Relays
- horn relay — remove and refit 86.55.09
- night dimming relay — contacts adjust 86.55.14
- night dimming relay — data and description 86.55.00
- overdrive relay — remove and refit 86.55.03
- starter solenoid — data and description 86.55.04
- starter solenoid — remove and refit 86.55.05

Seat belt warning system
- buzzer — remove and refit 86.55.13
- description 86.57.00
- diode — remove and refit 86.57.10
- drivers belt switch — remove and refit 86.65.31
- gearbox switch — remove and refit 86.65.28
- passengers belt switch — remove and refit 86.65.32
- passengers seat switch — remove and refit 86.65.29
- warning light — remove and refit 86.45.75

Starter motor
- data and description 86.60.00
- inertia drive — remove and refit 86.60.06
- overhaul 86.60.13
- remove and refit 86.60.01

Switches
- brake line failure switch — remove and refit 86.65.47
- column light switch — remove and refit 86.65.17
- data 86.65.00
- door switch — remove and refit 86.65.14
- driver's seat belt switch — remove and refit 86.65.31
- hazard switch — remove and refit 86.65.50
- heater switch — remove and refit 80.10.10
- horn push — remove and refit 86.65.18
- ignition/starter switch — remove and refit 86.65.02
- key switch — remove and refit . . . . See 57.40.31
- master light switch — remove and refit 86.65.09
- oil pressure switch — remove and refit 86.65.30
- overdrive gearbox switch — remove and refit 86.65.33
- overdrive gear lever switch — remove and refit 86.65.34
- passenger's seat belt switch — remove and refit 86.65.32
- passenger's seat switch — remove and refit 86.65.29
- reverse lamp switch — remove and refit 86.65.20
- Seat belt warning system gearbox switch — remove and refit . . . 86.65.28
- stop lamp switch — remove and refit 86.65.51
- turn signal switch — remove and refit 86.65.54
- windscreen wiper switch — remove and refit 86.65.38

** Wiring diagram chart . . . . 86.00.03 **

ELECTRICAL

BULB CHART

	Watts	Unipart No.	Stanpart No.
Headlamps:			
L.H. dip—Normal	60/45		512231
R.H. dip—Normal	60/50	GLU 101	215735 †
France	45/40		510219
U.S.A.	50/40		— †
Front parking lamps	5	GLB 207	57591
Front flasher lamps	21	GLB 382	502379
Front marker lamps	4		501436
Rear marker lamps	4		
Tail/stop lamps	5/21	GLB 380	502287
Rear flasher lamps	21	GLB 382	502379
Reverse lamp	21	GLB 207	57591
Plate illumination lamp	5	GLB 987	59492
Instrument illumination	2·2	GLB 987	59492
Courtesy light	2·2	GLB 987	57591
Warning lights	2·2	GLB 281	513000 **
Seat belt warning light	2		

† — Sealed beam light unit
** — Warning lights

WIRING DIAGRAMS

Spitfire Mark 4 vehicles are built with variations in electrical equipment according to market specification requirements.

To provide all wiring diagram information seven wiring diagrams are featured. Each is identified by a steering condition and a diagram No.

By referring to the chart below and the appropriate diagram service personnel will be able to obtain wiring diagram information for any specific vehicle.

	RIGHT HAND STEER		LEFT HAND STEER				
			NORMAL		U.S.A.		SWEDEN
	Up to the end of the 1972 model year	From the introduction of the 1973 model year	Up to the end of the 1972 model year	From the introduction of the 1973 model year	Up to the end of the 1971 model year	1972 model year	1973 model year	From the introduction of the 1974 model year**
Right Hand Steer Diagram 1	X							
Right Hand Steer Diagram 2		X						
Left Hand Steer Diagram 1			X	X				
Left Hand Steer Diagram 2					X			
Left Hand Steer Diagram 3								X
Left Hand Steer Diagram 4						X		
Left Hand Steer Diagram 5							X	
Left Hand Steer Diagram 6								** X **

WIRING DIAGRAM – SPITFIRE MARK 4
RIGHT HAND STEER – DIAGRAM 1

KEY TO WIRING DIAGRAM – SPITFIRE MARK 4
RIGHT HAND STEER – DIAGRAM 1

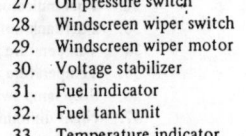

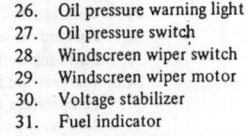

Please see page 86.00.03

1. Alternator
2. Ignition warning light
3. Battery
4. Ignition/starter switch
5. Starter solenoid
6. Starter motor
7. Ballast resistor
8. Ignition coil – 6 volt
9. Ignition distributor
10. Master light switch
11. Fuse
12. Front parking lamp
13. Night dimming relay winding
14. Tail lamp
15. Plate illumination lamp
16. Instrument illumination
17. Column light switch
18. Dip beam
19. Main beam warning light
20. Main beam
21. Courtesy light
22. Door switch
23. Horn relay
24. Horn push
25. Horn
26. Oil pressure warning light
27. Oil pressure switch
28. Windscreen wiper switch
29. Windscreen wiper motor
30. Voltage stabilizer
31. Fuel indicator
32. Fuel tank unit
33. Temperature indicator
34. Temperature transmitter
35. Stop lamp switch
36. Night dimming relay
37. Stop lamp
38. Reverse lamp switch
39. Reverse lamp
40. Turn signal flasher unit
41. Turn signal switch
42. L.H. flasher lamp
43. R.H. flasher lamp
44. Turn signal warning light
45. Heater motor
46. Heater rheostat
47. Heater switch
48. Radio facility
A. Overdrive (optional extra)
49. Overdrive relay
50. Overdrive gearbox switch
51. Overdrive gear lever switch
52. Overdrive solenoid
a. From ignition/starter switch – terminal 3.
b. From ignition/starter switch – terminal 2.

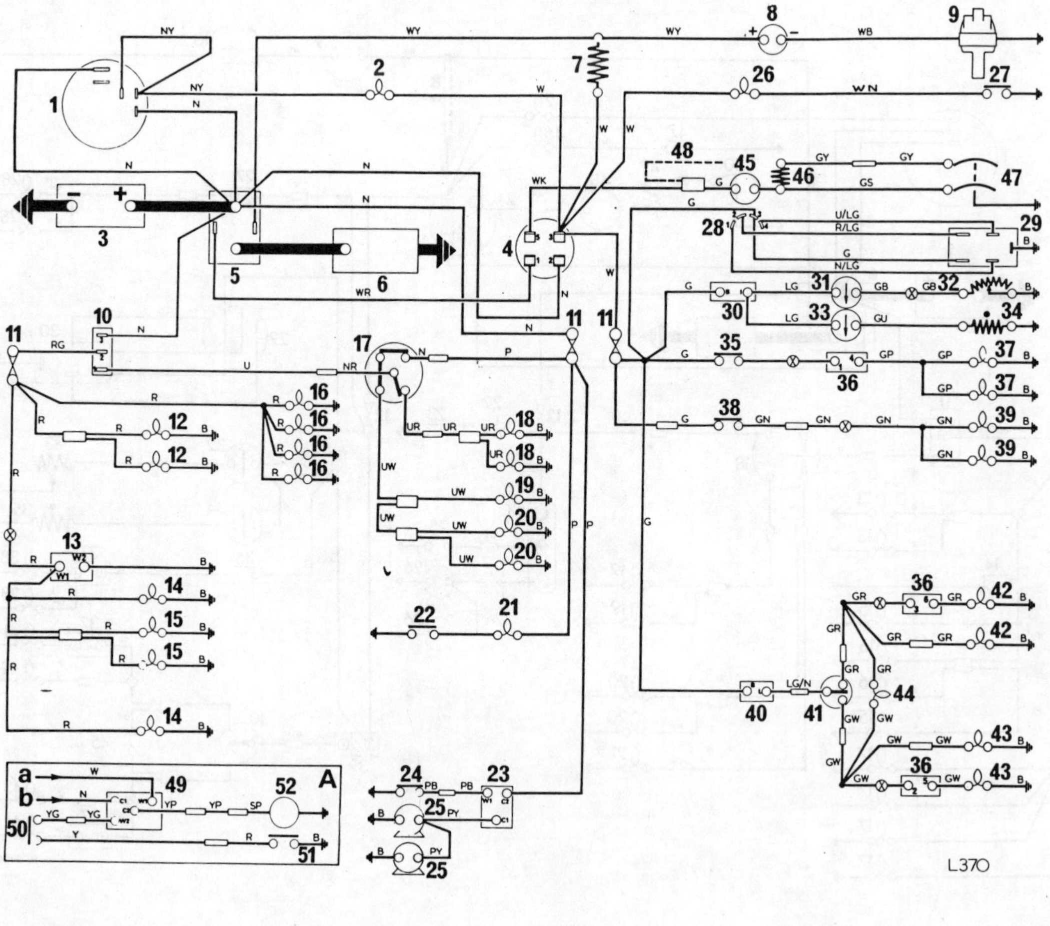

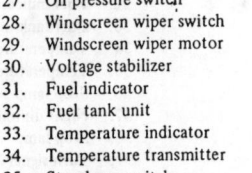

WIRING DIAGRAM – SPITFIRE MARK 4
RIGHT HAND STEER – DIAGRAM 2

KEY TO WIRING DIAGRAM – SPITFIRE MARK 4
RIGHT HAND STEER – DIAGRAM 2
Please see page 86.00.03

1. Alternator
2. Ignition warning light
3. Battery
4. Ignition/starter switch
5. Radio supply
6. Starter solenoid
7. Starter motor
8. Ballast resistor wire
9. Ignition coil – 6 volt
10. Ignition distributor
11. Master light switch
12. Fuse
13. Front parking lamp
14. Night dimming relay winding
15. Tail lamp
16. Plate illumination lamp
17. Instrument illumination
18. Column light switch
19. Dip beam
20. Main beam
21. Main beam warning light
22. Key light
23. Door switch
24. Horn relay
25. Horn push
26. Horn
27. Reverse lamp switch
28. Reverse lamp
29. Windscreen wiper switch
30. Windscreen wiper motor
31. Voltage stabilizer
32. Fuel indicator
33. Fuel tank unit
34. Temperature indicator
35. Temperature transmitter
36. Stop lamp switch
37. Night dimming relay contacts
38. Stop lamp
39. Turn signal flasher unit
40. Turn signal switch
41. L.H. rear flasher lamp
42. L.H. front flasher lamp
43. R.H. front flasher lamp
44. R.H. rear flasher lamp
45. Turn signal warning light
46. Oil pressure warning light
47. Oil pressure switch
48. Heater motor
49. Heater resistor
50. Heater switch

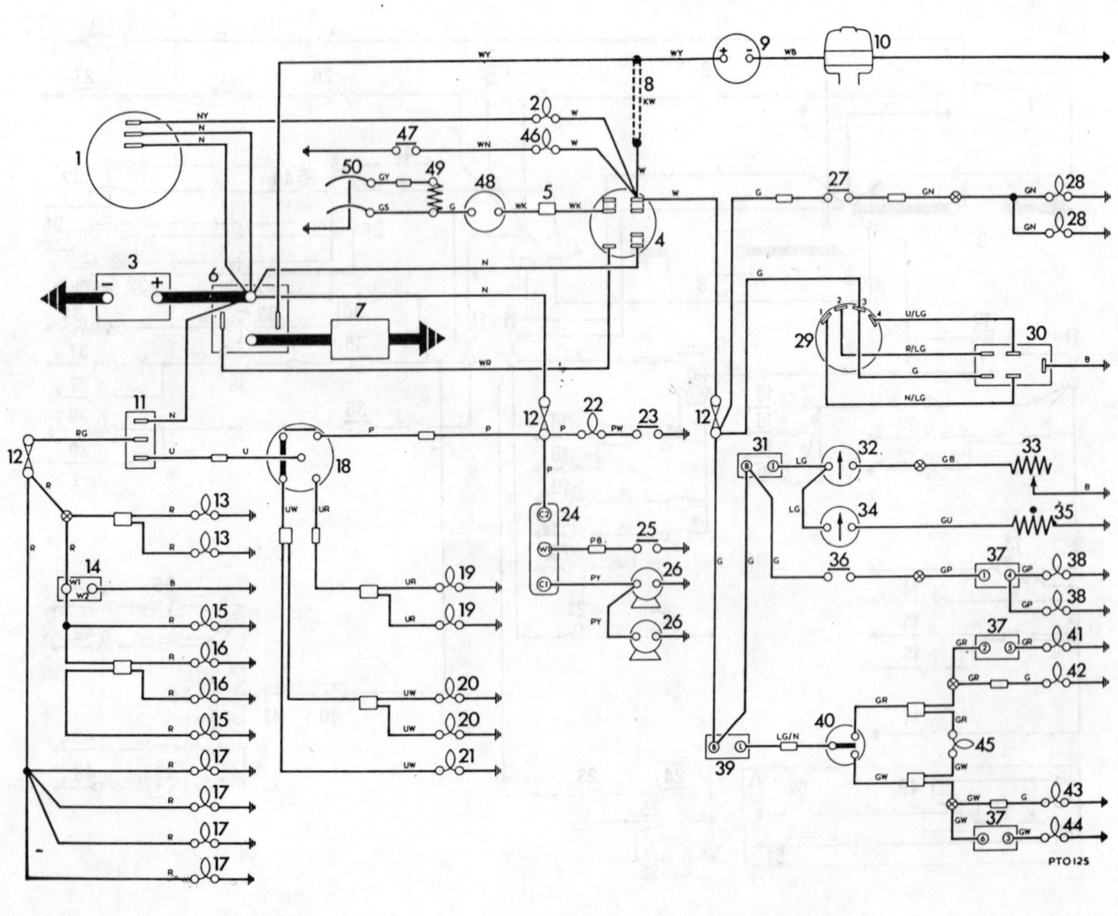

WIRING DIAGRAM – SPITFIRE MARK 4
LEFT HAND STEER – DIAGRAM 1

KEY TO WIRING DIAGRAM – SPITFIRE MARK 4
LEFT HAND STEER – DIAGRAM 1
Please see page 86.00.03

1. Alternator
2. Ignition warning light
3. Battery
4. Ignition/starter switch
5. Starter solenoid
6. Starter motor
7. Ballast resistor
8. Ignition coil – 6 volt
9. Ignition distributor
10. Master light switch
11. Fuse
12. Front parking lamp
13. Front marker lamp
14. Rear marker lamp
15. Tail lamp
16. Plate illumination lamp
17. Instrument illumination
18. Column light switch
19. Dip beam
20. Main beam warning light
21. Main beam
22. Door switch
23. Buzzer
24. Key switch
25. Key light
26. Horn relay
27. Horn push
28. Horn
29. Brake warning light
30. Brake line failure switch
31. Oil pressure warning light
32. Oil pressure switch
33. Windscreen wiper switch
34. Windscreen wiper motor
35. Voltage stabilizer
36. Fuel indicator
37. Fuel tank unit
38. Temperature indicator
39. Temperature transmitter
40. Stop lamp switch
41. Stop lamp
42. Reverse lamp switch
43. Reverse lamp
44. Turn signal flasher unit
45. Turn signal switch
46. L.H. flasher lamp
47. R.H. flasher lamp
48. Turn signal warning light
49. Hazard flasher unit
50. Hazard switch
51. Hazard warning light
52. Heater motor
53. Heater rheostat
54. Heater switch
55. Radio facility
56. Line fuse – 25 amp (Italy only)

A. Overdrive (optional extra)
57. Overdrive relay
58. Overdrive gearbox switch
59. Overdrive gear lever switch
60. Overdrive solenoid
a. From ignition/starter switch – terminal 3
b. From ignition/starter switch – terminal 2

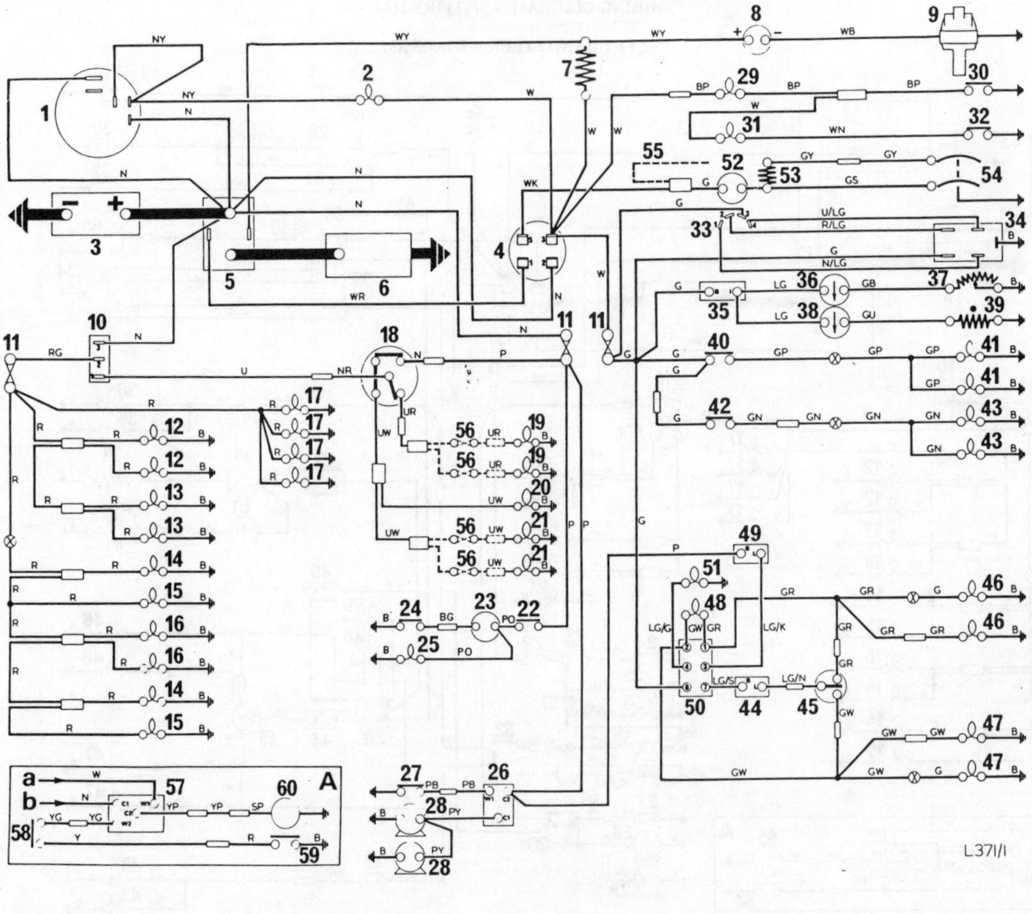

ELECTRICAL

WIRING DIAGRAM – SPITFIRE MARK 4
LEFT HAND STEER – DIAGRAM 2

KEY TO WIRING DIAGRAM – SPITFIRE MARK 4
LEFT HAND STEER – DIAGRAM 2

Please see page 86.00.03

1.	Alternator	24.	Key switch	47.	R.H. flasher lamp
2.	Ignition warning light	25.	Key light	48.	Turn signal warning light
3.	Battery	26.	Horn relay	49.	Hazard flasher unit
4.	Ignition/starter switch	27.	Horn push	50.	Hazard switch
5.	Starter solenoid	28.	Horn	51.	Hazard warning light
6.	Starter motor	29.	Brake warning light	52.	Belt warning gearbox switch
7.	Ballast resistor	30.	Brake line failure switch	53.	Drivers belt switch
8.	Ignition coil – 6 volt	31.	Oil pressure warning light	54.	Passengers seat switch
9.	Ignition distributor	32.	Oil pressure switch	55.	Passengers belt switch
10.	Master light switch	33.	Windscreen wiper switch	56.	Belt warning light
11.	Fuse	34.	Windscreen wiper motor	57.	Diode
12.	Front parking lamp	35.	Stop lamp switch	58.	Heater motor
13.	Front marker lamp	36.	Stop lamp	59.	Heater rheostat
14.	Rear marker lamp	37.	Voltage stabilizer	60.	Heater switch
15.	Tail lamp	38.	Temperature indicator	61.	Radio facility
16.	Plate illumination lamp	39.	Temperature transmitter		
17.	Instrument illumination	40.	Fuel indicator		
18.	Column light switch	41.	Fuel tank unit		
19.	Dip beam	42.	Reverse lamp switch	A.	Overdrive (optional extra)
20.	Main beam warning light	43.	Reverse lamp	62.	Overdrive relay
21.	Main beam	44.	Turn signal flasher unit	63.	Overdrive gearbox switch
22.	Door switch	45.	Turn signal switch	64.	Overdrive gear lever switch
23.	Buzzer	46.	L.H. flasher lamp	65.	Overdrive solenoid

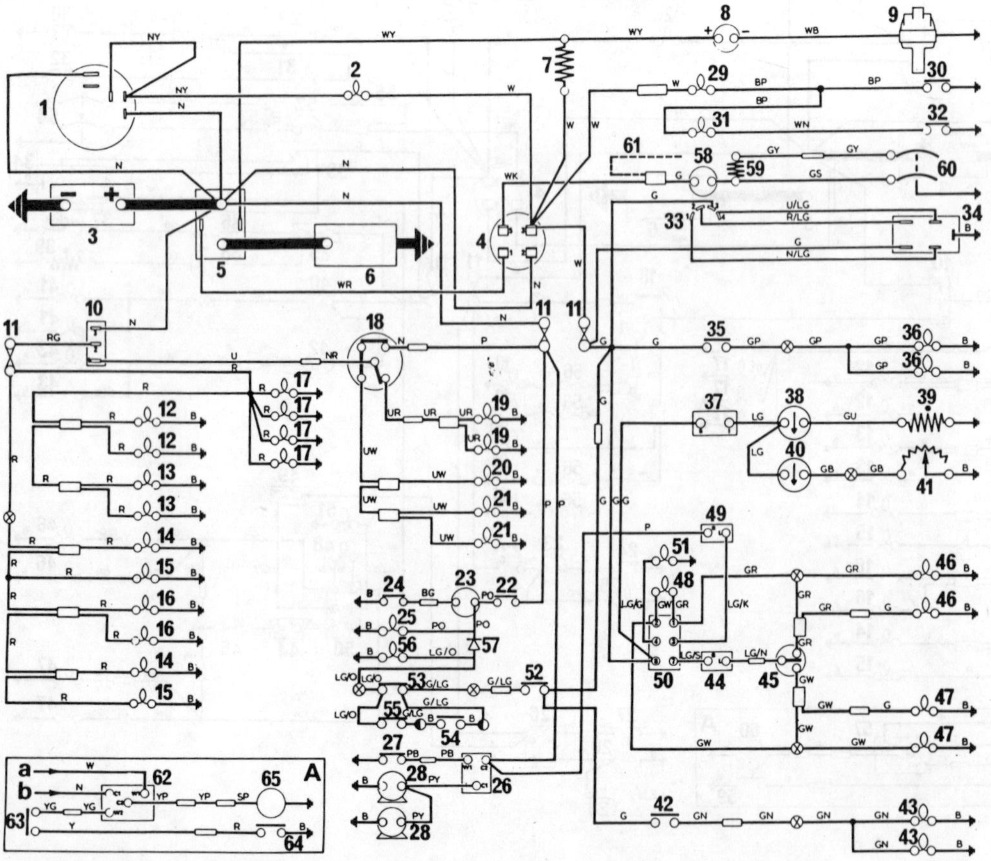

ELECTRICAL

KEY TO WIRING DIAGRAM – SPITFIRE MARK 4
LEFT HAND STEER – DIAGRAM 3

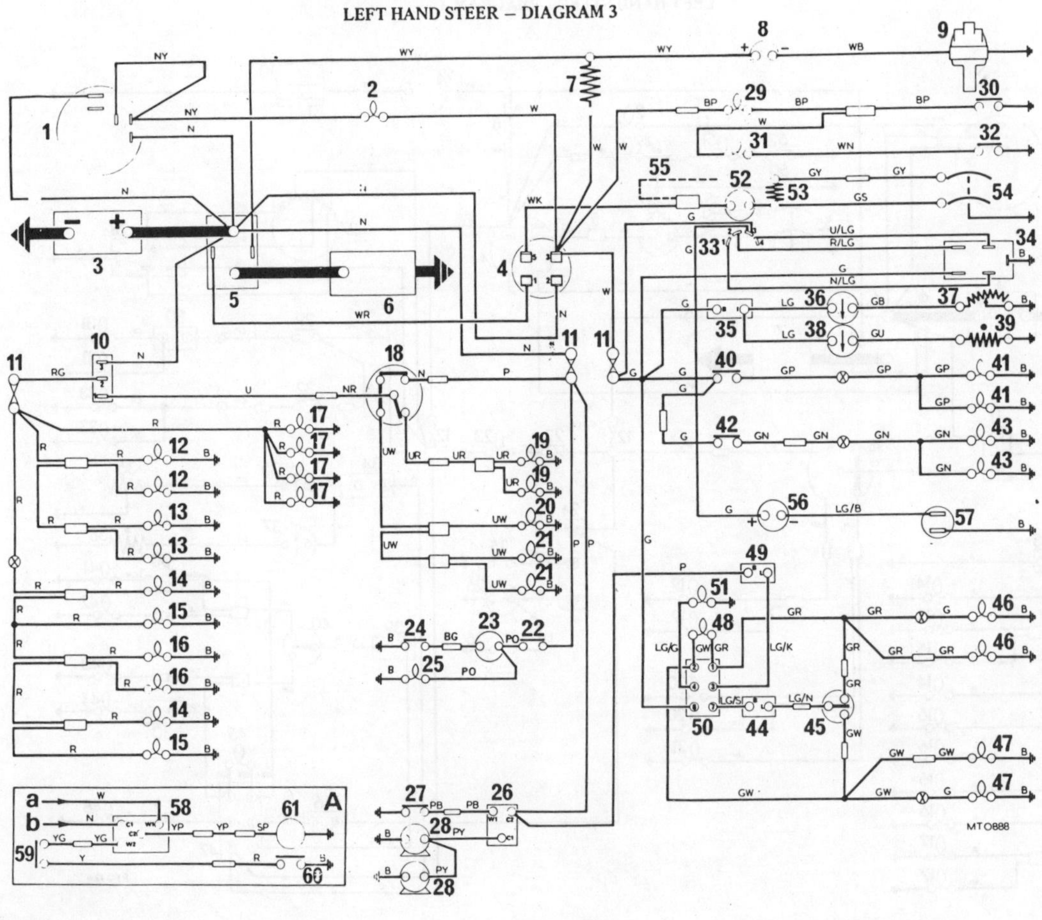

Please see page 86.00.03

1. Alternator
2. Ignition warning light
3. Battery
4. Ignition/starter switch
5. Starter solenoid
6. Starter motor
7. Ballast resistor
8. Ignition coil – 6 volt
9. Ignition distributor
10. Master light switch
11. Fuse
12. Front parking lamp
13. Front marker lamp
14. Rear marker lamp
15. Tail lamp
16. Plate illumination lamp
17. Instrument illumination
18. Column light switch
19. Dip beam
20. Main beam warning light
21. Main beam
22. Door switch
23. Key warning buzzer
24. Key switch
25. Key light
26. Horn relay
27. Horn push
28. Horn
29. Brake warning light
30. Brake line failure switch
31. Oil pressure warning light
32. Oil pressure switch
33. Windscreen wiper switch
34. Windscreen wiper motor
35. Voltage stabiliser
36. Fuel indicator
37. Fuel tank unit
38. Temperature indicator
39. Temperature transmitter
40. Stop lamp switch
41. Stop lamp
42. Reverse lamp switch
43. Reverse lamp
44. Turn signal flasher unit
45. Turn signal switch
46. L.H. flasher lamp
47. R.H. flasher lamp
48. Turn signal warning light
49. Hazard flasher unit
50. Hazard switch
51. Hazard warning light
52. Heater motor
53. Heater rheostat
54. Heater switch
55. Radio facility
56. Windscreen washer pump
57. Windscreen washer switch

A. Overdrive (optional extra)
58. Overdrive relay
59. Overdrive gearbox switch
60. Overdrive gear lever switch
61. Overdrive solenoid
a. From ignition/starter switch – terminal 3
b. From ignition/starter switch – terminal 2

ELECTRICAL

WIRING DIAGRAM – SPITFIRE MARK 4
LEFT HAND STEER – DIAGRAM 4

KEY TO WIRING DIAGRAM – SPITFIRE MARK 4
LEFT HAND STEER – DIAGRAM 4
Please see page 86.00.03

1. Alternator
2. Ignition warning light
3. Battery
4. Ignition/starter switch
5. Radio supply
6. Starter solenoid
7. Starter motor
8. Ballast resistor wire
9. Ignition coil – 6 volt
10. Ignition distributor
11. Master light switch
12. Fuse
13. Night dimming relay winding
14. Tail lamp
15. Plate illumination lamp
16. Instrument illumination
17. Front parking lamp
18. Column light switch
19. Dip beam
20. Main beam
21. Main beam warning light
22. Door switch
23. Key light
24. Horn relay
25. Horn push
26. Horn
27. Windscreen wiper switch
28. Windscreen wiper motor
29. Stop lamp switch
30. Night dimming relay contacts
31. Stop lamp
32. Reverse lamp switch
33. Reverse lamp
34. Voltage stabilizer
35. Fuel indicator
36. Fuel tank unit
37. Temperature indicator
38. Temperature transmitter
39. Turn signal flasher unit
40. Turn signal switch
41. L.H. rear flasher lamp
42. L.H. front flasher lamp
43. R.H. front flasher lamp
44. R.H. rear flasher lamp
45. Turn signal warning light
46. Hazard flasher unit
47. Hazard switch
48. Hazard warning light
49. Brake line failure warning light
50. Brake line failure switch
51. Oil pressure warning light
52. Oil pressure switch
53. Heater motor
54. Heater resistor
55. Heater switch

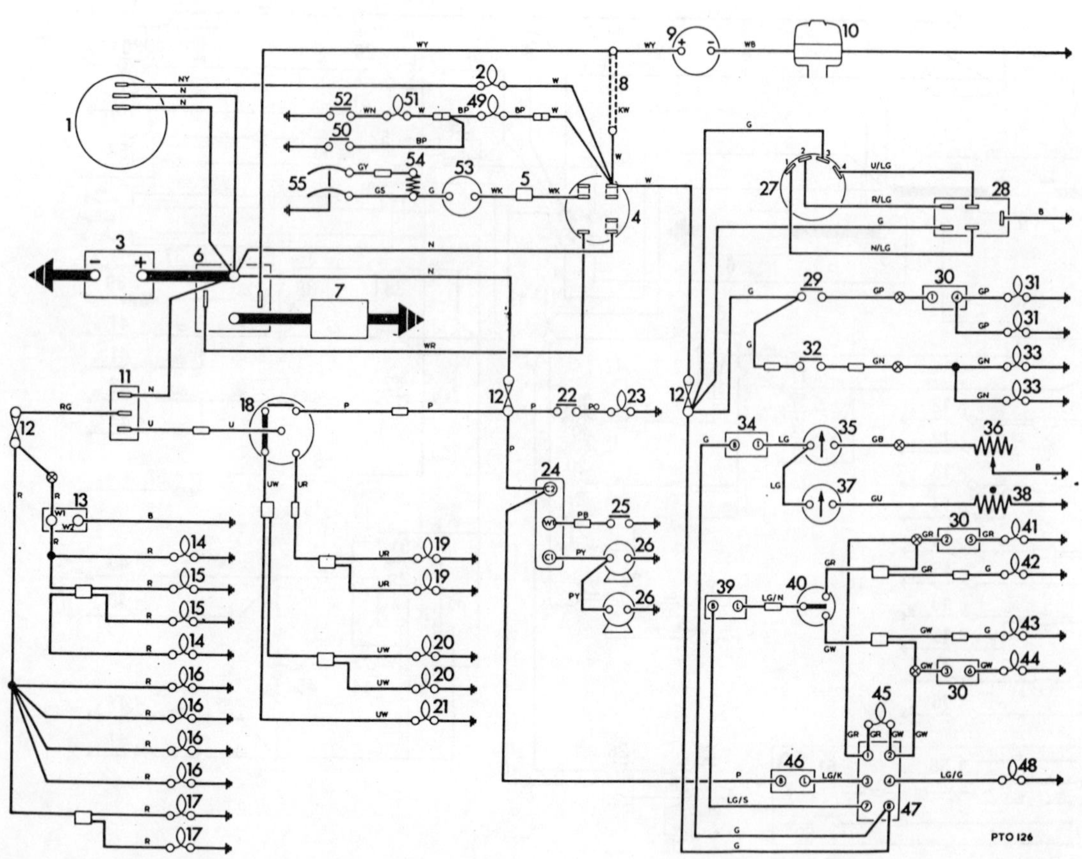

ELECTRICAL

WIRING DIAGRAM – SPITFIRE MARK 4
LEFT HAND STEER – DIAGRAM 5

KEY TO WIRING DIAGRAM – SPITFIRE MARK 4
LEFT HAND STEER – DIAGRAM 5

Please see page 86.00.03

1. Alternator
2. Ignition warning light
3. Battery
4. Ignition/starter switch
5. Starter solenoid
6. Starter motor
7. Ballast resistor wire
8. Ignition coil – 6 volt
9. Ignition distributor
10. Master light switch
11. Fuse
12. Wipe/wash switch identification light
13. Rear marker lamp
14. Tail lamp
15. Plate illumination lamp
16. Instrument illumination
17. Hazard switch identification light
18. Heater control identification light
19. Front parking lamp
20. Front marker lamp
21. Column light switch
22. Dip beam
23. Main beam
24. Main beam warning light
25. L.H. door switch
26. Buzzer
27. Key switch
28. Key light
29. Belt warning gearbox switch
30. Drivers belt switch
31. Passengers seat switch
32. Passengers belt switch
33. Fasten belts warning light
34. Diode
35. Horn relay
36. Horn push
37. Horn
38. Windscreen wiper switch
39. Windscreen wiper motor
40. Stop lamp switch
41. Stop lamp
42. Reverse lamp switch
43. Reverse lamp
44. Voltage stabilizer
45. Fuel indicator
46. Fuel tank unit
47. Temperature indicator
48. Temperature transmitter
49. Turn signal flasher unit
50. Turn signal switch
51. L.H. flasher lamp
52. R.H. flasher lamp
53. Turn signal warning light
54. Hazard flasher unit
55. Hazard switch
56. Hazard warning light
57. Brake warning light
58. Brake line failure switch
59. Oil pressure warning light
60. Oil pressure switch
61. Anti run on valve
62. Radio facility
63. Heater motor
64. Heater rheostat
65. Heater switch
A. Overdrive (optional extra)
66. Overdrive gear lever switch
67. Overdrive gearbox switch
68. Overdrive solenoid

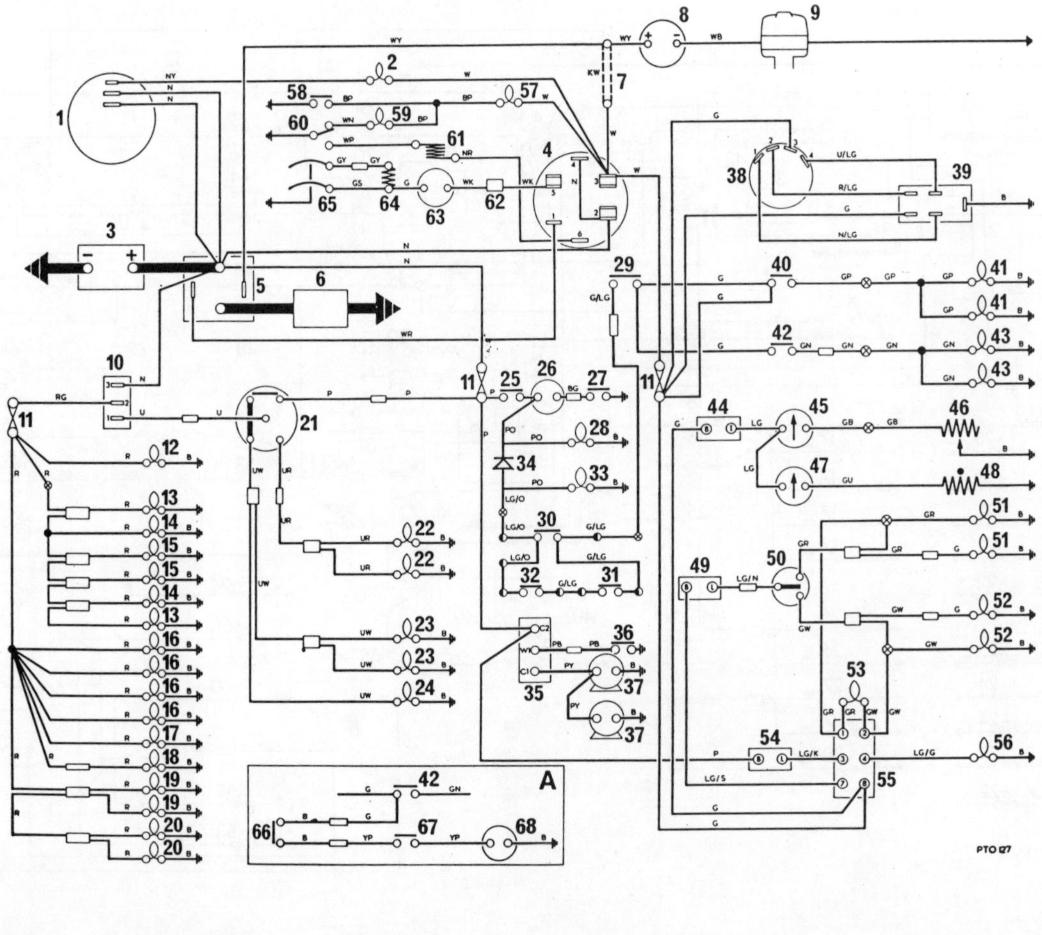

ELECTRICAL

WIRING DIAGRAM – SPITFIRE MARK 4
LEFT HAND STEER – DIAGRAM 6

KEY TO WIRING DIAGRAM – SPITFIRE MARK 4
LEFT HAND STEER – DIAGRAM 6
Please see page 86.00.03

1. Alternator
2. Ignition warning light
3. Battery
4. Ignition/starter switch
5. Radio supply
6. Seat belt interlock module
7. Starter solenoid relay
8. Starter solenoid
9. Starter motor
10. Ballast resistor wire
11. Ignition coil
12. Ignition distributor
13. Master light switch
14. Fuse
15. Panel rheostat
16. Wipe/wash switch identification light
17. Instrument illumination
18. Hazard switch identification light
19. Heater control identification light
20. Front parking lamp
21. Front marker lamp
22. Rear marker lamp
23. Tail lamp
24. Plate illumination lamp
25. Column light switch
26. Dip beam
27. Main beam
28. Main beam warning light
29. Drivers seat switch
30. Passengers seat switch
31. Drivers belt switch
32. Passengers belt switch
33. Seat belt interlock gearbox switch
34. Fasten belts warning light
35. Key light
36. Drivers door switch
37. Key switch
38. Horn relay
39. Horn push
40. Horn
41. Heater motor
42. Heater rheostat
43. Heater switch
44. Windscreen wiper motor
45. Windscreen wiper switch
46. Stop lamp switch
47. Stop lamp
48. Overdrive gear lever switch (optional extra)
49. Overdrive gearbox switch (optional extra)
50. Overdrive solenoid (optional extra)
51. Reverse lamp switch
52. Reverse lamp
53. Voltage stabilizer
54. Fuel indicator
55. Fuel tank unit
56. Temperature indicator
57. Temperature transmitter
58. Turn signal flasher unit
59. Turn signal switch
60. L.H. front flasher lamp
61. L.H. rear flasher lamp
62. R.H. front flasher lamp
63. R.H. rear flasher lamp
64. Turn signal warning light
65. Hazard flasher unit
66. Hazard switch
67. Hazard warning light
68. Brake warning light
69. Brake line failure switch
70. Oil pressure warning light
71. Oil pressure switch
72. Anti run on valve

COLOUR CODE
B   Black
G   Green
K   Pink
LG Light green
N   Brown
O   Orange
P   Purple
R   Red
S   Slate
U   Blue
W   White
Y   Yellow

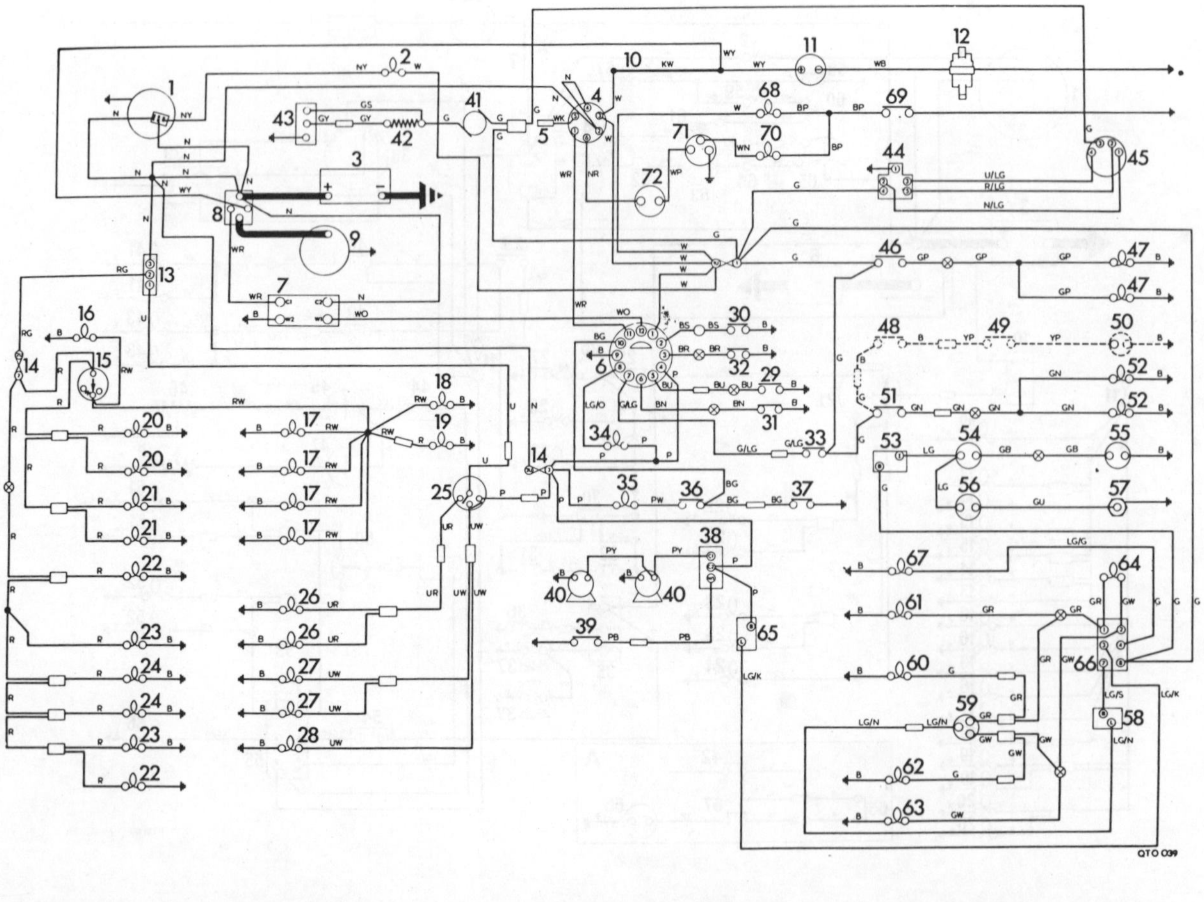

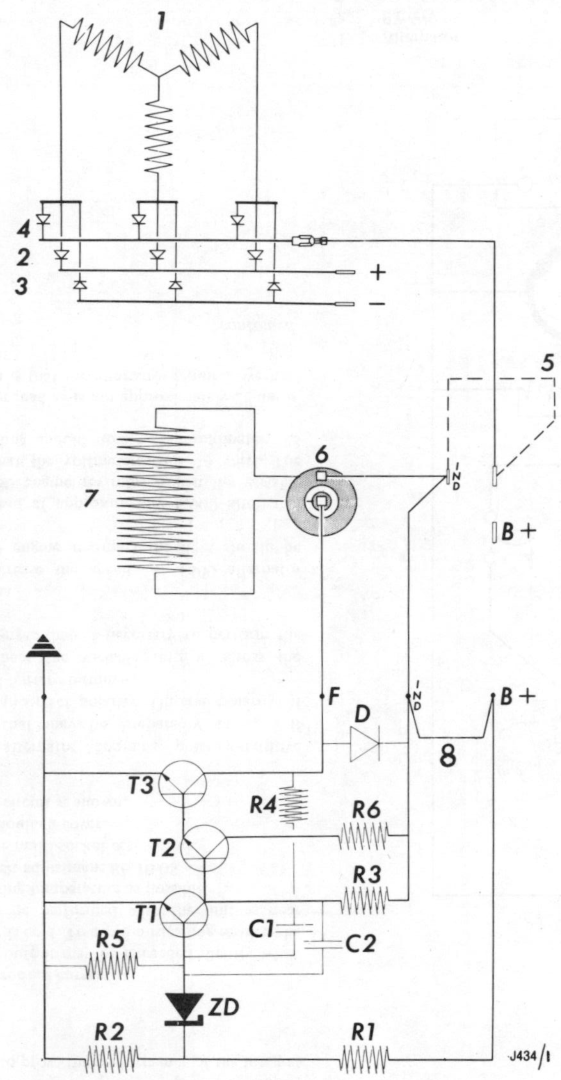

ELECTRICAL

KEY TO ALTERNATOR WIRING DIAGRAM

1.	Stator windings	
2.	Live side output diodes	
3.	Earth side output diodes	
4.	Field winding supply diodes	
5.	Harness loop	Circuit is made when multi-socket connector is fitted and broken when connector is removed.
6.	Brushes and slip rings	
7.	Field winding	
8.	Internal B+ connection	
R3.	Resistor	Restricts T2 base current supplied from 'field winding supply' diodes.
R6.	Resistor	Controls T3 base current direct.
T2.	Intermediate transistor	Restricts T3 base current supplied from 'field winding supply' diodes.
T3.	Output transistor	Controls field winding earth return circuit.
R1 and R2.	Potential divider	Senses battery reference voltage.
ZD.	Zener diode	Voltage sensitive component. Opposes passage of current until breakdown voltage — approximately 8 volts — is reached. Controls T1 base current direct.
T1.	Input transistor	Controls T2 base current by diverting current passing through R3 to earth when ZD is conducting.
C1 and R4.	Capacitor and Resistor	Prevents transistor overheating by providing a positive feed back circuit to ensure quick switching of transistors from 'fully on' to 'fully off'.
R5.	Resistor	Path for small leakage current which may pass through ZD at high temperatures.
D.	Surge quench diode	Connected across field winding. Protects T3 from field winding high induced voltage surge and smoothes field winding current.
C2.	Condenser	Radio interference suppression.

ELECTRICAL

ALTERNATOR

— Functional check   86.10.01

This operation must be performed in two parts. The first to prove the alternator's capacity to produce current, while the second is to prove the performance of the integral control unit.

Check capacity to produce current

NOTE: The stated output may be exceeded slightly when the alternator is cold. To avoid misleading results, the check should be performed with the unit as near to its normal operating temperature as possible.

1. Check drive belt adjustment 86.10.05
2. Disconnect the multi-socket connectors.
3. Remove the moulded cover.
4. Provide a test circuit as shown.

CAUTION: The alternator contains polarity-sensitive components that may be irreparably damaged if subjected to incorrect polarity. Observe polarity of alternator and battery terminals.

5. Do not connect the variable resistor across the battery for longer than is necessary to perform the check.
6. Run the engine.
7. Gradually increase the speed. At 1500 alternator rev/min (620 engine rev/min) the light should be extinguished.
8. Hold the speed at approximately 6,000 alternator rev/min (2,480 engine rev/min) Adjust the variable resistor so that the voltmeter reads 14 volts. The ammeter reading should now be approximately 28 amps.
9. If the ammeter reading is not approximately 28 amps, the indication is that the alternator requires overhaul or replacement.

continued

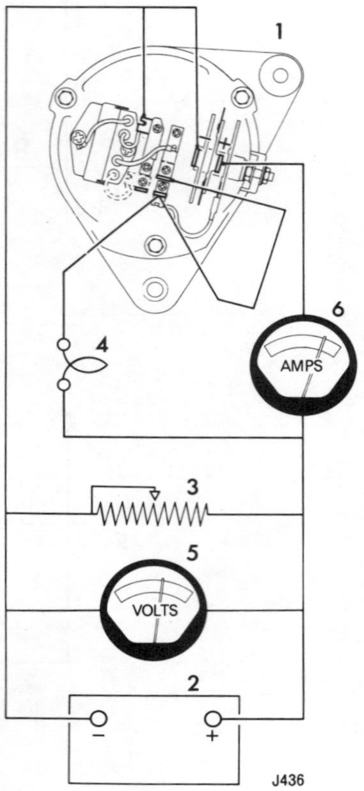

1. Alternator
2. Battery
3. Variable resistor . . . . 0–15 ohm – 35 amp
4. Light . . . . 12 volt – 2·2 watt
5. Voltmeter . . . . 0–20 volt
6. Ammeter . . . . 0–40 amp

Check control unit

NOTE: The stated output may be exceeded slightly when the alternator is cold. To avoid misleading results, the check should be performed with the unit as near to its normal operating temperature as possible.

10. Check drive belt adjustment 86.10.05.
11. Disconnect multi-socket connectors.
12. Provide test circuit as shown.

CAUTION: The alternator contains polarity-sensitive components that may be irreparably damaged if subjected to incorrect polarity. Observe polarity of alternator and battery terminals.

13. Run the engine.
14. Gradually increase the speed. At 1,500 alternator rev/min (620 engine rev/min) the light should be extinguished.
15. Hold the speed at approximately 6,000 alternator rev/min (2,480 engine rev/min). The voltmeter reading should now be steady at 140 to 144 volts.
16. If the voltmeter reading is not steady at the above figure – and a satisfactory check of capacity to produce current has been performed – the indication is that the control unit should be replaced.

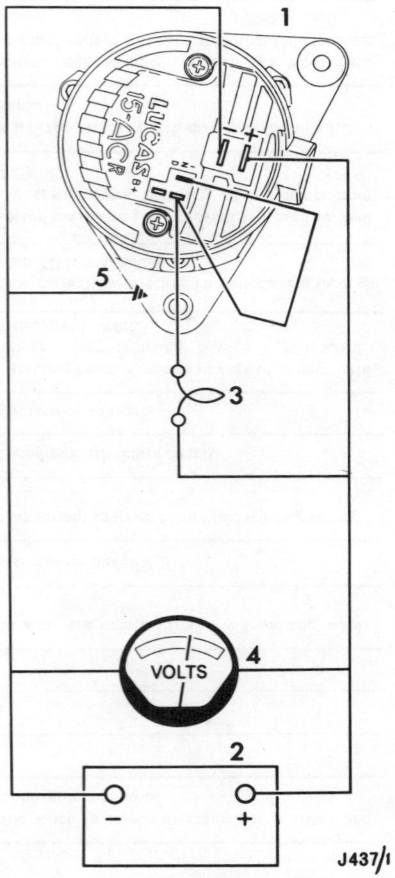

1. Alternator
2. Battery
3. Light . . . . 12 volt – 2·2 watt
4. Voltmeter . . . . 0–20 volt
5. Earth connection to alternator body.

ELECTRICAL

ALTERNATOR

— Remove and refit   86.10.02

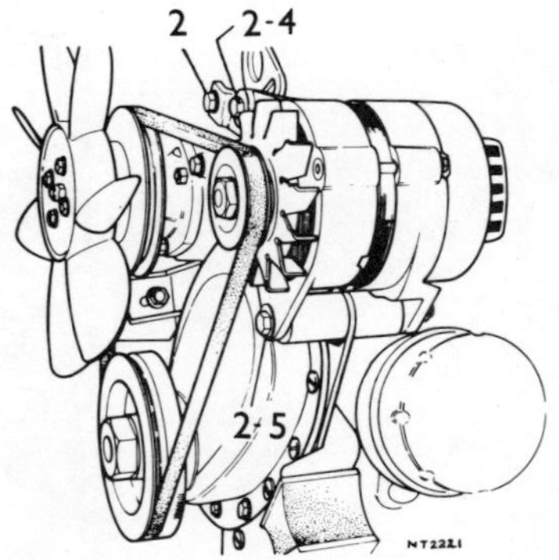

Removing

1. Disconnect the multi-socket connectors.
2. Slacken the main mounting bolt and the two adjustment bracket bolts.
3. Push the alternator towards the engine and remove the drive belt from the pulley.
4. Remove the outer adjustment bracket bolt.
5. Support the weight of the alternator and remove the main mounting bolt and spacer.

Refitting

6. Position the alternator. Fit the main mounting bolt and spacer.
7. Fit the outer adjustment bracket bolt.
8. Push the alternator towards the engine and fit the drive belt to the pulley.
9. Adjust the drive belt 26.20.01
10. Connect the multi-socket connectors.

ALTERNATOR

— Overhaul   86.10.08

Dismantling

1. Remove the moulded cover.
2. Remove the brush box and control unit assembly by disconnecting the Lucar type connector from the rectifier pack and unscrewing three screws.
3. If required, the control unit may be detached from the assembly. Note the position of the three wire eyelets. Withdraw the screw to release the control unit and three screws to release the wire eyelets.
4. Note the position of the three stator wires on the rectifier pack.
5. Unsolder the three stator wire connections. Do not overheat the diodes or bend the diode pins. Solder quickly and provide a heat sink by gripping the diode pin with pliers.
6. Slacken the nut and withdraw the rectifier pack.
7. Remove the through bolts.
8. Provide an extractor tool as shown.
9. To remove the slip ring end bracket, position the extractor tool to engage with the outer journal of the slip ring end bearing. Employ a second operator to support the slip ring end bracket by hand. Carefully tap the extractor tool to drive the bearing from the housing.

NOTE: It may be necessary to carefully file away surplus solder from the two field winding connections on the slip ring moulding if the extractor tool will not pass over the moulding.

10. The rubber 'O' ring fitted in the slip ring end bracket bearing housing may remain in situ unless replacement is contemplated.
11. Remove the stator windings from the drive end bracket.
12. Prevent the rotor turning by wrapping a scrap fan belt round the pulley and retaining by hand or vice. Remove the nut, spring washer, pulley and fan. If necessary, use a suitable extractor.
13. Remove the key.
14. Using a suitable press, remove the rotor from the drive end bracket.

CAUTION: Do not attempt to remove the rotor by applying hammer blows to the shaft end. Such action may burr over and damage the thread.

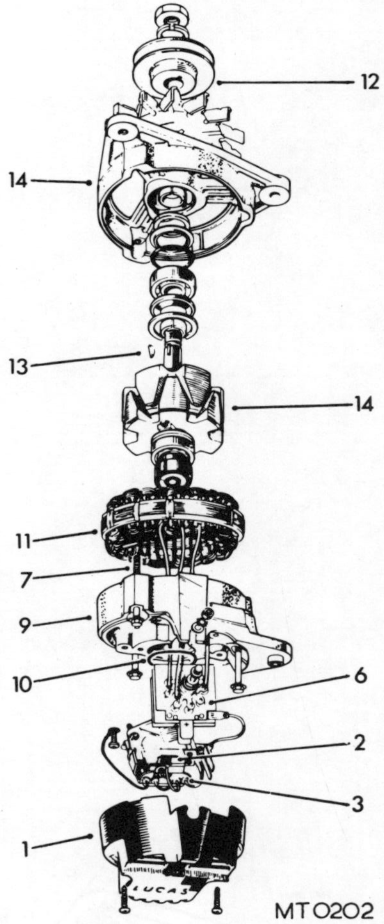

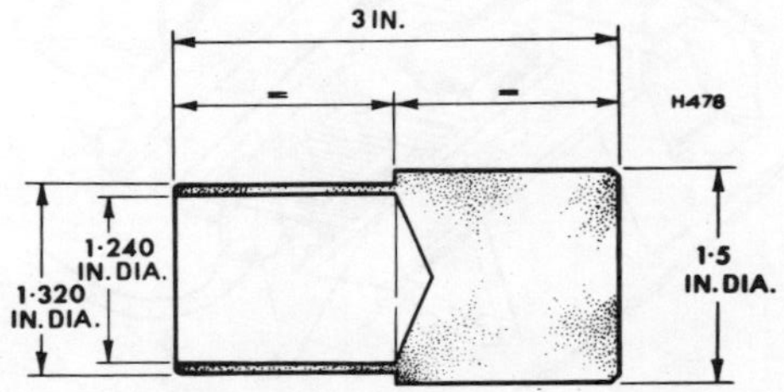

ELECTRICAL

Reassembling

15. Using the spacer (arrowed) and a suitable tube, fit the rotor to the drive end bracket by applying pressure to the bearing inner journal.

    CAUTION: Do not use the drive end bracket as a support while fitting the rotor. If the spacer is not employed, the felt ring may be damaged.

16. Fit the key.
17. Fit the fan, pulley, spring washer and nut. Prevent the rotor turning by wrapping a scrap fan belt round the pulley and retaining by hand or vice. Torque load the nut to 25 to 30 lbf ft. (3·46 to 4·15 kgf. m).
18. Observe the relationship of the stator windings to the drive end bracket determined by the stator wire connections, the rectifier pack position on the slip ring end bracket, the alignment of the mounting lugs on the end brackets and the through bolt clearances on the stator windings.
19. Position the stator windings to the drive end bracket.
20. Ensure that the rubber 'O' ring is fitted correctly in the slip ring end bracket bearing housing.
21. Fit the slip ring end bracket by carefully pushing the bearing into the housing.
22. Fit the through bolts, tightening evenly.
23. Ensure that the rubber locating piece is correctly fitted to the rectifier pack. Position the rectifier pack and secure it with the nut.
24. Position the three stator wires on rectifier pack as noted operation 4.
25. Solder the three stator wire connections. Note the precautions stated in operation 5 and use 'M' grade 45-55 tin-lead solder.
26. If required, attach the control unit to the brush box. Position the three wire eyelets on the brush box as noted in operation 3. Insert the screw to secure the control unit and three screws to secure the wire eyelets.
27. Ensure that the brushes are entered correctly in the brush box. Fit the brush box and control unit assembly by inserting three screws and connecting the Lucar type connector to the rectifier pack.
28. Fit the moulded cover.

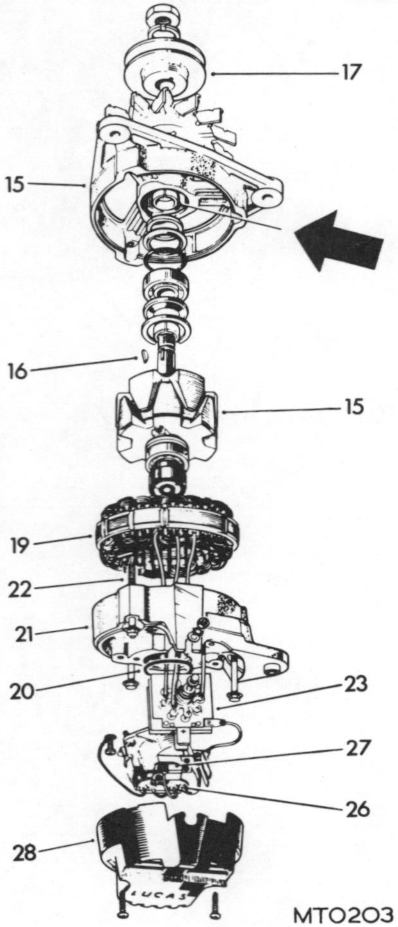

ELECTRICAL

BATTERY

— Remove and refit 86.15.01

Removing

1. Remove the battery leads.
2. Slacken the nuts and swing down the battery retaining assembly.
3. Lift the battery from the vehicle.

Refitting

4. Lift the battery into the tray.
5. Swing up the battery retaining assembly. Tighten the nuts.
6. Fit the battery leads. Do not hammer the terminals on to the terminal posts.
7. Coat the terminals with petroleum jelly (Vaseline) to prevent corrosion.

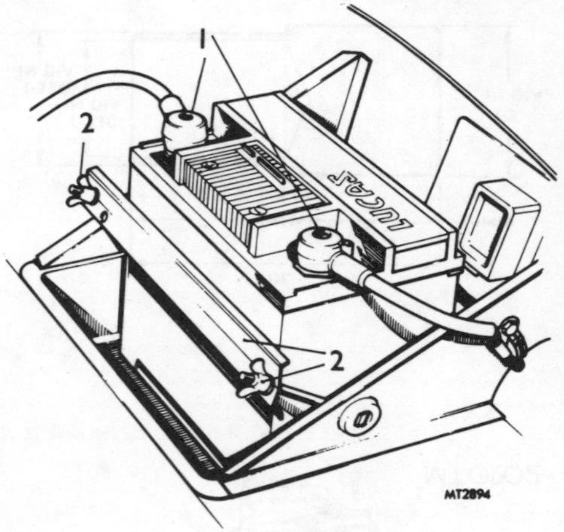

ELECTRICAL

The Spitfire Mark 4 model range is equipped with Delco Remy distributor. These vehicles are built with variations in power unit according to current market specification requirements. Distributor units are employed with different centrifugal advance, vacuum advance and retard unit characteristics to match each power unit.

An 'Ignition distributor applicability, ignition timing and features chart is provided below. Data information for each unit is given on the following pages.

IGNITION DISTRIBUTOR APPLICABILITY, IGNITION TIMING AND FEATURES CHART

	NORMAL		U.S.A.		SWEDEN
Ignition distributor Stanpart No.	214088	218099	311761	312222	311761	218099
	Fitted up to Engine No. FH 25000 HE or LE	Fitted from Engine No. FH25001 HE or LE	Fitted up to Engine No. FK25000 HE or LE	Fitted from Engine No. FK25001 HE	Fitted up to Engine No. FL 2 HE	Fitted from Engine No. FH 25001 HE
Ignition timing – static	6 degree B.T.D.C.	8 degree B.T.D.C.	6 degree A.T.D.C.	8 degree A.T.D.C.	6 degree A.T.D.C.	8 degree B.T.D.C.
Ignition timing – at idle	—	—	2 degree A.T.D.C.	2 degree A.T.D.C.	2 degree A.T.D.C.	—
Idle speed	—	—	800 to 850 rev/min	800 to 850 rev/min	800 to 850 rev/min	—
Centrifugal advance	X	X	X	X	X	X
Vacuum advance	X	X	X	X	X	X
Retard unit				X		
Micrometer adjustment nut	X	X	X	X	X	X

Use the static adjustment only to start the engine if the ignition timing setting has been lost. A dynamic adjustment is necessary to produce the accuracy of ignition timing required to meet the legal requirements in respect of air pollution throughout the speed range.

The above statement is especially true of these distributors. This is because to meet the legal requirements in respect of air pollution the timing is exceptionally retarded at idle. At cruising speeds normal timing is required. To meet these two demands the distributor features an exceptionally steep advance curve below 1000 rev/min.

ELECTRICAL

IGNITION DISTRIBUTOR

Data
Manufacturer	Delco Remy
Series	D 204
Delco Remy part No.	7953460
Stanpart No.	214088
Contact gap	0·016 ± 0·001 in (0·38 to 0·43 mm)
Rotation – viewed on rotor	Anticlockwise
Firing angles	90 ± 1 degree
Dwell angle	39 ± 1 degree
Open angle	51 ± 1 degree
Moving contact spring tension	19 to 24 ozf (540 to 680 g)
Condenser capacity	0·18 to 0·23 microfarad
Engine firing order	1–3–4–2

Centrifugal advance

Distributor r.p.m.	Degs. distributor advance		Crankshaft r.p.m.	Degs. crankshaft advance	
	Minimum	Maximum		Minimum	Maximum
400	0	1·90	800	0	3·8
725	6·00	8·00	1450	12·0	16·0
1100	7·50	9·50	2200	14·0	19·0
1500	9·00	11·00	3000	18·0	22·0
2250	11·25	13·25	4500	22·5	26·5
2500	13·25	13·25	5000	26·5	26·5

Vacuum advance

Inches of mercury vacuum	Degs. distributor advance		Degs. crankshaft advance	
	Minimum	Maximum	Minimum	Maximum
4·0	0	No advance to occur	0	
6·2	5·5	3·1	11·0	6·2
10·7	7·5	7·5	15·0	
20·0	7·5	7·5		

ELECTRICAL

IGNITION DISTRIBUTOR

Data

Manufacturer	Delco Remy
Series	D 204
Delco Remy part No.	7992128
Stanpart No.	218099
Contact gap	0·016 ± 0·001 in (0·38 to 0·43 mm)
Rotation — viewed on rotor	Anticlockwise
Firing angles	90 ± 1 degree
Dwell angle	39 ± 1 degree
Open angle	51 ± 1 degree
Moving contact spring tension	19 to 24 ozf (540 to 680 g)
Condenser capacity	0·18 to 0·23 microfarad
Engine firing order	1–3–4–2

Centrifugal advance

Distributor r.p.m.	Degs. Distributor advance Minimum	Degs. Distributor advance Maximum	Crankshaft r.p.m.	Degs. crankshaft advance Minimum	Degs. crankshaft advance Maximum
400	No advance to occur	No advance to occur	800	No advance to occur	No advance to occur
700	3·00	5·00	1400	6·00	10·00
750	4·00	6·00	1500	8·00	12·00
1250	5·40	7·49	2500	10·80	14·98
2000	7·71	9·71	4000	15·42	19·42
2500	10·00	10·00	5000	20·00	20·00

Vacuum advance

Ins. of mercury vacuum	Degs. distributor advance Minimum	Degs. distributor advance Maximum	Degs. crankshaft advance Minimum	Degs. crankshaft advance Maximum
3	0	0·84	0	1·68
5	1·52	3·52	3·04	7·04
8				
10	3·20	5·20	6·40	10·40
15	4·00	6·00	8·00	12·00
20	6·00	6·00	12·00	12·00

86.35.00 Sheet 3

Triumph Spitfire Mk IV Manual. Part No. 545254.

ELECTRICAL

IGNITION DISTRIBUTOR

Data

Manufacturer	Delco Remy
Series	D 204
Delco Remy part No.	7953944
Stanpart No.	311761
Contact gap	0·016 ± 0·001 in (0·38 to 0·43 mm)
Rotation — viewed on rotor	Anticlockwise
Firing angles	90 ± 1 degree
Dwell angle	39 ± 1 degree
Open angle	51 ± 1 degree
Moving contact spring tension	19 to 24 ozf (540 to 680 g)
Condenser capacity	0·18 to 0·23 microfarad
Engine firing order	1–3–4–2

Centrifugal advance

Distributor r.p.m.	Degs. distributor advance Minimum	Degs. distributor advance Maximum	Crankshaft r.p.m.	Degs. crankshaft advance Minimum	Degs. crankshaft advance Maximum
300	0	1·00	600	0	2·00
600	6·20	8·20	1200	12·40	16·40
750	9·80	11·80	1500	19·60	23·60
1000	10·58	12·58	2000	21·16	25·16
1600	12·44	14·44	3200	24·88	28·88
2100	14·00	16·00	4200	28·00	32·00
2500	16·00	16·00	5000	32·00	32·00

86.35.00 Sheet 4

Triumph Spitfire Mk IV Manual. Part No. 545254.

ELECTRICAL

IGNITION DISTRIBUTOR

Data

Manufacturer	Delco Remy
Series	D 204
Delco Remy part No.	7992115
Stanpart No.	312222
Contact gap	0·016 ± 0·001 in (0·38 to 0·43 mm)
Rotation — viewed on rotor	Anticlockwise
Firing angles	90 ± 1 degree
Dwell angle	39 ± 1 degree
Open angle	51 ± 1 degree
Moving contact spring tension	19 to 24 ozf (540 to 680 g)
Condenser capacity	0·18 to 0·23 microfarad
Engine firing order	1–3–4–2

Centrifugal advance

Distributor r.p.m.	Degs. distributor advance Minimum	Degs. distributor advance Maximum	Crankshaft r.p.m.	Degs. crankshaft advance Minimum	Degs. crankshaft advance Maximum
400	No advance to occur	No advance to occur	800	No advance to occur	No advance to occur
700	3·0	5·0	1400	6·0	10·0
750	4·0	6·0	1500	8·0	12·0
1600	6·6	8·6	3200	13·2	17·2
2400	9·0	11·0	4800	18·0	22·0
2800	11·0	11·0	5600	22·0	22·0

Retard unit

Ins of mercury vacuum	Degs distributor retard Minimum	Degs distributor retard Maximum	Degs. crankshaft retard Minimum	Degs. crankshaft retard Maximum
4	No advance to occur	No advance to occur	No advance to occur	No advance to occur
6	0	2	0	4
10	4	6	8	12
15	4	6	8	12
20	6	6	12	12

86.35.00 Sheet 5

Triumph Spitfire Mk IV Manual. Part No. 545254

ELECTRICAL

IGNITION COIL AND BALLAST RESISTOR

	Early	Later
Ignition coil		
Manufacturer	Lucas	Lucas
Type	16C6	15C6
Lucas part No.	45232	45243
Stanpart No.	154272	158830
Primary winding resistance	1·43 to 1·58 ohms	1·30 to 1·45 ohms

Ballast resistor unit — Early vehicles only

Manufacturer	Lucas
Type	3BR
Lucas part No.	47170
Stanpart No.	134176
Resistance	1·3 to 1·4 ohms

Ballast resistor wire — Later vehicles only

Resistance	1·3 to 1·5 ohms
Wire length	63 in (160 cm)

Early vehicles only:—
This system is designed to assist engine starting under adverse conditions. A ballast resistor is positioned in series in the normal supply to the ignition coil. This unit causes a voltage drop in the circuit so that the 12-volt supply from the ignition switch may be employed to power the nominally rated 6-volt ignition coil.

Later vehicles only:—
This system is designed to assist engine starting under adverse conditions. A ballast resistor wire built into the harness between two crimped joints is electrically positioned in series in the normal supply to the ignition coil. This wire causes a voltage drop in the circuit so that the 12 volt supply from the ignition switch may be employed to power the nominally rated 6 volt ignition coil.

All vehicles:—
During engine start the resistor is by-passed and the battery voltage (reduced from 12-volt by the starter motor load) is applied to the coil direct from the starter solenoid. This slight voltage overload provides an increased high tension voltage at the spark plugs.

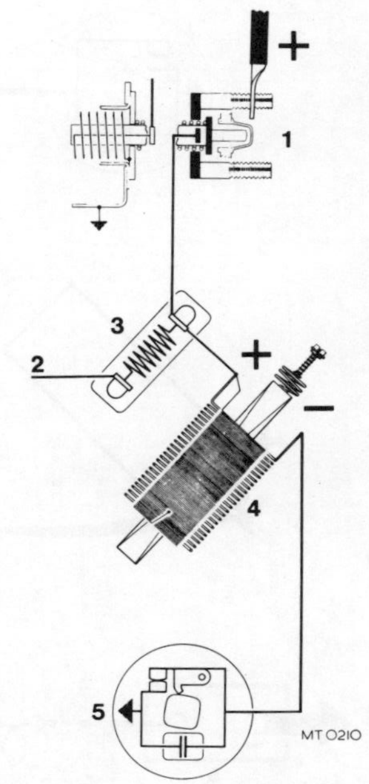

1. Starter solenoid
2. Normal ignition supply
3. Ballast resistor unit – shown
   or
4. Ballast resistor wire – not shown
5. Ignition coil – 6 volt
6. Ignition distributor

86.35.00 Sheet 6

Triumph Spitfire Mk IV Manual. Part No. 545254

ELECTRICAL

IGNITION DISTRIBUTOR

Contact assembly   86.35.13

— Remove and refit

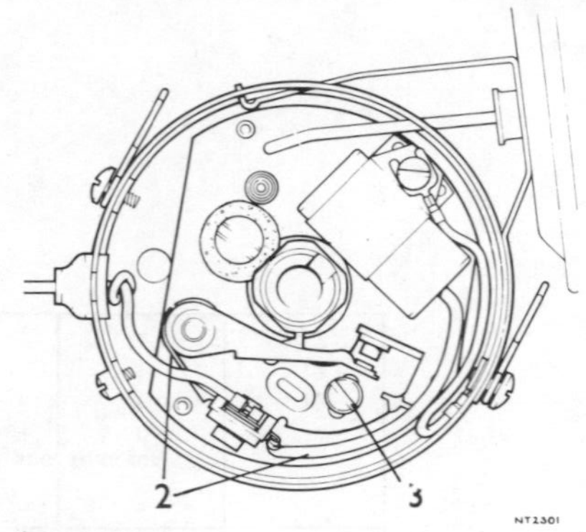

Removing

1. Remove the distributor cover and rotor.
2. Push the moving contact spring away from the terminal post and detach the two leads.
3. Remove the screw securing the fixed contact and lift out the contact assembly.

Refitting

4. Wipe preservative from new contact faces.
5. Reverse instructions 1 to 3.
6. Adjust contact gap 86.35.14

IGNITION DISTRIBUTOR

— Contact gap   86.35.14

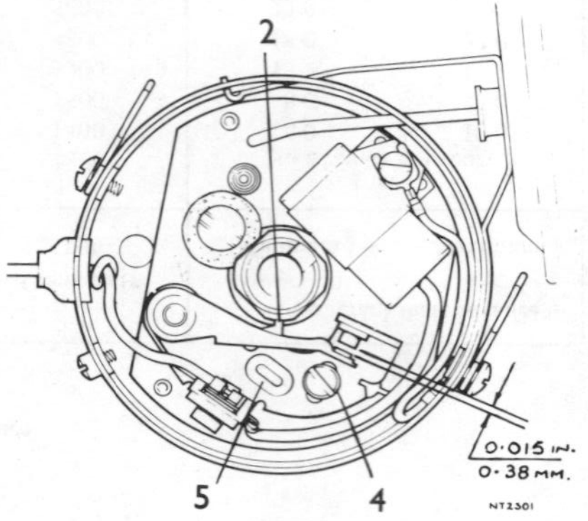

Adjust

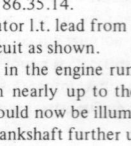

1. Remove the distributor cover and rotor.
2. Rotate the crankshaft to position the contact heel on a cam peak.
3. If the contact gap is correct, an 0·015 in (0·38 mm) feeler gauge will just slide between the contacts.
4. If correction is required, slacken the screw securing the fixed contact.
5. Move the fixed contact to obtain the correct gap.
6. Retighten the fixed contact securing screw.
7. Refit the rotor and distributor cover.

IGNITION DISTRIBUTOR

— Ignition timing — adjust   86.35.15

For normal market vehicles a static adjustment is satisfactory.

For all U.S.A. market vehicles, also Swedish market vehicles up to Engine No. FL2 HE use the static adjustment only to start the engine if the ignition timing setting has been lost. A dynamic adjustment is necessary to produce the accuracy of ignition timing required to meet the legal requirements in respect of air pollution throughout the speed range.

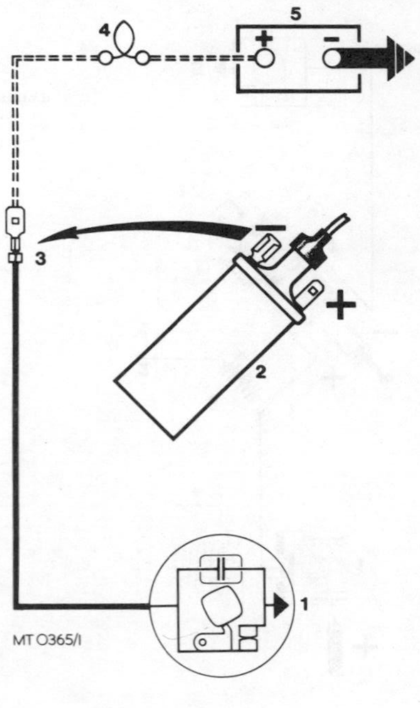

Static

1. Adjust the contact gap 86.35.14.
2. Disconnect the distributor l.t. lead from the coil.
3. Provide a test lamp circuit as shown.
4. Rotate the crankshaft in the engine run direction to bring the pulley notch nearly up to the edge of the scale. The test lamp should now be illuminated.
5. Carefully rotate the crankshaft further until the lamp just goes out.
6. If the timing is correct the pulley notch will be aligned with the scale at the static figure given in the chart 86.35.00.
7. If correct operations 8 to 10 may be ignored.
8. Distributor fitted with micrometer adjustment nut only — if a small correction is required rotate the micrometer adjustment nut to advance or retard the timing and repeat operation 4 onwards. If a large correction is required centre the micrometer adjustment nut and perform operation 9 onwards.
9. Slacken the clamp bolt. Align the pulley notch with the scale at the static figure given in the chart 86.35.00. Rotate the distributor body anticlockwise past the test lamp illumination position. Carefully rotate clockwise until the lamp just goes out. Tighten the clamp bolt with the unit in this position.
10. Repeat operation 4 onwards.

continued

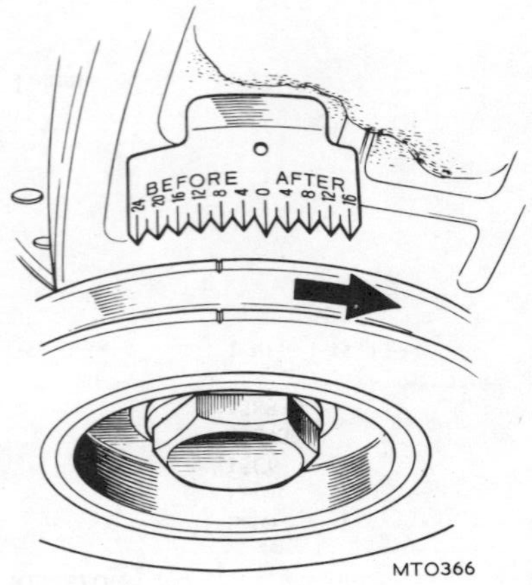

1. Distributor — diagrammatic layout
2. Ignition coil
3. Distributor lead removed from coil
4. Test lamp — 12 volt
5. Vehicle battery

ELECTRICAL

Dynamic

U.S.A. market vehicles only

11. Adjust the contact gap 86.35.14.
12. Connect timing light as instructed by the manufacturer. The engine is timed on No. 1 cylinder which is located at the front of the engine.
13. Run the engine at idle speed 800 to 850 revs/min.
14. Position timing light to illuminate crankshaft pulley and scale.
15. If the timing is correct the equipment will show the 'at idle' figure given in the chart 86.35.00.
16. If correct operation 17 may be ignored.
17. With the engine still running at 800 to 850 revs/min use a second operator to slacken the clamp bolt and carefully rotate the distributor body as required until the equipment shows the 'at idle' figure given in the chart 86.35.00. Tighten the clamp bolt with the unit in this position.

IGNITION DISTRIBUTOR

— Lubrication   86.35.18

1. Remove the distributor cover and rotor.
2. Apply a few drops of thin oil to the felt plug, oil holes and contact mounting post. Carefully wipe off any excess oil.
3. Lightly grease the cam (or lubricator pad, if fitted) with Shell Alvania No. 2 grease or equivalent.

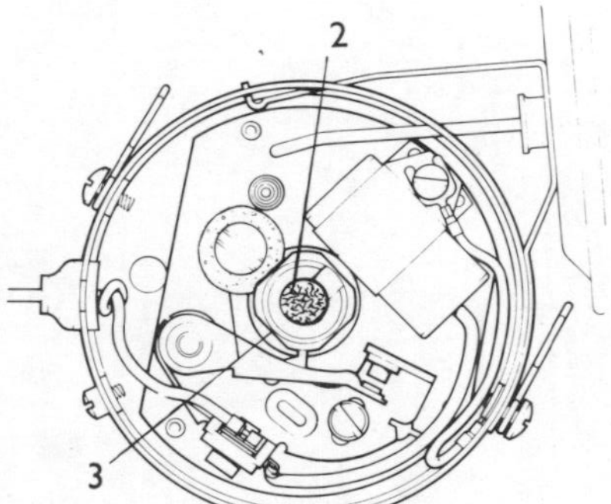

IGNITION DISTRIBUTOR

— Remove and refit   86.35.20

Removing

1. Remove the distributor cover.
2. Pull off the distributor l.t. connector from the coil.
3. Pull off the vacuum control pipe (if fitted).
4. Unscrew the knurled connector securing the tachometer drive.
5. Remove one bolt and spring washer securing clamp bracket to pedestal.
6. Withdraw the distributor.

NOTE: To facilitate re-timing do not slacken the clamp bolt.

Refitting

7. Rotate the crankshaft until No. 1 piston is at T.D.C. and the offset distributor drive gear slot is in the position shown.
8. Reverse instructions 1 to 6.
9. Adjust ignition timing if necessary 86.35.16.

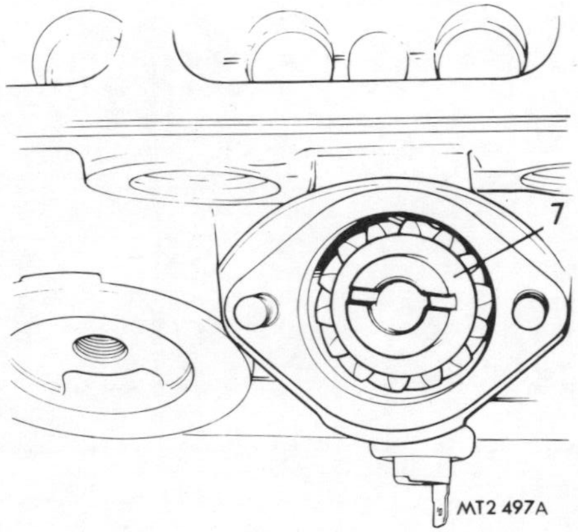

86.35.15 Sheet 2
86.35.20

ELECTRICAL

IGNITION DISTRIBUTOR

— Overhaul   86.35.26

Dismantling

1. Remove the contact assembly 86.35.13.
2. Remove the capacitor — one screw and spring washer.
3. Pull off the cam lubricator pad if fitted.
4. Remove the screws and detach the earth lead and the cap securing clips if fitted.
5. Withdraw the contact breaker base plate and detach the vacuum control if fitted.
6. Pierce the staked plug and prise it out.
   CAUTION: Do not perform this operation unless a new plug is available.
7. Withdraw the tachometer drive gear and thrust washer.
8. File and tap out the coupling pin. Remove the coupling and thrust washer.
   CAUTION: Do not perform this operation unless a new coupling pin is available.
9. Withdraw the shaft assembly and thrust washer.
10. Remove the control springs.

Reassembling

11. Fit new control springs.
    CAUTION: Do not over extend the springs.
12. Lubricate and install the shaft assembly and thrust washer.
    NOTE: If fitting a new undrilled shaft, install and drill so that the end float is 0·002 to 0·005 in (0·02 mm to 0·13 mm) and relationship of the coupling offset key to the rotor locating slot is as shown viewed from the coupling end.
13. Lubricate the tachometer drive gear with Shell Alvania No. 2 grease or equivalent. Install the gear and thrust washer.
14. Fit a new plug and stake in six equidistant positions.
15. Reverse instructions 1 to 5.

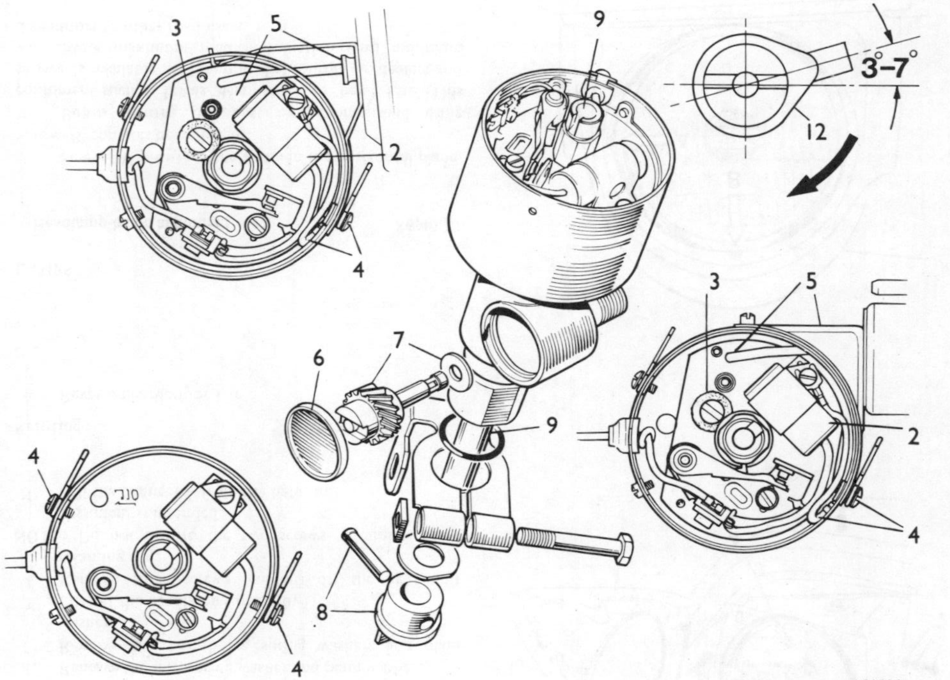

86.35.26

ELECTRICAL

IGNITION COIL AND BALLAST RESISTOR

— Ignition coil — remove and refit   86.35.32

Removing

1. Disconnect the two low tension Lucar connectors.
2. Pull off the high tension lead.
3. Remove the two screws, spring washers and washers, and lift out the coil.

Refitting

4. Position the coil and secure it with two washers, spring washers and screws. Include in the left hand screw assembly the ballast resistor lug.
5. Push on the high tension lead.
6. Connect the two low tension Lucar connectors as follows:
   White/yellow wire to positive terminal.
   White/black wire to negative terminal.

IGNITION COIL AND BALLAST RESISTOR

Ballast resistor — remove and refit   86.35.33

Earlier Vehicles only.

Removing

1. Locate the ballast resistor on the left hand engine bay valance adjacent to the ignition coil.
2. Disconnect the Lucar connectors.
3. Remove the screw, spring washer and washer and lift out the ballast resistor.

Refitting

4. Position the ballast resistor and secure it with the washer, spring washer and screw.
5. Connect the Lucar connectors as follows:
   White wire to rear terminal
   White/yellow wire to front terminal.

ELECTRICAL

LAMPS

Headlamp — Remove and refit   86.40.02

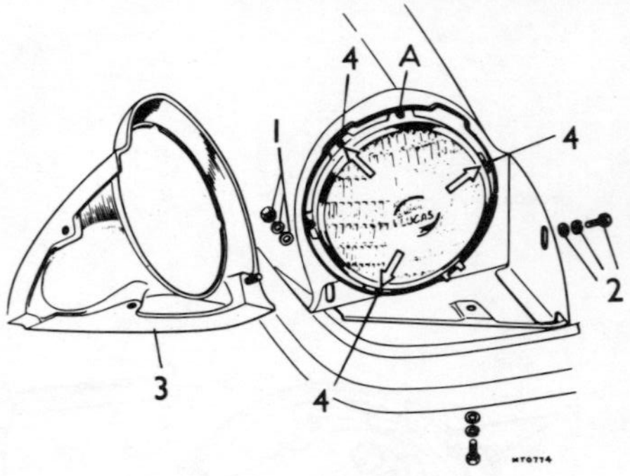

Removing

1. Remove the nut, spring washer and plain washer.
2. Remove the two bolts, spring washers and plain washers.
3. Lift off the headlamp surround.
4. Remove three screws and lift off the light unit retaining rim.
NOTE: Do not disturb the two screws 'A' unless beam alignment is intended.
5. Pull the connector from the light unit.

Refitting

6. Reverse instructions 1 to 5.

LAMPS

— Headlamp beam alignment   86.40.17

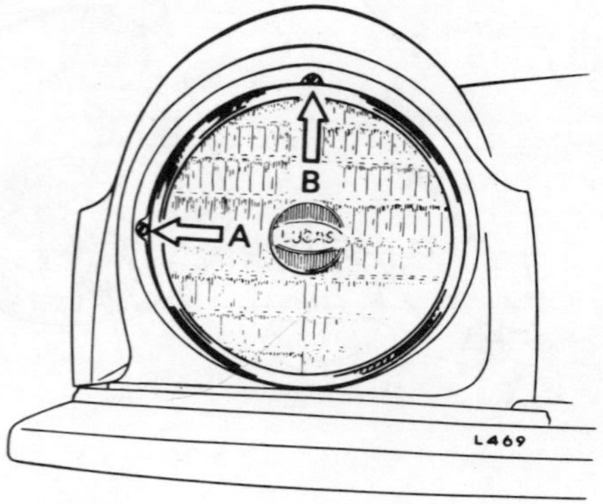

Screw 'A' positions the beam in the horizontal plane.
Screw 'B' controls beam height.
Beam aiming can best be accomplished using equipment such as Lucas 'Beam-setter' or 'Lev-L-Lite'. This service is available at Triumph distributors or dealers and will ensure maximum road illumination with minimum discomfort to other road users.

ELECTRICAL

LAMPS

— Front parking and flasher lamp — remove and refit 86.40.26

Removing
1. Remove the two screws and withdraw the rim, two lenses and gasket.
2. Remove the two bulbs from the bayonet fittings.
3. Remove the two screws and withdraw the lamp base and gasket.
4. Disconnect the earth wire from the lamp base.
5. Disconnect the two wires from the snap connectors.

Refitting
7. Reverse instructions 1 to 5.

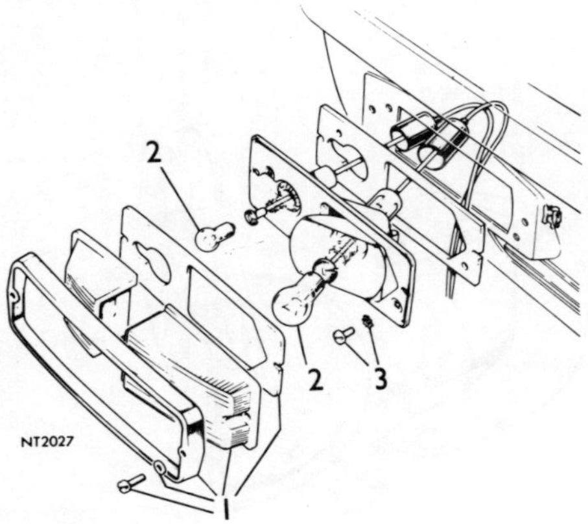

LAMPS

— Front parking and flasher lamp (U.S.A. only) — remove and refit
86.40.26

Removing
1. Remove the two screws and withdraw the rim and lens.
2. Remove the bulb from the bayonet fitting.
3. Remove the two screws and withdraw the lamp base and gasket.
4. Disconnect the earth wire from the lamp base.
5. Disconnect the two wires from the snap connecters.

Refitting
6. Reverse instructions 1 to 5.

86.40.26

Triumph Spitfire Mk IV Manual. Part No. 545254.

LAMPS

Front marker lamp (U.S.A. only)
— Remove and refit
86.40.59

Removing
1. Using a screwdriver, carefully prise the rim out of the lamp base.
2. Carefully pull out the lamp lens.
3. Remove the bulb from the bayonet fitting.
4. Carefully pull out the reflector lens.
5. Raise the bonnet.
6. Disconnect the red wire from the snap connector centrally located at the front of the bonnet.
7. Disconnect the black wire from the lamp.
8. Remove the three nuts, plain and rubber washers.
9. Withdraw the lamp base together with the bulb holder, wire and reflector base.
10. Remove the reflector base.
11. Remove the bulb holder and wire.

Refitting
12. Reverse instructions 1 to 11.

LAMPS

Rear marker lamp (U.S.A. only)
— Remove and refit
86.40.64

Removing
1. Using a screwdriver, carefully prise the rim out of the lamp base.
2. Carefully pull out the lamp lens.
3. Remove the bulb from the bayonet fitting.
4. Carefully pull out the reflector lens.
5. Open the luggage compartment lid.
6. Disconnect the red wire from the snap connector.
7. Disconnect the black wire from the lamp.
8. Remove the three nuts, plain washers and rubber washers.
9. Withdraw the lamp base together with the bulb holder, wire and reflector base.
10. Remove the reflector base.
11. Remove the bulb holder and wire.

Refitting
12. Reverse instructions 1 to 11.

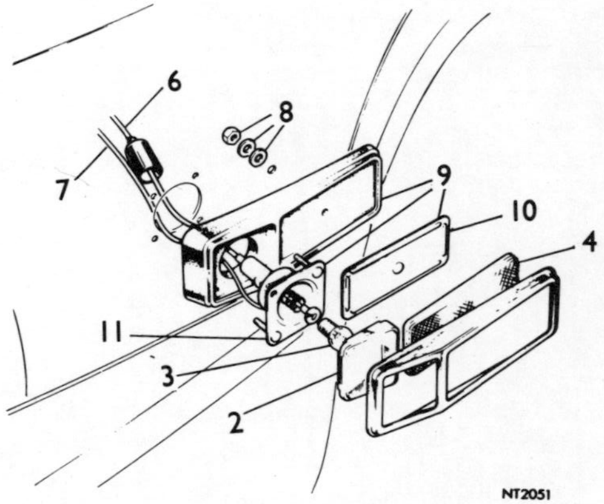

86.40.59
86.40.64

Triumph Spitfire Mk IV Manual. Part No. 545254.

ELECTRICAL

LAMPS

— Rear tail/stop, flasher and reverse lamp
— remove and refit   86.40.70

Removing

1. Remove the two screws and plain washers securing the lamp cover.
2. Disconnect the Lucar connector.
3. Pull out the three bulbholders.
4. Remove the three bulbs from the bayonet fittings.
5. Remove the five nuts, spring washers and plain washers securing the lamp to the body.
6. Detach the cover mounting bracket and withdraw the lamp.
7. Remove the flasher lamp lens — three screws.
8. Remove the tail/stop lamp lens — two screws.
9. Remove the reverse lamp lens — two screws.
10. Remove the lens seating gasket.

Refitting

11. Reverse instructions 1 to 10.

REAR NUMBER PLATE LAMP

— Remove and refit   86.40.86

Removing

1. Disconnect the two leads from inside the luggage compartment and pull them through the panel grommet.
2. Remove two screws and lift off the cover.
3. Remove the lenses.
4. Remove the bulbs.
5. Remove the two nuts, spring washers and plain washers.
6. Remove the lamp base from the bumpers.

Refitting

7. Reverse instructions 1 to 6.

Removing (later U.S.A. cars only)

1. Remove two screws and washers and withdraw the lens assembly.
2. If required — carefully remove the festoon bulb.
3. Disconnect two leads behind the lamp in the luggage compartment.
4. Remove two nuts and plain washers and withdraw the lamp from the car.

Refitting (later U.S.A. cars only)

5. Reverse instructions 1 to 4 ensuring a good weather resistant seal.**

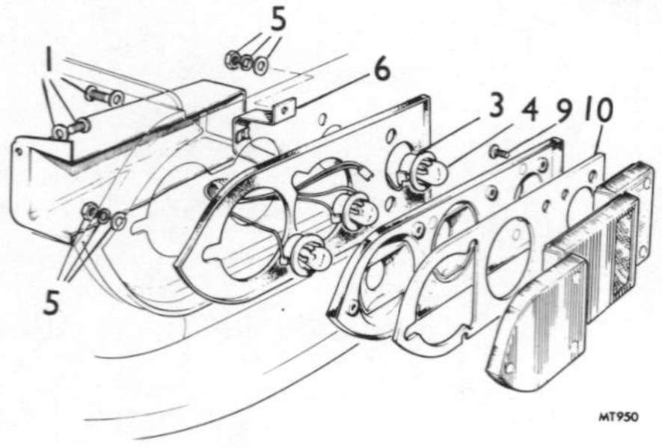

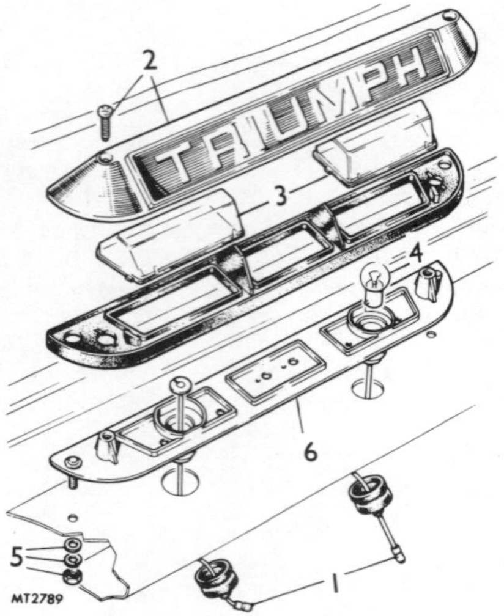

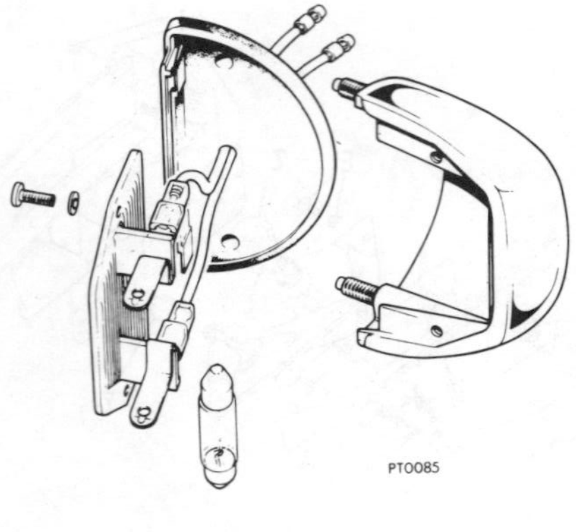

86.40.70
86.40.86

ELECTRICAL

LAMPS

— Seat belt — warning light — remove and refit   86.45.75

Later U.S.A. market vehicles only.

Removing

1. Isolate the battery.
2. Working from behind the fascia, pull out the bulb holder from the projection of the 'FASTEN BELTS' unit.
3. If required remove the bulb from the bayonet fitting.
4. Push out the 'FASTEN BELTS' unit from the fascia.

Refitting

5. Reverse instructions 1 to 4.

LAMPS

— Key light — remove and refit   86.45.78

Later U.S.A. market vehicles only.

Removing

1. Locate the key light adjacent to the steering column lock assembly.
2. Pull out the bulb holder from the bracket.
3. If required unscrew the bulb from the holder.

Refitting

4. Reverse instructions 2 to 3.

86.45.75
86.45.78

ELECTRICAL

RELAYS
— Night dimming relay   86.55.00

Data and description

Manufacturer	Lucas
Type	11RA
Lucas part No.	33329
Stanpart No.	217177
Body colour	Yellow
Winding resistance	36 ohm
Pull in voltage	4 to 10 volt
Release voltage	0 to 1 volt
R1 resistance	3 ohm
R2 resistance	3 ohm
R3 resistance	30 ohm
R4 resistance	1.5 ohm

This relay dims stop lamps and rear flasher lamps when the parking lamps are illuminated. At night minimum discomfort to other road users is ensured. During daylight the safety of full intensity is provided.

The relay winding is controlled by the parking lamp circuit. Three sets of normally closed contacts with associated resistors permanently connected in parallel are featured. The pair of stop lamps, the left hand rear flasher lamp and the right hand rear flasher lamp are each associated with one contact/resistor set.

When the relay is not energized the contacts are closed and the lamps operate at full intensity. When the relay is energized the contacts are open. The resistors are positioned in series with the lamps which then operate at reduced voltage.

To maintain the correct frequency of operation of the turn signal flasher unit the current must be kept constant. To provide current compensation for either flasher circuit a fourth resistor is used. This resistor is brought into circuit by the double contact set between terminals 2 and 5. The switching is such that when either flasher circuit is selected, a parallel path exists through R3, the resistor of the unselected flasher circuit and across the filament of the unselected rear flasher lamp to earth. While providing compensation, this current is not large enough to illuminate the unselected lamp.

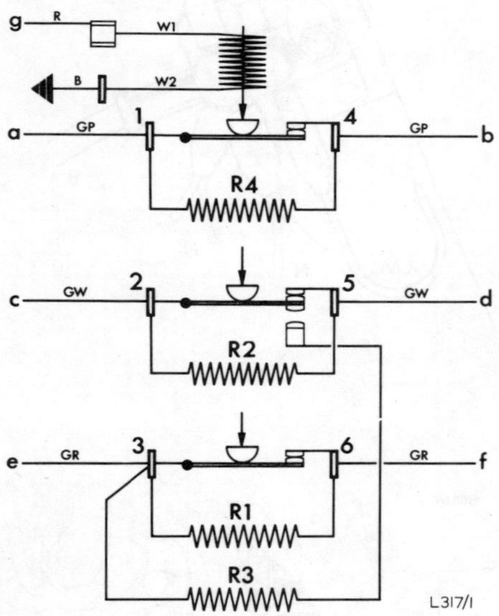

a. From stop lamp switch
b. To pair of stop lamps
c. From turn signal switch
d. To L.H. rear flasher lamp
e. From turn signal switch
f. To R.H. rear flasher lamp
g. From master light switch

RELAYS
— Remove and refit   86.55.03

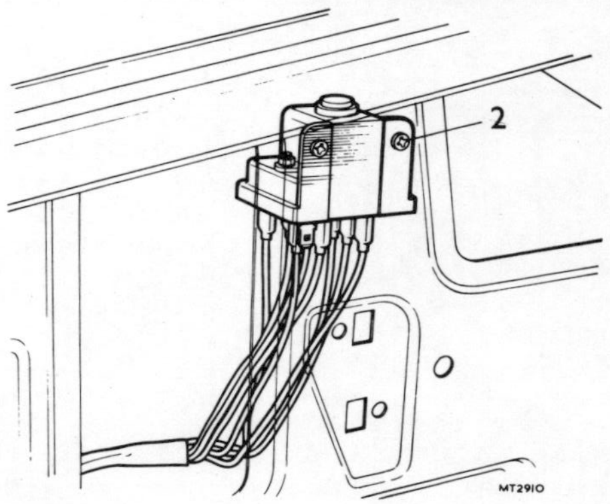

Removing
1. Open the luggage compartment lid and locate the relay behind the left hand wheelarch outer panel.
2. Remove the two screws and withdraw the relay.
3. Disconnect the eight Lucar connectors.

Refitting
4. To ensure the correct operation of the compensation circuit the following test is necessary to establish which green/red wire is from the turn signal switch and which is to the left hand rear flasher lamp. The pair of green/white wires must similarly be identified.
5. In order to perform the test a positive supply may be obtained in the area by connecting a short slave wire to the red wire and switching on the side lamp circuit. Using the live slave wire touch each green/red wire in turn. Illumination of the left hand rear flasher lamp will identify the wire to be connected to terminal 6. Connect the remaining green/red wire to terminal 3.
6. Using the live slave wire touch each green/white wire in turn. Illumination of the right hand rear flasher lamp will identify the wire to be connected to terminal 5. Connect the remaining green/white wire to terminal 2.
7. Connect the green/purple wires to terminals 1 and 4.
8. They may be fitted either way round.
9. Remove the slave wire and connect the red wire to terminal W1.
10. Connect the black wire to terminal W2.
11. Reverse instructions 1 and 2.

ELECTRICAL

RELAYS

— Overdrive relay

Remove and refit 86.55.04

Removing

1. Disconnect the four Lucar connectors.
2. Remove the two nuts, bolts and plain washers securing the horn and overdrive relays to the bulkhead.

Refitting

3. Reverse instructions 1 and 2. Connect the Lucar connectors as follows:
   Brown wire to terminal C1.
   Yellow/purple wire to terminal C2.
   White wire to terminal W1.
   Yellow/green wire to terminal W2.

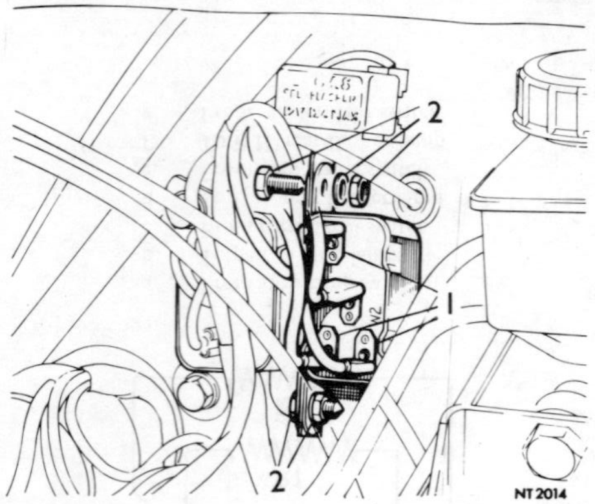

RELAYS

— Starter solenoid — remove and refit 86.55.05

Removing

1. Isolate the battery.
2. Note the four wire colour codes and positions.
3. Disconnect the four Lucar connectors.
4. Note the position of the battery lead and starter motor lead. This is important to ensure correct operation of the ballast resistor starter system.
5. Pull back the rubber protector.
6. Remove the two nuts and spring washers. Disconnect the battery lead and starter motor lead.
7. Note the position of the solenoid.
8. Remove the two screws, washers and spring washers, and lift the solenoid from the vehicle.

Refitting

9. Reverse instructions 1 to 8. Ensure that the battery lead, starter motor lead and four Lucar connectors are positioned as shown. Ensure good electrical contact between the solenoid and the vehicle body.

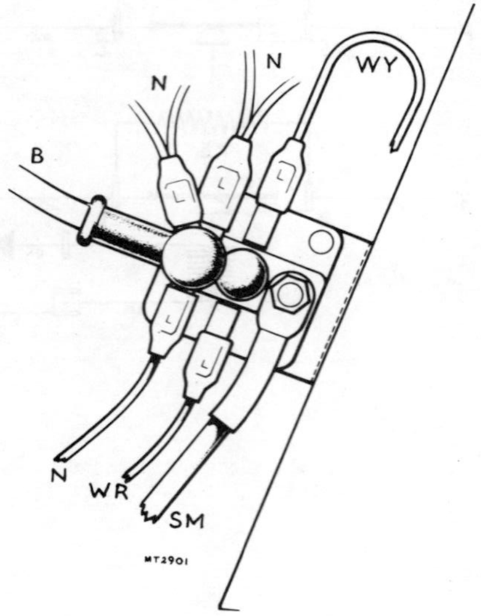

B Battery lead
N Brown wire
WY White/Yellow wire
N Brown wire
WR White/Red wire
SM Starter motor lead

ELECTRICAL

RELAYS

— Horn relay — remove and refit 86.55.09

Removing

1. Disconnect the three Lucar connectors.
2. Remove the two bolts, spring washers and plain washer securing the relay to the bulkhead.

Refitting

3. Reverse instructions 1 and 2. Connect the Lucar connectors as follows:
   Purple/yellow wire to terminal C1
   Purple wires to terminal C2
   Purple/black wires to terminal W1

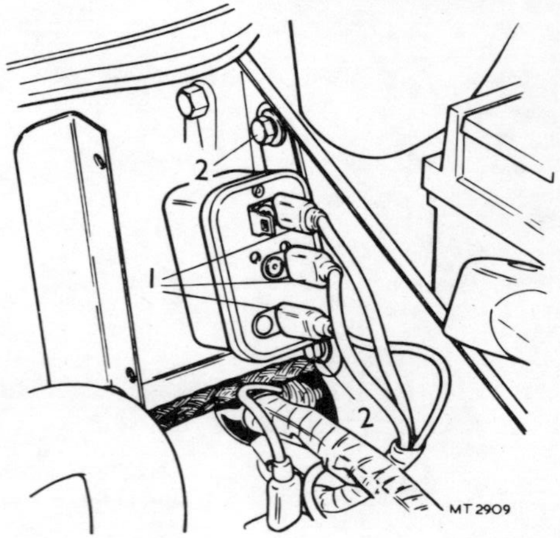

FLASHER UNIT

— Turn signal flasher unit — remove and refit 86.55.11

Removing

1. Locate the flasher unit mounted in clip on the forward face of the fascia panel beneath the speedometer on right hand steer cars.
2. Pull the flasher unit from the clip.
3. Disconnect the two Lucar connectors.

Refitting

4. Connect the Lucar connectors: Green wire to terminal 'B'. Light green/brown wire to terminal 'L'.
5. Fit the flasher unit to the clip.

FLASHER UNITS

Hazard flasher unit — remove and refit 86.55.12

The hazard flasher unit (if fitted) is located on the left hand side of the bulkhead.

ELECTRICAL

BUZZERS

— Key warning buzzer — remove and refit   86.55.13

Removing

1. Locate the buzzer on the extreme left hand side of the fascia panel.
2. Remove the nut, bolt and plain washers.
3. Disconnect the two Lucar connectors.

Refitting

4. Reverse instructions 1 to 3. Connect the Lucar connectors as follows:
   Purple/Orange wire to terminal W1
   Black/Green wire to terminal C1

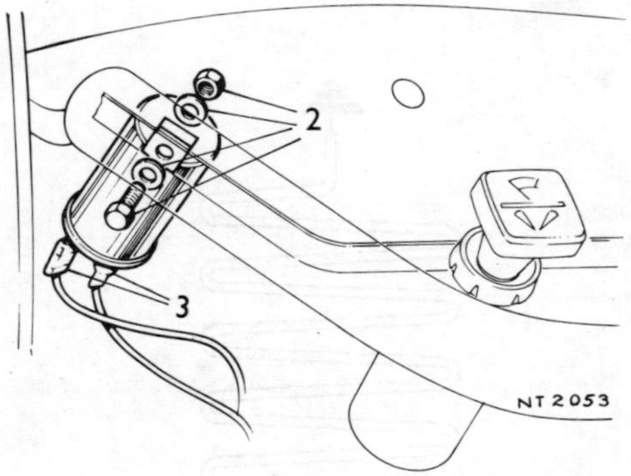

NIGHT DIMMING RELAY

— Contacts adjust   86.55.14

The contacts are set during production and normally require no attention in service. If the relay cover has been removed and the hexagon rotated, re-set as follows:

1. Remove the cover.
2. Provide a test circuit as shown.
3. With the winding not energised rotate the hexagon by hand fully clockwise.
4. Check that the three contact sets are correctly closed.
5. Energise the winding by applying 12 volts between W1 and W2.
6. Rotate the hexagon anticlockwise until the test lamp just illuminates.
7. Rotate the hexagon a further 90 degrees anticlockwise.
8. Observe the recess for the hexagon in the cover. If necessary rotate the hexagon a little further anticlockwise to achieve alignment.
9. Fit the cover.

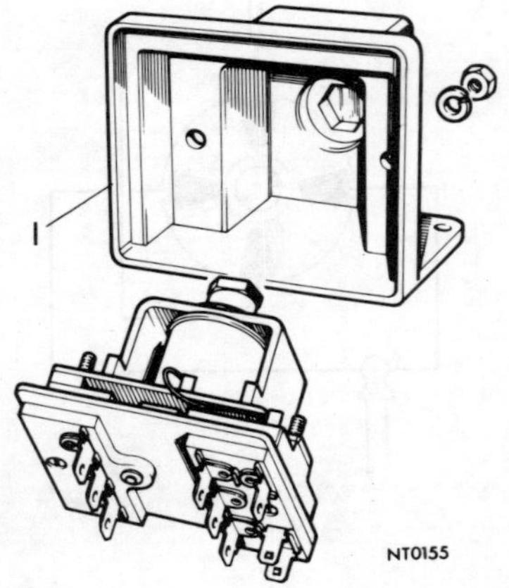

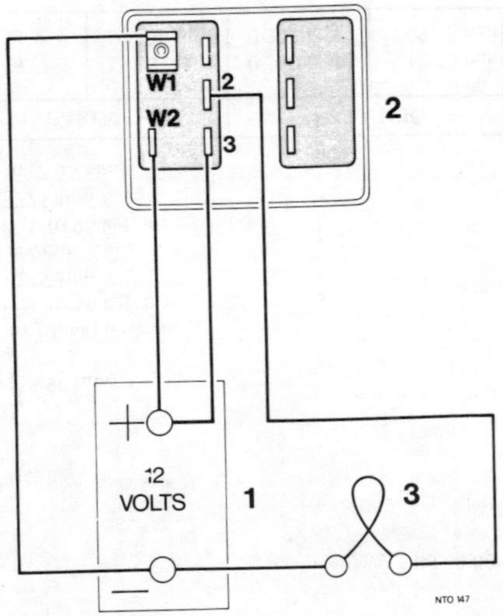

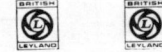

SEAT BELT WARNING SYSTEM

— Description   86.57.00

Later U.S.A. market vehicles only.

This system is designed to discourage driving the vehicle without the seat belts being in use.

The system is actuated by selection of any gear other than neutral. When the system is actuated a 'FASTEN BELTS' warning light on the fascia illuminates and a buzzer provides audible warning.

With the driver only in the vehicle the system is cancelled when the drivers seat belt is fastened.

With the driver and a passenger in the vehicle, a switch built into the passengers seat is actuated. The system is then cancelled when both the drivers and passengers seat belts are fastened.

A diode in the circuit (see appropriate wiring diagram) enables the seat belt warning system and the key warning system to use the same audible buzzer unit.

DIODE

— Remove and refit   86.57.10

Later U.S.A. market vehicles fitted with seat belt warning system only.

Removing

1. Isolate the battery.
2. (Pre 1973 cars only). Lower the centre fascia to the service position see 76.46.02 operations 1 to 4.
3. (Pre 1973 cars only). Locate the diode behind the centre fascia.
4. Disconnect two Lucar connectors. Remove the diode from the vehicle.
5. Remove the insulating sleeve.

Refitting

6. Fit the insulating sleeve over the female connector.
7. Position the diode the correct way round indicated by the connectors. Connect two Lucar connectors as follows:
   Light green/orange wire to diode male connector.
8. Refit the centre fascia (Pre 1973 cars only).
9. Connect the battery.

NOTE: On 1973 cars the diode, formerly located behind the centre fascia, will be found at the left hand end of the fascia above the parcel shelf.

KEY WARNING SYSTEM

— Description   86.58.00

Later U.S.A. market vehicles only.

This system is designed to discourage leaving the ignition key in the lock with the vehicle unattended. While it should discourage theft it is not a comprehensive anti-theft device.

The system is actuated by opening the drivers door when the ignition key is still in the lock. When the system is actuated a buzzer provides an audible warning.

The system is cancelled when the ignition key is removed from the lock or when the drivers door is closed.

The drivers door switch in the circuit controls the electrical supply to the key warning circuit and key light circuit.

The key switch is built into the steering column lock unit. Failure of the switch would necessitate replacement of the steering column lock.

A diode in the circuit enables the key warning system and the seat belt warning system to use the same audible buzzer unit.

86.55.13
86.55.14

86.57.00
86.58.00

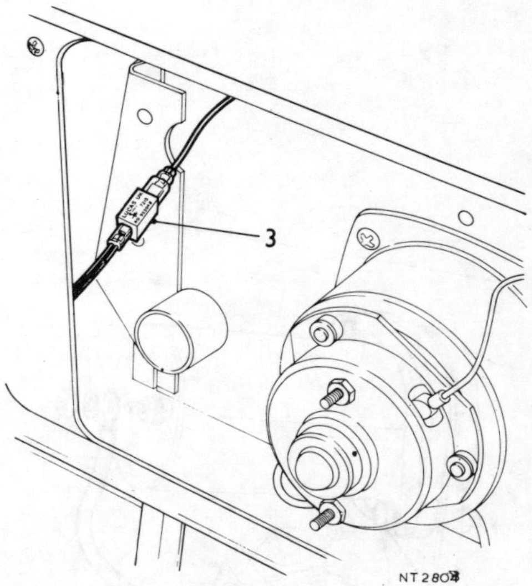

ELECTRICAL

STARTER MOTOR

— Data and description

Manufacturer	Lucas
Type	M35J
Lucas Part No.	25149
Stanpart No.	200535
Yoke diameter	3·5 in (88·90 mm)
Light running — current	65 amp
— speed	8,000 to 10,000 rev/min
Running torque — force	4·4 lbf. ft. (0·60 kgf. m)
— current	260 to 275 amp
— speed	1,000 rev/min
Lock torque — force	7·0 lbf. ft. (0·95 kgf. m)
— current	350 to 375 amp
Commutator minimum skimming thickness	0·080 in (2·03 mm)

	EARLY		LATER	
Brush length — new	0·625 in	15.88 mm	0·500 in	12·70 mm
— renew if less than	0·375 in	9.53 mm	0·375 in	9.53 mm

Brush spring pressure .... 28 oz (800 g)

A series-wound, four-pole, four-brush motor with an extended shaft which carries a conventional inertia drive.

The armature shaft rotates in two porous bronze bushes. A squared extension of the shaft protrudes to enable the shaft to be rotated to clear any jamming between the inertia drive and engine flywheel ring gear. The armature features a face-type moulded commutator.

A plastic brush box is riveted to the commutator end bracket. It holds four wedge-shaped brushes and captive coil springs. The brushes are keyed to ensure correct fitting.

The field winding is a continuously wound strip with no joints. One end is attached to two brush flexibles, while the other is attached to a single flexible which is earthed to the yoke.

The yoke is windowless and has no through-bolts.

The commutator end bracket is secured by four screws which align with tappings in the yoke. The drive end bracket is attached by two slot-headed bolts which screw into tappings provided in the end faces of two of the pole-shoes.

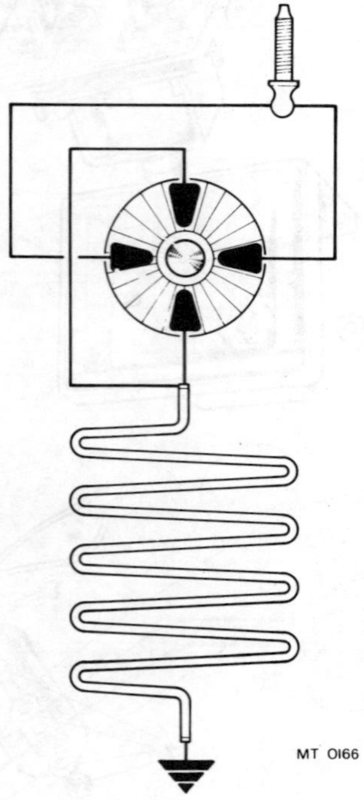

STARTER MOTOR

— Remove and refit   86.60.01

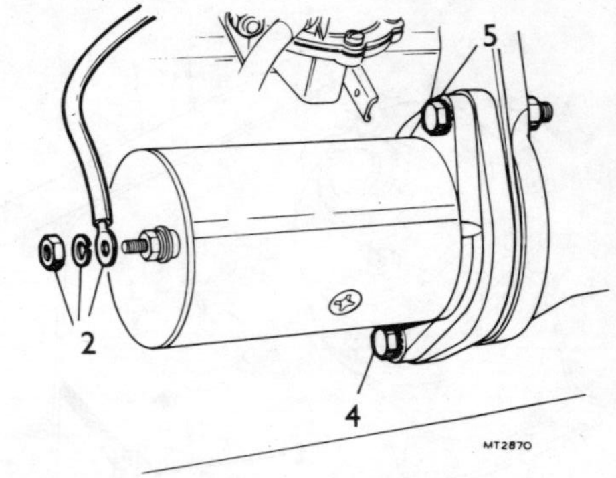

Removing

1. Isolate the battery.
2. Remove the nut and spring washer. Disconnect the lead from the terminal post.
3. Note the relationship between the starter motor, shims if fitted, packing and clutch housing.
4. Working from below the engine, remove the lower mounting bolt.
5. Working from above the engine, remove the upper mounting bolt.
6. Working from below the engine, withdraw the starter motor downwards from the vehicle complete with the packing and shims if fitted.

Refitting

7. Reverse instructions 1 to 6.

STARTER MOTOR

— Inertia drive — remove and refit   86.60.06

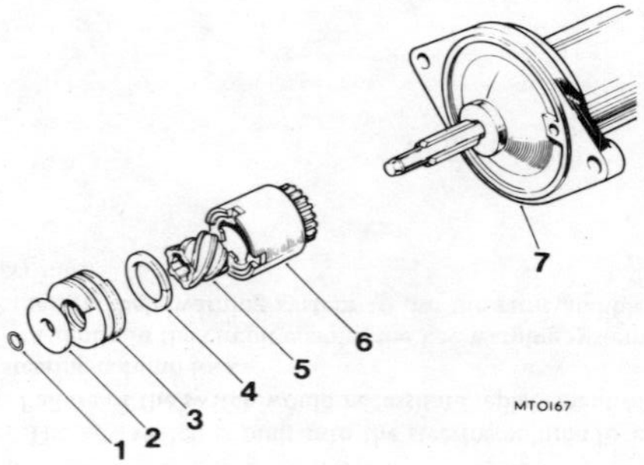

Removing

1. Dismantle the starter motor 86.60.13 operations 1 to 5.
2. Using a suitable press, compress the main spring and ease the jump ring from the shaft. Churchill hand press S4221A and adaptor S4221A-14 may be employed to perform this operation.
3. Withdraw the inertia drive components from the shaft.

Refitting

4. Lightly lubricate the drive and bracket bush with thin engine oil. Position the drive end bracket.
5. Fit the inertia drive components to the shaft as shown. The screwed sleeve may be fitted either way round.
6. Using a suitable press, compress the main spring and fit the jump ring to the shaft.
7. Reassemble the starter motor. 86.60.13 operations 22 to 26.

1. Jump ring
2. Shaft collar
3. Main spring
4. Buffer washer
5. Screwed sleeve
6. Pinion and barrel
7. Drive end bracket

ELECTRICAL

STARTER MOTOR 86.60.13

– Overhaul

Dismantling

1. Remove the two drive end bracket bolts and spring washers.
2. Withdraw the drive end bracket, armature and inertia drive assembly complete from the yoke.
3. Remove the thrust washer.
4. Remove the four 4B.A. bolts and lift aside the commutator end bracket.
5. Lift out the two field winding brushes from the brush box to separate the commutator end bracket from the yoke.

continued

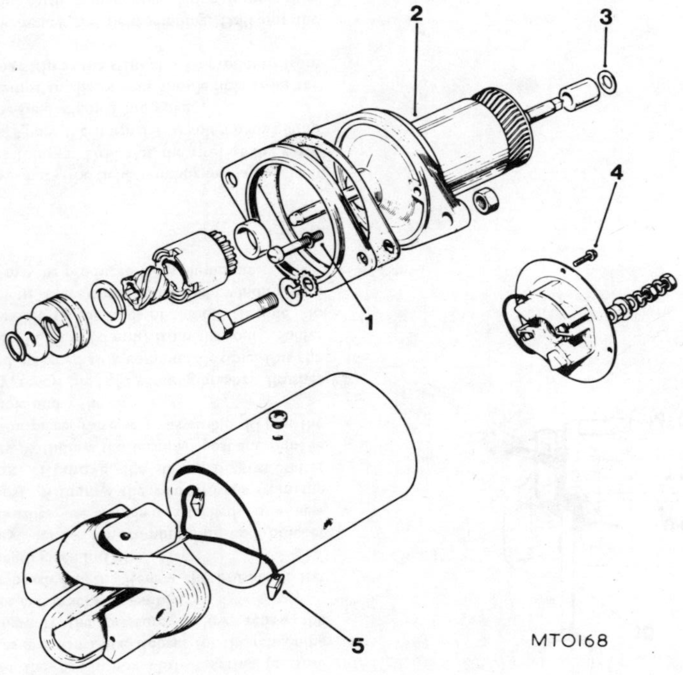

Armature

6. To separate the armature from the drive end bracket and inertia drive, perform the following: Remove the inertia drive, 86.60.06 and slide the drive end bracket from the shaft.
7. Inspect the laminations for score marks. These may indicate a bent shaft, worn bearings or a loose pole-shoe.
8. Clean the commutator with a petrol-moistened cloth. If the commutator is in good condition it will be smooth and free from pits or burned spots.
9. If necessary, polish the commutator with fine glass-paper.
10. If necessary, skim the commutator. Mount the armature in a lathe and rotate at high speed. Using a very sharp tool, take a light cut. Polish with fine glass-paper. Do not cut below the minimum skimming thickness given in Data. Do not undercut insulators between segments.

Bearings

11. Inspect the porous bronze bearing bushes for wear.
12. If necessary, renew the commutator end bracket bush. Drill out the two rivets and discard the plate and felt seal. Screw a ½ in tap squarely into the bush and withdraw. Prepare the porous bronze bush by immersing it in thin engine oil for 24 hours. Using a highly polished, shouldered mandrel suitably dimensioned and a suitable press, fit the bush. Do not ream the bush after fitting or its porosity may be impaired. Assemble the brush box, commutator end bracket, felt seal and plate. Secure with two rivets.
13. If necessary, renew the drive end bracket bush. Remove the inertia drive, 86.60.06, and slide the drive end bracket from the shaft. Support the bracket and press out the bush. Prepare the porous bronze bush by immersing it in thin engine oil for 24 hours. Using a highly polished, shouldered mandrel suitably dimensioned and a suitable press, fit the bush. Do not ream the bush after fitting or its porosity may be impaired.

continued

ELECTRICAL

Brushes

14. Clean the brushes and brush box with a petrol-moistened cloth.
15. Check that the brushes move freely in the brush box.
16. Check the brush spring pressure as shown. Position a new brush so that the top protrudes 0·060 in (1·50 mm) above the brush box. Brush spring pressure should be as given in Data. Repeat for the remaining three springs. If the pressure is low, renew the commutator end bracket assembly.
17. Check the brush length. Renew the brushes if less than the length given in Data.
18. If necessary, renew the commutator end bracket brushes. Brushes are supplied attached to a new terminal post. Withdraw the two brushes from the brush box. Remove the terminal post and remove attachments. Withdraw the terminal post and remove the insulation piece. Reverse to assemble. Retain the longer flexible under the clip.
19. If necessary, renew the field winding brushes. Brushes are supplied attached to a common flexible. Cut the old flexibles 0·250 in (6 mm) from the joint. Solder the new flexible to the ends of the old flexible. Do not attempt to solder direct to the field winding strip as the strip may be produced from aluminium.

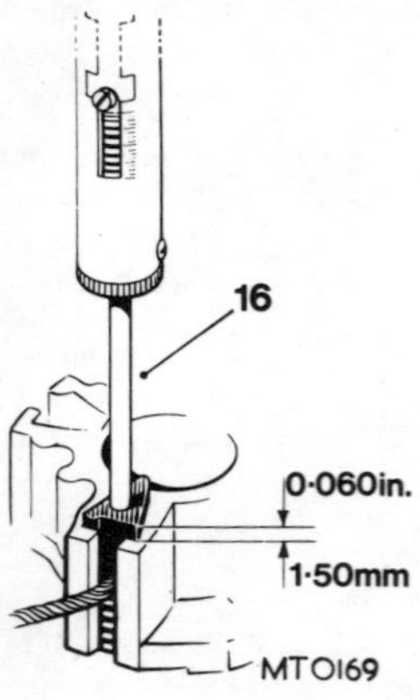

Field winding

20. If necessary, check the fields winding insulation from the yoke as follows: Drill out the rivet at the earth connection. Apply the normal 110 volt a.c. test lamp circuit to the field winding and yoke. Do not attempt to disconnect the flexible from the field winding strip as the strip may be produced from aluminium.
21. If necessary, renew the field winding. Drill out the rivet at the earth connection. Using a pole-shoe screwdriver, slacken the four pole-shoe screws. Remove the two diametrically opposite screws and pole-shoes. Slacken the remaining two screws sufficient to allow the field winding to be withdrawn from the yoke. Reverse to assemble.

Reassembling

22. Insert the two field winding brushes into the brush box with the flexibles positioned as shown.
23. Position the commutator end bracket and secure it with four 4 B.A. bolts.
24. Fit the thrust washer.
25. Insert the drive end bracket, armature and inertia drive assembly complete into the yoke.
26. Fit the two drive end bracket bolts and spring washers.

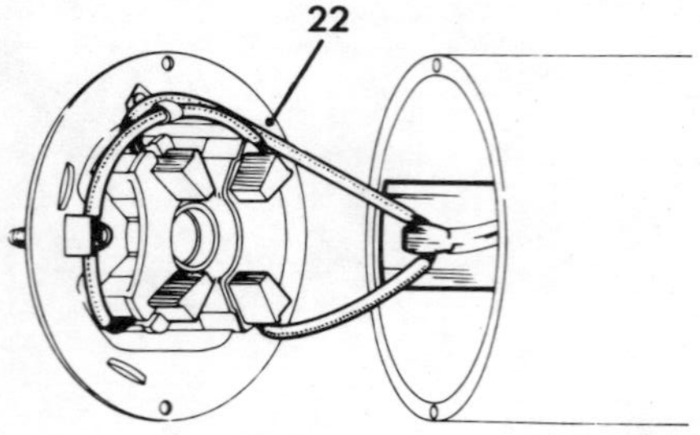

ELECTRICAL

SWITCHES

Data

Ignition/starter switch

Position 0	Off	No connections
Position 1	Auxiliary	2 to 5
Position 2	Ignition	2 to 5 to 3
Position 3	Start	2 to 3 to 1

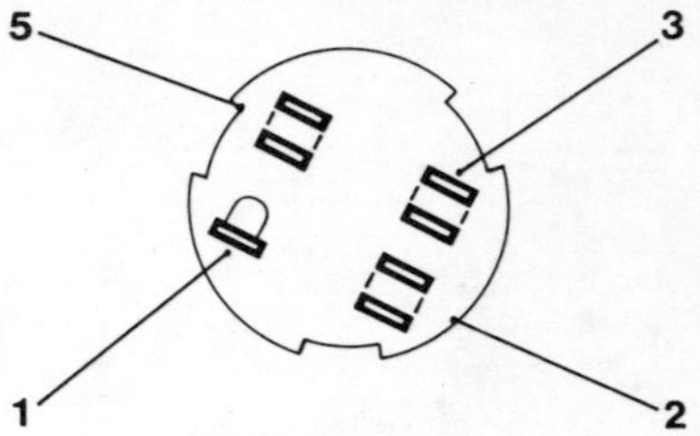

Master light switch

Position	Off	No connections
Position	Side	3 to 2
Position	Head	3 to 2 to 1

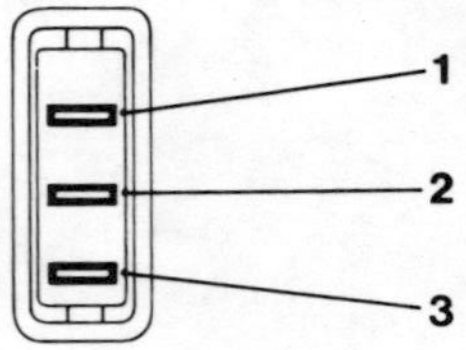

Column light switch

Position	Head main	U to UW
Position	Head dip	U to UR
Position	Head flash	P to UW

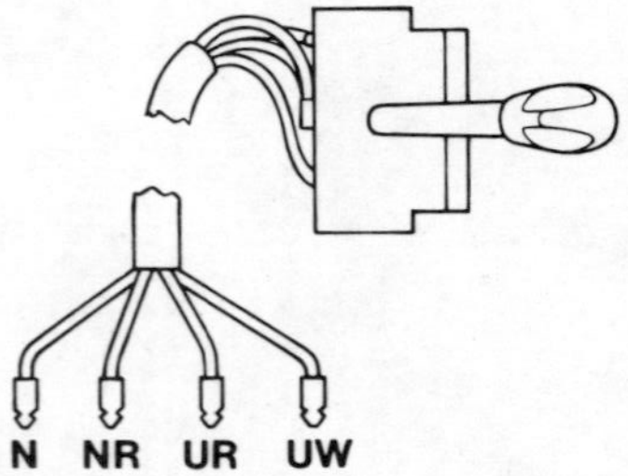

Windscreen wiper switch

Used when manual windscreen washer system is fitted to vehicle.

Position	Park	1 to 2
Position	Normal speed	3 to 2
Position	High speed	3 to 4

continued

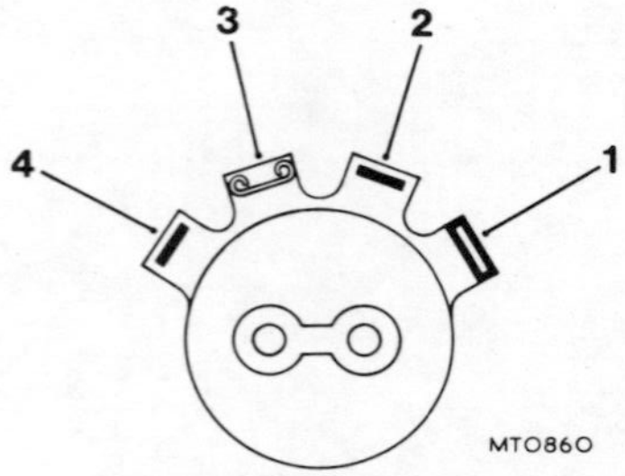

ELECTRICAL

Heater switch

Position	Off	No connections
Position	Low speed	GY to earth
Position	High speed	GS to earth

Turn signal switch

Position	Central	No connections
Position	L.H. turn signal	LG/N to GR
Position	R.H. turn signal	LG/N to GW

Hazard switch
Used when hazard warning system is not fitted to vehicle.

| Position | Off | 8 to 7 |
| Position | Hazard | 3 to 1 to 2 to 4 |

Door switch
Used when key warning system is not fitted to vehicle.

| Position | Door closed | No connections |
| Position | Door open | Terminal to earth |

continued

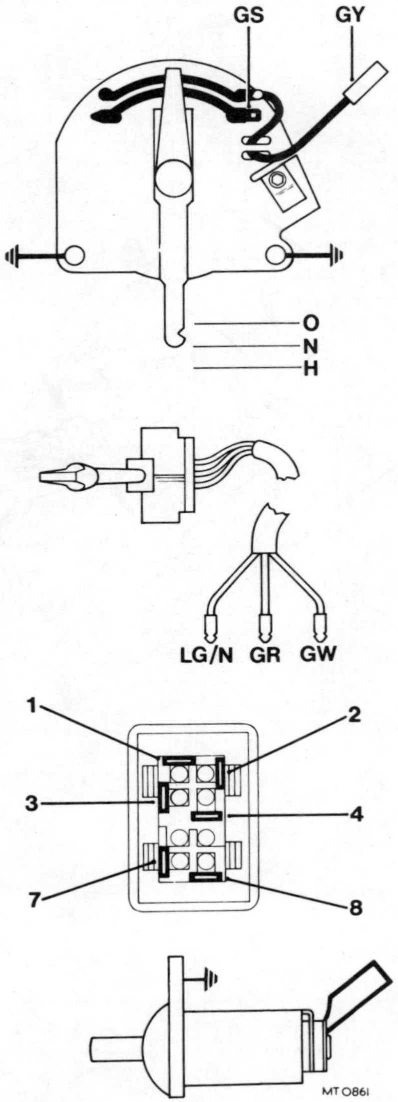

ELECTRICAL

Door switch
Used when key warning system is fitted to vehicle.

| Position | Door closed | No connections |
| Position | Door open | Two Lucar blades connected |

Windscreen washer/wiper switch
Used when electric washer pump is fitted to vehicle.

Position	Park	1 to 2
Position	Normal speed	3 to 2
Position	High speed	3 to 4
Position	Wash	Two centre terminals connected

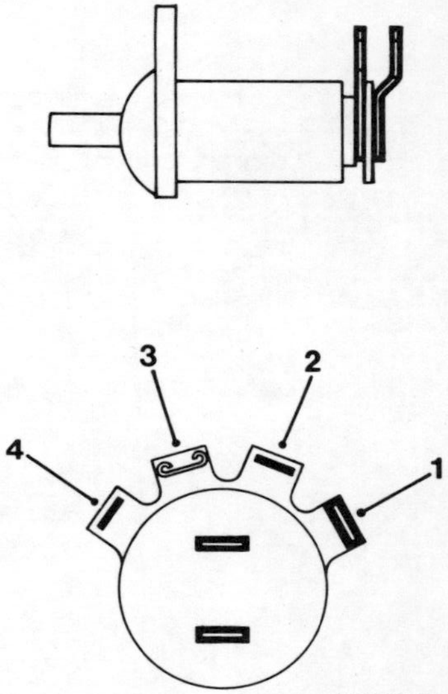

ELECTRICAL

SWITCHES
— Ignition/Starter switch — remove and refit   86.65.02

Removing
1. Isolate the battery.
2. Pull back the switch cover.
3. Withdraw the switch.
4. Disconnect the five Lucar connectors.

Refitting
5. Reverse instructions 1 to 3. When inserting the switch into the steering column lock assembly, note the keyway and ensure that the lock shaft and switch are aligned for correct engagement.
6. Connect the wires as follows:
   White/red to terminal 1
   Brown to terminal 2
   White to terminal 3
   White/pink to terminal 5

SWITCHES
Master light switch
— Remove and refit   86.65.09

Removing
1. Lower the centre fascia to the service position 76.46.02 operations 1 to 4.
2. Disconnect the three Lucar connectors.
3. Compress the springs and push out the switch.

Refitting
4. Reverse instructions 1 to 3.

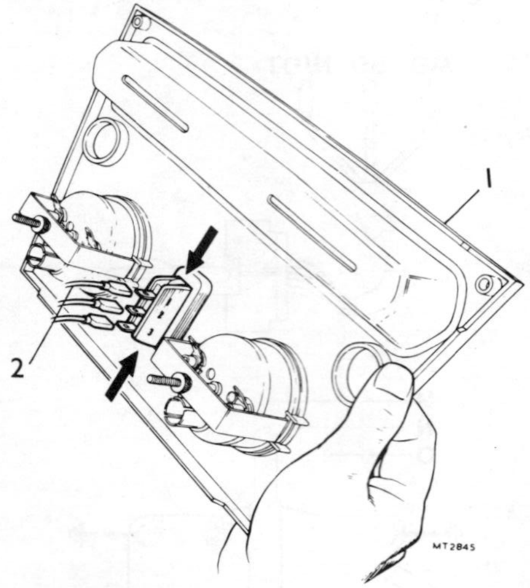

SWITCHES
— Door switch — remove and refit   86.65.14

Removing
1. Isolate the battery.
2. Remove the screw.
3. Remove the switch.
4. Disconnect the terminal(s).

Refitting
5. Reverse instructions 1 to 4.

SWITCHES—
Column light switch
— Remove and refit   86.65.17

Removing
1. Isolate the battery.
2. Remove the switch fairings — two screws.
3. Remove the two Allen screws and spring washers securing the steering column clamp. Remove the clamp and the harness cover.
4. Disconnect the four snap connectors.
5. Remove the two screws and spring washers.
6. Carefully withdraw the switch and leads.

Refitting
7. Reverse instructions 1 to 6. Ensure that the wires are connected as follows:-
   Blue/Red to Blue/Red
   Blue/White to Blue/White
   Brown/Red to Blue
   Brown to Purple
   The inconsistencies enable a common switch to be used on different circuits.

ELECTRICAL

SWITCHES —
Horn push
— Remove and refit
86.65.18

Removing

1. Pull off the steering wheel centre pad.
2. Prise out the horn push.
3. Withdraw the horn brush.

Refitting

4. Reverse instructions 1 to 3, ensuring that the horn push contact strip is positioned over the horn brush.

SWITCHES
— Reverse lamp switch — remove and refit
86.65.20

Removing

1. Remove the gearbox tunnel cover. 76.25.07.
2. Remove the top cover extension. 37.12.10.
3. Disconnect the two Lucar connectors.
4. Unscrew the reverse lamp switch.
5. Remove the packing washers.

Refitting

6. Reverse instructions 1 to 5.

SWITCHES
— Seat belt — gearbox switch — remove and refit
86.65.28

Later U.S.A. market vehicles only.

Removing

1. Remove the gearbox tunnel cover 76.25.07
2. Locate the required switch.
3. Disconnect two Lucar connectors.
4. Using a spanner on the hexagon, unscrew the switch.
5. Collect up the fibre washer/washers if fitted.

Refitting

6. Assemble with the same number of fibre washers as originally fitted. Use new fibre washer/washers if available.
7. Fit the switch and fibre washer/washers to the gearbox.
8. Connect two Lucar connectors. The connectors may be fitted either way round.
9. Perform a functional check of the seat belt warning circuit.
10. Refit the gearbox tunnel cover 76.25.07

86.65.18
86.65.28

Triumph Spitfire Mk IV Manual. Part No. 545254.

SWITCHES
Seat belt — passengers seat switch — remove and refit
86.65.29

Later U.S.A. market vehicles only.

Removing

1. Remove the passengers seat from the vehicle 76.70.05.

NOTE: To assist refitting, note the wire run through the seat.

2. Release the fabricated rivets and withdraw the switch and leads

Refitting

3. Reverse instructions 1 and 2.

SWITCHES
— Oil pressure switch — remove and refit
86.65.30

Removing

1. Disconnect Lucar connector.

NOTE: On later U.S.A. Market cars there are three Lucar connectors to the oil pressure switch. Note the relative positions of these connectors before attempt to seat switch shoulder.

Refitting

3. Screw switch into block and tighten to 11 to 14 lbf. ft (1·5 to 2·0 kg. m). Thread is tapered. Do not attempt to seat switch shoulder.
4. Connect Lucar connector.

SWITCHES
Seat belt — drivers belt switch — remove and refit
86.65.31

Seat belt — passengers belt switch — remove and refit
86.65.32

Later U.S.A. market vehicles only.

Removing

1. Lift the carpet at the rear of the seatwell and disconnect the electrical harness plug.
2. Remove single bolt and spring washer. Lift out the buckle and switch unit.

Refitting

3. Reverse instructions 1 to 3. If the sealing has been disturbed seal the large plain washer to the floor panel with an approved sealer to ensure a waterproof joint.

86.65.29
86.65.32

Triumph Spitfire Mk IV Manual. Part No. 545254.

ELECTRICAL

SWITCHES

— Overdrive gearbox switch — remove and refit 86.65.33

Removing

1. Remove the gearbox tunnel cover. 76.25.07.
2. Disconnect the two Lucar connectors.
3. Unscrew the switch.

Refitting

4. Reverse instructions 1 to 3.

SWITCHES

— Overdrive gear lever switch — remove and refit 86.65.34

Removing

1. Prise the switch from the gear lever knob (a slot at the reat of the knob enables a blade to be inserted).
2. Disconnect the two wires from the switch.

Refitting

3. Connect the two wires.
4. Clip the switch onto the gear lever knob.

SWITCHES —
Windscreen wiper switch
— Remove and refit 86.65.38

Removing

1. Isolate the battery.
2. Depress the retainer by inserting a suitable probe into the hole in the underside of the knob and pull the knob from the shaft.
3. Slacken the bezel using a suitable tool. Support the switch behind the fascia and unscrew the bezel.
4. Withdraw the switch and lower it into a visible position.
5. Disconnect the four Lucar connectors noting colour codes and positions for reconnection.
6. Pull off the two pipes, noting positions for reconnection.

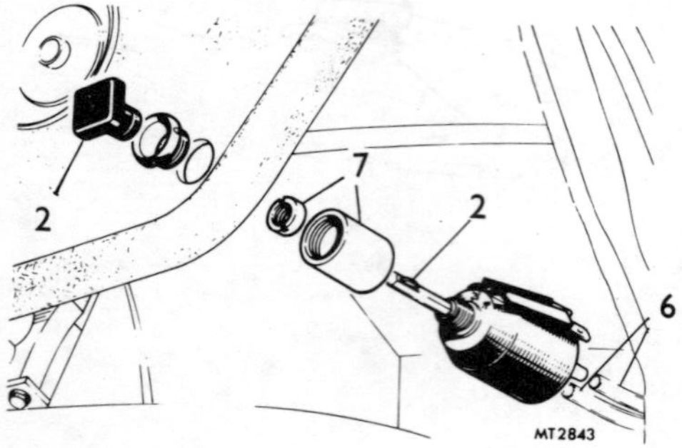

Refitting

7. Ensure that the switch is securely attached to the spacer. If not tighten the slotted ring.
8. Reverse instructions 1 to 6.

ELECTRICAL

SWITCHES

Brake line failure switch — remove and refit 86.65.47 **

Removing

1. Pull back the retaining clips and withdraw the socket from the switch.
2. Unscrew the switch.

Refitting

3. Reverse instructions 1 and 2. Ensure that the earth connection spring is correctly located with the outer end pointing in an anti-clockwise direction as shown.

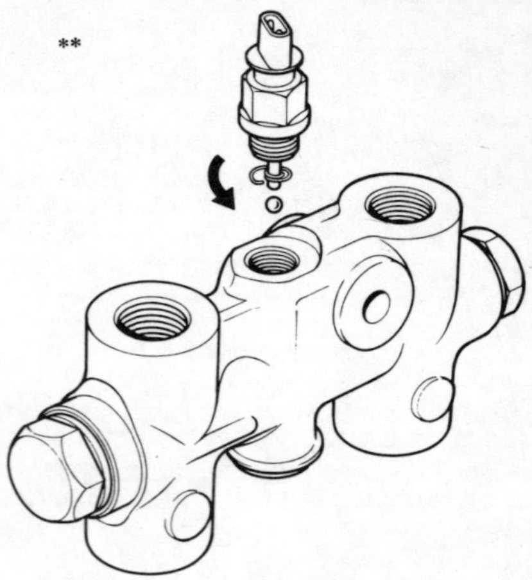

SWITCHES

— Hazard switch — remove and refit 86.65.50

Left hand steer vehicles only.

Removing

1. Isolate the battery.
2. To gain access remove either the speedometer 88.30.01 or the tachometer 88.30.21. The choice depends entirely on which operation is preferred by the individual fitter.
3. Push inwards two plastic clips on the switch and withdraw the switch from the panel.
4. Disconnect the Lucar connectors.

Refitting

5. Reverse instructions 1 to 4.

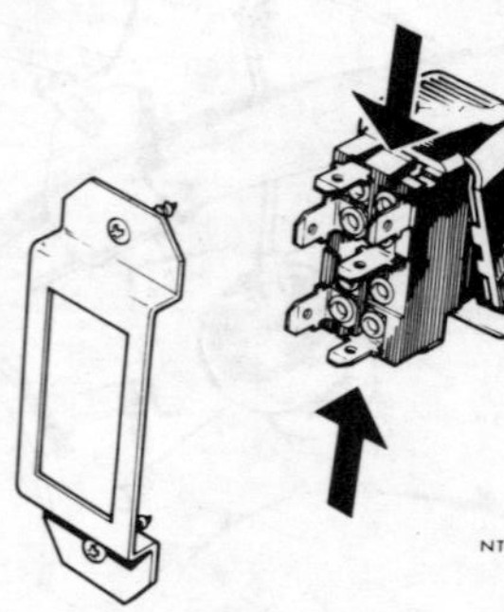

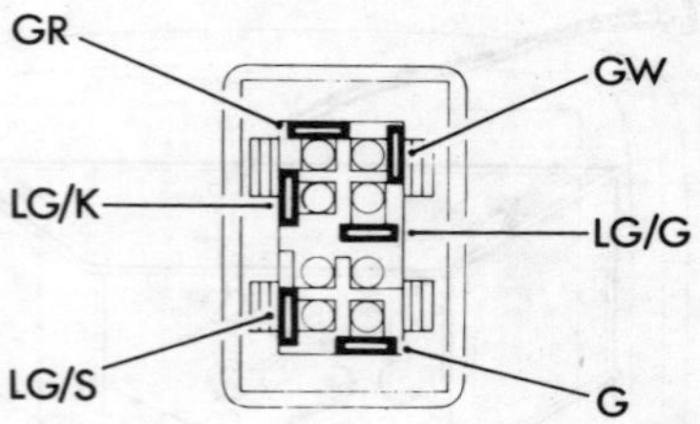

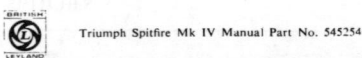

ELECTRICAL

SWITCHES

Stop lamp switch — remove and refit   86.65.51

Removing

1. Disconnect the two Lucar connectors.
2. Remove the nut and plain washer.
3. Withdraw the switch from the mounting bracket.

Refitting

4. Reverse instructions 1 to 3.

**SWITCHES

Turn signal switch — remove and refit   86.65.54 **

Removing

1. Remove the switch fairings — two screws.
2. Remove the two Allen screws and spring washers securing the steering column clamp. Remove the clamp and the harness cover.
3. Disconnect the three snap connectors.
4. Remove the two screws and spring washers.
5. Carefully withdraw the switch and leads.

Refitting

6. Reverse instructions 1 to 5.

FUSE SYSTEM

— Fuse — remove and refit   86.70.02

Removing

1. Lift the bonnet and locate the fusebox on the left hand side of the bulkhead.
2. Pull off the plastic cover.
3. Identify the defective fuse.
4. Carefully lever the fuse from the contacts.

Refitting

5. Reverse instructions 1 to 4.

NT2026

86.65.51
86.70.02

INSTRUMENTS

INSTRUMENTS OPERATIONS

Fuel indicator – remove and refit	88.25.26
Fuel tank unit – remove and refit	88.25.32
Speedometer – remove and refit	88.30.01
Speedometer cable – complete – remove and refit	88.30.06
Speedometer cable – inner – remove and refit	88.30.07
Tachometer – remove and refit	88.30.21
Tachometer cable – complete – remove and refit	88.30.23
Tachometer cable – inner – remove and refit	88.30.24
Temperature indicator – remove and refit	88.25.14
Temperature transmitter – remove and refit	88.25.20
Voltage stabilizer – remove and refit	88.20.26

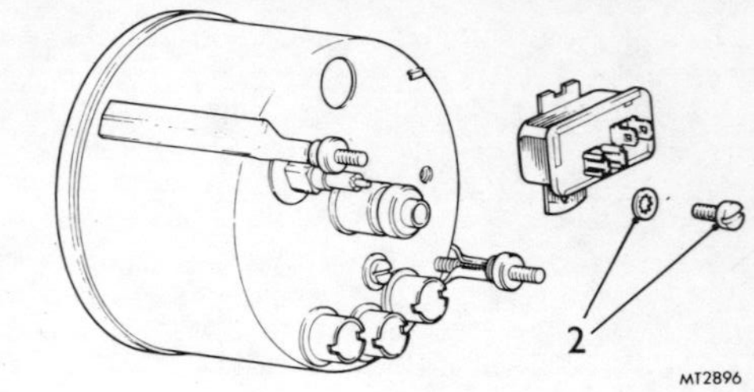

88.1

VOLTAGE STABILISER
88.20.26

— Remove and refit

Removing
1. Remove the speedometer 88.30.01.
2. Remove one screw and lift off the voltage stabiliser.

Refitting
3. Reverse instructions 1 and 2. Connect the Lucar connectors as follows:
Green wire to terminal B. Light green wire to terminal I.

TEMPERATURE INDICATOR
88.25.14

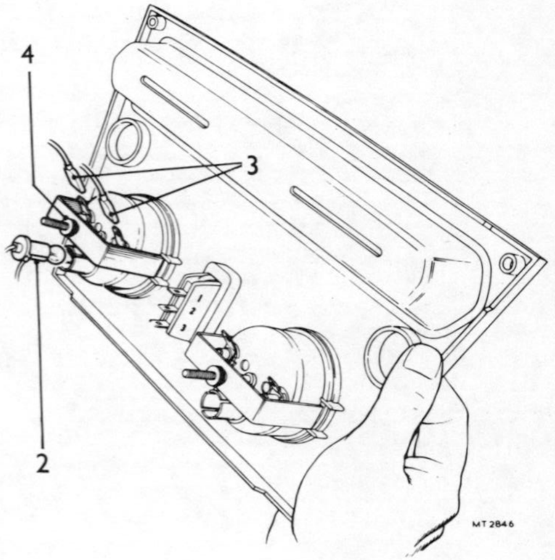

— Remove and refit

Removing
1. Lower the fascia centre to the service position 76.46.02, operations 1 to 4.
2. Pull out the panel light bulb holder.
3. Disconnect the two Lucar connectors.
4. Remove the knurled nut and spring washer.
5. Withdraw the indicator from the fascia centre.

Refitting
6. Reverse instructions 1 to 5.

TEMPERATURE TRANSMITTER
88.25.20

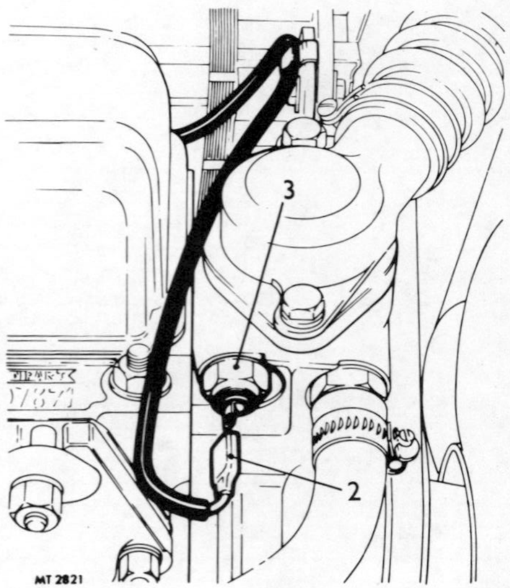

— Remove and refit

Removing
1. Drain part of the coolant 26.10.01.
2. Disconnect the Lucar connector.
3. Unscrew the transmitter.

Refiting
4. Reverse instructions 1 to 3.

88.20.26
88.25.20

INSTRUMENTS

FUEL INDICATOR 88.25.26
— Remove and refit

Removing
1. Lower the fascia centre to the service position 76.46.02, operations 1 to 4.
2. Pull out the panel light bulb holder.
3. Disconnect the two Lucar connectors.
4. Remove the knurled nut and spring washer.
5. Withdraw the indicator from the fascia centre.

Refitting
6. Reverse instructions 1 to 5.

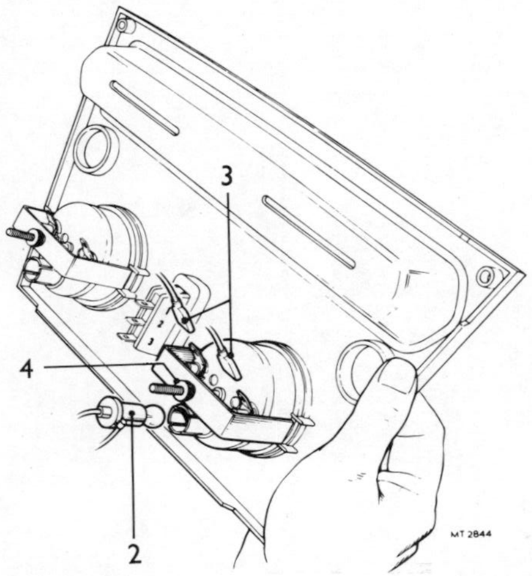

FUEL TANK UNIT 88.25.32
— Remove and refit

Removing
1. Isolate the battery and extinguish all naked lights.
2. Siphon the fuel out of the tank.
3. Remove the petrol tank rear casing board — seven screws, spring washers and plain washers.
4. Disconnect the two Lucar connectors noting positions for reconnection.
5. Release the locking ring by tapping anti-clockwise.
6. Remove the locking ring.
7. Carefully withdraw the tank unit.

Refitting
8. Reverse instructions 1 to 7.

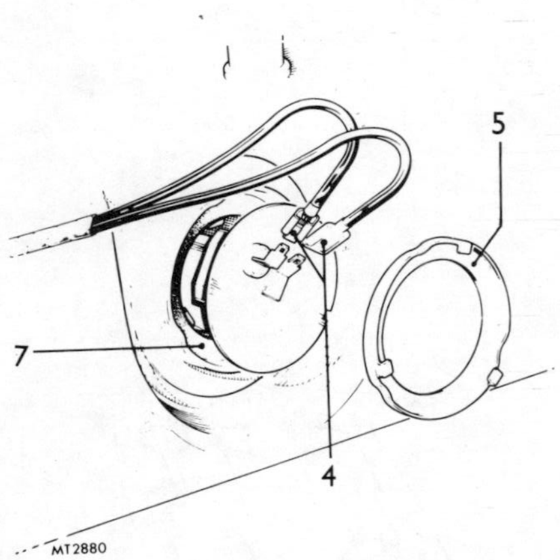

88.25.26
88.25.32

Triumph Spitfire Mk IV Manual. Part No. 545254.

INSTRUMENTS

SPEEDOMETER 88.30.01
— Remove and refit

Removing
1. Remove the centre fascia for access to the rear of the speedometer 76.46.02.
2. Remove the tachometer for access to the rear of the speedometer 88.30.21.
3. Depress the lever to release the catch from the annular groove in the boss. Detach the speedometer cable from the instrument.
4. Unscrew the trip reset knurled nut.
5. Remove the two knurled nuts, spring washers and clamp legs. Detach the earth wire.
6. Disconnect the two Lucar connectors from the voltage stabiliser.
7. Pull out the three warning light bulb holders.
8. Pull out the panel light bulb holder.

Refitting
9. Reverse instructions 4 to 8.
10. Using long nosed pliers, withdraw the inner cable about 1 in (25 mm).
11. Engage the inner cable to the instrument.
12. Push the outer cable over the boss, ensuring that the catch engages in the annular groove.
13. Refit the tachometer 88.30.21.
14. Refit the centre fascia.

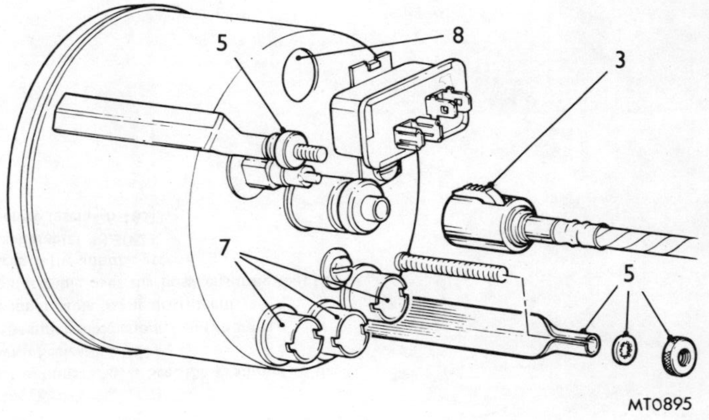

88.30.01

Triumph Spitfire Mk IV Manual. Part No. 545254.

INSTRUMENTS

SPEEDOMETER CABLE – COMPLETE

– Remove and refit (non-overdrive models only) 88.30.06

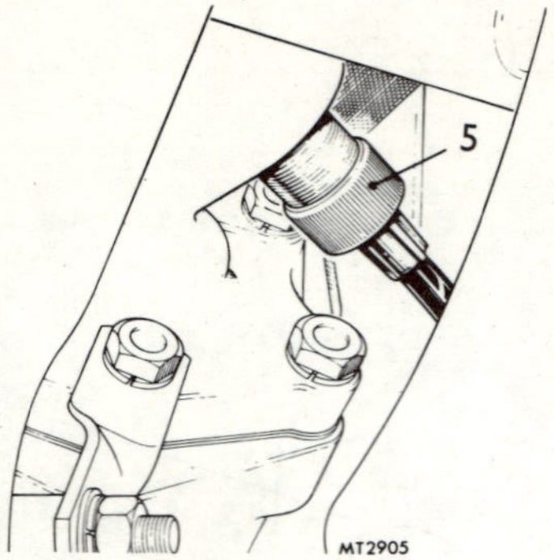

Removing

1. Place the vehicle on a ramp.
2. Remove the centre fascia for access to the rear of the speedometer 76.46.02.
3. Remove the tachometer for access to the rear of the speedometer 88.30.21.
4. Depress the lever to release the catch from the annular groove in the boss. Pull the speedometer cable from the instrument.
5. Working from below the vehicle, unscrew the speedometer cable knurled nut from the gearbox extension.
6. To assist refitting, carefully note the cable position relative to the other components.
7. Manoeuvre the cable downwards through the grommet aperture and detach it from the vehicle.

Refitting

8. Reverse instructions 5 to 7. Seal the grommet to the bulkhead with Seelastik SR51.
9. Withdraw the inner cable about 1 in (25 mm).
10. Engage the inner cable to the instrument.
11. Push the outer cable over the boss, ensuring that the catch engages in the annular groove.
12. Refit the tachometer 88.30.21.
13. Refit the centre fascia 76.46.02.

INSTRUMENTS

SPEEDOMETER CABLE – COMPLETE

– Remove and refit (overdrive models only) 88.30.06

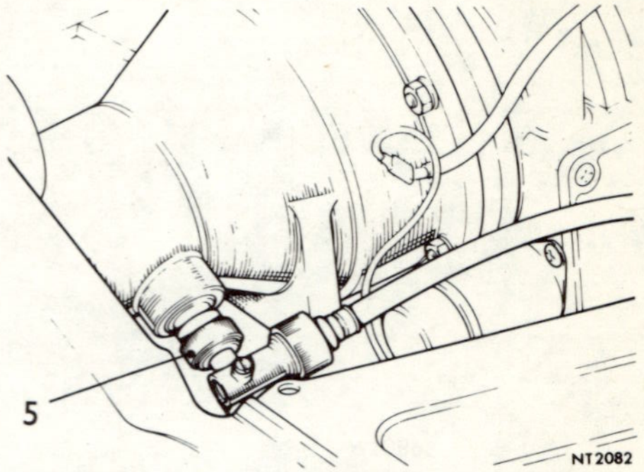

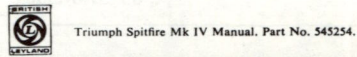

Removing

1. Remove the centre fascia for access to the rear of the speedometer 76.46.02.
2. Remove the tachometer for access to the rear of the speedometer 88.30.21.
3. Depress the lever to release the catch from the annular groove in the boss. Pull the speedometer cable from the instrument.
4. Remove the gearbox tunnel cover 76.25.07.
5. Unscrew the speedometer cable knurled nut from the gearbox extension.
6. To assist refitting, carefully note the cable position relative to the other components.
7. Manoeuvre the cable downwards through the grommet aperture and detach it from the vehicle.

Refitting

8. Reverse instructions 5 to 7. Seal the grommet to the bulkhead with Seelastik SR51.
9. Withdraw the inner cable about 1 in (25 mm).
10. Engage the inner cable to the instrument.
11. Push the outer cable over the boss, ensuring that the catch engages in the annular groove.
12. Refit the tachometer 88.30.21.
13. Refit the centre fascia 76.46.02.

INSTRUMENTS

SPEEDOMETER CABLE – INNER   88.30.07

— Remove and refit

Removing

1. Remove the centre fascia for access to the rear of the speedometer 76.46.02.
2. Remove the tachometer for access to the rear of the speedometer 88.30.21.
3. Depress the lever to release the catch from the speedometer cable from the instrument.
4. Using long nosed pliers, withdraw the inner cable. Take care not to contaminate the upholstery or fittings with grease.

Refitting

5. Sparingly grease the inner cable. Do not use oil.
6. Feed the inner cable into the outer cable, rotating it slightly to assist operation.
7. Withdraw the inner cable about 8 in (200 mm) and wipe off surplus grease. Re-insert the inner cable, rotating it slightly to assist engagement of the squared end to the drive gear.
8. Withdraw the inner cable about 1 in (25 mm).
9. Engage the inner cable to the instrument.
10. Push the outer cable over the boss, ensuring that the catch engages in the annular groove.
11. Refit the tachometer 88.30.21.
12. Refit the centre fascia, 76.46.02.

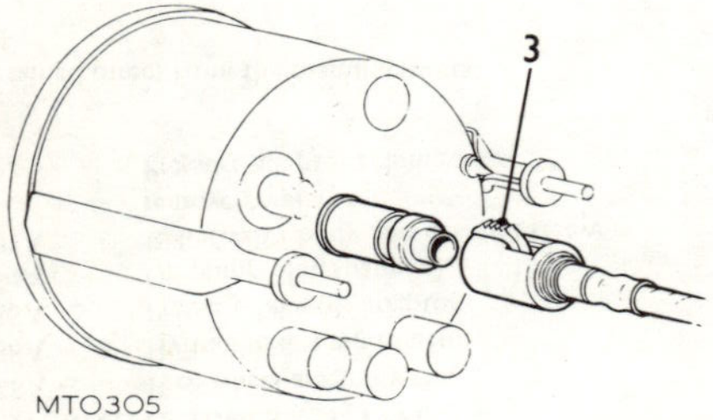

TACHOMETER   88.30.21

— Remove and refit

Removing

1. Remove the two knurled nuts, spring washers and clamp legs.
2. Pull out the bulb holder.
3. Unscrew the knurled retainer securing the cable to the tachometer.
4. Withdraw the tachometer from the fascia.

Refitting

5. Reverse instructions 1 to 4.

TACHOMETER CABLE – COMPLETE   88.30.23

— Remove and refit

Removing

1. Unscrew the knurled retainer securing the cable to the tachometer.
2. Unscrew the knurled retainer securing the cable to the distributor.
3. To assist refitting, carefully note the cable position relative to other components.
4. Manoeuvre the cable downwards through the grommet aperture and detach it from the vehicle.

Refitting

5. Reverse instructions 1 to 4. Seal the grommet to the bulkhead with Seelastik SR51.

TACHOMETER CABLE – INNER   88.30.24

— Remove and refit

Removing

1. Unscrew the knurled retainer securing the cable to the tachometer.
2. Using long nosed pliers, withdraw the inner cable. Take care not to contaminate the upholstery or fittings with grease.

Refitting

3. Sparingly grease the inner cable. Do not use oil.
4. Feed the inner cable into the outer cable, rotating it slightly to assist operation.
5. Withdraw the inner cable about 8 in (200 mm) and wipe off surplus grease. Re-insert the inner cable, rotating it slightly to assist engagement of the squared end to the drive gear.
6. Engage the inner cable to the tachometer.
7. Refit the knurled retainer.

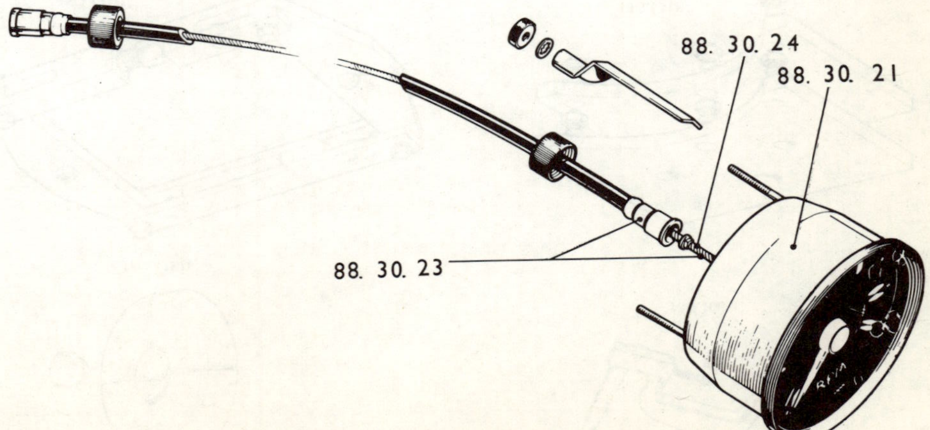

SERVICE TOOLS

SERVICE TOOLS

Tool No.	Description	
18G.47	Hand Press	S.4221A Hand Press
18G.47BD	Differential Bearing Carrier Remover	S.4221A-5 I.F.S. Coil Spring Remover/Replacer Adaptor
18G.106	Valve Spring Compressor	S.4221A-7B Inner Axle Shaft Bearing Remover/Replacer Adaptor
18G.131C	Differential Case Spreader	
18G.131E	Differential Case Spreader Adaptor Set	S.4221A-14 Rear Hub Bearing Remover/Replacer Adaptor
18G.134DH	Differential Bearing Replacer	S.4221A-17 Pinion Head Bearing Remover/Replacer Adaptor
18G.191	Pinion Height Gauge	
18G.191M	Dummy Pinion	S.4221A-19 Gearbox Mainshaft Ball Race Remover/Replacer Adaptor
60A	Valve Guide Remover/Replacer	4235A Slide Hammer
S.60A-2A	Valve Guide Remover/Replacer Adaptor	S.4235A-2 Constant Pinion Remover Adaptor
S.101	Differential Case Spreader	6118B Valve Spring Compressor
S.109C	Rear Hub Remover	S.6118B-1 Valve Spring Compressor Adaptor
S.144	Gearbox Mainshaft Circlip Remover	
S.145	Gearbox Mainshaft Circlip Replacer	**OVERDRIVE TOOLS — 'D' TYPE**
S.160	Ball Joint Separator	L.178 Freewheel Assembly Ring
S.300A	Rear Hub Needle Bearing Remover/Replacer	L.183A Pump Barrel Remover
S.304	Rear Hub Bearing Replacer	L.183A-2A Adaptor
S.306	Brake Adjusting Tool	L.188 Hydraulic Test Equipment
S.314	Mainshaft Ball Bearing Replacer	L.201 Dummy Drive Shaft
335	Con Rod Aligning Jig	L.202A Tailshaft Ballrace Remover
S.336-4	Con Rod Arbor Adaptor	L.206A Oil Pump Body Replacer
S.337	Flange Holder	L.213 Oil Pump Body Key
S.341	Rack Mounting Compressor	
S.353	Carburetter Adjusting Compressor	**** OVERDRIVE TOOLS — 'J' TYPE**
RG.421	Adjusting Flange Holding Wrench	L178A Free wheel assembly ring
550	Driver Handle	L188A Hydraulic test equipment
3072A	Slide Hammer	L188A-2 Pressure take-off adaptor
		L354A Oil pump plug spanner
		L401A Relief valve body and dashpot sleeve remover/replacer
		L402 Pressure adaptor spline release **

All Service Tools mentioned in this Manual must be obtained direct from the manufacturers:

Messrs. V.L. Churchill & Co. Ltd.
P.O. Box No. 3
London Road,
Daventry, Northants

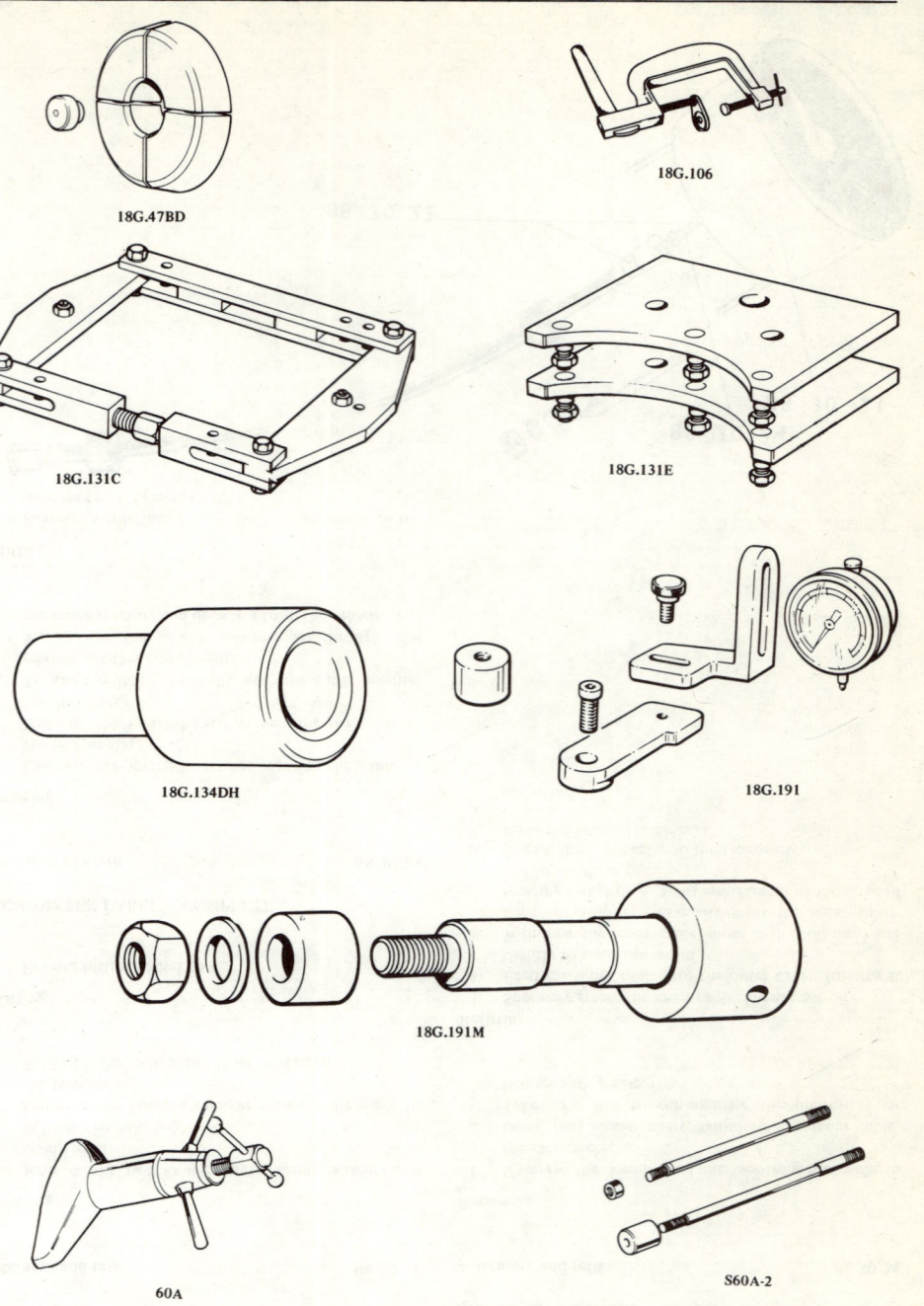

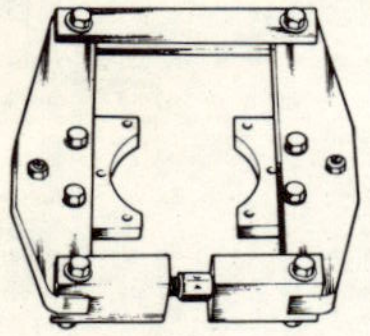

SERVICE TOOLS

S.101
S.144 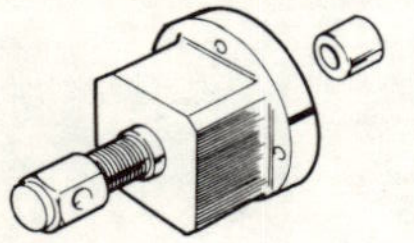
S.300A
S.314
S.145
S.306
335
S.109C
S.304
S.160
S.336-4

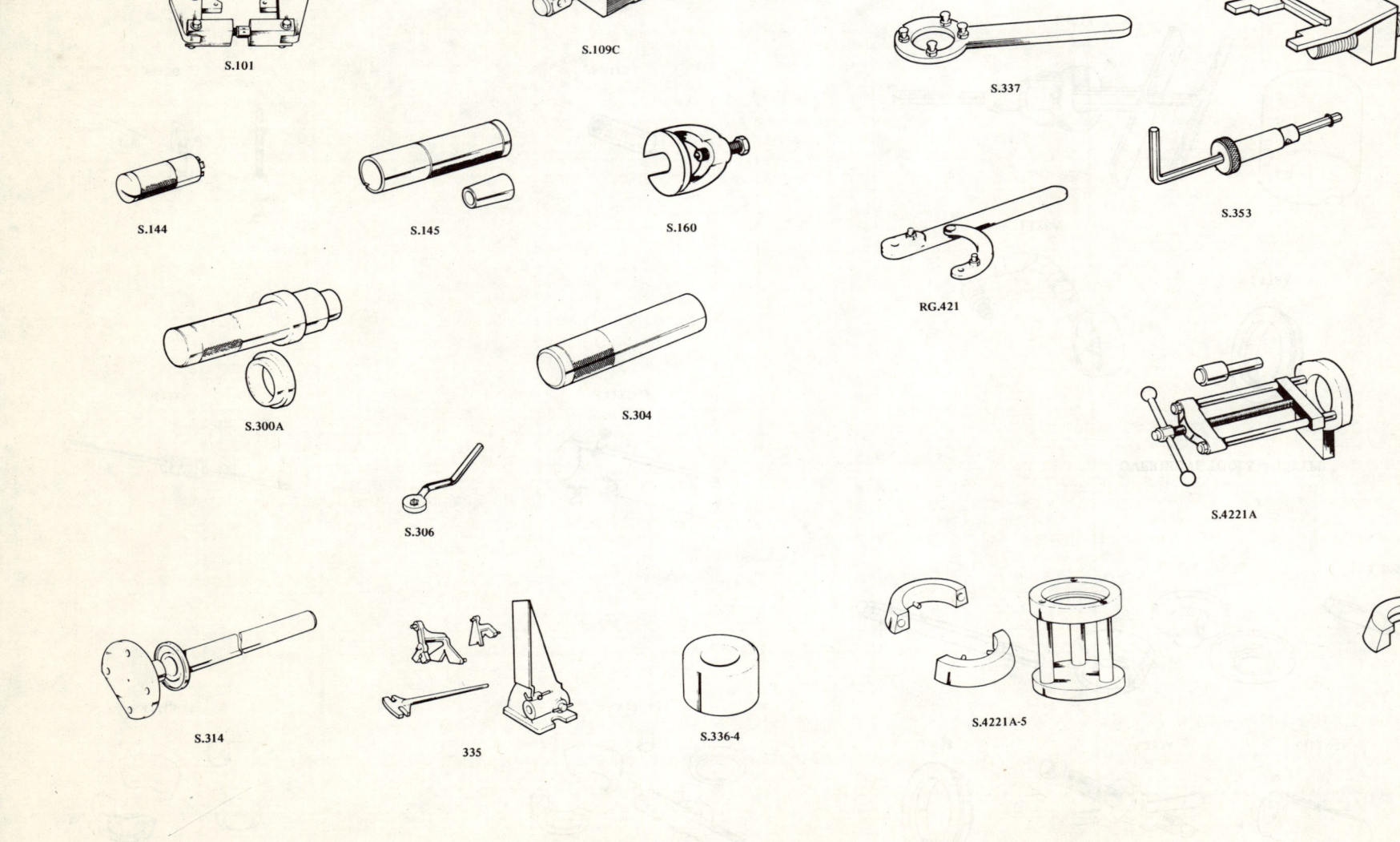

S.337
RG.421
S.4221A-5
S.353
S.4221A
S.341
550
S.4221A-7B

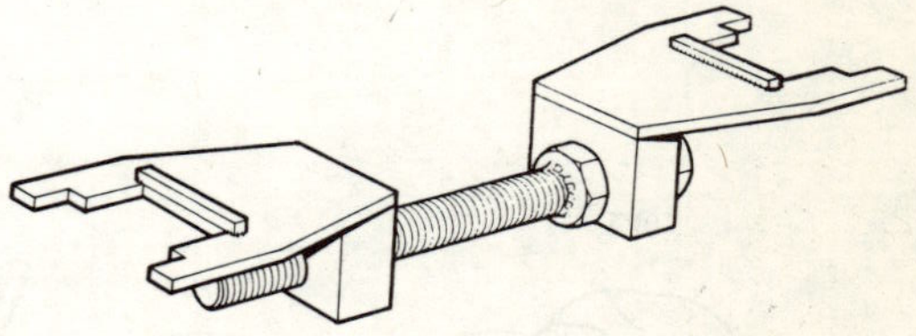

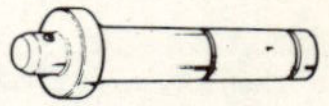

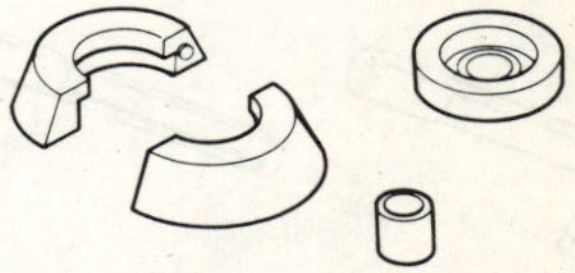

SERVICE TOOLS

SERVICE TOOLS

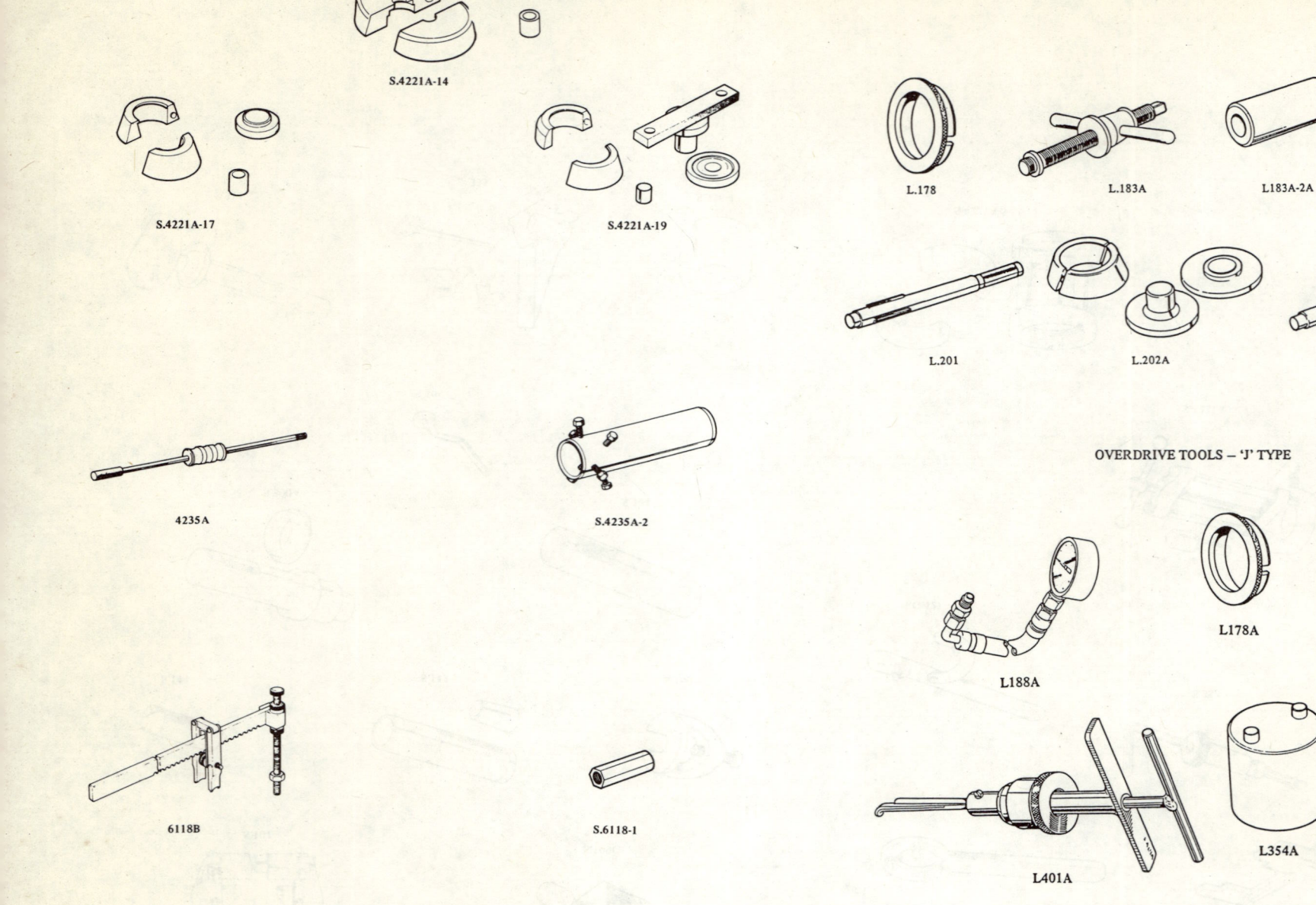

** OVERDRIVE TOOLS — 'D' TYPE **

S.4221A-17
S.4221A-14
S.4221A-19

4235A
S.6118-1
S.4235A-2

6118B

L.178
L.201
L.183A
L.202A
L.183A-2A 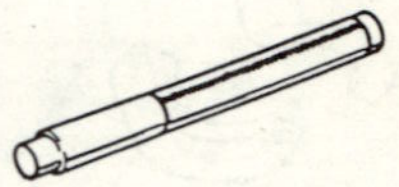
L.206A
L.188
L.213

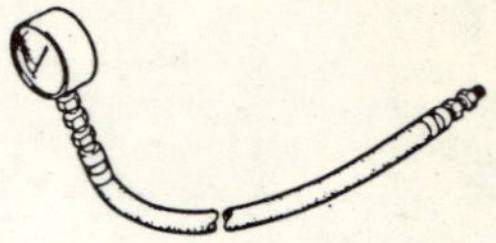

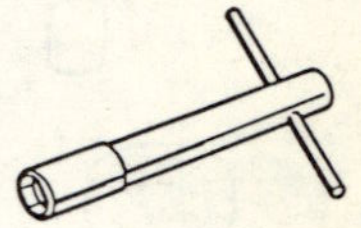

OVERDRIVE TOOLS — 'J' TYPE

L401A
L188A
L178A 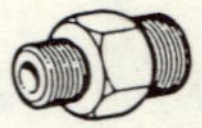
L354A
L188A-2
L402

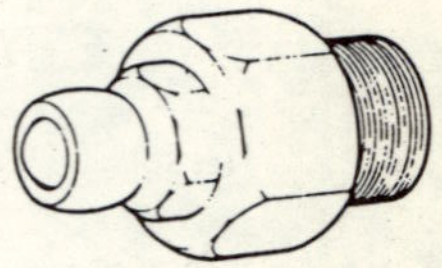